PARIS 1919

PARIS

SIX MONTHS THAT CHANGED THE WORLD

1919

Margaret MacMillan

RANDOM HOUSE/NEW YORK

The author and publisher would like to thank the following for permission to
reproduce illustrations: Plates 1 and 7, Princeton University Library; 2, 4, 5, 8, 9,
11, 12, 13, 16, 17, 20, 21, 22, 23, 24, 27 and 28, Hulton Getty; 3 and 29, The Trustees
of the Imperial War Museum, London; 10, 14, 18, 25 and 26, *The Illustrated
London News* Picture Library; 15, 19 and 30, Mary Evans Picture Library.

Library of Congress Cataloging-in-Publication Data

MacMillan, Margaret Olwen.
[Peacemakers]
Paris 1919 : six months that changed the world / Margaret MacMillan.—1st U.S. ed.
p. cm.
Originally published: Peacemakers. London : J. Murray, 2001.
Includes bibliographical references and index.
ISBN 0-375-50826-0
1. Paris Peace Conference (1919–1920)   2. World War, 1914–1918—Peace.
3. Treaty of Versailles (1919)   4. Germany—History—1918–1933.
5. Wilson, Woodrow, 1856–1924.   6. Germany—Boundaries.   I. Title.
D644 .M32 2002
940.3′141—dc21   2002023707

Random House website address: www.atrandom.com

Printed in the United States of America on acid-free paper

24689753

First U.S. Edition

Book design by Casey Hampton

To Eluned and Robert MacMillan

Foreword

Richard Holbrooke

In diplomacy, as in life itself, one often learns more from failures than from successes. Triumphs will seem, in retrospect, to be foreordained, a series of brilliant actions and decisions that may in fact have been lucky or inadvertent, whereas failures illuminate paths and pitfalls to be avoided—in the parlance of modern bureaucrats, lessons learned. With this in mind, it is time to look again at what happened in Paris in 1919. Margaret MacMillan's engrossing account of that seminal event contains some success stories, to be sure, but measured against the judgment of history and consequences, it is a study of flawed decisions with terrible consequences, many of which haunt us to this day.

In the headline version of history, the road from the Hall of Mirrors to the German invasion of Poland only twenty years later is usually presented as a straight line. But as MacMillan forcefully demonstrates, this widely accepted view of history distorts the nature of the decisions made in Paris and minimizes the importance of actions taken in the intervening years.

The manner in which the war ended—with an "armistice" and no fighting on German soil—played a significant role in subsequent events. "Things might have been different," MacMillan writes, "if Germany had been more thoroughly defeated." Most Germans outside the High Command did not realize that Germany was finished militarily, and therefore did not regard November 11, 1918, as a day of surrender. Hitler would capitalize on this; his promise to undo the Treaty of Versailles was a potent and popular theme during his rise to power. But MacMillan corrects the widely held view that the reparations payments imposed by the victors were so onerous as to have caused the wreck of the German economy that paved the way for Hitler.

By any standard, the cast of characters that assembled in Paris in 1919 was remarkable, from Lawrence of Arabia to a small Vietnamese kitchen hand later known as Ho Chi Minh. And for the first time in history, an American stood at the center of a great world drama. Woodrow Wilson inspired tens of millions who never met him, and frustrated those who worked with him. He was idealistic and remote, naïve and rigid, noble and conflicted. His strengths and weaknesses, his health, even the influence of his overbearing and ignorant wife, were all critical factors in events of historic importance.

In the eighty years since he left office, Wilson's reputation has risen and fallen regularly—but he remains as fascinating and central to an understanding of modern American foreign policy as ever. His many supporters, from Herbert Hoover to Robert McNamara, have argued that his enemies in both Paris and the United States Senate were responsible for the undoing of one of history's noblest dreams. Others, including Senator Jesse Helms, have viewed Wilson's determined adversary, Senator Henry Cabot Lodge, as a principled protector of American sovereignty and charged Wilson with seeking to undermine the American Constitution. Another school of thought, especially prevalent in the latter years of the Cold War, criticized Wilson for unrealistic, overly moralistic goals; among its best-known practitioners are George F. Kennan and Henry Kissinger, who accused Wilson of "extraordinary conceit," even while conceding that he "originated what would become the dominant intellectual school of American foreign policy." (To Kissinger's horror, *his* president, Richard Nixon, placed Wilson's portrait in the place of honor in the Cabinet Room.)

Through the fog of this never-ending debate, one thing is clear: as Wilson arrived in France in December 1918, he ignited great hopes throughout the world with his stirring Fourteen Points—especially the groundbreaking concept of "self-determination." Yet Wilson, often ill-informed or badly prepared for detailed negotiations, seemed vague as to what his own phrase actually meant. "When I gave utterance to those words," he admitted later, "I said them without the knowledge that nationalities existed, which are coming to us day after day."

Even at the time it was recognized that the concept of self-determination was, as MacMillan puts it, "controversial and opaque." "When the President talks of 'self-determination,'" Secretary of State Robert Lansing asked, "what unit has he in mind? Does he mean a race, a territorial area, or a community? . . . It will raise hopes which can never be realized. It will, I fear, cost thousands of lives. In the end it is bound to be discredited, to be called the dream of an idealist who failed to realize the danger until it was too late."

Lansing was one of the first to recognize a dilemma that lies at the core of many of today's bitterest disputes. Still, it was not Wilson's dreams but his decision to compromise them (by letting Japan take the Shantung peninsula in China, for example) that cost the world so dearly. Ironically, when Wilson returned home, he made the opposite mistake: by refusing to make relatively minor compromises with Senate moderates, he lost his chance to get the treaty (and American membership in the League of Nations) ratified.

Some of the most intractable problems of the modern world have roots in decisions made right after the end of the Great War. Among them one could list the four Balkan wars between 1991 and 1999; the crisis over Iraq (whose present borders resulted from Franco-British rivalries and casual mapmaking); the continuing quest of the Kurds for self-determination; disputes between Greece and Turkey; and the endless struggle between Arabs and Jews over land that each thought had been promised them.

As the peacemakers met in Paris, new nations emerged and great empires died. Excessively ambitious, the Big Four set out to do nothing less than fix the world, from Europe to the far Pacific. But facing domestic pressures, events they could not control, and conflicting claims they could not reconcile, the negotiators were, in the end, simply overwhelmed—and made deals and compromises that would echo down through history.

Even then, they sensed that they were laying the seeds for future problems. "I cannot say for how many years, perhaps I should say for how many centuries, the crisis which has begun will continue," predicted Georges Clemenceau, whose own behavior contributed to the failure. "Yes, this treaty will bring us burdens, troubles, miseries, difficulties, and that will continue for long years."

MacMillan brings back to life some great dramas: the Italian walkout after the failure of their effort to gain control of much of the Yugoslav coast; the Japanese grab of the Shantung peninsula, which launched the May Fourth Movement in China and started the path to war and revolution in Asia; the dismemberment of Hungary, which left millions of Hungarians permanently outside their own country's borders; the inability of the Big Four to deal with the new Soviet government, other than by sending a feckless expeditionary force into the Russian civil war; the dissolution of the Ottoman empire and the rise of one of the twentieth century's most remarkable leaders, Kemal Atatürk; and last but not least, the creation of Yugoslavia (originally, the Kingdom of the Serbs, Croats, and Slovenes) out of the disparate peoples of the south Balkans. This state would survive under Marshal Tito's communist dictatorship for decades, but when the patchwork put together in 1919 fell apart in the early 1990s, four wars followed—first Slovenia, then Croatia, then Bosnia-Herzegovina, and finally Kosovo. (A fifth, in Macedonia, was barely averted.)

As our American negotiating team shuttled around the Balkans in the fall of 1995 trying to end the war in Bosnia, the Versailles treaty was not far from my mind. Reading excerpts from Harold Nicolson's *Peacemaking 1919,* we joked that our goal was to undo Woodrow Wilson's legacy. When we forced the leaders of Bosnia, Croatia, and the Federal Republic of Yugoslavia to come together in Dayton, Ohio, in November 1995 and negotiate the end of the war, we were, in effect, burying another part of Versailles. In the spring of 2002, the last two parts of the Versailles creation still linked as "Yugoslavia" took another step, moving to the brink of a full and final divorce by agreeing to rename their country "Serbia and Montenegro"—probably a way station on the path to full separation.

At Dayton we were working on only one small part of the puzzle; in Paris they worked on the world. Margaret MacMillan's brilliant portrait of the men of Paris, what they tried to do, where they succeeded, and why they failed, is especially timely now. This story illuminates, as only great history can, not only the past but also the present. It could help guide us in the future. I only regret that it was not available a decade ago. But here it is: an irresistible voyage through history.

Acknowledgments

This book has my name on the title page, but it would not exist without the great many people who encouraged me to tackle such a huge subject, who prodded me on when I got discouraged and who bore with me when I only wanted to talk about the League of Nations. I must single out some for particular thanks. Sandra Hargreaves, Avi Shlaim, Peter Snow and Lord Weidenfeld helped turn an idea into a serious project. Grant McIntyre and Matthew Taylor provided invaluable and meticulous editing in London, matched only by the outstanding work of Joy de Menil and her team in New York. I owe an immeasurable intellectual debt to my colleague and friend Bob Bothwell, who over the years helped me to clarify my ideas not just on the Peace Conference but on the writing of history. Orde Morton, Thomas Barcsay, David MacMillan, Catharina MacMillan, Thomas MacMillan, Alex MacMillan, Megan MacMillan, Ann MacMillan, Peter Snow, Daniel Snow and Barbara Eastman read parts and gave me much-needed advice. My parents, Eluned and Robert MacMillan, read every word, often several times, without complaint. I had two outstanding researchers: Rebecca Snow, who found the illustrations, and John Ondrovcik, who checked the text and compiled the bibliography. Bob Manson, Al Wargo and Errol Aspevig provided support for my research at different stages.

For their consent to quote from material in their collections or for which they hold copyright, I am grateful to the following: the National Archives of Scotland for the Lothian Papers (GD 40/17); Nigel Nicolson for Harold Nicolson, *Peacemaking, 1919* (London: Methuen, 1964); the Clerk of the Records, House of Lords Record Office, acting on behalf of the Beaverbrook Foundation Trust for the Lloyd George Papers; Princeton University Press for Arthur S. Link, ed., *The Deliberations of the Council of Four,* 2 volumes (Princeton, N.J.: Princeton University Press, 1992); and the Trustees of the British Library for the Balfour Papers. Every effort has been made to trace copyright holders, but in the event of any omissions the author would be glad to hear from them.

I am grateful as well to my former employer, Ryerson University, for giving me time and to St. Antony's College, Oxford, for a wonderful term as a Senior Associate Member. The Snows and MacMillans in London and the Daniel-Shlaims in Oxford offered unstinting hospitality and encouragement. If this book does not reflect all this, the fault is mine.

Contents

NOTE ON PLACE-NAMES

Many of the places mentioned in this book have several names. For example, L'viv (in present-day Ukraine) is variously Léopol, Lemberg, Lwów or Lvov. I have generally given the names currently used, but where there is a familiar name in English, for example Munich, I have used that. In the case of particular controversies at the Peace Conference, I have followed the usage of 1919: Danzig (Gdańsk), Fiume (Rijeka), Memel (Klaipėda), Shantung (Shandong), Teschen (Cieszyn or Těšín), Tsingtao (Qingdao).

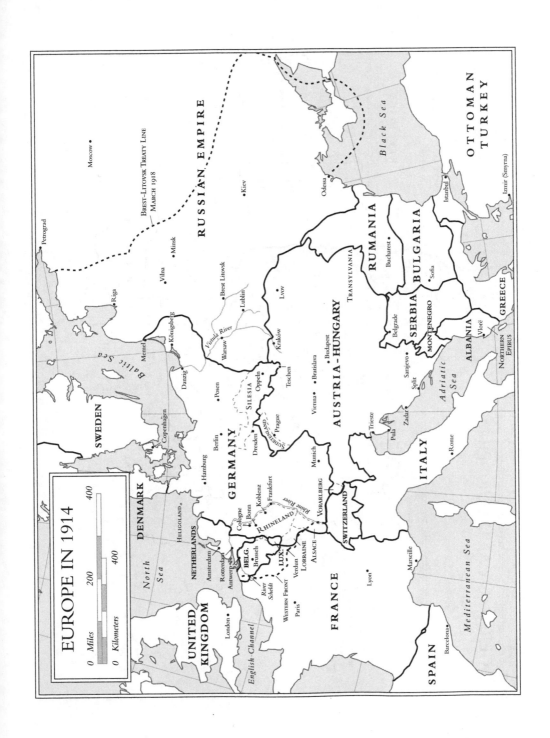

EUROPE IN 1914

Miles
0   200   400

Kilometers
0   400

UNITED KINGDOM
London

English Channel

North Sea

NETHERLANDS
Amsterdam
Rotterdam
Antwerp

BELG.
Brussels

River Scheldt

WESTERN FRONT
Paris

FRANCE

Lyon

Marseille

SPAIN
Barcelona

LUX.
Verdun
LORRAINE
ALSACE

RHINELAND
Cologne
Bonn
Koblenz
Frankfurt

Rhine River

VORARLBERG
SWITZERLAND

Mediterranean Sea

DENMARK
Copenhagen
HELIGOLAND

SWEDEN

Baltic Sea

Hamburg
Berlin
Dresden

GERMANY

Memel
Königsberg
Danzig
Posen
SILESIA
Oppeln
SUDETENLAND
Prague

Munich

Vienna

AUSTRIA-HUNGARY

Bratislava
Budapest

Teschen
Kraków

Warsaw
Vistula River

Riga

Vilna
Minsk

RUSSIAN EMPIRE

Petrograd

Moscow

BREST-LITOVSK TREATY LINE
MARCH 1918

Brest Litowsk
Lublin

Lvov

Kiev

TRANSYLVANIA

RUMANIA
Bucharest

Odesa

Black Sea

BULGARIA
Sofia

SERBIA
Belgrade

MONTENEGRO

Sarajevo
Split
Zadar

Trieste
Pola

Adriatic Sea

ITALY

Rome

ALBANIA
Vlorë

NORTHERN EPIRUS

GREECE

Istanbul

OTTOMAN TURKEY

Izmir (Smyrna)

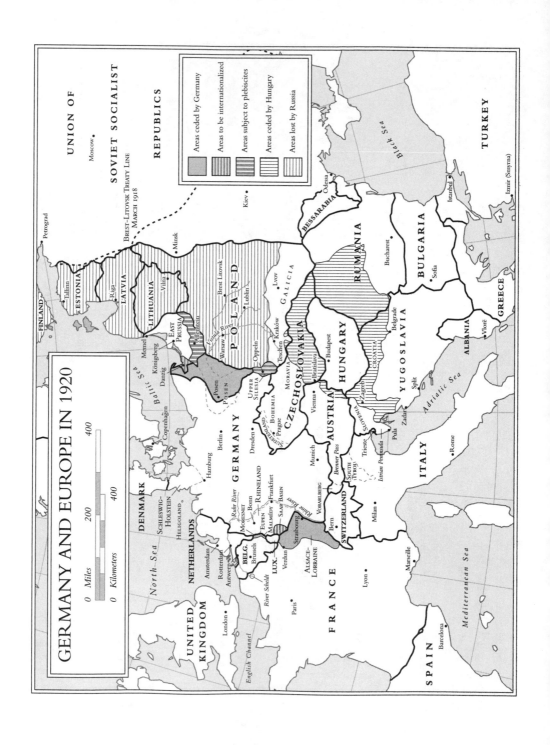

GERMANY AND EUROPE IN 1920

Areas ceded by Germany
Areas to be internationalized
Areas subject to plebiscites
Areas ceded by Hungary
Areas lost by Russia

UNION OF SOVIET SOCIALIST REPUBLICS

BREST-LITOVSK TREATY LINE
MARCH 1918

FINLAND

ESTONIA

LATVIA

LITHUANIA

EAST PRUSSIA

P O L A N D

Petrograd

Moscow

Tallinn

Riga

Vilna

Minsk

Brest Litovsk

Lublin

Kiev

Odessa

BESSARABIA

RUMANIA

Bucharest

BULGARIA

Sofia

TURKEY

Istanbul

Izmir (Smyrna)

GREECE

ALBANIA

Vlorë

YUGOSLAVIA

Belgrade

CROATIA

Split

Zadar

SLOVENIA

Zagreb

Pula

Adriatic Sea

Black Sea

GALICIA

Lvov

Kraków

Teschen

Oppeln

UPPER SILESIA

POSEN

Posen

Warsaw

Vistula River

Allenstein

Memel

Königsberg

Danzig

Copenhagen

Baltic Sea

DENMARK

SCHLESWIG-HOLSTEIN

HELIGOLAND

North Sea

Hamburg

Berlin

Dresden

G E R M A N Y

Prague

BOHEMIA

MORAVIA

SUDETENLAND

CZECHOSLOVAKIA

Bratislava

Vienna

Budapest

HUNGARY

AUSTRIA

Munich

Brenner Pass

SOUTH TIROL

VORARLBERG

SWITZERLAND

Bern

Milan

Trieste

Istrian Peninsula

ITALY

Rome

Marseille

Lyon

Ruhr River

RHINELAND

Bonn

MOERSNET

EUPEN

MALMÉDY

Frankfurt

SAAR BASIN

Rhine River

Strasbourg

ALSACE-LORRAINE

Verdun

LUX.

BELG.

Brussels

Antwerp

Rotterdam

Amsterdam

NETHERLANDS

River Scheldt

London

UNITED KINGDOM

Paris

F R A N C E

English Channel

SPAIN

Barcelona

Mediterranean Sea

0   Miles   200   400

0   Kilometers   400

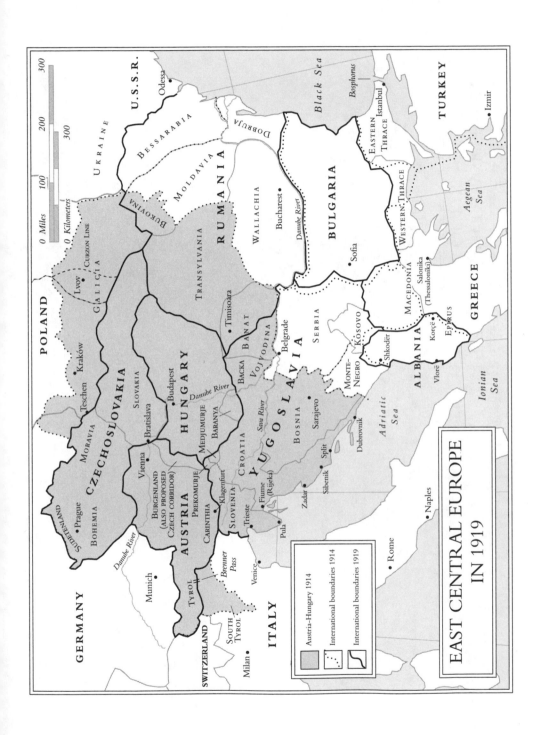

EAST CENTRAL EUROPE
IN 1919

Legend:
Austria-Hungary 1914
International boundaries 1914
International boundaries 1919

Scale:
0 Miles 100 200 300
0 Kilometers 300

GERMANY

POLAND

U.S.S.R.

UKRAINE

Odessa

BESSARABIA

Munich

SWITZERLAND

Milan

ITALY

Rome

Naples

Venice

SOUTH TYROL

Brenner Pass

TYROL

Danube River

AUSTRIA

Vienna

BURGENLAND (ALSO PROPOSED CZECH CORRIDOR)

Bratislava

CZECHOSLOVAKIA

SUDETENLAND

Prague

BOHEMIA

MORAVIA

Teschen

Kraków

SLOVAKIA

CURZON LINE

Lvov

GALICIA

BUKOVINA

MOLDAVIA

RUMANIA

TRANSYLVANIA

Timișoara

BANAT

WALLACHIA

Bucharest

Danube River

DOBRUJA

Budapest

HUNGARY

Danube River

MEDJUMURJE

BARANYA

PREKOMURJE

CARINTHIA

Klagenfurt

SLOVENIA

Trieste

Fiume (Rijeka)

Pula

Zadar

Šibenik

Split

CROATIA

VOJVODINA

BAČKA

Belgrade

Sava River

BOSNIA

Sarajevo

Dubrovnik

YUGOSLAVIA

SERBIA

KOSOVO

MONTE-NEGRO

Shkodër

ALBANIA

Vlorë

Korçë

EPIRUS

MACEDONIA

Salonika (Thessaloniki)

GREECE

BULGARIA

Sofia

WESTERN THRACE

EASTERN THRACE

Istanbul

Bosphorus

TURKEY

Izmir

Black Sea

Aegean Sea

Ionian Sea

Adriatic Sea

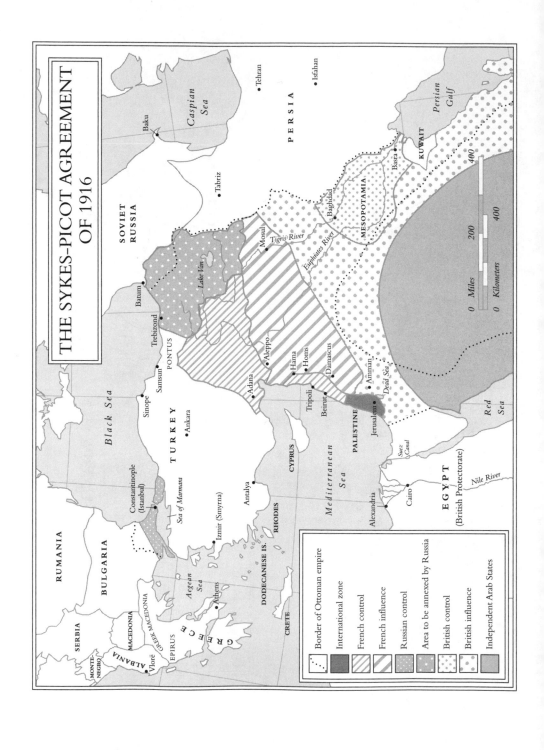

THE SYKES-PICOT AGREEMENT OF 1916

Legend:
- Border of Ottoman empire
- International zone
- French control
- French influence
- Russian control
- Area to be annexed by Russia
- British control
- British influence
- Independent Arab States

SOVIET RUSSIA

PERSIA

Caspian Sea

- Tehran
- Isfahan
- Baku
- Tabriz

Persian Gulf

KUWAIT

MESOPOTAMIA

- Basra
- Baghdad
- Mosul

Tigris River
Euphrates River

Lake Van
- Batum
- Trebizond
PONTUS
- Samsun
- Sinope

Black Sea

TURKEY
- Ankara

- Aleppo
- Adana
- Hama
- Homs
- Damascus
- Amman

Dead Sea

Red Sea

- Tripoli
- Beirut
- Jerusalem
PALESTINE

Suez Canal

Mediterranean Sea

CYPRUS

- Constantinople (Istanbul)
Sea of Marmara

- Izmir (Smyrna)
- Antalya

RHODES
DODECANESE IS.

Aegean Sea

- Athens

CRETE

GREECE

EPIRUS
- Vlorë
ALBANIA
MONTE-NEGRO
SERBIA
MACEDONIA
GREEK MACEDONIA
BULGARIA
RUMANIA

EGYPT
(British Protectorate)

- Alexandria
- Cairo

Nile River

0   200   400 Miles
0   400 Kilometers

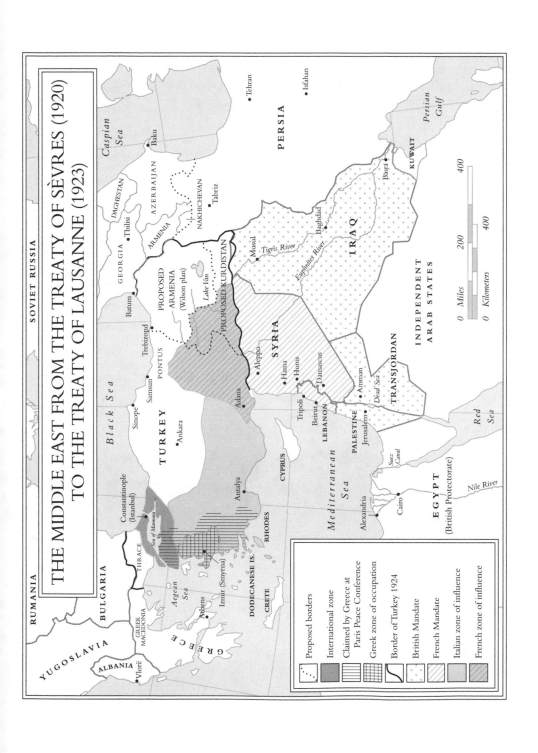

THE MIDDLE EAST FROM THE TREATY OF SÈVRES (1920) TO THE TREATY OF LAUSANNE (1923)

RUMANIA

YUGOSLAVIA

BULGARIA

ALBANIA

Vlorë

THRACE

GREEK MACEDONIA

G R E E C E

Athens

Aegean Sea

CRETE

DODECANESE IS.

RHODES

CYPRUS

SOVIET RUSSIA

Caspian Sea

Baku

DAGHESTAN

GEORGIA

Tbilisi

ARMENIA

AZERBAIJAN

NAKHICHEVAN

Tabriz

Batum

Trebizond

PROPOSED ARMENIA (Wilson plan)

Lake Van

PROPOSED KURDISTAN

Samsun

Sinope

PONTUS

Black Sea

TURKEY

Ankara

Adana

Antalya

Constantinople (Istanbul)

Sea of Marmara

Izmir (Smyrna)

Mediterranean Sea

PERSIA

Tehran

Isfahan

Persian Gulf

KUWAIT

Basra

Baghdad

Mosul

Tigris River

Euphrates River

I R A Q

S Y R I A

Aleppo

Hama

Homs

Damascus

Tripoli

Beirut

LEBANON

PALESTINE

Jerusalem

Amman

TRANSJORDAN

Dead Sea

I N D E P E N D E N T
A R A B   S T A T E S

Red Sea

Suez Canal

E G Y P T
(British Protectorate)

Alexandria

Cairo

Nile River

0   200   400   Miles

0   400   Kilometers

Proposed borders

International zone

Claimed by Greece at Paris Peace Conference

Greek zone of occupation

Border of Turkey 1924

British Mandate

French Mandate

Italian zone of influence

French zone of influence

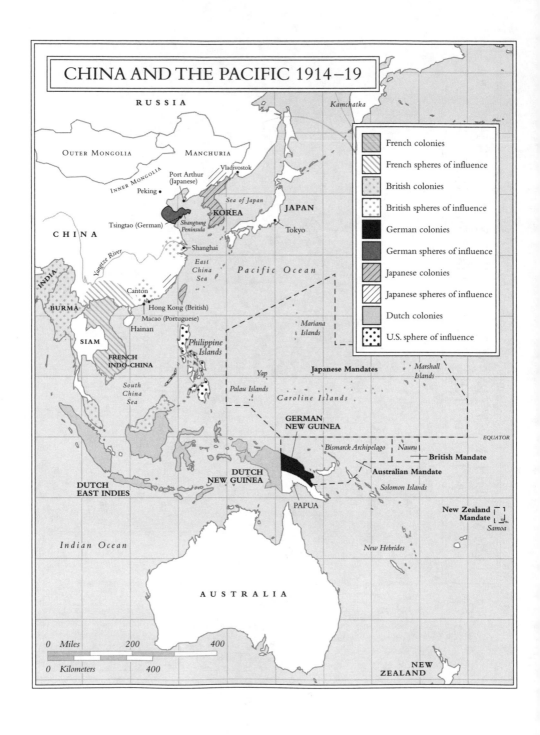

CHINA AND THE PACIFIC 1914–19

RUSSIA

Kamchatka

OUTER MONGOLIA · MANCHURIA

INNER MONGOLIA

Vladivostok

Port Arthur (Japanese)

Peking

Tsingtao (German)

Sea of Japan

KOREA

Shantung Peninsula

JAPAN

Tokyo

CHINA

Yangtze River

Shanghai

East China Sea

Pacific Ocean

Canton

Hong Kong (British)

Macao (Portuguese)

Hainan

INDIA

BURMA

SIAM

FRENCH INDO-CHINA

Philippine Islands

South China Sea

Yap

Palau Islands

Caroline Islands

Mariana Islands

Japanese Mandates

Marshall Islands

GERMAN NEW GUINEA

Bismarck Archipelago · *Nauru*

EQUATOR

+ British Mandate

DUTCH NEW GUINEA

Australian Mandate

DUTCH EAST INDIES

Solomon Islands

PAPUA

New Zealand Mandate

Samoa

Indian Ocean

New Hebrides

AUSTRALIA

0 Miles   200   400

0 Kilometers   400

NEW ZEALAND

Legend

	French colonies
	French spheres of influence
	British colonies
	British spheres of influence
	German colonies
	German spheres of influence
	Japanese colonies
	Japanese spheres of influence
	Dutch colonies
	U.S. sphere of influence

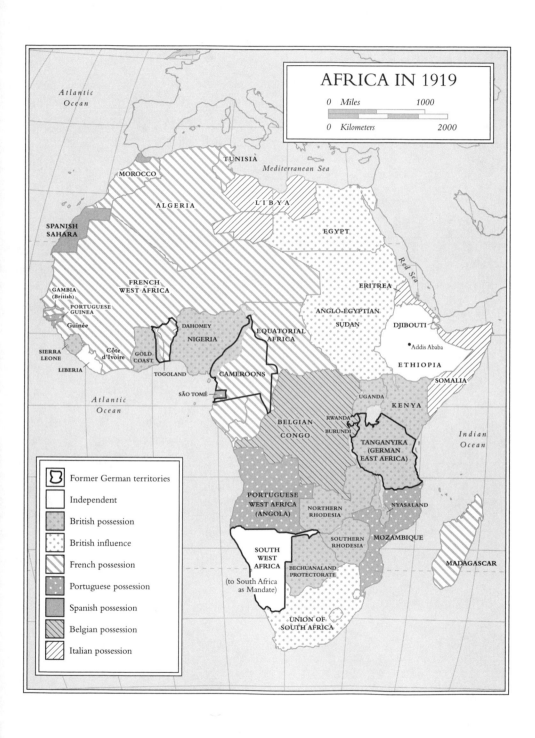

AFRICA IN 1919

0 Miles   1000

0 Kilometers   2000

Atlantic Ocean

Mediterranean Sea

MOROCCO
TUNISIA
ALGERIA
LIBYA
EGYPT

SPANISH SAHARA

Red Sea

GAMBIA (British)
PORTUGUESE GUINEA
Guinée
SIERRA LEONE
LIBERIA
Côte d'Ivoire
GOLD COAST
TOGOLAND
DAHOMEY
NIGERIA

FRENCH WEST AFRICA

ERITREA

ANGLO-EGYPTIAN SUDAN

DJIBOUTI

•Addis Ababa

ETHIOPIA

SOMALIA

EQUATORIAL AFRICA

CAMEROONS

SÃO TOMÉ

Atlantic Ocean

UGANDA
KENYA

BELGIAN CONGO

RWANDA
BURUNDI

TANGANYIKA (GERMAN EAST AFRICA)

Indian Ocean

PORTUGUESE WEST AFRICA (ANGOLA)

NORTHERN RHODESIA

NYASALAND

SOUTHERN RHODESIA

MOZAMBIQUE

MADAGASCAR

SOUTH WEST AFRICA

(to South Africa as Mandate)

BECHUANALAND PROTECTORATE

UNION OF SOUTH AFRICA

Legend

- Former German territories
- Independent
- British possession
- British influence
- French possession
- Portuguese possession
- Spanish possession
- Belgian possession
- Italian possession

Introduction

FOR SIX MONTHS IN 1919, Paris was the capital of the world. The Peace Conference was the world's most important business, the peacemakers its most powerful people. They met day after day. They argued, debated, quarreled and made it up again. They created new countries and new organizations. They dined together and went to the theater together, and between January and June, Paris was at once the world's government, its court of appeal and its parliament, the focus of its fears and hopes. Officially, the Peace Conference lasted into 1920, but those first six months are the ones that count, when the key decisions were taken and the crucial chains of events set in motion. The world has never seen anything quite like it and never will again.

The peacemakers were there because proud, confident, rich Europe had torn itself to pieces. A war that had started in 1914 over a squabble for power and influence in the Balkans had drawn in all the great powers, from tsarist Russia in the east to Britain in the west, and most of the smaller ones. Only Spain, Switzerland, the Netherlands and the Scandinavian countries had managed to stay out. There had been fighting in Asia, in Africa, in the Pacific islands and in the Middle East, but most had been on European soil, along the crazed network of trenches that stretched from Belgium in the north down to the Alps in the south, along Russia's borders with Germany and its ally Austria-Hungary, and in the Balkans themselves. Soldiers had come from around the world: Australians, Canadians, New Zealanders, Indians, Newfoundlanders to fight for the British empire; Vietnamese, Moroccans, Algerians, Senegalese for France; and finally the Americans, maddened beyond endurance by German attacks on their shipping.

Away from the battlefields, Europe still looked much the same. The great cities remained, the railway lines were more or less intact, ports still functioned. It was not like the Second World War, when the very bricks and mortar were pulverized. The loss was human. Millions of combatants—for the time of massive killing of civilians had not yet come—died in those four years: 1,800,000 Germans, 1,700,000 Russians, 1,384,000 French, 1,290,000 from Austria-Hungary, 743,000 British (and another 192,000 from the empire) and so on down the list to tiny Montenegro, with 3,000 men. Children lost fathers, wives husbands, young women the chance of marriage. And Europe lost those who might have been its scientists, its poets and its leaders, and the children who might have been born to them. But the tally of deaths does not include those who were left with one leg, one arm or one eye, or those whose lungs had been scarred by poison gas or whose nerves never recovered.

For four years the most advanced nations in the world had poured out their men, their wealth, the fruits of their industry, science and technology, on a war that may have started by accident but was impossible to stop because the two sides were too evenly balanced. It was only in the summer of 1918, as Germany's allies faltered and as the fresh American troops poured in, that the Allies finally gained the upper hand. When the war ended on 11 November, everywhere people hoped wearily that whatever happened next would not be as bad as what had just come to an end.

Four years of war shook forever the supreme self-confidence that had carried Europe to world dominance. After the Western Front, Europeans could no longer talk of a civilizing mission to the world. The war toppled governments, humbled the mighty and upturned whole societies. In Russia the revolutions of 1917 replaced tsarism, with what no one yet knew. At the end of the war Austria-Hungary vanished, leaving a great hole at the center of Europe. The Ottoman empire, with its vast holdings in the Middle East and its bit of Europe, was almost done. Imperial Germany was now a republic. Old nations—Poland, Lithuania, Estonia, Latvia—came out of history to live again, and new nations—Yugoslavia and Czechoslovakia—struggled to be born.

The Paris Peace Conference is usually remembered for producing the German treaty, signed at Versailles in June 1919, but it was always about much more than that. The other enemies—Bulgaria, Austria and Hungary, now separate countries, and the Ottoman empire—had to have their treaties. New borders had to be drawn in the center of Europe and across the Middle East. Most important of all, the international order had to be re-created on a new and different basis. Was the time now ripe for an International Labour Organization, a League of Nations, for agreements on international telegraph cables or international aviation? After such a great catastrophe, the expectations were enormous.

Even before the guns fell silent in 1918 the voices, plaintive, demanding, angry, had started. "China belongs to the Chinese." "Kurdistan must be free." "Poland must live again." They spoke in many languages. They made many demands. The United States must be the world's policeman; or, The Americans must go home. The Russians need help; no, They must be left to their own devices. They complained: Slovaks about Czechs; Croats about Serbs; Arabs about Jews; Chinese about Japanese. The voices were worried, uncertain whether the new world order would be an improvement on the old. In the West, they murmured about dangerous ideas coming from the East; in the East, they pondered the threat of Western materialism. Europeans wondered if they would ever recover and how they would manage their brash new American ally. Africans feared that the world had forgotten them. Asians saw that the future was theirs; it was only the present that was the problem.

We know something of what it is to live at the end of a great war. The voices of 1919 were very like the voices of the present. When the Cold War ended in 1989 and Soviet Marxism vanished into the dustbin of history, older forces, religion and nationalism, came out of their deep freeze. Bosnia and Rwanda have reminded us of how strong those forces can be. In 1919, there was the same sense of a new order emerging as borders suddenly shifted and new economic and political ideas were in the air. It was exciting but also frightening, in a world that seemed perilously fragile. Today, some argue, resurgent Islam is the menace. In 1919, it was Russian Bolshevism. The difference is that we have not held a universal peace conference. There is not the time. The statesmen and their advisers meet in brief meetings, for two, perhaps three days, and then take flight again. Who knows which is the better way of settling the world's problems?

To struggle with the great issues of the day and try to resolve them, statesmen, diplomats, bankers, soldiers, professors, economists and lawyers came to Paris from all corners of the world: the American president, Woodrow Wilson, and his secretary of state, Robert Lansing; Georges Clemenceau and Vittorio Orlando, the prime ministers of France and Italy; Lawrence of Arabia, wrapped in mystery and Arab robes; Eleutherios Venizelos, the great Greek patriot who brought disaster on his country; Ignace Paderewski, the pianist turned Polish politician; and many who had yet to make their mark, among them two future American secretaries of state, a future prime minister of Japan and the first president of Israel. Some had been born to power, such as Queen Marie of Rumania; others, such as David Lloyd George, the prime minister of Britain, had won it through their own efforts.

The concentration of power drew in the world's reporters, its businessmen, and spokesmen and spokeswomen for a myriad of causes. "One only meets people off to Paris," wrote the French ambassador in London. "Paris is going to become a place of amusement for hundreds of English, Americans, Italians and shady foreign gentlemen who are descending on us under the pretext of taking part in the peace discussions."[1] Votes for women, rights for blacks, a charter for labor, freedom for Ireland, disarmament: the petitions and the petitioners rolled in daily from all quarters of the world. That winter and spring, Paris hummed with schemes, for a Jewish homeland, a restored Poland, an independent Ukraine, a Kurdistan, an Armenia. The petitions poured in, from the Conference of Suffrage Societies, the Carpatho-Russian Committee in Paris, the Serbs of the Banat, the anti-Bolshevik Russian Political Conference. The petitioners came from countries that existed and ones that were just dreams. Some, such as the Zionists, spoke for millions; others, such as the representatives of the Åland islands in the Baltic, for a few thousand. A few arrived too late; the Koreans from Siberia set out on foot in February 1919 and by the time the main part of the Peace Conference ended in June had reached only the Arctic port of Archangel.[2]

From the outset the Peace Conference suffered from confusion over its organization, its purpose and its procedures. The Big Four—Britain, France, Italy and the United States—had planned a preliminary conference to hammer out the terms to be offered, after which they intended to hold a full-scale peace conference to negotiate with the enemy. Immediately there were questions. When would the other allied powers be able to express their views? Japan, for example, was already an important power in the Far East. And what about the smaller powers such as Serbia and Belgium? Both had lost far more men than Japan.

The Big Four gave way, but the plenary sessions of the conference became ritual occasions. The real work was done by the Four and Japan in informal meetings, and when those in turn became too cumbersome, by the leaders of the Four alone. As the months went by, what had been a preliminary conference imperceptibly became the real thing. In a break with diplomatic precedent that infuriated the Germans, their representatives were eventually summoned to France to receive their treaty in its final form.

The peacemakers had hoped to be brisker and better organized. They had carefully studied the only available example—the Congress of Vienna, which wound up the Napoleonic Wars. The Foreign Office commissioned a distinguished historian to write a book on the Congress for guidance in Paris. (He later conceded that his work had almost no impact.[3]) The problems faced by the peacemakers in Vienna, large though they were, were straightforward by comparison with those in Paris. The

British foreign secretary at the time, Lord Castlereagh, took just fourteen staff with him to Vienna; in 1919 the British delegation numbered nearly four hundred. In 1815 matters were settled quietly and at leisure: Castlereagh and his colleagues would have been appalled at the intense public scrutiny of 1919. There were also many more participants: more than thirty countries sent delegates to Paris, including Italy, Belgium, Rumania and Serbia, none of which had existed in 1815. The Latin American nations had still been part of the Spanish and Portuguese empires. Thailand, China and Japan had been remote, mysterious lands. Now their diplomats appeared in Paris in pinstriped trousers and frock coats. Apart from a declaration condemning the slave trade, the Congress of Vienna paid no attention to the non-European world. In Paris, the subjects covered by the Peace Conference ranged from the Arctic to the Antipodes, from small islands in the Pacific to whole continents.

The Congress of Vienna also took place when the great upheavals set off by the French Revolution in 1789 had subsided. By 1815 its effects had been absorbed, but in 1919 the Russian Revolution was only two years old, its impact on the rest of the world unclear. Western leaders saw Bolshevism seeping out of Russia, threatening religion, tradition, every tie that held their societies together. In Germany and Austria, soviets of workers and soldiers were already seizing power in the cities and towns. Their own soldiers and sailors mutinied. Paris, Lyon, Brussels, Glasgow, San Francisco, even sleepy Winnipeg on the Canadian prairies had general strikes. Were these isolated outbreaks or flames from a vast underground fire?

The peacemakers of 1919 believed they were working against time. They had to draw new lines on the maps of Europe, just as their predecessors had done in Vienna, but they also had to think of Asia, Africa and the Middle East. "Self-determination" was the watchword, but this was not a help in choosing among competing nationalisms. The peacemakers had to act as policemen and they had to feed the hungry. If they could, they had to create an international order that would make another Great War impossible. And, of course, they had to draw up the treaties. Clearly Germany had to be dealt with, penalized for starting the war (or was it just for losing, as many suspected?), its future set on more pacific lines, its boundaries adjusted to compensate France in the West and the new nations in the East. Bulgaria had to have its treaty. So did the Ottoman empire. Austria-Hungary presented a particular problem, for it no longer existed. All that was left was a tiny Austria and a shaky Hungary, with most of their territory gone to new nations. The expectations of the Peace Conference were enormous; the risk of disappointment correspondingly great.

The peacemakers also represented their own countries, and since most of these were democracies, they had to heed their public opinion. They were bound to think ahead to the next election and to weigh the costs of appeasing or alienating important sections of opinion. They were thus not completely free agents. It was also a time to bring out the old demands and the new ones. Clemenceau complained to a colleague: "It is much easier to make war than peace."[4]

In their months in Paris the peacemakers were to achieve much: a peace treaty with Germany and the bases for peace with Austria, Hungary and Bulgaria. They drew new borders through the middle of Europe and the Middle East. Much of their work, it is true, did not last. People said at the time, as they have ever since, that the peacemakers took too long and that they got it wrong. It has become a commonplace to say that the peace settlements of 1919 were a failure, that they led directly to the Second World War. That is to overestimate their power.

There were two realities in the world of 1919, and they did not always mesh. One was in Paris and the other was on the ground, where people were making their own decisions and fighting their own battles. True, the peacemakers had armies and navies, but where there were few railways, roads or ports, as in the interior of Asia Minor or the Caucasus, moving their forces was slow and laborious. The new aircraft were not yet big enough or strong enough to fill that gap. In the center of Europe, where the tracks were already laid, the collapse of order meant that even if tracks, engines and cars were available, the fuel was not. "It really is no use abusing this or that small state," Henry Wilson, one of the cleverest of the British generals, told Lloyd George. "The root of evil is that the *Paris writ does not run*."[5]

Power involves will, as the United States and the world are discovering today: the will to spend, whether money or lives. In 1919 that will had been spent in Europe. The leaders of France, Britain and Italy no longer had the capacity to order their peoples to pay a high price for power. Their armed forces were shrinking day by day and they could not rely on the soldiers and sailors who were left. Their taxpayers wanted an end to expensive foreign adventures. The United States alone had the capacity to act, but it did not see itself as having that role, and its power was not yet great enough. It is tempting to say that the United States lost an opportunity to bend Europe to its will before the competing ideologies of fascism and communism could take hold. That is to read back into the past what we know about American power after another great war. In 1945, the United States was a superpower and the European nations were much weakened. In 1919, however, the United States was not yet significantly stronger than the other powers. The Europeans could ignore its wishes, and they did.

Armies, navies, railways, economies, ideologies, history: all these are important in understanding the Paris Peace Conference. But so, too, are individuals because, in the end, people draw up reports, make decisions and order armies to move. The peacemakers brought their own national interests with them, but they also brought their likes and dislikes. Nowhere were these more important than among the powerful men—especially Clemenceau, Lloyd George and Wilson—who sat down together in Paris.

PART ONE

GETTING READY
FOR PEACE

1

Woodrow Wilson Comes to Europe

O N DECEMBER 4, 1918, the *George Washington* sailed out of New York with the American delegation to the Peace Conference on board. Guns fired salutes, crowds along the waterfront cheered, tugboats hooted and Army planes and dirigibles circled overhead. Robert Lansing, the American secretary of state, released carrier pigeons with messages to his relatives about his deep hope for a lasting peace. The ship, a former German passenger liner, slid out past the Statue of Liberty to the Atlantic, where an escort of destroyers and battleships stood by to accompany it and its cargo of heavy expectations to Europe.[1]

On board were the best available experts, combed out of the universities and the government; crates of reference materials and special studies; the French and Italian ambassadors to the United States; and Woodrow Wilson. No other American president had ever gone to Europe while in office. His opponents accused him of breaking the Constitution; even his supporters felt he might be unwise. Would he lose his great moral authority by getting down to the hurly-burly of negotiations? Wilson's own view was clear: the making of the peace was as important as the winning of the war. He owed it to the peoples of Europe, who were crying out for a better world. He owed it to the American servicemen. "It is now my duty," he told a pensive Congress just before he left, "to play my full part in making good what they gave their life's blood to obtain." A British diplomat was more cynical; Wilson, he said, was drawn to Paris "as a debutante is entranced by the prospect of her first ball."[2]

Wilson expected, he wrote to his great friend Edward House, who was already in Europe, that he would stay only to arrange the main outlines of the peace settlements. It was not likely that he would remain for the formal Peace Conference with the enemy.[3] He was wrong. The preliminary conference turned, without anyone's intending it, into the final one, and Wilson stayed for most of the crucial six months between January and June 1919. The question of whether or not he should have gone to Paris, which exercised so many of his contemporaries, now seems unimportant. From Franklin Roosevelt at Yalta to Jimmy Carter or Bill Clinton at Camp David, American presidents have sat down to draw borders and hammer out peace agreements. Wilson had set the conditions for the armistices which ended the Great War. Why should he not make the peace as well?

Although he had not started out in 1912 as a foreign policy president, circumstances and his own progressive political principles had drawn him outward. Like many of his compatriots, he had come to see the Great War as a struggle between the forces of democracy, however imperfectly represented by Britain and France, and those of reaction and militarism, represented all too well by Germany and Austria-Hungary. Germany's sack of Belgium, its unrestricted submarine warfare and its audacity in attempting to entice Mexico into waging war on the United States had pushed Wilson and American public opinion toward the Allies. When Russia had a democratic revolution in February 1917, one of the last reservations—that the Allies included an autocracy—vanished. Although he had campaigned in 1916 on a platform of keeping the country neutral, Wilson brought the United States into the war in April 1917. He was convinced that he was doing the right thing. This was important to the son of a Presbyterian minister, who shared his father's deep religious conviction, if not his calling.

Wilson was born in Virginia in 1856, just before the Civil War. Although he remained a Southerner in some ways all his life—in his insistence on honor and his paternalistic attitudes toward women and blacks—he also accepted the war's outcome. Abraham Lincoln was one of his great heroes, along with Edmund Burke and William Gladstone.[4] The young Wilson was at once highly idealistic and intensely ambitious. After four very happy years at Princeton and an unhappy stint as a lawyer, he found his first career in teaching and writing. By 1890 he was back at Princeton, a star member of the faculty. In 1902 he became its president, supported virtually unanimously by the trustees, faculty and students.

In the next eight years Wilson transformed Princeton from a sleepy college for gentlemen into a great university. He reworked the curriculum, raised significant amounts of money and brought into the faculty the brightest and the best young men from across the country. By 1910, he was a national figure and the Democratic party in New Jersey, under the control of conservative bosses, invited him to run for governor. Wilson agreed, but insisted on running on a progressive platform of controlling big business and extending democracy. He swept the state and by 1911 "Wilson for President" clubs were springing up. He spoke for the dispossessed, the disenfranchised and all those who had been left behind by the rapid economic growth of the late nineteenth century. In 1912, at a long and hard-fought convention, Wilson got the Democratic nomination for president. That November, with the Republicans split by Teddy Roosevelt's decision to run as a progressive against William Howard Taft, Wilson was elected. In 1916, he was reelected, with an even greater share of the popular vote.

Wilson's career was a series of triumphs, but there were darker moments, both personal and political, fits of depression and sudden and baffling illnesses. Moreover, he had left behind him a trail of enemies, many of them former friends. "An ingrate and a liar," said a Democratic boss in New Jersey in a toast. Wilson never forgave those who disagreed with him. "He is a good hater," said his press officer and devoted admirer Ray Stannard Baker.[5] He was also stubborn. As House said, with admiration: "Whenever a question is presented he keeps an absolutely open mind and welcomes all suggestion or advice which will lead to a correct decision. But he is receptive only during the period that he is weighing the question and preparing to make his decision. Once the decision is made it is final and there is an absolute end to all advice and suggestion. There is no moving him after that." What was admirable to some was a dangerous egotism to others. The French ambassador in Washington saw "a man who, had he lived a couple of centuries ago, would have been the greatest tyrant in the world, because he does not seem to have the slightest conception that he can ever be wrong."[6]

This side of Wilson's character was in evidence when he chose his fellow commissioners—or plenipotentiaries, as the chief delegates were known—to the Peace Conference. He was himself one. House, "my alter ego," as he was fond of saying, was another. Reluctantly he selected Lansing, his secretary of state, as a third, mainly because it would have been awkward to leave him behind. Where Wilson had once rather admired Lansing's vast store of knowledge, his meticulous legal mind and his apparent readiness to take a back seat, by 1919 that early liking had turned to irritation and contempt. Lansing, it turned out, did have views, often strong ones which contradicted the president's. "He has," Wilson complained to House, who noted it down with delight, "no imagination, no constructive ability, and but little real ability of any kind." The fourth plenipotentiary, General Tasker Bliss, was already in France as the American military representative on the Supreme War Council. A thoughtful and intelligent man who loved to lie in bed with a hip flask reading Thu-

cydides in the original Greek, he was also, many of the junior members of
the American delegation believed, well past his prime. Since Wilson was
to speak to him on only five occasions during the Peace Conference, perhaps that did not matter.

The president's final selection, Henry White, was a charming, affable
retired diplomat, the high point of whose career had been well before the
war. Mrs. Wilson was to find him useful in Paris on questions of eti-
quette.[7]

Wilson's selection caused an uproar in the United States at the time
and has caused controversy ever since. "A lot of cheapskates," said William
Taft. "I would swear if it would do any good." Wilson had deliberately
slighted the Republicans, most of whom had supported the war enthusi-
astically and many of whom now shared his vision of a League of Na-
tions. "I tell you what," the humorist Will Rogers had him saying to the
Republicans, "we will split 50–50—I will go and you fellows can stay."
Even his most partisan supporters had urged him to appoint men such as
Taft or the senior Republican senator on the important Committee on
Foreign Relations, Henry Cabot Lodge. Wilson refused, with a variety of
unconvincing excuses. The real reason was that he did not like or trust
Republicans. His decision was costly, because it undercut his position in
Paris and damaged his dream of a new world order with the United States
at its heart.[8]

Wilson remains puzzling in a way that Lloyd George and Clemenceau,
his close colleagues in Paris, do not. What is one to make of a leader who
drew on the most noble language of the Bible yet was so ruthless with
those who crossed him? Who loved democracy but despised most of his
fellow politicians? Who wanted to serve humanity but had so few personal
relationships? Was he, as Teddy Roosevelt thought, "as insincere and cold-
blooded an opportunist as we have ever had in the Presidency"? Or was
he, as Baker believed, one of those rare idealists like Calvin or Cromwell,
"who from time to time have appeared upon the earth & for a moment, in
burst of strange power, have temporarily lifted erring mankind to a higher
pitch of contentment than it was quite equal to"?[9]

Wilson wanted power and he wanted to do great works. What brought
the two sides of his character together was his ability, self-deception perhaps, to frame his decisions so that they became not merely necessary, but
morally right. Just as American neutrality in the first years of the war had
been right for Americans, and indeed for humanity, so the United States'
eventual entry into the war became a crusade, against human greed and
folly, against Germany and for justice, peace and civilization. This conviction, however, without which he could never have attempted what he did

in Paris, made Wilson intolerant of differences and blind to the legitimate concerns of others. Those who opposed him were not just wrong but wicked.

Like the Germans. The decision to go to war had been agony for Wilson. He had worked for a peace of compromise between the Allies and the Central Powers. Even when they had rejected his offer to mediate, when German submarines had sunk American ships, when opponents such as Roosevelt had attacked his cowardice and when his own cabinet had been unanimous for war, he had waited. In the end he decided to intervene because, as he saw it, Germany left him no alternative. "It is a fearful thing," he told Congress in April 1917, when he went before it to ask for a declaration of war, "to lead this great peaceful people into war, into the most terrible and disastrous of all wars, civilization itself seeming to be in the balance."[10] In Wilson's view Germany, or at the very least its leaders, bore a heavy burden of guilt. The Germans might be redeemed, but they also must be chastised.

The photographs taken in 1919 make him look like an undertaker, but in the flesh Wilson was a handsome man, with fine, straight features and a spare, upright frame. In his manner he had something of the preacher and of the university professor. He placed great faith in reason and facts, but he saw it as auspicious that he landed in Europe on Friday, December 13. Thirteen was his lucky number. A deeply emotional man, he mistrusted emotion in others. It was good when it brought people to desire the best, dangerous when, like nationalism, it intoxicated them. Lloyd George, who never entirely got his measure, listed his good qualities to a friend— "kindly, sincere, straightforward"—and then added in the next breath "tactless, obstinate and vain."[11]

In public, Wilson was stiff and formal, but with his intimates he was charming and even playful. He was particularly at ease with women. He was usually in perfect control of himself, but during the Peace Conference he frequently lost his temper. (It is possible he suffered a stroke while he was in Paris.) He loved puns and limericks and he liked to illustrate his points with folksy stories. He enjoyed doing accents: Scottish or Irish, like his ancestors, or Southern black, like the people who worked for him in Washington. He was abstemious in his habits; at most he would drink a small glass of whisky in an evening. He loved gadgets and liked the new moving pictures. On the voyage to Europe he generally went to the after-dinner picture shows. To general consternation the feature one evening was a melodrama called *The Second Wife*.[12]

Wilson's relations with women had always caused a certain amount of gossip. During his first marriage he had close, possibly even romantic, friendships with several women. His first wife, whom he had loved deeply if not passionately, had died in 1914; by the end of 1915, he was married again, to a wealthy Washington widow some seventeen years his junior. That this caused gossip bewildered and infuriated him. He never forgave a British diplomat for a joke that went around Washington: "What did the new Mrs. Wilson do when the President proposed? She fell out of bed with surprise." Wilson's own family and friends were more charitable. "Isn't it wonderful to see Father so happy," exclaimed a daughter. House, who was later to become Mrs. Wilson's bitter enemy, wrote in his diary that it was a relief that Wilson had someone to share his burdens: "his loneliness is pathetic."[13]

Edith Bolling, the new Mrs. Wilson, accompanied the president to Europe, a privilege not allowed lesser wives. She was warm and lively and laughed a great deal. She loved golf, shopping, orchids and parties. She had, everyone agreed, wonderful eyes, but some found her a bit plump and her mouth too large. She wore, they thought in Paris, her clothes a little too tight, the necks too low, the skirts too short. Wilson thought she was beautiful. Like him, she came from the South. She did not want to spoil her maid by taking her to London, she told a fellow American, because the British treated blacks too well. Although she had the easy flirtatious ways of a Southern woman, she was a shrewd businesswoman. After her first husband's death she had run the family jewelry store. When she married Wilson, he made it clear that he expected her to share his work. She took up the offer with enthusiasm. No intellectual, she was quick and determined. She was also ferociously loyal to her new husband. Wilson adored her.[14]

On board the *George Washington,* the Wilsons kept to themselves, eating most of their meals in their stateroom and strolling on the deck arm in arm. The American experts worked away on their maps and their papers, asking each other, with some disquiet, what their country's policies were to be. Wilson had said much about general principles but had mentioned few specifics. A young man called William Bullitt boldly went up to the president and told him that they were all confused by his silence. Wilson was surprised but agreed pleasantly to meet with a dozen of the leading experts. "It is absolutely the first time," said one afterward, "the president has let anyone know what his ideas are and what his policy is." There were to be few other such occasions. The experts left the meeting heartened and impressed. Wilson was informal and friendly. He spoke about the heavy task ahead and how he was going to rely on them to provide him with the best information. They must feel free to come to him at any time. "You tell me what's right and I'll fight for it." He apologized for talking about his own ideas: "they weren't very good but he thought them better than anything else he had heard."[15]

When it came to making peace, Wilson said, their country would rightly hold the position of arbiter. They must live up to the great American traditions of justice and generosity. They would be, after all, "the only disinterested people at the Peace Conference." What was more, he warned, "the men whom we were about to deal with did not represent their own people." This was one of Wilson's deep convictions, curious in a man whose own Congress was now dominated by his political opponents. Throughout the Peace Conference he clung to the belief that he spoke for the masses and that, if only he could reach them—whether French, Italian or even Russian—they would rally to his views.[16]

He touched on another favorite theme: the United States, he assured his audience, had not entered the war for selfish reasons. In this, as in so much else, it was unlike other nations, for it did not want territory, tribute or even revenge. (As a sign that American participation in the war was different from that of the Europeans, Wilson had always insisted on the United States being an Associate and not an Ally.) The United States generally acted unselfishly, in its occupation of Cuba, for example. "We had gone to war with Spain," he insisted, "not for annexation but to provide the helpless colony with the opportunity of freedom."[17]

Wilson tended to draw on Latin American examples, since most of his formative experiences in foreign relations had been there. He had recast, at least to his own satisfaction, the Monroe Doctrine, that famous defiance hurled at the Europeans in 1823 to warn them off attempting to colonize the New World again. The doctrine had become a fundamental precept in American foreign policy, a cloak, many said, for U.S. dominance of its neighbors. Wilson saw it rather as the framework within which all the nations of the Americas worked peacefully together, and a model for the warring European nations. Lansing was dubious, as he often was of Wilson's ideas: "the doctrine is exclusively a *national* policy of the United States and relates to its national safety and vital interests."[18]

Wilson paid little attention to what he regarded as niggling objections from Lansing. He was clear in his own mind that he meant well. When the American troops went to Haiti or Nicaragua or the Dominican Republic, it was to further order and democracy. "I am going to teach," he had said in his first term as president, "the South American Republics to elect good men!" He rarely mentioned that he was also protecting the Panama Canal and American investments. During Wilson's presidency, the United States intervened repeatedly in Mexico to try to get the sort of government it wanted. "The purpose of the United States," Wilson said, "is solely and singly to secure peace and order in Central America by seeing to it that the processes of self-government there are not interrupted or set aside." He was taken aback when the Mexicans failed to see the landing of American troops, and American threats, in the same light.[19]

The Mexican adventure also showed Wilson's propensity, perhaps unconscious, to ignore the truth. When he sent troops to Mexico for the first time, he told Congress that it was in response to repeated provocations and insults to the United States and its citizens from General Victoriano Huerta, the man who started the Mexican Revolution. Huerta in fact had taken great care to avoid provocations. At the Paris Peace Conference Wilson was to claim that he had never seen the secret wartime agreements among the Allies, promising Italy, for example, enemy territory. The British foreign secretary, Arthur Balfour, had shown them to him in 1917. Lansing said sourly of his president: "Even established facts were ignored if they did not fit in with this intuitive sense, this semi-divine power to select the right."[20]

As the Mexican imbroglio demonstrated, Wilson was not afraid to use his country's considerable power, whether financial or military. And by the end of the Great War the United States was much more powerful than it had been in 1914. Then it had possessed a minuscule army and a middle-sized navy; now it had over a million troops in Europe alone, and a navy that rivaled Britain's. Indeed, Americans tended to assume that they had won the war for their European allies. The American economy had surged ahead as American farmers and American factories poured out wheat, pork, iron and steel for the Allied war effort. As the American share of world production and trade rose inexorably, that of the European powers stagnated or declined. Most significant of all for their future relations, the United States had become the banker to the Europeans. Together the European allies owed over $7 billion to the American government, and about half as much again to American banks. Wilson assumed, overconfidently as it turned out, that the United States would get its way simply by applying financial pressure. As his legal adviser David Hunter Miller said, "Europe is bankrupt financially and its governments are bankrupt morally. The mere hint of withdrawal by America by reason of opposition to her wishes for justice, for fairness, and for peace would see the fall of every government in Europe without exception, and a revolution in every country in Europe with one possible exception."[21]

In that meeting on the *George Washington,* Wilson also talked briefly about the difficulties that lay ahead with the nations emerging from the wreckage of central Europe: Poland, Czechoslovakia, Yugoslavia and many more. They could have whatever form of government they wanted, but they must include in their new states only those who wanted to be there. "Criterion not who are intellectual or social or economic leaders but who form mass of people," a member of his audience wrote down. "Must have liberty—that is the kind of government they want."[22]

Of all the ideas Wilson brought to Europe, this concept of self-determination was, and has remained, one of the most controversial and opaque. During the Peace Conference, the head of the American mission in Vienna sent repeated requests to Paris and Washington for an explanation of the term. No answer ever came. It has never been easy to determine what Wilson meant. "Autonomous development," "the right of those who submit to authority to have a voice in their own governments," "the rights and liberties of small nations," a world made safe "for every peace-loving nation which, like our own, wishes to live its own life, determine its own institutions": the phrases had poured out from the White House, an inspiration to peoples around the world. But what did they add up to? Did Wilson merely mean, as sometimes appeared, an extension of democratic self-government? Did he really intend that any people who called themselves a nation should have their own state? In a statement he drafted, but never used, to persuade the American people to support the peace settlements, he stated, "We say now that all these people have the right to live their own lives under governments which they themselves choose to set up. That is the American principle." Yet he had no sympathy for Irish nationalists and their struggle to free themselves from British rule. During the Peace Conference he insisted that the Irish question was a domestic matter for the British. When a delegation of nationalist Irish asked him for support, he felt, he told his legal adviser, like telling them to go to hell. His view was that the Irish lived in a democratic country and they could sort it out through democratic means.[23]

The more Wilson's concept of self-determination is examined, the more difficulties appear. Lansing asked himself: "When the President talks of 'self-determination' what unit has he in mind? Does he mean a race, a territorial area, or a community?" It was a calamity, Lansing thought, that Wilson had ever hit on the phrase. "It will raise hopes which can never be realized. It will, I fear, cost thousands of lives. In the end it is bound to be discredited, to be called the dream of an idealist who failed to realize the danger until it was too late to check those who attempt to put the principle into force." What, as Lansing asked, made a nation? Was it a shared citizenship, as in the United States, or a shared ethnicity, as in Ireland? If a nation was not self-governing, ought it to be? And in that case, how much self-government was enough? Could a nation, however defined, exist happily within a larger multinational state? Sometimes Wilson seemed to think so. He came, after all, from a country that sheltered many different nationalities and which had fought a bitter war, which he remembered well, to stay in one piece.

Initially, he did not want to break up the big multinational empires such as Austria-Hungary and Russia. In February 1918, he had told Congress that "well-defined" national aspirations should be satisfied without, however, "introducing new or perpetuating old elements of discord and antagonism that would be likely in time to break the peace of Europe, and consequently of the world."[24]

That led to another series of questions. What was a "well-defined" nationalism? Polish? That was an obvious one. But what about Ukrainian? Or Slovak? And what about subdivisions? Ukrainian Catholics, for example, or Protestant Poles? The possibilities for dividing up peoples were unending, especially in central Europe, where history had left a rich mix of religions, languages and cultures. About half the people living there could be counted as members of one national minority or another. How were peoples to be allocated to one country or another when the dividing lines between one nation and another were so unclear?

One solution was to leave it to the experts. Let them study the history, collect the statistics and consult the locals. Another, more apparently democratic solution, which had been floating around in international relations since the French Revolution, was to give the locals a choice through a plebiscite, with a secret vote, administered by some international body. Wilson himself does not seem to have assumed that self-determination implied plebiscites, but by 1918 many people did. Who was to vote? Only men, or women as well? Only residents, or anyone who had been born in the disputed locality? (The French firmly rejected the idea of a plebiscite on their lost provinces of Alsace and Lorraine on the grounds that the vote would be unfair because Germany had forced French speakers out and brought in Germans.) And what if the locals did not know which nation they belonged to? In 1920, when an outside investigator asked a peasant in Belarus, on the frontier where Russians, Poles, Lithuanians, Byelorussians and Ukrainians all mingled, who he was, the only answer that came back was "I am a Catholic of these parts." What do you do, asked American experts in Carinthia in the Austrian Alps, when you have people "who do not want to join the nation of their blood-brothers, or else are absolutely indifferent to all national questions"?[25]

At the end of 1919, a chastened Wilson told Congress, "When I gave utterance to those words [that 'all nations had a right to self-determination'], I said them without the knowledge that nationalities existed, which are coming to us day after day." He was not responsible for the spread of national movements looking for their own states—that had been going on since the end of the eighteenth century—but, as Sidney Sonnino, the Italian foreign minister, put it, "the War undoubtedly had had the effect of over-exciting the feeling of nationality. . . . Perhaps America fostered it by putting the principles so clearly."[26]

Wilson spent most of his time in the meeting with his experts on the matter closest to his heart: the need to find a new way of managing international relations. This did not come as a surprise to his audience. In his famous Fourteen Points of January 1918, and in subsequent speeches, he had sketched out his ideas. The balance of power, he told the U.S. Congress in his "Four Principles" speech of February 1918, was forever discredited as a way to keep peace. There would be no more secret diplomacy of the sort that had led Europe into calculating deals, rash promises and entangling alliances, and so on down the slope to war. The peace settlements must not leave the way open to future wars. There must be no retribution, no unjust claims and no huge fines—indemnities—paid by the losers to the winners. That was what had been wrong after Prussia defeated France in 1870. The French had never forgiven Germany for the monies paid over and for the loss of their provinces of Alsace and Lorraine. War itself must become more difficult. There must be controls on armaments—general disarmament, even. Ships must sail freely across the world's seas. (That meant, as the British well knew, the end of their traditional weapon of strangling enemy economies by blockading their ports and seizing their shipping; it had brought Napoleon down, and, so they thought, hastened the Allied victory over Germany.) Trade barriers must be lowered so the nations of the world would become more interdependent.

At the heart of Wilson's vision was a League of Nations to provide the collective security that, in a well-run civil society, was provided by the government, its laws, its courts and its police. "Old system of powers, balance of powers, had failed too often," one expert jotted down, as the president spoke. The League was to have a council that could "butt in" in case of disputes. "If unsuccessful the offending nation to be outlawed—'And outlaws are not popular now.' "[27]

Wilson's was a liberal and a Christian vision. It challenged the view that the best way to preserve the peace was to balance nations against each other, through alliances if necessary, and that strength, not collective security, was the way to deter attack. Wilson was also offering a riposte to the alternative being put out by the Russian Bolsheviks, that revolution would bring one world, where conflict would no longer exist. He believed in separate nations and in democracy, both as the best form of government and as a force for good in the world. When governments were chosen by their people, they would not, indeed they could not, fight each other. "These are American principles," he told the Senate in 1917. "We could stand for no others. And they are also the principles and policies of forward looking men and women everywhere, of every modern nation, of every enlightened community. They are the principles of mankind and they must prevail." He was speaking, he thought, for humanity. Americans tended to see their values as universal ones, and their government and society as a model for all others. The United States, after all, had been founded by those who wanted to leave an old world behind, and its revolution was, in part, about creating a new one. American democracy, the American constitution, even American ways of doing business, were examples that others should follow for their own good. As one of the younger Americans said in Paris: "Before we get through with these fellows over here we will teach them how to do things and how to do them quickly."[28]

The Americans had a complicated attitude toward the Europeans, a mixture of admiration for their past accomplishments, a conviction that the Allies would have been lost without the United States and a suspicion that, if the Americans were not careful, the wily Europeans would pull them into their toils again. As they prepared for the Peace Conference, the American delegates suspected that the French and the British were already preparing their traps. Perhaps the offer of an African colony, or a protectorate over Armenia or Palestine, would tempt the United States—and then suddenly it would be too late. The Americans would find themselves touching pitch while the Europeans looked on with delight.[29]

American exceptionalism has always had two sides: the one eager to set the world to rights, the other ready to turn its back with contempt if its message should be ignored. The peace settlement, Wilson told his fellow passengers, must be based on the new principles: "If it doesn't work right, the world will raise hell." He himself, he added half-jokingly, would go somewhere to "hide my head, perhaps to Guam." Faith in their own exceptionalism has sometimes led to a certain obtuseness on the part of Americans, a tendency to preach at other nations rather than listen to them, a tendency as well to assume that American motives are pure where those of others are not. And Wilson was very American. He came to the Peace Conference, said Lloyd George, like a missionary to rescue the heathen Europeans, with his "little sermonettes" full of rather obvious remarks.[30]

It was easy to mock Wilson, and many did. It is also easy to forget how important his principles were in 1919 and how many people, and not just in the United States, wanted to believe in his great dream of a better world. They had, after all, a terrible reference point in the ruin left by the Great War. Wilson kept alive the hope that human society, despite the evidence, was getting better, that nations would one day live in harmony. In 1919, before disillusionment had set in, the world was more than ready to listen to him.

What Wilson had to say struck a chord, not just with liberals or pacifists but also among Europe's political and diplomatic élites. Sir Maurice Hankey, secretary to the British War Cabinet and then the Peace Conference itself, always carried a copy of the Fourteen Points in the box he kept for crucial reference material. They were, he said, the "moral background." Across Europe there were squares, streets, railway stations and parks bearing Wilson's name. Wall posters cried, "We Want a Wilson Peace." In Italy, soldiers knelt in front of his picture; in France, the left-wing paper *L'Humanité* brought out a special issue in which the leading lights of the French left vied with each other to praise Wilson's name. The leaders of the Arab revolt in the desert, Polish nationalists in Warsaw, rebels in the Greek islands, students in Peking, Koreans trying to shake off Japan's control, all took the Fourteen Points as their inspiration. Wilson himself found it exhilarating but also terrifying. "I am wondering," he said to George Creel, his brilliant propaganda chief, who was on board the *George Washington,* "whether you have not unconsciously spun a net for me from which there is no escape." The whole world was turning to the United States but, he went on, they both knew that such great problems could not be fixed at once. "What I seem to see—with all my heart I hope that I am wrong—is a tragedy of disappointment."[31]

The *George Washington* reached the French port of Brest on December 13, 1918. The war had been over for just a month. While the president stood on the bridge, his ship steamed slowly in through a great avenue of battleships from the British, French and American navies. For the first time in days, the sun was shining. The streets were lined with laurel wreaths and flags. On the walls, posters paid tribute to Wilson, those from right-wingers for saving them from Germany and those from the left for the new world he promised. Huge numbers of people, many resplendent in their traditional Breton costumes, covered every inch of pavement, every roof, every tree. Even the lampposts were taken. The air filled with the skirl of Breton bagpipes and repeated shouts of "Vive l'Amérique! Vive Wilson!" The French foreign minister, Stéphen Pichon, welcomed him, saying, "We are so thankful that you have come over to give us the right kind of peace." Wilson made a noncommittal reply and the American party boarded the night train for Paris. At three in the morning, Wilson's doctor happened to look out the window of his compartment. "I saw not only men and women but little children standing with uncovered head to cheer the passage of the special train."[32]

Wilson's reception in Paris was an even greater triumph, with even greater crowds: "the most remarkable demonstration," said an American who lived in Paris, "of enthusiasm and affection on the part of the Parisians that I have ever heard of, let alone seen." His train pulled into the Luxembourg station, which had been festooned with bunting and flags and filled with great masses of flowers. Clemenceau, the French prime minister, was there with his government and his longtime antagonist, the president Raymond Poincaré. As guns boomed across Paris to announce Wilson's arrival, the crowds started to press against the soldiers who lined the route. The president and his wife drove in an open carriage through the Place de la Concorde and on up the Champs-Elysées to their residence, to the sound of wild cheers. That night, at a quiet family dinner, Wilson said he was very pleased with his reception. "He had carefully watched the attitude of the crowd," he reportedly told the table, "and he was satisfied that they were most friendly."[33]

2

First Impressions

THE AFTERNOON of his arrival in Paris, Wilson had a reunion with his most trusted adviser. Colonel Edward House did not look like the rich Texan he was. Small, pale, self-effacing and frail, he often sat with a blanket over his knees because he could not bear the cold. Just as the Peace Conference was starting, he came down with flu and nearly died. House spoke in a soft, gentle voice, working his small delicate hands, said an observer, as though he were holding some object in them. He invariably sounded calm, reasonable and cheerful. People often thought of one of the great French cardinals of the past, of Mazarin perhaps.

He was not really a colonel; that was only an honorary title. He had never fought in a war but he knew much about conflict: the Texas of his childhood was a world where men brought out their guns at the first hint of an insult. House was riding and shooting by the time he was three. One brother had half his face shot off in a childish gunfight; another died falling off a trapeze. Then House too had an accident when he fell from a rope and hit his head. He never fully recovered. Since he could no longer dominate others physically, he learned to do so psychologically. "I used to like to set boys at each other," he told a biographer, "to see what they would do, and then try to bring them around again."[2]

He became a master at understanding men. Almost everyone who met him found him immediately sympathetic and friendly. "An intimate man," said the son of one of his enemies, "even when he was cutting your throat." House loved power and politics, especially when he could operate behind the scenes. In Paris, Baker called him, only half in admiration, "the small knot hole through which must pass many great events." He rarely gave interviews and almost never took official appointments. This, of course, made him the object of intense speculation. He merely wanted, he often said, to be useful. In his diary, though, House himself carefully noted the powerful and importunate who lined up to see him. He also faithfully recorded every compliment, no matter how fulsome.[3]

He was a Democrat, like most Southerners of his race, but on the liberal, progressive side of the party. When Wilson moved into politics, House, already a figure in Texas politics, recognized someone he could work with. The two men met for the first time in 1911, as Wilson was preparing to run for president. "Almost from the first our association was intimate," House remembered years later, when the friendship had broken down irrevocably, "almost from the first, our minds vibrated in unison." He gave Wilson the unstinting affection and loyalty he required, and Wilson gave him power. When his first wife died, Wilson became even more dependent on House. "You are the only person in the world with whom I can discuss everything," he wrote in 1915. "There are some I can tell one thing and others another, but you are the only one to whom I can make an entire clearance of mind." When the second Mrs. Wilson appeared on the scene, she watched House carefully, her eyes sharpened with jealousy.

When the war broke out, Wilson sent House off to the capitals of Europe in fruitless attempts to stop the fighting; as the war came to an end, he hastily dispatched him to Paris to negotiate the armistice terms. "I have not given you any instructions," Wilson told him, "because I feel that you will know what to do." House agreed with all his heart that Wilson's new diplomacy was the best hope for the world. He thought the League of Nations a wonderful idea. He also thought he could do better than Wilson in achieving their common goals. Where the president was too idealistic, too dogmatic, he, House, was a fixer, with a nod here, a shrug there, a slight change of emphasis, a promise first to this one and then that, smoothing over differences and making things work. He had not really wanted Wilson to come to the Peace Conference. In his diary, during the next months, the loyal lieutenant was to list Wilson's mistakes methodically: his outbursts of temper, his inconsistencies, his clumsiness in negotiations and his "one-track" mind.[5]

Clemenceau liked House enormously, partly because he was amused by him, but also because he seemed to understand France's concerns so well. "I can get on with you," Clemenceau told him, "you are practical. I understand you but talking to Wilson is something like talking to Jesus Christ!" Lloyd George was cooler: House "saw more clearly than most men—or even women—to the bottom of the shallow waters which are to be found here and there in the greatest of oceans and of men." A charming man, in Lloyd George's opinion, but rather limited—"essentially a salesman and not a producer." House would have been a good ambassador, but never a foreign minister. "It is perhaps to his credit," Lloyd George concluded kindly, "that he was not nearly as cunning as he thought he was." House could not bear Lloyd George, "a mischief maker who changes his mind like a weather-cock. He has no profound knowledge of any of the questions with which he is dealing." But Lloyd George knew how to keep his eye on the ends. House, who thought every disagreement could be worked out, did not. "He is a marvellous conciliator," was Baker's opinion, "but with the faults of his virtue for he conciliates over . . . minor disagreements into the solid flesh of principle." House had already done this during the armistice discussions.[6]

The Great War had begun with a series of mistakes and it ended in confusion. The Allies (and let us include their Associate the United States in the term) were not expecting victory when it came. Austria-Hungary was visibly collapsing in the summer of 1918, but Germany still looked strong. Allied leaders planned for at least another year of war. By the end of October, however, Germany's allies were falling away and suing for armistices, the German army was streaming back toward its own borders and Germany itself was shaking with revolutionary outbursts. The armistice with Germany, the most important and ultimately the most controversial of all, was made in a three-cornered negotiation between the new German government in Berlin, the Allied Supreme War Council in Paris and Wilson in Washington. House, as Wilson's personal representative, was the key link among them. The Germans, calculating that their best chance for moderate peace terms was to throw themselves on Wilson's mercy, asked for an armistice based on the Fourteen Points. Wilson, who was eager to push his somewhat reluctant European allies to accept his principles, agreed in a series of public notes.

The Europeans found this irritating. Furthermore, they had never been prepared to accept the Fourteen Points without modification. The French wanted to make sure that they received compensation for the enormous damage done to their country by the German invasion. The British could not agree to the point about freedom of the seas, for that would prevent them from using the naval blockade as a weapon against their enemies. In a final series of discussions in Paris, House agreed to the Allied reservations, and so the Fourteen Points were modified to allow for what later came to be called reparations from Germany and for discussions on freedom of the seas at the Peace Conference itself. In addition, the military terms of the armistice, which called for not just the evacuation of French and Belgian territory but also the withdrawal of German troops from the western edge of Germany itself, went a long way toward disarming Germany, something the French devoutly wished.[7]

The way the armistice was made left much room for later recrimination. The Germans were able to say that they had only accepted it on the basis of the original Fourteen Points and that the subsequent peace terms were therefore largely illegitimate. And Wilson and his supporters were able to blame the wily Europeans for diluting the pure intentions of the new diplomacy.

When House and Wilson had their first conversation in Paris on the afternoon of December 14, 1918, they were already suspicious of European intentions. Although the Peace Conference was not to start officially for another few weeks, the maneuvering had begun. Clemenceau had already suggested to the British that they come up with a general agreement on the peace terms, and the Europeans, including the Italians, had met in London at the beginning of the month. Wisely, Clemenceau took out insurance. He visited House on his sickbed to assure him that the London meetings had no importance whatsoever. He himself was only going over because it might help Lloyd George in his forthcoming general election. As it turned out, between disagreements over Italy's territorial demands in the Adriatic and squabbling between Britain and France over the disposition of the Ottoman empire, the meetings failed to produce a common European approach. All three European powers also hesitated, not wishing to give Wilson the impression that they were trying to settle things before he arrived.[8]

House, who shared Wilson's view that the United States was going to be the arbiter of the peace, believed, without much evidence, that Clemenceau was likely to be more reasonable than Lloyd George. Conveniently, Wilson met Clemenceau first. The wily old statesman listened quietly as Wilson did most of the talking, intervening only to express approval of the League of Nations. Wilson was favorably impressed, and House, who hoped that France and the United States would make a common front against Britain, was delighted. The Wilsons spent Christmas Day with General John Pershing at American headquarters outside Paris and then left for London.[9]

In Britain, Wilson was again greeted by large and adoring crowds, but his private talks with British leaders did not initially go well. The president was inclined to be stiff, offended that Lloyd George and senior British ministers had not rushed over to France to welcome him and annoyed that the British general election meant the start of the Peace Conference would have to be delayed. Wilson was, like many Americans, torn in his attitude to Great Britain, at once conscious of the United States' debt to its great liberal traditions but also wary and envious of its power. "If England insisted on maintaining naval dominance after the war," Wilson told André Tardieu, Clemenceau's close colleague, "the United States could and would show her how to build a navy!" At a gala reception at Buckingham Palace, Wilson spoke bluntly to a British official (who at once passed on the remarks to his superiors): "You must not speak of us who come over here as cousins, still less as brothers; we are neither." It was misleading, he went on, to talk of an Anglo-Saxon world, when so many Americans were from other cultures; foolish, also, to make too much of the fact that both nations spoke English. "No, there are only two things which can establish and maintain closer relations between your country and mine: they are community of ideals and of interests." The British were further taken aback when Wilson failed to reply to a toast from the king to American forces with a similar compliment to the British. "There was no glow of friendship," Lloyd George commented, "or of gladness at meeting men who had been partners in a common enterprise and had so narrowly escaped a common danger."[10]

Lloyd George, who recognized the supreme importance of a good relationship with the United States, set out to charm Wilson. Their first private conversation began the thaw. Lloyd George reported with relief to his colleagues that Wilson seemed open to compromise on the issues the British considered important, such as freedom of the seas and the fate of Germany's colonies. Wilson had given the impression that his main concern was the League of Nations, which he wanted to discuss as soon as the Peace Conference opened. Lloyd George had agreed. It would, he said, make dealing with the other matters much easier. The two leaders had also talked about how they should proceed at the Peace Conference. Presumably, they would follow the customary practice and sit down with Germany and the other defeated nations to draw up treaties.[11]

Past practice offered little guidance, though, for the new order that Wilson wanted. The rights of conquest and victory were woven deeply into European history, and previous wars—the Napoleonic, for example—had ended with the victors helping themselves to what they wanted, whether land or art treasures. Moreover, the defeated had been expected to pay an indemnity for the costs of the war and sometimes reparations for damages as well. But had they not all turned their backs on that in the recent war? Both sides had talked of a just peace without annexations. Both had appealed to the rights of peoples to choose their own rulers, the Allies more loudly and persuasively than the Central Powers. And even before the United States had come into the war, terms such as "democracy" and "justice" had peppered Allied war aims. Wilson had taken hold of the Allied agenda and made it into a firm set of promises for a better world. True, he had allowed for some recompense for the victors: France to get its lost provinces of Alsace and Lorraine, or Germany to make good the damage it had caused Belgium. The French wanted more, though: land from Germany possibly, guarantees of security against attack certainly. The British wanted certain German colonies. The Italians demanded part of the Balkans, and the Japanese part of China. Could that be justified in terms of the new diplomacy? Then there were all the nations, some already formed but some still embryonic, in the center of Europe, who demanded to be heard. And the colonial peoples, the campaigners for women's rights, the labor representatives, the American blacks, the religious leaders, the humanitarians. The Congress of Vienna had been simple by comparison.

In their first discussions with Wilson, both Clemenceau and Lloyd George pointed out the need for the Allies to sort out their own position on the peace, in a preliminary conference. Wilson was unhelpful. If they settled all the peace terms in advance, then the general peace conference would be a sham. On the other hand, he was prepared to have informal conversations to work out a common Allied position. "It really came to the same thing," Lloyd George reported to his colleagues, "but the President insisted definitely on his point of view." It was agreed that they would meet in Paris, have their preliminary discussions—a few weeks at the most—and then sit down with the enemy. Wilson, or so he thought, would probably go back to the United States at that point.[12]

After these first encounters with the men who were going to become his closest colleagues in Paris, Wilson continued on to Italy, to more ecstatic welcomes. But the cheers, the state receptions, the private audiences, could not conceal that time was passing. He began to wonder whether this was not deliberate. The people, he thought, wanted peace; their rulers seemed to be dragging their feet, for who knew what sinister motives. The French government tried to arrange a tour of the battlefields for him. He refused angrily. "They were trying to force him to go to see the devastated regions," he told his small circle of intimates, "so that he might see red and play into the hands of the governments of England, France and Italy." He would not be manipulated like this; the peace must be made calmly and without emotion. "Even if France had been entirely made a shell hole it would not change the final settlement."[13] The French resented his refusal bitterly and were not appeased when he finally paid a fleeting visit in March.

Wilson was coming to the conclusion that he and the French were not as close in their views as House had encouraged him to believe. The French government had drawn up an elaborate agenda which placed the League of Nations well down the list of important issues to be decided. Paul Cambon, the immensely experienced French ambassador in London, told a British diplomat, "The business of the Peace Conference was to bring to a close the war with Germany." The League was something that could easily be postponed. Many in the French official establishment thought of a league that would be a continuation of the wartime alliance and whose main role would be to enforce the peace terms. No matter, said an internal memorandum, that much of the French public thought in more idealistic terms: "that can help us." Clemenceau was publicly skeptical. The day after Wilson had made a speech in London reiterating his faith that a League of Nations was the best way to provide security for its members, Clemenceau had spoken in the Chamber of Deputies. To loud cheers he asserted: "There is an old system of alliances called the Balance of Power—this system of alliances, which I do not renounce, will be my guiding thought at the Peace Conference." Wickedly, he had referred to Wilson's noble *candeur,* a word that can mean either candor or pathetic naïveté. (The official record transformed it into *grandeur.*) The American delegation saw Clemenceau's speech as a challenge.[14]

In that speech and the American reaction to it were sown the seeds of what grew into a lurid and enduring tableau, especially in the United States. On the one hand, the Galahad, pure in thought and deed, lighting the way to a golden future; on the other, the misshapen French troll, his heart black with rage and spite, thinking only of revenge. On the one side, peace; on the other, war. It makes a good story, and it is not fair to either man. Both were liberals with a conservative skepticism of rapid change. What divided them was temperament and their own experience. Wilson believed that human nature was fundamentally good. Clemenceau had his doubts. He, and Europe, had been through too much. "Please do not misunderstand me," he once said to Wilson, "we too came into the world with the noble instincts and the lofty aspirations which you express so often and so eloquently. We have become what we are because we have been shaped by the rough hand of the world in which we have to live and we have survived only because we are a tough bunch." Wilson had lived in a world where democracy was safe. "I have lived," Clemenceau explained, "in a world where it was good form to shoot a democrat." Where Wilson believed that the use of force ultimately failed, Clemenceau had seen it succeed too often. "I have come to the conclusion that *force* is right," he said over lunch one day to Lloyd George's mistress, Frances Stevenson. "Why is this chicken here? Because it was not strong enough to resist those who wanted to kill it. And a very good thing too!" Clemenceau was not opposed to the League; he simply did not put much trust in it. He would have liked to see greater international cooperation, but recent history had shown all too clearly the importance of keeping the powder dry and the guns primed just in case. In this he faithfully reflected French public opinion, which remained overwhelmingly suspicious of Germany.[15]

By the second week of January Wilson was back in Paris, waiting for the preliminary conference to start. He was living in great state at the Hôtel Murat, a private house provided by the French government. (One of Wilson's little jokes was that the Americans were paying indirectly through their loans to France.) The hotel was owned by descendants of the great soldier Joachim Murat, who had married one of Napoleon's sisters, and lent by them to the French government. Later, when relations soured between France and the United States, the Princesse Murat asked for it back again. The presidential party, which included Wilson's personal physician, Admiral Cary T. Grayson, and Mrs. Wilson's social secretary, settled uneasily into the cold and gleaming rooms, filled with treasures from the past reflected back endlessly in huge mirrors. A British journalist who came to interview the president found him in a gray flannel suit sitting at a magnificent Empire desk with a great bronze eagle above his head.[16]

The rest of the American delegation was housed some distance away, also in considerable luxury, at the Hôtel Crillon. "I was assigned an enormous room," wrote an American professor to his wife, "high ceiling, white paneling, fireplace, enormous bathroom, very comfortable bed, all done in rich old rose." The Americans were delighted with the food, impressed by the meticulous service and amused by the slow old hydraulic elevators, which sometimes hung suspended between floors until enough water had moved from one tank to another. Because the hotel itself was small, their offices were scattered nearby, some in what had once been private dining rooms at Maxim's and which still smelled of stale wine and food. Over the months, the Americans added their own touches to the Crillon: a barbershop, a network of private phone lines and a hearty American breakfast in place of the French one. And, of course, the guards at the doors, and the sentries who paced back and forth on the flat roof. "The whole place is like an American battleship," said Harold Nicolson, the young British diplomat who left one of the most vivid descriptions of the Peace Conference, "and smells odd." British visitors were also struck by how seriously the Americans took rank: unlike their own delegation, the important men never sat down to meals with their juniors.[17]

Lansing and his fellow plenipotentiaries White and Bliss had rooms on the second floor, but the true hub of power was on the floor above them, where House had his large suite of heavily guarded rooms—more, he smugly noticed, than anyone else. There he sat, as he loved to do, spinning his plans and drawing in the powerful. Prime ministers, generals, ambassadors, journalists: they almost all came by to see him. His most important relationship was always that with his president. The two men talked daily, either in person or on the direct private line the Army engineers had installed. Sometimes Wilson strolled down to the Crillon; he never stopped on the second floor, but always went directly upstairs.[18]

3

Paris

PARIS WAS SAD and beautiful as the peacemakers began to assemble from all parts of the world in January 1919. Its people were subdued and mournful but its women were still extraordinarily elegant. "Again and again," wrote a Canadian delegate to his wife, "one meets a figure which might have stepped out of *La Vie Parisienne,* or *Vogue* in its happier moments." Those with money could still find wonderful clothes and jewels. The restaurants, when they could get supplies, were still marvelous. In the nightclubs, couples tripped the new fox-trots and tangos. The weather was surprisingly mild. The grass was still green and a few flowers still bloomed. There had been a lot of rain and the Seine was in flood. Along the *quais* the crowds gathered to watch the rising waters, while buskers sang of France's great victory over Germany and of the new world that was coming.[1]

Signs of the war that had just ended were everywhere: the refugees from the devastated regions in the north; the captured German cannon in the Place de la Concorde and the Champs-Elysées; the piles of rubble and boarded-up windows where German bombs had fallen. A gaping crater marked the Tuileries rose garden. Along the Grands Boulevards the ranks of chestnuts had gaps where trees had been cut for firewood. The great windows in the cathedral of Notre-Dame were missing their stained glass, which had been stored for safety; in their place, pale yellow panes washed the interior with a tepid light. There were severe shortages of coal, milk and bread.

French society bore scars, too. While the flags of victory fluttered from the lampposts and windows, limbless men and demobilized soldiers in worn army uniforms begged for change on street corners; almost every other woman wore mourning. The left-wing press called for revolution, the right-wing for repression. Strikes and protests came one after the other. The streets that winter and spring were filled with demonstrations by men and women in the customary blue of French workers, and with counterdemonstrations by the middle classes.

Neither the British nor the Americans had wanted the Peace Conference to be in Paris. As House confided to his diary, "It will be difficult enough at best to make a just peace, and it will be almost impossible to do so while sitting in the atmosphere of a belligerent capital. It might turn out well and yet again it might be a tragedy." The French were too excitable, had suffered too much and were too bitter against the Germans to provide the calm atmosphere needed. Wilson had preferred Geneva until alarmist reports coming from Switzerland persuaded him that the country was on the verge of revolution and riddled with German spies. Clemenceau did not waver in his insistence on Paris. "I never," said Lloyd George later on, when he was particularly annoyed, "wanted to hold the Conference in his bloody capital. Both House and I thought it would be better to hold it in a neutral place, but the old man wept and protested so much that we gave way."[2]

It may be only a legend that Clemenceau asked to be buried upright, facing Germany. It was certainly true that he had been on guard against France's great neighbor for most of his life. He was only twenty-eight when the Franco-Prussian War started, and he was part of the group of young left-wing republicans who fought on in Paris after the French armies were defeated. He saw the city starve, the French government capitulate and the new German empire proclaimed in the Hall of Mirrors at Versailles. As a newly elected deputy, he voted against the peace terms with Germany. As a journalist, writer, politician and finally prime minister, he sounded the same warning: Germany was a menace to France. "My life hatred," he told an American journalist shortly before he died, "has been for Germany because of what she has done to France." He did not actively seek war after 1871; he simply accepted it as inevitable. The problem, he said, was not with France: "Germany believes that the logic of her victory means domination, while we do not believe that the logic of our defeat is serfdom."[3]

To have a chance, Clemenceau had always recognized, France needed allies. Before 1914, the new Germany had been a formidable opponent, its industry, exports and wealth all growing while France's were static and its birthrate was declining. Today, when sheer numbers of soldiers matter less in battle, it is difficult to remember how important it was to be able to put huge armies into the field. As Clemenceau told the French senate during the ratification debate, the treaty with Germany "does not specify that the French are committed to have many children, but that would have been the first thing to include." Those disadvantages were why France had reached out to its hereditary enemies, tsarist Russia in the east and Britain across the Channel, for Russian manpower and British industry and maritime power to balance against Germany. Much had changed by 1918, but not the underlying imbalance. There were still more Germans than French. How long would it take the German economy, with its largely intact infrastructure, to recover? And now France could not count on Russia.[4]

During the Peace Conference, France's allies became exasperated with what they saw as French intransigence, French greed and French vindictiveness. They had not suffered what France had suffered. The war memorials, in every city, town and village, with their lists of names from the First World War, the handful from the Second, tell the story of France's losses. A quarter of French men between eighteen and thirty had died in the war, over 1.3 million altogether out of a prewar population of 40 million. France lost a higher proportion of its population than any other of the belligerents. Twice as many again of its soldiers had been wounded. In the north, great stretches of land were pitted with shell holes, scarred by deep trenches, marked with row upon row of crosses. Around the fortress of Verdun, site of the worst French battle, not a living thing grew, not a bird sang. The coal mines on which the French economy depended for its power were flooded; the factories they would have supplied had been razed or carted away into Germany. Six thousand square miles of France, which before the war had produced 20 percent of its crops, 90 percent of its iron ore and 65 percent of its steel, were utterly ruined. Perhaps Wilson might have understood Clemenceau's demands better if he had gone early on to see the damage for himself.[5]

At the Peace Conference, Clemenceau was to keep all the important threads in his own hands. The French delegation drew on the best that France had to offer, but it did not meet at all for the first four months of the conference. Clemenceau rarely consulted the Foreign Ministry professionals at the Quai d'Orsay, much to their annoyance. Nor did he pay much attention to the experts from the universities he had asked to draw up reports on France's economic and territorial claims and to sit on the commissions and committees that proliferated over the course of the conference. "No organization of his ideas, no method of work," complained clever old Paul Cambon from London, "the accumulation in himself of all duties and all responsibilities, thus nothing works. And this man of 78 years, sick, for he is a diabetic . . . receives fifty people a day and exerts himself with a thousand details which he ought to leave to his ministers. . . . At no moment in the war was I as uneasy as I am for the peace."[6]

Stéphen Pichon, Clemenceau's foreign minister, was an amiable, lazy and indecisive man who received his instructions every morning and would not have dreamed of disobeying. Clemenceau was rather fond of him in an offhand way. "Who is Pichon?" he asked one day. "Your minister of Foreign Affairs," came the reply. "So he is," said the old Tiger, "I had forgotten it." On another occasion, Pichon and a party of experts were waiting patiently in the background for a meeting to start when Clemenceau teased Balfour about the number of advisers he had. When Balfour replied, "They are doing the same thing as the greater number of people with you," Clemenceau, infuriated to be caught out, turned around. "Go away all of you," he told Pichon. "There is no need for any of you!"[7]

If Clemenceau discussed issues at all, it was in the evening at his house, with a small group that included his faithful aide General Henri Mordacq, the brilliant gadfly André Tardieu and the industrialist Louis Loucheur. He kept them on their toes by having the police watch them. Each morning he would give them a dossier with details of their previous day's activities. As much as possible he ignored Raymond Poincaré, his president, whom he loathed.[8]

Throughout his long life Clemenceau had gone his own formidable way. His enemies claimed that his slanting eyes and his cruelty were a legacy from Huns who had somehow made it to the Vendée. He was born in 1841, to minor gentry in a lovely part of France with a violent history. Generally, the people of the Vendée chose the wrong side: in the wars of religion, which the Catholics won, they were Protestants; during the French Revolution they were Catholic and royalist. The Clemenceau family was a minority within a minority; republican, radical and resolutely anticlerical. Clemenceau himself thought snobs were fools, but he always went back to the gloomy family manor house, with its stone floors, its moat and its austere furnishings.[9]

Like his father, Clemenceau trained as a doctor; but, again like his father, he did not practice. His studies in any case always took second place to writing, politics and his love affairs. Like other bright young men, he was drawn to Paris and the world of radical intellectuals, journalists and artists. In the late 1860s he spent much time in the United States, widely admired by republicans as a land of freedom. His travels left him with fluent English, peppered with out-of-date New York slang, in an accent that mingled a Yankee drawl with rolling French "r"s. He also gained a wife, Mary Plummer, a lovely, stupid and very conventional New England girl whom he had met while he was teaching French in a girls' school. He brought her back to France and deposited her for long periods of time with his parents and unmarried aunts in the Vendée. The marriage did not last but Mary Plummer lived on in Paris, supplementing her modest annuity by taking American tourists to museums. She rarely saw Clemenceau after their separation but she faithfully collected his press cuttings. Unfortunately, she could not read them because she had never learned French. After her death in 1917 Clemenceau expressed mild regret: "What a tragedy that she ever married me."[10]

The Clemenceau family kept the three children from the marriage, and Clemenceau never married again. He preferred to travel through life alone. There were women, of course, as friends and as lovers. "Never in my life," he said, "has it been necessary for me to make appeals to women." And on the whole it was true. In 1919 he complained sardonically that, just when he was too old to take advantage of it, women were throwing themselves at him.[11]

Politics and, above all, France were his great passion. With the collapse of Napoleon III's empire in 1870 and the rise of the Third Republic, the way was open to him and other radical politicians to participate in public life. Clemenceau was elected to the French parliament in 1876. He was a republican like most of those who dominated the Third Republic but he did not belong to a political party in the modern sense (indeed such things did not exist then). In the loose and shifting groupings before the Great War, he was invariably found on the left, just this side of the socialists and those who rejected constitutional, democratic politics. Clemenceau made a name for himself as an incisive and witty orator and a tenacious opponent, happiest when he was attacking governments he saw as too conservative. With his old friend Emile Zola, for example, he helped to reopen the guilty verdict against Alfred Dreyfus, the Jewish army officer falsely accused of selling French secrets to the Germans.[12] But he was not trusted even on the left; there were too many dubious financiers in his life, women with shady reputations, creditors asking for their money. His duels left an impression of someone who belonged in the pages of Dumas. In his relentless attacks on authority he was prepared to do almost anything to win. "He comes from a family of wolves," said a man who knew him well. Clemenceau did not help himself by his contempt for convention and his profound cynicism. Lloyd George once said of him, "He loved France but hated all Frenchmen." In 1906, when he was already in his sixties, he became a government minister. He was brought in as minister of the interior perhaps because France's president at the time owed him a political debt, more likely because, as one of his new colleagues argued, it would be too dangerous to leave him out. Later that year when what was a weak government fell, Clemenceau to the surprise of many emerged as the new prime minister and an effective one at that.

His intimates saw another side. Clemenceau was loyal to his friends and they to him. He was kind and generous with both time and money. He loved his garden, although, according to one visitor, "it was a helter-skelter survival of mixed-up seeds hurled about recklessly in all directions." For years Clemenceau had a country place close to Giverny and Claude Monet, a great friend. In Paris he frequently dropped in to see the great panels of the water lilies. "They take my breath away whenever I enter that room." (He could not bear Renoir's painting: "It's enough to disgust you with love forever after. Those buttocks he gives those wenches ought not to be allowed."[13])

Clemenceau was also extraordinarily brave and stubborn. When the Germans advanced on Paris in 1914, the French parliament debated leaving. Clemenceau, who had resigned office in 1909 and was back to his familiar role in opposition, agreed: "Yes, we are too far from the front." In the dark days of 1917, when the French armies had been shattered on the Western Front and there was talk of collapse at home, Clemenceau the Father of Victory, as the French called him, finally came into his own. As prime minister, he held France together until the final victory. When the Germans made their last great push toward Paris in the spring of 1918, Clemenceau made it clear that there would be no surrender. If the Germans took the city, he intended to stay until the last moment and then escape by plane. When he heard that the Germans had agreed to an armistice, for once in his life he was speechless. He put his head in his hands and wept. On the evening of November 11, he walked through Paris with his favorite sister, Sophie. "The war is won," he said when he saw the crowds starting to pull captured German guns to pieces. "Give them to the children to play with." Later, with Mordacq, he talked of the work to come: "Yes, we have won the war and not without difficulty; but now we are going to have to win the peace, and that will perhaps be even more difficult."[14]

France, of all the Great Powers, had the most at stake in the German peace terms. Britain already had most of what it wanted, with the German fleet and the major German colonies safely in its hands, and the United States, protected from Germany by the Atlantic Ocean, was eager to pack up and go home. France not only had suffered the most; it also had the most to fear. Whatever happened, Germany would still lie along its eastern border. There would still be more Germans than French in the world. It was an ominous sign that even the souvenir penknives engraved with "Foch" and "La Victoire" being sold in France in 1919 had been made in

German factories. France wanted revenge and compensation, but above all, it wanted security. No one was more aware of this than its prime minister.

Clemenceau was convinced that the only safety for France was in keeping the wartime alliance alive. As he told the Chamber of Deputies in December 1918, "To preserve this entente, I will make any sacrifice." During the Peace Conference he held firm to that, even through the worst disagreements. The French public must remember, he told his closest advisers, that "without America and England, France would perhaps no longer actually exist." As he remarked to Lloyd George, when the two were engaged in one of their many quarrels, "my policy at the conference, as I hope you will acknowledge, is one of close agreement with Great Britain and America."[15]

Clemenceau's policy was one thing; persuading the rank and file of French officials to follow it was another. "I find them full of intrigue and chicanery of all kinds," complained Hankey, the British secretary to the conference, "without any idea of playing the game." Memories of past greatness, a conviction of the superiority of French civilization, resentment of Anglo-Saxon prosperity and fears of Germany did not make the French easy to deal with. "One could not help feeling," wrote a British expert when he visited the French occupation forces in the Rhineland, "that in a moment all that has happened in the last fifty years was wiped away; the French soldiers were back again in the place where they used to be under the Monarchy and the Revolution; confident, debonair, quick, feeling themselves completely at home in their historical task of bringing a higher civilization to the Germans." The Americans, like the British, found the French intensely irritating at times. "Fundamental trouble with France," wrote an American expert in his diary, "is that as far as she was concerned the victory was wholly fictitious and she is trying to act as if it were a real one and to make herself believe that it was." American officers clashed repeatedly with their French counterparts and the ordinary soldiers brawled in the streets and cafés.[16]

It was unfortunate, perhaps, that Clemenceau himself did not establish good personal relations with the leader of either country. Where Wilson and Lloyd George frequently dropped in on each other and met over small lunches or dinners during the Peace Conference, Clemenceau preferred to eat alone or with his small circle of advisers. "That has its disadvantages," said Lloyd George. "If you meet for social purposes, you can raise a point. If you find that you are progressing satisfactorily, you can proceed, otherwise you can drop it."[17] Clemenceau had never cared for ordinary social life at the best of times. In Paris in 1919, he saved his flagging energies for the negotiations.

Clemenceau was the oldest of the three and, although he was robust for his age, the strain told. The eczema on his hands was so bad that he wore gloves to hide it. He also had trouble sleeping. He woke up very early, often at three, and read until seven, when he made himself a simple breakfast of gruel. He then worked again until his masseur and trainer arrived for his physical exercises (which usually included his favorite, fencing). He spent the morning in meetings but almost always went home for his standard lunch of boiled eggs and a glass of water, worked again all afternoon, and after an equally simple supper of milk and bread, went to bed by nine. Very occasionally, he took tea at Lloyd George's flat in the Rue Nitot, where the cook baked his favorite, *langues de chat*.[18]

Clemenceau did not much like either Wilson or Lloyd George. "I find myself," he said in a phrase that went round Paris, "between Jesus Christ on the one hand, and Napoleon Bonaparte on the other." Wilson puzzled him: "I do not think he is a bad man, but I have not yet made up my mind as to how much of him is good!" He also found him priggish and arrogant. "What ignorance of Europe and how difficult all understandings were with him! He believed you could do everything by formulas and his fourteen points. God himself was content with ten commandments. Wilson modestly inflicted fourteen points on us . . . the fourteen commandments of the most empty theory!"[19]

Lloyd George, as far as Clemenceau was concerned, was more amusing but also more devious and untrustworthy. In the long and acrimonious negotiations over control of the Middle East, Clemenceau was driven into rages at Lloyd George's attempts to wriggle out of their agreements. The two men shared certain traits—both had started out as radicals in politics, both were ruthlessly efficient—but there were equally significant differences. Clemenceau was an intellectual, Lloyd George was not. Clemenceau was rational, Lloyd George intuitive. Clemenceau had the tastes and values of an eighteenth-century gentleman; Lloyd George was resolutely middle-class.

Clemenceau also had problems closer to home. "There are only two perfectly useless things in the world," he quipped. "One is an appendix and the other is Poincaré!" A small, dapper man, France's president was fussy, legalistic, pedantic, very cautious and very Catholic. He was a republican, but a conservative one. Clemenceau came to despise him during the Dreyfus affair, when Poincaré carefully avoided taking a stand. "A lively little beast, dry, disagreeable, and not courageous," Clemenceau told an American friend. "This prudence has preserved it up to the present day—a somewhat unpleasant animal, as you see, of which, luckily, only one specimen is known." Clemenceau had been attacking Poincaré for years and even spread rumors about Poincaré's wife. "You wish to sleep with Madame Poincaré?" he would shout out. "OK, my friend, it's fixed." During the war, Clemenceau, who like many leading French politicians had his own newspaper, criticized the president, often unfairly, for the failings of the French military. *L'Homme Libre* (renamed *L'Homme Enchâiné* after the censors got busy on its pages) carried editorial after editorial, written by Clemenceau himself, castigating the inadequate medical care for wounded soldiers and the shortages of crucial munitions. The conduct of the war was a disaster, those in charge utterly incompetent. Poincaré was outraged. "He knows very well that he is not telling the truth," he complained, "that the constitution leaves me no rights."[20]

Poincaré returned the hatred. "Madman," he wrote in his diary. "Old, moronic, vain man." But on crucial issues, curiously, the two men tended to agree. Both detested and feared Germany. Poincaré had also fought against the defeatists during the darkest period of the war and had brought Clemenceau in as prime minister because he recognized his will to defeat Germany. For a brief period there had been something of a truce. "Now, Raymond old chum," Clemenceau had said before his first cabinet meeting in November 1917, "are we going to fall in love?" Six months later, Poincaré was complaining bitterly that Clemenceau was not consulting him. After the victory the two men embraced publicly in Metz, capital of the recovered province of Lorraine, but their relations remained difficult. Poincaré was full of complaints about Clemenceau's conduct of affairs. The armistice had come too soon: French troops should have pushed farther into Germany. France was being heavy-handed in Alsace and Lorraine. As a native of Lorraine, Poincaré still had contacts there, who warned him that many of the inhabitants were pro-German and that the French authorities were handling them tactlessly. Clemenceau was neglecting France's financial problems. He was also making a mess of foreign policy, giving away far too much to the British and the Americans and expressing little interest in German colonies or the Middle East. Poincaré was infuriated when Clemenceau conceded that English would be an official language at the Peace Conference alongside French. And he couldn't bear his rival's popular adulation. "All Frenchmen believe in him like a new god," he wrote. "And me, I am insulted in the popular press. . . . I am hardly talked about other than to be insulted."[21]

To the dismay of Poincaré and the powerful colonial lobby Clemenceau cared little about acquiring Germany's colonies, and was not much interested in the Middle East. His few brief remarks about war aims before the conference opened were deliberately vague, enough to reassure the French public but not to tie him down to any rigid set of demands. Official statements during the war had referred merely to the liberation of

Belgium and the occupied French territories, freedom for oppressed peoples and, inevitably, Alsace-Lorraine. His job, as he told the Chamber of Deputies, was to make war. As for peace, he told a journalist, "Is it necessary to announce ahead of time all that one wants to do? No!" On December 29, 1918, Clemenceau was pressed by his critics in the Chamber to be more precise. He refused. "The question of the peace is an enormous one," he said. The negotiations were going to be tricky. "I am going to have to make claims, but I will not say here what they are." He might well have to give way on some in the greater interest of France. He asked for a vote of confidence. It went 398 to 93 in his favor. His main challenge now was his allies.[22]

4

Lloyd George and the
British Empire Delegation

O N JANUARY 11, David Lloyd George bounded with his usual energy onto a British destroyer for the Channel crossing. With his arrival in Paris the three key peacemakers, on whom so much depended, were finally in one place. Although he was still feeling his way with Wilson, Lloyd George had known Clemenceau on and off since 1908. Their first meeting had not been a success. Clemenceau found Lloyd George shockingly ignorant, both of Europe and the United States. Lloyd George's impression was of a "disagreeable and rather bad-tempered old savage." He noticed, he said, that in Clemenceau's large head "there was no dome of benevolence, reverence, or kindliness." When the two men crossed paths again during the war, Lloyd George made it clear that there was to be no more bullying. In time, he claimed, he came to appreciate Clemenceau immensely for his wit, his strength of character and his passionate devotion to France. Clemenceau, for his part, developed a grudging liking for Lloyd George, although he always complained that he was badly educated. He was not, said the old Frenchman severely, "an English gentleman."[1]

Each of the Big Three at the Peace Conference brought something of his own country to the negotiations: Wilson the United States' benevolence, a confident assurance that the American way was the best, and an uneasy suspicion that the Europeans might fail to see this; Clemenceau France's profound patriotism, its relief at the victory and its perpetual apprehension of a revived Germany; and Lloyd George Britain's vast web of colonies and its mighty navy. Each man represented great interests, but each was also an individual. Their failings and their strengths, their fatigue and their illnesses, their likes and dislikes were also to shape the peace settlements. From January to the end of June, except for the gap between mid-February and mid-March when Wilson was back in the United States and Lloyd George in Britain, the three met daily, often morning and afternoon. At first they were accompanied by their foreign ministers and advisers, but after March they met privately, with only a secretary or two or an occasional expert. The intensity of these face-to-face meetings forced them to get to know each other, to like each other and to be irritated by each other.

Lloyd George was the youngest of the three, a cheerful rosy-faced man with startling blue eyes and a shock of white hair. ("Hullo!" a little girl once asked him. "Are you Charlie Chaplin?") He was only two when the American Civil War—something Wilson remembered clearly—ended. When a twenty-year-old Clemenceau was witnessing the birth of the new Germany in the aftermath of France's defeat by Prussia, Lloyd George was still in primary school. He was not only younger; he was also fitter and more resilient. Wilson worried himself sick trying to live up to his own principles, and Clemenceau lay awake at nights going over and over France's needs. Lloyd George thrived on challenges and crises. As Lord Robert Cecil, an austere Conservative who never entirely approved of him, said with reluctant admiration, "Whatever was going on at the Conference, however hard at work and harried by the gravest responsibilities of his position, Mr. Lloyd George was certain to be at the top of his form—full of chaff intermingled with shrewd though never ill-natured comments on those with whom he was working."[2]

Lloyd George had known tragedy with the death of a much-loved daughter, as well as moments of considerable strain when personal scandals and political controversies had threatened to ruin his career. He had worked under enormous pressure during the previous four years, first as minister of munitions and then as war minister. At the end of 1916, he had taken on the burden of the prime ministership, at the head of a coalition government, when it looked as though the Allies were finished. Like Clemenceau in France, he had held the country together and led it to victory. Now, in 1919, he was fresh from a triumphant election but led an uneasy coalition. He was a Liberal; his supporters and key cabinet members were predominantly Conservative. Although he had a solid partnership with the Conservative leader, Andrew Bonar Law, he had to watch his back. His displaced rival, the former Liberal prime minister Herbert Asquith, sat brooding in his tent, ready to pounce on any slip. Many of the Conservatives remembered his radical past as the scourge of privilege and rank, and as they had with their own leader Disraeli, they wondered if he were not too clever, too quick, too foreign. He also faced formidable enemies in the press. The press baron Lord Northcliffe, who had chosen his title because it had the same initial letter as Napoleon, was moving rapidly from megalomania to paranoia, perhaps an early sign of the tertiary syphilis that was to kill him. Northcliffe had been convinced that he had made Lloyd George prime minister by putting his papers, which included *The Times* and the *Daily Mail,* behind him. Now he was angry when his creation refused to appoint him either to the War Cabinet or to the British delegation in Paris. He wanted revenge.

Lloyd George had on his hands a country ill prepared for the peace, where the end of the war had brought huge, and irrational, expectations: that making peace would be easy; that wages and benefits would go up and taxes down; that there would be social harmony, or, depending on your point of view, social upheaval. The public mood was unpredictable: at moments vengeful, at others escapist. The most popular book of 1919 was *The Young Visiters,* a comic novel written by a child. While he was in Paris, Lloyd George had to take time out for labor unrest, parliamentary revolts and the festering sore of Ireland. Yet he entered into the negotiations in Paris as though he had little else on his mind.

If anyone was like Napoleon it was not the poor deluded Northcliffe but the man he hated. Napoleon once said of himself, "Different subjects and different affairs are arranged in my head as in a cupboard. When I wish to interrupt one train of thought, I shut that drawer and open another. Do I wish to sleep? I simply close all the drawers and there I am—asleep." Lloyd George had those powers of concentration and recuperation, that energy and that fondness for the attack. "The Englishman," he told a Welsh friend, "never respects any fellow unless that fellow beats him; then he becomes particularly affable towards him."[3]

Like Napoleon, Lloyd George had an uncanny ability to sense what other people were thinking. He told Frances Stevenson that he loved staying in hotels: "I am always interested in people—wondering who they are—what they are thinking about—what their lives are like—whether they are enjoying life or finding it a bore." Although he was a wonderful conversationalist, he was also a very good listener. From the powerful to the humble, adults to children, everyone who met him was made to feel that he or she had something important to say. "One of the most admirable traits in Mr. Lloyd George's character," in Churchill's view, "was his complete freedom at the height of his power, responsibility and good fortune from any thing in the nature of pomposity or superior airs. He was always natural and simple. He was always exactly the same to those who knew him well: ready to argue any point, to listen to disagreeable facts even when controversially presented." His famous charm was rooted in this combination of curiosity and attention.[4]

Lloyd George was also a great orator. Where Clemenceau drove home his points with devastating clarity and sarcasm, and Wilson preached, Lloyd George's speeches, which he prepared so carefully and which sounded so spontaneous, were at once moving and witty, inspiring and intimate. Like a great actor, he was a skillful manipulator of his audience. "I pause," he once told someone who asked him about his technique, "I reach out my hand to the people and draw them to me. Like children they seem then. Like little children."[5]

John Maynard Keynes, who went to Paris as the Treasury's representative and did so much to create myths about the Peace Conference, wove a special one for Lloyd George. "How can I convey to the reader," the great economist asked, "any just impression of this extraordinary figure of our time, this syren, this goat-footed bard, this half-human visitor to our age from the hag-ridden magic and enchanted woods of Celtic antiquity?" There spoke the voice both of intellectually superior Cambridge and of stolid John Bull, but it spoke romantic nonsense. The real Wales in which Lloyd George grew up was a modest sober little land, with slate mines and shipbuilding, fishermen and farmers.[6]

Lloyd George liked to talk of his origins in a humble cottage, but in fact he came from the educated artisan class. His father, who died when he was very young, was a schoolmaster; the uncle who brought him up was a master cobbler and lay preacher, a figure of stature in his small village. Wales was always important to Lloyd George as a reference point, if only to measure how far he had come, and also for sentimental reasons (although he grew quickly bored if he had to spend too much time there). He had early on seen himself on a larger stage. And what larger stage than the capital of the world's biggest empire? As he wrote to the local girl who became his wife, "My supreme idea is to get on."[7]

He was fortunate in his uncle, who gave him unstinting devotion and support. When, as a boy, he discovered that he had lost his belief in God, the lay preacher forgave him. When he decided to go into the law, his uncle worked through a French grammar book one step ahead of him so that he could get the language qualification that he required. And when he decided to go into politics, a huge gamble for someone without money or connections, his uncle again supported him. The old man lived just long enough to see his nephew become prime minister.[8]

Lloyd George was made for politics. From the hard work in the committee rooms to the great campaigns, he loved it all. While he enjoyed the cut and thrust of debate, he was essentially good-natured. Unlike Wilson and Clemenceau, he did not hate his opponents. Nor was he an intellectual in politics. Although he read widely, he preferred to pick the brains of experts. On his feet there was no one quicker: he invariably conveyed a mastery of his subject. Once during the Peace Conference Keynes and a colleague realized that they had given him the wrong briefing on the Adriatic. They hastily put a revised position on a sheet of paper and rushed to the meeting, where they found Lloyd George already launched on his subject. As Keynes passed over the paper, Lloyd George glanced at it and, without a pause, gradually modified his arguments until he ended up with the opposite position to the one he had started out with.[9]

He made his mark early on as a leading radical politician. Where Wilson attacked the big banks and Clemenceau attacked the church, Lloyd George's favorite targets were the landowners and aristocracy. He rather liked businessmen, especially self-made ones. (He also frequently liked their wives.) As chancellor of the exchequer, he pushed through radical budgets, introducing an income tax for the rich along with benefits for the poor, but he was not a socialist. Like Wilson and Clemenceau, he disliked collectivism, but he was always prepared to work with moderate socialists just as he was prepared to work with Conservatives.[10]

Over the course of his career he became a superb, if unconventional, administrator. He shook established procedures by bringing in talented and skilled men from outside the civil service to run government departments, and he ensured the success of his bills by inviting all the interested parties to comment on them. He settled labor disputes by inviting both sides to sit down with him, normal enough procedure today but highly unusual then. "He plays upon men round a table like the chords of a musical instrument," said a witness to his settlement of a railway dispute, "now pleading, now persuasive, stern, playful and minatory in quick succession."[11]

Naturally optimistic, he was always sure that solutions could be found to even the most difficult problems. "To Lloyd George," said a friend of his children, "every morning was not a new day, but a new life and a new chance."[12] Sometimes the chances he took were risky, and he engaged in some dubious transactions—a mine in Argentina or the purchase of shares where he had inside knowledge—but he seems to have been motivated more by the desire for financial independence than by greed. He was equally careless in his private life. Where Clemenceau's affairs with women enhanced his reputation, Lloyd George came close to disaster on more than one occasion when angry husbands threatened to name him in divorce actions. His wife, a strong-willed woman, stuck by him, but the couple grew apart. She preferred to stay in north Wales with her beloved garden; he got used to a part-time marriage. By 1919 he had settled down, as much as was in his nature, with a single mistress, a younger woman who had originally come into his household to tutor his youngest daughter. Frances Stevenson was an educated, efficient and intelligent woman who gave him love, intellectual companionship and a well-run office.

People often wrote Lloyd George off as a mere opportunist. Clemenceau once dismissed him as an English solicitor: "All arguments are good to him when he wishes to win a case and, if it is necessary, he uses the next day arguments which he had rejected or refuted the previous day." Wilson, sharp-eyed where the failings of others were concerned, thought Lloyd George lacked principle: he wished that he had "a less slippery customer to deal with than L.G. for he is always temporizing and making concessions." In fact, Lloyd George was a man of principle; but he was also intensely pragmatic. He did not waste his energies on quixotic crusades. He opposed the Boer War, when Britain waged war on the small South African republics, because he thought it was wrong and wasteful. His tenacious public opposition took courage and nearly cost him his life when an angry mob in Birmingham stormed the platform where he was speaking. But it paid off politically. As the British government blundered its way through to a hard-won peace, Lloyd George emerged as a national leader.[13]

When the Great War broke out, it was inevitable that he would play an important part in the British war effort. As Churchill, an increasingly close friend, wrote: "L.G. has more true insight and courage than anyone else. He really sticks at nothing—no measure too far-reaching, no expedient too novel." He hated war, Lloyd George told a Labour delegation in 1916, but "once you are in it you have to go grimly through it, otherwise the causes which hang upon a successful issue will perish." The wise old Conservative Arthur Balfour had seen leaders come and go. "He is impulsive," he said of Lloyd George, "he had never given a thought before the War to military matters; he does not perhaps adequately gauge the depths of his own ignorance; and he has certain peculiarities which no doubt make him, now and then, difficult to work with." But there was no one else, in Balfour's opinion, who could successfully lead Britain.[14]

Although Lloyd George had come a long way from his village in north Wales, he never became part of the English upper classes. Neither he nor his wife liked visiting the great country houses, and he positively disliked staying with the king and queen. When George V, as a mark of honor, invited him to carry the sword of state at the opening of Parliament, Lloyd George privately said, "I won't be a flunkey," and begged off. Most of his friends were, like him, self-made men. Balfour, who was a Cecil, from an old and famous family, was a rare exception. And Balfour, with his affable willingness to take second place, suited him very well as a foreign minister.[15]

In Paris, Lloyd George ignored the Foreign Office wherever he could and used his own staff of bright young men. The bureaucrats particularly resented his private secretary, the high-minded, religious and arrogant Philip Kerr. Because Lloyd George hated reading memoranda, Kerr, who dealt with much of his correspondence, was the gatekeeper to the great man. Even Balfour was moved to mild reproof when he asked Kerr whether the prime minister had read a particular document and was told no, but that Kerr had. "Not quite the same thing, is it, Philip—yet?" The professional diplomats muttered among themselves, and Lord Curzon, who had been left behind in London to mind the shop while Balfour and Lloyd George were in Paris, was pained. The prime minister paid no attention.[16]

Was this a bad thing for Britain? He clearly did not have a grasp on foreign affairs equal to that of his predecessor, Lord Salisbury, or his later successor Churchill. His knowledge had great gaps. "Who are the Slovaks?" he asked in 1916. "I can't seem to place them." His geography was equally sketchy. How interesting, he told a subordinate in 1918, to discover that New Zealand was on the east side of Australia. In 1919, when Turkish forces were retreating eastward from the Mediterranean, Lloyd George talked dramatically of their flight toward Mecca. "Ankara," said Curzon severely. Lloyd George replied airily, "Lord Curzon is good enough to admonish me on a triviality." Yet he often came to sensible conclusions (even if his disdain for the professionals and his own enthusiasms also led him into mistakes, such as support for a restored Greater Greece). Germany, he told a friend in the middle of the war, must be beaten, but not destroyed. That would not do either Europe or the British empire any good, and would leave the field clear for a strong Russia. He understood where Britain's interests lay: its trade and its empire, with naval dominance to protect them and a balance of power in Europe to prevent any power from challenging those interests.[17]

He recognized that Britain could no longer try to achieve these goals on its own. Its military power, though great, was shrinking rapidly as the country moved back to a peacetime footing. During 1919, the size of the army was to drop by two thirds at a time when Britain was taking on more and more responsibilities, from the Baltic states to Russia to Afghanistan, and dealing with more and more trouble in its empire—India, Egypt and, on its own doorstep, Ireland. "There are no troops to spare," came the despairing answer from the general staff to repeated requests.[18] The burden of power was also weighing heavily in economic terms. Britain was no longer the world's financial center; the United States was. And Britain owed huge amounts to the Americans, as the prime minister was well aware. With his usual optimism, he felt that he could build a good relationship with the United States which would help to compensate for British weaknesses. Perhaps the Americans would take on responsibility for such strategically important areas as the straits at Constantinople.

Britain went into the Peace Conference with a relatively good hand, certainly a better one than either France or Italy. The German fleet, which had challenged British power around the world, was safely in British hands, the surface ships in Scapa Flow in the Orkneys and most of the submarines in Harwich on the southeast coast of England. Its coaling stations, harbors and telegraph stations had been taken by Japan or the British empire. "If you had told the British people twelve months ago," Lloyd George said in Paris, "that they would have secured what they have, they would have laughed you to scorn. The German Navy has been handed over; the German mercantile shipping has been handed over, and the German colonies have been given up. One of our chief trade competitors has been most seriously crippled and our Allies are about to become her biggest creditors. That is no small achievement."

There was more: "We have destroyed the menace to our Indian possessions." Russia, whose southward push throughout the nineteenth century had so worried generations of British statesmen, was finished as a power, at least in the short run, and all along its southern boundaries, in Persia and the Caucasus, were British forces and British influence.[19]

So much of prewar British policy had been devoted to protecting the routes to India across the Mediterranean, the Suez Canal and down the Red Sea, either by taking direct control, as in the case of Egypt, or by propping up the shaky old Ottoman empire. That empire was finished, but thanks to a secret agreement with France, Britain was poised to take the choice bits it wanted. There were new routes, at least in the dreams of the Foreign Office and the military, perhaps across the Black Sea to the Caucasus and then south, or by air via Greece and Mesopotamia, but these, too, could be protected if Britain moved quickly enough to seize the territory it needed.

People have often assumed that, because Lloyd George opposed the Boer War, he was not an imperialist. This is not quite true. In fact, he had always taken great pride in the empire, but he had never thought it was being run properly. It was folly to try to manage everything from London and, he argued, an expensive folly at that. What would keep the empire strong was to allow as much local self-government as possible and to have an imperial policy only on the important issues, such as defense and a common foreign policy. With home rule—he was thinking of Scotland, his own Wales and the perennially troublesome Ireland as well—parts of the empire would willingly take on the costs of looking after themselves. ("Home Rule for Hell," cried a heckler at one of his speeches. "Quite right," retorted Lloyd George, "let every man speak up for his own country.") The dominions—Australia, Canada, New Zealand, Newfoundland and South Africa—were already partly self-governing. Even India was moving slowly to self-government; but with its mix of races, which included only the merest handful of Europeans, and its many religions and languages, Lloyd George doubted it would ever be able to manage on its own. (He never visited India and knew very little about it but, in the off-hand way of his times, he considered Indians, along with other brown-skinned peoples, to be inferior.[20])

In 1916, shortly after he became prime minister, Lloyd George told the House of Commons that the time had come to consult formally with the dominions and India about the best way to win the war. He intended, therefore, to create an Imperial War Cabinet. It was a wonderful gesture. It was also necessary. The dominions and India were keeping the British war effort going with their raw materials, their munitions, their loans, above all with their manpower—some 1,250,000 soldiers from India and another million from the dominions. Australia, as Billy Hughes, its prime minister, never tired of reminding everyone, had lost more soldiers by 1918 than the United States.[21]

By 1916 the dominions, which had once tiptoed reverentially around the mother country, were growing up. They and their generals had seen too much of what Sir Robert Borden, the Canadian prime minister, called "incompetence and blundering stupidity of the whiskey and soda British H.Q. Staff." The dominions knew how important their contribution was, what they had spent in blood. In return, they now expected to be consulted, both on the war and the peace to follow. They found a receptive audience in Britain, where what had been in prewar days a patronizing contempt for the crudeness of colonials had turned into enthusiasm for their vigor. Billy Hughes became something of a fad when he visited London in 1916; women marched with signs saying "We Want Hughes Back," and a popular cartoon showed the Billiwog: "No War Is Complete Without One." And then there was Jan Smuts, South Africa's foreign minister, soldier, statesman and, to some, seer, who spent much of the later part of the war in London. Smuts had fought against the British fifteen years previously; now he was one of their most trusted advisers, sitting on the small committee of the British cabinet which Lloyd George set up to run the war. He was widely admired: "Of his practical contribution to our counsels during these trying years," said Lloyd George, "it is difficult to speak too highly."[22]

In the last days of the war Hughes and Borden were infuriated to discover that the British War Cabinet had authorized Lloyd George and Balfour to go to the Supreme War Council in Paris to settle the German armistice terms with the Allies without bothering to inform the dominions. Hughes also strongly objected to Wilson's Fourteen Points being accepted as the basis for peace negotiations—"a painful and serious breach of faith." The dominion leaders were even more indignant when they discovered that the British had assumed they would tag along to the Peace Conference as part of the British delegation. Lloyd George attempted to mollify them by suggesting that a dominion prime minister could be one of the five British plenipotentiaries. But which one? As Hankey said, "The dominions are as jealous of each other as cats." The real problem over representation, as Borden wrote to his wife, was that the dominions' position had never been properly sorted out. Canada was "a nation that is not a nation. It is about time to alter it." And he noted, with a certain tone of pity, "The British Ministers are doing their best, but their best is not good enough." To Hankey he said that if Canada did not have full representation at the conference there was nothing for it but for him "to pack his trunks, return to Canada, summon Parliament, and put the whole thing before them."[23]

Lloyd George gave way: not only would one of the five main British delegates be chosen from the empire, but he would tell his allies that the dominions and India required separate representation at the Peace Conference. It was one of the first issues he raised when he arrived in Paris on January 12, 1919. The Americans and the French were cool, seeing only British puppets—and extra British votes. When Lloyd George extracted a grudging offer that the dominions and India might have one delegate each, the same as Siam and Portugal, that only produced fresh cries of outrage from his empire colleagues. After all their sacrifices, they said, it was intolerable that they should be treated as minor powers. A reluctant Lloyd George persuaded Clemenceau and Wilson to allow Canada, Australia, South Africa and India to have two plenipotentiaries each and New Zealand one.[24]

The British were taken aback by the new assertiveness in their empire. "It was very inconvenient," said one diplomat. "What was the Foreign Office to do?" Lloyd George, who had been for home rule in principle, discovered that the reality could be awkward, when, for example, Hughes said openly in the Supreme Council that Australia might not go to war the next time Britain did. (The remark was subsequently edited out of the minutes, but South Africa raised the question again.) Britain's allies watched this with a certain amount of satisfaction. They might be able to use the dominions against the British, the French realized with pleasure, when it came to drawing up the German peace terms. House took an even longer-term view: separate representation for the dominions and India in the Peace Conference, and in new international bodies such as the League of Nations and the International Labour Organization, could only hurry along "the eventual disintegration of the British Empire." Britain would end up back where it started, with only its own islands.[25]

It was a British empire delegation (and the name was a victory in itself for the fractious dominions) that Lloyd George led to Paris. With well over four hundred officials, special advisers, clerks and typists, it occupied five hotels near the Arc de Triomphe. The largest, and the social center, was the Hôtel Majestic, in prewar days a favorite with rich Brazilian women on clothes-buying trips. To protect against spies (French rather than German), the British authorities replaced all the Majestic's staff, even the chefs, with imports from British hotels in the Midlands. The food became that of a respectable railway hotel: porridge and eggs and bacon in the mornings, lots of meat and vegetables at lunch and dinner and bad coffee all day. The sacrifice was pointless, Nicolson and his colleagues grumbled, because all their offices, full of confidential papers, were in the Hôtel Astoria, where the staff was still French.[26]

Security was something of an obsession with the British. Their letters to and from London went by a special service that bypassed the French post office. Detectives from Scotland Yard guarded the front door at the Majestic, and members of the delegation had to wear passes with their photographs. They were urged to tear up the contents of their wastepaper baskets into tiny pieces; it was well known that at the Congress of Vienna, Prince Talleyrand, the French foreign minister, had negotiated so successfully because his agents assiduously collected discarded notes from the other delegations. Wives were allowed to take meals in the Majestic but not to stay—yet another legacy of the Congress of Vienna, where, according to official memory, they had been responsible for secrets leaking out.[27]

Lloyd George chose to stay in a luxurious flat in the Rue Nitot, an alleyway that had once been the haunt of ragpickers. Decorated with wonderful eighteenth-century English paintings—Gainsboroughs, Hoppners and Lawrences—the flat had been lent him by a rich Englishwoman. With him he had Philip Kerr and Frances Stevenson, as well as his youngest daughter and favorite child, the sixteen-year-old Megan. Frances was her chaperone, or perhaps it was the other way around. Balfour lived one floor above and in the evenings he could hear the sounds of Lloyd George's favorite Welsh hymns and black spirituals drifting up.[28]

At the Majestic each inhabitant was given a book of house rules. Meals were at set hours. Drinks had to be paid for unless, and this was a matter for bitter comment, you came from one of the dominions or India, in which case the British government footed the bill. Coupons were available, but cash was also accepted. There was to be no running up of accounts. Members of the delegation were not to cook in their rooms or damage the furniture. They must not keep dogs. A doctor (a distinguished obstetrician, according to Nicolson) and three nurses were on duty in the sick bay. A billiard room and a *jardin d'hiver* were available in the basement for recreation. So were a couple of cars, which could be booked ahead. There was a warning here: windows had already been broken "through violent slamming of doors." There was another warning too: "All members of the Delegation should bear in mind that telephone conversations will be overheard by unauthorised persons."[29]

"Very like coming to school for the first time" was the opinion of one new arrival. "Hanging about in the hall, being looked at by those already arrived as 'new kids,' picking out our baggage, noting times for meals, etc., to-morrow—very amusing."[30] If the British were the masters and the matrons, the Canadians were the senior prefects, a little bit serious perhaps, but reliable; the South Africans were the new boys, good at games and much admired for their sporting instincts; the Australians the cheeky ones, always ready to break bounds; the New Zealanders and Newfoundlanders the lower forms; and then, of course, the Indians, nice chaps in spite of the color of their skin, but whose parents were threatening to pull them out and send them to a progressive school.

The Canadians, well aware that they were from the senior dominion, were led by Borden, upright and handsome. They took a high moral tone (not for the first time in international relations), saying repeatedly that they wanted nothing for themselves. But with food to sell and a hungry Europe at hand, the Canadian minister of trade managed to get agreements with France, Belgium, Greece and Rumania. The Canadians were also caught up in the general feeling that borders had suddenly become quite fluid. They chatted away happily with the Americans about exchanging the Alaska panhandle for some of the West Indies or possibly British Honduras. Borden also spoke to Lloyd George about the possibility of Canada's taking over the administration of the West Indies.[31]

The main Canadian concern, however, was to keep on good terms with the United States and to bring it together with Britain. Part of this was self-interest: a recurring nightmare in Ottawa was that Canada might find itself fighting on the side of Britain and its ally Japan against the United States. Part was genuine conviction that the great Anglo-Saxon powers were a natural alliance for good. If the League of Nations did not work out, Borden suggested to Lloyd George, they should work for a union between "the two great English speaking commonwealths who share common ancestry, language and literature, who are inspired by like democratic ideals, who enjoy similar political institutions and whose united force is sufficient to ensure the peace of the world."[32]

South Africa had two outstanding figures: its prime minister, General Louis Botha, who was overweight and ailing, and Jan Smuts. Enthusiastic supporters of the League and moderate when it came to German peace terms, they nevertheless had one issue on which they would not compromise: Germany's African colonies. Smuts, who helped to draw up Britain's territorial demands, argued that Britain must keep East Africa (what later became Tanganyika and still later part of Tanzania) so that it could have the continuous chain of colonies from south to north Africa which the Germans had so inconveniently blocked. He also spoke as a South African imperialist. His country must keep German Southwest Africa (today's Namibia). Perhaps, he suggested, Portugal could be persuaded to swap the southern part of its colony of Mozambique on the east side of Africa for a bit of German East Africa. South Africa would then be a nice compact shape with a tidy border drawn across the tip of the continent.[33]

Australia was not moderate on anything. Its delegation was led by its prime minister, Billy Hughes, a scrawny dyspeptic who lived on tea and toast. A fighter on the Sydney docks, where he became a union organizer, and a veteran of the rough-and-tumble of Australian politics, Hughes made Australia's policies in Paris virtually on his own. He was hot-tempered, idiosyncratic and deaf, both literally and figuratively, to arguments he did not want to hear. Among his own people, he usually listened only to Keith Murdoch, a young reporter whom he regarded as something of a son. Murdoch, who had written a report criticizing the British handling of the landings at Gallipoli, where Australian troops had been slaughtered, shared Hughes's skepticism about British leadership. (Murdoch's own son Rupert later carried on the family tradition of looking at the British with a critical eye.) On certain issues, Hughes probably spoke for public opinion back home: he wanted leeway to annex the Pacific islands which Australia had captured from Germany, and nothing in the League covenant that would undermine the White Australia policy, which let white immigrants in and kept the rest out.[34]

Lloyd George, always susceptible to the Welsh card, which Hughes played assiduously, generally found the Australian prime minister amusing. So did Clemenceau. He thought that Hughes, who stood for firmness with Germany, would be a good friend to France. Most people found Hughes impossible. Wilson considered him "a pestiferous varmint." Hughes in return loathed Wilson: he sneered at the League and jeered at

Wilson's principles. New Zealand shared Australia's reservations about the League, although less loudly, and it, too, wanted to annex some Pacific islands. Its prime minister, William Massey, was, according to one Canadian, "as thick headed and John Bullish as his appearance would lead one to expect and sidetracked the discussion more than once."[35]

Then there was India. (It was always "the dominions and India" in the official documents.) India had been included in the Imperial War Cabinet along with the self-governing dominions thanks to its participation in the war. But its delegation did not look like that of an independent nation. It was headed by the secretary of state for India, Edwin Montagu, and the two Indian members, Lord Satyendra Sinha and the Maharajah of Bikaner, were chosen for their loyalty. In spite of the urgings of various Indian groups, the Indian government had not appointed any of the new Indian nationalist leaders. And in India itself, Gandhi's transformation of the Indian National Congress into a mass political movement demanding self-government was rapidly making all the debate about how to lead India gently toward a share of its own government quite academic.

The British were to find the presence of so many dominion statesmen in Paris a mixed blessing. While Borden faithfully represented the British case in the committee dealing with the borders of Greece and Albania, and Australia did the same with respect to Czechoslovakia, it was not quite such smooth sailing when the dominions had something at stake. Lloyd George had already confronted his Allies on behalf of his dominions and he would have to confront them again. It was not a complication he needed as the laborious negotiations began.

PART TWO

A NEW WORLD ORDER

5

We Are the League of the People

ON JANUARY 12, the day after his arrival in Paris, Lloyd George met Clemenceau, Wilson and the Italian prime minister, Vittorio Orlando, at the French Foreign Ministry on the Quai d'Orsay for the first of well over a hundred meetings. Each man brought his foreign secretary and a bevy of advisers. The following day, in deference to British wishes, two Japanese representatives joined the group. This became the Council of Ten, although most people continued to refer to it as the Supreme Council. The smaller allies and neutrals were not invited, an indication of what was to come. At the end of March, as the Peace Conference reached its crucial struggles, the Supreme Council was to shed the foreign ministers and the Japanese to become the Council of Four: Lloyd George, Clemenceau, Wilson and Orlando.

The great staterooms at the Quai d'Orsay have survived the passage of time and a later German occupation surprisingly well. They were given their present shape in the middle of the nineteenth century, when Napoleon III ruled a France that still dreamed of being a great world power. Important visitors still go in the formal entrance overlooking the Seine, past the massive branching staircase which leads up to the private apartments, and into the series of reception rooms and offices with their parquet floors, Aubusson carpets and massive fireplaces. Huge windows stretch up toward the high decorated ceilings and elaborate chandeliers. The heavy tables and chairs stand on fat gilded legs. The predominant colors are gold, red and ebony.

The Supreme Council met in the inner sanctum, the office of France's foreign minister, Stéphen Pichon. Today it is white and gilt; in 1919 it was darker. The same carved-wood paneling still decorates the walls, and the faded seventeenth-century tapestries still hang above the paneling. The double doors open out to a rotunda and there is still a rose garden beyond. Clemenceau, as the host, presided from an armchair in front of the hearth with its massive log fire. His colleagues, each with a little table for his papers, faced him from the garden side, the British and Americans side by side, then the Japanese and the Italians off in a corner. Wilson, as the only head of state, had a chair a few inches higher than anyone else's. The prime ministers and foreign ministers had high-backed, comfortable chairs, and in clusters behind them were the lesser advisers and secretaries on little gilt chairs.

The Supreme Council rapidly developed its own routine. It met once, sometimes twice, occasionally three times a day. There was an agenda of sorts, but the council also dealt with issues as they came up. It heard petitioners, a procession that did not end until the conference's conclusion. As the afternoons closed in, the green silk curtains were drawn and the electric lights were switched on. The room was usually very hot, but the French reacted with horror to any suggestion of opening a window. Clemenceau slouched in his chair, frequently looking at the ceiling, with a bored expression; Wilson fidgeted, getting up from time to time to stretch his legs; Lansing, his foreign minister, who had little enough to do, made caricatures; Lloyd George chatted in a loud undertone, making jokes and comments. The official interpreter, Paul Mantoux, interpreted from French to English and back again, throwing himself into each speech with such verve that one might have thought he was himself begging for territory. Since Clemenceau spoke English well and the Italian foreign minister, Sidney Sonnino, spoke it reasonably, conversations among the Big Four were often in English. The assistants tiptoed about with maps and documents. Every afternoon the doors opened and footmen carried in tea and macaroons. Wilson was surprised and somewhat shocked at first that they should interrupt discussing the future of the world for such a trivial event, but, as he told his doctor, he realized that this was a foreign custom that he might as well accept.[1]

From their first meeting, the men on the Supreme Council knew that as their armed forces demobilized, their power was shrinking. "Three hundred and twelve thousand will be sent this month," the commander of the American forces in Europe, General Pershing, told House that spring. "The record last month was 300,000. At this rate all our troops will be in the United States by August 15."[2] The peacemakers had to impose peace terms on the enemy while they could. Meanwhile, they had to worry about issues at home that had been postponed during the war. They were also racing, or so they believed, against another sort of enemy. Hunger, disease—typhoid, cholera and the dreadful influenza—revolutionary insurrections in one city after another, and small wars, some dozen of them in 1919 alone, all threatened to finish off what was left of European society.

It was already two months since the end of the war, and people were wondering why so little had been accomplished. Part of the reason was that the Allies were not really ready for the sudden end of the fighting. Nor could they have been. All their energies had been devoted to winning the war. "What had we to do with peace," wrote Winston Churchill, "while we did not know whether we should not be destroyed? Who could think of reconstruction while the whole world was being hammered to pieces, or of demobilisation when the sole aim was to hurl every man and every shell into battle?" Foreign offices, it is true, colonial ministries and war offices had dusted off old goals and drawn up new demands while the fighting went on. There had been attempts to think seriously about the peace: the British special inquiry, established in 1917, the French Comité d'Etudes and the most comprehensive of all, the American Inquiry, set up in September 1917 under House's supervision. To the dismay of the professional diplomats, they had called on outside experts, from historians to missionaries, and had produced detailed studies and maps. The Americans had produced sixty separate reports on the Far East and the Pacific alone, which contained much useful information as well as such insights as that, in India, "a great majority of the unmarried consist of very young children."[3] The Allied leaders had not paid much attention to any of their own studies.

In the first week of the Peace Conference, the Supreme Council spent much time talking about procedures. The British Foreign Office had produced a beautiful diagram in many colors of a hexagon within which the conference, its committees and subcommittees fitted together in perfect symmetry, while outside, the Allies' own committees floated like minor planets. Lloyd George burst out laughing when it was shown to him. The French circulated a detailed agenda with lists of guiding principles and problems to be addressed, ranked in order of importance. Since the settlement with Germany came first and the League of Nations barely rated a mention, Wilson, with support from Lloyd George, rejected it. (Tardieu, its author, saw this as "the instinctive repugnance of the Anglo-Saxons to the systematized constructions of the Latin mind."[4])

The Supreme Council managed to choose a secretary, Henri Dutasta, a junior French diplomat who was rumored to be Clemenceau's illegitimate son. (The extraordinarily efficient British official, Hankey, who became the deputy secretary, soon took over most of the work.) After much wrangling it was decided that French and English would both be the official languages for documents. The French argued for their own language alone, ostensibly on the grounds that it was more precise and at the same time capable of greater nuance. French, they said, had been the language of international communication and diplomacy for centuries. The British and the Americans pointed out that English was increasingly supplanting it. Lloyd George said that he would always regret that he did not know French better (he scarcely knew it at all), but it seemed absurd that English, spoken by more than 170 million people, should not have equal status with French. The Italians said, in that case, why not Italian as well? "Otherwise," said Sonnino, "it would look as if Italy was being treated as an inferior by being excluded." In that case, said Lloyd George, why not Japanese as well? The Japanese delegates, who tended to have trouble following the debates whether they were in French or English, remained silent. Clemenceau backed down, to the consternation of many of his own officials.[5]

In December the French Foreign Ministry had sent out invitations to every country, from Liberia to Siam, that could claim, however improbably, to be on the Allied side. By January there were twenty-nine countries represented in Paris, all expecting to take part. How would their role be defined? Would they all sit together, with the British empire having the same vote as Panama? None of the Great Powers wanted that, but where Clemenceau was willing to start the delegates from the lesser powers on relatively harmless questions such as international waterways, Wilson preferred as little structure as possible. "We ought to have," he said, "no formal Conferences but only conversations." Clemenceau found this exasperating: if the Allies waited until they had agreed on all the main issues, it would be months before the Peace Conference proper could begin, and public opinion would be very disappointed. Anyway, he added, they had to give all the other powers, who were assembling in Paris, something to do. Lloyd George proposed a compromise, as he was to do on many occasions: there would be a plenary session at the end of the week; in the meantime, the Supreme Council would get on with other matters.[6]

The members of the Supreme Council, even Wilson, had no intention of relinquishing control of the conference agenda, which promised to be huge. The rejected French list included the League of Nations, Polish affairs, Russian affairs, Baltic nationalities, states formed from the late Austro-Hungarian monarchy, the Balkans; the Far East and the Pacific, Jewish affairs, international river navigation, international railways, legislation to guarantee people's self-determination; protection for ethnic and religious minorities, international legislation on patents and trademarks, penalties for crimes committed during the war, reparations for war damages and economic and financial questions. The list was prescient.[7]

The Supreme Council also faced intense scrutiny from the public. In the weeks leading up to the start of the proceedings, hundreds of journalists had arrived in Paris. The French government created a lavish press club, in a millionaire's house. The press, men mainly but also including a handful of women, such as the great American muckraker Ida Tarbell, were ungrateful. They sneered at the vulgarity of the décor, and the Americans nicknamed it "The House of a Thousand Teats." More important, the press complained about the secrecy of the proceedings. Wilson had talked in his Fourteen Points about "open covenants openly arrived at." As with many of his catchphrases, its meaning was not clear, perhaps not even to Wilson himself, but it caught the public imagination.[8]

Wilson certainly meant there should be no more secret treaties, such as those that he and many others saw as one of the causes of the Great War, but did he mean that all the negotiations would be open for public scrutiny? That is what many of the journalists and their readers expected. Press representatives demanded the right to attend the meetings of the Supreme Council, or at least get daily summaries of their discussions. He had always fought for the freedom of the press, Clemenceau told his aide General Mordacq, but there were limits. It would be "a veritable suicide" to let the press report on the day-to-day discussions of the Supreme Council. If that were to happen, Lloyd George commented, the Peace Conference would go on forever. He proposed that they release a statement to the press, saying that the process of reaching decisions among the powers was going to be long and delicate, and that they had no wish to stir up unnecessary controversy by publicizing their disagreements. Wilson agreed. American journalists complained bitterly to Baker, Wilson's press adviser, who went, according to one, pale with anxiety. Wilson, they told him, was a hypocrite and a naïve one at that. Lloyd George and Clemenceau, safe from the spotlight of public scrutiny, would tie him in knots. The journalists threatened to leave Paris, but few did.[9]

The lesser powers were also full of complaints and demands. Portugal, which had contributed 60,000 soldiers to the Western Front, thought it was outrageous that it should have only one official delegate while Brazil, which had sent a medical unit and some aviators, had three. Britain supported Portugal, an old ally, the United States Brazil. Recognition in Paris, the center of world power, was important for established states, and crucial for what the peacemakers christened "states in process of formation." With the collapse of Russia, and the disintegration of Austria-Hungary and the Ottoman empire, there were many of these. Just standing in front of the Supreme Council to present a case was validation of a sort—and good for reputations back home.[10]

For the next five months, until the signing of the German treaty in June at Versailles, Paris housed a virtual world government. "We are the league of the people," said Clemenceau the day before that momentous ceremony.

Wilson replied, "We are the State." And even in those very first meetings, the members of the Supreme Council were starting to act as a cabinet, within a representative system of government. Indeed, it was an analogy that they themselves used.[11]

Paris may have housed a world government, but that government's power was never as great as most people, both then and since, have assumed. By the time the Supreme Council first met on January 12, Poland had been re-created, Finland and the Baltic states were well on their way to independence and Czechoslovakia had been pieced together. In the Balkans, Serbia had joined with Austria-Hungary's South Slav territories of Croatia and Slovenia. The new entity did not yet have a name but some people were talking of a Yugoslav state. "The task of the Parisian Treatymakers," Lloyd George commented, "was not to decide what in fairness should be given to the liberated nationalities, but what in common honesty should be freed from their clutches when they had overstepped the bounds of self-determination."[12]

But what were those bounds? There was no clear answer—or rather, every competing nationality had a different answer. "You see those little holes?" a local asked an American visitor to Lvov, on the disputed borders between Russia and Poland. "We call them here 'Wilson's Points.' They have been made with machine guns; the big gaps have been made with hand grenades. We are now engaged in self-determination, and God knows what and when the end will be." At its first meetings the Supreme Council had to deal with fighting between Poland and its neighbors. When the Peace Conference officially ended a year later, the fighting was still going on, there and elsewhere. Tasker Bliss, the American military adviser, wrote gloomily to his wife from Paris predicting another thirty years of war in Europe. "The 'submerged nations' are coming to the surface and as soon as they appear, they fly at somebody's throat. They are like mosquitoes—vicious from the moment of their birth."[13]

It is tempting but misleading to compare the situation in 1919 to that in 1945. In 1919 there were no superpowers, no Soviet Union with its millions of soldiers occupying the center of Europe and no United States with its huge economy and its monopoly of the atomic bomb. In 1919, the enemy states were not utterly defeated. The peacemakers talked expansively about making and unmaking nations, but the clay was not as malleable and the strength to mold it not as great as they liked to think. Of course, the peacemakers had considerable power. They still had armies and navies. They had the weapon of food if they chose to use it against a starving Europe. They could exert influence by threats and promises, to grant or withhold recognition, for example. They could get out the maps and move borders this way or that, and most of the time their decisions would be accepted—but not always, as the case of Turkey was to show in spectacular fashion. The ability of the international government in Paris to control events was limited by such factors as distance, usable transportation and available forces—and by the unwillingness of the Great Powers to expend their resources.

In 1919 the limits were not yet clear—to the peacemakers themselves, or to the world. Consequently, many people believed that, if only they could catch the attention of the Supreme Council, past wrongs would be righted and their futures assured. A young kitchen assistant at the Ritz sent in a petition asking for independence from France for his little country. Ho Chi Minh—and Vietnam—were too obscure even to receive an answer. A Korean graduate of Princeton University tried to get to Paris but was refused a passport. After the Second World War, Syngman Rhee became the president of a newly independent South Korea.[14]

Women's suffrage societies met in Paris, chaired by the formidable Englishwoman Millicent Fawcett, and passed resolutions asking for representation at the Peace Conference and votes for women. Wilson, who had a certain sympathy for their cause, met their delegation and talked vaguely but encouragingly about a special commission of the conference, with women members, to look into women's issues. In February, just before he left on a short trip back to the United States, he hesitantly asked his fellow peacemakers whether they would support this. Balfour said he was a strong supporter of votes for women but he did not think they should be dealing with such a matter. Clemenceau agreed. The Italians said it was a purely domestic issue. As Clemenceau whispered loudly, "What's the little chap saying?," the Japanese delegate expressed appreciation for the great part women had played in civilization but commented that the suffrage movement in Japan was scarcely worth notice. The matter was dropped, never to be taken up again.[15]

The peacemakers soon discovered that they had taken on the administration of much of Europe and large parts of the Middle East. Old ruling structures had collapsed and Allied occupation forces and Allied representatives were being drawn in to take their place. There was little choice; if they did not do it, no one would—or, worse, revolutionaries might. The men on the spot did what they could. In Belgrade, a British admiral scraped together a small fleet of barges and sent them up and down the Danube carrying food and raw materials. He brought about a modest revival in trade and industry, often in the face of obstruction from the different governments along the river, but it was a stopgap measure. As he told Paris, the long-term solution was international control of the Danube and the other great European waterways. There were other schemes and other enthusiasts, but was there the political will? Or the money?[16]

The economic responsibilities alone were daunting. The war had disrupted the world's economy and it would not be easy to get it going again. The European nations had borrowed huge amounts of money—in the case of the Allies, increasingly from the United States. Now they found it almost impossible to get the credit to finance their reconstruction and the revival of trade. The war had left factories unusable, fields untilled, bridges and railway lines destroyed. There were shortages of fertilizer, seeds, raw materials, shipping, locomotives. Europe still depended largely on coal for its fuel, but the mines in France, Belgium, Poland and Germany were flooded. The emergence of new nations in central Europe further damaged what was left of the old trading and transportation networks. In Vienna, the electric lights flickered and the trams stopped running because the coal which had once come from the north was now blocked by a new border.

From all quarters of Europe, from officials and private relief agencies, alarming reports came in: millions of unemployed men, desperate housewives feeding their families on potatoes and cabbage soup, emaciated children. In that first cold winter of the peace, Herbert Hoover, the American relief administrator, warned the Allies that some 200 million people in the enemy countries and almost as many again among the victors and the neutral nations faced famine. Germany alone needed 200,000 tons of wheat per month and 70,000 tons of meat. Throughout the territories of the old Austria-Hungary, hospitals had run out of bandages and medicines. In the new Czechoslovak state, a million children were going without milk. In Vienna, more babies were dying than were surviving. People were eating coal dust, wood shavings, sand. Relief workers invented names for things they had never seen before, such as the mangel-wurzel disease, which afflicted those who lived solely on beets.[17]

The humanitarian case for doing something was unanswerable. So was the political one. "So long as hunger continued to gnaw," Wilson warned his colleagues, "the foundations of government would continue to crumble."[18] They had the resources. The Canadians, Australians, New Zealanders and the Americans all had surplus food and raw materials which they were eager to sell. The ships could be found to carry them. But where was the money to come from? Germany had gold reserves, but the French, who were determined those should go toward reparations, did not want to see them used up financing imports. The European Allies could not finance relief on the scale that was needed, and the defeated nations, except Germany, were bankrupt. That left the United States, but Congress and the American public were torn between an impulse to help and a sense that the United States had done enough in winning the war. After the Second World War, their mood was very much the same, but with a crucial difference: in place of the diffuse threat of revolution there was a single clear enemy, in the Soviet Union. The equivalent of the Marshall Plan, which contributed so much to the revival of Europe in those circumstances, was not possible in 1919.

The United States, moreover, did not have the preponderance of power that it had after the Second World War. Its European allies were not exhausted and desperate, prepared to take American aid, even at the price of accepting American suggestions. In 1919, they still saw themselves as, and indeed were, independent actors in world affairs. Before the war ended, Britain, France and Italy drew up a plan for pooling Allied credit, food, raw materials and ships to undertake relief and reconstruction under an inter-Allied board. The Americans resisted. They suspected that their allies wanted to control the distribution of resources, even though the bulk would come from the United States, as a lever to pressure the enemy states into accepting peace terms. When Wilson insisted that Hoover be placed in charge of Allied relief administration, the Europeans objected. Hoover, Lloyd George complained, would become the "food dictator of Europe" and American businessmen would take the opportunity to move in. The Europeans only gave way reluctantly, and did their best to make Hoover's job difficult.[19]

To Wilson, as to many Americans, Hoover was a hero, a poor orphan who had worked his way through Stanford University to become one of the world's leading engineers. During the war he had organized a massive relief program for German-occupied Belgium, and when the United States became a belligerent in 1917 he took charge of saving food for the war effort. "I can Hooverize on dinner," said Valentine cards. "But I'll never learn to Hooverize, When it comes to loving you." He was efficient, hardworking and humorless. Lloyd George found him tactless and brusque. The Europeans resented his reminders that the United States was supplying the bulk of Europe's relief and the way in which he promoted American economic interests, unloading, for example, stockpiled American pork products and severely undercutting European producers.[20]

Although the Allies had a number of economic agencies, supervised loosely by the Supreme Economic Council, Hoover's food and relief section was by far the most effective. With $100 million from the United States and about $62 million from Britain, he established offices in thirty-two countries, opened soup kitchens that fed millions of children, and moved tons of food, clothes and medical supplies into the hardest-hit areas. By the spring of 1919, Hoover's organization was running railways and supervising mines. It had its own telegraph network. It waged war on lice, with thousands of hair clippers, tons of soap, special baths and stations manned by American soldiers. Travelers who did not have a "deloused" certificate were seized and disinfected. In the summer of 1919 Hoover infuriated the Europeans yet again. He argued that the United States had done enough; it was now up to the Europeans. With hard work, austerity and savings they should be all right. His views met with approval in an increasingly isolationist Washington, and American aid and loans fell off sharply.[21]

In fact, it took Europe until 1925 to get back to prewar levels of production; in some areas, recovery was much slower. Many governments resorted to such measures as borrowing, budget deficits and trade controls to keep their countries afloat. Europe's economy as a whole remained fragile, adding to political strains at home in the 1920s and tensions abroad as governments turned to protectionist measures. Perhaps with American money and European cooperation a stronger Europe could have been built, more able to resist the challenges of the 1930s.[22]

6

Russia

O N JANUARY 18, 1919, the Peace Conference officially opened. Clemenceau made sure that the opening took place on the anniversary of the coronation in 1871 of Wilhelm I as kaiser of the new Germany. To the delegates assembled in the sumptuous Salle d'Horloge at the Quai d'Orsay, President Poincaré spoke of the wickedness of their enemies, the great sacrifices of the Allies and the hopes for a lasting peace. "You hold in your hands," he told them, "the future of the world." As they walked out, Balfour turned to Clemenceau and apologized for his top hat. "I was told," he said, "that it was obligatory to wear one." "So," replied Clemenceau, in his bowler, "was I."[1]

Observers noticed some absences: the Greek prime minister, Venizelos, annoyed that Serbia had more delegates than his own country; Borden, the Canadian prime minister, offended that the prime minister of little Newfoundland had been given precedence; and the Japanese, who had not yet arrived. But the most striking absence of all was that of Russia.

An Ally in 1914, Russia had probably saved France from defeat when it attacked Germany on the Eastern Front. For three years, Russia had battled the Central Powers, inflicting huge losses but absorbing even more. In 1917 it had finally cracked under the strain and, in eight months, had gone from autocracy to liberal democracy to a revolutionary dictatorship under a tiny extreme faction of Russian socialists, the Bolsheviks, whom most people, including the Russians themselves, had never heard of. As Russia collapsed, it spun off parts of a great empire: the Baltic states, Ukraine, Armenia, Georgia, Azerbaijan and Daghestan. The Allies had sent in troops in a vain attempt to bolster their disintegrating ally against the Germans, but at the start of 1918 the Bolsheviks made peace with Germany. The Allied soldiers remained on Russian soil, but to do what? Topple the Bolsheviks and their Soviet regime? Support their heterogeneous opponents, the royalists, liberals, anarchists, disillusioned socialists, nationalists of various sorts?

In Paris it was not easy to tell what was happening in the east or who was on which side. Stories drifted westward of a social order turned upside down, civil wars, nationalist uprisings, a cycle of atrocities, retribution and more atrocities: the last tsar and his family murdered and their bodies thrown down a well; the mutilated body of a British naval attaché lying unburied on a St. Petersburg street. Russian soldiers had shot their officers, and sailors had commandeered their ships. Across the huge Russian countryside, peasants, driven by an ancient hunger for land, were killing their landlords. In the cities, teenagers swaggered with guns and the poor crept out of their slums to occupy the great mansions. It was hard to tell how much was true (most of it was) because Russia had become an unknown land. The new regime was under a virtual blockade. The powers had cut off trade with the Bolsheviks and had withdrawn their diplomats by the summer of 1918. Almost all foreign newspaper correspondents had gone by the start of 1919. The land routes were cut by fighting. Telegrams took days or weeks, if they got through at all. By the time the Peace Conference assembled, the only sure conduit for messages was through Stockholm, where the Bolsheviks had a representative. During the conference, the peacemakers knew as much about Russia as they did about the far side of the moon.[2] As Lloyd George put it: "We were, in fact, never dealing with ascertained, or perhaps, even ascertainable facts. Russia was a jungle in which no one could say what was within a few yards of him."[3] His shaky grasp of geography did not help him; he thought Kharkov (a city in the Ukraine) was the name of a Russian general.

Legally, perhaps, there was no need to invite Russian representatives. That was Clemenceau's view: Russia had betrayed the Allied cause, leaving France to the mercy of the Germans.[4] The Bolshevik leader, Lenin, at once a realist and a fanatic, had given away land and resources to Germany at Brest-Litovsk (today Brest in Poland) in return for peace so that he could conserve the vital spark from which the Marxist millennium would come. Germany gained access to the materials it so desperately needed and the chance to switch hundreds of thousands of its troops to the Western Front. Lenin's action, certainly for Clemenceau, released the Allies from all their promises to Russia, including the promise of access to the vital straits leading from the Black Sea to the Mediterranean.

On the other hand, Russia was technically still an Ally and still at war with Germany. After all, the Germans had been obliged to renounce the Treaty of Brest-Litovsk, the peace treaty they had signed with Russia, when they made their own armistice in November 1918. In any case, Russia's absence was inconvenient. "In the discussions," wrote a young British adviser in his diary, "everything inevitably leads up to Russia. Then there is a discursive discussion; it is agreed that the point at issue cannot be determined until the general policy towards Russia has been settled; having agreed to this, instead of settling it, they pass on to some other subject."[5] Finland, the emerging Baltic states of Estonia, Latvia and Lithuania, Poland, Rumania, Turkey and Persia all came up at the Peace Conference, but their borders could not finally be set until the future shape and status of Russia were clear.

The issue of Russia came up repeatedly during the Peace Conference. Baker, later an apologist for Wilson, claimed that Russia and the fear of Bolshevism shaped the peace. "Russia," he cried, "played a more vital part at Paris than Prussia!" This, like much of what he has to say, is nonsense. The peacemakers were far more concerned with making peace with a still intact Germany and with getting Europe back onto a peacetime footing. They worried about Russia just as they worried about social unrest closer to home, but they did not necessarily see the two as sides of the same coin. Destroying the Bolsheviks in Russia would not magically remove the causes of unrest elsewhere. German workers and soldiers seized power because the kaiser's regime was discredited and bankrupt. Austria-Hungary collapsed because it could no longer keep itself afloat and its nationalities down. The Russian Revolution sometimes provided encouragement—and a vocabulary. "Bolshevism is having its day," wrote Borden in his diary, but he was talking about labor unrest, not revolution. "Bolshevism" (or its fellow, "communism") was a convenient shorthand in 1919. As Bliss, Wilson's military adviser, said, "If we replaced it by the word 'revolutionary,' perhaps that would be clearer."[6]

Of course, the peacemakers were concerned about the spread of revolutionary ideas, but not necessarily Russian ones. The survivors of the Great War were weary and anxious. Apparently solid structures, empires, their civil services and their armies, had melted away and in many parts of Europe it was not clear what was to take their place. Europe had been a place of unsatisfied longings before the war—of socialists hoping for a better world, of labor for better conditions, of nationalists for their own homes—and those longings emerged again with greater force because in the fluid world of 1919 it was possible to dream of great change—or have nightmares about the collapse of order. The Portuguese president was assassinated. Later in 1919, in Paris, a madman would try to kill Clemenceau.

In Bavaria and Hungary, communist governments took power, for a few days in Munich, but much longer in Budapest. In Berlin in January, and Vienna in June, communists tried, unsuccessfully, to do the same. Not everything could be blamed on the Russian Bolsheviks.

Many, and not just those on the left, refused to panic. Over lunch in the Hôtel Majestic one day, a Canadian delegate, Oliver Mowat Biggar, chatted cheerfully with a group that included Philip Kerr, Lloyd George's personal assistant. "The feeling of all of us was that money had too much to say in the world—selfish money that is. The logical conclusion is communism, and we shall no doubt all arrive there in a quarter of a century or so." In the meantime, as Biggar wrote to his wife in Canada, he was having a wonderful time: Saturday evening dances at the Majestic, *Faust* and *Madame Butterfly* at the Opéra, the music halls where he was struck, he told her, by the beauty of the prostitutes. The French, he noted, certainly had different standards from Canadians. In one comic opera, the lead actress "had nothing on above the hips except a few chains and in the other nothing on either above or below except ribbons and shoes. As a dancer she was dismal." When his wife suggested that she come immediately from Canada to join him, Biggar had serious reservations. Of course, he wanted to see her but even now the flats in Paris were terribly expensive, and they had appalling bathrooms. And he had been told, by a senior politician, that revolution was about to sweep across Germany and possibly into France. There would be serious shortages of food and fuel. The lights would go out, the taps would run dry. "You must, however, make up your own mind to discomfort with, very remotely, danger." Mrs. Biggar remained in Canada.[7]

Bolshevism had its uses. When Rumania claimed the Russian province of Bessarabia or Poland advanced into the Ukraine, it was to stop Bolshevism. Italy's delegates warned of revolution at home if they did not get most of the Dalmatian coast. The peacemakers used it as a threat to each other. Germany, said Lloyd George and Wilson, would go Bolshevik if they imposed too harsh a peace.

Western reactions to the new regime in Russia itself were deeply divided. Lack of information did not, of course, prevent people from having strong views. If anything, it made it easier. Both left and right projected their own fears and hopes into the black hole in the east. The radical American journalist Lincoln Steffens, who unusually actually got to Russia in 1919, crafted his famous "I have seen the future and it works" on the journey out. Nothing he witnessed in Russia changed his mind. On the right, every horror story was credited. The British government published reports, allegedly from eyewitnesses, claiming that the Bolsheviks had nationalized women and set them up in "commissariats of free love."

Churches had been turned into brothels. Special gangs of Chinese executioners had been imported to work their ancient Oriental skills on the Bolsheviks' victims.[8]

Churchill, Britain's secretary of state for war during the Peace Conference, was one of the few to grasp that Lenin's Bolshevism was something new on the political scene, that beneath the Marxist rhetoric was a highly disciplined, highly centralized party grasping at every lever of power it could secure. Motivated by the distant goal of a perfect world, it did not care what methods it used. "The essence of Bolshevism as opposed to many other forms of visionary political thought," Churchill asserted, "is that it can only be propagated and maintained by violence." Lenin and his colleagues were prepared to destroy whatever stood in the way of that vision, whether the institutions of Russian society or the Russians themselves. "Of all tyrannies in history," Churchill told an audience in London, "the Bolshevik tyranny is the worst, the most destructive, the most degrading." Lloyd George was unkind about Churchill's motives: "His ducal blood revolted against the wholesale elimination of Grand Dukes in Russia." Others, and they included many of his colleagues and the British public, wrote Churchill off as erratic and unreliable. The shadow of the disastrous Gallipoli campaign still hung over him, and his florid language sounded hysterical. "Civilisation," he said in an election speech in November 1918, "is being completely extinguished over gigantic areas, while Bolsheviks hop and caper like troops of ferocious baboons amid the ruins of cities and the corpses of their victims." After one outburst in cabinet Balfour told him coolly, "I admire the exaggerated way you tell the truth."[9]

While most Western liberals in 1919 were inclined to give the Bolsheviks the benefit of the doubt, the revolutionists' seizure of power from a democratically elected assembly, their murders—most notoriously of the tsar and his family—and their repudiation of Russia's foreign debts shocked public opinion. (The French were particularly irritated by the debt issue because a great many among the middle classes had bought Russian government bonds.) But, as good liberals reminded themselves, both the United States and France were the products of revolution. Wilson initially thought that Bolshevism was about curbing the power of big business and big government to provide greater freedom for the individual. His personal doctor, Grayson, noted that Wilson found much to approve of in the Bolshevik program: "Of course, he declared, their campaign of murder, confiscation and complete disregard for law, merits the utmost condemnation. However, some of their doctrines have been developed entirely through the pressures of the capitalists, who have disregarded the rights of the workers everywhere, and he warned all of his colleagues that if the Bolsheviks should become sane and agree to a policy of law and order they would soon spread all over Europe, overturning existing governments." Progressive thinkers such as himself and Wilson, said Lloyd George, thought that the old order—"inept, profligate and tyrannical"—deserved what it had got: "it had been guilty of exactions and oppressions which were accountable for the ferocity displayed by the Revolutionaries." There was still something, too, in Lloyd George of the bold young solicitor in north Wales who had taken on the powerful local interests. "The trouble with the P.M.," Curzon complained to Balfour, "is that he is a bit of a Bolshevist himself. One feels that he sees Trotsky as the only congenial figure on the international scene."[10]

The Russian Bolsheviks would, many believed, eventually settle down and become bourgeois. If Bolshevik ideas were permeating Western societies, it was because people were fed up. Remove the causes of Bolshevism, both Wilson and Lloyd George argued, and you would take away its oxygen. Farmers without land, workers without jobs, ordinary men and women without hope, all were fodder for visionaries promising the earth. There was a dangerous gulf, said Wilson, even in his own country, between capital and labor. "Seeds need soil, and the Bolshevik seeds found the soil already prepared for them." They could defeat Bolshevism, he assured the American experts on the voyage to Paris, by building a new order. Lloyd George, too, was inclined to be optimistic. "Don't you think Bolshevism will die out of itself?" he asked a British journalist. "Europe is very strong. It can resist it."[11]

Lloyd George would have preferred to include Russia in the Peace Conference. As he told Clemenceau at their meeting in London in December 1918, they could not proceed as if the country did not exist. He had, he said, great sympathy for the Russian people. "Their troops had fought without arms or munitions; they had been outrageously betrayed by their Government, and it was little to be wondered at if, in their bitterness, the Russian people had rebelled against the Alliance." Russia was a huge country, stretching from Europe to Asia, with almost 200 million people. If the nations with claims on Russian territory were to be allowed to come to Paris, then surely the Russians themselves deserved the right to be heard. That might mean inviting the Bolsheviks. He did not like them, Lloyd George told the Supreme Council, but could they refuse to recognize them? "To say that we ourselves should pick the representatives of a great people was contrary to every principle for which we had fought." The British government had made the same mistake after the French Revolution, when it had backed the émigré aristocrats. "This," Lloyd George said dramatically, "led them into a war which lasted about twenty-five years."[12]

His arguments did not go down well with Clemenceau, who loathed the Bolsheviks, partly because he saw them as tools of the Germans and partly because he abhorred their methods. For Clemenceau revolution was sublime when it was the one of 1789, despicable when it fell into the hands of the Jacobins, with their Robespierres and Lenins, who used the guillotine and the noose to create perfection. He had lived through the mob violence and the bloody suppression of the radical Commune of Paris at the end of the Franco-Prussian War. From that moment on he had broken with the extreme left. In 1919 he, like the other Allied leaders, also had to heed his own public opinion. If the Bolsheviks sent representatives to Paris, he told Balfour in a private interview, the extreme radicals would be encouraged and the middle classes would panic. There would be rioting in the streets, which his government would have to put down with force. That would not be a good atmosphere for the Peace Conference. If his allies insisted on going ahead with such an invitation, Clemenceau warned, he would be obliged to resign.[13]

And did the Bolsheviks speak for all the Russian people? They controlled only the core Russian lands, along with the great cities of St. Petersburg (soon to become Leningrad) and Moscow. They faced rival governments: that of the White Russians, as they were commonly known, in the south, under General Anton Denikin, one of the better tsarist generals, and another in Siberia under Admiral Aleksandr Kolchak. In Paris itself, Russian exiles, from conservatives to radicals, had formed the Russian Political Conference to speak for all non-Bolshevik Russians. Sergei Sazonov, who had been a foreign minister under the tsar, found himself working with Boris Savinkov, a famous terrorist. Sleek, fashionably dressed, a gardenia in his buttonhole, Savinkov was much admired in Paris. Lloyd George, who always liked efficiency, said: "His assassinations had always been skilfully arranged and had been a complete success."[14] Unfortunately, the Russian Political Conference got only grudging support from the rival governments of Denikin and Kolchak (which also spent much time trying to outmaneuver each other) and none at all from the Bolsheviks.

On January 16, Lloyd George brought the whole question of Russia before the Supreme Council. It seemed to him that they had three choices: first, to destroy Russian Bolshevism; second, to insulate the outside world from it; or third, to invite the Russians, Bolsheviks included, to meet the peacemakers. They had already taken steps towards the first two options: there were Allied soldiers on Russian soil, and the Allies had a blockade on Russia. Neither of these appeared to be working. He himself therefore preferred the last option. In fact, they could do the Russians a good turn by persuading the different factions to talk to each other and try to work out a truce. It was, he said privately, what the Romans had done when they sent for the barbarians and told them to behave.[15]

The peacemakers did not find it easy to make up their minds. There were objections to each course of action. Intervention to overthrow the Bolsheviks was risky and expensive; isolating Russia would hurt the Russian people; and bringing Bolshevik representatives to Paris or anywhere else in the West ran the risk of giving them a chance to spread their message, to say nothing of infuriating the conservatives. Wilson supported Lloyd George. The French and Italian foreign ministers, Pichon and Sonnino, demurred. At the least, suggested Pichon, they should listen to the French and Danish ambassadors, who had just returned from Russia. The two duly appeared, with alarming tales of the Red Terror, which Lloyd George cavalierly dismissed as exaggerations.[16] The Supreme Council found itself unable to come to any decision.

Throughout the Peace Conference, Allied policy toward Russia remained inconsistent and incoherent, not firm enough to overthrow the Bolsheviks but sufficiently hostile to convince them, with unfortunate consequences, that the Western powers were their implacable enemies. Churchill, who begged repeatedly for a clear policy line from his own government, was bitter in his memoirs about Allied indecision. "Were they at war with Soviet Russia? Certainly not; but they shot Soviet Russians at sight. They stood as invaders on Russian soil. They armed the enemies of the Soviet Government. They blockaded its ports, and sunk its battleships. They earnestly desired and schemed its downfall. But war—shocking! Interference—shame!"[17]

Churchill, of course, was for intervention. So was Marshal Ferdinand Foch, the senior French soldier and Allied commander-in-chief. And so were Tory members of Parliament in London and embittered French investors. Against them were ranged an equally vociferous group: the unions in solidarity with a working-class movement, humanitarians of various stripes, and the pragmatists who, with the popular London *Daily Express,* simply said, "We are sorry for the Russians, but they must fight it out among themselves."[18]

That tended to be Wilson's view. "I believe in letting them work out their own salvation," he told a British diplomat in Washington just before the end of the war, "even though they wallow in anarchy for a while. I visualize it like this: A lot of impossible folk fighting among themselves. You cannot do business with them, so you shut them all up in a room and lock the door and tell them that when they have settled matters among themselves you will unlock the door and do business." Wilson assumed that the shape of the room would remain much the same. He did not contemplate, as the British sometimes did, the breakup of the Russian empire. Self-determination, as he saw it, meant the Russian peoples running their own huge country. The only exception he made, on the basis of the same principle, was for Russia's Polish territory, which he felt should be part of a restored Poland. Curiously, he did not see Ukrainian nationalism in the same light (possibly because his great Republican opponent Senator Henry Cabot Lodge favored an independent Ukraine) and he staunchly resisted Allied recognition of the Baltic states. Otherwise his policy toward Russia was largely negative: nonintervention and nonrecognition. The sixth of his Fourteen Points called for the evacuation of Russian territory by foreign armies (he had the Japanese in mind, in particular) so that the Russian people could work out the institutions that best suited them. When the Russians had sorted out who was governing them (he hoped that it would not be the Bolsheviks), the United States would extend recognition. This, Wilson liked to point out, was what the United States had done in the Mexican civil war.[19]

The trouble was that the Allies had already intervened. In the spring of 1918, British troops had landed at the northern ports of Archangel and Murmansk, and the Japanese had seized Vladivostok on the Pacific and spread westward into Siberia to keep the Germans from getting their hands on Russian raw materials such as grain and oil, as well as on ports, railways and munitions. To keep an eye on the Japanese (and perhaps on the British) and to protect a legion of Czechs who had got themselves stuck in Siberia from Russian prisoner-of-war camps, the Americans had reluctantly landed their own troops. ("I have been sweating blood," Wilson complained to House that summer, "over the question of what is right and feasible to do in Russia. . . . It goes to pieces like quicksilver under my touch.") The British then prevailed on the Canadians to supply a force to balance the Americans and the Japanese. Down in the south another British force moved into the oil-rich mountains of the Caucasus. When, at the end of the war, Britain decided not only to keep its troops in place but to offer support to anti-Bolshevik White Russians, it was quite clear that an intervention that had started out against the Germans had slipped into something quite different.[20]

The defeated Germany, on Allied instructions, started to pull its troops out of the Ukraine and the Baltic states. The Allies struggled to fill the vacuum. By the end of 1918, there were over 180,000 foreign troops on Russian soil and several White Russian armies receiving Allied money and Allied guns. People were starting to talk about a crusade against Bolshevism. But there was strong opposition to any more military adventures. The slogan from the left, "Hands Off Russia," was gaining in popularity.

If they were not careful, Lloyd George told his cabinet, they would spread Bolshevism simply by trying to put it down. The prospect of being sent to Russia was hugely unpopular among British and American soldiers. The Canadians, who had been supplying troops for the Siberian expedition and for Murmansk, wanted to pull out by the summer; there was "great anxiety" over the issue in Canada, Borden told his colleagues in the British empire delegation.[21]

The French, who talked a strong line on intervention, could actually do very little. They did not have the manpower or the resources. Under an agreement with Britain, France was in theory responsible for the southern Ukraine and the Crimea, and Britain for the Caucasus and central Asia. (What that meant, beyond supporting local anti-Bolshevik forces, was never clearly spelled out.) But only a handful of French soldiers had arrived in Russia before the end of the war. The French general in the Near East, Louis Franchet d'Esperey, complained bitterly, "I do not have enough forces to settle into this country, all the more so since it would not appeal to our men to experience Russia in winter when all their comrades are resting." His warnings were unwisely ignored.

The French government moved a mixed force, with French, Greek and Polish troops, to the Black Sea port of Odessa. The expedition promptly found itself fighting a heterogeneous collection of enemies, from Bolsheviks to Ukrainian nationalists to anarchists. Morale plummeted during the long winter of 1918–19 and the Bolsheviks found easy pickings when they sent in French speakers to work on the troops. As one French officer reported, "not one French soldier who saved his head at Verdun and the fields of the Marne will consent to losing it on the fields of Russia." In April 1919, the French authorities abruptly gave up what was becoming a debacle and hastily pulled out, abandoning Odessa and its people to the Bolsheviks. Civilians lined the waterfront, vainly begging the French to take them with them. A smaller French expedition left the Crimean port of Sebastopol in somewhat better order, taking with it some 40,000 Russians, including the mother of the murdered tsar. Two weeks later the French Black Sea fleet mutinied.[22]

Although France remained vociferous in opposing the Bolsheviks and their ways, it played no further part in the Allied intervention. Foch came up with a series of increasingly improbable plans to march into Russia with armies variously made up of Poles, Finns, Czechoslovaks, Rumanians, Greeks and even the Russian prisoners of war still in Germany, all of which came to nothing, partly because his cast of extras mostly refused the parts assigned them, but also because of strong opposition from the British and the Americans.[23]

French policy became by default the second of the options Lloyd George had outlined: to isolate Bolshevism within Russia. At the Peace Conference and in subsequent years, France did its best to build up states around Russia such as Poland to form, in the old medieval phrase, a cordon sanitaire around the carriers of the plague. This had the advantage, even more important to the French, of providing counterweights to Germany and a barrier in the unlikely event that Germany and Russia should try to join forces. Foch and Churchill were among the few in Paris who took that possibility seriously. Churchill warned about a future combination of a Bolshevik Russia with a nationalist Germany and Japan. "In the ultimate result we could contemplate a predatory confederation stretching from the Rhine to Yokohama menacing the vital interests of the British Empire in India and elsewhere, menacing indeed the future of the world."[24]

"We should continue to keep an eye on them," a weary Clemenceau said of the Bolsheviks to Lloyd George at the end of 1919, "surrounding them, as it were, by a barbed wire entanglement, and spending no money." Money was always a problem in 1919. Lloyd George tried to dampen Churchill's enthusiasm for intervention by reporting a conversation with the chancellor of the exchequer, Austen Chamberlain: "We cannot afford the burden. Chamberlain says we can barely make both ends meet on a peace basis, even at the present crushing rate of taxation." The British spent perhaps £100 million on their Russian adventure; the French under half that amount. "How much will France give?" asked Lloyd George when the question of expanding military intervention came up in February 1919. "I am sure she cannot afford to pay; I am sure we cannot. Will America bear the expense? Pin them down to the cost of any scheme before sanctioning it."[25]

Much of the aid to the White Russians was being wasted through inefficiency and corruption. Petty officials behind the lines took the uniforms intended for the soldiers; their wives and daughters wore British nurses' skirts. While Denikin's trucks and tanks seized up in the cold, antifreeze was sold in the bars. Although the Bolsheviks were later able to paint a propaganda picture of world capitalism in all its might arrayed against their revolution, in fact Allied help did very little to stave off White defeat.[26]

The Allied intervention in Russia was always muddled by differing objectives and mutual suspicions. The Americans were officially against intervention, yet they kept their troops in Siberia after the end of the war, to block Japanese designs. Where the French before 1914 had relied on a strong Russia to keep Germany in line, the British had worried about the

Russian threat to India. In 1919 France would have preferred a restored White Russia, but Britain could have lived with a weak Red one. Curzon, who loathed everything the Bolsheviks stood for, was delighted that the Russians had lost control of the Caucasus; the British must, he told Churchill, be careful that Denikin, the White Russian leader in the south, did not get his hands on the area again. The British tended to be suspicious of French motives. The French government, complained Lloyd George, was unreasonably swayed by its own middle classes, who had lost their savings in Russia. "There is nothing they would like better," he said, "than to see us pull their chestnuts out of the fire for them."[27]

While the Allies dabbled fitfully with intervention in Russia, they also explored the option favored by Lloyd George: that of negotiation. On January 21, 1919, Wilson and Lloyd George suggested a compromise to the Supreme Council. The Russians would be encouraged to agree on a common position on the peace settlements for discussion with the Allies. Since the French did not want the Bolsheviks to come to Paris, why not meet them, along with other Russian representatives, somewhere nearer Russia? As long as they refused to speak to the Bolsheviks, Wilson added, the Russian people would believe Bolshevik propaganda that the Allies were their enemies. Clemenceau, supported by Sonnino, objected that the very act of speaking to the Bolsheviks would give them credibility. He was not prepared to break with his Allies over this and so, reluctantly, he would go along. Only Sonnino held out. They must, he urged, collect all the White Russians together and give them enough soldiers or at least the weapons to destroy the Bolsheviks. Lloyd George had a practical question. How many soldiers could they each provide? There was an awkward pause. None, came the answer. It was agreed to proceed with negotiations. Wilson immediately sent for a typewriter. "We conjured up visions of a beautiful American stenographer," a British journalist recalled, but a messenger appeared with Wilson's battered old machine, and the president sat in a corner tapping out an invitation. As Clemenceau left the room he snarled to a waiting French journalist, "Beaten!"[28]

Wilson's draft, which talked of the Allies' sincere and unselfish desire to help the Russian people, was duly sent to the representatives of the major Russian factions, inviting them to meet on the Princes Islands—Prinkipo—in the Sea of Marmara between the Black Sea and the Mediterranean. The islands were a favorite picnic spot for the inhabitants of Constantinople. They had also been used by the Turkish authorities just before the war as a place to dump the city's thousands of stray dogs; for weeks, desperate barks and yaps had echoed back across the waters.

An invitation was sent off to the Bolsheviks by shortwave radio, and Paris waited for a reply. It was difficult to gauge what the response would be. Already the Bolsheviks had established what was to become a familiar pattern of rudeness and civility, utmost hostility and grudging cooperation. Lenin believed that the Russian Revolution would set fire to Europe, then the world. Borders, flags, nationalism, the tools of a doomed capitalism for keeping the workers of the world apart, would be swept away. His first commissar for foreign affairs, the great revolutionary theorist Leon Trotsky, saw his new post as a simple one: "I will issue a few revolutionary proclamations to the peoples of the world and then shut up shop." (In an unconscious parallel to Wilson's call for open diplomacy, he had much fun rummaging through the old tsarist files and publishing, to the considerable embarrassment of the Allies, secret wartime agreements carving up, for example, the Middle East.) The only question for Lenin and Trotsky was one of tactics. If world revolution was going to happen immediately, there was no need to deal with the enemy. If there was a delay, however, it might become necessary to play off one capitalist nation against another. In 1917, the Bolsheviks assumed the first was true; by 1919, even though Lenin summoned a founding congress for a world revolutionary headquarters, the Communist International, they were starting to have doubts.[29]

The Soviet foreign policy, which reflected this ambivalence, did much to deepen the Allies' suspicions. In October 1918 Georgi Chicherin, a disheveled, obsessive scholar who had just replaced Trotsky as commissar for foreign affairs, sent a sarcastic note to Wilson, mocking his cherished principles. The Fourteen Points called for leaving Russia alone to work out its own fate; curious, then, that Wilson had sent troops to Siberia. The American talked of self-determination; how odd that he had not mentioned Ireland or the Philippines. He promised a League of Nations to end all war; was this some sort of joke? Everyone knew that the capitalist nations were responsible for creating wars. At that very moment, the United States and its partners in crime Britain and France were plotting to spill more Russian blood and extort more money from Russia. The only true league was one of the masses.[30]

Yet the Bolsheviks also struck conciliatory notes. Maxim Litvinov, Chicherin's deputy, was smooth and agreeable. He had lived in London for several years, eking out a living as a clerk and marrying a novelist, Ivy Low, from the fringes of Bloomsbury. On Christmas Eve 1918, he sent Wilson a telegram from Stockholm. It spoke of peace on earth, of justice and humanity. The Russian people, Litvinov went on, shared Wilson's great principles. They had been the first to cry out for self-determination and open diplomacy. All they wanted now was peace to build a better society. They were anxious to negotiate, but Allied intervention and the Allied blockade were causing terrible misery. The Bolsheviks found themselves obliged to use terror to keep the country afloat. Would not Wilson help them?

Wilson was deeply impressed. So, when he saw the telegram, was Lloyd George. An American diplomat, William Buckler, was dispatched to talk to Litvinov. Buckler's report, which Wilson brought to the Supreme Council on January 21, was encouraging. The Soviet government, as it was now calling itself, was ready to do much for the sake of peace, whether that meant paying at least part of the repudiated foreign debts or granting new concessions to foreign enterprises. It would drop its calls for worldwide revolution; it had only been forced to use such propaganda as a way of defending itself first against Germany and more recently the Allies.[31]

Wilson and Lloyd George had some reason, then, to expect that the Bolsheviks would welcome the invitation to Prinkipo. The two statesmen chose their delegates: a liberal journalist and a defrocked clergyman for the United States, and for Britain a delighted Borden—"a great honour to Canada." (He did not know that Lloyd George was having trouble finding someone to go.) They all waited. The Soviet government's reply arrived on February 4. Not for the last time the Bolsheviks misjudged the West. They craftily, but transparently, avoided agreeing to a cease-fire, one of the preconditions laid down by the Supreme Council. They did not bother to comment on the appeal to high principles in the invitation. Clearly thinking that capitalists understood only one thing, they offered significant material concessions, such as raw materials or territory. After all, it had worked with the Germans at Brest-Litovsk. Wilson was taken aback: "This answer was not only uncalled for, but might be thought insulting." Lloyd George agreed. "We are not after their money or their concessions or their territory."[32]

At the same time the other invitees, with quiet support from the French and from friends such as Churchill, were digging in their heels. The news of the Prinkipo proposal had deeply shocked the White Russians. In Paris, the exile community turned out in a huge demonstration; far away in Archangel, pictures of Wilson were hurriedly taken down. Sazonov, the former foreign minister, asked a British diplomat how the Allies could expect him to meet the people who had murdered his family.[33]

If the British and the Americans had put pressure on them, the White Russians would probably have caved in, but neither Wilson nor Lloyd George was prepared to do so. Prinkipo was becoming a political problem for both men. The press and some of their own colleagues were increasingly critical. Lloyd George, who depended on Conservative support for his coalition government, had already been warned by Bonar Law, the Conservative leader, and his deputy that the government might well break up over the issue. By February 8, Clemenceau, in a rare communicative mood, told Poincaré that the Prinkipo meeting was in trouble. Wilson showed no signs of wanting to respond to the Bolsheviks' partial acceptance. Just to make sure, Clemenceau begged Balfour to delay discussion until the president left for his brief visit to the United States. By the time the White Russians sent their refusal on February 16, Wilson was at sea, Lloyd George was back in London dealing with a threatened general strike and Prinkipo was already dead.[34]

That left the whole question of Russia as undecided as ever. In London, Churchill was demanding that Lloyd George make a clear decision, either to intervene in force or to withdraw from Russia once and for all. Lloyd George was not prepared to do either: full-scale intervention would create trouble on his left; withdrawal would make trouble on his right. And so, as he did on other occasions at the Peace Conference, he proceeded indirectly, testing out first one approach and then another without exposing himself.

He told Churchill that any decision on Russia had to be made in Paris, with Wilson's participation. Churchill dashed across the Channel on the morning of February 14, the day the president was due to leave for the United States. (In his memoirs, Lloyd George expressed pious horror that Churchill had "adroitly" slipped over to Paris on his own initiative.) After a hectic drive to Paris—and a crash which left his car's windshield shattered—Churchill rushed into the Supreme Council just as Wilson was getting to his feet. The president listened courteously as Churchill pointed out that the uncertainty over Allied intentions was bad for the troops in Russia and for the White Russians. His own view was that withdrawal would be a disaster. "Such a policy would be equivalent to pulling out the linch-pin from the whole machine. There would be no further armed resistance to the Bolsheviks in Russia, and an interminable vista of violence and misery was all that remained for the whole of Russia." Wilson, as Lloyd George must have known, refused to be drawn. Allied troops were doing no good in Russia, he admitted, but the situation was confusing.[35]

Churchill remained in Paris for a couple more days, trying to prod the Supreme Council into at least a clear policy; but with Wilson and Lloyd George absent this was difficult. Lloyd George, who was getting daily reports from the faithful Kerr, directed matters from a distance. "Winston is in Paris," he told a friend cheerfully. "He wants to conduct a war against the Bolsheviks. That *would* cause a revolution! Our people would not permit it."[36] He sent Churchill mixed signals, hinting that Britain might supply weapons and volunteers for the White Russians but then, in the next cable, warning him against planning military action against the Bolsheviks. The War Office, Lloyd George claimed, felt that the presence of Allied soldiers in Russia was a mistake. He agreed: "Not merely is it none of our business to interfere with its internal affairs, it would be positively mischievous: it would strengthen and consolidate Bolshevik opinion." Lloyd George made sure that Kerr gave copies of his message to other members of the British empire delegation as well as to House. From the middle of the Atlantic, Wilson sent his warning: "Greatly surprised by Churchill's Russian suggestion," he wired, "it would be fatal to be led further into the Russian chaos." He need not have worried. On February 19, the day chosen to renew the discussion on Russia at the Supreme Council, Clemenceau was shot and wounded in an assassination attempt, and any decision was postponed indefinitely. Allied troops remained on Russian soil, but there was no great crusade.[37]

Perhaps, as Wilson was fond of suggesting, the peacemakers needed more information. Several of the younger Americans, including the radical journalist Lincoln Steffens and William Bullitt, a young Russian expert with the American delegation who was known to oppose intervention, were already suggesting a mission of inquiry. Lloyd George agreed that it might be a good idea, not least as a way of postponing an awkward decision.[38]

On February 17, House told Bullitt that he had been chosen to lead a small secret mission to talk to the Bolshevik leaders about what sort of conditions they might accept to make peace with the Allies. Bullitt was delighted. His job in Paris had been routine; now, as he saw it, he was moving onto center stage. A product of the privileged, insular world of the Philadelphia upper classes, he had enormous confidence in himself and his own judgment. Something of a prodigy, or so his doting mother thought, he had sailed through Yale University. His contemporaries thought him brilliant, although some also noticed that there was something cold and calculating in the way he used and discarded people. He admired Wilson and his principles tremendously, but wondered if the president was up to defending them.[39]

Together House and Kerr outlined a list of subjects the mission was to discuss. "Bullitt was going for information only," House assured other American delegates. He failed to make this sufficiently clear to Bullitt himself, who maintained, even when his expedition came to grief, that he had a mandate from both House, speaking on Wilson's behalf, and Lloyd

George to negotiate conditions of peace with the Bolsheviks. Steffens, who went on the mission, concurred: "Bullitt's instructions were to negotiate a preliminary agreement with the Russians so that the United States and Great Britain could persuade France to join them in an invitation to a parley, reasonably sure of some results." Steffens, not for the first time, was wrong. Neither House nor Lloyd George had given up hope of some sort of settlement, but they were not about to alienate either the French or their own domestic opinion if the Bolsheviks proved recalcitrant. A small mission headed by an insignificant twenty-eight-year-old might bring back good news. It was expendable if it did not.[40]

Bullitt and Steffens spent a wonderful week in Moscow: accommodation in a confiscated palace, piles of caviar, nights at the opera in the tsar's old box and during the day discussions with Lenin and Chicherin themselves. The Bolsheviks, Steffens believed, were getting rid of the causes of poverty, corruption, tyranny and war. "They were not trying to establish political democracy, legal liberty, and negotiated peace—not now. They were at present only laying the basis for these good things." Bullitt agreed that a great work had been started in Russia. Both men were deeply impressed with Lenin. He was "straightforward and direct," said Bullitt, "but also genial and with a large humor and serenity." Steffens asked about the terror against the Bolsheviks' opponents and was moved when Lenin expressed regret; he was, thought Steffens, "a liberal by instinct."[41]

By the end of the week Bullitt had, he thought, a deal. There would be a cease-fire and then concessions on both sides. The Allies would withdraw their troops, but the Bolsheviks would not insist on an end to the various White governments in Russia. (Since the terms called for an end to Allied assistance to the Whites, the Bolsheviks could afford to be generous.) It is doubtful that the Bolsheviks were negotiating in good faith; Lenin had shown with the Germans at Brest-Litovsk that he was prepared to make concessions only to buy time. Bullitt and Steffens were "useful idiots," their mission helpful at least for propaganda.

Bullitt proudly bore his agreement, and Steffens his rosy picture of the future, back to Paris. House, as usual, was encouraging, but other members of the American delegation had their doubts. Wilson himself, by now back from the United States, was simply too distracted by the difficult negotiations over the German treaty to pay much attention. He would not make time to see Bullitt. Lloyd George, who had him to breakfast on March 28, was getting very cold feet indeed. Béla Kun's seizure of power in Hungary the weekend before had reawakened fears about Bolshevism spreading westward. News had leaked out about Bullitt's mission; rumors were circulating that Britain and the United States were about to recognize the Soviet government. Lloyd George's Conservative backbenchers were watching him like a hawk; so were Northcliffe's papers. That morning, the *Daily Mail* had carried a savage leading article by Henry Wickham Steed, the new editor of its sister paper *The Times,* who hated Lloyd George as much as Northcliffe did. The Prinkipo "intrigue" was being resurrected, thanks to the machinations of international Jewish financiers and possibly German interests. Lloyd George held the newspaper out toward Bullitt over the breakfast table. "As long as the British press is doing this kind of thing, how can you expect me to be sensible about Russia?"[42]

In the next weeks, the pressure on Lloyd George grew. On April 10 more than two hundred Conservative members of Parliament signed a telegram urging him not to recognize the Soviet government. Lloyd George, who was also under attack over the German peace terms, knew when to cut his losses. When he faced the House of Commons on April 16, he said firmly that recognition had never been discussed in Paris and was out of the question. When he was asked specifically about Bullitt's mission, he said airily, "There was a suggestion that there was some young American who had come back." He could not say whether the young man had brought back any useful reports.[43]

Bullitt was shattered. No one in Paris wanted to hear about his mission, not even the president he admired so much. His disillusionment with Wilson was complete when the terms of the German treaty came out in May. He sent an angry and hurt letter of resignation and headed for the Riviera, "to lie on the sand and watch the world go to hell." That autumn he returned to the United States and helped to seal the fate of Wilson and the Treaty of Versailles by testifying before the Senate that he, and many others in the American delegation, disapproved of many of its clauses. He also managed to get his report on his mission to Russia into the record. In 1934, he returned to Moscow as the first American ambassador to the Soviet Union. This time the experience turned him into a fervent anticommunist.[44]

Lloyd George and Wilson drew back from contact with the Soviet government after this, although they continued to hope for some miraculous transformation of the Bolsheviks into good democrats. The two even toyed briefly with the idea of using food shipments to calm the Bolsheviks down, a scheme that Hoover, as head of the Allied relief administration, had been pushing. Hoover's own views on the Bolsheviks were close to Wilson's: that they were an understandable response to appalling conditions. They were dangerous, though, their propaganda attractive even in strong societies such as America. The Allies should let the Bolsheviks know, indirectly, that if they stopped trying to spread their revolution,

Russia would receive substantial help. With time and food, the Russian people would swing away from radical ideas. To avoid any hint of Allied recognition and to forestall objections from the French, Hoover suggested using a prominent figure from a neutral country to run the whole operation.[45]

As it happened, he had someone in mind, "a fine, rugged character, a man of great physical and moral courage"—Fridtjof Nansen, the famous Norwegian Arctic explorer, who happened to be in Paris with the vague idea of doing something for the League of Nations. In the middle of April, the Council of Four approved Hoover's plan. A group of neutral countries, including Nansen's own Norway, were to collect food and medicines for Russia, which they would deliver if the Bolsheviks arranged a cease-fire with their enemies. Nansen tried to dispatch a telegram to Lenin to tell him the good news, but neither the French, who saw the scheme as a ploy by British, American, perhaps even German interests to gain concessions in Russia, nor the British, who were wary of anything that looked like recognition of the Bolsheviks, would send it. The telegram finally went from Berlin.[46]

The Soviet reply, drafted by Chicherin and Litvinov, came back via radio and cable on May 15. "Be extremely polite to Nansen, *extremely insolent* to Wilson, Lloyd George and Clemenceau," Lenin had instructed them. As for the scheme itself, "use it *for propaganda* for clearly it can serve *no other* useful purpose." His colleagues followed his advice, mixing stinging attacks on the Allies with a categorical refusal to consider a cease-fire unless there was a proper peace conference. In Paris, the peacemakers shook their heads sadly and abandoned all further discussion of humanitarian relief. The episode showed yet again the bankruptcy of Allied policy toward Russia.[47]

There was one last glimmer of hope: that the Russians themselves might solve their dilemma. Just before the spring thaw turned Russia's roads to mud, the White Russians managed to coordinate an attack on the Bolsheviks. From his base in eastern Siberia, the White admiral Kolchak struck along a wide front. One force moved north toward Archangel and managed to link up with a small advance guard from a beleaguered White Russian and British force. Another pushed west toward the Ural Mountains. A third went south to join up with Denikin and his armies. By mid-April Kolchak and his allies had pushed the Bolsheviks back out of 300,000 square kilometers of territory. But this was the high point of their fortunes.

The Bolsheviks possessed two crucial advantages: their unity and their location. They controlled the center of Russia, while their heterogeneous opponents were widely dispersed around the periphery. Often, none of the White Russian commanders, mutually suspicious and separated from one another by miles of often hostile country, had any idea of what the others were doing. The Bolsheviks had three times the manpower and most of Russia's arms factories.[48]

On May 23, 1919, the Allies decided to extend partial recognition to Kolchak's government. "The moment chosen," wrote Churchill later, "was almost exactly the moment when that declaration was almost certainly too late." A dispatch asking for assurances that democratic institutions would be introduced made its tortuous way out to Siberia and in due course a partly garbled answer came back that seemed to provide the necessary guarantees. What also came back from Russia shortly afterward were reports of defeats. By late June, Red armies had broken through Kolchak's center and the Whites were falling back hundreds of kilometers.[49]

By this time, however, the Peace Conference was drawing to a close and the Germans were about to sign the Treaty of Versailles. There was no time to do anything more about Russia. A brief clause was drawn up for the treaty which simply said that any treaties made in the future between the Allies and Russia, or any parts of it, must be recognized. Another clause left open the possibility of Russia's claiming reparations. Otherwise policy toward Russia remained as confused as it had been all along. The blockade against the Bolsheviks remained in force, but support for the Whites gradually dwindled. Britain and France abandoned Kolchak as a lost cause. (The admiral put himself under the protection of the Czech Legion, still in eastern Siberia; the Czechs handed him over to the Bolsheviks, and he was shot in February 1920.) By October 1919, Denikin was in full retreat in the south. In January 1921, with much prodding from Britain, the European Allies agreed to end military intervention and abandon their blockade. In March 1921, Britain signed a trade agreement with the Soviet government. Even Conservative businessmen, who feared they were losing an opportunity in Russia, supported it. In 1924 Britain and the Soviet Union established full diplomatic relations. France followed reluctantly. America would wait another decade, until FDR.

With hindsight, Churchill and Foch were right about the Bolsheviks and Lloyd George and Wilson were wrong. The governing party in Russia did not become like Swedish Social Democrats. Lenin had established a system of terrible and unfettered power which gave Stalin free rein for his paranoid fantasies. The Russian people, and many more beyond, paid a dreadful price for the Bolshevik victory in the civil war, while in Paris the peacemakers were brought up against the limits of their own power.

The League of Nations

O N JANUARY 25, the peace conference formally approved the setting up of a commission on the League of Nations. A couple of the younger members of the American delegation thought it would make a wonderful inspirational film. They would show, they thought, the old diplomacy doing its evil work. Animated maps would illustrate how the seeds of war had been sown in the past: the secret alliances, the unjust wars, the conferences at which the old, selfish European powers drew arbitrary lines on the maps. The Paris Peace Conference and the League would shine out in "bold contrast." The film would also, they were sure, make lots of money.[1]

It is hard today to imagine that such a project could have been taken seriously. Only a handful of eccentric historians still bother to study the League of Nations. Its archives, with their wealth of materials, are largely unvisited. Its very name evokes images of earnest bureaucrats, fuzzy liberal supporters, futile resolutions, unproductive fact-finding missions and, above all, failure: Manchuria in 1931, Ethiopia in 1935 and, most catastrophic of all, the outbreak of the Second World War a mere twenty years after the first one had ended. The dynamic leaders of the interwar years— Mussolini, Hitler, the Japanese militarists—sneered at the League and ultimately turned their backs on it. Its chief supporters—Britain, France and the smaller democracies—were lukewarm and flaccid. The Soviet Union joined only because Stalin could not, at the time, think of a better alternative. The United States never managed to join at all. So great was the taint of failure that when the powers contemplated a permanent association of nations during the Second World War, they decided to set up a completely new United Nations. The League was officially pronounced dead in 1946. It had ceased to count at all in 1939.

At its last assembly, Lord Robert Cecil, who had been there at its creation, asked, "Is it true that all our efforts for those twenty years have been thrown away?" He answered his own question bravely: "For the first time an organisation was constructed, in essence universal, not to protect the national interest of this or that country . . . but to abolish war." The League had been, he concluded, "a great experiment." It had put into concrete form the dreams and hopes of all those who had worked for peace through the centuries. It had left its legacy in the widespread acceptance of the idea that the nations of the world could and must work together for the collective security of them all. "The League is dead: Long live the United Nations!"[2]

Cecil was right. The League did represent something very important: both a recognition of the changes that had already taken place in international relations and a bet placed on the future. Just as steam engines had changed the way people moved about the surface of the earth, just as nationalism and democracy had given them a different relationship to one another and to their governments, so the way states behaved toward one another had undergone a transformation in the century before the Peace Conference met. Of course power still counted, and of course governments looked out for their countries, but what that meant had changed. If the eighteenth century had made and unmade alliances, and fought and ended wars, for dynastic advantage, even matters of honor, if it was perfectly all right to take pieces of land without any regard for their inhabitants, the nineteenth century had moved toward a different view. War increasingly was seen as an aberration, and an expensive one at that. In the eighteenth century someone's gain was always someone's loss; the overall ledger remained balanced. Now war was a cost to all players, as the Great War proved. National interests were furthered better by peace, which allowed trade and industry to flourish. And the nation itself was something different, no longer embodied by the monarch or a small élite but increasingly constituted by the people themselves.

In diplomacy, the forms remained the same: ambassadors presented credentials, treaties were signed and sealed. The rules, however, had changed. In the game of nations it was no longer fashionable, or even acceptable, for one nation to seize territory that was full of people of a different nationality. (Colonies did not count, because those peoples were assumed to be at a lower stage of political development.) When Bismarck created Germany, he did so in the name of German unity, not conquest for his master's Prussia. When his creation took Alsace-Lorraine from France in 1871, the German government did its best to persuade itself and the world that this was not for the sake of old-fashioned spoils of war but because the peoples of those provinces were really German at heart.

Another factor also now entered into the equation: public opinion. The spread of democracy, the growth of nationalism, the web of railway lines and telegraphs, the busy journalists and the rotary presses churning out the mass circulation newspapers, all this had summoned up a creature that governments did not much like but which they dared not ignore. At Paris, it was assumed that negotiations would be conducted under public scrutiny.

For idealists this was a good thing. The people would bring a much needed common sense to international relations. They did not want war or expensive arms races. (This faith had not been shaken by the fact that many Europeans seemed enthusiastic about war in the decades before 1914, and positively passionate in 1914 itself.) The prosperity and progress of the nineteenth century encouraged the belief that the world was becoming more civilized. A growing middle class provided a natural constituency for a peace movement preaching the virtues of compulsory arbitration of disputes, international courts, disarmament, perhaps even pledges to abstain from violence as ways to prevent wars. The opponents of war took as models their own societies, especially those in Western Europe, where governments had become more responsive to the will of their citizens, where public police forces had replaced private guards and where the rule of law was widely accepted. Surely it was possible to imagine a similar society of nations providing collective security for its members?[3]

In Paris, Wilson insisted on chairing the League commission, because for him the League of Nations was the centerpiece of the peace settlements. If it could be brought into being, then everything else would sooner or later fall into place. If the peace terms were imperfect, there would be plenty of time later for the League to correct them. Many new borders had to be drawn; if they were not quite right, the League would sort them out. Germany's colonies were going to be taken away; the League would make sure that they were run properly. The Ottoman empire was defunct; the League would act as liquidator and trustee for the peoples who were not yet ready to rule themselves. And for future generations the League would oversee general prosperity and peace, encouraging the weak, chiding the wicked and, where necessary, punishing the recalcitrant. It was a pledge that humanity was making to itself, a covenant.

The picture sometimes painted of Wilson sailing across the Atlantic bearing the gift of the League of Nations from the new world to the old is compelling but, alas, false. Many Europeans had long wanted a better way of managing international relations. The war they had just survived made sense only if it produced a better world and an end to war. That was what their own governments had promised in the dark days, and that was what had kept them going. In 1919, as Europeans contemplated those catastrophic years, with the scarcely imaginable outpouring of blood, as they realized that European society had been horribly damaged, perhaps fatally, the League struck many, and not only liberals and left-wingers, as their last chance. Harold Nicolson spoke for many of his generation when he said: "We were journeying to Paris, not merely to liquidate the war, but to found a new order in Europe. We were preparing not Peace only, but Eternal Peace. There was about us the halo of some divine mission. We must be alert, stern, righteous and ascetic. For we were bent on doing great, permanent and noble things."[4]

Lloyd George went along with Wilson's insistence that the League should be the first task of the Peace Conference, not merely out of a cynical desire to keep the Americans happy. He was, after all, a Liberal, the leader of a party with a strong history of opposition to war. A consummate politician, he also knew the British public. "They regard with absolute horror," he told his colleagues on Christmas Eve 1918, "the continuance of a state of affairs which might again degenerate into such a tragedy." It would be political disaster to come back from the Peace Conference without a League of Nations. But the League never caught his imagination, perhaps because he doubted whether it could ever truly be effective. He rarely referred to it in speeches and never visited its headquarters while he was prime minister.[5]

In France, where memories of past German aggression and apprehension about the future were painfully alive, there was deep pessimism about international cooperation to end war. Yet there was a willingness, especially among liberals and the left, to give the League a try. Clemenceau would have preferred to deal with the German peace first, but he was determined that it would not be said that France had blocked the League. He himself remained ambivalent, not, as is sometimes said, hostile. As he famously remarked, "I like the League, but I do not believe in it."[6]

Public opinion provided general support for the League but no clear guidance as to its shape. Should it be policeman or clergyman? Should it use force or moral suasion? The French, for obvious reasons, leaned toward a League with the power to stop aggressors by force. Lawyers, especially in the English-speaking world, put their faith in international law and tribunals. For pacifists, there was still another remedy for international violence: general disarmament and a promise from all members of the League to abstain from war. And what was the League going to be like? Some sort of superstate? A club for heads of state? A conference summoned whenever there was an emergency? Whatever shape it took, it would need qualifications for membership, rules, procedures and some sort of secretariat.

The man who had put the League at the heart of the Allied peace program kept an enigmatic silence on such details during the war. Wilson spoke only in generalities, albeit inspiring ones. His League would be powerful because it would represent the organized opinion of humanity. Its members would guarantee, he said in his Fourteen Points, each other's independence and borders. It might use force to protect these, but would probably not need to. The war had shown that ordinary people longed for such an organization; it was what they had fought for. "The counsels of plain men," he told a huge audience in the Metropolitan Opera House in New York just before the war ended, "have become on all hands more simple and straightforward and more unified than the counsels of sophisticated men of affairs, who still retain the impression that they are playing a game of power and playing for high stakes."[7]

Wilson thought it was a mistake to get down to specifics while the war was still on. That would only cause dissension among the Allies and it might give the enemy countries the impression that the League was somehow directed against them. To him it was so eminently a rational idea, the need for it so widely accepted, that it would grow on its own into a healthy organism. Even in Paris, while the League's covenant was being drafted, he resisted what he saw as excessive detail. "Gentlemen," he told his colleagues on the League commission, "I have no doubt that the next generation will be made up of men as intelligent as you or I, and I think we can trust the League to manage its own affairs."[8]

Wilson's casual attitude alarmed even his supporters. Fortunately, perhaps, there were several detailed plans floating about. As the war had dragged on, it had inevitably provoked much discussion about ways to forestall conflict. In the United States, the League to Enforce Peace brought Democrats and Republicans together. In Britain, a League of Nations Society drew a respectable middle-class, liberal membership. To their left, the Fabians sponsored a full-scale study of the matter by Leonard Woolf. At the beginning of 1918, the French and British governments decided that they had better get in on the act since, thanks to Wilson, a League of Nations was now an explicit Allied war aim. In France a commission under the prominent liberal statesman Léon Bourgeois drew up an elaborate scheme for an international organization with its own army. In Britain a special committee under a distinguished lawyer, Sir Walter Phillimore, produced a detailed set of recommendations that incorporated many of the prewar ideas on, for example, compulsory arbitration of disputes. Its approach was cautious, rejecting both utopian ideas of a world federation and the pragmatic suggestion that a league should be merely a continuation of the wartime alliance. When the British government sent him a copy of the Phillimore report, Wilson said unhelpfully that he found it disappointing and that he was working on his own scheme, which he would unveil in due course. His main principles, he allowed the British to learn, were two: "There must be a League of Nations and this must be virile, a reality, not a paper League." The war ended with no more definite word than that from Washington.[9]

It was at this point that one of the luminaries of the British empire decided to try his hand at drafting a scheme. Tall, thin, with hard blue eyes, General Jan Smuts, the South African foreign minister, was not particularly imposing at first glance. (In London, Borden's secretary thought he had come to fix the electric light and curtly told him to wait outside.) He had, however, precisely the sort of personal qualities to appeal to Wilson, because they were so much like his own: a fondness for dealing with the great questions, deep religious and ethical convictions, and a desire to make the world a better place. Both men had grown up in stable, happy families in small communities, Wilson in the American South, Smuts in the settled Boer farming community of the Cape. Both had fond memories of happy black servants (although both doubted that blacks would ever be the equals of whites) and unhappy memories of war, civil in Wilson's case and Boers against the British in Smuts's. Both were sober and restrained on the surface, passionate and sensitive underneath. Both combined vast self-righteousness with huge ambition. Both were quick to see the inconsistencies in others while remaining blind to their own.[10]

Smuts sailed through school and Stellenbosch University and then, like many bright young men from the colonies, headed off to England. At Cambridge he worked assiduously, collecting prizes and a double first in law. In London, where he prepared for the bar, he never, as far as is known, visited a play or a concert or an art gallery. In his limited spare time he read poetry: Shelley, Shakespeare, but above all Walt Whitman, whose deep love of nature he shared. If Wilson could inspire his audience with his sober prose, if Lloyd George could lift them up with his golden speeches, Smuts could, above all the other peacemakers, sing to them.[11] Smuts had advised on the great issues of the war; it was natural that he would also advise on the peace.

Smuts had greeted Wilson's appearance on the world stage with enthusiasm. "It is this moral idealism and this vision of a better world which has up-borne us through the dark night of this war," he told a group of American newspapermen. The world was shattered but there now lay before it a gigantic opportunity. "It is for us to labour in the remaking of that world to better ends, to plan its international reorganization on lines of universal freedom and justice, and to re-establish among the classes and nations that good-will which is the only sure foundation for any enduring international system." The words, and the exhortations, poured out. "Let us not underrate our opportunity," he cried to a weary world. "The age of miracles is never past." Perhaps they had come to the moment when they could end war itself forever.[12]

What Smuts said less loudly was that the League of Nations could also be useful to the British empire. In December 1918 he prepared one of his dazzling analyses of the world for his British colleagues. With Austria-Hungary gone, Russia in turmoil and Germany defeated, there were only three major powers left in the world: the British empire, the United States and France. The French could not be trusted. They were rivals to the British in Africa and in the Middle East. (The French returned Smuts's antipathy, especially after he inadvertently left some of his confidential papers behind at a meeting in Paris.) It made perfect sense, Smuts argued, for the British to look to the United States for friendship and cooperation. "Language, interest, and ideals alike" had marked out their common path. The best way to get the Americans to realize this was to support the League. Wilson, everyone knew, thought the League his most important task; if he got British support, he would probably drop awkward issues such as his insistence on freedom of the seas.[13]

Smuts set himself to put what he described as Wilson's "rather nebulous ideas" into coherent form. Working at great speed, he wrote what he modestly called "A Practical Suggestion." A general assembly of all member nations, a smaller executive council, a permanent secretariat, steps to settle international disputes, mandates for peoples not yet ready to rule themselves: much of what later went into the League covenant was in his draft. But there was also much more: the horrors of the recent war, a Europe reduced to its atoms, ordinary people clinging to the hope of a better world, and the great opportunity lying before the peacemakers. "The very foundations have been shakened and loosened, and things are again fluid. The tents have been struck, and the great caravan of humanity is once more on the march." Smuts wrote proudly to a friend: "My paper has made an enormous impression in high circles. I see from the Cabinet Minutes that the Prime Minister called it 'one of the ablest state papers he had ever read.'" It was immediately published as a pamphlet.[14]

It was, commented an American legal expert, "very beautifully written" but rather vague in places. Smuts had carefully avoided, for example, discussing mandates for Germany's former colonies in Africa. (This was deliberate; he was determined that his own country should hang on to German Southwest Africa.) Wilson, to whom Lloyd George gave a copy, liked it, not least because Smuts insisted that the making of the League must be the first business of the Peace Conference. Back in Paris after his tour of Europe, Wilson set himself to the task he had so long postponed, of getting his own ideas down on paper. The result, which he showed the British on January 19, borrowed many of Smuts's ideas. He did not mind, Smuts told a friend: "I think there is a special satisfaction in knowing that your will is quietly finding out the current of the Great Will, so that in the end God will do what you ineffectively set out to do." Wilson pronounced Smuts "a brick."[15]

Wilson also came to approve of Robert Cecil, the other British expert on the League. Thin, stern, reserved, Cecil often reminded people of a monk. He rarely smiled, and when he did, said Clemenceau, it was like "a Chinese dragon." He was a devout Anglican by conviction, a lawyer by training, a politician by profession and an English aristocrat by birth. His family, the Cecils, had served the country since the sixteenth century. Balfour was a cousin and his father was the great Lord Salisbury, Conservative prime minister for much of the 1880s and 1890s. The young Robert met Disraeli and Gladstone, visited Windsor Castle and was taken to call on the crown prince of Prussia. His upbringing, at once privileged and austere, created in him a strong sense of right and wrong and an equally strong sense of public duty. When the war broke out, he was fifty, too old to fight, so he volunteered to work for the Red Cross in France. By 1916 he was in charge of the blockade against Germany.[16]

By this point he had come to the firm conviction that the world must establish an organization to prevent war, and he welcomed Wilson's pronouncements enthusiastically. His first encounter with the president, in December 1918, was sadly disappointing. The two men were able only to exchange a few remarks at a large reception. When they finally had a proper conversation, in Paris on January 19, Cecil found Wilson's ideas on the League largely borrowed from the British. Wilson himself, Cecil wrote in his diary, "is a trifle of a bully, and must be dealt with firmly though with the utmost courtesy and respect—not a very easy combination to hit off." Wilson assigned David Hunter Miller to meet Cecil and come up with a common draft, a sign of the growing cooperation between the Americans and the British.[17]

On January 25, when the Peace Conference created the Commission on the League of Nations, the room resounded with noble sentiments. The mood was somewhat spoiled when representatives of the smaller nations, already restive about their role in Paris, grumbled that the commission was made up only of representatives, two apiece, from the Big Five—the British empire, France, Italy, Japan and the United States. They too, said the prime minister of Belgium, had suffered. Clemenceau, in the chair, was having none of this. The Five had paid for their seats at the Peace Conference with their millions of dead and wounded. The smaller powers were fortunate to have been invited at all. As a concession, they would be allowed to nominate five representatives for the League commission. The flurry of revolt subsided, but the resentment did not. When the British and Americans unveiled their plan for a League with an executive council of the Five, the small powers made such a fuss that they were eventually given the right to vote four additional members.[18]

Cecil thought Wilson was mad when he talked of writing the League covenant in two weeks, but in fact the work went extraordinarily quickly, thanks partly to the fact that the British and the Americans had come to substantial agreement beforehand. The first meeting was held on February 3, and by February 14 a comprehensive draft was ready. The commission's nineteen members met almost daily, in House's rooms at the Crillon, seated around a large table covered with a red cloth. Behind them sat their interpreters murmuring quietly in their ears. The British and the Americans were beside each other, consulting each other continually. The French were separated from them by the Italians. The Portuguese and the Belgians were inexhaustible; the Japanese rarely uttered. Wilson, in the chair, was brisk, discouraging speeches and discussions of details and pushing the League in the direction he wanted. "I am coming to the conclusion," Cecil wrote, "that I do not personally like him. I do not know quite what it is that repels me: a certain hardness, coupled with vanity and an eye for effect." House, the other American representative, was always there at the president's elbow, although he rarely spoke. Behind the scenes he was, as usual, busy: "I try to find out in advance where trouble lies and to smooth it out before it goes too far."[19]

Neither Lloyd George nor Clemenceau put himself on the commission. Baker saw this as more proof, if any were needed, that the Europeans did not take the League seriously. They were happy, he said darkly, to see Wilson occupied while they shared out the spoils of war in their customary fashion. But Wilson continued to attend the Supreme Council and shared in all its major decisions. Lloyd George, as he had done throughout his political career, chose men he trusted—in this case Smuts and Cecil—gave them full authority and generally left them to it. Clemenceau appointed two leading experts, whom he equally typically treated badly, Professor Ferdinand Larnaude, dean of the faculty of law at the University of Paris, and Léon Bourgeois.[20]

A man of great learning and cultivation, Bourgeois was an expert in the law, a student of Sanskrit and a connoisseur of music, as well as a passable sculptor and caricaturist. After entering politics as a liberal, he had risen rapidly to the top: minister of the interior, of education, of justice, foreign minister, prime minister. His interest in international order dated back long before the war; he had represented France at the Hague peace conferences, which tried, without success, to put limits on war. When Wilson outlined his hopes for the League, Bourgeois wept for joy. In 1919, however, he was old and tired. His eyesight was failing and he suffered terribly from the cold.[21]

He labored, moreover, under considerable handicaps. Many French officials persisted in seeing the League as a continuation of the wartime alliance, still directed against Germany. Clemenceau made no secret that he thought Bourgeois a fool. When House asked why Bourgeois had ever been prime minister, Clemenceau replied, "When I was unmaking Cabinets, the material ran out, and they took Bourgeois." The British and the Americans regarded him as something of a joke with his prolix speeches in mellifluous French which, on occasion, put them to sleep. Wilson took a positive dislike to him, in part because he had heard that Clemenceau had given him instructions to delay proceedings as much as possible. This was probably true. Bourgeois did very little without consulting Clemenceau, who was hoping to squeeze concessions out of Wilson over the German peace terms. "Let yourselves be beaten," he told Bourgeois and Larnaude. "It doesn't matter. Your setbacks will help me to demand extra guarantees on the Rhine." Bourgeois was bitter but resigned. "In other words," he told Poincaré, "he asks me simply to get myself killed in the trenches, while he fights elsewhere."[22]

In the League commission meetings, the French representatives fought against both the British and the Americans to give the League teeth, something, after all, Wilson had once said he wanted. Bourgeois argued that the League should operate like the justice system in any modern democratic state, with the power to intervene where there were breaches of the peace and forcibly restore order. In other words, if there were disputes among League members, these would automatically be submitted to compulsory arbitration. If a state refused to accept the League's decision, then the next step would be sanctions, economic, even military. He advocated strict disarmament under a League body with sweeping powers of inspection and an international force drawn from League members.[23] The British and the Americans suspected that such proposals were merely another French device to build a permanent armed coalition against Germany. In any case, they were quite out of the question politically. The U.S. Congress, which had enough trouble sharing the control of foreign policy with the president, was certainly not going to let other nations decide when and where the United States would fight. The Conservatives in

Lloyd George's government, the army and the navy and much of the Foreign Office preferred to put their faith in the old, sure ways of defending Britain. The League, said Churchill, is "no substitute for the British fleet." It was all "rubbish" and "futile nonsense," said Henry Wilson, chief of the Imperial General Staff. Britain could be dragged into conflicts on the Continent or farther afield in which it had no interest.[24]

British reservations were echoed by several of the dominion delegates in Paris, something Lloyd George and his colleagues could not easily ignore. Alight with malice like a small imp, Billy Hughes was predictably vehement. He liked the French and hated the Americans, not least because Wilson had snubbed him during a visit to Washington. The League, he said, was Wilson's toy: "he would not be happy till he got it." Speaking for Australia and himself, he did not want to see the British empire dragged behind Wilson's triumphal chariot. Borden added his more sober and tactful criticisms. He liked the idea of a League, but he would have preferred one without too many Europeans. His real dream was always a partnership between the United States and the British empire. The Canadians, who had just won from Britain a measure of control over their own foreign policy, did not intend to turn around and hand it back to another superior body.[25]

French attempts to sharpen the League's teeth irritated the other Allies and threatened to hold up the Peace Conference. As the commission on the League rushed to get the first draft finished before Wilson went back to the United States for his brief visit, enough leaked out of its secret meetings to cause alarm. "Dark clouds are gathering in conference quarters," wrote the American correspondent of the Associated Press, "and there is a general atmosphere of distrust and bitterness prevailing, with the fate of the League Covenant still very much in doubt." It did not help that the French press was starting to attack Wilson or that Clemenceau gave an interview in which he warned that France must not be sacrificed in the name of noble but vague ideals. Rumors circulated that in retaliation Wilson was going to move the whole Peace Conference from Paris or perhaps give up the attempt to get a League altogether.

On February 11, three days before Wilson was due to sail, the League commission met for most of the day. The French brought up amendments to create a League army. "Unconstitutional and also impossible," said Wilson. The meeting adjourned without a decision. The next day, David Hunter Miller recorded in his diary, Cecil coldly pointed out their predicament to the French: "In his view they were saying to America, and to a lesser extent to Great Britain, that because more was not offered they would not take the gift that was at hand, and he warned them very frankly that the alternative offer which we have made, if the League of Nations was not successful, was an alliance between Great Britain and the United States." Bourgeois backed down, but he did make one last, futile attempt a month later, when he suggested that the League should have its own general staff. This, he said mildly, could give the League council information and prepare plans so that it would not be caught flat-footed when wars came. Wilson was enraged. "The French delegates seem absolutely impossible," he told Grayson, his physician. "They talk and talk and talk and desire constantly to reiterate points that have already been thoroughly thrashed out and completely disposed of." Bourgeois returned the antipathy. He told Poincaré that Wilson was both authoritarian and deeply untrustworthy: "He conducted everything with the goal of personal exaltation in mind."[26]

By February 13, the first draft was ready. Wilson was delighted, both with the auspicious date and with the fact that the articles numbered twenty-six, twice thirteen. The main outlines of the League were in place: a general assembly for all members, a secretariat and an executive council where the Big Five would have a bare majority (the failure of the United States to become a member of the League vitiated that clause). There would be no League army and no compulsory arbitration or disarmament. On the other hand, all League members pledged themselves to respect one another's independence and territorial boundaries. Because the Great Powers worried that the smaller powers might get together and outvote them, there was also a provision that most League decisions had to be unanimous. This was later blamed for the League's ineffectiveness.[27]

Germany was not allowed to join right away. The French were adamant on this, and their allies were prepared to give way. Indeed, Wilson was all for treating Germany like a convict in need of rehabilitation: "The world had a moral right to disarm Germany and to subject her to a generation of thoughtfulness." And so Germany was to be in the curious position of agreeing in the Treaty of Versailles to a club that it could not join. Both the British and Americans came to think this rather unfair.[28]

The covenant also reflected several other causes dear to internationalists and humanitarians. It contained an undertaking that the League would look into setting up a permanent international court of justice, provisions against arms trafficking and slavery and support for the spread of the international Red Cross. It also established the International Labour Organization to work for international standards on working conditions.

This was something middle-class reformers, left-wing parties and unions had long wanted. (The eight-hour day was their great rallying cry.)

The most they had been able to achieve before the war, however, had been limits on women working at night and a ban on phosphorus in match-making. The Bolshevik revolution helped to work a miraculous change of attitude among the Western ruling classes. The workers, even in the victorious democracies, were restless. Who knew how far they would go down the path toward revolution? European labor representatives were threatening to hold a conference in Paris at the same time as the Peace Conference, with delegates from the defeated nations as well as the victors. While the Allies managed to deflect this to Berne in Switzerland, Lloyd George and Clemenceau both thought that a clause on labor in the covenant of the League would be very helpful in calming their workers down. In any case, their own political leanings, like Wilson's, made them sympathetic to the labor movement, at least when it steered clear of revolution.[29]

The day the League of Nations commission was appointed, another was set up on international labor. Under the chairmanship first of the fierce little head of the American Federation of Labor, Samuel Gompers, and then of the British labor leader George Barnes, it worked away quietly. Barnes complained to Lloyd George that the peacemakers took only a "languid interest" in its work.[30] This was probably a good thing: the International Labour Organization came into existence with a minimum of fuss and held its first conference before the end of 1919. Unlike the League of Nations, to which it was attached, it included German representatives from the very beginning. And unlike the League, it has survived to the present day.

On February 14, Wilson presented the draft of the League covenant to a plenary session of the Peace Conference. The members of the commission had produced a document, at once practical and inspirational, of which they were all proud. "Many terrible things have come out of this war," he concluded, "but some very beautiful things have come out of it." That night he left Paris for the United States, confident that he had accomplished his main purpose in attending the conference.[31]

The covenant was not quite finished, though. The French still hoped to get in something about military force; the Japanese had warned that they intended to introduce a controversial provision on racial equality; and the mandates over the former German colonies and the Ottoman empire still had to be awarded. There was also the tricky matter of the Monroe Doctrine, underpinning U.S. policy toward the Americas. Would the League have the power, as many of Wilson's conservative opponents feared, to override the doctrine? If so, they would oppose the League, which might well lead to its rejection by Congress. Although Wilson hated to make concessions, especially to men he loathed, he agreed on his return to Paris to negotiate a special reservation saying that nothing in the League covenant invalidated the Monroe Doctrine.[32]

He found himself embroiled, this time with the British, in the sort of diplomatic game that he had always regarded with contempt. Although Cecil and Smuts sympathized with his predicament and were prepared to support him, Lloyd George had scented an opportunity. He had been trying without success to get an agreement with the United States to prevent a naval race; he now hinted that he might oppose any reservation on the Monroe Doctrine. There was also a difficulty with the Japanese, who, it was feared, might ask for recognition of an equivalent doctrine for Japan warning other nations off the Far East. That in turn would upset the Chinese, already highly nervous about Japanese intentions.[33]

On April 10, with the naval issue thrashed out and the British back onside, Wilson introduced a carefully worded amendment to the effect that nothing in the League covenant would affect the validity of international agreements such as the Monroe Doctrine, designed to preserve the peace. The French, resentful over their failure to get a League with teeth, attacked with impeccable logic. There was already a provision in the covenant saying that all members would make sure that their international agreements were in accordance with the League and its principles. Was the Monroe Doctrine not in conformity? Of course it was, said Wilson; indeed, it was the model for the League. Then, said Bourgeois and Larnaude, why did the Monroe Doctrine need to be mentioned at all? Cecil tried to come to Wilson's rescue: the reference to the Monroe Doctrine was really a sort of illustration. Wilson sat by silently, his lower lip quivering. Toward midnight he burst out in a spirited defense of the United States, the guardian of freedom against absolutism in its own hemisphere and here, much more recently, in the Great War. "Is there to be withheld from her the small gift of a few words which only state the fact that her policy for the past century has been devoted to principles of liberty and independence which are to be consecrated in this document as a perpetual charter for all the world?" The Americans who heard him were deeply moved; the French were not.[34]

On April 28, as a freak snowfall covered Paris, a plenary session of the conference approved the covenant. A delegate from Panama made a very long and learned speech, which started with Aristotle and ended with Woodrow Wilson, about peace. The delegate from Honduras spoke in Spanish about the Monroe Doctrine clause but, since few people understood him, his objections were ignored. Clemenceau, as chairman, moved matters along with his usual dispatch, limiting discussion of hostile amendments, even when they came from his own delegates, with a sharp bang of his gavel and a curt "Adopté."[35]

Wilson had every reason to be pleased. He had steered the covenant in the direction he wanted; he had blocked demands for a military force; and he had inserted a reservation on the Monroe Doctrine that should ensure its passage in the United States. The League, he felt confident, would grow and change over the years. In time, it would embrace the enemy nations and help them to stay on the paths of peace and democracy. Where the peace settlements needed fixing, as he told his wife, "one by one the mistakes can be brought to the League for readjustment, and the League will act as a permanent clearinghouse where every nation can come, the small as well as the great."[36] In concentrating on the League, Wilson allowed much else to go by at the Peace Conference. He did not fight decisions that, by his lights, were wrong: the award of the German-speaking Tyrol to Italy, or the placing of millions of Germans under Czechoslovak or Polish rule. Such settlements once made were surprisingly durable, at least until the start of the next war. It would have been difficult in any case for the League to act, because its rules insisted on unanimity in virtually all decisions.

8

Mandates

E VEN BEFORE the League commission got down to work, the issue of mandates had come up at the Supreme Council. None of the victorious powers thought Germany should get back its colonial possessions, which included several strings of Pacific islands and pieces of Africa, and Wilson had made it clear that he expected the League to assume responsibility for their governance. Wilson's attitude came as an unwelcome shock in certain quarters. The French wanted Togoland and Cameroon and an end to German rights in Morocco (leaving France the latter's sole protector). The Italians had their eyes on, among other things, parts of Somalia. In the British empire, South Africa wanted German Southwest Africa, Australia wanted New Guinea and some nearby islands, and New Zealand wanted German Samoa. The British hoped to annex German East Africa to fill in the missing link between their colonies to the north and south. They had also made a secret deal with the French to divide up the Ottoman empire. The Japanese too had their secret deals, with the Chinese to take over German rights and concessions, and with the British to keep the German islands north of the equator.

Wilson's new world order called for some arrangement other than annexation or colonization for those parts of the world not yet ready to govern themselves. Mandates, a form of trusteeship either directly under the League of Nations or under powers to be mandated by the League, were proposed as a possible solution. The length of the mandate would depend on the progress made by their wards. Wilson was maddeningly imprecise. Clearly, Africa would need outside control, but what about the pieces of territory which were flaking off from the defeated empires: the Arab Middle East, or Armenia, Georgia and the other Caucasian republics? In the confusion that was central Europe, there were also peoples who did not seem ready to look after themselves. Here Wilson would only say that he did not approve of mandates for European peoples.[1]

The idea itself, of the strong protecting the weak, was not a new one. Imperialists, frequently quite sincerely, had made much of their mission before the Great War. Germany, said the leading American expert on Africa, was exceptional in never having properly understood its duty: "The native was almost universally looked upon as a means to an end, never as an end in himself, and his welfare and that of the colony were completely subordinated to the interests of the German on the spot and of Germany at a distance."[2]

The British, realizing that there was no point in antagonizing the Americans by talking of adding Germany's territory, or anyone else's, to their empire, supported the idea of mandates. Smuts applied his usual eloquence. Great empires were being liquidated, he wrote in the memorandum on the League of Nations which so impressed Wilson, and the League must step in. "The peoples left behind by the decomposition of Russia, Austria and Turkey are mostly untrained politically; many of them are either incapable or deficient in the power of self-government; they are mostly destitute, and will require much nursing towards economic and political independence." Where Europeans—Finns, for example, or Poles—could stand on their own feet almost at once, it would take longer in the Middle East. The former German colonies in the Pacific and Africa would probably never be able to look after themselves. Their inhabitants were barbarians "to whom it would be impracticable to apply any ideas of political self-determination in the European sense." It would be much the best thing if the British empire took them over directly. If the Americans objected, he told his British colleagues, then Britain could graciously concede and ask in return for control under general, and minimal, League supervision. That in turn would oblige other nations, in particular France, Smuts's bugbear, to accept similar conditions for their colonies. Cecil saw a practical advantage: British traders and investors might finally be able to get into French and Portuguese colonies in Africa.[3]

The very word "mandate" had a benevolent and pleasing sound. Initially it also caused considerable confusion when it was produced at the Peace Conference. Was it merely a bit of window dressing, as cynics thought, to describe old-fashioned land grabbing, or was it a new departure in international relations? Would the League leave the mandatory powers alone to administer their assigned territories or would there be constant interference? When a bewildered Chinese delegate was told that the former German territories in his country would receive a new ruler, he was heard to ask, "Who is Mandatory?"[4]

The French reacted to the whole idea with hostility and apprehension.

Clemenceau exclaimed to Poincaré: "The League of Nations guaranteeing the peace, so be it, but the League of Nations proprietor of colonies,
no!" Colonies were a mark of power; they also held what France badly
needed: manpower. There were always going to be more Germans than
French, but with colonies in Asia and Africa the French had some hope of
restoring the balance with what they liked to call "our distant brothers."[5] If
France received mandates under the League, would there be niggling restrictions on the recruitment of native soldiers for duty overseas? Unfortunately both the Americans and the British appeared to be thinking along
these lines. Their proposed terms for mandates had the responsible powers doing humanitarian work, putting down slave trafficking, for example,
but they also prohibited the military training of inhabitants for anything
except police and "defence of territory."

When the mandates issue came up in the Supreme Council, Clemenceau and Pichon launched an attack. Why should France spend time and
money on looking after its mandates if it could not ask for volunteers to
defend it when the time came? It was all very well for the United States
and Britain to take a detached view, protected as they were from Germany
by geography, but France would not have survived the German attack
without its colonial soldiers. Lloyd George tried to find a compromise.
The clause that so upset the French was really directed against the sort of
thing the Germans used to do, raising big native armies to attack other colonies. The French would be perfectly free to defend themselves and whatever territories were under their wing. Clemenceau was mollified: "If this
clause meant that he had a right of raising troops in case of general war, he
was satisfied." Lloyd George cheerfully agreed: "So long as M. Clemenceau did not train big nigger armies for the purposes of aggression, that
was all the clause was intended to guard against." Wilson said he agreed
with Lloyd George's interpretation. The trouble was that no one was quite
clear what the clause meant. Could the French use soldiers from their
mandates in a European war, or not? Several months later, in May, the
French tried quietly to introduce their own clarification when they
slipped in a phrase about defense "of the mother country" to the mandates
clause in the final version of the covenant of the League as it was being
prepared for printing. The British secretary to the Peace Conference,
Hankey, who spotted the change late one night, did not believe French assurances that the other powers had approved it. He rushed round, catching Wilson already in bed and Lloyd George as he was getting undressed.
"As I suspected, it was a 'try-on.' " An agitated Wilson made Clemenceau
remove the phrase.[6]

·   ·   ·

The British watched the French maneuverings with smug disapproval, but they had their own difficulties with the Americans. Or rather, they were forced into a confrontation by South Africa, Australia and New Zealand, who because of their own territorial ambitions wanted nothing to do with mandates. Lloyd George found himself putting a case that he knew would be opposed by the United States. On January 24, he argued, somewhat halfheartedly, in the Supreme Council that annexation made administrative sense. He left it to the dominion leaders to supply the other arguments.

Smuts and Botha presented South Africa's case for the annexation of German Southwest Africa. Both men had fought in the brief victorious campaign of 1915, planned by Botha. They were asking to keep a huge stretch of territory, the size of England and France combined, widely regarded as without much value. (Its rich deposits of minerals had yet to be discovered.) The Atlantic coast was desert, the bulk of the interior scrub land, suitable mainly for grazing. A few thousand Germans, many of them rumored to be fleeing scandal in Germany, had built themselves imitation castles, cozy German villages and a neat little capital at Windhoek. The first German imperial commissioner, Ernst Goering (father of Hermann), had set the tone for German rule over the much larger African population with his authoritarian and brutal administration.[7]

Smuts and Botha made much of German cruelty toward the natives. White South Africans by contrast, said Smuts, understood the natives; indeed, they had done their best to give them a form of self-government. "They had established a white civilization in a savage continent and had become a great cultural agency all over South Africa." Now there was a chance for the peoples of Southwest Africa to share in these benefits. The territory was already tied to South Africa by geography; on all grounds, it made sense simply to make one country out of two. Wilson listened sympathetically. He liked both men, Smuts in particular, and, while he was not prepared to back down, he made it clear that he felt a South African mandate would be so successful that the inhabitants of Southwest Africa would one day freely choose to unite with South Africa.[8]

Clemenceau, the chair, then invited the "cannibals"—a little running joke he had with Hughes—to present the case for Australia and New Zealand. Waving a grossly distorted map which showed the lands he wanted—New Guinea and nearby islands such as the Bismarck Archipelago—practically touching Australia, Hughes demanded outright annexation. He cited defense (the islands were "as necessary to Australia as water to a city") and Australia's contribution in the war, the 90,000 casualties, the 60,000 killed and the war debt of £300 million. "Australia did not wish to be left to stagger under this load and not to feel safe." Although he could not say so openly, the future enemy Hughes had in mind was Japan. The Australians had also considered using the argument that the locals welcomed them with open arms, but when the Australian government carried out some inquiries in New Guinea it found that the inhabitants much preferred German officials, who had let them go their happy head-hunting way. There would be unlimited access for missionaries, Hughes said in reply to an earnest question from the president: "There are many days when the poor devils do not get half enough missionaries to eat."[9]

Massey, brandishing his own map, made a long and rambling speech on behalf of New Zealand's claim to Samoa. New Zealand troops, at "great risk," had occupied the islands at the start of the war. (In fact, the greatest risk came from boredom as the occupiers sat for the next few years downing huge quantities of beer.) The Samoans were not savages but very sensible people, and they wanted New Zealand rule. (Meanwhile, the Samoans were presenting the local New Zealand administrator with a petition demanding American rule, rule from London, rule by any power except New Zealand.[10])

Wilson, who could not bear Hughes in particular, listened with an obvious lack of sympathy. The French watched with amusement. They did not like mandates and they did not mind seeing disarray in the British empire. "Poor little Hughes is swelling up with pseudo importance," wrote a member of the Australian delegation. "Of course he is being used as a Catspaw by the French who want the Cameroons, Togo Land & Syria."[11]

A few days later, the French minister of colonies, Henri Simon, was moderation itself when he spoke to the Supreme Council. France only wanted two little pieces of territory in Africa: Togoland, which ran inland along France's West African colony of Dahomey (Benin), and the Cameroons, also in West Africa, which Germany had managed to pry out of France in 1911. (In addition, France wanted an exclusive protectorate over Morocco, but there was no need to mention that.) He preferred annexation, said Simon, as being more efficient and better for the natives. All France wished was to be able to continue its work of spreading civilization in tropical Africa. Clemenceau, who did not care at all about colonial possessions, undercut the effect of all this by saying that he was quite ready to compromise.[12]

Wilson dug in his heels. "If the process of annexation went on," he told the Supreme Council, "the League of Nations would be discredited from the beginning." The world expected more of them. They must not go back to the old games, parceling out helpless peoples. If they were not careful, public opinion would turn against them. They would see further upheavals in a Europe already troubled by revolution. He would not stand, he said privately, for "dividing the swag." If necessary, and this was a favorite threat, he would take the whole issue to the public. On the other hand, he was eager to move on from mandates. The fate of Europe—of Germany, Austria-Hungary, Russia—was the important question.[13]

Behind the scenes, a number of people were working to ease the confrontations. The Canadians, who always feared the consequences of tension between Britain and the United States, urged Hughes and Massey to be reasonable. House, now recovered from his illness, told the British that they must back down. Smuts and Cecil worked out a proposal which House thought the basis of a deal. There would be three types of mandates: "A" for nations, such as those in the Middle East, which were nearly ready to run their own affairs; "B" where the mandatory power would run them; and "C" for territories that were contiguous or close to the mandatory power, which would administer the territory as part of its own, subject only to certain restrictions, such as on the sale of alcohol and firearms. "C" mandates, in other words, conveniently covered Southwest Africa and the islands Australia and New Zealand wanted. A 999-year lease, said Hughes, instead of outright freehold. He was not prepared, however, to give way gracefully.[14]

On January 29, a meeting of the British empire delegation produced, in Borden's words, a "pretty warm scene." Lloyd George outlined the three types of mandate, which he thought the Americans would accept. Hughes, fighting "like a weasel," quibbled over every point until Lloyd George lost his temper and told him that he had been arguing his case with the United States for three days but that he did not intend to quarrel with the Americans over the Solomon Islands.[15]

Unfortunately, the next morning the *Daily Mail,* which published a Paris edition during the Peace Conference, came out with a story clearly inspired by Hughes. The article accused Britain of truckling to the United States, and claimed that the interests of the British empire were being sacrificed to satisfy Wilson's impractical ideals. That morning, the Supreme Council saw "a first-class row." Lloyd George was angry with Hughes, and Wilson, always sensitive to criticism, was furious. He delivered a rambling and muddled criticism of the proposed compromise and suggested that the whole question of mandates be postponed until the League had been settled. He was noticeably rude to the Australian prime minister. "Mr Hughes," said Lloyd George, who was despairing of ever getting an agreement, "was the last man I should have chosen to handle in that way." Wilson brusquely asked Hughes: "Am I to understand that if the whole civilised world asks Australia to agree to a mandate in respect of these islands, Australia is prepared still to defy the appeal of the whole civilised world?" Hughes, who was fiddling with his cumbersome hearing aid, claimed he had not heard the question. Wilson repeated himself. "That's about the size of it, President Wilson." There was a grunt of agreement from Massey. In fact, Hughes was not as adamant as he sounded. He was shaken by the reaction to the article and was to spend the next few days trying to avoid Lloyd George.[16]

At this point Botha, who was widely respected, lumbered to his feet. He thought the newspaper article was disgusting. As gentlemen, they must keep their disagreements to themselves. Speaking for himself, he wholeheartedly supported the great ideals expressed by President Wilson. Surely they all did. "He hoped that they would try in a spirit of co-operation, and by giving way on smaller things, to meet the difficulties and make the bigger ideal more possible." Wilson, who was ashamed of his outburst, was deeply moved. Massey made conciliatory noises, while Hughes said nothing. The proposal, with its three classes of mandate, went through. The awkward question of who got what was put to one side.[17]

It was the most difficult moment of a grueling week. The Supreme Council was also grappling with other matters: whether to negotiate with the Bolsheviks; Poland and its needs; Czechoslovakia's borders; the German peace terms. It had heard from the Chinese, who wanted German concessions in China back, and from the Japanese, who hoped to keep them; from the Belgians, who also wanted territory in Africa; and from the Rumanians and the Yugoslavs, who were arguing over territory. That Friday evening, Clemenceau complained to his aide Mordacq that he was at the end of his tether. His mind was racing with all the questions that they had been discussing; what he needed was to relax. The two men went off together to the Opéra-Comique.[18]

In all the discussions, there had been much talk of how glad the colonies were to get away from German rule. Yet although the fifth of Wilson's Fourteen Points had talked about taking the interests of the indigenous populations into account, no one had actually bothered to consult the Africans or the Pacific islanders. True, no Samoans or Melanesians had made their way to Paris, but there were Africans at hand. Indeed, a black French deputy from Senegal, Blaise Diagne, and the great American black leader W.E.B. Du Bois were busy organizing a Pan-African Congress. This duly took place in February with the grudging consent of the peacemakers. None of the leading figures from the Peace Conference attended. A member of the Belgian delegation spoke enthusiastically about the reforms that were taking place in the Congo, and a former minister of foreign affairs from Portugal praised his own country's management of its colonies. The handful of delegates from French Africa demonstrated the success of the *mission civilisatrice* by eulogizing the achievements of the Third Republic. The Congress passed resolutions calling for the Peace Conference to give the League direct control of the former German colonies. House received Du Bois with his customary courtesy but said nothing about the resolutions.[19]

As the months passed, the powers made quiet deals behind the scenes. Some merely confirmed arrangements made during the war. Japan, for example, got its islands north of the equator. To the south, New Zealand and Australia also got their islands. Partners when it came to defying Wilson, they then squabbled briskly for the next few months over Nauru, which had not been allocated. The island was only 20 square kilometers, but since it was composed mainly of bird droppings, it was an extremely valuable source of phosphates, used to make fertilizer. Without Nauru, both Hughes and Massey argued, their agriculture would collapse. The British settled the matter by taking over the mandate for Nauru themselves and doling out a meager royalty to the few thousand locals. (When Nauru became independent in 1968 and took over the phosphate business, its inhabitants had one of the highest per capita incomes in the world and a homeland that was vanishing under their feet. A trust fund which may be worth around $1 billion has gone into buying property abroad, and into the pockets of highly respectable Australian advisers. The phosphates are about to run out, but Nauru has today found a fresh source of income in money laundering for the Russian mafia.[20])

Britain and France had agreed in secret on a preliminary division of the German colonies in Africa during the war. At the Peace Conference, Lord Milner, the British colonial secretary, met with his French counterpart, Henri Simon, to work out the details of their control of some thirteen million people. France duly got most of Togoland and the Cameroons, Britain a small strip of each next to its colonies of the Gold Coast and Nigeria, and almost the whole of German East Africa. The Portuguese complained; they hoped to add a piece of German East Africa to their colony of Mozambique. Portugal, one of its delegates told Clemenceau, was owed something for "its unforgettable services to Humanity and Civilization above all in Africa, which it has watered with its blood since the 14th century." The Portuguese also suspected, correctly, that their allies were planning to transfer a bit of Angola to Belgium in order to give the Belgian Congo a proper Atlantic coast. In the end Portugal kept its colonies intact and gained a minuscule piece of land for Mozambique.[21]

The Belgians were less easily ignored. On May 2, they complained to
the Council of Four that they were being left out and put in a demand for
part of German East Africa. "A most impudent claim," said Lloyd George.
"At a time when the British Empire had millions of soldiers fighting for
Belgium, a few black troops had been sent into German East Africa."
Lloyd George was being unfair. Congolese troops under Belgian command had played an important part in pushing the Germans back in East
Africa. At the end of the war, Belgian forces occupied about a third of the
country. The Belgian government had no interest in keeping this; it intended to use East Africa to bargain for Portuguese territory along the Atlantic. The British, who were unable to persuade the Portuguese to play
along, found themselves in an awkward position. Belgium would not give
up its gains without something in return. Unfortunately, that occupied
territory included what looked like the best possible route for the
north–south railway linking the Cape to Cairo that British imperialists
had so long dreamed of building.[22]

On May 7, just after the Germans had received their terms, Clemenceau, Lloyd George, Wilson and Orlando met in a room at Versailles and
agreed on the final distribution of mandates over the former German colonies. (They still were haggling over the wreckage of the Ottoman empire
in the Middle East.) When word leaked out into the press that Belgium
was to get nothing, the Belgians, who were already feeling shortchanged,
were enraged.[23] In the end, Britain decided it could spare a bit of territory
(and that there were other routes for the railway) and so two provinces
next to the Congo's borders were detached from East Africa. Belgium
took the mandates for Rwanda and Burundi.

When the League finally came into existence in 1920, it confirmed what
had long since been decided. In the interwar years, the mandates in Africa
and the Pacific did look, as Hughes had predicted, very much like direct
annexation. The mandatory powers sent in annual reports to the League
but otherwise went their own way. At the end of the Second World War,
the United Nations took over the mandates and, as the great colonial empires melted away, gave independence to the territories it had inherited—
with one exception. South Africa refused to give up Southwest Africa.
Only in 1990 did it welcome its new neighbor, the independent state of
Namibia. In 1994, the last mandate ended when Palau, which had been
placed under Japan in 1919 and then under the United States after 1945, became independent. The 999-year leases had run out ahead of their time.

PART THREE

THE BALKANS AGAIN

Yugoslavia

WHILE THE GREAT POWERS had been preoccupied with the League, the smaller powers had been busy polishing up their demands. On the evening of February 17, 1919, a telephone call came to the Hôtel de Beau-Site, near the Etoile. Would the delegation of the Serbs, Croats and Slovenes please be ready to attend the Supreme Council the following afternoon? This sudden and typically capricious attention from the powers came as something of a relief. The delegation had been in Paris since the beginning of January, but its leaders had only appeared once before the council, on January 31, to counter Rumanian claims to the whole of the rich Banat, which lay between their two countries.

The Hôtel de Beau-Site had not been a happy place during those long weeks. The delegation, almost a hundred strong, comprised Serbs, Croats, Slovenes, Bosnians and Montenegrins, university professors, soldiers, former deputies from the parliament in Vienna, diplomats from Belgrade, lawyers from Dalmatia, radicals, monarchists, Orthodox, Catholics and Muslims. Many of its members did not know each other; indeed, as subjects of Serbia or of Austria-Hungary, they had fought on opposite sides during the war. The delegation faithfully reflected the great dividing lines that ran through the Balkans: between Roman Catholicism in the west, and Eastern Orthodoxy; between Christianity in the north, and Islam to the south. The delegates from the Adriatic side, mainly Slovene and Croat, cared passionately about security from Italy and control over ports and railways that had once belonged to Austria-Hungary, but were indifferent to border changes in the east. The Serbs from Serbia, meanwhile, were prepared to trade away Dalmatia or Istria to get more territory to the north and east.

They were together in Paris because of an idea, one of those so popular in nineteenth-century Europe, that a common language meant a common nationality. They all spoke a South Slav (Yugoslav) language. While Slovenian had become a distinct language over the centuries, Serbian and Croatian were virtually the same except for one striking difference. Serbian, like Russian and Bulgarian, was and is written in the Cyrillic alphabet, borrowed from the Greek of the Byzantine empire, while Croatian reflected the Catholic and Western orientation of its people and used the Latin alphabet. While separate nationalisms had been growing in the Balkans before the war—Serbian, for example, or Croatian—so too had the dream that all South Slavs, whether still under Ottoman rule, inside Austria-Hungary, or already independent in Serbia and Bulgaria, belonged together in one great nation. What started with a few mainly Croat intellectuals and priests along the Dalmatian coast grew by the 1860s into *jugoslovjentsvo*—Yugoslavism—with a Yugoslav academy, schools, journals, all to promote unity among South Slavs. But was that going to be stronger than all the other forces, from history to religion, that marked them out, one from the other? The Yugoslav idea was always strongest among the South Slavs, especially the Croats, inside Austria-Hungary who feared that they were being made into Germans or Hungarians.[1] Those outside, in Serbia, for example, had an alternative and equally compelling vision, of a large nation-state built around themselves.

The state of the South Slavs—cobbled together from Serbia and the southern parts of the vanished Austria-Hungary—that emerged in 1919 was the result of both accident and hasty, often desperate choices. It was not even clear what the delegation or the new country it claimed to represent should be called. Made up of Serbia and the southern parts of the vanished Austria-Hungary, it eventually took the name Yugoslavia. The Peace Conference, contrary to what many people have believed since, did not create Yugoslavia—it had already created itself by the time the first diplomats arrived in Paris. Seventy years later, the powers were equally unable to prevent its disintegration. But the peacemakers in Paris had the ability to withhold territory from the new state, perhaps even destroy it. They were wary, with good reason, of ambitious nations in the Balkans. It would be a mistake to give the South Slav state a navy, Wilson thought: "It will be a turbulent nation as they are a turbulent people, and they ought not to have a navy to run amuck with."[2]

In February 1919 the peacemakers had not yet decided whether to be good or bad fairy godmothers. Except for one. The Italian government would have preferred to strangle the infant state in its cradle. Italian nationalists were quick to cast Yugoslavia as their main enemy, the role having been left empty by the disappearance of Austria-Hungary. "To our

hurt and embarrassment," complained Prime Minister Orlando, "Yugoslavia will have taken the place of Austria, and everything will be as unsatisfactory as before." Britain and France at first reluctantly went along with
Italy and refused to recognize the new state. The United States, which had
no love for Italy and Italian ambitions in the Balkans, recognized Yugoslavia in February; Britain and France did so only in June, partly in reaction to Italy's intransigence, which at that point was threatening to break
up the Peace Conference.[3]

Nicola Pašić, for many years prime minister of Serbia, headed the delegation. In his mid-seventies, with clear blue eyes and a long white beard
that fell to his waist, he looked like a benevolent old monk. His private life
was exemplary: he was deeply religious, and, although he had married a
rich woman, he lived simply. He loved to sit in the evenings singing old
Serbian folk songs with his wife and daughters. When he spoke in public,
which he did rarely, he was slow and deliberate. (His Serbian was said to
be full of mistakes.) He spoke only rudimentary French and German and
no English at all. Perhaps because of this, he had a reputation for great
wisdom. Lloyd George thought him "one of the craftiest and most tenacious statesmen in South Eastern Europe." Like another Serb leader, in
the 1990s, Pašić was a devious, dangerous old man who loved two things:
power and Serbia. Few of his colleagues trusted him; he was, however,
adored in the countryside, where most Serbs lived.[4]

Many people in Paris found the Balkans confusing. At his first meeting
with Pašić, Lloyd George inquired whether Serbs and Croats spoke the
same language.[5] Only a handful of specialists, or cranks, had made it their
business to study the area. What most people knew was that the Balkans
were dangerous for Europe; they had caused trouble for decades as the
Ottoman empire disintegrated and Austria-Hungary and Russia vied for
control; and they had sparked off the Great War when Serb nationalists assassinated the heir to the Austrian throne in Sarajevo.

Pašić had been born when Serbia was already free, with its own prince,
but he had grown up in a world marked by those long years of Ottoman
rule. From Rumania south to Greece, the Ottomans had left their cook-
ing, their customs, their bureaucracy, their corruption and, to a certain extent, their Islam. "Balkan" had become shorthand for a geographic area
but also for a state of mind, and for a history marked by frequent war and
intrigue. Their past had taught the peoples of the Balkans, as the proverb
had it, that "the hand that cannot be cut off, must be kissed." The cult of
the warrior coexisted with admiration for another sort of man, like Pašić,
who never trusted anyone, never revealed his true intentions and never
took advice.[6]

Besides the Serbs, Croats, Slovenes, Albanians, Bulgarians and Macedonians, the Balkan peoples also included the Greeks (who preferred to think of themselves as a Mediterranean race) and, depending on your definition, Rumanians (who preferred to talk about their Roman ancestry), as well as a host of minorities left behind by the tides of the past. The Jewish merchants of Sarajevo, the Italian colonies on the Dalmatian coast, the descendants of German settlers in the north, and the Turks in the south— these were also part of the Balkan reality.

At the heart of the region was Serbia. In Pašić's childhood it was a simple place. Railways and telegraphs had not yet linked the little principality, as it then was, with the wider world. Apart from Belgrade, the capital, which had only 20,000 inhabitants, its towns were large villages. Its people lived, much as they had always done, from farming and trading. Pašić was one of the handful in his generation who had traveled abroad, in his case to Zurich, for higher education. His little country had great dreams, which he came to share: of a greater Serbia, reaching east and west toward the Black Sea and the Adriatic, sitting astride the great land routes leading down from central Europe to the Aegean. With the spread of nationalism in the nineteenth century, Serb historians rummaged the past to bolster their claims and bring all Serbs into the fold. "We got the children," a schoolmaster told a traveler in Macedonia when it was still under Ottoman rule. "We made them realize they were Serbs. We taught them their history." All over the Balkans, teachers, artists and historians were at work, reviving memories, polishing national myths, spreading a new sort of consciousness.[7]

The trouble was that it was not only Serbs who were awakened. As Churchill observed, the Balkans produce more history than they can consume. Where the blind Serb musicians sang of the great fourteenth-century kingdom of Stephen Dušan, stretching from the Danube to the Aegean, the Bulgarians looked to the tenth century, when King Simeon's empire controlled much of the same land. And the Greeks had the grandest memories of all, going all the way back to classical times, when Greek influence spread east to Asia Minor and the Black Sea, and west to Italy and the Mediterranean. Even the brief possession of a piece of land centuries ago could be hauled out to justify a present claim. "We might as justly claim Calais," the traveler pointed out to the nationalist schoolmaster. "Why don't you?" he replied. "You have a navy."[8]

Pašić was a founding member of the Serbian National Radical Party, founded in 1880, which advocated the liberation and union of all Serbs, including those in Austria-Hungary. Like so many Serb nationalists, he cared little about the Croats or Slovenes; they were Roman Catholic and looked to the West, while the Serbs were Orthodox.[9] If Croats and

Slovenes were to join Serbia, they would do so on Serbian terms, under Serbian leadership.

One by one, in little wars, simple and straightforward as they now seemed from the perspective of 1919, the Balkan nations had freed themselves from the lethargic embrace of the Turks. By 1914, all that was left of the European part of the empire that had once menaced Vienna was a toehold in Thrace and the great capital of Constantinople (today's Istanbul). The new countries acquired the trappings of statehood: newspapers, railways, colleges, academies of arts and science, anthems, postage stamps, armies and kings, most of whom came from Germany.

In the turbulent world of Serbian politics, Pašić managed to survive, a triumph in itself. Death sentences, exile, plots, assassination attempts, car accidents: he outlasted them all. And he returned the favors to his enemies. The English writer Rebecca West airily dismissed rumors, probably true, that he had known about the plot to assassinate the archduke in Sarajevo: "Politicians of peasant origin, bred in the full Balkan tradition, such as the Serbian Prime Minister, Mr. Pashitch, could not feel the same embarrassment at being suspected of complicity in the murder of a national enemy that would have been felt by his English contemporaries, say Mr. Balfour or Mr. Asquith."[10]

In 1919, when the question of appointing a leader for the delegation going to Paris came up, Prince Alexander of Serbia, who was acting as regent for his senile old father, insisted on Pašić, perhaps to keep him away from Belgrade. To his considerable annoyance, Pašić found that he had to share power with a Croat, Ante Trumbić, the new foreign minister. Serbs and Croats tended to irritate each other. As a Serbian official once complained to a British visitor, "for the Serbs everything is simple; for the Croats everything is complicated." And Trumbić was very Croatian. Fluent in Italian, with a deep love of Italian culture, he came from the cosmopolitan Dalmatian coast. While Pašić had been dreaming of destroying Austria-Hungary, Trumbić had sat in its parliaments. He had learned there to love precedents and quibbles and reasons why things could not be done. Although he spent much of his life working to create a Yugoslav state which would include Serbia, he regarded the Serbs as barbarians, deeply scarred by their long years under Ottoman rule. "You are not going to compare, I hope," he told a French writer, "the Croats, the Slovenes, the Dalmatians whom centuries of artistic, moral and intellectual communion with Austria, Italy and Hungary have made pure occidentals, with these half-civilised Serbs, the Balkan hybrids of Slavs and Turks."[11]

By 1914, Trumbić was becoming convinced that the future for his people lay outside Austria-Hungary. In 1915, in company with a journalist and a young sculptor, he set up the Yugoslav National Committee in London to work for a federation of South Slavs, this time including Serbia. It seemed like yet another of the strange self-appointed committees pursuing lost causes that dotted the capitals of Europe. None of the powers contemplated the disintegration of Austria-Hungary (and they were not going to do so until 1918). Serbians had no interest in a federation, only a greater Serbia. If the South Slav lands of Austria-Hungary entered into Allied thinking at all, it was for use in bargaining. In 1915, in the secret Treaty of London, Britain, France and Russia promised Italy a large chunk of Slovenia and the northern part of the Dalmatian coast. Serbia, it was hinted, would get the rest of Dalmatia and Bosnia-Herzegovina, perhaps even part of Croatia.[12]

Trumbić, now backed financially by the prosperous Croatian and Slovenian communities in North America, complained bitterly. Pašić and the Serbs refused to commit themselves to an alliance of equals. Trumbić was so discouraged that he talked of giving it all up and becoming a taxi driver in Buenos Aires. In London, however, his cause had attracted a small but powerful body of supporters, including Robert Seton-Watson, an independently wealthy scholar and linguist, and Wickham Steed, who had been *The Times*'s correspondent in Vienna before the war. Both men viewed Austria-Hungary with irritation; it was a corrupt and incompetent anomaly and they made it their self-appointed task to put it out of its misery. Wickham Steed had a particular enthusiasm for the Yugoslav cause. According to the British ambassador in Rome, this was because he had lived for years, "filially I believe rather than maritally," with a very clever South Slav woman.[13]

Croatia and Slovenia, and Bosnia as well, remained part of Austria-Hungary during the war, and many of their soldiers fought loyally for the old empire until the very end. There were Croats, Slovenes and Bosnians, even Serbs, in the Austrian armies which bombarded Serbia's capital, Belgrade, into ruins, which defeated the Serbian army and sent the Serbian government into exile, which occupied Serbia and which raped and brutalized the civilian population. Whatever their complicity in the murder of Archduke Franz Ferdinand in Sarajevo, the Serbians paid a very heavy price. More than 120,000 died in the war, out of a population of 4.5 million. By the war's end, no matter how much Trumbić and his committee in London talked of South Slav unity, it was not easy for such recent enemies to see each other as brothers and sisters. On the other hand, it was not clear what alternative they had.

As Austria-Hungary stumbled from one military disaster to the next, its South Slavs turned, many with reluctance, toward independence. The Serbians, temporarily chastened by defeat and by the collapse of their great protector, Russia, were more receptive to the idea of a Yugoslav state. In exile in Corfu, Pašić met with Trumbić and, in July 1918, the two men agreed that Serbs, Croats and Slovenes, including those in Bosnia, whether Muslim or not, would be united into Yugoslavia, with the king of Serbia as ruler. Union with Serbia, whatever its drawbacks, seemed less frightening than independence as, at best, a country cobbled together from Slovenia, Croatia and Bosnia and, at worst, two or three weak little states. Unwisely, the two sides put off discussing a constitution; the issue of federation (which the Croats and Slovenes wanted) or a unitary state (which of course Pašić wanted) was never settled. Trumbić can have had few illusions about how the Serbians saw the process of bringing together the different peoples. As one Serbian government official told him cheerfully, there would be no difficulty in managing the Bosnian Muslims. The Serbian army would give them twenty-four hours—no, perhaps even forty-eight—to return to the Orthodox faith. "Those who won't, will be killed, as we have done in our time in Serbia." Trumbić gasped. "You can't be serious." "Quite serious."[14]

In the months after the Corfu declaration Pašić quietly slid away from any real union. He worked behind the scenes to make sure that the Allies did not recognize Trumbić and the Yugoslav Committee as the voice of the South Slavs from Austria-Hungary. In October, just as the war was ending, he had a meeting in London with Wickham Steed, who still thought that he could sort out the remnants of Austria-Hungary into nice, rational patterns. Pašić would not be managed. He told Wickham Steed that Serbia had liberated the South Slavs from Austria-Hungary, that the Corfu Declaration had been intended only for propaganda, and that Serbia was going to be in control of any new state. Croats or Slovenes who did not like it were perfectly free to go elsewhere. "He alone was entitled to determine what policy should be followed; and those whom he employed had to obey orders." Wickham Steed angrily accused Pašić of acting like a sultan, and the two men never spoke to each other again.[15]

Apart from self-appointed experts such as Wickham Steed, few on the Allied side had given much thought to the future of central Europe and even less to the Balkans. The sudden disintegration of the Habsburg empire in the last weeks of the war raised huge issues. Would there still be some sort of rump state, with Austria and Hungary presided over perhaps by a different set of Habsburgs? Perhaps Croatia could become a new kingdom under an English prince. More practically, who was going to own the railway lines and the ports? What about Austria-Hungary's fleet? The young Emperor Karl, in one of his last acts, handed it over to his rapidly departing South Slav subjects. Possibly because the Balkans had caused so much trouble already, the powers tacitly agreed that the borders settled with so much difficulty before 1914 would not be touched.

Well before the Peace Conference opened, the South Slavs had taken matters into their own hands. In Zagreb, capital of Croatia, a National Council of Croats, Serbs and Slovenes declared its independence from Austria-Hungary on October 29, 1918. The next step was not clear. Many still hoped for their own separate South Slav state. Many Serbs, on the other hand, were for simply joining Serbia. Trumbić and his supporters preferred a federation, but a considerable number of Croats wanted an independent Croatia. In that moment the choices all seemed open.

In reality, circumstances were closing them off. Although Pašić was forced by Allied pressure into forming a coalition government with Trumbić and representatives of the National Council in Zagreb in the second week of November, he made sure that the new government was stillborn. "The old man," reported Seton-Watson, "changes his mind every few hours and cannot be trusted for five minutes with his word of honour or anything else." Meanwhile, on the ground, the Serbian army, as an Allied force, was fanning out into Austrian territory, first to the north and south and then, by November, into Croatia and Slovenia. French authorities, nominally responsible for the sector, watched benevolently. France had no objection to a strong Yugoslavia, which could act as a brake on Italy. When the Yugoslav Volunteers, some 80,000 soldiers from Austria-Hungary now fighting on the Allied side, tried to win Allied recognition as an occupation force, Pašić, to the dismay of Trumbić and other Croats, made sure that this did not happen. With Serbian encouragement, self-appointed assemblies in the Banat and in Bosnia-Herzegovina voted, hastily, for union with Serbia. In Montenegro, with Serbian troops in occupation, a national assembly, apparently made up only of those with the correct views, voted equally hastily to depose their king and to unite with Serbia.[16]

In Zagreb, the National Council started to panic. It had no forces of its own, and law and order were collapsing as peasants attacked the landlords and gangs of looters ransacked shops and businesses. Along the Adriatic, Italian troops were seizing the major ports. Demonstrators began to appear in the streets of Zagreb demanding union forthwith with Serbia. On November 25, the National Council hastily resolved to ask Serbia for a union. Crucial details, such as the constitution, were to be settled later. A Croat nationalist leader warned in vain against scuttling to Belgrade like

"drunken geese in the fog." Surely, many thought, the powers would protect them. An American military man reported from Slovenia in early
1919: "The government and the people emphasize their almost pathetic
confidence in the United States as their champion in Paris. They constantly refer to President Wilson and his doctrines, and believe that their
national claims and their national security, like those of other small states,
can only be gained if these doctrines are accepted and carried out as the
basis of the peace settlement."[17]

On December 1, 1918, Prince Alexander of Serbia proclaimed the
Kingdom of Serbs, Croats and Slovenes. The name itself was a problem;
non-Serbians generally preferred "Yugoslavia" because it implied a true
union of equals. Serbians wanted a name that enshrined the central importance of Serbia. It was an uneasy marriage, among peoples who had
been divided by years of history, religion, cultural influences and war.
Were the claims of a common ethnicity and similar languages enough to
make it last? Outsiders were dubious; as an American military observer
wrote in the spring of 1919, "while the Government officials all take pains
to protest ('too well') that the Serbs and Croats are one people, it is absurd
to say so. The social 'Climate' is quite different. The Serbs are soldier-
peasants; the Croats are passive intellectuals in tendency. The Public Pros-
ecutor, from whom one would expect a certain robustness of mind, told
me frankly that the Croats had given up struggling against their Magyar
oppressors long ago, and had devoted themselves to the arts." He noticed
that the Serbian army was increasingly unpopular throughout Croat territories.[18]

Matters were not helped by the conviction of many Serbians that they
had simply increased Serbian territory rather than founded a new country,
and by their suspicion that the Croats and Slovenes and Bosnian Muslims
had not tried very hard to liberate themselves from Habsburg rule. Although Serbs made up less than half of the population, they ran the new
country. The Serbian army became the Yugoslav army; Croatian units
from the old Austrian-Hungarian army were disbanded. In the bureaucracy and government, Serbs held almost all the important posts. Belgrade
remained the capital and the kings of Serbia became kings of the new
state. Alexander took an oath of allegiance to the constitution on June 28,
1921, the anniversary of the Battle of Kosovo, the most important day in
Serb history.[19] It was a beginning from which Yugoslavia never recovered.

At its very first meeting in Paris, the Supreme Council found itself dealing
with the fallout from Yugoslavia's sudden appearance. Should Montenegro be treated as a separate country or not? The hasty vote to unite with

Serbia and depose the royal family had produced an armed struggle between the Greens, who refused to recognize the union and who were
largely monarchist, and the Whites, who did. (The colors, and the divisions, appeared again after the collapse of Tito's Yugoslavia in 1991.) Sonnino, speaking for the Italians, objected to separate representation on the
grounds that Serbs and Montenegrins were virtually the same. Italy clearly
did not want Serbia to have any more voice than it already had. (The Italians were quite content to see Montenegro swallowed up by Serbia, hoping that the mouthful would be particularly indigestible.) Lloyd George
and Wilson were for hearing both sides. Wilson was particularly worried
about Montenegro's rights to self-determination: "The action of Serbia
had gone some way toward prejudicing his mind against Serbia. It was absolutely against all principle that the processes of self-government should
be forced." The difficulty, as the statesmen all agreed, was to find anyone,
in the existing circumstances, who could speak for the Montenegrins.
Should the Allies recognize the king? Balfour said mordantly, "We pay for
him." (Britain and France had subsidized Nicholas during the war and
had not yet got around to withdrawing recognition from him.) Wilson
objected that the king could speak only for himself and not for Montenegro.[20]

Much greater problems were waiting for the peacemakers, but there
was something fascinating about Montenegro. The country, a spot on the
map between Croatia and Albania so small that few people could find it,
was absurd and heroic, remote and beautiful. According to Montenegrin
legend, when God was creating the world he had its mountains in a sack
which broke and rained them down in a crazy jumble on what became
their homeland. The Montenegrins themselves matched their mountains.
They were perhaps the tallest people in Europe, handsome, proud, brave
and indolent, given to endless drinking of coffee and the rehashing of old
victories and blood feuds. The intrepid traveler Edith Durham took
against them when she inadvertently looked into the bag of one noble
warrior to discover his booty of sixty human noses; from that point on she
transferred her considerable loyalties to the Albanians.[21]

Their legends had it that Montenegrins were descended from the
Serbs who had fled from the invading Turks in the fourteenth century, and
it is true that they were Orthodox like the Serbs and spoke a version of
Serbian. From their mountains they had fought the Turks to a standstill
and so had remained an autonomous Christian island in the Turkish Muslim sea. Their rulers, until the middle of the nineteenth century, had been
warrior bishops. The modern dynasty was established by the last bishop of
the line in 1851, when he tired of being celibate and married. His nephew,
Nicholas II, had been on the throne since the 1860s.

Nicholas himself, as it happened, was in Paris, living on a dwindling pension from Britain while his daughters worked as dressmakers. Opinion was divided as to whether he was a cunning buffoon (Rebecca West's view) or a great warrior king (the opinion of Edith Durham, who spent a happy evening with him before the war swapping toasts). There was a whiff of the Middle Ages about King Nicholas: his insistence on leading his own troops into battle, on dispensing justice from his seat under an ancient tree, even the magnificent medals he awarded himself and his friends so copiously. His capital, Cetinje, was a large village, the Bank of Montenegro a small cottage, and the Grand Hotel a boardinghouse. The Biljarda, his old palace, was named after its much prized English billiard table, which had been hauled up the mountainside, and looked like an English country inn. His new palace was more like a German pension, with the royal children in folk costume doing their lessons with their Swiss tutor while the king sat on the front steps waiting for visitors. Franz Lehár used Montenegro as the model for Pontevedria in *The Merry Widow*.[22]

In fact, Nicholas was not quite the quaint figure he seemed. He had been educated, in France, among other places, and he had maneuvered with such success in the tangle of Balkan politics before the war that he had enlarged the size of his tiny state four times. He had also married his children well, two daughters to Russian royal dukes, one to the king of Italy and yet another to the king of Serbia. He had dreamed of Montenegro's absorbing Serbia; it was not meant to happen the other way round. He still hoped, in 1919, that he could regain the throne he had lost during the war.

Montenegro had been dragged into war when Austria invaded in 1916; Nicholas fled to Italy with what many on the Allied side thought was surprising alacrity. The suspicion that he had done a quiet deal with the Austrians followed him to Paris. The British Foreign Office regarded him as a treacherous ally, who probably was guilty as charged. It soon became clear in the discussion of Montenegro's representation that no one in Paris had any idea what the state of affairs on the ground was, and so it was decided to hold the question of Montenegro's representation open. It remained so until the Peace Conference ended.[23]

Nicholas did what little he could. He tried to give Colonel House one of his most magnificent orders; he wrote to Wilson; he issued optimistic memoranda claiming part of Bosnia for Montenegro. He did not get any response: there were, after all, more pressing issues than the fate of a country of 200,000 people. Fresh votes were held, under Serbian supervision, which seemed to show that Montenegrins wanted to be part of Yugoslavia. At the end of 1920, France withdrew its support for Nicholas; in the spring of 1921, Britain did likewise. Nicholas died, still in exile, in the spring of 1921. His grandson, an architect in France, has said that he has no interest in reclaiming the throne. Montenegro remains, as it has done since 1918, an uneasy part of Yugoslavia.

When the Yugoslav delegation finally got its chance to speak to the Supreme Council in February 1919, it brought a set of demands that had been put together with as much haste as the nation itself, and with as much wrangling. In an attempt to satisfy everyone, six out of the country's seven borders were open for discussion. Only the border with Greece, in the former Ottoman territory of Macedonia, was left alone. In the west, Slovenes insisted on Klagenfurt, on the north side of the southern spur of the Alps, as security against what was left of Austria. Otherwise they would be satisfied with the old boundaries between Austria-Hungary and Italy. Pašić, as usual, played his own game. His main interest, and that of the other Serbs, was to push eastward into Bulgaria and north of the Danube, taking a swath of Hungarian territory. Among other things, this would protect their capital, Belgrade, which had been in a uniquely exposed position, separated from a hostile Austria-Hungary by the width of a river. The Serbians had chosen it despite this drawback because it lay at the intersection of the Danube as it swept down from the north and the Sava River, which flowed from the west, at one of the most important strategic points in southern Europe. From the north and the west traders, pilgrims or armies had to pass by Belgrade if they wanted to go on to Greece and the great port at Salonika, or eastward through Bulgaria and on to Constantinople. The city had been besieged, defended, taken, sacked and fought over by Romans, Huns, Crusaders, Turks, Austrians and of course the Serbians themselves.[24]

On the afternoon of February 18, Milenko Vesnić, a Serb, started by apologizing that he did not yet have a full memorandum to lay before the powers. There were "certain difficulties," he murmured. Vesnić, easily the best speaker in the delegation, was smooth, affable and well traveled. His rich, attractive wife was friendly with the new Mrs. Wilson. Putting up a map, he laid out the basis for Yugoslav claims: reward for virtue (Serbia was a loyal ally, and the South Slavs within Austria-Hungary had done their best to disrupt the enemy war effort), self-determination, security. Slovene and Croat colleagues followed to explain away the contentious claims: to the largely Italian town of Trieste, the Hungarian provinces of the Backa and the Baranya north of the traditional boundaries of Croatia, the Rumanian-speaking parts of the Banat and the German-speaking areas around Klagenfurt. They denied that they were asking for non-Slav areas: the old censuses were unreliable, and in any case the Austrians and the Hungarians had deliberately suppressed Slavic schools and culture. Why, a man had been arrested in the old empire for asking for a railway ticket in Slovene. Even Yugoslavia's supporters were troubled. "Have they lost all sense of proportion and good sense?" asked a friend of Seton-Watson.[25]

Yugoslavia was already in possession of much of what it wanted in Austria-Hungary by the time the Peace Conference started—Bosnia-Herzegovina, the Slovene heartland in the old Austrian province of Carniola, much of Dalmatia and of course the old kingdom of Croatia—but it wanted still more. The delegation asked for two little scraps in the west known as the Medjumurje and the Prekomurje, where Croatia met Austria and Hungary, and, further east, the Baranya and the Backa, part of the rich southern Hungarian plain. Hungary had few friends in Paris: it was not only a defeated enemy but looked about to fall into revolution. The main question to be determined by the Peace Conference was how much of Hungary Yugoslavia could reasonably have. The Medjumurje and the Prekomurje were largely Croat and Slovene (although the Hungarians tried to claim otherwise) and, after some discussion, were handed over. The fate of Baranya and Backa, however, became tangled up in the dispute between Rumania and Yugoslavia and took much longer to settle.

To all the Balkan nations, the disappearance of Austria-Hungary was as exhilarating an opportunity as the defeats of the Ottoman empire before the war. Each wanted as much as it could get: self-determination for itself but not for its neighbors. Already during that confused period in October 1918 when Austria-Hungary sued for peace and then vanished from history, Balkan governments had started to stake out possession, moving their armies in. New bodies popped up like mushrooms after a storm: workers' councils, soldiers' councils, councils of Croats, Macedonians, Greeks. It was not clear who was behind them, but there seemed no end to them and no limit to their demands.

Greece wanted the rest of European Turkey; so did Bulgaria. Both Greece and Yugoslavia contemplated a division of Albania. Rumania and Bulgaria could not agree on ownership of the Dobrudja, which stretched along the west coast of the Black Sea. Serbia, Greece and Bulgaria all wanted more of Macedonia. There was fine talk of saving civilization and fighting for right and honor; underneath were the calculations of realpolitik. In the heady atmosphere of 1919, it was madness not to grab as much as possible. Balkan statesmen claimed to admire Wilson; they talked the language of self-determination, justice and international cooperation, and they produced petitions, said to represent the voice of the people, to bolster their old-style land grabbing. They showed beautifully drawn maps.

"It would take a huge monograph," wrote an American expert, "to contain an analysis of all the types of map forgeries that the war and peace conference called forth. . . . It was in the Balkans that the use of this process reached its most brilliant climax."[26]

The peacemakers had little to guide them in adjudicating all the claims. Wilson had mentioned the Balkans in the Fourteen Points, indirectly when he talked of the "freest opportunity of autonomous self-development" of the peoples of Austria-Hungary, and more directly when he said that Rumania, Serbia and Montenegro should be set on their feet again. He also promised that Serbia should have access to the sea, without specifying how, and that the Balkan states, under the benevolent eye of the powers, should all become friends "along historically established lines of allegiance and nationality." What that last meant was not clear but it suggested a disregard of both recent history and the national mix in the Balkans.

There was also a feeling that loyal allies should be rewarded. Serbia ought to have something for its sufferings—ports on the Adriatic, perhaps, or, at the very least, access to the Aegean. Greece and Rumania ought to collect on some of the promises handed out so freely during the war. Bulgaria and Ottoman Turkey deserved to pay the penalty for joining the wrong side. What they could pay was another matter. The Ottoman empire did not have much left in the Balkans, and Bulgaria was broke and had already lost a great swath of territory in 1913.

The British were largely indifferent to what happened in the Balkans, as they were to most of Central Europe, so long as British interests, whether commercial or naval, were protected. They preferred strong and stable states because those would act as a barrier to a revived Germany or Russia. While "gallant little Serbia" had its devoted admirers, as did Montenegro and Albania, the British government was not prepared to spend British force or British money to secure its well-being.[27] France, by contrast, was guided, as always, by its need for protection against Germany. Ideally, an enlarged Serbia and Rumania and, to the north, Czechoslovakia and Poland would provide such a forceful counterbalance that Germany would never dare to attack France again. And if a strong Serbia kept Italy honest, so much the better.

Geography forced Italy to think seriously about the Balkans. While Italians were generally delighted to see the end of their hereditary enemy Austria-Hungary, and the liberals, at least, sympathized with the small nations struggling to gain their freedom, Italian nationalists did not want any other power to achieve dominance in the Balkans, whether a Bolshevik Russia or a new South Slav state. The nationalists would shape Italian policy in an increasingly belligerent and expansionist direction. Because it feared a strong South Slav state, Italy was prepared to back the demands of its neighbors Rumania, Austria and Bulgaria. In Paris, Sonnino insisted that the competing claims of Italy and Yugoslavia must be discussed only by the Supreme Council. He feared, with reason, that a committee of experts would worry about the fairness of the frontiers, not about what Italy had been promised during the war. That story is part of the wider dispute between Italy and its allies which nearly wrecked the whole Peace Conference.

The Americans, in the Balkans as elsewhere, saw their role as that of honest broker, cutting through the thickets of the old diplomacy to apply the brave new standard of self-determination.[28] Unfortunately, the truth about populations in the Balkans was not easily discovered. The practice of defining oneself by nationality was so new that many inhabitants of the Balkans still thought of themselves primarily in terms of their region or clan or, as they had done under the Turks, of their religion. Were Serbs and Croats alike because they spoke virtually the same language, or different because the former were mainly Orthodox and used the Cyrillic script and the latter were Catholic and used the Latin? Where did the Macedonians belong—with the Greeks because of their history, or with the Slavs because of their language? How could you draw neat boundaries where there was such a mixture of peoples? How could you leave people together who had come to fear each other? On the population maps of the Balkans the patterns were rather pretty, a pointillist scattering of colors and an occasional bold blob. On the ground it was less pretty, a stew of suspicions and hatreds bubbling away.

The borders drawn through the region left in their wake unhappy minorities and resentful neighbors. And at its heart was the new Yugoslavia. It had formed itself, but the peacemakers recognized it and padded out its borders in a series of separate committees. The result was a country three times bigger than the old Serbia but with even more enemies. The new state took in Montenegro, Slovenia and Bosnia from Austria; Croatia and part of the Banat from Hungary; and pieces of Albania and Bulgaria. What was involved, as so often at the Peace Conference, was not merely the land and the fate of its inhabitants, but the future web of alliances on which the peace of Europe would depend.

Austria, Hungary and Bulgaria, the defeated, mourned their losses, both of territory and of their people. Only Greece in the south was friendly to the new country. Within Yugoslavia, peoples who had little in common except language never agreed on a common interpretation of what the country meant. Yugoslavia paid a heavy penalty for its gains during the Second World War, when its neighbors, with much help from Germany, seized back the land it had won at the Peace Conference and its peoples turned on each other. Although the communist leader Tito managed to put the pieces back together again, seventy years after the Paris Peace Conference had first recognized its existence Yugoslavia started to decompose into its separate components, disappearing for perhaps good as a country in March 2002. Its neighbors watched it uneasily, as they had been doing since 1919.

10

Rumania

A FEW DAYS before the Peace Conference officially opened, a rumor reached Rumania that only Belgium and Serbia among the smaller powers would be invited to participate. Ion Brătianu, the Rumanian prime minister, in the grip of "violent emotion," summoned the Allied ambassadors and complained. "Rumania is treated like a poor wretch deserving pity," he said, "and not like an Ally who has a right to justice." He instructed them to tell their governments that Rumania had always been a loyal ally (a dubious statement); he obliquely criticized Serbia for entering the war only because it was attacked; he muttered darkly about people who had lost touch with their own countries (his political enemies, some of whom had made their way to Paris); he warned that if the Allies were not careful, they would lose all influence in Rumania; and he threatened to withdraw (from what, it was not clear). The Allied ambassadors passed on this curious statement to their governments with a warning of their own: it would not do to alienate Rumania, because it was a useful buffer against Russia and Russian Bolshevism.[1] Since the Great Powers fully intended that Rumania should be represented, both performance and warning were unnecessary.

The Rumanians had a high opinion of their own importance; they also had large expectations of the Peace Conference. Early on January 8, Harold Nicolson, from the British delegation, had a brief meeting with two Rumanian delegates: "They say they are 'too ashamed to speak of internal questions.' On external questions, however, they show no shame at all, demanding most of Hungary."[2] Rumania also wanted a slice of Russia, Bessarabia, which it was already occupying, and the Bukovina from Austria in the north. Its demands were exorbitant, but it was particularly well placed to achieve them. There was no Russian force capable of stopping it, and Hungary and Austria were humbled. Rumania moved to occupy Hungarian Transylvania and the Bukovina pending a final decision in Paris. That had to wait until the Austrian and Hungarian treaties were drawn up.

Rumania faced a more difficult task with its claim to the Banat—also on Yugoslavia's list. Sloping westward down from the foothills of the Transylvanian Alps to the southern end of the Hungarian plain, this bucolic backwater caused much controversy in 1919. It was a rich prize: its 11,000 square miles, with their industrious farmers, rich black soil and abundant rivers and streams poured out corn and wheat. Herds of long-haired cows grazed on its pastures, and fat chickens and pigs scratched in its farmyards. The Banat had almost no industry to speak of, no towns of over 100,000, and few great monuments. It was picturesque rather than grand.

On January 31, 1919, Rumanian and Yugoslav representatives came before the Supreme Council. The Chinese, Czechs and Poles had appeared earlier in the week to present their respective cases, a precedent that worried Lloyd George—and he was by no means alone. The day before, he had asked whether there should be a firmer agenda. "He thought the discussion on Czecho-Slovakia and Poland the other day was absolutely wrong. He would not use the term 'a waste of time' because that was a very provocative one, and he could already see the glare in the President's eye! At the same time he thought it was not quite the best method of dealing with the business." If they were starting to deal with territorial issues, Lloyd George argued, they should get on with it and actually make some decisions. After an inconclusive discussion, the council accepted Balfour's suggestion that they might as well hear the Rumanians and Serbs out because it would make them happier.[3] Like many of Balfour's solutions, it was more elegant than practical.

As the light faded on that cold afternoon, Brătianu presented Rumania's case. Rich and polished to the point of absurdity, Brătianu had a profound sense of his own importance. He had been educated in the Hautes Ecoles in Paris, and never let anyone forget it; he loved to be discovered lying on a sofa with a book of French verse in a languid hand. Nicolson, who met him at a lunch early on in the conference, was not impressed: "Bratianu is a bearded woman, a forceful humbug, a Bucharest intellectual, a most unpleasing man. Handsome and exuberant, he flings his fine head sideways, catching his own profile in the glass. He makes elaborate verbal jokes, imagining them to be Parisian." Women rather liked him. "The eyes of a gazelle and the jaw of a tiger," said one. Queen Marie of Rumania, who knew all about seductions, demurely recalled an evening when the full moon had made him "sentimental." In a less charitable mood, she told Wilson that he was "a tiresome, sticky and tedious individual."[4]

Throwing open his briefcase with what Nicolson described as "histrionic detachment," he claimed the whole of the Banat. "He is evidently convinced that he is a greater statesman than any present. A smile of irony and self-consciousness recurs from time to time. He flings his fine head in profile. He makes a dreadful impression."[5] His arguments ran from the strictly legalistic (Rumania had been promised the Banat in the secret clauses of the Treaty of Bucharest of 1916 with which the Allies had enticed Rumania into the war) to the Wilsonian (Rumanians ought to be in one nation). In the course of his peroration he called in ethnology, history, geography and Rumania's wartime sacrifices. He also hinted that the Serbians had tilted toward Austria-Hungary in the past. (The Serbians were to make the same accusation about the Rumanians.)

Vesnić and Trumbić replied. They pointed out that Serbia was asking for only the western part of the Banat. While they could not call on secret treaties, they could otherwise use the same sorts of arguments as the Rumanians. "Since the Middle Ages," said Vesnić, "the portion of the Banat claimed by Serbia had always been closely connected with the Serbian people." Historically, he went on, "as the Isle of France was to France, and Tuscany to Italy, so was the Banat to Serbia." It had given birth to the Serb Renaissance and later Serbian nationalism. And when the Serbian royal family had been exiled, it had naturally taken refuge there. (To this Brătianu replied, reasonably enough, that the vagaries of Serbian politics had occasionally driven its rulers into Rumania proper, but this was scarcely reason for Serbia to claim that as well.[6])

In the discussion Wilson noted, with some surprise, that the delegates from the Balkan nations did not "represent their facts in the same way, and there would always be something that was not quite clear." The United States was always ready, he said, to approve a settlement based on facts. Balfour, who had been half asleep, intervened to ask an apparently simple question: Were there any figures as to the ethnic mix of the Banat? Yes, said the Yugoslavs; the western part, which they were claiming, was predominantly Serb and, moreover, so were monasteries and convents all over the Banat. There were, of course, large numbers of Germans and Hungarians, but they would much rather be part of Serbia than Rumania. No, said Brătianu, Rumanians were in the majority if you took the Banat as a unit (for political and historical reasons the only thing to do); monasteries were neither here nor there because everyone knew the Serbs, like all Slavs, tended to be religious; and, as for the Germans and Hungarians, the Serbs would have trouble managing such large minorities.[7]

On February 1, Brătianu produced the full list of Rumania's demands:

the Banat, Transylvania, Bessarabia on the Russian border, and the Bukovina in the north, all of which he claimed were historically and ethnically
part of Rumania. The Allies acquiesced on Bessarabia and the Bukovina;
they had little enthusiasm for handing the one back to a Bolshevik Russia
and the other over to what looked then like a Bolshevik Hungary. Transylvania was a much larger piece of land and a more complicated issue. The
Allies assumed that they would deal with that at their leisure when they
got around to doing the Hungarian treaty.

Brătianu warned that the Great Powers must settle Rumania's claims
before matters got out of hand and "serious developments" took place.
"Roumania was in need of the moral support of the Allies, if she was to
remain what she had been hitherto—a rallying point for Europe against
Bolshevism."[8] This, of course, was a popular argument in Paris, but in the
case of Rumania, which lay between the new Bolshevik Russia and revolutionary Hungary, a powerful one. Geography helped Rumania in another way: it was too far away for the Allies to enforce their will. Rumania
had been an ally during the war, although a notoriously unreliable one,
and promises, as awkward now as those to Italy, had been made by Britain
and France.

The Rumania that Paris knew was the cultivated and worldly one of
Princess Marthe Bibesco, whose salon was famous in Paris before the war,
or of her beautiful young cousin, who married into an ancient French
aristocratic family and as Anna de Noailles became one of the most famous poets of her generation. The Rumanian upper classes loved France:
they bought educations in Paris for their children, and clothes and furniture for themselves. And the French reciprocated in their own offhand
way; Rumania, it was said, was a fellow Latin country, the Rumanians descendants of Roman legionaries and Rumanian a Latin language. In the
nineteenth century, France had supported the cause of Rumanian independence from the Ottomans; in 1919, the French government envisaged
a strong Rumania as both a counterbalance against Germany and as a crucial link in the cordon sanitaire against Russian Bolshevism. The Rumanians themselves made much of their Western connections: they were the
heirs of the Roman empire, part of Western civilization. Conveniently for
the peace negotiations, they could argue that all the old Roman province
of Dacia including part of Transylvania, which belonged to Hungary,
should be restored to them.

There was another Rumania, though, with a more complicated history: the Rumania that had been invaded and settled over the centuries by
peoples from the east; that had been divided up among the kingdoms that

had come and gone in the center of Europe, and that, as Moldavia and Wallachia, had been under the sway of the Ottoman empire since the early sixteenth century. The Rumanian aristocrats who spoke such beautiful French and who came to Paris to buy their clothes had portraits of their grandparents in caftans and turbans.

Their society was deeply marked by the years under corrupt Ottoman rule. Rumanians had a saying: "The fish grows rotten from the head." In Rumania almost everything was for sale: offices, licenses, passports. Indeed, a foreign journalist who once tried to change money legally instead of on the black market was thrown into jail by police who thought he must be involved in a particularly clever swindle. Every government contract produced its share of graft. Although Rumania was a wealthy country, rich in farmland and, by 1918, with a flourishing oil industry, it lacked roads, bridges and railways because the money allocated by government had been siphoned off into the hands of families such as Brătianu's own. Rumanians tended to see intrigues everywhere. In Paris they hinted darkly that the Supreme Council had fallen under the sway of Bolshevism or, alternatively, that it had been bribed by sinister capitalist forces.[9]

Visitors to Rumania from Western Europe were struck by its exotic, even Oriental, flavor, from the onion domes of the Orthodox churches to which most of the inhabitants belonged, to the cabdrivers who wore blue velvet caftans and came from a sect where men were castrated after they had produced two children. Before the war Bucharest, the capital, was charming but backward. Most of its buildings were low and rambling, its unpaved streets busy with street vendors selling live birds, fruit, pastries or carpets. Dark-eyed Gypsy girls hawked their flowers; in the nightclubs their men played Gypsy music or the popular "Tu sais que tu es jolie." Well-to-do families lived with their own livestock in compounds guarded by Albanians.[10]

Rumania, for all its claims to an ancient past, was a relatively new country. Moldavia and Wallachia had gained a limited independence from the Ottomans by the mid-nineteenth century and complete independence by 1880. Together they formed a reverse L, with the richer, more developed province of Wallachia running east–west along the south side of the Transylvanian Alps, and Moldavia to the east of the Carpathians. In 1866 they had gained their own German prince, later King Carol, who had dodged the Austrian attempts to stop him by taking a Danube steamer disguised as a traveling salesman. His wife was a famous mystic who wrote poetry and romances under the pen name Carmen Sylva.

The Rumanians themselves were the Neapolitans of central Europe. Both sexes loved strong scents. Among the upper classes, women made up heavily, and men rather more discreetly, but even so the military authorities had to restrict the use of cosmetics to officers above a certain rank. Even after Rumania entered the war, foreign observers were scandalized to see officers strolling about "with painted faces, soliciting prostitutes or one another." Noisy, effusive, melodramatic, fond of quarreling, Rumanians of all ranks threw themselves into their pastimes with passionate enthusiasm. "Along with local politics, love and love-making are the great occupation and preoccupation of all classes of society," said a great Rumanian lady, adding: "Morality has never been a strong point with my compatriots, but they can boast of charm and beauty, wit, fun, and intelligence." Even the Rumanian Orthodox Church took a relaxed view of adultery; it allowed up to three divorces per individual on the grounds of mutual consent alone.[11]

Before Brătianu arrived in Paris, Rumania's spokesman had been the distinguished and charming Take Ionescu. Cheerful, dapper and well fed, he had studied law at the Sorbonne and spoke excellent French. His equally cheerful English wife, Bessie, was the daughter of a boardinghouse keeper in Brighton. Ionescu had been pro-Ally since the start of the war and played a considerable part in bringing Rumania in on the Allied side. On Rumania's claims, he was more moderate than his prime minister. "His attitude," reported an American delegate, "is very friendly towards the Serbs: the Bulgars, he says, have behaved very badly; of the 28,000 Rumanian prisoners taken by the Bulgarians only 10,000 survived captivity." On the Banat, Ionescu was for doing a deal: "they must be friends with Serbia and he does not want to hog the whole Banat, but will give them the southwestern portion."[12]

And in fact a deal had been made in October 1918. Ionescu had met with the Yugoslavs and hammered out an agreement, actually close to the one that was reached months later, giving Rumania the largest part of the Banat and Serbia the rest. The deal had been attacked in the Rumanian press as a betrayal of the Rumanian nation and was finally scuppered by Brătianu, partly at least because he hated Ionescu. When Rumania's delegation was chosen for the Peace Conference, Brătianu made sure that Ionescu was omitted.[13]

The Rumanian claim to the Banat stressed, inevitably, ethnic factors. It also laid heavy emphasis on Rumania's record in the war. This was not perhaps the wisest choice. Rumania, sensibly, had stood aside when the war started. Brătianu, who was then prime minister, told his colleagues that they must wait for the most favorable bid. Less sensibly, the Brătianu government had made this too obvious, behaving, said a French diplomat, "like a peddler in an oriental bazaar." When the Allies appeared to be gaining the upper hand in the summer of 1916, Rumania finally decided to enter the war, extracting as its price a promise that it would get the whole of the Banat, Transylvania and most of the Bukovina. Privately the Russians and the French agreed that they would review the whole package when peace came.[14]

Rumania's timing was bad; by the time its troops were ready to move, the Central Powers had rallied. By the end of 1916 over half the country was occupied by Germans and Austrians; during that winter, 300,000 Rumanians out of a total of six million died from disease and starvation. Its allies, unfairly perhaps, blamed Rumania itself for the disaster. Under a new Treaty of Bucharest with the Central Powers in May 1918, Rumania dropped out of the war, an understandable move but one that had implications for its territorial claims. Since in the earlier Treaty of Bucharest in 1916, Rumania had promised not to make a separate peace, the Allies now considered themselves no longer bound by their promises. Clemenceau never forgave Brătianu for his treachery. Brătianu dealt with the awkwardness by resigning and letting his successors (whom he had chosen) take responsibility. He managed to delay ratification of the new treaty in parliament and on November 10, 1918, declared war again on Germany. This, he announced cheerfully, meant that the deal with the Allies still stood. Rumania had made peace only in order to conserve its strength for war: "neither legally, practically, nor morally, were the Rumanians ever really at peace with the enemy." Just in case, though, he quietly arranged with the Italians, themselves anxious to limit Serbia's gains, that their two countries would stand together on the need to adhere to wartime treaties.[15]

The Supreme Council found Rumania's demands excessive and the wrangling with Yugoslavia over the Banat tedious. (Brătianu complained that some of them had slept during his presentation.) It was with obvious relief that the peacemakers adopted Lloyd George's recommendation to refer Rumania's claims, including those to the Banat, to a subcommittee of experts for a just settlement. When it had studied the matter, he added optimistically, and teased out the truth, only a few issues would have to come back before the council. Wilson agreed, with the reservation that the experts should not look at the political side of the problem. (What was "political" was never defined.) Clemenceau, perhaps as a result of Wilson's intervention, remained virtually speechless and Orlando made an ineffectual plea to settle the borders then and there. And so the future of the Banat, along with other prize pieces of territory in south-central Europe, was shipped off to a special territorial commission, the first of many, which was to have no more success in bringing the different sides together. In time, the Commission on Rumanian and Yugoslav Affairs dealt with all of Yugoslavia's boundaries, except the ones with Italy which, on Italian insistence, were reserved for the Supreme Council.[16]

Although the experts on the territorial commissions (eventually there were six in all) could not know it, almost all their recommendations were to go into the various peace treaties unchanged because their leaders simply did not have the time to consider them in detail. The Rumanian commission eventually broadened its scope until its experts determined the future shapes of Yugoslavia, Rumania, Greece and Bulgaria and the future balance of power in the Balkans, between Hungary and its neighbors and between Soviet Russia and south-central Europe. "How fallible one feels here!" Nicolson, one of the British experts, wrote. "A map—a pencil—tracing paper. Yet my courage fails at the thought of the people whom our errant lines enclose or exclude, the happiness of several thousands of people."[17]

The Supreme Council did not explain what made a just settlement. Did it mean providing defensible borders? Railway networks? Trade routes? In the end the experts agreed only that they would try to draw boundaries along lines of nationality. The Banat, the piece of land that triggered the process, also gave warning as to its difficulties. It held a rich mix of Serbs, Hungarians, Germans, Russians, Slovaks, Gypsies, Jews, even some scattered French and Italians. And there was always the problem of how to count heads in an area where the whole notion of national identity was as slippery as the Danube eels. In the gilt and tapestries of the banqueting room at the Quai d'Orsay, the Rumanian commission got out the maps, read the submissions, heard the witnesses and tried to impose a rational order on an irrational world.[18]

They also, in the case of the Europeans, kept their own national interests in mind. The French, looking for allies in central Europe, wanted both Rumania and Yugoslavia to be strong and friendly. The Italians split hairs and quibbled over procedure, all with the aim of blocking Yugoslav demands, and then appalled the Americans by hinting that they might agree to some of them in return for Italy's own claims in the Adriatic being accepted. Even where they could have made a magnanimous, and better still a cost-free, gesture in accepting Yugoslavia's claim on the Klagenfurt area of Austria, they would not. "Poor diplomacy," in the opinion of Charles Seymour, a young historian from Yale University. A French colleague was blunter: "He did not mind the Italian's crookedness, but he did object to the gaucherie." The Americans tried valiantly to pin down the elusive just settlement, and the British tried to reconcile the Americans and the French. "There was a good deal of jockeying to begin with," reported Seymour, "and a good deal of rather dirty work in maneuvering for position, so to speak. The British stood firm with us in killing this and in getting down to honest work."[19]

Brătianu made a poor impression, refusing to compromise, showing his temper and sulking when questioned too closely. He made the curious argument that granting the whole of the Banat to Rumania would actually improve relations with Yugoslavia, like "a tooth which has to be extracted." He also made threats: if he did not get the Banat, he would resign and let the Bolsheviks take over in Rumania. He tried to appeal over the experts' heads to Wilson, who sent him along to see House, who had to endure a drunken harangue about how Rumania had been betrayed by its allies. Brătianu also accused Hoover of holding up loans and food supplies until American interests, Jewish ones at that, got concessions to Rumania's oil. The news coming in from Central Europe did not help his case. Rumania was advancing beyond the armistice lines into Hungary and Bulgaria; its troops were massing on the northern edge of the Banat; it was making wild accusations that Serbs were murdering Rumanian civilians. The Yugoslavs by comparison appeared reasonable.[20]

At the beginning of March the Rumanian delegation received a reinforcement when Queen Marie, accompanied by three plump daughters, arrived on the royal train. Colette described her for *Le Matin:* "The morning was grey, but Queen Marie carried light within her. The glitter of her golden hair, the clarity of her pink and white complexion, the glow in her imperious yet soft eyes—such an apparition renders one speechless." The queen spoke charmingly of her longing to help her country; she called attention to her war work. "I simply went, My God!, I simply went wherever they called for me, and they needed me everywhere." She was, she said modestly, "a sort of banner raised for my country."[21]

She was indeed. It was fortunate that the heir to the Rumanian throne had married the one grandchild of Queen Victoria who had no difficulty in shaking off her English upbringing and adopting the ways of her new country. Ferdinand was deadly dull, shy and stupid; she was lovely, vivacious and adulterous. Her new subjects found this endearing. Her lovers included Joe Boyle, the dashing Canadian millionaire miner from the Klondike, and Brătianu's brother-in-law, who fathered, it was said, all of her children except the disastrous one who became King Carol. She was also very extravagant. Her trip to Paris was as much about shopping for herself as about her country. "Rumania," she cried, "has to have Transylvania, Bessarabia too. And what if for the lack of a gown, a concession should be lost?" She talked constantly of "my" ministers, country and army. Her husband, the king, she ignored; she claimed that a letter of advice he sent to Paris was "almost impossible to read but as the first sentence began that he had complete confidence in her she never attempted to read any of the rest."[22]

From her suite at the Ritz Hotel, she set out to conquer the powerful. She entreated Foch, with some success, to send weapons to Rumania, ostensibly for its fight against Bolshevism. She flattered House, who found her "one of the most delightful personalities of all the royal women I have met in the West." The British ambassador in Paris dined with her: "She really is a most amusing woman and if she was not so simple you would think she was very conceited." She asked Balfour prettily whether she should talk about her recent purchases or the League of Nations with Wilson. "Begin with the League of Nations," he advised, "and finish up with the pink chemise. If you were talking to Mr. Lloyd George, you could begin with the pink chemise!" Lloyd George found her "very naughty, but a very clever woman." Clemenceau was amused by her. He spoke to her frankly, though, about his displeasure with Rumania for having made a separate peace with the enemy, and about his dislike of Brătianu. When he accused Rumania of wanting the lion's share of the Banat, Marie answered archly, "that is just why I came to see his first cousin, the Tiger." Clemenceau shot back, "A tiger never had a child by a lioness."[23]

Her great failure was Wilson. She shocked him at their first meeting by talking about love. Grayson, Wilson's doctor, agreed: "I have never heard a lady talk about such things. I honestly did not know where to look I was so embarrassed." Marie then invited herself to lunch, "with one or two of my gentlemen." She arrived half an hour late with an entourage of ten people. "Every moment we waited," another guest noticed, "I could see from the cut of the president's jaw that a slice of Rumania was being lopped off." The queen thought the lunch went off very well; indeed, she felt that her time in Paris had done much to help her people. "I had pleaded, explained, had broken endless lances in their defense. I had given my country a living face."[24]

She might have been better advised to spend more time on the subordinates of the great men. On March 18, the Rumanian commission divided up the prize of the Banat, with the western third going to Yugoslavia and most of the rest to Rumania. It also gave Yugoslavia about a quarter of the Baranya and well over half the Backa on the western end of the Banat. The American experts, concerned as always with ethnic fairness, insisted on a predominantly Hungarian area near the city of Szeged remaining with Hungary. On June 21, in spite of passionate protests from the Rumanians, the Supreme Council accepted the recommendations. The Yugoslavs briefly caused problems by refusing to evacuate an island in the

Danube that had been awarded to Rumania, and in the autumn of 1919 there was tension between Rumania and Yugoslavia in the Banat. It was not until 1923 that the two countries grudgingly agreed to respect the award.

Yet the new line on the map could not tidy up the population. Almost 60,000 Serbs were left in Rumania, while 74,000 Rumanians and almost 400,000 Hungarians remained in Yugoslavia. In the new world of ethnic states which had triumphed in the center of Europe, the situation of such minorities was uneasy; they were too often treated as interlopers, even though they had been there for centuries. Rumania and Yugoslavia both pursued policies of assimilation. Yugoslavia eventually grouped its gains from Hungary together as the Vojvodina; Belgrade ruled, as it does today, with a heavy hand. Serbian was decreed the language of business; shop signs had to be in the Cyrillic alphabet, although the Latin script might be used as long as it came underneath; concerts had to include a stated number of Serb pieces; newspapers and school textbooks were strictly censored. In the 1930s, a foreign observer noticed that even Serbs in the Vojvodina were singing a sad little song:

I gave four horses
To bring the Serbs here—
I would give eight
To take them away.[25]

During the Second World War, Hitler's Germany and Hungary divided up the area; it then became a battleground between the occupiers and the resistance. Szeged, the town that the Americans had insisted on giving to Hungary, became the site of the camp where Jews from the Vojvodina, and indeed from all over that part of Europe, were killed. Today there are few Jews or Gypsies left in the Vojvodina, but the population is still mixed. Only half is Serb, and almost a quarter is Hungarian. Belgrade has fallen back on the familiar techniques of intimidation and repression to keep it under control. It is difficult to see a peaceful future.

Of all the victors at the Peace Conference, Rumania made by far the greatest gains, doubling in population and in size. Moreover, it has, unusually, managed to hang on to most of its gains. Bessarabia, it is true, went back to the Soviet Union after the Second World War. The Soviets also took about half of the Bukovina in the north, and the Bulgarians took back part of the disputed Dobrudja in the south. But Rumania still holds its greatest gain: Transylvania.

11

Bulgaria

WHILE THE BANAT was being discussed, the possibility of making it part of a complicated series of land deals was floated by, of all people, the Americans. If Rumania got more of the Banat, then it might be willing to give back some of the territory that it had seized in 1913 from Bulgaria, its neighbor to the southwest; Bulgaria might then be willing to give up some pieces of land to Yugoslavia, which would then be happier about losing some of the Banat.[1] Not surprisingly, this came to nothing. Rumania and Yugoslavia were in no mood to compromise.

Bulgaria, the one Balkan nation to have fought on the side of the Germans and Austrians, was of course not represented at the Peace Conference. Nevertheless, it came surprisingly close to gaining rather than losing territory. It had some friends, particularly in the United States, and even its enemies were halfhearted. Moreover, the principle of self-determination was in its favor; Bulgarians were in a majority in at least two areas outside the country: in the southern Dobrudja, along the west coast of the Black Sea; and in western Thrace at the top of the Aegean. It is also possible, as the Bulgarians argued, that they were in a majority in the parts of Macedonia belonging to Yugoslavia, but, as so often in the Balkans, establishing this was extraordinarily difficult.

It was not clear what made a Bulgarian. Not religion, because, while most Bulgarian speakers were Orthodox, some were Muslim. Race possibly, but were they Slavs, or nomads from Asia, or a mixture? And how were they different from Serbs and Macedonians? Their languages, after all, were very alike. Bulgarian nationalism was as new a growth as the others in the Balkans, newer perhaps because Bulgarians had lived under Ottoman rule since the fourteenth century, longer than any other Balkan nation. In the 1870s, they had finally revolted. Gladstone had made some of his greatest speeches when the Ottomans had massacred them by the thousands. But by 1919, Bulgarians were seen in western Europe less as victims than as unreliable thugs.[2]

From the time it first came into existence as a modern state, Bulgaria had been fluctuating like a Balkan amoeba. In 1878 a huge, autonomous Bulgaria had emerged out of the Ottoman empire, reaching westward to the borders of Albania and down to the head of the Aegean. That was too much, both for its neighbors and for the Great Powers. Serbia grabbed much of Macedonia, and Greece western Thrace. The Ottomans managed to hang on to eastern Thrace. After a short-lived expansion in 1912, Bulgaria lost the southern Dobrudja to Rumania. Recovering the losses became part of the Bulgarian national dream, along with that golden age in the tenth century when Bulgaria touched the Adriatic in the west and the Black Sea in the east.

If the Rumanians were the Neapolitans of the Balkans, the Bulgarians, some five million of them in 1919, were the lowland Scots. Dour, hardworking, thrifty and taciturn, they had a reputation for stubbornness. As a local proverb had it, "The Bulgarian will hunt the hare in an ox-cart, and catch him."[3] In the Great War, the hare Bulgaria wanted above all else was Macedonia, a goal that was shared by their king, an ambitious and wily German prince known to Europe as Foxy Ferdinand. Possession of Macedonia would give them control not only of the Aegean coast but also of the valleys and railways that linked central Europe with the south and the Middle East. After some calculation, Ferdinand and his government decided that the Central Powers offered the better deal and so in the autumn of 1915 Bulgaria attacked Serbia. The Allies declared war. Bulgaria enjoyed a brief period of success, during which it seized the southern Dobrudja and much of Macedonia, but by 1918 its armies, short of weapons and food, could no longer fight. Bulgaria was the first of the Central Powers to surrender.

With Bulgaria's defeat, Ferdinand abdicated and went back to his considerable estates in Austria-Hungary and to bird-watching, his one great passion in life apart from his mother. His successor was his son Boris, a thin and unhappy young man. Boris's main pleasure was driving trains; engine drivers on the Orient Express were warned not to let him anywhere near the cab. The young king's new subjects thought him a fool or worse; most observers did not think he would last long on the throne, a view he himself shared. The Allies fretted from a distance. Would Bulgaria go communist? What if it refused to sign a peace treaty? As the British military representative pointed out in the summer of 1919, "the Allies had no troops, and, if a national uprising were provoked, it would be impossible to stop it."[4]

Much depended on the flamboyant figure of Alexander Stamboliski, "like a brigand, moving through a blackberry bush" in the view of a British observer. The leading republican in Bulgaria, Stamboliski was the opposite of Boris in every way: powerful, crude, self-confident and energetic. He did an hour of gymnastics a day in his little farmhouse. Unlike Boris, he was not remotely in awe of Ferdinand. When Bulgaria was tilting toward Germany and Austria-Hungary, he had not only attacked the king in a private audience but had published the details in his paper, for which he was sent to prison.[5]

Stamboliski gloried in his peasant background. Although he had gone to university in Germany, his language was vivid with bulls mating and chickens clucking. He was not, as many suspected, a communist, but rather a peasant socialist, suspicious of both communism and capitalism; this was an appealing combination in a country where there were many small farmers. He articulated their suspicions of townspeople and the upper classes. "Who sent you to the trenches?" he asked. "They did. Who made you lose Macedonia, Thrace and Dobrudja?"[6]

In September 1918, as the Bulgarian armies collapsed, Ferdinand, in one of his last acts, sent for his old enemy. Stamboliski calmed the mutinous soldiers. By the following autumn he was prime minister. Curiously, he made no move to abolish the monarchy, perhaps because he had developed a soft spot for the "kinglet" Boris. The truth was, Bulgaria could not afford further upheavals. The Turks and the Bulgarians had loathed each other for years. Rumania had troops on the northern border and was preparing to move south. Greece was massing troops on the southern border and complaining about Bulgarian crimes, including the theft of cows. Only Yugoslavia offered some hope for friendship. An old dream that Serbia and Bulgaria might form a great South Slav state was not completely dead in either country. (Indeed, it was revived by Marshal Tito after the Second World War.) Still, it was an unpropitious time to talk of Slavic unity, given the way the Bulgarians had behaved during the war, first attacking Serbia in a pincer movement with Austria-Hungary and Germany, and then ravaging Serbian lands. At one point in 1919, the Serbians and the Greeks talked about waging a war against Bulgaria, an idea firmly vetoed by Clemenceau.[7]

Surprisingly, the Bulgarians awaited the start of the Peace Conference with considerable optimism. The American representative in Sofia found their view "peculiar": they somehow considered themselves one of the Allies. "They realize that they committed a 'crime,' as the Prime Minister called it, but once having admitted this fact, they seem to think that this is the end of the matter, and cannot seem to understand why there should be any hard feeling or resentment among the Allies towards Bulgaria, or why there is anything to prevent Bulgaria from resuming her pre-war position as 'The Spoiled Child of the Balkans.' " Artlessly, the Bulgarian prime minister admitted that his country had made a huge mistake in joining Germany and Austria: "Bulgaria would never have gone into the war if it had realized that it would have to come into conflict with England and the great powers." The Bulgarian people themselves had always opposed their wartime alliance, which had been imposed on them by "a small band of unscrupulous politicians in the pay of Germany." The victorious Allies, in fact, owed Bulgaria a debt of gratitude for suing for an armistice and thus starting the process that ended the war.[8]

The Bulgarian government put particular faith in one power: the United States. Wilson was, it was said, widely admired by Bulgarians; in particular, they liked his principle of self-determination. This was shrewd: Bulgaria was not formally at war with the United States, and Americans were generally sympathetic, encouraged by the enthusiastic lobbying of American missionaries from the Protestant Board. (It was suggested by a cynic that the latter were uniformly pro-Bulgarian because Bulgaria was the only Balkan country where they had enjoyed any success.) American experts favored giving Bulgaria access to the Aegean, the southern Dobrudja and perhaps part of Macedonia. Bulgaria itself would have settled for even more. Like the other defeated nations—Germany, Austria, Hungary and Turkey—it was anxious to see the terms of its treaty. The government sent a memorandum to Paris with its demands, which included the whole of Thrace; "unreal and unworthy of its subject" was the view in the British delegation.[9]

Bulgaria's southern boundaries could not be decided until a peace was worked out with the Ottoman empire, which was clearly not going to happen for some time. As far as Macedonia was concerned, the Allies eventually decided that they had enough to do without worrying about that unhappy, much disputed piece of territory. The British and the French agreed that it was dangerous to start meddling with borders established in the Balkans before 1914. Macedonia was left alone, even though this would leave a considerable number of Bulgarians under Yugoslav rule.

The British and the French might have been persuaded to break their own rule (as they later did when they took western Thrace from Bulgaria and gave it to Greece) if they had felt Bulgaria deserved it. They did not. When Yugoslavia claimed territory on Bulgaria's western frontier to protect crucial railway lines and Belgrade itself against future attack, the British and the French were prepared to listen. The Italians, hostile to Yugoslavia, objected. Italian soldiers in the Allied occupying forces apparently let Bulgarian prisoners escape, dragged their feet on disarming the Bulgarian army and even supplied it with weapons. Eventually, over Italian objections, four pieces of territory, mainly inhabited by Bulgars, were handed over to Yugoslavia—not as much as it wanted, but too much for Bulgaria, which complained bitterly that it had lost all the strategic points in the mountains dividing the two countries.[10]

The southern Dobrudja caused even greater bitterness. The Americans insisted that the Peace Conference deal with its ownership. On ethnic grounds, Bulgaria's claim was much stronger than Rumania's. The population was mixed: largely Tatars, Turks, Bulgarian-speaking Muslims and Christian Bulgarians, who were probably in a slight majority. There were fewer than 10,000 Rumanians out of a population of almost 300,000. Rumania nevertheless managed to hang on to it at the Peace Conference, partly because the issue was small and unimportant in the context of its other demands. And, as so often happened, facts had been created on the ground: by the time the Peace Conference opened, the French military authorities in the occupation forces had allowed Rumanian troops and civilian officials to take control of the area.[11]

The Bulgarian delegation, including Stamboliski, was summoned to Paris in July 1919 although their treaty was not ready. For two and half dreary months they sat in their hotel, an old castle in the suburb of Neuilly, under police guard. They were forbidden to go into Paris, their mail was censored and they were not allowed visitors. In a plaintive letter to Clemenceau they complained that the French press was attacking Bulgarians "as a barbarous people, unworthy of the confidence and friendship of civilized nations."[12] Sadly for Bulgaria, the United States, the only power to support its claim to the Dobrudja, was disengaging itself from Europe and European affairs by the time the issue came up for negotiation. The American delegates who stayed on in Paris after the signing of the Versailles treaty doggedly argued their case through the summer of 1919, but they no longer had much leverage over the European powers, who held, as Balfour put it in his usual detached fashion, that although Rumania should properly give up a piece of territory "which was clearly not Rumanian," it was not the time to make such a request.[13]

When the draft treaty was finally delivered in September, the delegation had much more to complain about. Bulgaria lost about 10 percent of its land, including the southern Dobrudja and what it still had of western Thrace, along with its access to the Aegean. (The Allies took over Thrace temporarily, but Greece, which had come to Paris with a long shopping list, had every hope of getting hold of it.) Bulgaria was to pay reparations of £90 million. (Since the annual payments taken together with the country's foreign debts were more than the annual budget, Bulgaria eventually defaulted on both.) Finally the armed forces were severely slashed; the army was to be a mere police force of 20,000. When the details of the treaty were published, there was a national day of mourning in Bulgaria.

The Bulgarian delegation begged for modifications, arguing that since the overthrow of Ferdinand it had become a new, democratic country, just like France after its revolution. The Allies paid little attention; almost their only concession was to allow Bulgaria to maintain a small flotilla of lightly armed boats on the Danube. There was talk in Bulgaria of resistance but Stamboliski, a realist, said that he would sign "even a bad peace." On November 27, 1919, a simple ceremony took place in the old town hall in Neuilly. Guards with fixed bayonets lined the stairway and a curious crowd waited for the Bulgarians to appear. Stamboliski, pale and apprehensive, entered alone. It looked, said a sympathetic American, "as if the office boy had been called in for a conference with the board of directors." Among the observers was the Greek prime minister, Venizelos, "endeavouring not to look too pleased." Clemenceau presided from a table covered in green baize, and the signing was over quickly. In Athens there was a public holiday. In Sofia there was glum resignation.[14]

Earlier that month, Stamboliski had made a desperate appeal to Venizelos for their two countries to cooperate: "Of all the statesmen in the Balkans, your excellency is the best able to appreciate the great efficacy of an understanding among the Balkan peoples."[15] Venizelos, bent on his dream of a greater Greece and secure in his support from Britain, did not listen. The following year, western Thrace was given to Greece. Bulgaria's southern boundaries were not finally settled until a lasting treaty with Turkey was signed in 1923, by which time Venizelos, and his dream, had run up against reality.

Stamboliski turned out to be something of a statesman. Bulgaria accepted its new borders and renounced its old expansionist policies, even in Yugoslavian Macedonia. He went further, mending relations with Yugoslavia and signing an agreement to cooperate against terrorists; he duly cracked down on the Macedonian terrorists who were turning Sofia into their fiefdom. He started to build a Green International of peasant parties to counter the new Communist International founded by the Soviet Russians. Bulgaria became an enthusiastic member of the League of Nations. But Stamboliski's foreign and domestic policies also made him many enemies: Bulgarian nationalists, army officers, Macedonian terrorists, the middle classes suffering from inflation and high taxes, possibly the king himself. In June 1923, there was a coup; Stamboliski was killed by Macedonian conspirators who first cut off the hand which had signed the antiterrorist agreement with Yugoslavia. "The poor great man," murmured the king when he heard.[16]

The moderate approach to foreign affairs taken by Stamboliski did not long outlast his death. Too many Bulgarians looked back longingly at the great Bulgaria of earlier decades; they resented the Treaty of Neuilly and were infuriated by the treatment of their compatriots by Rumania, Greece and Yugoslavia. The Macedonian terrorists continued to operate from Bulgarian soil with virtual impunity, worsening relations with both Greece and Yugoslavia. Attempts in the early 1930s to get a general Balkan agreement respecting existing boundaries foundered on Bulgaria's refusal. The result was an agreement among Yugoslavia, Greece, Turkey and Rumania that left Bulgaria isolated. As Europe drifted toward war again, Bulgaria tilted to the German camp. In 1940, under pressure from Germany, Rumania handed back the southern Dobrudja. In the spring of 1941, Bulgarian troops, fighting with the Germans and the Italians, occupied Macedonia and western Thrace. Bulgaria did not enjoy its recovered territories for long; under the settlements of 1947 it kept only the southern Dobrudja. By that time its new communist regime was firmly in place. Boris was long dead—poisoned, many believed, by the Nazis. Foxy Ferdinand, however, died peacefully in Germany in 1948, at the age of eighty-seven.[17]

12

Midwinter Break

B Y THE END of January 1919, the main outlines of the peace settlements were emerging. The Russian question, the League of Nations
and the new borders in central Europe had all come up, even if they had
not been completely settled. Progress had been made, too, on some of the
crucial details of the German treaty by special committees: on war damages and on Germany's capacity to make reparation; on Germany's borders, its colonies and its armed forces; on the punishment of German war
criminals; even on the fate of German submarine cables. The big question, though—how to punish Germany and how to keep it under control
in the future—had barely been touched on by Clemenceau, Lloyd George
and Wilson, the only men who could really settle it.

Also emerging was what a Swiss diplomat called the "great surprise at
the conference": a close partnership between the British and the Americans. True, there had been difficulties over the mandates, but at the Supreme Council, on the committees and commissions and in the corridors,
British and Americans found that they saw eye to eye on most issues. Wilson, who never wholeheartedly liked Lloyd George, had succumbed a
little to his charm, chatting away cheerfully as they went in and out of
meetings and even going out to the occasional lunch or dinner. He had
also come to recognize that he was better off dealing with a strong Liberal
as prime minister than a Conservative.[1]

On January 29, Wilson told House that he thought it would be a good
idea for the American experts to work closely with the British. House,
whatever his own reservations, obediently passed this on to both the
Americans and the British. Lloyd George, who valued good relations between Britain and the United States highly, was delighted. So were the

Canadians. "Our relations with the British, who are the only people here who are not playing chauvinistic politics (a fact that it took Wilson about a week to discover)," said Seymour, the American expert, "are so close that we are exchanging views with absolute frankness on the territorial settlement of Europe." Members from the two delegations fell into a pattern of frequent consultation, exchanging confidential memoranda and talking on the secure telephone lines that American army engineers rigged up to link the Crillon and the Majestic. "Our unanimity," wrote Nicolson later, "was indeed remarkable. There—in what had once been the *cabinets particuliers* of Maxim's—was elaborated an Anglo-American case covering the whole frontiers of Jugo-Slavia, Czecho-Slovakia, Rumania, Austria and Hungary. Only in regard to Greece, Albania, Bulgaria and Turkey in Europe did any divergence manifest itself. And even here the divergence was one of detail only, scarcely one of principle."[2]

As relations between Britain and the United States flourished, those of each country with France deteriorated. The British saw the French as competitors for Ottoman and Russian territory in the Middle East and Central Asia. They also suspected that once Wilson had left for his brief trip home, the French would try to shape the German terms to suit themselves. "I find them full of intrigue and chicanery of all kinds, without any idea of playing the game," wrote Hankey. When France faced a financial crisis, with downward pressure on the franc in February, the British reaction was cool. They could not, they told the French, make a loan to tide them over. It was only when House interceded with Lloyd George that some funds were made available. The French accepted the loan but remembered the delay. The British and the Americans shook their heads over what they saw as French incompetence and irresponsibility.[3]

Relations between the French and the Americans were especially poor. French diplomats blamed Wilson for holding up the real business of the conference—the punishment of Germany—with his League. The French finance minister, Louis-Lucien Klotz, told his colleagues that the Americans were trying to sell their excess food to Germany in return for cash payments, which would, of course, make it more difficult for the French to collect the reparations due to them. The Americans in return complained that the French were stinging them for their accommodation in Paris and for the expenses of their army. In the cinemas, French audiences, which had once cheered every appearance of Wilson on the screen, now stayed silent. French policemen and American soldiers brawled in the streets. Some of the Americans were overheard to say that they had been fighting on the wrong side. The Parisians made fun of Mrs. Wilson, and the French papers, which had been generally favorable to the American president, now started to criticize him.[4]

The attacks infuriated Wilson, who was convinced that they were or-
chestrated by the French government. His voice trembling with indignation, he showed a visitor a confidential document which told French
newspapers to exaggerate the chaos in Russia, to stress the strong possibility of a renewed offensive from Germany and to remind Wilson that he
faced a strong Republican opposition back home. Increasingly, in private,
Wilson poured out his bitterness: the French were "stupid," "petty," "insane," "unreliable," "tricky," "the hardest I ever tried to do business with."
He still thought the ordinary French people were all right, he told his doctor, but their politicians were leading them astray. "It was due entirely to
the fact that the French politicians had permitted so many apparent dis-
criminations against Americans that the rank and file of the people of the
United States had turned from being pro-French to being pro-British.
And the President also said that the British seemed to be playing the game
nobly and loyally."[5]

Like Franco-American relations, the weather turned colder. Wet snow
fell over Paris; American soldiers had snowball fights in the Champs-
Elysées. There was skating in the Bois de Boulogne and tobogganing at
Versailles. Because of the shortage of coal, even the grand hotels were icy.
People came down with colds or, more dangerously, fell prey to the flu
epidemic which had started in the summer of 1918. The military doctors
in the Crillon dispensed cough mixture and advice. Smoking, said one,
was an excellent preventative.[6]

Delegates—in the end, there were well over a thousand—continued to
arrive. The British issued each of theirs 1,500 visiting cards to leave with
their counterparts because that was what had been done at the Congress of
Vienna. After many complaints about the waste of time, Clemenceau
ruled that the practice be abandoned. Many delegates were diplomats and
statesmen; but, for the first time at a major international conference, many
were not. The British brought over virtually the whole of the Intelligence
Bureau from the Ministry of Information, including men such as the
young Arnold Toynbee and Lewis Namier, later among the most eminent
historians of their generation. The Americans had their professors from
House's Inquiry, and Wall Street bankers such as Thomas Lamont and
Bernard Baruch. The professional diplomats grumbled. "An improvisa-
tion," said Jules Cambon, the secretary-general at the Quai d'Orsay, but
such views did not bother Lloyd George or Wilson, or Clemenceau for
that matter. "Diplomats," in Lloyd George's view, "were invented simply
to waste time."[7]

Paris was also filling up with petitioners, journalists and the merely curious. Elinor Glyn, the romantic novelist, entertained prominent men at
her corner table at the Ritz and wrote articles asking "Are Women Chang-

ing?" and "Is Chivalry Dead?" Franklin Roosevelt, then assistant secretary of the Navy, persuaded his superiors that he had to supervise the sale of American naval property in Europe and arrived in Paris, a resentful and unhappy Eleanor in tow. Their marriage was already falling to pieces; now she found him too attentive to the Parisian women. William Orpen and Augustus John settled in to paint official portraits of the conference, although the latter spent much of his energy on riotous parties. British Cabinet ministers popped over for a day or two at a time. Bonar Law, the deputy prime minister, bravely flew back and forth, dressed in a special fur-lined flying suit. Lloyd George's eldest daughter, Olwen, a lively young married woman, came over for a brief visit. Clemenceau offered her a lift in his car one afternoon and, as they chatted, asked if she like art. Yes, she replied enthusiastically, and he whipped out a set of salacious postcards.[8]

Elsa Maxwell, not yet the doyenne of international café society that she would become, secured a passage from New York as companion to a glamorous divorced woman who was on the lookout for a new husband. The two women gave marvelous parties in a rented house. General Pershing supplied the drink; Maxwell played the latest Cole Porter songs on the piano; and the divorcée found her husband, a handsome American captain called Douglas MacArthur. Outside, early one morning, two young officers fought a duel with sabers over yet another American beauty.[9]

Attractive women had a wonderful time in Paris that year. Few delegates had brought their wives; indeed, it had been expressly forbidden most of the junior ranks. "All the most beautiful & well dressed society ladies appear to have been brought over by the various Departments," wrote Hankey to his wife. "I do not know how they do their work, but in the evening they dance and sing and play bridge!" The puritanical suspected that worse was going on than bridge. An American female journalist traveled "with complete frankness and tremendous enthusiasm" with an Italian general. In the hotels where the delegations stayed, women wandered freely into men's rooms. A couple of Canadian Red Cross nurses who made quite a career of mistaking the number on the door and then refusing to leave had to be sent home. The war appeared to have loosened the old inhibitions. "Vice is rampant in Paris," said Elinor Glyn severely. "Lesbians dine together openly, in groups of six sometimes, at Larue's. . . . Men are the same. Nothing is sacred, nothing is hidden, not even vice and avarice.[10]

Paris offered many distractions: the races at St. Cloud, excellent restaurants if you could afford the prices and could get in, and the Opéra, where there were productions of the great favorites: *Les Contes d'Hoffmann,*

Madame Butterfly, La Bohème. The theaters were gradually reopening, with everything from the classics to farces. Sarah Bernhardt appeared in a gala for a French charity, and Isadora Duncan's brother did interpretative dances. Ruth Draper came over from London to give her monologues, and Canadian delegates were slightly shocked by the musical *Phi Phi.* "We concurred, however," wrote one to his wife, "in thinking there was something to be said for the open eyes. I should like to know if, through greater knowledge, the French escape diseases of a kind which, there is no doubt, are prevalent with us." Even Wilson, who was usually in bed by ten P.M., went out to a revue; he found some of the jokes too crude but enjoyed "the decent parts." Elsa Maxwell carried Balfour off to a nightclub for the first time in his life. "Allow me to thank you," said the elder statesman with his usual courtesy, "for the most delightful and degrading evening I have ever spent."[11]

Other delegates found more innocent pastimes: early morning walks in the Bois de Boulogne, bridge games in the evening. Balfour tried to play tennis whenever he could. Lansing passed his evenings quietly reading philosophy. The chief Italian delegates, Sonnino and Orlando, kept to their hotel. Lloyd George went out occasionally in the evenings to restaurants or the theater, although Frances Stevenson found that his arrival always caused an unfortunate stir. She also complained one evening when he flirted with a young woman from the British delegation. "However, he was quite open about it & I think it did him good, so that I did not mind."[12]

Social life in Paris started to revive. When Prince Murat and Elsa Maxwell went together to a costume ball—Murat as Clemenceau, and Maxwell, who was rather plump, as Lloyd George—their car was stopped on the Champs-Elysées by a huge, cheering crowd. In the bar at the Ritz, people met to drink the new cocktails. Out at Versailles, in her famous villa, the decorator Elsie de Wolfe (later Lady Mendl) gave teas for the more prominent delegates. Mrs. Wilson tried to drag Wilson out to some of the parties and receptions, to the dismay of his admirers.[13]

At the Hôtel Majestic, Ian Malcolm, Balfour's private secretary, gave readings of his comic poems, "The Breaking Out of Peace" and "The Ballad of Prinkipo." There were amateur theatricals in the basement. After Orpen did posters for one production which showed two naked children, the next revue had a chorus singing "We are two little Orpens / Of raiment bereft." A British officer, who had come hundreds of miles to report on the situation in central Europe, went away in disgust. "Nobody at his level," he told an American colleague, "could be bothered to listen to his account of the appalling conditions in Poland because they were totally preoccupied with discussing whether the ballroom should be used for theatricals to the exclusion of dancing on Tuesdays and Thursdays or just on Tuesdays." Lloyd George's youngest daughter, the sixteen-year-old Megan, had the time of her life. The hotel, said the wits, should be called the Megantic. Her father finally put his foot down and she was shipped off to a finishing school.[14]

The dancing at the Majestic became famous. The young nurses and typists—"like nymphs," said an elderly diplomat—knew the latest dances, from the hesitation waltz to the fox-trot. Spectators were fascinated. "Why," asked Foch, who dropped in one day, "do the British have such sad faces and such cheerful bottoms?" The Saturday night dances, in particular, were so popular that the authorities grew concerned about the impression being made and considered putting a stop to them.[15]

The Paris Peace Conference had far fewer, however, of grand balls and extravagant entertainments than the Congress of Vienna. The most popular forms of social life were lunches and dinners, where the delegates got much useful work done. Lloyd George, more energetic than almost everyone else, had breakfast meetings as well. The supplicant nations laid on lavish meals where they poured out their demands. "I am beginning my work as social laborer again," wrote Seymour to his wife. "Dinner with Bratianu tomorrow, lunch with Italian liberals on Saturday, dinner with the Serbs in the evening, and dinner with Czechoslovaks—Kramarz [Karel Kramář] and Benes—on Monday." The Poles gave a lunch for the Americans that lasted until five in the afternoon; one after another, Polish historians, economists and geographers outlined the justice of Poland's claims. The Chinese invited the foreign press to a special dinner. As the courses followed, one after the other, hour after hour, their guests waited to hear their hosts' case. In impeccable English the Chinese chatted about this topic and that, everything but the Peace Conference. At 3:30 in the morning, the American correspondents went home, leaving one of their number to report. When he finally left, as dawn was breaking, the Chinese had still not explained the reason for the dinner.[16]

Some of the overseas delegates visited the battlefields. They tried, in letters home, to describe what they had seen: the splintered trees, the little wooden crosses with palm leaves dotting the fields, the shrapnel littering the road, the shell craters, the tangles of rusting barbed wire, the tanks and guns buried in the mud, the scraps of uniform, the unburied bones. "For miles and miles," wrote Gordon Auchincloss, House's son-in-law, "the ground is just a mass of deep shell craters, filled with water, and there are dozens of tanks, all shot to pieces, laying [sic] about the fields. I have never seen such horrible waste and such intense destruction." They ventured into the trenches and picked up German helmets and empty shell cases for souvenirs. One party found some new fuses, "lovely playthings for the children." They marveled at the mounds of rubble which had once been cities and towns. Like the ruins of Pompeii, said James Shotwell, an American professor, after he had visited the old cathedral city of Reims, although he was relieved to find a restaurant among the ruins serving sausages and sauerkraut.[17]

By the middle of February, the pace of work slackened as Wilson left on a quick trip back to the United States—officially, for the closing sessions of Congress; unofficially, to deal with the growing opposition to the League of Nations—and Lloyd George went back to London to cope with domestic problems. Balfour stood in for Lloyd George on the Supreme Council and Wilson, choosing yet again to ignore his own secretary of state, chose House as his deputy. Lansing, depressed and unwell—he was trying out a new treatment for his diabetes—felt the slight deeply. And it was by no means the first. When Lansing, an experienced international lawyer, had made some suggestions about the League of Nations at a meeting of the American delegation, Wilson had said curtly that he did not intend to have lawyers drafting the peace treaty. Since he was the only lawyer present, Lansing took this as an insult to both himself and his profession. Wilson repeatedly gave House the important jobs; Lansing was left to brief the press, something he hated. Wilson seems to have taken a malicious pleasure in stirring up trouble between House and Lansing and he was delighted when he heard anything to Lansing's discredit. "Everything Mr. L. does seems to irritate him," wrote Mrs. Wilson's secretary in her diary after a visit from a tearful Mrs. Lansing, "the fact that they go out to dinner so much, accept invitations from people he (the P.) doesn't like. He is simply intolerant of any form of life save the one he leads." Wilson's behavior was cruel and ultimately costly: Lansing would take his revenge when the peace settlements came up for approval back home.[18]

Both House and Balfour were anxious to speed up the work of the conference in the absence of their superiors. They decided to concentrate on getting at least general terms ready for Germany (the details, it was assumed, could be negotiated directly in what was still expected to be a full-blown peace conference). The special commissions and committees (in the end there were almost sixty) were told to have their reports ready by March 6. That would leave a week for tidying up before Wilson's return. The plan was to call the German delegation before the end of the month. This was wildly optimistic.[19]

The delegates groaned but plowed ahead. When Nicolson met Marcel

Proust—"white, unshaven, grubby, slip-faced"—at a dinner at the Ritz, he found the great writer fascinated by the details of the work. "Tell me about the committees," Proust commanded. Nicolson started by saying that they generally met at ten in the morning. Proust begged for more details. "You take a car from the Delegation. You get out at the Quai d'Orsay. You climb the stairs. You go into the room. And then? Be specific, my friend, be specific."[20]

By the time Wilson left Paris, the League's covenant had largely been drawn up, some progress had been made on the German terms and most of the territorial commissions had been created. But almost nothing had been decided on the Ottoman empire, and the treaties with Austria, Hungary and Bulgaria had scarcely been considered. There was less and less talk about a preliminary peace conference and more about the quantity of work that had to be got through before the enemy states could be summoned to Paris. Although it was not yet acknowledged, what was happening in Paris was now the Peace Conference proper. In the hotels and meeting rooms, there were gloomy speculations about whether a peace could be made before the world went up in flames.

On February 19, as Clemenceau was leaving his house in the Rue Franklin to drive to a meeting with House and Balfour at the Crillon, a man in work clothes who had been lurking behind one of the public urinals jumped out and fired several shots at the car. Clemenceau later told Lloyd George that the moment seemed to last forever. One bullet hit him between the ribs, just missing vital organs. (It was too dangerous to remove and he carried it for the rest of his life.) Clemenceau's assailant, Eugène Cottin, a half-mad anarchist, was seized by the crowd, which was waiting as usual to see the prime minister's comings and goings, and nearly lynched. Clemenceau was carried back into his house. When his faithful assistant Mordacq rushed in, he found him pale but conscious. "They shot me in the back," Clemenceau told him. "They didn't even dare to attack me from the front."[21]

"Dear, dear," said Balfour when the news reached the Crillon, "I wonder what that portends." Many people in Paris feared the worst, especially when news came in a couple of days later that the socialist chief minister of Bavaria had been assassinated. Lloyd George cabled Kerr from London. "If the attempt is a Bolshevist one it shows what lunatics these anarchists are for nothing would do them as much harm as a successful attempt on Clemenceau's life and even a failure will exasperate opinion in France and make it quite impossible to have any dealings with them."[22]

Clemenceau carried the whole thing off with his usual panache. Visitors found him sitting up in an armchair, complaining about Cottin's marksmanship—"a Frenchman who misses his target six times out of seven at point-blank range"—and arguing with his doctors: "Doctors, I know them better than anyone because I am one myself." To the nurse who said that his escape was a miracle, he replied that "if Heaven intended to perform a miracle, it would have been better to have prevented [my] aggressor from shooting at [me] at all!" He refused to allow Cottin to be condemned to death: "I can't see an old republican like me and also an opponent of the death penalty having a man executed for the crime of lèse-majesté." Cottin got a ten-year prison sentence but was released halfway through, much to Clemenceau's annoyance, after the left took up his cause.

Messages of sympathy poured in, from Lloyd George and King George in London, from Wilson out on the Atlantic, from Sarah Bernhardt—"just now Clemenceau is France"—and from the thousands of French who regarded Clemenceau as the father of their victory. The pope sent his blessing (the old anticlerical radical sent his own in return) and ordinary soldiers left their decorations on Clemenceau's doorstep. Poincaré, who had initially been as shocked as anyone, was furious. "Singular collective madness, strange legend which hides the reality and will falsify, no doubt, history." The day after the attempt, Clemenceau was walking in his garden; a week later he was back at work. He was severely shaken, though. Wilson, among others, felt that he never again had the same powers of concentration.[23]

Back in London, Lloyd George was having more success confronting his enemies. He jumped off the train on February 10 and went straight into meetings with Bonar Law and his chief adviser on labor questions. "I saw him a little later," reported the secretary of the cabinet to Hankey, "and he was extraordinarily cheerful and vigorous and happy about your doings in Paris and full of schemes of dealing with the miners and the railway men should they come out during the next week or two." In the end he managed to head off the threatened strikes, arranging for commissions of inquiry and bringing management and labor together as he had so often done before. In his four weeks in London he also created a new Ministry of Transport and introduced a whole array of parliamentary bills dealing with social issues.[24]

Wilson's trip home was much less successful. The *George Washington* ran into bad weather and, as it finally reached the coast of New England, nearly came to grief on a sandbar. And trouble was waiting on land. In Washington the last days of the old Congress were marked by partisan bitterness and a filibuster by Republicans who hoped, among other things, to delay important bills until after the recess when the newly elected Congress, with its Republican majority, would meet. Ominously, the Republicans were increasingly taking the opportunity to attack the League. In the country as a whole, support for the League remained strong but leading members of the influential League to Enforce Peace were privately contemplating revisions to build bridges to moderate Republicans.[25]

Wilson showed little interest in compromise. He landed in Boston on February 24 and immediately gave a rousing and partisan speech. He and the United States, he said, were carrying out a great work in Paris; those who questioned this were selfish and shortsighted. On their seats the audience found copies of the draft covenant for the League. The senators in Washington had not yet seen it. This was tactless, and it was not Wilson's only political blunder. Boston was the hometown of his great rival, the Republican senator from Massachusetts, Henry Cabot Lodge.

Lodge, of whom it was once said that his mind was like his native soil, "naturally barren, but highly cultivated," came from the New England aristocracy. He was short, bad-tempered and a tremendous snob. He shared Wilson's conviction that the United States had a mission to make the world a better place and was even prepared to contemplate some form of league to keep the peace. But he disagreed with Wilson's methods and scorned his conviction that the League could solve all the world's problems. And he loathed the man—not just, as is sometimes said, because they disagreed, but also because he thought him ignoble and a coward. Wilson's speech that day in Boston was further proof to Lodge not only of the president's folly, but also of his baseness. Wilson had asked him and the other members of the Senate's Foreign Relations Committee to hold off all discussion of the League until he had had a chance to explain it to them in person in Washington.[26]

The two men had been antagonists for years. They had disagreed over the start of the war, when Lodge had been for intervening on the Allied side at once and Wilson had opted for neutrality, and over its end, when Lodge would have marched on to Berlin and Wilson chose to sign an armistice. Now they disagreed over the peace. Wilson put his trust in the League and collective security as a way to end war. Lodge, a pessimist with little faith in the perfectibility of human nature, preferred to trust power. He wanted to hem Germany in with strong states, a renewed Poland, a solid Czechoslovakia and a France beefed up with Alsace and Lorraine and perhaps even the Rhineland. If the United States joined any association at all, it should be one with other democracies, where there was a community of interests, not a league which threatened to draw the country into vague and open-ended commitments.[27]

Lodge represented the moderate middle of the Republican party. On one wing stood those, mainly from the Midwest, who recoiled from any contact with wicked Europe, and on the other the internationalists, often from the East Coast, who supported the League enthusiastically. Wilson could have reached out to many in the Republican party but instead he drove them away, with his refusal to take any leading Republicans along to Paris, with his insistence that, in the congressional elections of November 1918, a vote for the Democrats was a vote for peace and a vote for the Republicans something quite different, and now with his actions on his return trip to the United States.

Unfortunately, at the same time he did little to conciliate the doubters in his own party. He refused to talk at all to a Southern senator who he said had been nothing but "an ambulance-chaser" in his law career. Even his little jokes now had a sour edge. His remark when he saw a new grandson for the first time made the rounds: "With his mouth open and his eyes shut, I predict that he will make a Senator when he grows up."

From Boston, Wilson hurried on to Washington. On February 26 at Colonel House's urging, he gave a dinner in the White House for the members of the key Senate and House Foreign Relations Committees. The evening did not go well. Lodge, seated next to Mrs. Wilson, had to listen to her happy chatter about the wonderful reception her husband had received in Boston. Some of the guests complained that, after dinner, they were not offered enough cigars or enough to drink. More seriously, they came away thinking that Wilson had hectored them, as one said, "as though they were being reproved for neglect of their lessons by a very frigid teacher in a Sunday School class." When he saw House again, the president was resentful. "*Your* dinner," he told him, "was not a success."[28]

As he was to do so often, Wilson found reassurance in telling himself that the people were with him even if their representatives were not. And he was probably right. When a leading American journal asked its readers whether they favored the League, more than two thirds said yes. Unfortunately the public did not vote on treaties but the Senate did—and there a two-thirds majority, which was necessary to ratify a treaty, was not so easily obtained. On March 4, as Wilson was preparing to head back to Europe, Lodge circulated a round-robin rejecting the covenant as it was drawn and asking the negotiators in Paris to postpone any further discussion of the League until the treaty with Germany had been finished. Thirty-nine Republican senators signed, more than a third of the total membership of the Senate. Wilson's initial reaction was to wonder if he might somehow bypass the Senate altogether.[29]

The Congress duly adjourned on March 4, in keeping with its calendar at the time, leaving much unfinished financial and other business. Wilson issued a public rebuke: "A group of men in the Senate have deliberately chosen to embarrass the administration of the Government, to imperil the financial interests of the railway systems of the country, and to make arbitrary use of the powers intended to be employed in the interests of the people." That afternoon he started north for the *George Washington* and Europe. On March 5, in one last speech, at the Metropolitan Opera House in New York, he wound up his brief stay in the United States with another attack on the opponents of the League: "I cannot imagine how these gentlemen can live and not live in the atmosphere of the world. I cannot imagine how they can live and not be in contact with the events of their times, and I cannot particularly imagine how they can be Americans and set up a doctrine of careful selfishness thought out in the last detail."[30]

When his train pulled into Paris on March 14, only a small group of French dignitaries greeted him at the station. As he drove to his new quarters, at the Place des Etats-Unis, just opposite Lloyd George's apartment, there were no ecstatic crowds as there had been the previous December. The house, the property of a wealthy banker, was not as grand or as large as the Hôtel Murat. The daisies were beginning to emerge, and so were the problems at the Peace Conference.

PART FOUR

THE GERMAN ISSUE

13

Punishment and Prevention

WILSON'S RETURN OPENED a period of intense work on the German treaty that ended only at the start of May, when the terms were finally agreed. The delay—the war had been over for four months by this point—raised the awkward question of what the German defeat really meant. How much power did Germany still have? How strong were the Allies? In November 1918, the victors had possessed an enormous advantage. If they had been ready to make peace then, if they had realized the extent of their victory, they could have imposed almost any terms they wanted.

The German army, despite what Generals Ludendorff and Hindenburg—and Corporal Hitler—later claimed, had been decisively defeated on the battlefield before the German government asked for an armistice, and before the old regime was toppled inside Germany. In the summer of 1918, as fresh troops and tons of equipment were pouring in from the United States, the Allies had attacked. On August 8, 1918, the "Black Day" to the German army, they smashed through the German lines. For four years, shifts in the lines on the Western Front had been measured in meters; now the Germans went back kilometer by kilometer, leaving behind guns and tanks and soldiers. Sixteen German divisions were wiped out in the first days of the Allied attack. On August 14, Ludendorff told the kaiser that Germany should think of negotiating with the Allies; by September 29 he was demanding peace at any price. The Allies were moving slowly but inexorably toward Germany's borders and there was little the German High Command could do to stop them. Germany was near the end of its manpower and its supplies, and the public was losing its appetite for the war. In the streets of Berlin, housewives marched with their empty pots and pans to show they could no longer feed their families; in the shipyards and factories, workers put down their tools; and in the Reichstag, deputies who had once submissively voted for the war demanded peace. One by one Germany's allies dropped away: Bulgaria at the end of September, Ottoman Turkey a month later, and then Austria-Hungary. By November, insurrections were breaking out in Germany. When the armistice was signed in a French railway carriage on November 11, Germany was reeling under the combination of its wartime losses and political upheaval. The terms left no doubt as to the extent of the Allied victory. Hindenburg collapsed into depression. Ludendorff, disguised in false whiskers and tinted glasses, fled in a panic to Sweden.

Germany relinquished all the territory it had conquered since 1914, as well as Alsace-Lorraine. Allied troops occupied the whole of the Rhineland as well as three bridgeheads on the east bank of the river. Germany also handed over the greater part of its machinery of war—its submarines, its heavy guns, its mortars, its airplanes and 25,000 machine guns. (This brought an anguished cry from the German negotiators: "Why, we are lost! How shall we defend ourselves against Bolshevism?") The great high seas fleet, which had done so much to alienate Britain from Germany, sailed out of port one last time. On a misty November day sixty-nine ships, from battleships to destroyers, passed between lines of Allied ships on their way to Scapa Flow in the British Orkneys. It was a surrender and the Allies treated it as such.[1]

The French ambassador saw Lloyd George the day after the armistice was signed: "The Prime Minister said that he had never hoped for such a rapid solution nor envisaged such a complete collapse of German power." Among the Allied leaders only General Pershing, the top American military commander, thought the Allies should press on, beyond the Rhine if necessary. The French did not want any more of their men to die. Their chief general, Marshal Foch, who was also the supreme Allied commander, warned that they ran the risk of stiff resistance and heavy losses. The British wanted to make peace before the Americans became too strong. And Smuts spoke for many in Europe when he warned gloomily that "the grim spectre of Bolshevist anarchy is stalking the front."[2]

The mistake the Allies made, and it did not become clear until much later, was that, as a result of the armistice terms, the great majority of Germans never experienced their country's defeat at first hand. Except in the Rhineland, they did not see occupying troops. The Allies did not march in triumph into Berlin, as the Germans had done in Paris in 1871. In 1918, German soldiers marched home in good order, with crowds cheering their way; in Berlin, Friedrich Ebert, the new president, greeted them with "No enemy has conquered you!"[3] The new democratic republic in Germany was shaky, but it survived, thanks partly to grudging support from what was left of the German army. The Allied advantage over Germany began to melt.

And the Allied forces were shrinking. In November 1918, there were 198 Allied divisions; by June 1919, only 39 remained. And could they be relied upon? There was little enthusiasm for renewed fighting. Allied demobilization had been hastened by protests, occasionally outright mutiny. On the home fronts there was a longing for peace, and lower taxes. The French were particularly insistent on the need to make peace while the Allies still could dictate terms. The Germans, Clemenceau warned, could not be trusted. They were already becoming "insolent" again; in Weimar, the constituent assembly had concluded its deliberations by singing "Deutschland über Alles." It was madness for the Allies to say to them, "Go on. Do as you like. Perhaps we shall some day threaten to break off relations; but just now we will not be firm." What would it be like by April, when American troops had gone home? "France and Britain would be left alone to face the Germans."[4]

While his pessimism was premature, it is true that by the spring of 1919 Allied commanders were increasingly doubtful about their ability to successfully wage war on Germany. The German army had been defeated on the battlefield, but its command structure, along with hundreds of thousands of trained men, had survived. There were 75 million Germans and only 40 million French, as Foch kept repeating. And the German people, Allied observers noticed, were opposed to signing a harsh peace. Who knew what resistance there would be as Allied armies moved farther and farther into the country? They would face, warned the military experts, a sullen population, perhaps strikes, even gunfire. It was very unlikely that the Allies could get as far as Berlin.[5]

The great Allied weapon of the blockade was also starting to look rather rusty. Although it still remained in force in 1919, and although Allied ships still patrolled the seas looking for contraband cargo heading for Germany, the blockade was increasingly halfhearted. In Britain, whose navy was primarily responsible for enforcing the ban on trade with Germany, the public was starting to ask awkward questions about the sufferings of German civilians. The general in charge of British troops in Germany told Frances Stevenson that "he could not be responsible for his troops if children in Germany were allowed to wander about the streets half starved." The admirals worried about the mood of their men. "If the final terms could be fixed at once," the first sea lord told the Supreme Council, "the Navies would no longer be tied down to their present employment as instruments of the blockade. The spirit of unrest did not leave the Naval Services untouched. A very calming influence on sea-faring folk as a whole would be effected by the settlement of naval peace terms at the next renewal of the Armistice."[6]

The terms of the armistice in fact allowed food to be shipped in to Germany, although Allied military advisers warned that Germany would build up stockpiles which might make it less willing to sign a peace treaty. The French, too, had been unenthusiastic. "It was proposed," said Clemenceau sarcastically, "to buy the good will of the Germans by offering them food and raw materials. A state of war still existed, and any appearance of yielding would be construed as evidence of weakness." Wilson and Lloyd George were more inclined to worry about a desperate Germany sliding further toward anarchy and Bolshevism, "a pool," said Lloyd George, "breeding infection throughout Europe."[7]

Food shipments to Germany moved slowly, something for which many Germans never forgave the Allies. Part of the problem was a shortage of shipping. The Allies insisted that Germany provide the ships, not as unreasonable a request as it might seem: much of the German merchant marine was safely in German ports. The German government, urged on by powerful shipowners, dragged its feet, fearing that if it let the ships go it would never get them back again. Germany also tried to get guarantees from the Allies about the quantities of food to be supplied and, with the lack of realism that was to mark its attitude toward the Allies in this period, suggested that it could pay for its food purchases with a loan from the United States. When it was made clear that there was no hope of getting such a loan through Congress, the German government agreed to use its gold reserves. This, however, alarmed the French, who wanted the German gold to go for reparations. It was only after a heated debate in the Supreme Council, enlivened by Lloyd George waving a telegram he claimed to have just received from the British army in Germany warning that the country was on the edge of a famine, that the French reluctantly backed down. By late March 1919, the first food shipments were arriving.[8]

The delay in drawing up the peace terms worked to the Allies' disadvantage in another way, too. Wartime coalitions usually fall apart in peacetime as the thrill of victory gives way to the more permanent realities of national interests and rivalries. By the spring of 1919, it was public knowledge that there were differing views among the Allies on what needed to be done with Germany. (The Germans studied the Allied press with close attention.) It was not, as has often been portrayed, a matter of the vindictive French against the forgiving Americans, with the British somewhere in between. Everyone agreed that the two provinces of Alsace and Lorraine, which France had lost to Germany in 1871, must be French again. And by a tacit understanding, no one raised the awkward issue of self-determination; there was no question of consulting the locals, many of whom might have disobligingly preferred to remain German. Everyone agreed that the damage done to Belgium and the north of France must be repaired. Everyone agreed that Germany, and the Germans, deserved punishment. Even Wilson, who had insisted during the war that his only quarrel was with the German ruling classes, now seemed to blame the whole of the German people. "They would be shunned and avoided like lepers for generations to come," he told his intimates in Paris, "and so far most of them had no idea of what other nations felt and didn't realize the Coventry in which they would be put."[9] Everyone agreed that Germany must somehow be prevented from dragging Europe into war again.

Almost everyone in Paris in 1919 believed that Germany had started the war. (Only later did doubts begin to arise.) Germany had invaded neutral Belgium, and German troops, to the horror of Allied and American opinion, had behaved badly. (Not all the atrocity stories were wartime propaganda.) Germany had also done itself great damage in Allied eyes by two punitive treaties, often forgotten today, which it imposed in 1918. The Treaty of Bucharest turned Rumania into a German dependency. And with the Treaty of Brest-Litovsk the new Bolshevik government of Russia gave Germany control of a huge swath of Russian territory stretching from the Baltic down to the Caucasus mountains and agreed to pay over a million gold rubles in reparations. Two decades later, Hitler set his sights on the same goal. Russia lost 55 million people, almost a third of its agricultural land and the greater part of its heavy industry and iron and coal. The Bolsheviks were also obliged to pay over millions of gold rubles. Germans might talk of peace, said Wilson in April 1918, but their actions showed their real intentions. "They nowhere set up justice, but everywhere impose their power and exploit everything for their own use and aggrandisement." Lloyd George and Wilson, both from religious backgrounds, both good liberals, believed firmly in chastising the wicked. They also believed in redemption; one day Germany would be redeemed.[10]

Punishment, payment, prevention—on these broad objectives there was agreement. It was everything else that was the problem. Should the kaiser and his top advisers be tried as war criminals? What items should be on the bill presented to Germany? War damages (whatever those were)? Civilian losses? Pensions to the widows and orphans of Allied soldiers? And there was also the related question of how much Germany *could* pay. What sort of armed forces should it have? How much territory should it lose? Were the Allies dealing with the old Germany or a new one that had emerged since the end of the war? Was it fair to punish a struggling democracy for the sins of its predecessors?

Punishment, payment, prevention—all were interconnected. A smaller Germany, and a poorer Germany, would be less of a threat to its neighbors. But if Germany was losing a lot of land, was it also fair to expect it to pay out huge sums? Striking a balance between the different sets of terms was not easy, especially since Wilson, Clemenceau and Lloyd George did not agree among themselves, or, frequently, with their own colleagues.

What made these questions even more complicated was that there were no clear principles to go on. It had been more straightforward in the past. The spoils of war, whether works of art, cannon or horses, went to the victor while the defeated nation paid an indemnity to cover the costs of the war and normally lost territory as well. At the Congress of Vienna, France had lost most of Napoleon's conquests and been liable for 700 million francs as well as the costs of its occupation. After the Franco-Prussian War of 1870–71, which many in Paris still remembered vividly, France had paid 5 billion gold francs and lost its provinces of Alsace and Lorraine. But 1919 was supposed to mark a new sort of diplomacy. "No annexations and no punitive peace" had been the cry from liberals and the left; and statesmen from Washington to Moscow had taken it up. Self-determination, not power politics, was supposed to settle borders.

Public opinion, that new and troubling element, was no help. There was a widespread feeling that someone must pay for such a dreadful war; but there was an equally strong longing for peace. The Allied publics spoke with loud and contradictory voices. In December 1918, the British public had wanted to string the kaiser up; four months later, it was not so sure. The French wanted to bring Germany low, but did they want to hand it over to Bolshevism? The Americans hoped to destroy German militarism but also to rehabilitate the German nation. The statesmen were feeling their way in Paris, trying at once to pay attention to their voters, stay true to their principles, and work out a deal they could all accept. It is perhaps not surprising, then, that they spent so much time in the early days on a relatively simple but highly symbolic issue: the fate of the kaiser.

In 1919 Kaiser Wilhelm, the third and last leader of the empire built by Bismarck, was a fidgety man in his early sixties living in a comfortable castle near Utrecht. At the end of the war, his armies melting away, he had uttered a few last boastful remarks about dying with his troops around him and then slipped away into exile in the Netherlands. Even his most loyal generals had been glad to see him go. His sudden enthusiasms and his equally sudden rages had always been hard to bear. Wilhelm had never grown up; the unloved, restless child had turned into a man who loved dressing up and playing cruel practical jokes. His erratic behavior and wild statements had done much to unsettle Europe before the Great War. He may have been clinically mad; from time to time before 1914 there was talk in Germany of declaring a regency.[11] Queen Victoria had other difficult grandchildren; none, perhaps, did so much damage as he did. Under the "operetta regime," as one critic put it, which ran Germany, the kaiser had a dangerous amount of power, especially over the military and foreign affairs. With a different personality, things might have turned out differently; as it was, the most powerful nation on the continent of Europe lurched and bullied its way toward the explosion of 1914.

The kaiser always made it clear that it was his Germany, his army and his navy. "He has utterly ruined his country and himself," wrote his cousin George V of Britain in November 1918. "I look upon him as the greatest criminal known for having plunged the world into this ghastly war which has lasted over 4 years and 3 months with all its misery."[12] The king spoke for many people. As a shattered world looked for someone to blame, who better than the kaiser, together with his weak, womanizing son and his military leaders?

In Britain, the coalition had started out the postwar election campaign in high-minded fashion. "We must not allow," said Lloyd George, "any sense of revenge, any spirit of greed, any grasping desire to over-rule the fundamental principles of justice." It rapidly became clear that the electorate preferred talk of hanging the kaiser. Lloyd George himself seems to have deplored the language but shared the sentiments. He amused himself, annoyed colleagues such as Churchill and infuriated the king by thinking up elaborate schemes for trying the kaiser publicly in London, or perhaps at Dover Castle, and then shipping him off, after the inevitable guilty verdict, to the Falkland Islands. A Foreign Office official commented to his diary: "The papers write the greatest rubbish about hanging the Kaiser. They are as mad about him as they once were over Jumbo the Elephant. We ought to have better things to think about."[13]

Sonnino, who had made and then abandoned Italy's treaty with the Central Powers, raised repeated objections. It would not do to establish precedents. Clemenceau had little patience for such arguments. "What is a precedent? I'll tell you. A man comes; he acts—for good or evil. Out of the good he does, we create a precedent. Out of the evil he does, criminals—individuals or heads of state—create the precedent for their crimes." There were no precedents for Germany's crimes—"for the systematic destruction of wealth in order to end competition, for the torture of prisoners, for submarine piracy, for the abominable treatment of women in occupied countries."[14]

In the London meetings before Wilson's arrival, talk of punishing the kaiser and his subordinates took up much time but all that was agreed in the end was that they should wait and see what Wilson thought. The American president was not sure. He loathed German militarism, of which the kaiser was such a potent symbol, but was it possible that Wilhelm had been coerced by his own general staff? The American experts, led by Lansing, were uneasy about the legality of proceeding against the Germans.

Wilson eventually agreed, unenthusiastically, to a commission to investigate responsibility for the war and appropriate penalties for the guilty. Its American members, who included Lansing, refused to agree that the Germans should be tried for crimes against humanity. Wilson warned his fellow peacemakers in the Council of Four that it would be much better to leave the kaiser alone with his disgrace: "Charles I was a contemptible character and the greatest liar in history; he was celebrated by poetry and transformed into a martyr by his execution." In a spirit of compromise (and perhaps to get the amendment on the Monroe Doctrine that he wanted in the League covenant), Wilson finally agreed to a clause accusing Wilhelm of "a supreme offence against international morality and the sanctity of treaties" and invited the government of the Netherlands to hand him over. The lesser German criminals were to be tried by special military tribunals once the German government had surrendered them. "The rabbit must first be caught" was the opinion of one of the American experts.[15]

By the spring of 1919, the public appetite for the chase was waning. When the Netherlands refused to give up the kaiser, the Allies, who could scarcely be seen to be bullying a small neutral country, acquiesced. On June 25, shortly before the signing of the Treaty of Versailles, the Council of Four discussed the matter one last time. The mood was jovial rather than vindictive. The kaiser should be brought to England, said Lloyd George. "Be careful not to let him sink," said Clemenceau. "Yes, judgement in England, execution in France." Where shall we send him afterward, wondered Lloyd George. Canada? Some island? "Please don't send him to Bermuda," cried Wilson. "I want to go there myself!"[16]

The kaiser lived on until 1941, writing his memoirs, reading P. G. Wodehouse, drinking English tea, walking his dogs and fulminating against the international Jewish conspiracy which, he had discovered, had brought Germany and himself low. He thrilled to "the succession of miracles" when Hitler started the war in 1939, and he died just before the

German invasion of the Soviet Union. The Allies eventually gave up the idea of trying any Germans themselves. They sent a list of names—including those of Hindenburg and Ludendorff—to the German government, which set up a special court. Out of the hundreds named, twelve were tried. Most were set free at once. A couple of submarine officers who sank lifeboats full of wounded received sentences of four years each; they escaped after a few weeks and were never found.[17]

Keeping Germany Down

T HE MILITARY CLAUSES of the treaty, which the Council of Four had started to look at even before the midwinter break, warned that dealing with Germany was infinitely more difficult than dealing with the kaiser. Most people agreed that militarism and huge armed forces, especially the German, were bad for the world; indeed, books arguing that the arms race had caused the Great War were already starting to appear. One of Wilson's Fourteen Points talked about reducing national armaments "to the lowest point consistent with domestic safety," and one of the selling points of the League was that it would provide such security that nations would willingly cut back on their armed forces. Lloyd George, who knew that conscription was deeply unpopular in Britain, seized on the idea with enthusiasm. Disarming the most powerful nation on the continent was clearly an important first step to the more general disarmament to be carried out by the League. Although it mattered much less, the Allies intended to impose stringent military conditions on the other defeated nations. They would also try, unsuccessfully, to persuade their friends in Europe, such as Czechoslovakia, Poland and Greece, to accept small armed forces.[1]

Disarmament was good in itself, but it was difficult to reach agreement on how much of an army Germany should be left with. The new German government had to be able to put down rebellion at home. Should it also be strong enough to hold off the Bolshevik threat from the east? The Allies could not do it for them. Neither could the states of central Europe. They were not only struggling to survive, but, as Hankey said severely, "there has not been the smallest sign of any serious attempt at combined effort to resist the Bolshevists among them. On the contrary, they show all the worst qualities that we have become accustomed to in the Balkan states." The Germans, for all their flaws, were at least "a solid, patriotic, reliable and highly-organised people." From the French point of view, however, German forces were always a danger. Foch in particular argued from the first that the Allies must confiscate German military equipment, occupy the Rhineland and its bridgeheads, destroy German fortifications along its frontiers with France and limit the German army to 100,000 men. These demands, he said implausibly, were merely military.[2]

One of the few top French generals to come out of the war with his reputation enhanced, Foch liked to refer to himself as a simple soldier. He was short, fair-haired, unassuming and rather sloppy in appearance. "At a distance of 15 feet," in the opinion of an American expert, "one would never pick him for the generalissimo." Born into a modest family in the Pyrenees, Foch was a devout Catholic and irreproachable family man who liked gardening and shooting and the theater (as long as it was nothing too modern) and hated politicians and Germans. The English general Henry Wilson, a great friend, revered his courage and refusal to give up, even in the darkest moments of the war. Foch, he said, had "an uncanny instinct as to the right thing to be done. He cannot always give you reasons." On the other hand, the American commander, General Pershing, who clashed with him in the last days of the war, saw only "a narrow, small, self-opinionated man." President Wilson grew to see him as the embodiment of French vengefulness and blindness. He also found him dull.[3]

Clemenceau, who had known him for years, was always ambivalent. "He was a great General," he told the Supreme Council in 1919, but "not a military Pope." During the war he had weighed General Pétain against Foch as supreme Allied commander. "I found myself between two men, one of whom told me we were finished and the other who came and went like a mad man and who wanted to fight. I said to myself 'Let's try Foch!' " And Clemenceau felt he had been right. "I always see him," he said, "in March 1918, more confident, more fervent than ever, showing himself truly like a great leader, and having only one idea: to fight, and to go on until the enemy gave up." But Clemenceau had reservations. "During the war," he said, "it was necessary for me to see Foch practically every day in order to keep him from doing something foolish."[4]

Clemenceau never could trust any soldier entirely, especially not a religious one. He did not name Foch as a French delegate to the Peace Conference and made it clear that Foch would attend its meetings only when he was invited. Foch never forgave him: "It is really extraordinary that M. Clemenceau did not think of me in the first place as a suitable person to overcome the resistance of President Wilson and Lloyd George." When Foch and his supporters nevertheless tried to influence the peace negotiations, Clemenceau became increasingly impatient. There were dreadful scenes. During one, in the Supreme Council, Foch marched out and sat in the anteroom. When his colleagues tried to persuade him to go back in, his shouts of "Never, Never, Never" could be heard clearly within. Clemenceau thought of dismissing him from time to time, but could never quite bring himself to do so. "Leave the people their idols," he said, "they have to have them."[5]

Foch had insisted on writing strict provisions into the initial armistice agreement of November 11, 1918. During the Peace Conference, he warned that the Germans were not complying with the clauses of the armistice; they were not demobilizing fast enough, not handing over their weapons. The Allies, he said, must keep large armies in existence, especially in the Rhineland, or they would not be able to enforce the peace terms. The British and the Americans were skeptical. Wilson thought the French "hysterical," and when Pershing told him that Foch was exaggerating German strength, he promptly passed the opinion on to Lloyd George.[6]

When the armistice came up for renewal, which it did at monthly intervals, Foch tried to insert new provisions. "It was not sportsmanlike," said Wilson. "Little and irritating secondary demands were continually being added to the armistice conditions whilst at the same time reports were being received to the effect that the previously accepted terms were not being fulfilled." How could they persuade the Germans to accept them? Foch's answer was blunt: "By war." Clemenceau, a little reluctantly, backed him up. "He knew the German people well. They become ferocious when any one retires before them." On February 12, after considerable debate, the Supreme Council came to a compromise: the armistice was to be renewed indefinitely, without the addition of any significant changes, and Foch was put in charge of a committee to draw up detailed military terms for the peace treaty. In the continuing confusion over whether they were drawing up a preliminary treaty or the final one, no one was sure whether the military terms were going to be presented first, on the installment plan, or incorporated in some comprehensive and final document.[7]

When Foch's committee reported back on March 3, it recommended a small German army with basic equipment but no frills such as a general staff or tanks. Foch asked the Supreme Council for an immediate decision. He wanted to be able to start negotiations with German representatives within three weeks. Given the rate of demobilization of the Allied armies, he and his Allied colleagues could not guarantee that they would have the upper hand for much longer. The British and the American peacemakers were unsympathetic. "This," said Balfour, "was equivalent to holding a pistol at the head of the Council." Nor did he want to make a decision in Lloyd George's absence, since some of Foch's proposals were controversial.[8]

Where Foch wanted a German army of 140,000 conscripts who would serve for one year only, the British representative on his committee, Henry Wilson, favored 200,000 volunteers who would serve for a number of years. The British tried to persuade the French that training thousands of men per year would produce a huge pool of experienced soldiers. He would hate, said Lloyd George, to leave France facing that threat. Foch replied that he was not worried about quantity but about quality. Long-serving soldiers could easily become the nucleus of a much larger force. The Germans, "flocks of sheep," would end up with lots of officers to drive them.[9]

Lloyd George took Clemenceau aside and persuaded him to abandon a conscript German army. Foch only discovered this at the next meeting of the Supreme Council; he remonstrated furiously with Clemenceau, who refused to budge. All he achieved was a lower cap, of 100,000, on the German army. "So," wrote Henry Wilson, "I got my principle, but not my numbers, and Foch got his numbers but not his principle. An amazing state of affairs."[10] The military clauses were put aside to await Woodrow Wilson's return.

Foch, like many of his compatriots, wanted far more than a disarmed Germany. He wanted a much smaller one. Germany, all the peacemakers agreed, must shrink. Where and by how much was the problem. Poland was demanding Upper Silesia, with its coalfields, and the port of Danzig (now Gdańsk). Lithuania, if it survived, wanted the Baltic port of Memel (now Klaipėda) and a slice of territory stretching inland. Those borders in the east, which were part of the much larger settlement of Central Europe, were to cause much trouble.

On the northwest, Germany's borders were settled relatively easily. Neutral Denmark put in a claim to the northern part of Schleswig-Holstein, a pair of duchies whose fate had much disturbed Europe in the middle of the previous century. With a mixed population of Germans and Danes and a legal status of great antiquity and bewildering complexity (Bismarck always said that only two men in Europe understood the issue—he was one and the other was in an asylum), they had been seized by Prussia as it began the creation of modern Germany. The German government had done its best to make the inhabitants German, but despite its best efforts an overwhelming majority in the northern part still spoke Danish. The Danish government beseeched the Peace Conference to act quickly. The collapse of the old German regime had produced revolutionary councils in Schleswig-Holstein as elsewhere, but they were still behaving as Germans. Danish speakers were being prevented from holding meetings, their windows were being smashed and, perhaps worst of all in such a prosperous farming area, their cows were being confiscated.[11] No one wanted to reopen the old legal questions, but fortunately there was the new principle of self-determination to hand. The Supreme Council decided that the question should be referred to the committee examining Belgium's claims against Germany. It duly reported back in favor of two plebiscites, the first of the handful ordered by the peacemakers. In February 1920, an international commission supervised a vote by all men and women over the age of twenty. The results closely mirrored the language divisions; the northern zone voted for incorporation in Denmark, the southern to stay with Germany. The border remains unchanged today.

It was not so easy to settle Germany's borders in the west, when France's need for compensation and security ran up against the principle of self-determination and the old British fears of a strong France dominating the Continent. At the northern tip of Alsace lay the rich German coalfields of the Saar. France needed coal, and its own mines had largely been destroyed by the Germans. Besides, as Clemenceau reminded the British ambassador just after the armistice, Britain had once thought of giving the Saar to the French at the end of the Napoleonic Wars; why not take the opportunity now to erase "any bitter recollection they might have of Waterloo"?

The Saar, however, was only a small piece of the much larger territory on the west bank of the Rhine that stretched north from Alsace-Lorraine to the Netherlands. The Rhineland, Clemenceau argued, should be removed from German control to ensure France's security. "The Rhine was the natural boundary of Gaul and Germany." Perhaps the Allies could create an independent state with its neutrality guaranteed, just as Belgium's had been done, by the powers. "I can see," reported the British ambassador, "that he intends to press for that very strongly." Clemenceau in fact was prepared to compromise on many of France's demands as long as the overriding goal of security was met. Indeed, he was even willing to consider, though little came of it, limited cooperation with Germany, with the two countries working together on rebuilding the devastated areas of France and perhaps developing fruitful economic links.[12]

Foch did not think in such terms and spoke with the authority of a military man who had spent his life facing the menace across the Rhine. France needed that river barrier; it needed the time that a Rhineland under its control would buy in the face of an attack from the east; and it needed the extra population. "Henceforward," he insisted in a memoran-

dum to the Peace Conference in January 1919, "Germany ought to be deprived of all entrance and assembling grounds, that is, of all territorial
sovereignty on the left bank of the river, that is, of all facilities for invading quickly, as in 1914, Belgium, Luxembourg, for reaching the coast of
the North Sea and threatening the United Kingdom, for outflanking the
natural defences of France, the Rhine and the Meuse, conquering the
Northern provinces and entering upon the Paris area."[13]

If Germany attacked, he told Cecil, it could strike deep into France
long before the United States and Britain responded. "If there were any
other natural features which could be made an equally good line of defence he would not have asked for the Rhine frontier, but there were absolutely none." His preference was an independent Rhineland which
could be grouped together with Belgium, France and Luxembourg in a
defensive confederation. "I think Foch is going too far," said his friend
Henry Wilson, "but it is at the same time clear to me that neutrals like the
Luxembourgs and the Belgians unduly expose the flank of the poor
French, and that therefore some precaution must be taken, such as that no
Boche troops should be quartered over the Rhine, and possibly no Boche
conscription in the Rhenish provinces." Foch's second choice was a neutral and demilitarized state, or perhaps states, in the Rhineland. Its inhabitants, he felt, were naturally inclined toward France; in time, they would
recognize that their best interests lay in looking westward rather than to
the east.[14]

French troops made up the majority of the occupying forces in the
Rhineland, and the French commanders there shared Foch's views completely (including Marshal Pétain, who was to take a rather different view
of Germany in the Second World War). The Rhineland, said General
Charles Mangin, was the symbol of "immortal France which has become
again a great nation." Mangin, whose career had been spent mainly in
France's colonies, saw the local inhabitants as natives to be won over, with
festivals, torchlit processions, fireworks and a firm hand. The French also
wooed the Rhinelanders with economic concessions, exempting them
from the continuing blockade of Germany.[15]

For an exhilarating few months in 1919, it looked as though powerful
separatist forces were stirring among the largely Catholic Rhinelanders,
who after all had never really settled down comfortably under Prussian
rule. But were they ready to throw themselves into the arms of France?
The mayor of the great Rhine city of Cologne, a cautious and devious
politician, spoke for the moderates. Konrad Adenauer toyed with sepa-
ratism but gave it up as a lost cause by the spring.[16] The diehard separatists
remained a small minority.

Clemenceau chose not to know what his military was up to. Nor did he directly forbid it from intriguing with the separatists. He himself did not care so much how the Rhineland was managed, as long as it did not become, yet again, a platform for attacks on France. He wanted the Allied occupation to continue; indeed, he wanted it extended to the eastern side of the Rhine to protect the bridgeheads. If he could get this guarantee for France's security, he was prepared to back down on other French demands, such as reparations. He urged his allies to keep the peace terms together as a package. As he told Balfour in February, he did not want the disarmament terms, even though nearly ready, to be given to the Germans because they would feel that they had nothing left to bargain with and so be difficult on everything else.[17]

Clemenceau had to move carefully on the Rhineland: his critics at home were watching him closely. From the Elysée Palace, Poincaré warned: "The enemy is picking herself up and if we do not remain united and firm, everything is to be feared." Poincaré's view that France should have direct control of the Rhineland had much support in France. While the government had been careful during the war, for propaganda reasons, not to talk publicly about annexing parts of Germany, private French citizens had set up committees and rushed into print with their aspirations (without the censors making any effort to stop them). The river had always been the boundary between Western civilization and something darker, more primitive. France had civilized the Rhineland, they wrote. Charlemagne's capital had been there; Louis XIV had conquered it; and French revolutionary armies had conquered it again. (The much longer periods when the Rhineland was ruled by German-speaking princes were skipped over hastily.) The people of the Rhine were really French in their genes and their hearts. Their love of good wine, their joie de vivre, their Catholicism (as even anticlerical French writers pointed out) were proof of this. Get rid of the Prussians, and the Rhineland would revert to its true, French, nature. And—perhaps this argument was the most compelling of all—the Rhineland was fair compensation for France's losses.[18]

The Americans were unmoved. The League, not the Rhineland, would solve France's security problems. As House put it, "If after establishing the League, we are so stupid as to let Germany train and arm a large army and again become a menace to the world, we would deserve the fate which such folly would bring upon us." Lloyd George was undecided. Perhaps the Rhineland could be a small neutral state. On the other hand, as he repeatedly said, he did not want to create new Alsace-Lorraines to disrupt the peace of Europe for yet another generation.[19]

French officials floated various ingenious schemes: a permanent occupation by Allied troops; a customs union with France that left the Rhineland technically in Germany; a plan to make the Rhineland part of France militarily and of Germany legally. Some dreamed of something more dramatic. "To assure a durable peace for Europe," said the French Foreign Ministry, "it is necessary to destroy Bismarck's work, which created a Germany without scruples, militarized, bureaucratic, methodical, a formidable machine for war, which blossomed out of that Prussia, which has been defined as an army which has a nation."[20] To see an independent Bavaria again, a Saxony, above all a chastened Prussia, in the center of Europe would quiet French nightmares.

Clemenceau himself was rather more realistic. He was convinced that Germany would survive and that France would have to deal with it. He could not forget that France's future security depended on its allies as much as on its own efforts. The Rhineland was only a piece of what France wanted. If he went all out to gain it, would his allies support France's bill for reparations? Would they be as sympathetic on disarming Germany? The full extent of his maneuvers and his real thoughts will never be known, and that is as he preferred. When the French Foreign Ministry tried to prepare a summary of the 1919 negotiations on the Rhineland a few years later, it could not find a single document in its files.[21] Clemenceau destroyed most of his own papers before he died.

In the early months of the Peace Conference, Clemenceau did his best to build up a reserve of goodwill among his allies by cooperating, for example, on the League of Nations. He kept silent on the Rhineland in the Supreme Council, sounding out his allies privately on the alternatives of outright annexation or an autonomous Rhine state. He found some sympathy among the Americans, particularly from House. The British, he felt, would be harder to win over. He did not apparently talk to Wilson before the president's departure for the United States. As Lloyd George put it, with his usual disregard of geography, "the old tiger wants the grizzly bear back in the Rocky Mountains before he starts tearing up the German hog!"[22]

On February 25, André Tardieu, one of the official French delegates, finally presented a formal statement on the Rhineland to the Peace Conference. It was his usual dazzling performance. Tardieu, who came from a family of Paris engravers, was a distinguished intellectual (he had been top of his class at the élite Ecole Normale Supérieure), diplomat, politician and journalist. In 1917, Clemenceau sent him to the United States as his special representative. He was very clever, energetic and charming. Lloyd George could not abide him, and Wilson never forgave him for his close contacts with the Republicans in Washington. Clemenceau was fond of him and trusted him as much as he did anyone. He also kept him firmly under control. When Tardieu made the mistake of standing in front of him at a meeting of the Supreme Council, the old man rapped sharply on the table. "S'il vous plaît, Monsieur." Tardieu slunk back to his seat in a fury, but dared not answer back.[23]

Tardieu's memorandum of February 25, which he had drawn up on Clemenceau's instructions, asked for Germany's western borders to stop at the Rhine and for Allied forces to occupy the bridgeheads permanently. France, he insisted, did not have the slightest interest in annexing any part of the Rhineland, but Tardieu did not say how it was to be governed. The response from France's allies was firm. "We regarded it," said Lloyd George, "as a definite and dishonourable betrayal of one of the fundamental principles for which the Allies had professed to fight, and which they blazoned forth to their own people in the hour of sacrifice." Always the realist, he also pointed out that trying to divide Germany up probably would not work in the long run; "meanwhile it would cause endless friction and might provoke another war." Wilson, in the United States, was equally firm. "This could not be," he told Grayson. "The desires of the people were German in character. Taking this territory away from Germany would simply give a cause for hatred and a determination for a renewal of the war throughout Germany that would always be equal to the bitterness felt by France against Germany over the lost provinces." The president ordered House not to make any commitments on the Rhineland. He would deal with the issue in person when he returned to Paris.[24]

In an attempt to come up with a compromise, Lloyd George, Clemenceau and House set up a secret committee a few days before Wilson's boat docked. Tardieu, who represented France, now came out openly for an independent Rhine state. "France," he said, "would never be content unless it was secured against a repetition of 1914 and . . . this security could only be given by drawing the frontier along the Rhine. France had the right to expect that if there was to be another war, it should not take place on French soil." Kerr replied that Britain could not see either separating the Rhineland from Germany or stationing troops there permanently. British public opinion was against it; so were the dominion governments, whose wishes could not be ignored. On the other hand, British forces would, of course, come to France's aid if Germany attacked again. Tardieu pointed out that they would probably not arrive in time. (The French did not take seriously Lloyd George's offer to build a tunnel under the Channel.) The American representative said very little. The talks produced nothing useful.[25]

·   ·   ·

By the time Wilson was due back in Paris, considerable progress had been made on the military clauses of the Germany treaty, but Germany's borders, including the Rhineland, were far from settled and the tricky issue of reparations was completely deadlocked. When Wilson's ship reached Brest on the evening of March 13, House came down to meet him. He brought discouraging news. There was only the outline of a German treaty.

The colonel thought he had simply briefed the president. Mrs. Wilson and her supporters, who had never liked House, declared that the president was shattered. "He seemed to have aged ten years," she said twenty years after the event, "and his jaw was set in that way it had when he was making a superhuman effort to control himself." He exclaimed, according to Mrs. Wilson, "House has given away everything I had won before we left Paris." Grayson later added his embellishment: the president was horrified to discover that House had not only agreed to the establishment of a separate Rhine republic but had gone along with the nefarious scheme of the British and the French to play down the significance of the League of Nations by taking the covenant out of the German treaty. House had done neither, but Wilson's suspicions were aroused, and those around him were happy to keep them alive.[26]

We will never know what happened between the president and the man he had once called an extension of himself, but certainly that night a crack appeared in their friendship. They continued to see each other and House continued to act for the president, but it was rumored that he no longer had his master's ear. Lloyd George thought the main trouble came later, in April, when he, Clemenceau and House were meeting in the latter's room at the Crillon. House was trying to smooth over a dispute, this time between Wilson and the Italians over Italy's claims in the Adriatic. The president walked in unexpectedly and clearly felt that something was going on behind his back. "He had at least one divine attribute," said Lloyd George; "he was a jealous god; and in disregarding what was due to him House forgot that aspect of his idol and thus committed the unforgivable sin."[27]

What House may have done at Brest is put to Wilson a suggestion coming from Foch, among others, to present a preliminary treaty to Germany with the military terms and perhaps some financial ones, leaving the difficult issues such as borders and reparations for later. Wilson certainly heard of it almost as soon as he arrived back. He immediately scented a plot to delay the covenant of the League of Nations. On March 15 he spoke "very frankly" to Lloyd George and Clemenceau. "There were so many collateral questions which must be referred to the League of Nations when created that its creation must be the first object, and that no treaty could be agreed upon that would deal only with military, naval and financial matters." Wilson refused to go to that afternoon's meeting of the Supreme Council, which was meant to approve the military terms; he needed time, he claimed, to read them. "Impudence," said the British general Henry Wilson. Two days later, when the question finally came up, the president contemplated opposing the provision for a German volunteer army. Lloyd George, irritated at the delay, threatened in return that he would refuse to approve the League of Nations covenant. The terms went through.[28]

Germany was left, as even the Allies admitted, with something closer to a police force than an army. When the promise of reductions in all armies failed to materialize in later years, it added to British unease about the German treaty, and to German resentment. With an army of 100,000 men and a navy of 15,000, and with no air force, tanks, armored cars, heavy guns, dirigibles or submarines, Germany was to be put in a position where it could not wage an aggressive war. Most of its existing stocks of weapons, and all its fortifications west of the Rhine and along its eastern bank, were to be destroyed. Only a few factories in Germany would be allowed to produce war materials, and all imports were forbidden. To make sure that Germany did not train men surreptitiously, public services, such as the police, had to be kept at prewar levels, and private societies—touring clubs, for example, or veterans' associations—were not allowed to do anything of a military nature. In Germany's high schools and universities, students were no longer to be cadets. All this would be enforced by the Germans themselves, supervised by an Inter-Allied Commission of Control. It was, in retrospect, like the ropes of the Lilliputians over Gulliver.[29]

The difficulties over the military terms were not yet over. Wilson now found himself in a serious quarrel with the British over the naval terms, a quarrel that reflected both older rivalries and the newer one that was developing as the United States became a world naval power. To begin with, the British Admiralty longed to destroy the Kiel Canal, which linked the Baltic and the North Sea and thus enabled Germany to move even its largest ships without sending them through the straits by Copenhagen. The admirals feared, with good reason, that commercial shipping interests and the American government might object. The alternative of handing over the canal to the Danes was out of the question; they showed no enthusiasm for such a poisoned chalice. The best that could be done was to take it out of German control and let every nation's ships use it. The Americans objected even to that. "A punitive measure," said Admiral William Benson, the American naval representative and chief of naval operations. With the new Panama Canal firmly under their control, the Americans did not want precedents for international management of waterways. Benson also objected in general to imposing harsh terms on Germany, which he argued would drag the United States into endless efforts to enforce them. The compromise, which went into the treaty, simply allowed free passage for all countries at peace with Germany.[30]

The Americans had similar reservations about British proposals to raze the fortifications along Germany's coasts. "Naval armaments were being limited," Lansing complained. "Why then should Germany not be permitted to defend her own coasts?" Lloyd George came up with a solution; defensive fortifications were acceptable, offensive ones were not. In the end, all German fortifications conveniently turned out to be defensive except the ones that the British really cared about.

Out in the North Sea were two tiny low-lying islands, Heligoland (Helgoland) and Dune, which the British had given to Germany in 1890, in what seemed like an excellent deal, for Zanzibar. Unfortunately, time had produced airplanes, submarines and long-range guns—and the Anglo-German naval race. The useless specks of land became formidable bases. The Admiralty had a simple solution: "The key of the mad dog's kennel must be in our pocket," said an admiral, "for there is no knowing when the evil beast will get another attack of hydrophobia." If the Americans objected, an alternative was to blow them both to smithereens. From his retirement in England, the half-blind Sir Edward Grey put in his suggestion, to turn Heligoland into a sanctuary: "For some reason this, humanly speaking, unattractive and barren spot is a resting place for millions of birds on migration." Why not give it to Hughes of Australia? suggested Clemenceau. The final British position, which the French supported, was that only the fortifications and harbors should be destroyed. President Wilson "was entirely in sympathy with the destruction of the fortifications on the Islands of Heligoland and Dune, but he thought the destruction of the breakwaters was rather a serious matter from a humane point of view, as those formed havens for fishermen in case of storms in the North Sea." He did not, he added, want to give "an impression of gratuitous violence." The fishermen, according to the British, could easily find shelter in natural harbors. The British got their way on this, but the islands remained German. In the 1930s, with the Nazis in power, the fortifications were rebuilt, only to be blown up again after the Second World War.[31]

When it came to Germany's submarines, the British and the Americans found themselves on the same side. "These pests ought to be disposed of," said Lloyd George when the matter came up for discussion. The American secretary of the navy, Josephus Daniels, spoke for many when he compared them to poison gas: "I believe all submarines should be sunk and no more should be built by any nation, if and when the League of Nations becomes a fact." The French and Italians objected. "There is no treacherous weapon," said the French minister of marine, "there can only be treachery in the way the weapon is used." And if the submarines were to be destroyed, they would like a share in the work and in the profits from the scrap. In the end, the French navy took ten submarines; the remainder were broken up.[32]

The real tension between the British and the Americans came over Germany's surface ships. Initially both had taken the same view: their admirals did not want them; it would be expensive and difficult to incorporate them into their own fleets. Although Wilson thought it foolish to destroy perfectly good ships, Lloyd George rather liked the idea of sinking them ceremoniously in the middle of the Atlantic. The French and the Italians objected. France, said a French admiral, had thrown all its resources into winning the war on land. "Our fleet suffered losses which could not be repaired, while the fleets of our allies increased in considerable proportion." It would make more sense, in his view, to divide the ships up. The Japanese suggested diffidently that they might take a few as well.

Britain was about to give way at the beginning of March when House told Lloyd George that the United States could not accept an increase in the British navy. The distribution of the German fleet had set off alarm bells in the mind of the excitable and Anglophobic American naval adviser. Admiral Benson pointed out that whether the distribution was done on the basis of contribution to the war effort or on that of losses, in either case Britain would come out with the greatest share. "In future her sole naval rival will be the United States, and every ship built or acquired by Great Britain can have in mind only the American fleet." Britain, he was convinced, was determined to dominate the world's seas and world trade.[33]

Lloyd George tried to defuse the issue by suggesting another of his sleights of hand: the ships would be given out, but the United States and Britain would go ahead and sink theirs. Unwisely, perhaps, he made this dependent "upon the understanding that we should not in the future enter into a building competition against each other." Otherwise the British navy would simply go ahead and keep its share of the German ships. Behind his proposal lay British concern over the continuing expansion of the American navy, which threatened to end Britain's naval dominance. Daniels had brought a second major building program before Congress at the end of 1918. The public justifications were reassuring: that the program was really just a continuation of the one of 1916 or that it was intended only to support the League of Nations. In Paris, however, Benson was saying firmly that the United States should not stop until its navy equaled Britain's. It was a fundamental of British policy that its navy must be larger than any other, ideally larger than any two other navies. But the British knew that they could not keep up financially in a naval race; moreover, they did not want to jeopardize their new relationship with the United States.[34]

Daniels came over to Paris in person to try to defuse the tension. "President," he told his diary, "hoped we would talk it over and reach some right understanding." The talks went badly. "The supremacy of the British Navy," Walter Long, the first lord of the Admiralty, told Benson and Daniels, "was an absolute necessity, not only for the very existence of the British Empire but even for the peace of the world." Benson replied briskly that the United States was quite capable of taking a share in keeping the peace. He and his British counterpart, "Rosie" Wemyss, quarreled so angrily that Daniels feared they were about to come to blows. "The British Admiral thought his country ought to have the right to build the biggest navy in the world and we ought to agree to it. To Benson that would have been treason to his own country." The British threatened to oppose the special amendment on the Monroe Doctrine in the covenant of the League. Lloyd George told Daniels over breakfast on April Fool's Day that the League would be useless if the United States continued its building. "They had stopped work on their cruisers, & we ought to stop work if we really trusted the League Wilson wanted."[35]

In the end, since neither side, admirals apart, really wanted a break, a truce was declared. The Americans promised to modify their building program (which they had to do in any case, because Congress was being difficult) and the British promised not to oppose the amendment or the League. Each side agreed it would continue to consult with the other. The new mood did not, however, produce an agreement on the German ships that remained at Scapa Flow. "We should like to see them sunk," Wemyss told a subordinate, "but I do see that they are a pawn in the game." The cooperation between the British and the Americans which had so struck observers was ruffled by what later came to be called "the naval battle of Paris." It was to be shaken even further by the question of German reparations.[36]

15

Footing the Bill

I N 1995, there was a faint echo of that most contentious issue in the German peace when a newly reunified Germany agreed that it would pay the interest still due on the loans it had received in the years between the wars to pay off the reparations imposed by the Treaty of Versailles. "The subject of reparations," said Thomas Lamont, the banker who represented the American Treasury in Paris in 1919, "caused more trouble, contention, hard feeling, and delay at the Paris Peace Conference than any other point of the Treaty."[1]

Reparations helped to poison relations between Germany and the Allies, and among the Allies themselves, for much of the 1920s and 1930s. The issue facing the peacemakers was at once very simple and very complicated. Simple, because, as Lloyd George put it, "Somebody had to pay. If Germany could not pay, it meant the British taxpayer had to pay. Those who ought to pay were those who caused the loss."[2] Complicated, because that involved drawing up the bill and working out how much Germany could actually afford. The very mention of reparations caused disagreements. Were they simply compensation for damages or were they really a disguised fine, an indemnity for war costs for the victors? Should these costs include uncollected taxes or earnings lost because of invasion, death or damage? Pensions to widows and orphans? Compensation for animals that had died when their owners fled? Were they in essence an acknowledgment by Germany and whichever of its allies could still be found of their moral responsibility for the whole catastrophic war?

France, Britain and the United States, which worked out the final agreement, had different needs and different views. The United States took a high moral line. It did not want anything for itself, but it expected the Europeans to pay back the money they had borrowed during the war. For the Europeans, reparations promised a way to pay off their debts and to reconstruct their societies. What should be included in the reparations bill therefore assumed great importance because it affected sharing out the spoils. France had suffered the most direct damage, Belgium the next most, but Britain had spent the most. There were also intense debates over the question of how much Germany could pay. If the figure were set too high, the German economy might collapse, which would not help British exporters. If too low, Germany would be getting away lightly; it would also recover more quickly, a prospect that worried the French. Getting clear figures was not easy then and since, because it was in almost everyone's interest to exaggerate and obfuscate: in the Allies', to exaggerate how much they were due, and in the Germans', how much they were paying. Because the peacemakers could not agree on a final figure, the German treaty merely included a provision for a special commission, made up of Allied representatives, which would have two years to determine what Germany should pay. This understandably brought charges from the Germans that they were being asked to sign a blank check.

Although historians are increasingly coming to the conclusion that the burden was never as great as Germany and its sympathizers claimed, reparations remain the preeminent symbol of the peace made in Paris.[3] While most of the 440 clauses of the Treaty of Versailles have long been forgotten, the handful dealing with reparations stand, in what is still the received view, as evidence of a vindictive, shortsighted and poisonous document. The new Weimar democracy started life with a crushing burden and the Nazis were able to play on understandable German resentment. Responsibility for the disastrous consequences, so the argument goes, begins with the peacemakers of 1919: the vengeful, grasping Clemenceau, the pusillanimous, vacillating Lloyd George and the pathetic, broken Wilson, who allowed himself, as John Maynard Keynes put it, to be bamboozled.

Keynes did not create the picture on his own, of course, but he painted it most persuasively and most persistently. A very clever, rather ugly young man, he had sailed through Eton and Cambridge, collecting prizes and attention. His membership in the Bloomsbury circle only enhanced his propensity to moral superiority. He was a terrifying subordinate because he never bothered to hide his contempt for virtually all his superiors. Keynes went to the Peace Conference as chief Treasury adviser. In *The Economic Consequences of the Peace,* written immediately after the German treaty was signed, he spoke, therefore, with his usual authority.

Wilson, said Keynes, was the victim of the Europeans' grisly blindman's buff. "He allowed himself to be drugged by their atmosphere, to discuss on the basis of their plans and of their data, and to be led along their paths." Wilson betrayed his own principles, his country and the hopes of all those who wanted a better world. Lloyd George was the chief enchanter who had come out of the mists of the Welsh mountains to entice the good and the gullible into the swamps. "One catches in his company," said Keynes in a piece he left out of the book, "that flavour of final purposelessness, inner irresponsibility, existence outside or away from our Saxon good and evil, mixed with cunning, remorselessness, love of power, that lend fascination, enthralment, and terror to the fair-seeming magicians of North European folklore."[4]

Clemenceau, dried up, old and bitter, cared only for France and its security. Keynes had come to loathe the French and what he saw as their inordinate greed. He fought with their representatives over relief for Germany and over the loans France needed from Britain. The German representatives whom he met on the armistice commission were quite a different matter. In a memoir he wrote for his Bloomsbury friends he described the prominent Hamburg banker Carl Melchior as "exquisitely clean, very well and neatly dressed, with a high stiff collar . . . his eyes gleaming straight at us, with extraordinary sorrow in them, yet like an honest animal at bay." Keynes's declaration that he felt a sort of love for Melchior need not be taken too seriously. It was a rhetorical flourish for old friends who knew his complicated sexual past.[5]

The peacemakers appalled Keynes. They fretted about revenge while European civilization tottered on the brink of collapse.

> In Paris where those connected with the Supreme Economic Council received almost hourly the reports of the misery, disorder, and decaying organisation of all Central and Eastern Europe, allied and enemy alike, and learnt from the lips of the financial representatives of Germany and Austria unanswerable evidence of the terrible exhaustion of their countries, an occasional visit to the hot, dry room in the President's house, where the Four fulfilled their destinies in empty and arid intrigue, only added to the sense of nightmare.[6]

What did they achieve in their gilded rooms? According to Keynes, a peace that completed the economic destruction done to Europe by the war. They were drawing new lines on the map when they should have been setting up a free trade area; they were haggling about the debts they owed one another when they should have canceled them all; and, the criticism that reverberated most in Germany, they imposed crippling reparations. Quoting extensively from his own memoranda written for the Peace Conference, Keynes argued that Germany could pay at the most £2 billion

($10 billion). Anything more would drive it to despair, and probably revolution, with dangerous consequences for Europe.[7]

While he was in Paris, Keynes produced a scheme to solve Europe's economic problems and the problem of reparations in one neat, clever package. The European Allies needed to raise money, to repair war damage and to pay back their debts to each other and to the United States. The defeated nations would issue bonds for their reparations, but those bonds would be guaranteed by both enemy and Allied nations. The financial rivers would start to flow again and Europe's nations would be linked together to their common benefit. Ultimately, all depended on the participation of the United States. While on paper Britain was still a creditor nation, and France had an overall debt of $3.5 billion, the reality was rather different. Both France and Britain had lent large amounts to Russia, which had defaulted on its debts, and to other Allies such as Italy and Rumania, which were in no position to start paying them back. Britain owed the United States $4.7 billion, and France owed it $4 billion as well as $3 billion to Britain. "The economic mechanism of Europe is jammed," Lloyd George told Wilson in April 1919, when he forwarded Keynes's memorandum. "A proposal which unfolds future prospects and shows the peoples of Europe a road by which food and employment and orderly existence can once again come their way, will be a more powerful weapon than any other for the preservation from the danger of Bolshevism of that order of human society which we believe to be the best starting point for future improvement and greater well-being."[8]

The idea that the United States should use its financial resources to get Europe going again after the war had been around for some time in various forms. The French, deeply in debt to their allies and facing huge repair bills, were particularly enthusiastic about prolonging and strengthening Allied wartime economic cooperation. Their minister of commerce and industry, Etienne Clémentel, a hardworking, earnest man from a farming family, drew up an elaborate plan for a "new economic order," where organization and coordination would replace wasteful competition, resources would be pooled and shared out as needed, and the whole would be directed by clever technocrats. When Germany had put its own political house in order, it too could be part of the new order, safely enmeshed in a strong organization. The scheme languished because of active opposition from the United States and indifference from Britain and was finally turned down by the Allies in April 1919. The effort bore unexpected fruit after the Second World War, when Jean Monnet, who had been Clémentel's assistant in 1919, founded the economic organization that grew into the European Union.[9]

The British preferred to hint that the United States should cancel the interest on its loans for a few years. Alternatively, the whole expense of the war could be added up and the United States could take a large proportion. Lloyd George, with his enthusiasm for big ideas, preferred an even more dramatic solution, that of simply canceling all intra-Allied debts outright. The Americans, however, were determined not to let that happen. "I realize the efforts that are being made to tie us to the shaky financial structure of Europe," wrote Wilson to the financier Bernard Baruch, who was one of his main advisers, "and am counting upon your assistance to defeat the efforts." Most of his experts agreed, as did the Treasury in Washington. It was up to the Europeans to sort out their own problems; the more the United States helped them, the less likely they were to stand on their own feet. In any case, there was not much chance of Congress, dominated as it now was by Republicans, approving massive financial support for the Europeans. Keynes's scheme was turned down flat like all the others, and he watched with increasing gloom as the peacemakers tried to move ahead on reparations.[10]

"There is no doubt," said Lloyd George in reply to a worried query from a member of his cabinet in April, "it would be better to fix a sum if we could agree on the figure. The difficulty is first of all to ascertain it; the next is to secure agreement amongst the Allies as to the amount, and in the third place to secure an arrangement as to the proportions in which it is to be distributed. If you have any plan that will meet these three difficulties you will have solved the most baffling problem in the Peace Treaty." Shortly after the opening of the conference the Supreme Council had set up a Commission on the Reparation of Damage, which was to look at the related questions of how much the enemy countries (which mainly meant Germany) should pay, how much they could pay, and how payment should be made. The subcommittee for the last point rarely met, but the other two subcommittees were in session day and night, producing little beyond mounds of paper. By the time Wilson left for the United States on February 14, the commission was deadlocked, with the Americans holding out for a relatively moderate figure and the British and the French demanding more. "They play with billions as children play with wooden blocks," said a journalist cynically, "but whatever we agree to will largely be a figure of speech, for the Germans will never be able to pay such a vast sum." The British were asking for £24 billion ($120 billion), the French for £44 billion ($220 billion); the American experts recommended £4.4 billion ($22 billion).[11]

The Americans also wanted to include a fixed amount in the treaty. This, their experts argued, would help to end the financial uncertainty that was holding back Europe's recovery. The Europeans disagreed. As Montagu, one of the British cabinet ministers involved in the discussions, said: "If too low a figure were given Germany would pay out cheerfully and the Allies would get too little, while, on the other hand, if too high a figure were given, she would throw up the sponge and the Allies would get nothing.[12]

It is easy with hindsight to say that the victors should have been less concerned with making Germany pay and should have concentrated more on getting Europe going again. But after a war that had brought destruction on such a scale and shaken European society so deeply, how could political leaders speak of forgetting? In any case, public opinion would simply not allow them to do so. "Make the Hun pay," said the British. "Let Germany Pay First," said the posters covering the walls of Paris.[13]

The European leaders saw danger even in assessing Germany's capacity to pay, because the figure was bound to be lower than the public expected. The British and the French pointed out that it was very difficult to judge how much Germany—or whatever was to be left of it—would be able to pay. The country was in a bad way, its economy and its government equally shaky. The Germans could not provide reliable statistics, even if they had wanted to. Foreign trade had evaporated, and with it an important source of revenue. Government finances were in a mess. Taxes had been kept low for political reasons and the war costs had been paid for largely through the issue of huge amounts of war bonds and special notes. The plan had always been for Germany to settle accounts for the war when it had won and could transfer its costs to the defeated enemy. In the last year of the war this had in fact started to happen; the treaties of Brest-Litovsk with Russia and of Bucharest with Rumania had transferred control of huge resources to Germany. The Bolsheviks had also been obliged to start payments on an indemnity of $600 million. In the defeated Germany of 1919, conservatives protested loudly against any attempts to raise taxes or to default on government bonds, while the left pushed for benefits for veterans and widows and orphans, subsidized food and increased wages. The government meekly acquiesced to both, and Germany's deficit climbed until, by 1921, it amounted to two thirds of the budget. There was little incentive to cut expenditures or raise taxes merely to pay reparations.[14]

Nor was it easy to determine the Allied bill. "In my poor country France," said the French minister of the liberated regions, "there are hundreds of villages into which no one has yet been able to return. Please understand: it is a desert, it is desolation, it is death." The American army engineer and his team of assistants who made what was probably the most detailed study of the war-torn parts of France and Belgium estimated in January 1919 that it would take at least two years to come up with a reliable estimate of the costs of repairing the damage. The British unkindly suspected their allies of inflating their claims, in Belgium's case for more than its total prewar wealth and in France's for about half. "Almost incredible," said Lloyd George sternly. The more his allies claimed, of course, the less there would be for Britain.[15]

There was also much disagreement over what counted as damage. Wilson had said firmly that he would consider only restitution for damage done by unlawful acts of war and not for war costs themselves. His Fourteen Points had talked merely of "restoration" of invaded territories, and he had promised that there would be "no annexations, no contributions, no punitive damages." When Germany had signed the armistice agreement, it had done so on that understanding. Germany would thus be liable for repairing the battlefields in France and Belgium but not for the money Allied governments had spent on, for example, munitions or feeding their soldiers. When Lloyd George tried to blur the line between reparations and indemnities, Wilson would have none of it: "Bodies of working people all over the world had protested against indemnities, and he thought the expression reparations would be sufficiently inclusive."[16]

Lloyd George, optimistic as always, told his colleagues that he did not really think Wilson had ruled out indemnities. The British were concerned that, if Wilson stuck to his guns, the British empire would end up with compensation largely for ships sunk by the Germans. France would get the lion's share, which, in the British view, it would probably waste with its usual inefficient financial management. The British also suspected that France was not trying very hard to repay its debts to Britain. As Churchill said severely, "France was going bankrupt as a nation, but the French were growing wealthy as individuals."[17]

Lloyd George tried persuasion with Wilson and then he tried threats. He might not be able to sign the treaty, he told him at the end of March 1919, unless some of Britain's costs were included. Fortunately, Smuts had come up with an ingenious solution. He pointed out that, when the armistice had been arranged, the European Allies had stated, and the Americans had accepted, that Germany was liable for all damage done to civilians by its aggression. Therefore, reparations must include separation allowances for soldiers' families, as well as pensions for widows and orphans. The effect was to double the potential bill. And this came from the same Smuts who four months earlier had warned Lloyd George against excessive claims, and who was to protest vigorously a month later that reparations would cripple Germany. High-minded, moralistic and clever,

Smuts persuaded himself that he had not been inconsistent. In his own defense, he claimed that he had simply expressed an opinion shared by most of the legal experts at the Peace Conference. More revealingly, he wrote that, if pensions had been excluded, France would have got most of the reparations.[18]

Wilson listened to Smuts where he would not have listened to Lloyd George. The American experts thought the argument absurd and illogical. "Logic! Logic!" Wilson told them. "I don't give a damn for logic. I am going to include pensions!"[19] His decision in the end affected only the distribution of reparations, because the final figure was to be determined by what Germany could actually pay.

Although Wilson has been blamed for backing down, Lloyd George has been blamed even more for, as Keynes would have it, bamboozling the Americans and allowing the British public to dream of exacting huge sums from Germany. At best, he has been seen, as he was by many at the time, as a liberal who did not have the courage to be true to his principles. Certainly, he was not consistent. When Hughes of Australia first talked in terms of millions of pounds, Lloyd George pointed out that Germany could raise the sum only by expanding its manufacturing and dumping cheap goods on world markets. "It would mean that for two generations we would make German workmen our slaves." What was more, it would damage British and imperial trade. Yet Lloyd George then turned around and made Hughes chairman of a committee packed with known hardliners to draw up a preliminary estimate for the British government of Germany's capacity to pay. The group—"altogether it was the oddest committee I ever served upon," said Sir George Foster, of Canada—made little attempt to collect evidence but relied on personal impressions and wishful thinking; as Foster put it, "to make the Hun pay to the utmost, whether it leads to a generation of occupancy and direction, or not, and forgetful of the results otherwise."[20]

As the weeks went by and the numbers floated around, Lloyd George continued to vacillate. He argued for high reparations with Wilson and Clemenceau but then talked of moderation in his famous Fontainebleau Memorandum at the end of March. He opposed putting a fixed figure in the treaty on the grounds that it might be too low; then he swung round in June after the Germans complained and said perhaps the Allies ought to set an amount. He appeared to listen sometimes to Keynes and Montagu, both of whom were moderates, at other times to Lord Cunliffe, a former governor of the Bank of England, and a judge, Lord Sumner. The Heavenly Twins, as Keynes nicknamed them, were widely seen as the two bad men of the conference; "they always go about together and are always

summoned when some particularly nefarious act has to be committed."
Lloyd George named the Twins as British representatives to the reparations commission but, when a special committee was set up in March to
try to resolve the impasse, he chose Montagu. "When he meant to do business," said an American, "he brought along Montagu and Keynes; when
he was going to hedge he brought in Sumner and Cunliffe." Keynes
loathed his rivals. Lloyd George later claimed that he too was appalled by
their lack of judgment. During the Peace Conference he disingenuously
intimated to the Americans that, while he would prefer lower reparations,
he could not get the Twins to agree.[21]

Both Cunliffe and Sumner believed they should get as good a deal as
possible for their own country, but they were prepared to compromise—
and to take direction from their prime minister. "We ought to act here like
statesmen," Sumner told his colleagues on the reparations commission,
when he argued against piling on the costs. Both would have gone for a
fixed amount in the treaty, and a lower figure, if Lloyd George had told
them to do so. Why did he not? His vacillation damaged his reputation
and caused much trouble with his colleagues in Paris. "I wish," said Lamont, the American expert, "Mr. Lloyd George could tell us just what he
finally wants, so that we could determine whether his ideas, and the President's as we understand them to be, are in reality far apart or close together." By exasperating the Americans, from Wilson on down, Lloyd
George was putting at risk a relationship he considered of supreme importance. The problem was that he was not sure himself what he, or the
British public, wanted.[22]

There was a side of him that wanted to see Germany punished. At his
moral core—and he had one, despite what his enemies said—Lloyd
George deplored war, and Germany had unleashed the worst one the
world had ever seen. He also saw the issue as a lawyer. "By every principle
of justice," he told the British empire delegation, "by the principles of justice which were recognized as applicable between individuals, the Germans were liable for the whole of the damages and the cost of recovering
them." Since he was acting, in a sense, for Britain, he had to make sure
that Germany's other creditors did not inflate their claims. "That is an old
device when claiming against a bankrupt estate."[23]

He was also, however, a statesman. He had been chancellor of the exchequer before the war, and he understood finance and trade. He knew
that sooner or later the British would have to sell their goods to the Germans again. He did not want to destroy Germany. At the beginning of
March, while the president was still in the United States, Lloyd George
discussed reparations with House over lunch. He needed to provide, he

told the American, "a plausible reason to his people for having fooled them about the question of war costs, reparations and what not. He admitted that he knew Germany could not pay anything like the indemnity which the British and French demanded." Wilson, when he heard this on his return, was unsympathetic. He urged Lloyd George to resist demands for high reparations. "Nothing would be finer," he said, "than to be put out of office during a crisis of this kind for doing what was right." Lloyd George would have the consolation of knowing that posterity would think well of him. "I could not wish," Wilson told him, "a more magnificent place in history."[24]

Lloyd George did not take this noble, and barren, way out. He was a politician, obliged to weigh what was just against what was practical. He also had to function in a world where the democratic voice of the people had to be heeded. The pressures on him in Paris were considerable. Parts of the liberal press were starting to talk of reconciliation, but the conservative papers were loudly demanding large reparations. Northcliffe had taken it upon himself to keep Lloyd George up to the mark. The press baron hinted darkly to the editors of the *Daily Mail* and *The Times* that the prime minister was under the sway of pro-German forces.[25]

Lloyd George also found himself hemmed in, to a certain extent, by the December 1918 election. Promises to squeeze Germany hard—in one memorable phrase, "until the pips squeaked"—went over very well. He had produced ever larger notional bills for Germany. "We will," he said, "search their pockets for it." The last coalition manifesto before the vote stated simply: "1. Punish the Kaiser 2. Make Germany pay." Many of the Conservatives who were elected in the resulting landslide were new to politics. "Hard-faced men who look as if they had done very well out of the war," in the words of a leading Conservative, they saw their mission primarily as making the German pips squeak. In April, as he was arguing with Wilson, Lloyd George received a telegram signed by 370 members of Parliament asking him to remain true to his election speeches and "present the bill in full." He rushed back to London and on April 16 demolished his critics with a tremendous speech in the House of Commons. He had no intention, he told his audience, of breaking his promises. They must not listen to an embittered, madly vain man—here he tapped his forehead significantly—but must trust to the world's statesmen to do the best for humanity and peace. He left to loud cheers. Back in Paris he told the faithful Frances Stevenson that he had won "complete mastery of the House, while telling them absolutely nothing about the peace conference."[26]

Pressure came as well from the empire. While the Canadians, as on much else, took the American position, the Australians were for getting the maximum from Germany. Hughes loathed the Germans, whom he, like most of his compatriots, had long seen as the chief threat to Australia, and he thought the American objection to high reparations unprincipled and self-serving. As he told Lloyd George, a neutral United States had made great profits in the early stages of the war, while the British empire poured out its blood and treasure. Without a huge settlement from Germany, Britain would lose in the coming competition with the United States for world economic supremacy.[27]

Lloyd George's handling of the reparations issue was actually more successful than it appeared. By persuading Wilson to include pensions in reparations, he increased Britain's share. By not mentioning a fixed sum in the treaty (for which there were sound technical reasons), he managed to keep public opinion at home and in the empire happy. (The impact on German opinion was another matter.) He also took out insurance of another sort when he privately urged a prominent European socialist to whip up a public outcry against treating Germany too harshly.[28] Finally, he managed to cast the French as the greedy ones, a role they have generally played ever since, with Louis-Lucien Klotz, the minister of finance, as chief villain.

Klotz, described by Clemenceau as "the only Jew I knew who knew nothing of finance," is supposed to have said in answer to all questions about France's future, "Germany will pay." (In fact, he warned that German reparations should not be expected to pay for everything.) Clemenceau treated him contemptuously, as he did so many of his colleagues. Lloyd George found him merciless: "His mind and heart were so stuffed with bonds that he had no room left for the humanities." Even Wilson was moved to a little joke about Klotz on the brain. Keynes has left a characteristically cruel sketch: "a short, plump, heavy-moustached Jew, well groomed, well kept, but with an unsteady, roving eye, and his shoulders a little bent in an instinctive deprecation" who tried to hold up food shipments to a starving Germany. Whatever Klotz did, though, he did as Clemenceau's subordinate. If Klotz stood publicly for high reparations, that kept the French right from attacking Clemenceau for not being tough enough on Germany. In private, Clemenceau admitted that France would never get what it hoped for and he sent Louis Loucheur, his most trusted economic adviser, to talk to the Americans in confidence about more moderate terms. In their conversations, Loucheur made it clear that he personally saw no long-term advantage for France in driving Germany into bankruptcy.[29]

Like Lloyd George, Clemenceau had to worry about public opinion.

Most French took a straightforward view. Germany had invaded Belgium, violating its own solemn undertaking to protect its neutrality, and France, not the other way around. And almost all the fighting had been on Belgian and French soil. "Who Ought to Be Ruined?" asked a headline in the conservative *Le Matin*, "France or Germany?"[30] Surely the aggressor and not the victim should pay for setting the damage right. The Americans might talk of the new diplomacy without indemnities or fines, but the old traditions where the loser customarily paid still ran strong. France had paid up in 1815, when Napoleon was finally defeated, and it had done so again after 1871. Both times Germany had collected; now it was going to pay out.

France, and Belgium, had argued from the start that claims for direct damage should receive priority in any distribution of reparations. Belgium had been picked clean. In the heavily industrialized north of France, the Germans had shipped out what they wanted for their own use and destroyed much of the rest. Even as German forces were retreating in 1918, they found time to blow up France's most important coal mines. As Clemenceau said bitterly: "The barbarians of whom history spoke took all that they found in the territories invaded by them, but destroyed nothing; they settled down to share the common existence. Now, however, the enemy had systematically destroyed everything that came in his way." Judging by captured German documents, it looked as though the Germans intended to cripple French industry and leave a clear field for their own.[31]

France and Belgium had hoped to include war costs in the final tally of reparations. Here Belgium, for once, was on firm ground: Wilson had made it clear that when he talked of Belgian restoration he meant all the harm done by Germany's initial, and illegal, invasion in August 1914. The French case was weaker. Clemenceau, who did not want to antagonize the Americans when he needed their support on the other issues so crucial to France's security, chose not to push this. He realized, although he did not say so publicly, that there was a limit to how much Germany could pay. Klotz admitted to the Foreign Affairs Commission of the French Chamber of Deputies that war costs would have produced a figure that even novelists in their wildest dreams would not come up with.[32]

The French also realized that, since Britain had spent more on the war than France, including war costs would boost the British share of whatever the Germans finally paid. The French quietly changed tack, arguing that only direct damages—for their destroyed towns and villages, their flooded coal mines, their torn-up railway lines—should be included. That would give France about 70 percent of all German payments, Britain perhaps 20 percent and other claimants—Belgium, Italy, Serbia—whatever was left. After intense bargaining, the British insisted on 30 percent, with the French getting 50 percent and the remaining 20 percent shared out among the smaller powers. It took until 1920 to get a final agreement on 28 percent for Britain and 52 percent for France.[33]

The French, it should be noticed, made the greatest concession. They were to follow a similar pattern on the total figure to be paid by Germany. Clemenceau, who always thought in terms of the overall settlement, may have set a high figure early on partly to persuade the Americans to consider the French proposals for continued Allied economic cooperation. At the end of February, when it was clear that the Americans were not interested, Loucheur came down to £8 billion ($40 billion), just over a quarter of what France had been demanding. Cunliffe, representing Britain, refused to go any lower than £9.4 billion ($47 billion). The British suspected that the French were siding with the Americans on a lower figure and leaving them to appear the most demanding. The picture painted so vividly by Keynes and others of a vindictive France, intent on grinding Germany down, begins to dissolve.[34]

In the end, mainly because of British resistance, it proved impossible to agree on a figure for the treaty. At the end of March the Allied leaders, now meeting as the Council of Four, decided on the alternative of the special commission. The postponement, one of the American experts wrote in his diary, "will relieve Great Britain and France from their troubles of making public the small amount they are to get from reparations because both Prime Ministers believe their government will be overthrown if the facts are known." He was right. By the time the commission set a final total of 132 billion gold marks (approximately £6.5 billion, or $34 billion) in 1921, emotions about Germany, especially in Britain, were cooling off.[35]

The German delegation that came to Versailles in May complained bitterly about the decision not to announce the final figures of the reparations until after the treaty had been signed. "No limit is fixed save the capacity of the German people for payment, determined not by their standard of life but solely by their capacity to meet the demands of their enemies by their labour. The German people would thus be condemned to perpetual slave labour." The emotion, given the general dismay over the terms, is understandable; the interpretation, however, unduly pessimistic. The special commission on reparations had to take into account Germany's capacity to pay; it also had to consult the Germans themselves. Furthermore, the categories of damage for which reparations were to be paid were specifically limited; not enough, perhaps, since they included pensions, but they were certainly not open-ended.[36]

Starting the section in the treaty on reparations were two articles—Articles 231 and 232—that came to be the object of particular loathing in Germany and the cause of uneasy consciences among the Allies. Article 231 assigned responsibility to Germany and its allies for all the damage caused by the war. Article 232 then restricted what was an unlimited liability by saying that since Germany's resources were in fact limited, it should be asked to pay only for the specified damages. The first clause—the war guilt clause, as it later came to be known—had been put in after much debate and many revisions, primarily to satisfy the British and the French that Germany's legal liability was clearly established. The Americans helpfully put one of their clever young lawyers on to it. John Foster Dulles, the future secretary of state, thought he had both established the liability and successfully limited it and that, on the whole, the treaty was pretty fair. The European Allies were happy with his formulation. Lloyd George, always sensitive to political considerations, said, "The English public, like the French public, thinks the Germans must above all acknowledge their obligation to compensate us for all the consequences of their aggression. When this is done we will come to the question of Germany's capacity to pay; we all think she will be unable to pay more than this document requires of her." If the Germans balked at paying a particular category of damages, Loucheur thought, the Allies could always threaten them with an unlimited claim. No one thought there would be any difficulty over the clauses themselves.[37]

Deadlock Over the German Terms

Reparations had still not been settled when Wilson arrived back in Paris on March 14—and neither had the Rhineland. The president had a quick private meeting with Lloyd George, who suggested that some sort of military guarantee, plus of course his beloved Channel tunnel, might satisfy the French. The two decided to offer to come to France's aid if Germany attacked. In return, France would have to drop its plans for a separate Rhine state. Clemenceau could be brought round, Wilson thought: "When you have hooked him, you first draw in a little, then give liberty to the line, then draw him back, finally wear him out, break him down, and land him."[1]

That afternoon Clemenceau joined the two men at the Crillon. He talked again of France's sufferings, its fears for the future, its need for Germany to stop at the Rhine. Lloyd George and Wilson produced their proposal. Clemenceau was delighted but asked for time to think it over. For two days Clemenceau and his closest advisers, including his foreign minister, Pichon, and Tardieu, mulled over the new proposal. He did not bother to consult his cabinet or Poincaré. Tardieu conceded that they would be criminal to turn it down, but there was still a problem: "A French Government satisfied with only this and nothing more would be equally guilty." France, said the official reply on March 18, needed other guarantees: an Allied occupation of the Rhineland and the bridgeheads for at least five years; no German troops there and none within fifty miles of the east bank of the river. Wilson was greatly irritated. Talking to the French was like handling a rubber ball: "You tried to make an impression but as soon as you moved your finger the ball was as round as ever." Even Balfour was moved from his customary calm. France, he told Lloyd

George, would be better off working for a strong international system, "the very possibility of which many of them regard with ill-concealed derision." Without that, "no manipulation of the Rhine frontier is going to make France anything more than a second-rate Power, trembling at the nod of its great neighbours on the East, and depending from day to day on the changes and chances of a shifting diplomacy and uncertain alliances."[2]

The next month saw memoranda and notes hurtling back and forth as the French tried to surround the Anglo-American guarantee with additional provisions. Day after day Clemenceau and his colleagues buttonholed the British and the Americans with new proposals: to enlarge the demilitarized zone on the east bank, to set up a commission of inspection with sweeping powers, or to give France the right to occupy the Rhineland if Germany violated any of the other provisions of the peace treaty, from disarmament to reparations payments.[3]

And they renewed their demand for the Saar, where the southwestern edge of the Rhineland met Alsace-Lorraine. What had been a quiet farming country with beautiful river valleys had become a major coal mining and manufacturing area in the nineteenth century. In 1919, when coal supplied almost all of Europe's fuel needs, that made the region very valuable. Inconveniently for France, almost all of the Saar's 650,000 inhabitants were German. The French tried historical arguments: the town of Saarlouis had been built by Louis XIV, the region had briefly been owned by the French during the French Revolution and the borders of 1814 gave most of it to France. "You base your claim," Wilson told Clemenceau, "on what took place a hundred and four years ago. We cannot readjust Europe on the basis of conditions that existed in such a remote period." The French did better when they spoke of reparations. Wilson had talked in his Fourteen Points about restitution to France for the damage done by Germany, and everyone agreed that the Germans had deliberately destroyed France's coalfields. The British and the American experts, who had been working privately together since February, advised that France should control the Saar's coal. The French held out for outright annexation.[4]

By the end of March, Lloyd George was seriously concerned about the way the German terms were shaping up. The French were insisting on elaborate controls of the Rhineland and annexation of the Saar. In the east, Poland was getting territory that included not only some three million Germans but also the huge coalfields in Silesia. His own public opinion appeared to be moving in favor of a rapid, reasonably moderate, peace. His military and financial experts were warning him about the costs of having large forces scattered about the globe. He was worried about labor unrest at home and about revolution in Europe. On March 21 word came in that communists had seized power in Hungary. The next day Lloyd George and several of his closest advisers, including Kerr, Hankey and Henry Wilson, took a break from negotiations over the German treaty to spend the weekend at the Hôtel de France et d'Angleterre in the charming Paris suburb of Fontainebleau. The party visited the palace with its lovely park, but its real purpose was to take a fresh look at the whole treaty and to come up with something Britain, France and the United States could accept.

That afternoon, Lloyd George called his team into his private sitting room and assigned each a role, as an ally or an enemy. As far as we know, no one played the United States. Hankey, who took Britain, argued that Germany deserved punishment and should certainly lose its colonies. The Allies, however, must not be vindictive, or they would deliver the center of Europe to the dreadful peril of Bolshevism. For the sake of Europe and its own people, Germany must be rehabilitated. It must become part of the League of Nations. This was in Britain's interest, since it did not want to keep troops on the Continent permanently. Hankey also reminded his audience that yet again the British navy had saved the country; they must look out for any threats to their seapower.

Henry Wilson threw himself into his two roles with enthusiasm. First, he turned his military cap back to front to play a German officer. "I explained my present situation, and my wish to come to an agreement with England and France, but saw no hope, for I read into the crushing terms they were imposing on me a determination on their part to kill me outright. As I could not stand alone I would turn to Russia, and in course of time would help that distracted country to recover law and order, and then make an alliance with her." Then he became a Frenchwoman, the significant factor, he said, in shaping French opinion. He painted a moving picture of "the losses of so many of their husbands, sons and men folk, the unbearable anxiety and long separations, the financial losses, and the desperate struggle and overwork to keep their homes going." Of course they wanted revenge and restitution from Germany, and they wanted assurance that Germany could never hurt them again.[5]

Lloyd George listened carefully and then gave his own views. His main point was that the peace terms must not destroy Germany. As the discussions continued, Kerr was given the job of making sense out of all this. By Monday morning, he had typed out a final draft—the Fontainebleau Memorandum. Lloyd George arrived back in Paris full of energy. "He means business this week," reported Frances Stevenson. "He will stand no more nonsense either from French or Americans. He is taking the long view about the Peace, & insists that it should be one that will not leave bitterness for years to come & probably lead to another war."[6] (She loyally overlooked his contribution to both the bitterness and the delay in drawing up the German terms.)

Lloyd George presented the memorandum to his colleagues on the Council of Four. It urged the peacemakers to make a moderate peace that would last. "You may strip Germany of her colonies, reduce her armaments to a mere police force and her navy to that of a fifth-rate power," he wrote; "all the same in the end if she feels that she has been unjustly treated in the peace of 1919 she will find means of exacting retribution from her conquerors." They must not leave Europe another poisoned legacy by placing millions of Germans or Hungarians or other minorities under alien rule. They must not stimulate the revolutionary forces burning their way through Europe. Above all, they must not drive Germany into a corner. "The greatest danger that I see in the present situation is that Germany may throw in her lot with Bolshevism and place her resources, her brains, her vast organising power at the disposal of the revolutionary fanatics whose dream it is to conquer the world for Bolshevism by force of arms." Lloyd George painted an alternative future, where Britain, the United States, France and Italy would agree to limit their naval building and their armies, and where the League of Nations, the guardian "of international right and international liberty throughout the world," would admit a new, democratic Germany, as soon as it was sufficiently stable.

How was this to be achieved? Germany should still lose territory, but not as much as some people wanted. Poland should still have its corridor to the sea, but as few Germans as possible should end up under Polish rule. The Rhineland, suitably demilitarized, should stay with Germany. Lloyd George was less categorical on the Saar; perhaps France could have the 1814 frontiers, or merely ownership of the coal mines. Germany must, of course, give up all its colonies. And, yes, it should pay reparations. Wilson approved on almost every count—after all, he could have written much of the Fontainebleau Memorandum himself. The French, however, were furious. "If you find the peace too harsh," Clemenceau wrote to Lloyd George, "let us give Germany back her colonies and her fleet, and let us not impose upon the continental nations alone—France, Belgium, Bohemia and Poland—the territorial concessions required to appease the beaten aggressor." It was, he added, "a sheer illusion" to think that Germany could be appeased by moderate terms.[7]

Illusion or not, the British were determined to disengage themselves from the Continent and its problems. A balance of power there had always served Britain well; intervention was needed only when a single nation threatened to dominate the whole. Germany had been that threat, but it would be foolish now to destroy it and leave France supreme. As passions cooled, the British remembered both their old rivalry with France and the potential for friendship between Germany and Britain. British industries needed markets; there were 70 million Germans. Britain wanted stability on the Continent, not the sort of chaos that could so clearly be seen farther east; a solid Germany at Europe's center could provide that.

In the short run, the Fontainebleau Memorandum accomplished little. The British and the French continued to squabble over their share of reparations. The French refused to produce an estimate of either their damages or what they wanted Germany to pay. "It was a crime," Wilson exclaimed to Grayson, "to waste time when every hour meant so much to the settlement of world conditions along proper lines." And yet he feared that, if he pushed his allies too hard, their governments might fall and the peace be delayed still further.[8]

Clemenceau now appeared to be hardening his position on Germany. Britain and the United States, he pointed out, were protected by the sea. "We must have an equivalent on land." He demanded the Saar and held out for a military occupation of the Rhineland. "The Germans are a servile people who need force to support an argument," he said. On March 31 he allowed Foch to present to the Council of Four an impassioned plea for a separate buffer state. "The peace," said Foch, "can only be guaranteed by the possession of the left bank of the Rhine until further notice, that is to say, as long as Germany has not had a change of heart." Lloyd George and Wilson listened politely but without paying close attention.[9]

Wilson felt the French were simply being obstructive. "I feel terribly disappointed," he told Grayson. "After arguing with Clemenceau for two hours and pushing him along, he practically agreed to everything, and just as he was leaving he swung back to where we had begun."[10] Wilson was showing the strain, but so were they all. The Council of Four was meeting virtually nonstop, the weather was frightful and the bad news kept coming in: from Hungary, where the communists were firmly in control; from Russia, where the Bolsheviks appeared to be winning the civil war; from Danzig, where the German authorities were refusing to allow Polish troops to land.

On March 28 Clemenceau yet again raised France's claim to the Saar. Wilson said, unfairly, that the French had never mentioned it as one of their war aims and that, in any case, giving it to France was contrary to the Fourteen Points. Clemenceau accused the president of being pro-German and threatened to resign rather than sign the peace treaty. Wilson said this was a deliberate lie and that it was quite clear that Clemenceau wanted him to go back to the United States. Clemenceau, equally angry, marched out of the room. He had not expected, he told Mordacq, such immovable opposition to French demands.

Lloyd George and Orlando, who had watched with consternation, did their best to smooth things over in that afternoon's meeting. Lloyd George chuckled appreciatively when Wilson replied to his apology for being late by saying, "I would hate to have to use the term the *late* Mr. Lloyd George." When Tardieu tactlessly went on at length about the ancient links between the Saar and France, Orlando pointed out that Italy, under such reasoning, could claim the lands of the former Roman empire; it would be awkward, though, for his good friend Lloyd George. Everyone laughed heartily, except Clemenceau. Lloyd George suggested a compromise: an autonomous Saar, with the French owning the coal mines. It was agreed that the experts would look into it. Clemenceau made an apology of sorts and spoke of the chains of affection that bound France to the United States; later, to his circle of advisers, he spoke of Wilson's extraordinary intransigence. Wilson made a graceful reference to the greatness of France. In private he complained bitterly that the French were holding up the whole Peace Conference. Clemenceau, he said, was like an old dog: "He turns slowly around & around, following his tail, before he gets down to it."[11]

Two days later it snowed. April in Paris that year started badly and rapidly got worse. Although the Council of Four was meeting in strictest secrecy, details of its discussions filtered out. Foch was in despair, Henry Wilson confided to his diary: "He prophesied that within a week from now the Paris Conference would crash." The rumors spread outward, "in a blue and sulphurous haze," said one American delegate. Germany would have a revolution, a Canadian wrote home. "Drifting to destruction," said the Paris edition of the *Daily Mail.* "The League of Nations is dead and the Peace Conference a failure," its correspondent cabled *The New York Times.*[12]

Wilson, said Baker, his press aide, looked "grayer & grimmer all the time." The president felt alone in his struggle to build a just peace. Lloyd George was too much the politician; Wilson longed to tell him that "he is to stay put when he agrees with me on a subject and that he is not going to be permitted to agree with me when he is with me and then to change his position after he leaves me and joins the opposition." Clemenceau had willfully refused to make a peace on the basis of the Fourteen Points. "I have never seen [Wilson] so irritated, so thoroughly in a rage," wrote Mrs. Wilson's secretary. "He characterized the attitude of the French and the delays as 'damnable.'" Wilson was maddened too by the attacks from the French press. "Just fancy," one paper had him saying, "I have discovered that Spring always follows Winter." With Lloyd George he had "a violent explosion" and said "he would never sign a French peace and would go home rather than do so."[13]

On April 3 Wilson took to his bed with a bad cold and House took his place at the Council of Four. Clemenceau was delighted: "He is *worse* today," he said to Lloyd George on April 5. "Do you know his doctor? Couldn't you get round him & bribe him?" In his sickroom, the invalid brooded. "I have been doing a lot of thinking," Wilson told Grayson, "thinking what would be the outcome on the world if these French politicians were given a free-hand and allowed to have their way and secure all that they claim France is entitled to. My opinion is that if they had their way the world would go to pieces in a very short while." He had come, he said, looking relieved, to a decision. He asked Grayson to arrange for the *George Washington* to be ready at Brest, on the Brittany coast. "I don't want to say that I am going as soon as I can get a boat; I want the boat to be here." The next day the news had leaked out, as no doubt Wilson intended it should. His threat caused a sensation. "Peace Conference at Crisis," said the *New York Times* headline.[14]

The French downplayed it. "Wilson acts like a cook," joked Clemenceau to a friend, "who keeps her trunk ready in the hallway. Every day he threatens to leave." A spokesman for the Quai d'Orsay talked rudely about "going home to mother." In fact, the French were extremely worried. The censors kept comment in the French papers to a minimum and *Le Temps,* well known to have close links to official circles, hastily printed a story saying that France had no intention of annexing any territory inhabited by Germans. Tardieu's assistant gave a statement to American correspondents saying that France had reduced its demands to a minimum and was perfectly content, as it had been all along, to accept the frontiers of 1871, which included Alsace-Lorraine but nothing more. (This caused a certain amount of amusement.[15])

These concessions came at a considerable cost politically. Deputies and senators urged Clemenceau to stand firm on France's legitimate demands. Foch inspired a press campaign demanding the occupation of the Rhineland. The generalissimo was coming perilously close to open defiance, refusing to transmit orders from the Council of Four and demanding to speak to the French cabinet. This, in a country with a lively tradition of attempted military coups, was alarming. It was also embarrassing. "I would not trust the American army," said Wilson after one incident, "to a general who does not obey his own government."[16]

Leading politicians, journalists and soldiers went to warn Poincaré that France was heading for disaster. Clemenceau was throwing away any chance of security against Germany. Perhaps Poincaré should resign in protest. Or was it his duty, as Foch and others urged, to use his powers under the constitution to take over the negotiations himself? Poincaré, as was typical of him, joined the criticism but hesitated to take action. Clemenceau, whose sources of information were always good, came to the Elysée Palace and made a tremendous scene, accusing the president of disloyalty. "All your friends are against me," he shouted. "I have had enough. I am in discussions every day, from morning to night. I am killing myself." He offered his resignation. Poincaré protested: "I have never stopped being loyal, that goes without saying; but, beyond that, I have been devoted, and, to say the word, filial." Clemenceau accused him of lying. Poincaré responded with outrage. "Well, you see," Clemenceau shot back, "you reply to me with insolence!" Somehow, at the end of the interview the two shook hands. Poincaré said in a statesmanlike manner, "Circumstances are serious, the future is dark, it is essential that the public officials are united." He immediately poured out his feelings in his diary. "In brief, this conversation showed me a Clemenceau who is scatterbrained, violent, conceited, bullying, sneering, dreadfully superficial, deaf physically and intellectually, incapable of reasoning, reflecting, of following a discussion."[17]

Only Lloyd George remained cheerful throughout the crisis. "We have made great progress," he told the newspaper magnate George Riddell. "We have settled practically all outstanding questions with the exception of that relating to breaches of the Laws of War. We shall begin next week to draft the Peace Treaty." He expected that the final peace terms would be drawn up in time for Easter Sunday, two weeks away. Lloyd George was particularly pleased that he had carried his point on reparations: the final figure would not be in the treaty.[18]

When Wilson was on his feet again on April 8, spring had finally arrived and the mood at the Peace Conference was markedly better. He was still rather "wabbly," he told Grayson, but he felt "very much better in his mind." Wilson found it useful, however, to keep the threat of the *George Washington* in reserve.[19] In his absence, much of the groundwork had been laid for the subsequent agreements. The Saar was finally settled on April 13. The experts had come up with a compromise under which France got ownership only of the mines. The League of Nations took over the Saar's administration with a commitment to hold a plebiscite after fifteen years, when the inhabitants could decide between independence, France and Germany. (In 1935 the attraction of Hitler's new Reich proved overwhelming and 90 percent of them voted to rejoin Germany.)

The package with the Rhineland and the Anglo-American guarantee to

France took only slightly longer to work out. Wilson, who felt that he had gone quite far enough in offering a guarantee, sent a stern message to Clemenceau on April 12 saying that he would have to settle for a demilitarized Rhineland and not a permanent Allied occupation. Clemenceau thought it over and two days later called on his old friend House. It was a pity, he said, that the conference was in crisis. The Italians (as we shall see) were threatening to leave without signing the German treaty. He himself was prepared, of course, to work with his colleagues. He accepted the American position, although it was not what he wanted, and he would fight Foch on it. In return, he asked only that Wilson accept a temporary French occupation of three zones around the main bridgeheads: the French would evacuate the first zone, in the north Rhineland (including the bridgehead around Cologne), after five years, the second zone, in the middle (including the bridgehead around Koblenz), after ten years, and the third, in the south (including the bridgehead around Mainz), after fifteen years.[20]

By April 15 the eczema on Clemenceau's hands was noticeably worse and he complained of dizzy spells. That evening, after House brought the news that Wilson had agreed to the temporary occupation, he was a different man. "I am no longer worried," he told Mordacq. "All the big questions concerning France are now almost settled. In another ten days, we will have, very probably, decided on the main lines of the treaty. Today, in particular, apart from the two treaties bringing military aid from America and England in case of a German attack, I obtained definitively the occupation of the Rhineland for fifteen years with a partial evacuation from five years to five years. Of course, in the case of Germany's not observing the treaty, no partial evacuation, no final evacuation." Cheerfully, he promised House a favor in return. Clemenceau told his private secretary that all attacks in the French press on Wilson must stop at once. The next day, even normally hostile papers were filled with praise of the president.[21]

When he arrived back from London, having triumphantly disposed of his parliamentary opposition, Lloyd George was annoyed. "Provocative incidents," he wrote years later, "are the inevitable consequence of any occupation of territory by foreign troops. The irritating and occasionally odious accompaniments of such an occupation of German towns by troops, some of whom were coloured, had much to do with the fierce outbreak of patriotic sentiment in Germany which finds its expression in Nazism." With some reluctance he agreed to the Rhineland clauses on April 22.[22]

On April 25 Clemenceau took the Rhineland clauses to his own cabinet, where he had to listen to heated criticism from Foch and others. Poincaré, to everyone's surprise, merely asked for clarification of certain points. "He is the leading critic in the republic," Clemenceau told Mordacq, "but all the times that I asked his advice on the innumerable delicate questions which we have been dealing with for three months and still are dealing with, I got only vague replies." The cabinet approved the deal unanimously and on May 4 it approved the peace terms as a whole, also unanimously. Foch said bitterly that Clemenceau was a criminal. Poincaré contemplated resigning, but, as so often before, thought better of it.[23]

Clemenceau always thought he had got the best possible deal for France, and he was right. He had won more from his allies than they had originally been prepared to give; he had kept the alliance with Britain and the United States alive; he had given France another measure of safety in the demilitarization and fifteen-year occupation of the Rhineland; and he had tied the ending of that occupation to Germany's fulfilling the other parts of the treaty. As he told the Chamber of Deputies in September 1919, during the debate on ratification, "The treaty, with all its complex clauses, will only be worth what you are worth; it will be what you make it. . . . What you are going to vote today is not even a beginning, it is a beginning of a beginning. The ideas it contains will grow and bear fruit. You have won the power to impose them on a defeated Germany."[24] The difficulty was always going to be enforcement. As Clemenceau's successors, among them Poincaré, discovered, France could do little without British and American support. That support was not there in the 1920s, and in the 1930s there was no Clemenceau to rally a demoralized France against the Nazi menace in Germany.

PART FIVE

BETWEEN EAST AND WEST

17

Poland Reborn

THE REBIRTH OF POLAND was one of the great stories of the Paris Peace Conference. It was also a source of endless difficulties. The commission on the borders of the new Poland had more meetings than any other at the conference. Should they be drawn to punish Germany for past wrongs and present defeat? Should there be a large Poland to act as a barrier against Bolshevism? What did it need for survival? Coal mines? Iron? Railways? A proper port on the Baltic? Wilson had promised, in the thirteenth of his Fourteen Points, that a reconstituted Poland should have "free and secure access to the sea": as with so many of his points, the meaning was elastic. He talked, too, of giving Poland territory "indisputably" Polish. Finding indisputable territory of any kind in central Europe was never easy. The Poles made matters worse by disagreeing among themselves over whether they wanted their new country to encompass the farthest reaches of their past glory (in which case they would find themselves with a great many non-Poles) or to limit itself to the Polish heartland (which would leave many Poles living outside the country). The peacemakers were reaching out hundreds of miles from Paris to impose order on a protean world of shifting allegiances, civil wars, refugees and bandit gangs, where the collapse of old empires had left law and order, trade and communications in shreds.

A couple of days before the Allied armistice with Germany, a grizzled Polish soldier with fierce blue eyes in a thin pale face had read the proposed terms with anguish and frustration. There was no mention of Poland and he was in a German jail. Józef Piłsudski had spent much of his life trying to re-create a country that had disappeared at the end of the eighteenth century. Now, with the destruction of its great enemies—Austria-

Hungary, Germany and Russia—Poland's chance had come. Germany's collapse gave Piłsudski back his freedom; on November 10, 1918, he arrived in the old Polish capital of Warsaw. Poland itself was a dream, not a reality. It had few friends but many enemies, no clearly defined borders, no government, no army, no bureaucracy. In the next three years Piłsudski made a country.

Piłsudski was probably the only man who could have survived and triumphed on such a mission. He had, in a way, been training for it all his life. He was born into the Russian part of Poland, in the town of Vilna (Polish: Wilno; now Vilnius, in Lithuania). His mother read him the Polish literature that the Russian censors had outlawed. She taught him the history of his tragic country, from the great days of the sixteenth and seventeenth centuries, when the Polish-Lithuanian commonwealth stretched from the Baltic almost to the Black Sea and included much of what later became Germany and Russia, and when Polish republican government, Polish learning, Polish cities were the admiration of Europe; to the partitions of the 1790s, when Poland vanished into the hands of its neighbors. He learned about the repeated hopeless uprisings, the executions, the imprisonments, the long lines of exiles sent off to Siberia and the attempts to root out Polish culture. From 1795, Poland had existed only in the memories of its patriots, in the work of its great writers and composers.

It had looked, to most rational observers, as though the passage of time was setting the division forever. The Poles of Germany, perhaps 3 million out of a total population of 56 million, shared in the prosperity of one of the most developed nations of Europe. They kept something of their language, but culturally, they were increasingly German.[1] The Poles of Austria-Hungary, concentrated in Austrian Galicia, lagged far behind. Corrupt, poor, the most backward part of a decaying empire, Galicia was a byword for misery. Those who could, emigrated, many of them to North America. The rest of Europe's Poles, about half the total number, lived under Russian rule, the most brutal, oppressive and incompetent of all.

Piłsudski, like other Polish boys in Russia, was forbidden to speak his language. Although a Catholic, like the overwhelming majority of Poles, he was forced to attend Orthodox services. He became a radical socialist, which raised apprehensions among the peacemakers about a Bolshevik Poland, but he was above all a nationalist. The day after he arrived back in Warsaw after the armistice, his old socialist friends came to see him and made the mistake of calling him comrade. "Gentlemen," he told them, "we both took a ride on the same red tram, but while I got off at the stop marked *Polish Independence,* you wish to travel on to the station *Socialism.* Bon voyage—but be so kind as to call me *Sir!*"[2]

Temperament and experience had made Piłsudski a lone wolf who found it difficult to trust anyone. He was arrested for the first time in 1887, for participating in a plot organized by Lenin's older brother to assassinate the tsar, and sent to Siberia for five years. (Lenin's brother was executed.) In 1900 he was arrested again, but escaped by feigning madness. He spent the years before the war in the socialist underground, as an organizer and fund-raiser. (He robbed banks and mail trains.) He married a fellow conspirator, but the marriage collapsed when he started an affair with a younger woman in the underground.[3]

When the war started, the Poles were caught in the middle, some fighting for Austria-Hungary and Germany, others for Russia. Sometimes they could hear Polish songs coming from the enemy trenches. Piłsudski threw in his lot with Austria-Hungary, yet another black mark against him in Paris. His calculation was quite straightforward: Russia was the chief obstacle to Polish hopes. When Russia collapsed in 1917 and Austria-Hungary grew shakier, he watched with alarm; the last thing he wanted was a powerful Germany. He refused to put his Polish Legions under German command and ended up in prison again.[4]

On his return to Warsaw in 1918, Piłsudski, who with his Legions possessed one of the few coherent forces left in central Europe, seized power from the German occupation authorities in the name of Poland. "It is impossible," said a Polish politician, "to express all the excitement and fever of enthusiasm which gripped Polish society at this moment. After one hundred and twenty years the cordons broke. 'They' are gone! Freedom! Independence! Our own statehood!" One noble family brought out wine from 1772, the date of the first partition, which they had kept to toast this moment. ("Strange to say it was drinkable," reported an English diplomat.[5])

Piłsudski had many opponents: conservatives afraid of his socialism, liberals who disliked his enthusiasm for violence, and those who looked to the Allies, even Russia, for help. Their spokesman was his great rival, Roman Dmowksi. Where Piłsudski came from the gentry, Dmowski was a poor boy from the city. A biologist, he loved science, reason and logic. Music, he told the great Polish pianist Paderewski, was "mere noise." He despised grandiose schemes, noble posturing and futile gestures, all of which he felt Polish nationalism had seen far too much of. He wanted Poles to become modern and businesslike. He had little nostalgia for the old Poland, for its tradition of religious tolerance or its attempts to compromise with other nationalities such as Lithuanians or Ukrainians or Jews. Like the Social Darwinists he admired, he held that life was struggle. The strong won and the weak lost. He was generally admired in western

Europe, although the British had reservations. "He was a clever man," said a diplomat who had to deal with him, "and clever men are distrusted: he was logical in his political theories, and we hate logic: and he was persistent with a tenacity which was calculated to drive everybody mad."[6]

Dmowski's Polish National Committee in Paris claimed to speak for the Poles, and in 1918 the French government agreed that an army of Polish exiles in France commanded by General Józef Haller should come under its control. When the war ended, Poland had two potential governments, one in Paris and one in Warsaw, and two rival leaders, each with his own armed forces. In contrast, the Czechs were already speaking with a single, clear voice.

Outsiders wondered whether Poland would make it. In 1919, all its borders were in question and there were enemies everywhere: the surviving units of the German army, many of them to the east, and Russians (Bolshevik or anti-Bolshevik, none wanted an independent Poland) and other nationalists competing for the same territory: Lithuanians in the north, Ukrainians to the east, and Czechs and Slovaks to the south. And Poland had few natural defenses. Between 1918 and 1920, Piłsudski was to fight six different wars. He also had to watch his back, with supporters of Dmowksi to his right and radicals to the left.

Piłsudski grew thinner and paler and more intense. He worked frantically, often through the night, keeping himself awake with endless tea and cigarettes. In those early months he often walked across from the palace he had commandeered to eat a simple meal alone in a cheap restaurant. His task was appalling. As much as 10 percent of Poland's wealth had been destroyed in the war. The Germans had ransacked the Polish territories during their occupation. Raw materials, manufactured goods, factories, machinery, even church bells had been fed into the German war effort. "I have nowhere seen anything like the evidences of extreme poverty and wretchedness that meet one's eye at almost every turn," wrote a British diplomat who arrived in Warsaw at the beginning of 1919. Piłsudski had to weld together different economies, different laws and different bureaucracies. He had to rationalize nine separate legislative systems. He had to reduce five different currencies to one, and he did not have even the means to print banknotes. Railways were a nightmare, with 66 kinds of rails, 165 types of locomotives and a patchwork of signaling systems.[7]

He was dealing too with a people whose ambitions, after a century of frustration, now far outstripped their strength. "The Poles are developing an appetite like a freshly hatched sparrow," reported a German emissary less than a month after the armistice. There was talk of the frontiers of 1772, when Poland included most of today's Lithuania and Belarus and much of Ukraine. In Paris, Dmowksi and his Polish National Committee promoted a huge Poland to act as a check on both Germany and Bolshevism. Their Poland would have significant minorities of Germans, Ukrainians, Byelorussians, Lithuanians—40 percent of the total population—all ruled firmly by the Poles. While Dmowski talked the language of self-determination to the Allies, there was to be no such nonsense at home.[8]

Piłsudski was more cautious. He, too, wanted a strong Poland but he was prepared to accept less than Dmowski. He was also willing to contemplate a federation, in which the Lithuanians, perhaps, or the Ukrainians, would work with Poles as equals. He recognized that he needed some help from the Allies. "All that we can gain in the west depends on the Entente, on the extent to which it may wish to squeeze Germany." In the east, the situation was different. "Here there are doors which open and close and it depends on who will force them open and how far."[9]

On one thing, though, all Poles agreed: the need for access to the Baltic. They were putting up with great hardships, reported an American officer from Warsaw, because they could foresee Poland being a great power again, with its trade flowing along the Vistula and the railways which ran to the sea. It was essential not to take that hope away: "Their confidence in the future rudely shaken, the acuteness of the present becomes more sharply defined and their patriotism is shaken to the foundation. Without this future why should they continue to resist Bolshevism?" Danzig, at the mouth of the Vistula, was the obvious choice for a port. It had once been a great free city under Polish rule. The Amsterdam of the East, people had called it, with its prosperous trade, its rich merchants and its elegant buildings. Since the 1790s, however, it had been under German rule. In 1919 its population was over 90 percent German, although much of the surrounding countryside was heavily Polish.[10]

The Allies agreed before the Peace Conference that Poland should be independent. The British, however, were not prepared to invest much to achieve this, since they had little national interest at stake. They also feared, with some reason, that Poland could become a liability. Who would defend it if its neighbors, Germany and Russia in particular, attacked? Moreover, the British did not particularly care for either Polish faction. Piłsudski had fought against them and was a dangerous radical. Dmowski and the Polish National Committee were too right-wing. "In fact the prevailing opinion," said a British diplomat in Warsaw, "which to a great extent influenced me at the time seemed to be that to do anything the Polish Committee asked for would be to fasten upon Poland a regime of wicked landlords who spent most of their time in riotous living, and establish there a Chauvinist Government whose object was to acquire territories inhabited by non-Polish populations." Dmowski did not help himself when he was in Britain during the war by making remarks, as he did, for example, at a dinner given by G. K. Chesterton, that "my religion came from Jesus Christ, who was murdered by the Jews." The British, who had their share of anti-Semitism, found him crude. Distinguished British Jews protested to the government about its dealings with the Polish National Committee. In the Foreign Office, Lewis Namier, himself of Polish and Jewish origin, waged a campaign against Dmowski and "his chauvinist gang."[11]

The French, by contrast, were not only great supporters of Dmowski; they took a profound interest in Poland. In the autumn of 1917 Pichon publicly promised France's support for an independent Poland, "a big and strong, very strong" Poland, several months before either Britain or the United States. French policy toward Poland was a mixture of the practical and the romantic. France no longer had Russia to counterbalance Germany, but a strong Poland, allied perhaps to Czechoslovakia and Rumania, could fill that role. Poland for the French was also memories of Maria Walewska, the beautiful mistress of Napoleon (their son had become foreign minister of France), of sad Polish exiles in Paris, of Frédéric Chopin, the lover of their own George Sand, of the Polish volunteers fighting for France against Prussia in 1870. Poland was a cause both for devout Catholics and good liberals. As a schoolboy, Clemenceau had chatted with Poles escaping tsarist repression. "Poland will live again," he wrote in his newspaper on the outbreak of the Great War. "One of the greatest crimes of history is going to be undone." During the war, the French gave money to Polish relief; during the Peace Conference, they ate dinners in Poland's honor.[12]

The United States lay somewhere in between. It too had memories of Poles: Tadeusz Kościuszko, a hero in the American War of Independence; the Poles on both sides in the Civil War; Paderewski packing the concert halls. By 1914, Poles were the largest single group of immigrants from Central Europe, perhaps 4 million of them, with their own newspapers, schools, churches and votes. The war awoke their latent patriotism but it also created divisions between pro-Allied and pro-German Poles, giving the impression that Poles were always quarreling with each other. But Americans were moved by the sufferings of Poland, just as they were by those of Belgium. Wilson gradually came around to supporting an independent Poland but he was noncommittal on its borders. "I saw M. Dmowski and M. Paderewski in Washington," he told his fellow peacemakers in Paris, "and I asked them to define Poland for me, as they understood it, and they presented me with a map in which they claimed a large part of the earth."[13]

When the French tried to get Dmowski's Polish National Committee recognized as the only representative of the Polish people, the British and Americans held back. They urged Dmowksi to build a coalition with Piłsudski. The world's most famous Pole, Ignace Paderewski, undertook to bring the two men together. In December 1918, the British arranged for him to travel back to Poland on HMS *Condor.* (He played the old ward-room piano for the officers on Christmas Eve.) His arrival in Posen (Poznan) on Christmas Day, 1918, produced immense excitement. Street demonstrations turned violent, and by the time he left for Warsaw on New Year's Day, Posen had risen against its German rulers. In the hand of a huge bronze statue of the great German chancellor Bismarck, a wit placed a fourth-class ticket to Berlin.[14]

Paderewski came from a modest family in Austrian Galicia, where his father worked for a great aristocratic landowner. "A remarkable man, a very remarkable man," the prince later reminisced to Nicolson. "Do you realise that he was born in one of my own villages? Actually at Chepe-towka? And yet, when I speak to him, I have absolutely the impression of conversing with an equal."[15] Paderewski became an international star. Burne-Jones sketched him, George Bernard Shaw praised his musical in-telligence, and women sent him love letters by the hundreds.

Voluble, untidy, he was a man of great learning with the open enthusi-asm of a child. During the war he had vowed not to perform until Poland was free again. He devoted himself to raising money for Polish relief and lobbying the world's leaders. In the summer of 1916 he played, Chopin of course, at a private party at the White House. "I wish you could have heard Paderewski's speeches for his country," Wilson told a colleague later, "he touched chords more sublime than when he moved thousands as he com-manded harmony from the piano." Paderewski's supporters later claimed that his efforts were responsible for Wilson's inclusion of Poland in his Fourteen Points.[16]

At their first meeting in Warsaw, Paderewski, the man of the world in his long fur coat, and Piłsudski, the thin pale revolutionary in his shabby tunic, circled each other with suspicion. Piłsudski needed both Paderew-ski's influence over the Polish National Committee in Paris and his con-tacts, while Paderewski wanted a Poland that spoke with one voice. The two men agreed that Piłsudski would remain head of state and com-mander-in-chief of the armed forces and Paderewski would become prime minister at the head of a coalition government as well as Poland's delegate to the Peace Conference alongside Dmowski. Together they attended the celebrations, dinners, plays, even a mass in Warsaw Cathedral, to mark the opening of Poland's newly elected parliament. Dmowski and Piłsudski remained as far apart as ever.[17]

Paderewski was still in Warsaw when the Peace Conference opened, so only Dmowski was on hand when Poland first came up at the Supreme Council in January. Piłsudski had sent an urgent request for supplies, particularly weapons and ammunition, to help Poland hold off its enemies. The French suggested sending back the Polish army in France under General Haller. The easiest way to do this, said Foch, was to ship the men to Danzig, still under German control, and then down the railway to Warsaw. The British and the Americans were doubtful. Haller's army was in Dmowski's camp; its return to Poland might well produce civil war. Wilson saw another danger in using Danzig: "With the object of sending Polish troops into Poland we were going to prejudge the whole Polish question." This, of course, was exactly what the French had in mind. When the Germans got wind of the proposal, they protested loudly. The army finally went back by land in April. Piłsudski did not press very hard for its return. He had no wish to irritate the Allies even further by insisting on the Danzig route as Dmowski was doing; he probably did not care passionately about Danzig itself.[18]

On January 29, Dmowski was invited to explain to the Supreme Council what was happening in Poland. He took the opportunity to outline Poland's claims, or at least the ones he supported. He was not, he said, going to claim everything Poland had once possessed. Parts of Lithuania and the Ukraine no longer had a Polish character. Poland was, however, quite willing to help them out since they were a long way from being able to manage their own affairs. On the other hand, Poland should take possession of the eastern part of Germany. True, much of this had never been Polish, but there were a great many Poles living there, far more than the German statistics indicated. "These Poles were some of the most educated and highly cultured of the nation, with a strong sense of nationality and men of progressive ideas." Even the local Germans looked up to them. Poland also needed the coalfields of Silesia and Teschen (Polish: Cieszyn; Czech: Těšín). Lloyd George listened with obvious impatience and Wilson studied the paintings on the walls.[19]

The Poles had a knack for irritating even their friends in Paris. People joked that when an Englishman wrote a book on the elephant, he dealt with its habitat and how to hunt it; a German wrote a treatise on its biology; but the Pole started with "The elephant is a Polish question." Even the French were alarmed by the extent of Polish demands in Russia, which, after all, might be an ally again one day. The British and the Americans complained about the rival delegations. Polish actions on the ground also raised suspicions. "The Poles," said Balfour, "were using the interval between the cessation of war and the decisions of the Peace Congress to make good their claims to districts outside Russian Poland, to which in many cases they had little right, although in others their claims were amply justified." Wilson agreed: moreover, the Rumanians, the Serbs and the Hungarians were doing exactly the same thing. Piłsudski was moving troops into German territory around Posen, north into Lithuania and south to Galicia. The difficulty was how to stop him. The Allies could withhold supplies, but they had not yet sent much anyway. They could threaten, but they had very little real power in the center of Europe. Indeed, they had been obliged to keep German troops in place along the frontier with Russia. They also hesitated to come down too hard on the Poles. As Wilson said in May when the Council of Four was considering, yet again, ways of getting the Polish army to stop attacking the Ukrainians, "If Paderewski falls and we cut off food supplies to Poland, won't Poland herself become Bolshevik? Paderewski's government is like a dike against disorder, and perhaps the only one possible." If the dike went, who could tell how far west the Bolshevik current might flow?

The peacemakers sent plaintive telegrams and fact-finding missions. "Action undertaken without further knowledge," said Lloyd George sagely, "might lead to a mess." They sent military experts, the French with a young Colonel Charles de Gaulle in their number, the British led by the war hero General Adrian Carton de Wiart. With only one arm, one eye and one foot, he impressed the Poles deeply with his complete disregard of danger and his willingness to fight duels.[20]

Otherwise the peacemakers left Polish matters largely to the experts. In February, the Supreme Council established a Commission on Polish Affairs, to receive the reports coming in from Poland. Two weeks later, Balfour, who was hoping to speed up the work of the Peace Conference in the absence of Wilson and Lloyd George, discovered that nothing was being done about Poland's borders. On his suggestion, the Polish commission took on the job. Its members, in the absence of any detailed instructions, assumed that they should base their decisions on ethnic factors and on Wilson's promise of access to the sea.[21] This was nearly impossible.

Poland's lack of natural barriers had let invaders in over the centuries; it had also let Poles flow out. In the east, Polish settlers had pushed north and south of the great forests and marshes lying across the border of what is today Belarus and Ukraine. The result was like a crescent moon, with a heavily Polish area around Vilna on its northern end, another around Lvov

(German: Lemberg; Polish: Lwów; today, Lviv in the Ukraine) in the south. In the north, Poles mingled with Lithuanians and Germans. In the middle, said one of the experts in Paris, was a huge region "with its enigmatic population, which may be White Russian or Ukrainian, but is certainly not Polish."[22] The towns were Polish or Jewish (many Jews identified with the Poles) and in the country there was a thin sprinkling of Polish landowners.

In the west there was a similar ethnic jumble. For centuries, the Poles had been pushing north to the Baltic, and the Germans had been moving eastward. Along the eastern shores of the Baltic the cities were largely German. In the countryside the big landowners were usually German—the Baltic Barons, as they were known—although toward the south some were Polish and Lithuanian. A Polish majority lay along the banks of the Vistula. East Prussia, tucked in the southeast corner of the Baltic, was largely German-speaking and Protestant. If Poland got access to the sea, should it have control of both the banks of the Vistula and of Danzig itself? That would leave hundreds of thousands of Germans living under Polish rule and perhaps cut off the land route from the western part of Germany to East Prussia.

Statistics were as unreliable as they were elsewhere in the center of Europe. In any case, even the inhabitants of that part of the world were not always sure who they were. Was identity religious or linguistic? Did Polish-speaking Protestants, a significant group in the southern part of East Prussia, identify with their coreligionists, who were German, or with the Poles, who were Catholic? Were Lithuanians a separate nationality or a variety of Pole? Were Ukrainians really Russian?

In the Polish commission the British and the American experts, meeting informally as they did on most matters, agreed that Poland's boundaries should be drawn on ethnic lines as much as possible but that other factors, such as access to the Baltic, control of railways or strategic considerations also had to be taken into account. The French, who were headed by the wise old diplomat Jules Cambon, generally accepted this but, when it came to disputes, were invariably for giving Poland the benefit of the doubt. Poland, they said, must have borders that could be defended against Germany and Russia even if that meant including non-Poles. The Italians generally sided with the French. The Japanese, as usual, said little.[23]

The commission produced its first report, on Poland's borders with Germany, which were going to be dealt with in the German treaty, a few days after Wilson arrived back from the United States. The experts had tried to keep rivers and lakes in one country, to make sure that railways did not wander back and forth across international borders, and to leave as few

Poles and Germans as possible on the wrong sides. In the end, Poland would have its access to the Baltic thanks to a long arm that would reach northward along the Vistula. The arm—the Polish Corridor, as it came to be called—would bend westward at the elbow to bring in the largely Polish province around Posen. East Prussia, with the port of Königsberg (where Kant had lived), would remain German. Almost two million Germans would end up under Polish rule. Only Allenstein (Polish: Olsztyn), the part of East Prussia nearest Poland, with its Polish-speaking Protestants, would have a plebiscite. When it was finally held in 1920, 363,000 to 8,000 voted to stay with East Prussia.

The Supreme Council considered the report on March 19, at a meeting that also addressed the fighting between Poles and Ukrainians. (More telegrams were sent out, ordering both sides to stop.) Lloyd George thought the recommendations generally good. He had only one question: "Was it necessary to assign so much German territory, together with the port of Dantzig?" He noticed that there was a district called Marienwerder, about fifty miles south of Danzig and abutting East Prussia, which had a clear German majority. Surely its inhabitants should be allowed to vote on their future? The proposed corridor was not fair, he went on; worse, it was dangerous. Germany might well decide not to sign such a treaty. "He feared that this demand, added to many others which would have to be made on Germany, would produce deplorable results on German public opinion. The Allies should not run the risk of driving the country to such desperation that no Government would dare to sign the terms." Were they not creating fresh Alsace-Lorraines and the seeds of future wars by leaving large numbers of Germans in Poland? The Poles, he added unkindly, did not have a high reputation as administrators. The commission was told to reconsider its report.[24]

Many Poles, both then and later, were convinced that Lloyd George had it in for them, perhaps because he wanted to appease Germany or even Bolshevik Russia, perhaps because he had an irrational hatred of all small nations. He was unprincipled and arrogant, overriding his own experts. He was also shockingly uninformed, for example about the amounts of traffic carried on the Vistula. Dmowski said baldly that Lloyd George was "the agent of the Jews." He spoke for all who believed that the British prime minister was the tool of sinister capitalist forces opposed to a strong Poland.[25]

Like most liberals, Lloyd George in fact sympathized strongly with Poland's sufferings. He liked and admired Paderewski, whom he saw socially during the Peace Conference. But he thought that some of the Polish demands were unreasonable and dangerous, creating enemies for

Poland and trouble for Europe. As Kerr wrote on his behalf to the British embassy in Warsaw, "Mr. Lloyd George has always said that the real thing for Poland was a settlement which both the German people and the Russian people would recognise to be just." It was true, as the Poles charged, that Lloyd George was preoccupied with getting the German treaty signed. This was not unreasonable. It was also true that Lloyd George had little faith that Poland would survive. This also was not unreasonable.[26]

When Lloyd George produced his memorandum on the German treaty after his weekend in Fontainebleau, he reiterated that Poland must have access to the sea but warned against placing over 2 million Germans under Polish rule. "My conclusion," he told the Council of Four on March 27, "is that we must not create a Poland alienated from the time of its birth by an unforgettable quarrel from its most civilized neighbour." Make Danzig itself a free city and draw the corridor to leave, as far as possible, Poles in Poland and Germans in Germany. Clemenceau, who wanted Poland to have Danzig outright and a generous corridor, attacked Lloyd George's reasoning. Let the Germans complain, he said. "We remember the children whipped for having prayed to God in Polish, peasants expropriated, driven from their lands to make room for occupants of the German race." Poland deserved recompense and needed the means to live again.[27]

Wilson said little in the meeting but he was coming to share Lloyd George's concern. He may also have been thinking of another issue that needed to be resolved: the dispute with Italy, which we will return to later, over Fiume. If he gave Danzig to the Poles, he might have to give Fiume to the Italians. The two men met privately and decided that Danzig should be an independent city and that Marienwerder in the corridor should also decide its own fate by plebiscite. On April 1 they persuaded a reluctant Clemenceau to agree. Lloyd George was reassuring; as Danzig's economic ties with Poland strengthened, its inhabitants would turn like sunflowers toward Warsaw, in just the same way, he expected, as the inhabitants of the Saar would eventually realize that their true interests lay with France and not Germany. The Poles were enraged when they heard the news. "Danzig is indispensable to Poland," said Paderewski, "which cannot breathe without its window on the sea." According to Clemenceau, who saw him privately, he wept. "Yes," said Wilson unsympathetically, "but you must take account of his sensitivity, which is very lively." The fact that "our troublesome friends the Poles," as Wilson called them, were continuing to fight around Lvov despite repeated calls from Paris for a cease-fire did not help Poland's cause.[28]

Under the revised terms of the treaty with Germany, the Polish Corridor shrank. A plebiscite was eventually held in Marienwerder, and its population voted overwhelmingly to join Germany. That left one of the railway lines joining Warsaw and Danzig under German control. Danzig itself became a free city under the League of Nations in a customs union with Poland. Poland and Germany were to sign a separate treaty, which they duly did, guaranteeing that Poland would have all the facilities it needed for its trade, from docks to telephones. A high commissioner, appointed by the League, would act as arbiter in cases of disputes. There were, unfortunately, plenty of these: over who controlled the harbor police, over taxes, even over whether Poland was allowed to set up its own mailboxes. Much of the trouble arose because Danzig, its industry, its administration and its population, remained very German. The corridor, too, produced friction; there were quarrels over the railways and, of course, over the fate of the Germans still living there and elsewhere in Poland. Germany never really accepted its loss of territory, and virtually all Germans, good liberals or right-wing nationalists, regarded Poland with contempt.[29] In September 1939, as he had promised, Hitler broke yet another of the links in what he called the chains of Versailles, and sent his troops storming across the border to seize Danzig and the corridor. In 1945, Poland got it back again, as Gdańsk. There are no longer any Germans living there and the city itself has fallen on hard times as its shipbuilding has languished.

Then there was the problem of Upper Silesia, an area of about 11,000 square kilometers (4,200 square miles) where Poland's borders met Germany's in the south. It was a rich prize, with mines and iron and steel mills. The Commission on Polish Affairs had awarded it to Poland on the grounds that about 65 percent of its inhabitants were Polish-speaking. The Germans protested. The Silesian mines were responsible for almost a quarter of Germany's annual output of coal, 81 percent of its zinc and 34 percent of its lead. The German government argued that the award also violated the principle of self-determination: the people of Upper Silesia were German and Czech and the local Poles, whose dialect was heavily influenced by German, had never demonstrated the slightest interest in the Polish cause. Upper Silesia had been separated from Poland for centuries; its prosperity owed everything to German industry and German capital. Poland already had enough coal; Germany, particularly with the loss of the Saar, did not. "Germany cannot spare Upper Silesia; Poland does not need it." If Germany lost Upper Silesia, the German note concluded, it would not be able to fulfill its other obligations under the treaty.[30]

On May 30 Lloyd George had his old friend Riddell, the newspaper magnate, to dinner. "Just read that," he said, handing him the note, "and tell me what you think of it." To get Riddell in the mood, he put a roll of Chopin into his player piano. When Riddell argued that there were strategic considerations for giving Upper Silesia to Poland, Lloyd George agreed but pointed out the threat to reparations. "If the Poles won't give the Germans the products of the mines on reasonable terms, the Germans say they cannot pay the indemnity. Therefore the Allies may be cutting off their noses to spite their faces if they hand the mines to the Poles without regard to the question of the indemnity." The two men went off to a singsong in Balfour's flat upstairs.[31]

The next day, Lloyd George brought key cabinet members over from London for an emergency meeting. On June 1, the British empire delegation authorized him to go back to the Council of Four and ask for modifications in the terms on reparations, on the Rhineland occupation and on Upper Silesia. Smuts was particularly firm on the need to revise the German-Polish borders. "Poland was an historic failure, and always would be a failure, and in this Treaty we were trying to reverse the verdict of history." He also said privately that putting Germans under Polish rule was as bad as handing them over to a lot of kaffirs. Balfour thought Smuts a bit hard on Poland, but agreed, as did everyone else, that there should be a plebiscite in Upper Silesia.[32]

Lloyd George's colleagues in the Council of Four did not relish changing the terms, which had taken so long to put together. In an acrimonious meeting on June 3, Clemenceau categorically opposed a plebiscite. Although Poles were in a majority, they could not possibly vote freely when the local administration was still German. Wilson agreed. His experts told him that the big landowners and capitalists were all German. Well then, said Lloyd George, the Allies would have to bring in troops to supervise the voting. It would be a small price to pay if it avoided trouble with Germany over the treaty. "It is better to send an American or English division to Upper Silesia than an army to Berlin." He quoted self-determination at the president. Wilson, who was fair-minded, began to back down. Clemenceau, considerably disturbed, saw no alternative but to do the same. A plebiscite would take place, but not until the Allies were convinced that it could be held fairly. Paderewski protested, to no avail. "Don't forget," Lloyd George said sharply, "your liberty was paid for with the blood of other peoples, and truly, if Poland, in these circumstances, should revolt against our decisions, she would be something quite other than we had hoped."[33]

Arranging the plebiscite took months, partly because the situation in Upper Silesia was deteriorating as Poles rose up against the Germans, partly because the Allies had trouble finding the troops. There were also disagreements over whether only those actually living in Silesia could vote (the choice of the Polish government) or whether former residents could vote as well (as the Germans preferred). The German government won that argument and on a Sunday in March 1921, as trainloads of German Silesians rolled in to the sound of band music, the vote finally took place. The north and west chose Germany, the south Poland, and the middle, which with all its industry was what both Poland and Germany wanted, divided almost evenly. Further months of negotiations, with the British backing Germany and the French Poland, produced only deadlock. The whole issue was finally turned over to the League, where four powers with no direct interest in the matter—Belgium, China, Spain and Brazil—drew a line that left 70 percent of the area in Germany but gave most of the industries and mines to Poland. In 1922, in one of the longest treaties ever seen, Germany and Poland agreed on economic and political cooperation and the protection of their respective minorities.[34] But the Germans resented the loss of Upper Silesia as much as that of Danzig and the corridor. In 1939, Hitler annexed the whole to Germany. In 1945, it went back to Poland and most, but not all, of the Germans living there fled or were expelled.

Settling Poland's borders in the east, where anarchists, Bolsheviks, White Russians, Ukrainians, Lithuanians, Latvians, Estonians and Baltic Germans were jostling for power, was even more difficult. The peacemakers did not know how many countries they would be dealing with, or which governments. The Commission on Polish Affairs was instructed to go ahead anyway and duly worked out a border that brought all the clearly Polish territories into Poland. In December 1919, what was left of the Supreme Council approved what came to be known as the Curzon Line (roughly the line of Poland's eastern border today). The Polish government did not have the slightest intention of accepting this. While the peacemakers had been busy with their maps, Polish forces had been equally busy on the ground. All along the disputed borderlands, Poland had staked out much greater claims, which were to be settled largely by success or failure in war.

Piłsudski's emotions were most deeply engaged in the northeast. On his father's side he came from a Polish-Lithuanian family; an ancestor had helped to create the union between Poland and Lithuania in the fifteenth century. Vilna was the only place where he truly felt at home.[35] He wanted his birthplace for Poland, together with a slice of southeastern Lithuania. This brought Polish demands up against those of the emerging Lithuanian nation and into the whole peace settlement in the Baltic.

A map of the eastern end of the Baltic in 1919 would have shown many question marks. Only Finland in the north had managed to establish a precarious sort of independence from Russia, after a vicious civil war between its own Whites and Reds. The Peace Conference recognized Finland in the spring of 1919. To its south the Estonians, Latvians and Lithuanians had also tried to declare themselves independent from Russia, but they had to deal with a German occupation and their own German or Russian minorities. None had secure borders or established governments, and what the Russians had not destroyed in their retreat, the Germans had requisitioned. White Russians, Red Bolsheviks, Green anarchists, the Baltic Barons, German freebooters, embryonic national armies and simple gangsters ebbed and flowed across the land. Cities and towns changed hands repeatedly. At sea, the remnants of the Russian Imperial Navy, now under Bolshevik command, darted out from Petrograd to spread revolution.

The Allies had concerns but no coherent policy. If they recognized the Baltic nations, they were, in a sense, interfering in Russia's internal affairs. The Americans were for self-determination but hesitated to accord full recognition because Wilson did not want to change Russia's borders unilaterally. The British and the French hoped, at least until the summer of 1919, that Admiral Kolchak would defeat the Bolsheviks, and Kolchak strongly opposed independence for any part of the Russian empire. The French preferred to let the British worry about the Baltic while they looked after Poland. The British sent a small naval force—all they could spare—to bottle up the Bolshevik fleet in Petrograd/Leningrad and to find, if it could, some local democratic forces to support. Its admiral was warned not to get caught by mines or ice and to resist Bolshevik attacks, but only at a safe distance from land. "The work of British naval officers in the Baltic," wrote the Admiralty to the Foreign Office in the spring of 1919, "would be much facilitated if they could be informed of the policy which they are required to support."[36]

As a stopgap measure, the Allies instructed the German government to leave its troops in the Baltic after the armistice. Rather humiliating, said Balfour, but there did not appear to be an alternative. This created its own problems. The German high command was delighted. Neither the military nor German nationalists wanted to give up their Baltic conquests, which they saw as a barrier against Bolshevism and the Slavic menace (often the same thing, in the lurid imaginings of the right). The Baltic lands were hallowed by the blood of the Teutonic Knights who had fought for them centuries ago; they were also a redoubt where Germany might regroup against the Allies.[37]

On Christmas Day, 1918, the provisional president of Latvia, an agricultural expert from the University of Nebraska, appealed, with the acquiescence of the local British naval commander, to the Germans for help. His pathetically weak forces were about to be overrun by Bolsheviks. His appeal opened the door to a new type of Teutonic Knight, the Freikorps, a group of private armies forming in Germany. Their members had volunteered in order to stop Bolshevism, to save civilization, for the promise of land or simply for adventure and a free meal.

By February 1919 the Freikorps were pouring into Baltic cities and towns. Some of the troops looked like soldiers; others grew their hair long and shot out windows and street lamps for target practice. They treated the locals, whom they had ostensibly come to save, with contempt. In April they overthrew the Latvian government and headed into Estonia, even though the Bolsheviks were withdrawing. The peacemakers, who had paid little attention to the Baltic, grew perturbed. "Odd," said Balfour, "given the chaos now reigning in those areas, the Germans, by preventing the formation of local armies, and by forcing the countries which they occupy to rely entirely upon their aid against the Bolshevik invasion, are working for the permanence of their influence and domination." In May the Allies sent a mission to help the Baltic governments organize their own armies.[38]

The difficulty now was to get the Freikorps to withdraw. Stern notes went from Paris to Berlin. The German government sent its own orders to the Freikorps commander, General Colmar von der Goltz, who ignored them. "It is a frightful confusion," complained Lloyd George. In August the German government finally managed to get von der Goltz back to Germany. His men remained behind, under the command of a braggart Russian aristocrat who dreamed of reconquering Russia. Since he announced that the Baltic states were Russian again and that he intended to recruit their inhabitants as slave labor, he failed to gain any support beyond the local Germans. By the end of 1919, the Freikorps had slunk back to Germany, where they fulminated against the Allies, the Slavs and their own government. Many, including von der Goltz himself, were to find a spiritual home with Hitler and the Nazis. The Allies finally recognized the independence of Estonia and Latvia in January 1921.[39]

Lithuania, the southernmost of the Baltic states, had an even more complicated birth, if possible, because it had also to deal with Poland. In 1919, the great majority of Poles wanted to restore the old union between Poland and Lithuania, but this time with Poland firmly in control. The Lithuanians, said Dmowski dismissively, were merely a tribe; much better for them to become Polish. Poland should absorb all areas with a Polish majority—self-determination, of course—but also those where there was a large Polish minority, which could act as the agent of civilization. The areas to the north where Lithuanians were the vast majority could be made into a little Lithuanian state. If it wanted to unite with Poland, it could have home rule. Piłsudski and the left were prepared to contemplate a looser federal arrangement. No one took account of the Lithuanians themselves, now in the grip of an awakening nationalism.[40]

Lithuanian national dreams were as extravagant as all the others in 1919, and included securing Vilna for their capital. In January 1919, as the Germans evacuated the area, a Bolshevik force made up of Lithuanians and Byelorussians seized the city; in April, the Polish army took over. Piłsudski issued a proclamation to the Lithuanian people with the magic word "self-determination." He was promptly attacked by Dmowski supporters, who wanted outright annexation. The Lithuanian prime minister exclaimed that his country would die without Vilna. In the city itself, a local Jew commented sardonically, "A new parade was announced—this time for Poles only. There were no more Greens, Whites or Reds. All and everybody became Poles overnight, except for the Jews. The Jews took it in their stride. They had served in their life under many flags."[41]

Both sides appealed to the Peace Conference. The Lithuanians sent delegates to Paris, who quarreled with the Poles and with each other. The peacemakers made sporadic demands for the fighting to stop and tried to draw a fair border. Lloyd George wondered idly whether Lithuania should be independent at all; after all, it had about the same population as Wales. On the other hand, the peacemakers saw the danger in letting Poland spread itself out over territory where Poles were in a minority. By the summer of 1919, Lloyd George had warmed to the idea of an independent Lithuania. Along with Estonia and Latvia, it could be a useful conduit for British trade into Russia when relations were finally established with the Bolsheviks, who appeared to be winning in the civil war. The French still preferred a large Poland. Very little of this actually made much difference as the armies kept marching.

A year later the Bolsheviks drove the Poles out of Vilna and handed it over to the Lithuanians. In October 1920, just after a truce between Poland and Lithuania which left the city in Lithuanian hands, units of the Polish army conveniently mutinied and seized the city. Two years later the area, still under Polish control, voted overwhelmingly for incorporation into Poland. After the Second World War the Soviet Union gave it to Lithuania, which was now a Soviet republic.[42]

At the time Lithuania eased its loss by seizing the sleepy little Baltic port of Memel and a strip of territory that ran inland. It was a foolish gesture, which alienated both the Allies, who had taken the area from Germany precisely to provide a free port for Lithuania, and Germany because the population was divided almost equally between Lithuanians and Germans. Memel itself was 92 percent German. In 1939 Hitler took it back, but after the war it became Lithuanian again, as Klaipėda. Memel was not enough to make Lithuania forgive Poland for the loss of Vilna. The two countries did not speak to each other for fifteen years. When they decided to try to mend their relationship in 1938, it was too late. Today Lithuania is still trying to get Poland to apologize for that old wrong.

Far away from Vilna to the south, Poland was also quarreling in 1919 with its other neighbors over what had been the Austrian province of Galicia. Everyone agreed that almost all of the western half, with its clear Polish majority, and the Polish city of Kraków, with its ancient university and its superb Renaissance buildings, should go to Poland. The rich little duchy of Teschen, though, on the western edge, was to lead to a costly clash with the new state of Czechoslovakia. And the eastern half of Galicia was much more difficult to sort out. As in the north, the cities were Polish, the countryside most decidedly not. Lvov was a Polish island, as was Tarnopol (Ternopol) even farther east. Overall, Poles made up less than a third of the population, and Jews, who might or might not see themselves as Polish, about 14 percent. The great majority were Catholic Ukrainians— Ruthenians, as they were sometimes called to distinguish them from the predominantly Orthodox Ukrainians of the old Russian empire. The Ruthenians, Dmowski told the Supreme Council, were a long way from being ready to rule themselves. They needed Polish leadership and Polish civilization. And, although Dmowski did not mention it, Poland also wanted the oilfields near Lvov. When Lloyd George hinted at this, Paderewski was outraged. Poles had been badly wounded defending Lvov against Ukrainian and Bolshevik forces. "Do you think that children of thirteen are fighting for annexation, for imperialists?" His eloquence had little impact; only the French were sympathetic.[43]

It was not clear where the Ruthenians belonged. Language and culture drew them east, toward their fellow Ukrainians; their past within the Austrian empire, and their religion, drew them west. In November 1918, one faction of Ruthenians had declared their independence from Austria-Hungary and formed a union with the Ukrainian republic in Kiev, which, unfortunately, promptly came under attack by local communists and Russian Bolsheviks. The Ruthenian delegates who managed to get to Paris by the spring of 1919 could not say what they wanted.[44]

In Galicia the declaration of independence marked the start of fighting with the local Poles in Lvov. The fighting spread as Polish and Ukrainian reinforcements came in, and the confusion deepened as Reds and Whites of both nationalities joined their own battles. The Allies tried, with little success, to arrange cease-fires. "It is very difficult," said Wilson in May, "for us to intervene without having a better understanding of our position vis-à-vis the Ukrainians or the Bolsheviks who are besieging Lemberg [Lvov]." The Poles did their best to drag out the armistice negotiations while they strengthened their position. This caused much annoyance in Paris, but the problem for the peacemakers was to enforce their will, once they had decided what that was.[45]

"I only saw a Ukrainian once," commented Lloyd George. "It is the last Ukrainian I have seen, and I am not sure that I want to see any more." As far as Ukraine itself was concerned, none of the Allies supported its independence. Both the British and the French, after all, still hoped for a single Russia under an anti-Bolshevik government. But they agreed that East Galicia, as the possession of a defeated enemy, ought to be settled by the Peace Conference. Lloyd George argued that self-determination required the wishes of the local inhabitants to be consulted. In grabbing East Galicia, Poland was doing exactly what they had all fought the war to prevent. "It fills me with despair the way in which I have seen small nations, before they have hardly leaped into the light of freedom, beginning to oppress other races than their own."[46]

After much fighting on the ground and much arguing in Paris, it was settled that Austria would hand over East Galicia to the powers for disposal, perhaps to Poland, or, as the British preferred, to Russia or even Czechoslovakia. The Poles, already deeply suspicious of the British government, were enraged. The cream of Warsaw society, who had been invited to a dance at the British ambassador's house just before Christmas in 1919, showed their contempt by eating the dinner but refusing to take to the dance floor. Carton de Wiart, head of the British military mission, went white with fury and told his hostess, "I should throw the whole lot out of the house if I were you." The challenges and counterchallenges to duels that followed were settled quietly the next morning. While the powers mulled over the fate of East Galicia for another three years, the Poles quietly went ahead and established their control. In 1923, Poland's possession was recognized. The Ruthenians complained bitterly but in the end they were more fortunate than their cousins across the border, who fell victim to Stalin.[47]

Poland's greatest struggle, from early 1919 to the autumn of 1920, was with the Russian Bolsheviks. Where the Poles, even relative moderates such as Piłsudski, wanted to push Poland's borders well to the east and gain control, directly or indirectly, over Byelorussia (Belarus) and Ukraine, the Bolsheviks wanted to spread their revolution into the industrial heartland of Europe. Their history had left the Poles wary of all Russians, even those talking the language of international brotherhood. The Bolsheviks for their part saw in Polish nationalism and Polish Catholicism an obstacle to revolution. Nationalism, in their view, was simply an excuse for feudal landowners, factory owners and reactionaries of various sorts to try to hang on to power. "While recognizing the right of national self-determination," wrote Trotsky, "we take care to explain to the masses its limited historic significance and we never put it above the interests of the proletarian revolution."[48] This was old-fashioned Russian imperialism in new clothes.

From February 1919, fighting between the Bolsheviks and the Poles spread along a wide front. The Poles pushed deep into Russian territory, taking much of Byelorussia in the north. Secret talks for a temporary truce in the summer of 1919 went nowhere when the Poles tried to insist on an independent Ukraine. On April 24, 1920, Piłsudski launched a fresh attack, driving toward Kiev, Ukraine's capital. By May Polish troops were in control of the city, but Piłsudski, deeply superstitious, was uneasy; Kiev was notoriously unlucky for its occupiers. A month later the Bolsheviks recaptured the city and started westward. "Over the corpse of White Poland," said the order to their troops, "lies the road to world-wide conflagration!" The British ambassador in Poland sent his wife and children home. By August the Soviet troops were outside the suburbs of Warsaw. "I have packed up all the plates, pictures, prints, lacquer objects, china, photographs, best books, best china and glass, carpets etc.," the ambassador wrote to his wife. "I wonder what will happen to all the nice furniture and good beds etc. which I could not pack up." The Poles appealed desperately for weapons or for pressure on the Bolsheviks to make a truce. None came. The French were drawing back. They did not like the Bolsheviks but they were by now tired of Polish ambitions. Lloyd George urged the Poles to open negotiations. The Poles were hopeless, he told C. P. Scott, the great editor of the liberal *Manchester Guardian,* and quite as bad as the Irish. "They have quarrelled with every one of their neighbours—Germans, Russians, Czecho-Slovaks, Lithuanians, Rumanians, Ukrainians—and they were going to be beaten." Lloyd George, fortunately, was wrong. "If Poland had become Soviet," Lenin later said, "the Versailles treaty would have been shattered, and the entire international system built up by the victors would have been destroyed."[49]

The battle for Warsaw was one of the great triumphs of Polish history. The army, which had been racked with jealousy and infighting among the officers, pulled itself together in the face of a common enemy. "I continue to marvel at the absence of panic," wrote a British diplomat, "at the apparent absence indeed of all anxiety." Piłsudski calmly planned a daring counterattack. On August 16 Polish forces attacked the Soviet forces in the rear, cutting their lines of communication. The Soviet commander began a hasty retreat. By the end of September 1920, Lenin asked for peace. The Treaty of Riga, signed on March 18, 1921, gave Poland a border in the east well beyond what the peacemakers had recommended and added even more minorities to its population: 4 million Ukrainians, 2 million Jews and a million Byelorussians.[50]

Piłsudski did not adjust well to peace or to democratic politics. In 1926 he seized power in a coup, and until his death in 1935 he did his best to run Poland on military lines. His great rival Dmowski never held office and moved even further to the right. Paderewski resigned as prime minister at the end of 1919, deeply hurt by the way he was blamed for the Allies' refusal to give Poland everything it wanted and by the attacks on his wife for being tactless and interfering (which she was).[51] He never lived in Poland again. In 1922, he tried a few notes on the piano and found to his amazement that he still enjoyed playing. His second career was as successful as the first. He died in New York in the summer of 1941, happy in the knowledge that Germany had invaded the Soviet Union and that there might again be hope for his country.

Poland itself survived its difficult birth and even flourished for a time. It had not won back all its historic territories, but it was still a big country and it had its window on the Baltic. These gains, however, came at a huge cost. The powers, even the French, thought the Poles greedy and feckless. And its neighbors had much to resent: Lithuania, the Vilna region; the Soviet Union, the 150-mile-wide strip of what had been Russian territory; Czechoslovakia, the conflict over Teschen; and Germany, the corridor and Danzig. In the summer of 1939 Poland disappeared from the map yet again. When it surfaced again at the end of the Second World War, it was a strangely altered and shrunken Poland, emptied of its Jews by the Nazis and of its Germans by the Soviets, and moved two hundred miles to the west.

Czechs and Slovaks

WHERE THE POLES tended to bring exasperated sighs, even from their supporters, the Czechs basked in general approval. The Poles were dashing and brave, but quite unreasonable; the Rumanians charming and clever, but sadly devious; the Yugoslavs, well, rather Balkan. The Czechs were refreshingly Western. "Of all the people whom we saw in the course of our journey," reported an American relief mission that traveled throughout the former Austria-Hungary in January 1919, "the Czechs seemed to have the most ability and common sense, the best organization, and the best leaders."[1]

The Czech delegates, its prime minister, Karel Kramář, and the foreign minister, Edvard Beneš, presented their case to the Supreme Council in February 1919. Beneš did most of the talking. Charles Seymour, the American expert, was deeply impressed: "He had done much to organize the revolution that swept aside the Habsburgs and to build up the Czecho-Slovak army in Siberia; his diplomatic skill had combined with the solid honesty of President Tomáš Masaryk to win the recognition of the Allies for the infant state."[2]

Everyone in Paris knew how Beneš and Masaryk had devoted their lives to freeing their people from the Austrian empire. Everyone knew the extraordinary story of the army of Czechs who had surrendered to the Russians only to find themselves in the middle of the revolution; how they were fighting their way thousands of miles across Siberia toward the Pacific and freedom. Almost everyone in Paris liked and admired the Czechs and their leaders. (Lloyd George, who referred to Beneš as "the little French jackal" and thought the Czech claims excessive, was an exception.) Beneš and Masaryk were unfailingly cooperative, reasonable and persuasive as they stressed the Czechs' deep-seated democratic traditions and their aversion to militarism, oligarchy, high finance, indeed all that the old Germany and Austria-Hungary had stood for.[3]

This being said, neither the British nor the Americans were particularly interested in the new little country, which looked like a tadpole with its head in the west and its tail tapering off in the east, sandwiched between Poland to the north and Austria and Hungary to the south. The French were interested, not for sentimental reasons but for security. France wanted a country strong enough to join with Poland and the new South Slav state to block both Bolshevism and Germany. That meant endowing Czechoslovakia with control of crucial railways, a position on the great central European waterway, the Danube, and adequate coal.[4]

Beneš presented Czechoslovakia's claims to the Supreme Council on February 5, the day after Venizelos presented Greek claims and the day before Feisal came to speak for Arab independence. He had an easier task than either, because Czechoslovakia had already been recognized by the powers, and most of the territory it wanted—the Austrian provinces of Bohemia, Moravia and Silesia, and the Hungarian province of Slovakia— was already in its possession. Much of this was due to Beneš himself and the help he got from France.

When he arrived in Paris in 1915, Beneš was an obscure sociology professor from Prague representing something called the Czechoslovak National Council. Four years later he was foreign minister of a new state. Not a romantic figure like Venizelos or Feisal or a great soldier like Piłsudski, Beneš was short, ordinary-looking and pedantic, a dull writer and an uninspiring speaker. (The French thought this should appeal to the Anglo-Saxons.) He had no apparent hobbies or vices, and few close friends. His relations with Masaryk, to whom he was devoted, were always curiously formal. But Beneš was enormously energetic and efficient. In Paris during the war he cultivated everyone, from Foreign Ministry officials to leading intellectuals, who might help the Czech cause. Where Beneš gained French attention, his charming, handsome colleague the Slovak Milan Štefánik won hearts. Štefánik, already well known before the war in Paris as an astronomer, made a huge impression when he took out French citizenship and become an ace in the French air force.[5]

As the nationalities of the collapsing Austria-Hungary scrambled to catch the eye of the powers, Beneš worked even harder. He assured the French that his country, unlike its neighbors, was ready for the fight against Bolshevism: "The Czechs alone can stop the movement." To the British he explained that his goal was "to form a State that would be thoroughly loyal ... especially to England and which would form a barrier between Germany and the East." Beneš had a significant bargaining chip: the Czech forces that had come out of prisoner-of-war camps to fight on the Allied side. "I want all your soldiers in France," Clemenceau told Beneš in June 1918, during the last great German attack. "You can count on me," Beneš replied, "I will go with you all the way."

In June the French foreign minister formally recognized the Czechoslovak National Council as the future government of an independent Czechoslovakia and put pressure on France's allies to do the same. The French also took the lead, then and later, in recognizing Czechoslovakia's borders, even the tricky ones. Beneš, and it was a measure of his achievement, was invited to sit in at the Supreme War Council to discuss the armistice with Austria-Hungary. Neither the Yugoslavs nor the Poles were invited to join him. By the time the Peace Conference opened, Beneš had established Czechoslovakia on the winning side, its past as part of Austria-Hungary to be mentioned only in passing and with regret. Unlike the Yugoslavs and the Poles, the Czechs had the advantage of speaking with one voice. Between Beneš and Masaryk there was an extraordinary collaboration, which endured until Masaryk's death.[6]

If Beneš was the workhorse, Masaryk was the man who gave Czechoslovakia life. He had the materials to hand: a people with its own Slavic language and literature, and many memories: of the fourteenth century, when the rich and powerful kingdom of Bohemia had reached north almost to the Baltic; of the few golden years when Prague was the capital of the Holy Roman Empire; and then the sadder story from 1526 on as, one by one, the last vestiges of independence were extinguished by the Habsburgs. But this history did not include the Slovaks, who may have spoken a similar language but had not been politically connected to the Czechs since the tenth century, when the Slovaks had fallen under Hungarian rule. And there they had remained even after the Habsburgs acquired Hungary. The Reformation, which had made the Czechs largely Protestant, had passed them by: the Slovaks remained firmly Catholic.

Masaryk was the son of a farm manager for big estates. He was born in 1850, just after the revolutions of 1848 ignited nationalism throughout central Europe. Pushed by his ambitious mother, he decided early on to escape rural life. Through sheer determination he got to the University of Vienna to study philosophy. He was a sober, hardworking, priggish young man with a striking confidence in his own opinions. At his first university posting he caused a sensation by disagreeing with a senior professor. When he moved into journalism and then politics, he showed the same propensity to challenge authority.[7]

When the war started, Masaryk slowly came to the conclusion that

Austria-Hungary no longer made sense and that the future for Czechoslovakia (he assumed from the first that it would include the Slovak lands) lay
in independence, possibly under Russian sponsorship. (That Slavs would
work together was a hope he pursued until his death.) By 1915 he was
safely in Switzerland. His family, unfortunately, were stuck in Prague. His
wife, an American, suffered a nervous breakdown, from which she never
really recovered, his eldest daughter was imprisoned, and his son Jan was
conscripted into the Austrian army. Masaryk moved on to Britain, where
he spent almost two years teaching at the University of London and making friends with a range of influential people, from diplomats to opinion
makers such as Wickham Steed of *The Times*.[8]

The overthrow of the tsar in February of 1917 drew Masaryk to St. Petersburg. He urged the shaky provisional government to renew its attack
on the Austrian armies and worked to transform Czech prisoners of war
into an army that would fight side by side with the Russians. The Bolshevik revolution in November 1917 and Lenin's decision to sue for peace
made those plans impossible. The Bolsheviks were nonetheless happy to
send the Czech Legion, now 50,000 strong, on its way to the Western
Front. The only feasible route was a roundabout one, six thousand miles
on the Trans-Siberian railway to the Pacific port of Vladivostok and then
by boat to France. With assurances from Bolshevik leaders, Masaryk left
first, in March 1918, confident that his troops would be right behind him.
Partway across Siberia, however, the Czech Legion clashed with Hungarians heading west to join the Bolsheviks. The fighting spread and the
Czechs found themselves at war with the Bolsheviks. By the end of the
summer Czech forces were effectively in control of most of the railway
and, by chance, the gold reserves of the tsarist government. By this time
the war was winding down in Europe, and the Czechs were more useful
where they were. The Allied forces that had landed at Vladivostok in
August might well want to move westward against the Bolsheviks. Caught
up now in the Allied intervention in the Russian civil war, the homesick
soldiers were condemned to another two years in Siberia. Beneš was not
sorry to see this; indeed, he extracted a promise from the grateful British
to recognize his Czechoslovak National Council as the official representative of Czechs and Slovaks. Masaryk agreed. "The dear boys will have to
stay a while alongside their allies," he said as he sailed off from Vladivostok to the United States to gather support.[9]

Masaryk crisscrossed the country—Chicago, Washington, Boston,
Cleveland, wherever there were Czech and Slovak immigrants. In New
York he lectured the experts of the Inquiry on self-determination in east-
ern Europe. He talked to representatives from Austria-Hungary's other

nationalities about working together in freedom and friendship. At a huge meeting in Carnegie Hall, he and Paderewski spoke of their profound admiration for each other and their common struggle against oppression. Three weeks before the war ended, the Mid-European Democratic Union, with Poles, Ukrainians, Czechs, South Slavs, Rumanians, Italians and even, improbably, Armenians and Zionists staged a four-day meeting in Philadelphia. Masaryk crafted a Declaration of Common Aims of the Independent Mid-European Nations. As the Liberty Bell rang, he was the first to sign it, dipping his pen in the inkwell used for the American Declaration of Independence.[10]

In Pittsburgh, Masaryk signed another agreement, this one with Czech and Slovak organizations, promising that, within the new democratic state, Slovaks would have considerable autonomy, with their own courts, a parliament and their own language. Although about a third of the world's Slovaks lived in the United States, they were not yet strongly nationalistic. Murmurs from their compatriots in Central Europe that not all Slovaks wanted union had not yet made their way across the Atlantic. Later on, when things started to go wrong between Czechs and Slovaks, Masaryk downplayed the agreement. "It was concluded in order to appease a small Slovak faction which was dreaming of God knows what sort of independence for Slovakia."[11]

The Pittsburgh Convention was useful in reassuring the Americans that self-determination would carry Slovakia into Czechoslovakia. And American support would be, as Masaryk knew, vital. Through Charles Crane, a well-traveled, inquisitive tycoon whose fortune came from making sinks and toilets, Masaryk met Lansing, House and finally, on June 18, Wilson. The meeting with the president did not go well. The two former professors lectured each other. More important, Masaryk discovered that Wilson was more interested in using the Czech Legion in Siberia than in supporting Czechoslovak independence. The Americans were not yet ready to admit publicly that Austria-Hungary was finished.[12]

By the autumn, it clearly was. Austrian forces had been smashed on the battlefields; inside the empire, the inexperienced young emperor watched impotently as Poles, South Slavs, Czechs, Germans talked of independence. In Prague, demonstrators cheered for Wilson and Masaryk. In Wilson's words, Austria-Hungary was "an old building whose sides had been held together by props." The time had come to take away those props. On September 3 the United States recognized the Czechoslovak National Council as a de facto belligerent government. Like the earlier British recognition, the statement did not specify the territory the new country would occupy.[13]

From Paris, Beneš decided to create facts on the ground. "A *fait accompli*," he wrote to his colleagues, "carried through without noise or struggle and the domination of the situation are now decisive." On October 28, in Prague, Czech politicians gently but firmly took power from the demoralized Austrian administration. Beneš urged the Allies to evacuate the German and Hungarian forces from the Czech lands and Slovakia and to bring in Allied forces. It was essential as well, he told the French, to occupy Teschen, on the border with Poland, and Bratislava (German Pressburg) in Hungary. Since the Allies had few troops to spare, the occupation was largely done by Czech forces acting under Allied command.[14]

The delay in starting the Peace Conference helped the Czechs considerably. By January 1919, Masaryk was back in Prague, installed as Czechoslovakia's first president and living in the palace that had once housed Bohemia's kings. In spite of complaints from the inhabitants, Czech troops had moved into the German-speaking borderlands, where Bohemia met Austria in the south and Germany in the north. In Slovakia the French military authorities had ordered the Hungarian government to withdraw its troops behind a line that, conveniently, coincided with the border the Czechs wanted.

Czechoslovakia's borders had been largely set by the time the peacemakers turned their attention to the new country. Above all, Beneš wanted recognition from the Peace Conference, but he also wanted to push the borders out in places. When he had his hearing at the Supreme Council on February 5, 1919, he laid claim to several morsels of Poland, as well as a slice of Hungary stretching along the Danube, and, where the great river bends south, pointing on toward the Carpathian mountains. He also asked for pieces of German and Austrian territory north and south of the old Bohemian and Moravian frontiers to give Czechoslovakia a smoother and more defensible border. These, Beneš claimed in private conversations, were not his demands; he was being pushed, he regretted, by nationalists such as his colleague Kramář.[15]

At Czechoslovakia's tail in the east, Beneš asked for the largely Ukrainian-speaking territory on the south side of the Carpathians on the grounds that the locals, largely Ruthenians, were very like the Slovaks. It would be unkind, he felt, to leave them under Hungarian rule when Czechoslovakia was prepared to take them under its wing. (Conveniently, Ruthenian immigrants in the United States had voted for joining Czechoslovakia.) Adding in that piece of territory would also give Czechoslovakia a border with Rumania, a friendly state.[16]

He had a couple of further requests, suggestions really. There were some Slavs living in the southern part of Germany, just east of Dresden, who had begged Czechoslovakia to protect them. This was essentially a moral question and he left it to the Peace Conference. Then there was Czechoslovakia's need for friends, surrounded as it was on three sides by Germans and Hungarians. Perhaps there could be a corridor of land running southward between Austria and Hungary to link his country with Yugoslavia. "Very audacious and indefensible," was Lloyd George's view. The corridor, which never materialized, reflected Masaryk's old dreams of a Slav federation. The Poles, Yugoslavs and Czechoslovaks, Beneš assured the French, were all aware of how much they had in common. Although a dispute over the territory of Teschen was already removing Poland from that happy equation, Czechoslovakia and Yugoslavia were to remain on friendly terms.[17]

The Czechs had many arguments to back their claims: their glorious past, their deep love of freedom, their sober, industrious virtues. They stood against Bolshevism when the lesser peoples around them were succumbing. They were at the same time the most advanced part of the Slavs and a bastion of Western civilization. His people, claimed Beneš, had always felt a special mission to defend democracy against the German menace. "Hence the fanatical devotion of the Czechs which had been noticed by all in this war." The Czech demands were modest and reasonable. "The Nation," said Beneš, "after 300 years of servitude and vicissitudes which had almost led to its extermination, felt that it must be prudent, reasonable and just to its neighbours; and that it must avoid provoking jealousy and renewed struggles which might again plunge it into similar danger." His government, he insisted, "wished to do all in their power to assist a just and durable peace." Lloyd George, almost alone, was unimpressed. "He larded his speech throughout with phrases that reeked with professions of sympathy for the exalted ideals proclaimed by the Allies in their crusade for international right." When Kramář, as second Czech delegate, asked to add his views, Clemenceau, despite his sympathy for Czechoslovakia, cut him short: "Oh, we'll appoint a special commission and you can talk to them for a couple of hours. Now we had better have a cup of tea."[18]

The Czechs passed lightly over any difficulties. Slovakia, they admitted, would contain some 650,000 Hungarians, but 350,000 Slovaks would still be left outside. The Hungarians could not complain; they had tried, with little success, to turn Slovaks into Hungarians and forced thousands to emigrate. Yes, Beneš said, there were German speakers living along the borders with Austria and Germany, in the west of old Bohemia (what the Germans themselves called the Sudetenland, "Southland"). But the prewar Austrian figures of several million were quite untrustworthy; the

Czech ones, by contrast very carefully done, showed only one and a half million Germans to probably three times as many Czechs. These Bohemian Germans knew that their future lay in Czechoslovakia. They did not want to see their businesses submerged by the more powerful German economy. If some of them talked of joining a greater Germany or perhaps even Austria, that was simply because they were being terrorized by outside agitators. Anyway, and this in his view was the strongest argument, Czechoslovakia could not survive without the Sudetenland's sugar refineries, glassworks, textile mills, smelters and breweries. And the Czechs needed the old frontiers, which ran along mountains and hills, to defend themselves. "In Bohemia," commented an American expert cynically, "they demand their 'historic frontiers' regardless of the protests of large numbers of Germans who do not wish to be taken over in this way. In Slovakia they insist on the rights of nationality and pay no heed to the ancient and well marked 'historic frontiers' of Hungary."[19]

Since the Allies had largely accepted the new state as it was, the commission set up to report on Czechoslovakia had a relatively easy job. Its members worked amicably, assisted, said Seymour, by the informality (which allowed them to smoke) and by the fact that the British and Americans met privately, as they were doing on most issues, to agree on common positions before the meetings. Occasionally they had trouble with the chief British representative, Sir Joseph Cook of Australia, whose complete lack of knowledge did not stop him from having very strong opinions. Nicolson spent much time coaching him. Because Italy's interests were not directly involved, the Italian representatives were not obstructive as they were over Yugoslavia's borders. Nor were they particularly helpful. Their chief representative, an old diplomat, was fond of saying, "I ask myself whether it is not wiser, at this stage, to put at least two possibilities before ourselves."[20]

The borders that caused everyone the most difficulty were between Slovakia and Hungary. The population, mainly Slovak and Hungarian, was very mixed; and east of the Danube there were no clear geographic features. The French supported Czech claims to territory that was primarily Hungarian; the British and the Americans did not. Everyone agreed that the corridor to Yugoslavia was impractical. After considerable bargaining and many compromises, the commission wound up its work at the end of the first week of March. The chairman asked for the final view of the British delegation. "Well," said Cook, "all I can say is that we *are* a happy family aren't we?" There was a silence as the interpreter provided a French translation.[21]

The report, which gave the Czechs some, but not all, of the additional territory they wanted from Germany, Austria and Hungary, was approved piecemeal as each of the treaties was drawn up. On April 4 the Council of Four, which was in the middle of strenuous disputes over the German terms, briskly agreed that it would be better on the whole to keep to the old boundaries of the Bohemian kingdom. On May 12, with equal dispatch, it approved the old boundaries between Czechoslovakia and Austria. Some of the peacemakers worried briefly about the German minority, three million strong, within Czechoslovakia. Lansing fretted about ignoring the principle of self-determination. Wilson is supposed to have exclaimed in surprise, "Why, Masaryk never told me that!" but in the end he gave the Sudeten Germans little thought. While Lloyd George later claimed to have had serious misgivings, he did not raise them at the time. Clemenceau had none: as he told the Council of Four, "the Conference has decided to call to life a certain number of new states. Without committing an injustice, may it sacrifice them by imposing on them unacceptable frontiers toward Germany?" No one, after all, much wanted to add the German territories to those of the defeated enemies. Most probably agreed with Masaryk when he said impatiently, "Whole nations are now oppressed by the Germans and the Magyars—is that nothing?" And the Czechs impressed the peacemakers by giving various guarantees to their minorities: their own schools, freedom of religion, even proportional representation, so they could have their own representatives. Czechoslovakia was going to be the Switzerland of central Europe.[22]

The Sudeten Germans themselves protested ineffectually in 1918 and 1919. Largely prosperous farmers and solid bourgeois, they were divided between despising their new Czech rulers and fearing the left-wing revolutions sweeping through Germany and Austria. Czechoslovakia at least offered stability. In any case, Germany, engrossed in its own problems, showed little interest in them at the time. The German delegation in Versailles mentioned them only once in passing in its written comments to the peacemakers. The German foreign minister, Count Ulrich von Brockdorff-Rantzau, offered the Sudeten Germans his sympathy but made it clear that Germany would not risk its negotiating position with the Allies by looking out for people who had, after all, never been part of Germany. Linking up with Austria was an equally unlikely solution for the Sudeten Germans in 1919, given the way the German speakers were situated in a crescent along the Austrian and German borders. Moreover, in 1919 Austria itself scarcely seemed likely to survive.[23]

The Czech government did keep many of its promises. In districts with significant numbers of Germans, they could use their own language for official matters. There were German schools, universities, newspapers. But Czechoslovakia was still a Slav state. Its banknotes showed young women dressed in folkloric Czech or Slovak costumes. Germans— along with Hungarians and Ruthenians—never felt they entirely belonged.[24] Perhaps that would not have mattered, if the Depression had not hit Sudetenland industries particularly hard and if Hitler had not made the cause of the lost Germans his own. At Munich in 1938, the Sudeten Germans provided him with the excuse to destroy Czechoslovakia.

Czechoslovakia's borders with Hungary took longer to settle, partly because the treaty with Hungary was delayed, first by the communist revolution at the end of March and then by the outbreak of more fighting. Assuring the peacemakers that their only intention was to combat Bolshevism, the Czechs moved in to seize Hungarian territory shortly after the revolution. With Foch's approval, their forces occupied crucial railways on Hungarian soil and then moved ahead, beyond what Foch had authorized, to take the last remaining Hungarian coalfield. The Hungarians counterattacked at the beginning of June. The Czechs immediately appealed to the peacemakers. They were amazed and hurt that anyone should think they had provoked the Hungarians. "I know nothing about a Czech offensive," said Kramář. "All I know relates to the advance of Hungarian Bolshevism, mixed and confused with Magyar chauvinism." Beneš painted a picture of a peaceful Czechoslovakia, unaware of the menace to the south: "We were busy with our domestic reforms and forthcoming elections." Czech forces had been concentrated largely on the German border, ready to leap into action if Germany refused to sign its treaty. "It was then that the Magyars, seeing Slovakia completely defenceless, advanced." The Czechs took the opportunity to make fresh demands on Hungarian territory: additional railway lines, for example, and a bridgehead on the south bank of the Danube. The Allies, by now seriously worried about the conflict, rejected most of these. "We must be fair even to the Hungarians," said Lloyd George, "they are only defending their country." The one exception was the largely German town of Bratislava on the Danube, which was given to Czechoslovakia on the grounds that it needed a river port. Even so, Czechoslovakia ended up with a substantial piece of what had been Hungary, and over a million ethnic Hungarians.[25]

Czechoslovakia also had trouble with Poland, over the little triangle of Teschen, where Upper Silesia met the western edge of Galicia. As part of Austria-Hungary, Teschen was up for grabs. It was a rich prize, partly because it lay at one end of the great Silesian coalfield, but also because it was a major railway junction, where the main north–south and east–west lines in the center of Europe met. In Paris, Dmowski claimed it for Poland on ethnic grounds. (Out of a total population of half a million, the Poles probably outnumbered the Czechs two to one.) The Polish majority, he said, were particularly well educated and consequently profoundly nationalistic. Beneš challenged his figures: a lot of the Poles were temporary inhabitants, drawn by a higher standard of living or so influenced by Czech language and culture as to be no longer Polish at all. He pointed to the costumes the people of Teschen wore, and their architecture. And Teschen's coal was essential for Czech industry, as was a railway line which, since it linked the two halves of Czechoslovakia, could not safely be left under Polish control. Delegates from Teschen itself who asked for an independent state never had a chance.[26]

Like many of the other issues that overloaded the agendas in Paris, this one could have been settled with relative ease. Masaryk and Paderewski had met the previous summer in Washington and agreed that it should be discussed in a friendly way once the war was over. In Teschen itself local Poles and Czechs worked out a division of responsibilities when the Austrian administration collapsed. The new Polish government, unwisely in retrospect, announced that elections to the new parliament in Warsaw would include the Polish part of Teschen. The Czech government in Prague overreacted and in late January 1919 ordered all Polish troops to leave Teschen at once. The Czechs, also unwisely, persuaded several Allied officers to give the impression that this order came from the Allies. Shots were fired and what had been a tense situation became a crisis as both governments rushed reinforcements in. An American professor who visited Masaryk in Prague found him tired and nervous. "Somehow," reported the American, "I gathered the impression that in the affair he had been led rather than he had taken the lead himself, and he was evidently unhappy about the whole matter."[27]

In Paris, where the peacemakers were busy with the League of Nations and the Russian question, this outbreak of hostilities between two friendly powers was an unwelcome interruption. "How many members ever heard of Teschen?" Lloyd George was famously to ask the House of Commons later that year. "I do not mind saying that I had never heard of it." The Supreme Council summoned the Poles and Czechs. Each side blamed the other, and Beneš used the occasion to produce all the reasons—"statistical, ethnological, historical and economic"—as to why Teschen belonged to Czechoslovakia. Lloyd George called him sharply to order. The peacemakers set up a special inter-Allied commission, which both sides accepted with reluctance.[28]

The commission managed to get a cease-fire of sorts, but finding a solution was more difficult. Lloyd George confessed that he rather sympathized with the Poles. So, said Wilson, did he. He had been touched when a group of Polish peasants appeared in his office to implore him not to make them part of Czechoslovakia. They had walked, they told him, sixty miles to the nearest railway station to get to Paris. The French, who generally backed Poland, on this occasion supported the Czechs, reasoning that Poland could survive easily without Teschen but Czechoslovakia, a crucial part of the cordon sanitaire against Bolshevism, could not. Beneš did his best to raise the Bolshevik specter; he warned that the cease-fire was only encouraging dark anti-Czechoslovak forces in Berlin, Vienna and Budapest. The Czech authorities had already unmasked their spies and agitators and discovered their leaflets and maps.[29]

The inter-Allied commission gave little useful advice to the peacemakers. An ethnic division of Teschen, it pointed out, would leave the border going right through the middle of the coalfields. It suggested alternatives that were bound to upset the Poles or the Czechs or both. In April the peacemakers encouraged Paderewski and Beneš to talk directly to each other. When those discussions failed to produce anything, the peacemakers fell back on a plebiscite. In the summer of 1919 the Polish government, thinking it would win, agreed; the Czechoslovak, for the opposite reason, did not. A year later the Czechs, who had been busy making propaganda in their part of Teschen, were all for consulting the inhabitants, but the Poles had changed their minds. Riots and strikes made a vote impossible and in July 1920 the powers finally made their decision. Czechoslovakia got the coal mines. The little city of Teschen was cut in two; the old part went to Poland and the suburbs with the railway station to Czechoslovakia. One state got the electric power plant, the other the gasworks. It was the sort of settlement being made all over Central Europe as modern ethnic nationalism superimposed itself on an older, different world. And two nations who should have been friends now resented each other.[30]

Poland thought briefly of seizing Teschen but all its resources were being poured into the war with Russia. It never forgave Czechoslovakia for taking advantage of that desperate struggle and for a conspicuous lack of sympathy—for example, the Czechs held up badly needed weapons being shipped from Austria. On October 1, 1938, the day after the Munich agreement dismembered Czechoslovakia, the Polish government demanded the return of Teschen. It was followed by Hungary with a demand for Slovakia and the Ruthenian territories on the south slopes of the Carpathians.[31]

The newborn democratic Czechoslovakia was based on shaky foundations. The Allies had created a state, according to the leader of the Austrian socialists, out of several nations, "all filled with hatred one against the other, arrested in their whole economic and social development and in the progress of their civilisation by hate and national strife, nourished by tyranny and poisoning their whole public life." There was some truth in what he said. Out of Czechoslovakia's population of some 14 million, 3 million were German, 700,000 Hungarian and 550,000 Ruthenian, with a sprinkling of Poles and Gypsies. Czechs and Slovaks together made up the other two thirds, but they had much to divide them. The Czech lands were indelibly marked by Austrian rule, as was Slovakia by Hungarian. The Czechs felt that they were bringing progress and civilization to a backwater, and the Slovaks resented this. The Czechs, who dominated the national government, resisted giving Slovakia the autonomy Masaryk had promised so freely in Pittsburgh, on the grounds that there were not enough educated Slovaks to run their own government; more important, they did not want to encourage the Germans, or the Ruthenians or the Hungarians, to ask for similar rights.[32]

Early in 1919 there was a warning of what was to come when Slovakia's economy took a sudden turn for the worse. It was now cut off from Hungarian markets and Hungarian coal. Sugar beets lay rotting in the fields; refineries closed down. Slovak farmers and workers were rioting, reported an American observer, saying, in effect, to their new government in Prague, "We thank you for nothing. You say you have rescued us from the political oppression of the Hungarians which was in fact pretty bad but now we are under martial law, we have no work, little food, we suffer from cold and our future is black." Local priests spoke of their fears for Catholicism at the hands of the Protestant Czechs. That summer, when Czechoslovakia and Hungary clashed, advancing Czech troops were attacked in the rear by Slovaks.[33]

In September, House's confidential aide Stephen Bonsal received a visit from two Slovaks, who complained that they had been prevented from leaving Czechoslovakia and had reached Paris only after an arduous journey through Yugoslavia, Italy and Switzerland. They begged him to see their leader, an ailing priest named Father Andrej Hlinka. The American and his Slovak escort rushed through Paris, doubling back on themselves to throw off pursuers, until they reached the secluded gate of a monastery. Inside, Bonsal found a wan Hlinka, lying in a monk's cell reading his prayer book. The priest talked of his disillusionment with Czechoslovakia. The Hungarians had not been so bad after all. "We have lived alongside the Magyars for a thousand years," he said. "All the Slovak rivers flow towards the Hungarian plain, and all our roads lead to Budapest, their great city, while from Prague we are separated by the barrier of the

Carpathians." Slovaks were true Catholics; Czechs, whatever they said, were infidels. Bonsal could not offer much hope that the peacemakers would undo what they had just done. "God has punished me," said Hlinka sadly, "but I shall continue to plead before God and man for my people who are innocent and without stain."[34]

In the 1920s, Father Hlinka built up a party, the Slovak Populists, which became the most important political force in Slovakia. In May 1938 a group of American Slovaks triumphantly bore back to Europe the original of the Pittsburgh agreement of 1918 and, at a huge meeting in Bratislava, Hlinka demanded that the government fulfill the promises Masaryk had made. Masaryk had died the year before and Hlinka was dead by the autumn, when the Munich agreement opened the door so long closed. Czechoslovakia, abandoned by its allies, harassed on all sides by enemies, capitulated to the demands of Hlinka's successor, Father Josef Tiso, and gave Slovakia full autonomy within what was left of the Czechoslovak state. Hitler, scenting blood, urged Tiso into claiming full independence. In March 1939, as Nazi armies marched into the Czech lands, a new state of Slovakia was born. Not all Slovaks welcomed the way this happened or the Nazi godfather who blessed it.[35]

Tiso barely outlived his creation. In 1946 he was executed for treason in a reconstituted Czechoslovakia, which, this time, had Stalin as a patron. The new country was smaller than, and different from, the one the peacemakers had approved in 1919; the Ruthenian parts had gone, swallowed up into the Soviet Union, and the Germans had fled, with considerable encouragement from the Czechs. As president, an old and sick Beneš struggled, and failed, to keep his country out of the Soviet web that was being constructed across the center of Europe. He died in September 1948, after the coup that carried the communists to power, but too early to witness the full misery to come. Masaryk's son Jan, who was foreign minister, died in that coup, probably pushed out a window by communist agents. On January 1, 1993, the rest of the construction of 1919 came to pieces as Slovakia and the Czech Republic announced their divorce.

19

Austria

O N JUNE 2, 1919, a brief ceremony took place in the great hall of the old royal château at St.-Germain-en-Laye on the outskirts of Paris. Delegates from Austria, representing a morsel of what had once been a great empire, received their peace terms at a table covered with a red carpet, as the rows of allied delegates stared at them. The Czech prime minister, who knew several of the Austrians from the time they had all been colleagues, ostentatiously turned his back. The walls were decorated with pictures of animals, now extinct, from the Stone Age. "Several among us," remarked Mordacq, Clemenceau's aide, "could not help but notice that."[1]

Austria-Hungary, the vast collection of territories painstakingly assembled since the thirteenth century by the Habsburgs, was already disintegrating before 1914. At its heart the link between the Austrian territories (which included Slovenia, Bohemia and Moravia as well as the German lands) and the kingdom of Hungary (which ruled over Slovakia and Croatia) had become as tenuous as the hyphen which joined their two names. The Habsburgs had always found it wise to compromise with Hungary. In 1867, weakened by defeat at the hands of Prussia, they made the greatest compromise of all: the empire was now the Dual Monarchy, a partnership between two states, each with its own parliament. They still had the same ruler in Franz Joseph but he was emperor in the Austrian territories and king in Hungary. They used the same postage stamps and coins, negotiated a common foreign policy and, with much wrangling between delegations from each parliament, they shared expenses. Otherwise, each ran its own affairs.

Hungarian nationalism was not the only nationalism buffeting the empire in the decades before 1914. In the north, the Poles and the Czechs were stirring and in the south Italians were agitating to join the newly unified Italy. Serbs, Slovenes and Croats talked of greater autonomy, perhaps even a South Slav state of their own. If Hungarians had autonomy, why shouldn't others? Franz Joseph, driven by the great but simple object of handing on what he had inherited to his successors, step-by-step gave way on nationalist demands to preserve the façade of imperial unity. In both his parliaments, the one in Vienna and the one in Budapest, the deputies increasingly organized themselves along national lines.

By the 1890s, the old emperor faced yet another challenge, from the new Austrian Social Democratic Party. Inspired by Karl Marx and drawing on the growing industrial working class as well as middle-class liberals in the great cities, it demanded universal revolution inside a reformed empire. Dr. Karl Renner, the affable and clever son of a Moravian peasant, who was the leading Socialist thinker on the national issue and a prominent Socialist deputy from 1907, downplayed the destructive threat of nationalism. He proposed an ingenious solution: each individual would be assigned to a nationality and each nationality would have an empire-wide body which would look after matters dear to nationalists such as culture and education. He was behind the times—or perhaps too far ahead of them. Nationalists in Austria-Hungary, as elsewhere, increasingly wanted their own states. Even his own party, the Social Democrats, for all its talk of working-class solidarity, was affected by nationalist rivalries.

In the last years of the peace, Austria-Hungary went from one political and constitutional crisis to the next. The Great War simply gave the final blow. "We were bound to die," said Count Ottokar Czernin, one of the empire's last foreign ministers. "We were at liberty to choose the manner of our death, and we chose the most terrible." The civilian and military bureaucracies, never efficient at the best of times, fell apart under the strain of war, and national rivalries turned to hatred: Germans for Hungarians and Slavs for both. From 1915 onward, desertions from the army grew sharply as Czechs, for example, asked themselves why they were fighting for German or Hungarian officers against fellow Slavs especially as the war was going badly for Austria-Hungary. In the second half of 1916, the Russians won a great victory in Galicia and the Rumanians entered the war on the Allied side, temporarily seizing Transylvania. German troops salvaged the situation but the result was to leave Austria-Hungary very much the junior partner in the alliance. When the Austrian government urged Germany to consider a negotiated peace, it was met with a contemptuous lack of interest.[2]

In November 1916, the old emperor, a faded symbol of better days, finally died. It was increasingly clear that the peoples of the empire were tired of the war and, more dangerous, tired of the old order. The news from Russia in February 1917 brought warning of where such moods could lead. "If the Monarchs of the Central Powers are not able to conclude peace *in the next few months,*" warned Czernin, "the people will do so over their heads."[3] The new emperor, Karl, a gentle and sickly young man, sent out peace feelers to the Allies, which he was careful to keep secret from Germany. These went nowhere largely because the Italians, who had much to gain from the complete defeat of Austria-Hungary, were adamantly opposed to a separate peace.

By 1918, the empire was near its end. Strikes brought the cities to standstill, parts of the navy mutinied in the Adriatic and the army hemorrhaged soldiers. The authorities watched helplessly as Czech and South Slav deputies openly demanded their own independent states and demonstrators took to the streets in support throughout the provinces. That August, Czechs, Poles and South Slavs met in the southern city of Ljubljana to demand their respective freedoms. The Allies, who had up to this point insisted that they had no intention of destroying Austria-Hungary, now gave up on it. The signs were there for friends and foe alike to see: Allied support for an independent Poland (most dramatically in Wilson's Fourteen Points), France's recognition in June 1918 of the Czechoslovak National Council, Wilson's statement the same month that "all branches of the Slav race must be completely liberated from German and Austrian domination." For Poles, Czechs, Rumanians, Slovaks, Slovenes or Croats, the prison doors were opening, whether or not they were prepared to escape.[4]

On September 15, 1918, his armies collapsing, Karl defied his German ally and issued a public appeal for a peace conference. The Allies, seeing victory at hand, rejected the offer. Two weeks later, after Bulgaria had dropped out of the war, Germany agreed that the Dual Alliance should ask for an armistice. On November 3 representatives of Austria-Hungary signed an armistice agreement. While Karl waited for an end to the fighting, the links that had bound his empire finally snapped. One by one the nationalities declared their independence: the Poles on October 15, the Ruthenes on October 19, and the South Slavs on October 29. On October 28 independent Czech and Hungarian governments took office in Prague and Budapest. Two days later, the German-speaking Austrian deputies in the parliament in Vienna appointed a German-Austrian government for what was left of the empire. The Social Democrats, who were particularly strong in what was an increasingly revolutionary Vienna, took the main offices. Renner became the first chancellor of the new republic of Austria.

Almost unnoticed, Karl renounced his part in the government of the two halves of his empire on November 11 and 13. In what was a forlorn attempt to keep the succession alive for his heirs, he did not formally abdicate. He kept his titles, the products of so many marriages, bargains and conquests: Emperor of Austria; King of Hungary, of Bohemia, of Dalmatia, Croatia, Slovenia, Lodomeria, Galicia, and Illyria; Archduke of Austria; Grand Duke of Tuscany and Kraków; Duke of Lothringia, of Salzburg, Styria, Carinthia, Carniola and Bukovina; Grand Duke of Transylvania; Margrave of Moravia; Duke of Upper and Lower Silesia, of Modena, Parma, Piacenza and Guastella, of Auschwitz and Sator, of Teschen, Friaul, Ragusa and Zara; Princely Count of Habsburg and Tyrol; and on and on. It was all gone, and he himself was to slip quietly from the world in 1922, when he died in Madeira of influenza. In March 1989, a few months before the division of Europe into East and West ended, his empress, Zita, died.

Preoccupied with satisfying Poland, Czechoslovakia, Yugoslavia and Rumania, the peacemakers had tended to overlook Austria and Hungary. The territorial commissions drawing new borders had assumed, like almost everyone else, that little Austria, reduced to its German-speaking territories, and Hungary, already shorn of the ancient kingdom of Croatia and of Slovakia, were lying inert, ready to be sliced into. What was fair to Austria and Hungary, according to the principles of self-determination, what was necessary if they were to survive, were questions that caused little concern in Paris. Neither country even had its own commission.

The greater part of the old empire had been transformed with the end of the war into friends. This raised an awkward question. Who was going to pay Austria-Hungary's reparations? Poland or Czechoslovakia or Yugoslavia? "We cannot," said Beneš firmly, "be held responsible for a war which we condemn."[5] The Allies agreed, which left as enemies only Austria and Hungary, two countries linked over the centuries at the core of the empire. Their representatives argued that they should not be seen as its heirs. As the Austrian prime minister, Karl Renner, reminded the peacemakers, the old empire had died in November 1918. "We stand before you," he said that day in June, "as one of the parts of the vanquished and fallen Empire." Austria was a new country. "In the same way as the other national States our new Republic too has sprung to life, consequently she can no more than the former be considered the successor to the late Monarchy." The British legal experts thought this made sense. The Italians, who hoped to make gains at Austria's expense, did not.[6]

Both Austria and Hungary appealed for mercy and understanding. They admitted that there had been faults, even wickednesses, committed in the past, but these were not theirs. Like Germany, they claimed to have undergone a rebirth and a cleansing. They had got rid of the old regimes and now embraced Wilson's sacred principles wholeheartedly. The Americans listened sympathetically. Wilson wanted to see Austria in the League of Nations as soon as it signed its treaty. The Europeans were sterner: Austria and Hungary must accept responsibility for the war, just as Germany had done, and on that basis be prepared to surrender war criminals and pay reparations. When Austria raised the awkward question of the responsibility of the other parts of the old empire, the Allies replied weakly that Austrians had supported the war more enthusiastically than anyone else: "Austria should be held to assume its entire share of responsibility for the crime which has unchained upon the world such a calamity."[7]

In reality, even the Europeans were prepared to go easier on Austria than on Hungary. Although Austria-Hungary bore as much responsibility as Germany for the fatal series of events that led to the outbreak of war in 1914, by 1918 even its enemies saw it as very much the junior partner, dragged along by and increasingly subordinate to an expansionist Germany hell-bent on the conquest of Europe. The well-meaning but abortive attempts in 1917 by the new emperor to open peace negotiations left a favorable impression at least on the British and the Americans.

Austria benefited more from this perception after the war than did Hungary. Lloyd George bore it no particular hostility at the peace conference. Clemenceau, whose brother was married to an Austrian, had spent much time there before the war. Like many of his compatriots, he thought Austria-Hungary had been mad to ally itself with Germany, but he had not actively promoted its disintegration until late in the war. Orlando talked dramatically about Austria being Italy's main enemy during the war, but Italian policy was ambivalent. Austria had been both enemy and ally in the past. Italy wanted to take Austrian territory, notably in the Tyrol, but it did not want Yugoslavia doing the same. Italian diplomats hinted to the Austrian government that, if there was no fuss over the Tyrol, their two countries might be able to form a close economic association.[8]

Hungary was another matter. Hungary went Bolshevik in 1919, while Austria remained socialist. It was fighting with most of its neighbors, while Austria was at peace. Hungary deserved punishment, Austria sympathy. It helped that, unlike Germany or Hungary, Austria was too small and too poor to be a threat. It had no strong sense of nationalism, for it had never been a country, only part of the Habsburg lands. In 1919 it was a strange misshapen orphan. Its picturesque and impoverished mountains and valleys clustered around the former imperial capital of Vienna, whose magnificent palaces, vast offices, grand avenues, parade grounds and cathedrals were built for the rulers of 50 million subjects, not 3 million. "We have thousands more officials than we need," the prime minister complained to a sympathetic American, "and at least two hundred thousand workmen. It is a fearful question to know what to do with them."[9] Half the population of Austria lived in Vienna, but there was little left to support them.

When the empire collapsed, so did an economic organism of which Austria had been at the heart. The Danube, navigable now from the Black Sea to southern Germany, ran through it. A huge Catherine wheel of railway lines revolved around it, linking up with other wheels around Budapest and Prague. In November 1918, the trade that carried food and raw materials into Austria and brought manufactured goods out stopped, as if, said a Vienna newspaper, by the blow of an ax. The coal and potatoes that once came from Bohemia and the beef and wheat from Hungary sat on the wrong side of new borders. Austria did not have the funds to buy them and its new neighbors were not inclined to be generous. Indeed, they were busy claiming their share of the imperial assets in Vienna: the works of art, the furniture, the collections of armor and scientific instruments, the books, the archives, even laboratories. The Italians chimed in with demands for works of art carried off to Vienna before Italy existed and the Belgians with a demand for a triptych taken by Maria Theresa.[10]

Alarming reports reached Paris about conditions in Austria: the countryside picked bare of its livestock; the empty shelves in the shops; the spread of tuberculosis; the men in ragged uniforms; the thousands of unemployed—125,000 in Vienna alone. Factories stood still and the trains and trams ran sporadically. The former commander-in-chief of the imperial armies ran a small tobacconist's shop, and lesser officers shined shoes. Starving children begged in the streets and there were long queues outside the soup kitchens. Girls from good middle-class families sold themselves for food and clothing. When several police horses were killed in one of the frequent violent demonstrations, the flesh was stripped from their bones within minutes.

The Viennese coffeehouses were still open and their orchestras still played, but their customers drank coffee made from barley and kept their overcoats on. Shops and restaurants shut early to save fuel and theaters were only allowed to open one night a week. The streets were dirty and uncared-for. Windows were boarded up because there was no glass to repair them. The Habsburg palaces had been ransacked and Schonbrünn was now a home for abandoned children, while the Hofburg was rented out for private parties. "Their whole attitude," said an American observer of the Viennese, "was very much like that of people who had suffered from some great natural calamity, such as a flood or famine. Their attitude and their arguments were very much like those of a delegation seeking help for the famine sufferers of India, and there was a complete assumption that we were free from resentment and filled with a sympathetic desire to put them on their feet."[11]

In January 1919, William Beveridge, a British civil servant (and later the father of the welfare state), was sent from Paris to assess Austria's needs. He warned that, without immediate relief, there was likely to be complete social collapse. Already the provinces were refusing to send food into Vienna. Voralberg, at the western tip of Austria, was agitating to join Switzerland. Other regions might well follow suit. The socialist government could do little and it had to share its power with a self-appointed people's militia. The peacemakers knew what these signs meant. They did not want Austria going the way of Russia or, later, Hungary. At the end of March, soon after the communists took over in Hungary, the Allies lifted their blockade and supplied credits to the Austrian government. They also shipped in food and clothing. Austria became the fourth largest beneficiary of Allied aid, after Germany, Poland and Belgium. By the spring of 1919, as a prominent Viennese journalist told an American, the situation was very serious but not yet hopeless. That June an attempt by the communists to seize power by force was put down relatively easily.[12]

The Austrian treaty was far from ready when the invitation went out to the Austrians to send their delegates to Paris; but, as Wilson said, it was a good idea to show that the Allies supported the Austrian government. They could not invite the Hungarians as well, when there was a communist government in Budapest, no doubt allied with the Russian Bolsheviks. Lloyd George was milder. He had heard that two hundred of the middle class had been killed in Budapest, but he could not vouch for the truth of that story. "We can't," he said, "refuse to make peace with the Hungarians because we don't like their government." In the end, it proved impossible to summon the Hungarians, because fighting broke out between Hungary and its neighbors.[13]

Austria's delegation was led by its prime minister, Karl Renner, a cheerful, portly man, fond of good food and drink, card games and dancing. Renner was a moderate and a realist. When he left for Paris, crowds at the railway station shouted, "Bring us a good peace." Renner replied, "Count on me to obtain all that is humanly possible for the good of our dear people. But we mustn't forget that our unhappy country did not win the victory, and we beg you not to nourish mad hopes." Along with his experts, he took with him a distinguished pacifist; a journalist who had friends in Paris from before the war, including Clemenceau; and Rudolf Slatin, a genuine British hero, who had been with General Gordon in the disastrous expedition in the Sudan (he was held prisoner by the Mahdi for years and then freed by Kitchener and given a knighthood). Slatin Pasha, as the British remembered him, wrote to his old friend Balfour, asking for Austria's delegates to be allowed to negotiate face-to-face with the peace-makers. Balfour regretted that it could not be done, but used Slatin as an unofficial means of communication.[14]

When his train arrived in Paris, Renner apologized, in French, for not speaking the language. He said how pleased he was to be visiting Paris for the first time. He smiled obligingly for the press. Another of his party managed a quiet dig when he was asked about the train journey through the battlefields: "Someone had the forethought to slow the passage of our train so that we could the better see France looking so lovely in this jolly month of May." The Austrians behaved impeccably, even when they were obliged to wait patiently for their terms because the Council of Four, which had summoned them in a burst of enthusiasm, as promptly forgot them. They played cards, read and went for long walks. "We got good French food and wines," recalled one, "which most of us enjoyed after the long hungry years." When it could be arranged, their Allied guards took them out for little expeditions. Renner asked especially to see a French agricultural college. The Austrians made a good impression—quite un-like, everyone said, the Germans, who had by then also arrived in Paris. In St. Germain the locals were particularly fond of a delegate from the Tyrol, in his chestnut hunting jacket and little green hat with its large black feather. They did not realize that he was dressed in mourning because the largely German-speaking southern part of the Tyrol had already been awarded to Italy.[15]

Enough was leaking out about the peace terms, mainly from the Ital-ians, to make the Austrians uneasy and depressed. Austria's borders had been largely left to the specialist committees, who had heard from coun-tries such as Czechoslovakia or Italy about what they wanted, but not of course from Austria itself. Galicia went to Poland, Bohemia to Czecho-slovakia. Some three million German-speaking Austrians went with them. Otto Bauer, Austria's cleverest socialist and its foreign minister, made an impassioned speech back in Vienna. "No less than two-fifths of our peo-ple are to be subjected to foreign domination, without any plebiscite and against their indisputable will, being thus deprived of their right of self-determination." He had a point, but few in Paris were prepared to listen.[16]

The Allies had also decided that Austria would not be allowed to join up with Germany. This was not something they had anticipated having to do. They had not after all expected that there would be an Austria at all. Nor had the German-speaking Austrians, apart from a handful of right-wing nationalists, shown much inclination to join Germany. They were after all the dominant group in a great empire. "God save the Emperor," the old anthem went, "Closely with the Habsburg throne, Austria's fate remains united." *Anschluss,* or union, never commanded widespread support until the last days of the Great War. On October 16, as Austria-Hungary was scrambling desperately to get out of the war and indeed to survive, Emperor Karl announced the creation of a new empire "in which every people would build its own political community in its own area of settlement." Unlike Czechs or Poles or Slovenes, German-speakers had never developed such a community. Who would need them when, as looked increasingly likely, there were no more emperors? How would they live among a Slavic majority? The German-Austrians faced a bleak future, whether or not Austria-Hungary survived, and it was out of that pessimism that the demand for *Anschluss* with Germany burgeoned.[17]

On October 21, German-speaking deputies in the Austrian parliament met as a Provisional National Assembly. They did not truly represent a nation as the Czech or Slovenian deputies did and, at that point, they asked not for union with Germany but for self-determination for Germans within the old Habsburg empire. By November 11, however, there was no longer either emperor or empire. It was also clear that the states emerging out of the wreckage of Austria-Hungary had no interest in any sort of political arrangement with German-speaking Austria. On November 12, the assembly, speaking in the name of all Austrian Germans, proclaimed the republic of Austria in one breath and asserted that it was part of the larger German republic in the next. It was an act born out of fear, much as Croatia's decision to join with Serbia was. Germany, the onetime enemy and the mistrusted ally, suddenly looked like a refuge. Unlikely political groups joined forces in those bewildering last days of the empire— anti-Semites, Jews, nationalists, socialists, liberals, Tyrolese and Styrians fearful of falling under Italian or Serbian rule—to demand union with Germany.[18]

Many Austrians, in fact, had reservations about *Anschluss:* Catholics, the great majority, who did not like North German Protestants; businessmen who feared German competition; and Viennese who did not want their city to take second place to Berlin or Weimar. Austrians of all classes remembered the long rivalry between Prussia and Austria for leadership of all Germans and the way in which Germany had refused to let Austria-Hungary make a separate peace during the war. But what alternative was there for them now?

By 1918, many Austrians saw *Anschluss* as the only hope for protection and prosperity for their little country. In the universities and coffeehouses, pan-German intellectuals talked dramatically of rejoining the severed branch to the great German tree. The Socialists were enthusiastic because, as Bauer argued, Germany was moving leftward. Joining the Austrian and German working classes would strengthen socialism everywhere. Renner's attitude was more pragmatic and more typical: "the fear of famine and unemployment and *Anschluss* as the only possible solution."[19]

The new provisional assembly in Vienna opened negotiations with Germany. The Austrians moved cautiously, making it clear to the Germans that any union must respect Austria's unique character. The Germans were equally cautious. Germany did not want to annoy the peacemakers unnecessarily, especially before its own terms were settled. As Brockdorff-Rantzau, the German foreign minister, made clear to Bauer, Germany had to think of itself. If the Allies thought that it was gaining territory in the south, they would be all the more inclined to take away its land in the west and east.[20]

These discussions were academic. The Allies had made up their minds, largely at France's insistence, to forbid any union between the two German-speaking countries. Briefly, at the end of the war, the French had toyed with the idea of encouraging Austria and Bavaria to unite, to form a strong Catholic bloc to counter Protestant Prussia. When it became clear that neither the British nor the Americans would support the breakup of Germany, French policy switched to preventing Austria from falling into Germany's arms. In Vienna, the French representative dropped heavy hints that if Austria wanted favorable peace terms, it should abandon all talk of *Anschluss*. France was for peace, said Clemenceau. "But if we reduce our armaments, and if, at the same time, Austria adds seven million inhabitants to the population of Germany, the power of our German neighbours will increase in a manner very threatening to us." Wilson worried that this might contradict Austrian self-determination, but in the end he and Clemenceau agreed in April that there would be a clause in the German treaty specifying that Germany must respect Austria's borders. Lloyd George suggested a face-saving compromise: that Austria could join Germany if the League of Nations approved. Wilson accepted the suggestion with relief, and clauses were inserted to that effect in both the German and Austrian treaties. Since the vote in the League Council had to be unanimous, this effectively gave France and Italy a veto.[21]

At the end of May the Austrian delegation complained gently that it was rather disturbed over the "incertitude" about its peace terms. The treaty for Austria, along with those for Hungary, Bulgaria and Turkey, still lay in bits and pieces around Paris, in this committee or that commission. The Council of Four, which had to approve the final drafts, had been occupied with last-minute negotiations on the German treaty and wrangling over Italy's claims. Austria and its problems came well down the list. As a British expert complained, "There is practically no one on the spot who has really sound knowledge and experience, and of course the Italians are very difficult."[22]

What the Austrian delegation finally saw on June 2 was a slapdash document—"a simulacrum of a Treaty," in Hankey's opinion. Some clauses had been lifted wholesale from the German treaty and there had been no time to check for accuracy and consistency. The Austrians were startled to learn, for example, that they were forbidden to have submarines. The terms were also, as Clemenceau explained with some embarrassment, incomplete. The Allies had not been able to agree on some of Austria's borders, especially those with Italy, in the Tyrol, and with Yugoslavia. Because of a last-minute disagreement, Clemenceau had been obliged to tear out the section on the Yugoslav borders just before he handed the terms to the Austrians.[23]

Although the peacemakers used the German treaty as a template, they went easier on Austria. On war guilt, for example: it was one thing to punish the kaiser, but, as Lloyd George pointed out, Emperor Karl had not been on the throne in 1914. As for reparations, the experts originally worked out an impossible scheme whereby Austria and Hungary would end up paying most of the old empire's war debt as well as reparations. "If a man were kept alive by charity," said Balfour, "he could not be asked to pay his debts." The job of setting the figures for reparations was eventually turned over to the reparation commission, which two years later admitted that Austria could not pay anything at all. Hungary, less fortunate, was scheduled to make annual payments in gold and materials. It actually met its obligations for several years, until its economic situation grew so bad that the Allies both advanced loans and suspended reparations. In 1930, during the Depression, Hungary's reparations were rescheduled, with payments to start in 1944.[24]

When he received the terms, which were made public once they were handed over, Renner made a dignified and conciliatory speech. "We know," he said, "that we have to receive peace out of your hands, out of the hands of victors. We are firmly resolved to conscientiously weigh each and any proposition laid before us, each and any advice offered by you to us." Back at their hotel, the Austrian delegation pored over the treaty, as one said, "very sad, bitter and depressed when we realized that Austria had received harsher terms than Germany while we had hoped they would be more favourable." In Austria itself, where there were three days of mourning, the shock and disillusionment were profound. "Never," said an editorial in a left-wing paper, "has the substance of a treaty of peace so grossly betrayed the intentions which were said to have guided its construction as is the case with this Treaty."[25]

The Austrians submitted their written comments and then waited while the peacemakers, depleted in July by the departure of many of the top statesmen, considered their own responses. "The contrast was great between the sunny gardens," recalled an Austrian financial expert, "our leisure, the good fare and our prolonged expectation of the punishment which we the defeated enemies had to expect from our conquerors." He passed the time by reading Alexandre Dumas and avoiding the nervous conversation of his fellow delegates. The Austrian strategy was to concentrate on several key issues rather than all the terms. They left the reparations clauses alone, on the sensible grounds that they would never be able to pay. They managed, however, to get some important concessions, including a clause prohibiting Austria's art treasures from being divided up among the successor states.[26]

The peacemakers also agreed to a plebiscite in the area around Klagenfurt in the south of Carinthia, which was also being claimed by Yugoslavia. Perhaps this was to compensate for ignoring the self-determination rights of the Germans going to Czechoslovakia in the north, perhaps because Yugoslavia did not inspire quite the same enthusiasm as Czechoslovakia, or perhaps simply to defuse what threatened to become another small war.

Klagenfurt, a peaceful country of lakes and hills on the northern slope of the Karawaken mountains, dotted with medieval monasteries, Gothic churches, Baroque palaces and whitewashed chalets, had once been on the front lines between the Austrian empire and the Ottoman Turks. The end of the war had left a makeshift Austrian administration in the north; in the south, a heavy-handed Yugoslav occupation soon stirred up resistance. Tension was high between Austrians and Yugoslavs along the armistice line and there was sporadic fighting. In 1919 Klagenfurt's population of about 150,000 was mixed; Slovene-speakers were in a majority, but the main towns were German. Most people switched easily between one language and the other. In February, an American mission drove through, stopping people at random to ask which nation they belonged to. The results surprised them: "The Slovene who does not want to be a Jugo-Slav is a curiosity we should never have believed in had we not seen him, and in large numbers."[27]

Italy was the main stumbling block to a decision, objecting in principle to Yugoslav claims but also anxious to prevent the railway line that linked its new port of Trieste with Vienna from running through Yugoslav territory. The Commission on Rumanian and Yugoslav Affairs threw the issue up to the Supreme Council, which simply bounced it back again. In May, the smaller problem of Klagenfurt got drawn into the bitter dispute between Italy and its allies over Italian borders on its east. The Yugoslavs sat on the sidelines worrying. The Austrians began to hope. As Wickham Steed reported, "a marked disposition to be very tender towards Austria had become noticeable among the 'Big Three.' The Southern Slavs began to fear that, while the Italians were driving a hard bargain with them in the Adriatic, the other Allies would support the Austrians in driving a hard bargain with them in the delimitation of the Slovene frontier in Carinthia."[28] The Yugoslav delegation reduced its demands slightly, a gesture that was vitiated when Yugoslav troops in Carinthia suddenly surged north at the end of May. The Council of Four ordered a cease-fire; it was a measure of the council's dwindling authority in Central Europe that fighting stopped only after several weeks. In the meantime, the Yugoslavs seized the whole area around Klagenfurt and much useful Austrian war matériel, and the Italians took part of a crucial railway line.

The Yugoslavs resisted the idea of partition, which was now being floated; they also strenuously objected to the proposal, mainly from the British and the Americans, for a plebiscite. (They suspected that they would lose.) They had some support from Clemenceau, who was always mindful that he might be asked to hold one in Alsace-Lorraine. Wilson, however, was determined that in this area, at least, the inhabitants would choose for themselves. On May 31 he emerged from the Council of Four and, as the French raised their eyebrows, announced, "If the experts will follow me, I am going to explain the matter to them." The Big Four and their experts crawled around a huge map on the floor. An irritated Orlando butted an American out of his way.[29]

The Yugoslavs muttered about boycotting the treaty with Austria but eventually agreed to a compromise. The part of Austria just to the north of Slovenia would have a plebiscite; if the inhabitants voted to join Yugoslavia, then the northern, more German part would also hold one. In October 1920 the vote, which all observers agreed was done in exemplary fashion, took place; a majority of 22,000 to 15,000 was for staying with Austria. The voters seemed to have been swayed by their economic links with Austria and a feeling that Austria was more advanced than the new Yugoslav state. For women voters, the knowledge that their sons were liable to conscription in Yugoslavia but not in Austria may also have played a part. If they could have seen into the future, when Austria became part of Nazi Germany, and Slovene children were forced into German schools and Slovene identity largely suppressed, would they have voted differently?[30]

The Yugoslav army made a dramatic march into the disputed zone immediately after the result was announced but withdrew without fuss two days later. The Slovenes in Yugoslavia complained bitterly about the "amputation" of national territory and suspected, probably correctly, that Serb leaders had never really been prepared to go to the wall, that they were far more concerned with Serbia's borders in the north and in the east.[31] Yet another grievance entered the catalog in the new Yugoslav state and yet another bitter memory was left between neighbors.

Austria asked for another concession from the Allies, a strip of territory from the western edge of Hungary. (In shape, it was close to the proposed corridor between Czechoslovakia and Yugoslavia, which the Peace Conference had turned down.) The Austrians argued that the inhabitants were mainly German. Unfortunately, they had never lived under Austrian rule and appeared to see themselves as part of Hungary. Of course, said a British expert, it was no use asking them because the communist revolution in Hungary had thoroughly confused them. (The Austrian government found this a useful argument when the question of a plebiscite was raised by Hungary.) Austria also used strategic grounds—Vienna, along with crucial roads and railways, was too close to the Hungarian border—and, rather plaintively, nutritional ones. The area had always supplied food to the Viennese, who had been lacking vegetables and milk ever since Hungary became an independent state. The Hungarians produced their counterarguments but the peacemakers listened to the Austrians. Most of the area, with the exception of one city, went to Austria. Hungary tried unsuccessfully to persuade Hitler to hand it back in 1938 as a reward for staying neutral during the *Anschluss*. Austria thus became the only defeated nation to gain new territory at the Peace Conference. It signed the Treaty of St. Germain in September 1919.[32]

Austria's first experience with independence was not happy. In the 1920s its economy staggered from crisis to crisis, tided over by parsimonious loans from the powers. Even before the Depression unemployment ran at well over 10 percent a year. In March 1938, when Hitler, with the connivance of the Austrian Nazis, moved in, Austrians, if they were not Jewish or communist, greeted *Anschluss* with relief. Hitler made a triumphal march from his birthplace just over the Austrian border to Vienna as ecstatic crowds cheered and threw flowers. Even rational men such as Renner were briefly swept up. In 1945 a chastened Austria regained its separate existence and an old Renner became its president. There has been little talk of *Anschluss* since.

20

Hungary

O N MARCH 23, 1919, as the first signs of spring were appearing, two American experts walked glumly in the Bois de Boulogne. "We had just learned," one wrote in his diary, "of the outbreak of troubles in Hungary, which, if they spread, may make waste paper of our conventions for a while to come."[1] If Austria had been causing mild concern in Paris, Hungary had been setting off alarm bells, especially when Béla Kun, an unknown communist, seized power in Budapest. Suddenly Bolshevism appeared to have taken a giant step into the rich Hungarian plain, with its key strategic position. With a short hop, it could be in Austria, already under a socialist government, or the Balkans, and with another step still, into Bavaria, where the communists were edging toward their brief moment in power. Kun himself sent out contradictory signals, with reassuring messages to the Allied leaders but fraternal greetings to their working classes. More worrying, he sent an offer eastward to Lenin, asking for a treaty. Perhaps the two communist states could establish a link through the disputed territory on the eastern edges of Poland and Czechoslovakia, where there were said to be local Bolshevik forces on the march.

Even before Kun arrived on the scene, the peacemakers were suspicious of Hungary. With its great landed magnates, its cowed peasantry and its history (the Magyars had stormed out of central Asia in the ninth century), there was something not quite European about Hungary. Liberals tended to blame the worst faults of the old empire on the Hungarian oligarchy. "There has been much talk of suppressing the revolution in Hungary," Lloyd George told his colleagues on the Council of Four when they first heard the news. "I don't see why we should do that: there are few countries so much in need of a revolution. This very day, I had a conversation with someone who has visited Hungary and who knows it well; he tells me that this country has the worst system of landholding in Europe. The peasants there are as oppressed as they were in the Middle Ages, and manorial law still exists there."[2]

This time Lloyd George was not far wrong. Budapest was an elegant, modern capital, but the countryside, which produced much of Hungary's wealth, was a different world. Serfdom had been finally abolished in 1848, but much of the land was still held in large estates, by aristocrats, the gentry or the church. In 1914 Prince Esterházy owned 230,000 hectares; one of his ancestors had had a uniform on which all the buttons were diamonds and the seams were marked out in pearls. The grand families were worldly and international, with houses in Vienna and Paris, English nannies and grooms, French cooks and German music masters. They spoke easily in French or Latin, less so in Hungarian. They produced the political leaders, the generals, occasionally even liberal reformers, but most were deeply conservative and uninterested in anything outside their own world. They distrusted Jews, although rich Jewish industrialists and bankers were starting to marry their children; they believed in keeping the non-Magyars, the Croats, Slovaks or Rumanians who probably made up more than half the population of prewar Hungary, firmly under control.[3]

The man Béla Kun overthrew in March 1919 was one of the greatest landowners of them all. Michael Károlyi, who took over in the last chaotic days of the war, owned 60,000 acres, a glass factory, a coal mine, a superb country house, a mansion in Budapest and several shooting lodges. When he tipped a Gypsy band in a restaurant the usual amount, his tutor, he recalled, reprimanded him. "I should pay at least double the amount given by anyone else, for I must never forget that I was a Count Károlyi." Fate had given him much but not everything. He was a lonely, ugly child with a cleft palate. Surrounded by protective relatives and servants, he was deeply hurt when, on his first forays into Hungarian society, people laughed at him and women rejected his timid advances.[4]

The young Károlyi reacted by throwing himself madly into various pursuits. He forced himself to become an orator and took up politics. He gambled, he drank, he drove fast cars very badly. He became the foremost dandy in Budapest, then the wildest man-about-town. He played polo recklessly, he fenced compulsively, he took one of the first flights over the city. He raised eyebrows by finding shooting parties boring, and doubts about his manhood when he refused the young peasant girl in his bed (supplied by custom to all male guests along with the game). His ideas, at least by the standards of his world, were radical. Before the war he was seen with strange people: socialists, middle-class politicians, intellectuals.[5]

When the war started, Károlyi joined up. (His regiment was h
from active service until his wife gave birth to their first child.) By 191₀,
was demanding a separate peace with the Allies and, finally, the end of the
union with Austria. On October 31 Károlyi became Hungary's prime
minister; two weeks later, he proclaimed a republic. "He seems a very
good fellow," reported an American, "but nervous and permanently worried, which is perhaps not surprising."[6] The army no longer obeyed orders, the civil administration had broken down, the transport system had
collapsed and money was rapidly losing its value.

The Hungarians, with their territory melting away, cast about for protection. A cousin of the emperor, now calling himself Joe Habsburg,
wrote to George V in London suggesting that Hungary become part of the
British empire. Perhaps, Hungarians hoped, they could borrow an English prince. Like the Germans and the Austrians, they also hoped that
their republican revolution would soften the Allies. The Hungarian Academy appealed to distinguished Allied scholars not to let Hungary be dismembered. Károlyi dispatched a prominent feminist as his representative
to contact the Allies in neutral Switzerland, calculating, wrongly as it
turned out, that this would demonstrate the new, liberal face of Hungary.
(She shocked the conservative Swiss and spent most of her time quarreling with her own staff.) A leading Budapest restaurant named a dish in
honor of Marshal Foch. (Unfortunately, in Hungarian it came out as
"diarrhea soup.")[7]

Like everyone else, the Hungarians looked to the Americans. His peace
platform, Károlyi assured American representatives in Budapest, was "Wilson, Wilson, Wilson." The city was festooned with Wilson's photograph
and the slogan "A Wilson Peace Is the Only Peace for Hungary." What that
meant, at least to Hungarians, was not self-determination for the minorities within Hungary but that their country should keep its historic boundaries. There was much talk of Switzerland, a favorite analogy in Central
Europe, of regional autonomy, and of language and other rights. The
Károlyi government set about passing laws to this effect.[8]

The Hungarian appeals were futile. The Allies remained suspicious of
Hungary. Was Károlyi really as liberal as he claimed? He was, after all, an
aristocrat, related to the men who had led Hungary into the war. If the
British and the Americans were cool, the French were actively hostile.
Only the Italians were sympathetic, simply because they hoped to use
Hungary against Yugoslavia. That both Czechoslovakia and Rumania
were able to present their demands as Allies did not help Hungary. Nor
did the fact that Hungary's borders were drawn piecemeal, in the Czechoslovak commission and the one on Rumania and Yugoslavia. As Nicol-

son, who represented Britain on both, admitted, "it was only too late that it was realised that these two separate Committees had between them imposed upon Hungary a loss of territory and population which, when combined, was very serious indeed."[9]

Thanks partly to the French, whose troops made up the bulk of Allied forces in Central Europe, Hungary had already lost control of much of its territory before the Peace Conference started. When Károlyi and his colleagues had arrived in Belgrade in November 1918 to surrender, they had come full of optimism, with postcards for the French general Louis Franchet d'Esperey to autograph. He had greeted them coldly, dismissing their claim to represent a new, liberal Hungary. "I know your history," he said. "In your country you have oppressed those who are not Magyar. Now you have the Czechs, Slovaks, Rumanians, Yugoslavs as enemies; I hold these people in the hollow of my hand; I have only to make a sign and you will be destroyed." The French allowed the Serbians to move north into Hungarian territory, the Czechs to take over Slovakia, and the Rumanians to advance westward into their coveted Transylvania. When the Hungarian government complained to Colonel Ferdinand Vix, the head of the French military mission in Budapest, he refused to pass on their complaints.[10]

The Hungarians feared that temporary occupations would harden into permanent possession. They had resigned themselves to the loss of Croatia, even Slovakia, although in both cases they had hoped for more generous boundaries than the ones they finally got. Transylvania was something else again. Over the hills dividing the Hungarian plain from the highlands, it lay sheltered within the arrowhead of the Carpathians where they point down toward the Black Sea. Transylvania was almost half the old kingdom of Hungary; it was rich; and it was woven into Hungarian history.

Geography gave Transylvania natural defenses, but over the centuries outsiders—Romans, Germans, Slavs, Magyars—found their way there. By the eleventh century, it was under Hungarian control and it remained so, in various forms, until 1918. Rumanian scholars dismissed this history, claiming that Rumanians had been there long before anyone else. "It was in this territory," Brătianu told the Supreme Council in February, "that the Rumanian nation had been constituted and formed; and all its aspirations for centuries had tended towards the political union of that territory." (Brătianu did not mention that the Rumanian claims went well beyond the old boundaries of Transylvania, into Hungary proper.) Rumania, he went on, had been promised Transylvania under the Treaty of Bucharest when it entered the war in 1916. This was not persuasive, because everyone remembered how Rumania had made a separate peace with Germany in 1918. In fact, Brătianu had a much better argument: even according to Hungarian statistics, Rumanians made up more than half the population in Transylvania; Hungarians constituted only 23 percent, with Germans and others accounting for the rest. At the end of the war, an assembly of Transylvanian Rumanians had voted overwhelmingly for union with Rumania. The local Germans eventually added their support. The Hungarians, of course, remained opposed. The peacemakers expressed some concerns over the Hungarian minority—Brătianu said they would be treated in the most liberal fashion—but did not question that Transylvania should go to Rumania. Indeed, the French had made up their minds long before they had heard the Rumanian case.[11]

The peacemakers asked the Commission on Rumanian and Yugoslav Affairs to draw the new border between Hungary and Rumania. The French and the Italians wanted to give Rumania a generous swath of Hungary as well, while the British and the Americans followed ethnic lines, which would have kept the border further east. As one of the British experts said, "The balance must naturally be inclined towards our ally Rumania rather than towards our enemy Hungary." The commission came up with a compromise report in March, which went a long way toward satisfying Rumania's demands. When rumors of its contents reached Hungary, they caused consternation. Posters with maps of a Hungary divided into four asked "Voulez-vous faire quatre Alsace-Lorraines?" ("Do you want to create four Alsace-Lorraines?") Before the Supreme Council could decide what to do, the revolution in Hungary broke out, adding the stigma of Bolshevism to the beleaguered country.[12]

Károlyi's government had been under attack from the right, which bitterly resented attempts at land reform, and the left, which felt it was not going far enough. The peacemakers did little to help. Where Austria received 288,000 tons of food and clothing for relief in the first six months of 1919, Hungary got only 635 tons. "Our difficulties," Károlyi recalled bitterly in exile, "were multiplied a thousand times by the ill-will and inefficiency of the different foreign missions in Budapest." On March 20, Colonel Vix delivered the final blow when he presented Károlyi with a decision from the Supreme Council establishing a neutral zone between Hungary and Rumania. Hungary had ten days to withdraw all its troops to the west of this area, while Rumania could advance to its eastern edge. This, according to the peacemakers, was to prevent clashes between the two nations. The Hungarians did not see it in that light.[13]

As Károlyi pointed out to Vix, the Hungarians were being asked to withdraw from almost exactly the territory claimed by Rumania, while

Rumanian troops were being allowed to move westward by a hundred kilometers. What was to stop them from going still farther into Hungary? If he agreed to the neutral zone, he added, there would be a revolution and his government would fall. Under his breath, he muttered: "As far as I am concerned, I should be glad to be rid of it." Vix was unmoved; it was not, he kept repeating, a matter of politics. The Hungarians must calm down and accept the ultimatum from Paris. He was sure that the Allies would keep Rumania in check. They might as well occupy the whole country now, said Károlyi: "Make it a French colony, or a Rumanian colony, or a Czechoslovak colony." Vix shrugged. The following day Károlyi's government fell and he went into exile.[14] He died on the French Riviera in 1955.

Károlyi's successor was, as he predicted, a revolutionary. Béla Kun came from a tiny village in Transylvania and was the son of a drunken, shiftless notary. (His father was a nonpracticing Jew, a fact later seized upon by anti-Semites as proof of a widespread Jewish-Marxist conspiracy.) A dandy and a poseur, Kun was vain, hot-tempered and self-centered. He was also, it was generally agreed, ugly, with a huge head supported on a wiry small body, a flat nose and enormous ears. Before the war he had made something of a name as a radical journalist. In 1914, he joined up and fought against the Russians on the Eastern Front, where he was captured and sent to a prisoner-of-war camp. The Russian Revolution of 1917 brought a rapid change in both his politics and his fortunes. By 1918 he was free and in Moscow, meeting with Lenin and the other Bolsheviks, and the leader of a new Hungarian communist movement. At the end of the war, provided with gold and fake documents by his new friends, Kun traveled back to Hungary to spread the revolution. His timing was perfect.[15]

Kun moved through Hungary's chaotic politics like a whirlwind, issuing manifestos and demands, calling strikes and demonstrations. When the police in Budapest beat him up, he achieved martyrdom. On March 21, the day after the Allied ultimatum, Károlyi's socialist allies in the government came to see Kun in prison; they were prepared to hand over power to the communists. Béla Kun got his freedom, his revolution and his power that day, all without a shot being fired. The next day he declared Hungary a Soviet republic.[16]

In the opinion of a young American officer in Budapest, the revolution was more nationalist than communist: "The Hungarians who are united in their conviction that Hungary must not be dismembered, have made use of Bolshevism as a last desperate resort to preserve the integrity of their country." In Paris the Council of Four hesitated. Clemenceau and his military advisers were for reinforcing the Rumanians and letting them loose on both the Russian and Hungarian Bolsheviks. Foch appeared with a large map to demonstrate how Rumania was the key to preventing a solid Bolshevik front in the center of Europe. Forget the White Russians in southern Russia, he said brutally; they were already lost. "This is why I tell you: build upon Rumania, because there you have not only an army, but also a government and a people." Wilson admitted that he was uncertain about the right course of action. "What exactly is our position with regards to the Bolsheviks?" Perhaps it had been unwise to establish the neutral zone between Rumania and Hungary: "It doesn't seem this method has produced the desired result." Should the Peace Conference be choosing sides? "Nominally we are friends of the Hungarians and even better friends of the Rumanians." Clemenceau responded sharply, "The Hungarians are not our friends but our enemies." Of all the peoples in Austria-Hungary, they had been the most reluctant to surrender.[17]

Lloyd George, who was now modifying his earlier hostility to Hungary, sided with Wilson. After all, the Croats and the Slovenes had also fought until the bitter end for Austria-Hungary, and the Allies were now friendly with them. "Why not enter into conversation with the Magyars as well?" The German peace terms should be a warning to them all; he had spent the previous weekend at Fontainebleau considering their flaws—the way, for example, they were leaving Germans under Polish rule. It was just as dangerous to the future peace of Europe to leave millions of Hungarians outside their country. He was also doubtful, as a result of their experience with Russia, about the prospects for a military solution to Bolshevism. "Let's not deal with Hungary as with Russia," he urged the others. "One Russia is enough for us." He suggested that they send some reliable person, Smuts perhaps, to report on Kun and his regime. Wilson agreed with enthusiasm, Clemenceau with reluctance. Under French pressure, the Council of Four also agreed to ship military supplies to Rumania.[18]

On the evening of April Fool's Day, Smuts and his aides, including Harold Nicolson, left Paris on a special train for Budapest. Ostensibly, Smuts's job was to persuade the Hungarians to accept the neutral zone between Hungary and Rumania; his real purpose was to assess Kun and decide whether he might be used as an informal conduit to Lenin. (The Allies still had not come up with a workable policy on Russia.) The British also hoped that the mission might counteract French influence in central Europe. The news caused tremendous excitement in Budapest, where it was seen as a sign that the Paris Peace Conference was prepared to recognize the new government. Kun hastily sold off Hungary's remaining assets—its stocks of fats—to Italy and ordered a huge amount of red velvet to drape the buildings leading from the railway station to Budapest's leading hotel, which itself was decorated with a giant Union Jack and a tricolor.[19]

When he arrived in Budapest, Smuts refused to play along. He remained firmly in his special train and Kun was obliged to come to him. (The miles of red velvet had to wait until May Day to make their appearance.) Nicolson, no friend to Hungary at the best of times, viewed the communist with all the hauteur of his class. "A little man of about 30: puffy white face and loose wet lips: shaven head: impression of red hair: shifty suspicious eyes: he has the face of a sulky and uncertain criminal." And the new Hungarian foreign minister, who accompanied Kun, was just as distasteful: "A little oily Jew—fur-coat rather moth-eaten—string green tie—dirty collar."[20]

The discussions, in the cramped quarters of the dining car, did not go well. Kun wanted recognition; Smuts was determined to withhold it. Kun wanted the Rumanians to withdraw to the east of the neutral zone; Smuts was only prepared to make minor concessions that would have left Rumania occupying Transylvania. Smuts decided that there was no point in further bargaining. "Well, gentlemen," he said at the end of the second day, "I must bid you good-bye." He politely shook hands and stepped back on his train, which, to the amazement of the Hungarians, slowly pulled out of the station.[21] Smuts concluded from his brief foray that Kun was a stupid man whose government was unlikely to last long.

Yet Smuts was willing, as he told the peacemakers in Paris, to follow up on the one useful suggestion Kun had made: that the nations of the former Austria-Hungary be called together to work out their common borders and common economic policies. Smuts even worked briefly with Keynes on a plan for an international loan to get the economies in the Danube basin going again. These were sensible ideas, but nothing came of them in Paris. The Italians were firmly against anything that smacked of a reborn Austria-Hungary, and none of the other Allies had a particular interest in implementing Kun's suggestions. Even if they had tried, the mutual hostilities among the successors to Austria-Hungary might have made the job impossible. There was to be precious little cooperation, economic or otherwise, along the Danube in the interwar years. The dream has never quite died, though. The son of the last emperor, Dr. Otto von Habsburg-Lothringen, as he is known in the European parliament, works indefatigably for cooperation among the nations that once belonged to his ancestors.[22]

In Hungary the communist-controlled newspapers claimed that Smuts's mission meant the Allies had recognized their regime. They did not report his sudden departure, but versions of what had taken place

leaked out, adding to public unease. It was rumored that the Allies were
sending an army to occupy Budapest, or that Trotsky and a Red Army
were approaching in the northeast to support the Hungarian revolution
and the one which had just occurred in Bavaria. The Austrian Reds were
about to seize Vienna. The communists were arresting thousands of the
middle and upper classes. There were right-wing plots to seize power,
left-wing plans to unleash mass terror. Not all the rumors were false.[23]

Trotsky was not on his way, but the Bolsheviks were hoping to link up
with their fellow communists. In Belgrade, Franchet d'Esperey was trying
to persuade the Yugoslavs to send part of their army north to Budapest
against Kun. In a palace in Vienna, exiled noblemen, including Károlyi's
relatives, were meeting secretly to plan a counterrevolution. (In a daring
raid on the Hungarian embassy, the conspirators seized a small fortune in
cash which Kun had sent out of the country; unfortunately, they immediately became immobilized with quarrels over how to spend it.) In the
Hungarian countryside, safely out of Budapest's reach, army officers led
by another one of Károlyi's cousins planned a military coup. They persuaded one of Austria-Hungary's few naval war heroes, Admiral Miklós
Horthy, to join them.[24]

Kun's regime made things easy for its opponents. In its 133 days in
power it announced dramatic and largely unenforceable reforms: prohibition of alcohol, socialization of the factories, distribution of the big estates,
the abolition of all titles, proletarian culture for all, compulsory baths and
sex education for schoolchildren, compulsory reallocation of housing and
furniture, the standardization of graves. They alienated almost every section of the population, from Catholics horrified by plans to turn churches
into cinemas, to liberals appalled by the censorship, the arbitrary arrests
and the secret police. Public opinion condemned the regime above all for
its failure to cope with inflation and shortages, and its own corruption.[25]

What finally finished off Kun's government, though, were its external
enemies. In April, a week after Smuts left Budapest, the Rumanian army,
with a nod and a wink from the French military, attacked through the neutral zone toward Budapest. The Czechs made their move in the north a
few days later. In Paris, the Rumanians, like the Czechoslovaks, claimed
that they were blameless. "I fear," Brătianu told the Council of Four, "that
you are not perfectly informed about the role of the Rumanian army and
the Hungarian provocations." Their moves were entirely defensive.
"They are all little brigand peoples," complained Lloyd George, "who only
want to steal territories." As the Rumanians moved well west of what they
were claiming, even Clemenceau found their demands excessive. And he
was worried about the political implications: his own left feared that he

was planning to intervene against the Hungarian communists. He was also getting alarming reports about the state of morale among French forces supervising the armistice in Eastern Europe.[26]

The Hungarians temporarily rallied. Even conservative army officers found Béla Kun preferable to the Rumanians. The regime, for its part, dropped the language of the proletarian revolution and appealed simply to patriotism. Volunteers rushed to join the army. The Italians, motivated largely by their hostility to Hungary's other hostile neighbor, Yugoslavia, sold Kun guns and ammunition. According to a British observer, they also passed on information about Allied plans. By the middle of May Hungarian forces had pushed the Czechs back and driven a wedge between them and the Rumanians.[27]

In Paris, the peacemakers failed to take this in at first. Wilson was inclined to think the Hungarians the innocent party but asked an awkward, and all too familiar, question: "Do we have a way of stopping the movement of the Rumanians?" Lloyd George and Clemenceau could only suggest talking firmly to Brătianu. They were, it must be admitted, distracted by the breach with the Italians over Fiume. When the Council of Four saw its experts' recommendations on Hungary's borders with Rumania and Czechoslovakia in the second week of May, it approved them with scarcely any discussion.[28]

The fighting went briskly on, forcing the peacemakers to take notice. In June a British journalist recently arrived from Hungary was invited to lunch with Lloyd George and his military adviser, Henry Wilson, to explain the situation. He found the British prime minister in a cheerful mood; together, they looked at a map of Central Europe. Lloyd George now blamed the Czechoslovaks and the Rumanians for the conflict. "I think," he added, "the Hungarians are the best of the lot out there. They are the most powerful race and have always kept the others in order." They talked about Allied intervention against Béla Kun. Henry Wilson asked gloomily, "Where are the troops to come from?" Lloyd George maintained that Bolshevism would die out of its own accord. He had enjoyed this chat; it would be helpful when he talked to his colleagues later that day. "It was quite obvious," the journalist concluded, "that the Big Four had hardly given the countries east of Germany a thought, being far too occupied with the principal offender to bother about the lesser minions."[29]

The Council of Four sent off its warnings and orders, just as it had done with the Poles, and with as little success. The Rumanians were told that they must not occupy Budapest. Brătianu took a high moral line: "We wanted in a spirit of solidarity with the Entente to march on Pest in order to help in the re-establishment of order." This was a familiar claim; so was his repeated charge that the Allies were treating Rumania with ingratitude after its great services during the war. The Hungarians were ordered to stop fighting. Kun replied that Hungary was willing to stop if Rumania and Czechoslovakia did.[30]

The Allies found it difficult to agree on what to do next. The French military were for sending in an army made up of Rumanian, Yugoslav and French troops to occupy what was left of Hungary; the Americans pointed out that, once in, the Rumanians might never leave. Lloyd George suggested that they might threaten to cut off supplies to Rumania. On June 12, the Council of Four settled for telegrams to Hungary, Czechoslovakia and Rumania, informing them of what their new borders were to be and ordering them to withdraw their troops into their own territory. There was to be no more land-grabbing; the Allies would not be induced to change their decisions "by the unscrupulous use of military methods." The American delegate, General Bliss, was deputed to make sure the various forces withdrew. "A nice job," he wrote to his wife, "to unload on a peaceful and peaceloving and somewhat tired man, isn't it?"[31]

Lloyd George warned Wilson and Clemenceau that "we must impose our will now; we can no longer hurl vain orders." But the fighting went on. The Rumanians refused to move back toward the east. Brătianu feared, he said, a simultaneous attack by Kun and the Russian Bolsheviks, perhaps even one from Bulgaria which, he claimed, was armed to the teeth. In July, the Hungarians provided him with an excuse to start advancing again when Kun, in a last desperate gamble, tried to throw the Rumanians back across the Tisza River, about a hundred kilometers east of Budapest. The Rumanians counterattacked in force. Several units of the Hungarian army that were in touch with the opposition around Admiral Horthy stopped fighting, and the Hungarian lines collapsed. Kun fled to Austria and then the Soviet Union. He was arrested there during Stalin's purges, charged with conspiring with the Rumanian secret police, and executed in the autumn of 1939.[32]

On August 3, 1919, Rumanian troops entered Budapest. The Yugoslavs and the Czechoslovaks took the opportunity to advance farther into Hungarian territory along their borders. In spite of repeated complaints from the Allies, all of Hungary's enemies stayed firmly where they were through the autumn of 1919. A series of weak Hungarian governments proved unable to deal either with them or with the Horthy forces, who were going from strength to strength in the countryside. "If the three great powers had been able to keep armies," the American military representative in Budapest wrote in his diary, "and could have sent them immediately to any place where trouble was brewing, it would have been entirely different, but the Supreme Council's prestige went aglimmering when a steady stream of ultimata had no effect whatever upon that miserable little nation of Rumania." The Peace Conference was by now winding down. Wilson was back in the United States, trying vainly to get the League approved by Congress, Lloyd George was spending most of his time in London, and Clemenceau was preparing to run for president of France.[33]

The Rumanians, who were now occupying most of Hungary, looted whatever Kun and his regime had left. Telephones, prized stallions, fire engines, shoes, carpets, automobiles, grain, cattle, and even railway cars and locomotives vanished eastward. Queen Marie cheerfully told an American officer, "You may call it stealing if you want to, or any other name. I feel that we are perfectly entitled to do what we want to." When the Allied military mission in Budapest objected, the Rumanians protested that they were only taking supplies for their army. After all, Brătianu said, Rumania had saved civilization from Bolshevism.[34]

By November the powers, mainly Britain and France, had had enough. Rumania, Czechoslovakia and Yugoslavia were all ordered to withdraw their troops immediately from territory designated as Hungarian under the peace terms. Rumania complied with bad grace and much procrastination. When a new, more stable government took office in Hungary, the Allies finally decided that they could make peace. On December 1, Hungary was invited to send its representatives to Paris, and on January 5, 1920, a train left Budapest. As it passed through the country, crowds waited beside the tracks to wish its passengers well.[35]

Count Albert Apponyi, the delegation's elderly leader, came from a family that traced its ancestry back to a migration from Central Asia in the twelfth century. His own political views were stuck somewhere in the eighteenth. He was kindly and courteous, enormously cultivated, deeply religious and a Hungarian patriot. He went to Paris with few hopes: "I could not refuse this saddest of duties, though I had no illusions as to there being any possibility of my securing some mitigation of our lot." Hungary had virtually nothing with which to bargain. By the time Kun fled, its borders had already been largely set and the Allies had already signed treaties with its neighbors.[36]

The Hungarians received a cold but correct welcome from the French and were taken off to the Château de Madrid, a resort hotel in the Bois de Boulogne. They were treated better than the Germans had been; they could wander through the Bois, even go to local restaurants. They received their peace terms in a brief ceremony at the Quai d'Orsay. Cle-

menceau curtly informed Apponyi that he could make a statement the following day but there would be no verbal negotiations, only written ones.
On leaving the room, the French prime minister gave a loud contemptuous laugh.[37]

Apponyi's statement was, in Lloyd George's opinion, a tour de force.
He spoke in fluent French, then switched to equally impeccable English
and concluded with flawless Italian. He pointed out that Hungary was
being punished more severely than any other of the defeated nations. It
was losing two thirds of its territory and its population, it was being cut off
from its markets and its sources of raw materials, and it was expected to
pay heavy reparations. Three and a half million Hungarians were going to
end up outside Hungary. If the principle of self-determination was a fair
one, and he thought it was, then surely it should apply to the Hungarians.
At the very least, there should be plebiscites held in the territories being
taken from Hungary. (Unwisely, the count weakened his case by complaining that Hungarians were being condemned to live under the rule of
inferior civilizations.[38])

In reply to a question from Lloyd George, Apponyi unfurled a large
ethnographic map that he had brought with him, and the peacemakers
gathered around. Lloyd George whispered to Apponyi, "You were very
eloquent." Even Clemenceau was polite. As the Hungarians went back to
their hotel to prepare their written commentary, there was some feeling of
hope. In Britain, critical questions were being asked in Parliament about
the Hungarian terms. Several important French businessmen were interested in reopening economic relations between France and Hungary and
informal talks had already started. The Italian government, under a new
prime minister, swung around from its previous hostility and urged its
allies to take Hungarian protests into account. It was not enough. In the
end, the British and the French were not prepared to redo the treaties; the
Italians were not willing to force the issue. The peacemakers may have
been influenced, too, by a memorandum from Rumania, Yugoslavia and
Czechoslovakia which argued that any attempt to redraw the borders
would be a betrayal. What ultimately weighed against Hungary was sheer
inertia. As a young English observer told Károlyi in 1919, "The Entente
governments had many more important things to worry about than the
fate of ten million people in Hungary."[39]

Hungary won only a few minor concessions: more patrol boats on the
Danube, for example. On June 4, 1920, in a brief ceremony at the Trianon
Palace, its representatives signed the treaty. In Hungary, the flags on public
buildings flew at half-mast. "Trianon" became shorthand for Allied cruelty
and its memory fueled an almost universal desire among Hungarians to

undo its provisions. The leading political figure in the interwar years was Horthy, now designated regent on the grounds that Hungary was still a monarchy. (It never managed to find a king again, which suited both the British and Horthy himself.) Horthy and his supporters toyed with improbable plans to restore Hungary to its prewar boundaries, for example by gassing Czech soldiers in their barracks in Slovakia and rushing in with Hungarian troops. Moderates would have settled for Transylvania.[40]

In the 1930s, Hungary cautiously drew closer to the other revisionist powers, Hitler's Germany and Mussolini's Italy. After the Munich settlement of 1938 left Czechoslovakia alone and exposed to Hitler, Hungary successfully demanded a slice of Slovakia and the whole of Ruthenia. In 1940 it was Rumania's turn, and in 1941 Yugoslavia's. With Hitler's support, Hungary got back about two fifths of Transylvania and part of the Banat in the south. It had only a short time to enjoy the restored territories. In 1945, the victorious Allies restored the boundaries of Trianon and there they remain, one of the arrangements from the Paris Peace Conference that has not been undone. Yet.

PART SIX

A TROUBLED SPRING

21

The Council of Four

S PRING CAME LATE to Paris in 1919, but by the middle of April the
magnolias were in full bloom and the chestnut trees along the boulevards were starting to flower. The Ethiopian delegates straggled in, tall and
handsome in their white robes. The great museums gradually reopened
and the children played in the parks. On May Day, the city closed down as
the left brought out thousands of demonstrators for the annual socialist
rally and the government responded by calling out the troops. All over the
center of Paris there were clashes; rumor had it that more than two thousand had been taken to hospital seriously injured.[1]

By May, the German terms were largely completed, many of the borders in Central and Southern Europe had been drawn, at least on paper,
and a start had been made on the treaties with Austria, Hungary, Bulgaria
and the Ottoman empire. A sour joke ran around Paris that they were
preparing a "just and lasting war."[2] At the heart of the conference was the
new Council of Four—Clemenceau, Lloyd George, Orlando and Wilson—which had been formed in the last week of March. The idea was to
meet without the customary entourage of experts and secretaries, to settle
the big questions among themselves. Lloyd George was concerned about
the repeated leaks from the Supreme Council and by the slowness of the
peacemaking. Clemenceau agreed: the conference had achieved little in
two months. So did Wilson, who had always preferred small, informal
groups where he could speak freely and, if necessary, change his mind.
Cynics said that the council was also a convenient excuse to get rid of the
Italian foreign minister, Sonnino, whose dour intransigence had antago-
nized everyone by this point, not excepting his own prime minister.[3]

The Four usually met twice a day, including on Sundays if there was a particular crisis. They occasionally sat in Clemenceau's dank, uncomfortable office at the Ministry of War, but most of the time they were in Wilson's study. There Wilson sat stiffly in an armchair, looking, said Tardieu, who was an occasional observer, "like a college professor criticizing a thesis." While Wilson spoke slowly and deliberately, Lloyd George, his knee clasped in his hands, dashed at his subject, sometimes angry, sometimes full of good humor, "wrapped in the utmost indifference to technical arguments, irresistibly attracted to unlooked-for solutions, but dazzling with eloquence and wit." Clemenceau lay back in his chair, his gloved hands lying by his side. He spoke less often than the other two, with more passion than Wilson and more logic than Lloyd George. Occasionally, to hear better, he perched on the padded fireguard. Orlando normally sat on one side of the fireplace, facing the other three. He was isolated in other ways; preoccupied with Italy's claims, he took little part in other discussions and often got lost when the others spoke English quickly together. Once, when a friend asked him about a recent meeting, he replied morosely that he had finally begun to understand a joke involving blacks that Wilson had told for the sixth time.[4]

The Japanese, who were now excluded, protested mildly. They were pushed off to the Council of Five, where they met with the foreign ministers of Britain, France, Italy and the United States to discuss the issues left them by the Four. The professional diplomats were scandalized at the disappearance of the Supreme Council and its replacement by the two new bodies. "Worthless schemes and improvised ideas," said Paul Cambon. The press, which was already chafing under restrictions on its reporting, were vociferous in complaint. The *Figaro* correspondent said the Peace Conference was like a canvas covered with black paint, entitled *A Battle of Negroes at Night in a Tunnel.* A cartoon in the *New York Herald* showed Wilson, "the new wrestling champion," hurling the press down to the floor.[5]

Hankey, the meticulous British secretary to the Peace Conference, worried about the Council of Four's decision not to keep records, "frightfully inconvenient from a secretarial point of view." After a couple of weeks the Four discovered that it was also inconvenient from the point of view of getting anything done. They could not remember what they had decided or who was supposed to do anything about it. By the middle of April, Hankey was back keeping notes. So, it later turned out, was the interpreter, the historian Paul Mantoux, who dictated his recollections of the previous day's meetings every morning in a confidential memo for Clemenceau. (Mantoux kept a copy for himself, which he left behind when the Germans entered Paris in 1940; it somehow survived the war.)

By the end of April, Orlando had brought in an Italian secretary. As a result, we have been left with an extraordinarily complete picture of four of the world's leading statesmen talking to one another day in and day out for three months in more than two hundred meetings. Where Hankey's version makes everyone sound like a discreet civil servant and smooths over the awkward exchanges, both Mantoux and Aldrovandi, the Italian, include the offhand remarks and the angry asides.[6]

The Four bickered, shouted and swore at each other, but they also, even Orlando, teased each other, told jokes, and commiserated. They pored over the maps and even crawled together over Wilson's huge map of Europe, which had to be unrolled on the floor. Lloyd George and Wilson talked about going to church; Clemenceau said he had never been in a church in his life. They compared notes on what upset them. Clemenceau told the others that he was never kept awake by abuse but had trouble sleeping when he felt he had made a fool of himself. Wilson and Lloyd George both knew exactly what he meant. The others listened politely to Wilson's homespun Southern jokes and ventured their own. "My dear friend," Wilson started to Clemenceau one day, who shot back, "I am always a bit afraid when you begin by calling us 'my dear friend.' " Wilson replied, "I can't do otherwise. But if you like, I shall say 'my illustrious colleague.' " Toward the end of their meetings, Clemenceau asked Lloyd George, "How do you like Wilson?" Lloyd George replied, "I like him and I like him very much better now than I did at the beginning." "So do I," said Clemenceau. They shared the loneliness of power, and they understood one another as no one else could.[7]

The volume of business kept growing. On the last day of March, for example, the Big Four discussed German reparations, the Saar coalfields, Allied occupation of the Rhineland, the possibility of a Channel tunnel, Belgium's claims, the revolution in Hungary, the armed clashes between Hungary and Rumania and the dispatch of the Smuts mission. Wilson also managed to find time to talk to his secretary of the navy about the Naval race with Britain. Lloyd George had breakfast with two advisers to discuss the Polish situation. Clemenceau had a crisis with Foch, and had to deal with a wave of strikes.[8]

Of the Four, Lloyd George held up best. He used to say later that the six months he spent in Paris were the happiest time of his life. He had seen Britain successfully through the war, and he enjoyed negotiating the peace. The day he left Paris, he told his old friend Riddell, "I felt I was closing a book that would never be reopened—a book of intense interest. It was an anxious time, but a pleasant time. I enjoyed it. I doubt if I shall ever spend such another. It was all so vivid."[9]

Wilson by contrast aged visibly, and the tic in his cheek grew more pronounced. He had been violently ill during the acrimonious discussions over the German terms; this may have been a minor stroke, a forerunner of the massive one he was to have four months later. "I have never seen the President look so worn & tired," wrote Baker, his press secretary, at the beginning of May. "He could not remember without an effort what the council had done in the forenoon." Wilson was emotionally exhausted. "I think if I could have a really good piece of news," he exclaimed one day, "I should fall dead." He was edgier, more unreasonable, more easily irritated. He fussed over the use of the official cars. He insisted, contrary to all evidence, that the French staff in his house spoke perfect English and that they must all be spies. He abruptly rearranged his study. "I don't like the way the colors of this furniture fight each other," he told his doctor. "The greens and the reds are all mixed up and there is no harmony." The American corner for the Council of Four meetings would be red, the British green, and the French could have the odds and ends.[10]

On April 14 the Council of Four precipitated fresh strains by inviting the German government to send its delegates to Paris. The German treaty, which still had to be approved by the whole Peace Conference, was a curious hybrid, in part traditional provision for a defeated enemy, in part a blueprint for a new world order. It talked of the trophies of war— Germany was to return all the flags taken from France in 1871 and the skull of an African ruler which had been taken to Berlin—but also of self-determination for nations such as Poland and Czechoslovakia. Clauses dealing with Germany's territorial losses and the punishment of those responsible for the war sat alongside provisions for a new world order— including the International Labour Organization, for example—and the whole started, as Wilson had insisted, with the covenant of the League of Nations. Because the German treaty was the first and most important one, Wilson and his supporters felt it must contain the essential principles and institutions of the new diplomacy.

A central drafting committee had been set up to collate the clauses and to make sure that the wording was clear and consistent. Baker's assistant dropped by to see it at the Quai d'Orsay. "The drafting commission was working itself to death," he reported, but "as very little of the material had been assembled when they took charge, most of it was very badly drafted, and much of it was conflicting, as for instance when reparations, ports, finance, and economics kept running across each other's tails." Changes and additions continued to stream out from the peacemakers until the moment the whole document was sent off to the printers. The Council of

Four discovered that it had forgotten to put in anything about opium traffic or Luxembourg. Lloyd George wanted something on poison gas; Borden, the Canadian prime minister, asked for a change in the International
Labour Organization clauses. Foch and his aides suspected the drafting
committee of weakening the disarmament clauses and so insisted in sitting in on its meetings.[11]

On the morning of April 29, like unwanted guests at a private party,
Belgian delegates appeared in Wilson's study to say that they could not
sign the treaty as it stood. In their country, public opinion was unanimous
that Belgium was being treated shabbily. Demonstrators in the streets
carried banners asking "Has England forgotten August 1914?" "Why does
Wilson not visit our ruins?" "Belgian heroes are buried in East Africa!
Who will guard their tombs?" A newspaper headline in Brussels declared
"Belgium Deserted and Humiliated by Its Allies." It did not exaggerate;
the country whose invasion had started the general European conflict had
been largely overlooked at the Peace Conference.[12]

Yet of all the Allies, Belgium had suffered the greatest material losses at
Germany's hands. Except for a tiny scrap extending inland from the coast
toward Ypres, the country had been completely occupied during the war.
While much of the Allied propaganda about German behavior in Belgium
was false, not all of it was. Germany had brutally and efficiently stripped
the country bare. Machinery, spare parts, whole factories including the
roofs, had disappeared eastward. Belgium had been a prosperous country
before 1914. In 1919, 80 percent of its workforce was unemployed. Steel
production was less than a tenth of what it had been. Farmers had no fertilizer and no implements, and very little livestock, because millions of
horses, cows, sheep and even chickens had also gone east. If it had not
been for Allied relief efforts, Belgians would have starved during that first
winter of peace.[13]

Unfortunately, Belgium had few champions. Wilson, who had made
the restoration of the country one of his Fourteen Points, was preoccupied with bigger issues. The French suspected the Belgians of trying to
annex the little duchy of Luxembourg, and the British thought they were
being greedy. Lloyd George had a furious scene with the Belgian prime
minister over Belgium's "preposterous" demands: "I had to tell him quite
plainly that the Belgians lost comparatively few men in the war, and that,
when all was said, Belgium had not made greater sacrifices than Great
Britain."[14]

Belgium's cause was not helped by its foreign minister. A neat, clever
little man, convinced of the justice of his cause, Paul Hymans lectured the
Council of Four and complained loudly and at length when he felt that he

or his country had been slighted. On one occasion, when he was in full spate, he exclaimed, "I wish there was something I could do for Belgium." Clemenceau roused himself. "The best thing you can do for Belgium is die or resign."[15]

The Belgians had hoped that the powers would put pressure on the Dutch to sort out unsatisfactory borders between their two countries, especially along the river Scheldt, which flowed out to the sea from the great Belgian port of Antwerp through Dutch territory. The Dutch, with their own port in Rotterdam, had done little before the war to improve navigation by, for example, dredging. The Netherlands, which as a neutral power was not taking part in the Peace Conference, firmly refused to give up an inch of its soil, even in return for gains elsewhere from Germany. The powers remained silent.[16]

Belgium also wanted to improve its borders with Germany. The Commission on Belgian Affairs recommended that Belgium get a scrap of land between the little towns of Eupen and Malmédy. It was not much, after all, under four hundred square miles with a population of about sixty thousand, but it did contain valuable forests to make up for Belgium's losses during the war. The experts also threw in an extra square mile known as neutral Moresnet, which had been floating in a legal limbo because the relevant clauses in a treaty of 1815 had been badly worded. The Council of Four agreed.[17]

The Four were not as sympathetic when it came to reparations. Belgium asked for special permission to include war costs in its demands. This was not as unreasonable as it sounded because, with most of its country occupied, the Belgian government had been obliged to finance itself entirely through borrowing. The Belgians also asked for priority when it came to handing out the payments received from Germany. The Americans were sympathetic. The British and the French, who had their own plans for reparations, were not. But on April 29, they backed down, and over the next few days a deal was hammered out. Belgium would get $500 million as soon as Germany paid up and a percentage, to be determined, of the total reparations. Britain and France did their best to whittle down Belgian claims in subsequent years, and Germany did its best not to pay at all. It took until 1925 for Belgium to get its priority payment in full; in the end, like its allies, it only received a fraction of what it had wanted.[18]

Italy Leaves

O N APRIL 20, nine days before the Belgian ultimatum, Frances Stevenson was at the window of Lloyd George's flat in the Rue Nitot looking across to Wilson's house to see whether an emergency meeting of the Council of Four was still going on. It was Easter Sunday, a lovely spring day, and Lloyd George had promised her a picnic. "Suddenly Orlando appeared at the window, leaned on the bar which runs across it, & put his head in his hands. I thought it looked as though he was crying, but could not believe it possible until I saw him take out his handkerchief & wipe his eyes and cheeks." Beside her, Lloyd George's valet exclaimed, "What have they been doing to the poor old gentleman?"

Inside Wilson's office, Clemenceau looked on coldly. The British were frozen with horror; Hankey said he would have spanked his own son for such a disgraceful display of emotion. The only person to make a move was Wilson, who went over to console the Italian prime minister, a particularly generous gesture given the animosity between the Americans and the Italians by this point.[1]

The most serious dispute to break out among the Allies at the Peace Conference had just reached an acute stage. This could not have happened at a worse time: with the German delegates about to arrive in Paris, it was essential that the peacemakers present a united front. Although Italy's demands at the conference covered three vast regions—Africa, the Middle East and Europe—it was the port of Fiume, in the Adriatic, that caused the problem. The quarrel was over territory but it was also over principle, since the Italians wanted what they had been promised under the old diplomacy, while the Americans stood firm on the new. And it was a clash of personalities, between Wilson and the Italians, especially Sonnino, their foreign minister. The question was whether the peace meant sharing the loot, as the Americans said contemptuously, or drawing borders based on ethnic lines. The territories Italy wanted had either been promised it by Britain and France under the secret Treaty of London (which Wilson loathed) or were inhabited largely by Slavs (which violated the principle of self-determination), or both.

Orlando had hoped to avoid a confrontation. A product of the murky world of Italian politics, with its deals, arrangements and doling out of patronage, he was a Sicilian by birth and a lawyer by training who had always found that difficulties could be papered over with the right words. A short, square man, much given to gesturing, he took a straightforward pride in both his country and his family. In Paris, he boasted to a table of Americans that he had produced three children in thirty-one months; impossible, he said, to do it any faster. Nicolson wrote him off, unfairly, as "a white, weak, flabby man," but Orlando had held his country together when it faced defeat.[2]

The war had been a tremendous strain for a society already divided between the prosperous, industrializing north and the agrarian, tradition-bound south. The great promise of the unification of the 1860s had not yet been realized. Italy's economy had grown slowly and its brief forays into foreign affairs had been embarrassing or, in the case of its defeat by the Ethiopians at Aduwa (Adwa) in 1896, humiliating. Like Germany, another new nation, Italy had a political system with many enemies: Catholics whose church had not accepted the new state, radical socialists who despaired of reform within the existing structures, and right-wing nationalists who longed to replace the corrupt and boring status quo.

In the war, Italy, the poorest of the Great Powers, spent money it did not have. By 1919 it owed its allies the equivalent of £700 million ($3.5 billion) and wartime inflation was higher than in any country except Russia. On the Austro-Hungarian front, Italian soldiers, badly led and ill equipped, had been slaughtered as they fought uphill into the Alps. The army had collapsed at Caporetto in 1917; Italians blamed their generals but also the system. Over half a million men had died by 1918 and as many more were seriously wounded. What had it all been for? Already a phrase that was to become a commonplace—"the mutilated victory"—was being heard in Italy, and so was talk of revolution.

Liberals and moderate socialists withdrew their support from the government, appalled at what they saw as its profound cynicism, and Orlando increasingly had to rely on the nationalist right. He badly needed a triumph, or the appearance of one, in Paris. If Sonnino and his conservative friends were going to insist on the letter of the Treaty of London, then they were going to have to have it. If some nationalists wanted even more territory than Italy had been promised on the eastern side of the Adriatic, Fiume for example, then he would have to produce that as well. It was Orlando who came up with the formula that excited the nationalists and so infuriated Italy's allies: "the Treaty of London plus Fiume." He was as much surprised as anyone when Fiume became a matter of life and death to Italian nationalists and a sticking point for Wilson.[3]

Sonnino, the other strong figure in the Italian delegation, stood behind the Treaty of London (after all, he had negotiated it) but he had little interest in Fiume. "He was apprehensive," in Lloyd George's opinion, "lest Italy should sacrifice bigger things in the frenzy for this trivial claim." He was to take the full blame, however, for Italy's disastrous diplomacy in Paris. Orlando got off lightly, partly because, unlike Sonnino, he did not speak English well; most of the Americans and British did not understand what he was saying. And, as Lloyd George said, "he had an attractive and amiable personality which made him an extremely pleasant man to do business with." Lloyd George also asserted, quite mistakenly, that "there was no fundamental difference of outlook or principle between him and President Wilson." Orlando was "exceedingly popular" with the Americans as well. "If Orlando were here I think I could do something," House wrote to Wilson, "but Sonnino is hopeless."[4]

In 1919 Sidney Sonnino was in his early seventies. With a shock of white hair, a large drooping mustache, deep-set eyes under beetling eyebrows, and a severe expression, he looked the very image of an old-style European statesman. In fact, he was something more: a Protestant in a largely Catholic country, an intellectual who wrote with passion about Dante's Beatrice, and a brilliant polemicist. Born in Egypt to an Italian Jewish businessman and his Welsh wife, Sonnino was an outsider who moved into the heart of Italian politics. An old-fashioned liberal, he moved rightward over the years. He believed in helping the masses, but not in trusting them to help themselves. Before the war he served twice, briefly, as prime minister, gaining a grudging respect even from his enemies as an honest and disinterested politician. In 1914 he became foreign minister.

"Dour, rigid and intractable," in Lloyd George's words, he spoke badly and made few friends in Paris. He took pride—to the point of obsession, said a man who was by no means an enemy—in not being like others: "When, as a young diplomat before the war, I used to see him fairly often in his beautiful solitary house near the Trajan Forum, I could not help being unpleasantly struck by this guileless superiority complex of which he was the first victim." Yet there was another side to Sonnino. He had loved deeply and unsuccessfully when he was young. "Who can and who should love this nonentity lacking all physical and moral attraction?" he wrote in his diary. "What I would not give for a bit of affection! Only affection can assuage this black fever that consumes me, that makes me hateful to myself, that renders me incapable of every serious and prolonged enterprise." When the negotiations in Paris went badly, he confided to his secretary that he felt physically sick.[5]

Sonnino's view of international relations was Bismarckian: he believed that nations were motivated by what another Italian foreign minister had called "sacred egoism" and that politics was above all about power. As an Italian nationalist, Sonnino wanted security for his country; that meant land, alliances, deals, the acquisition of friends against possible enemies. Clemenceau once reproached him for "remaining too faithful to the Italian method of which the grand master was Machiavelli and not presenting clear solutions."[6] Sonnino did not trust talk of principles or morality or openness in international relations, and he failed to grasp that others did.

When the war broke out, Italy was allied to its old enemy Austria-Hungary and to Germany. Under the terms of the Triple Alliance, however, Italy was only obliged to defend its allies if they were attacked first. The Italians used the fact that Austria-Hungary had declared war on Serbia as reason to remain neutral. There was little enthusiasm in Italy at that stage for entering a conflict that seemed to have little to do with Italy's interests. Sonnino, along with a small minority of his compatriots, inclined toward the Central Powers. He assumed that they would win, a reasonable enough assumption and, in any case, he preferred a Europe dominated by conservative powers. Most Italians, however, were for neutrality. It was only as the war dragged on that the great division opened up between those who kept to neutrality, mostly conservatives but also part of the radical left, and the increasing numbers who argued for intervention on the Allied side. The second group was a strange mix—liberals and republicans, but also socialists and rabid nationalists—and it was going to fall apart over Italy's war aims. After much deliberation, Sonnino decided that intervention on the Allied side was Italy's best option.

He changed his mind because it was the sensible thing to do. In 1915, when he started negotiations, the Allies appeared to be doing quite well. Moreover, they were prepared to offer Italy a better deal than the Central Powers, mainly because what Italy wanted was Austro-Hungarian territory. The Allies, for their part, were anxious to break the deadlock of the Western Front by attacking the enemy elsewhere. Italy's entry would shift the naval balance in the Mediterranean decisively in their favor and an attack by the Italian army against Austria-Hungary promised to inflict severe damage on the weaker partner in the Central Powers.

Sonnino did not want to see Austria-Hungary utterly defeated; indeed, he never imagined that it might disappear altogether. He felt no particular animosity to the Central Powers; he joined the Allies because that seemed the best way to get the territory that Italy needed. Sonnino always took care to distinguish Italy's war from the more general one. As he said in 1917: "If a lasting peace is to be assured, it is necessary that Italy obtain secure national frontiers—an indispensable condition for her full independence." In 1918, shortly after Wilson had announced his Fourteen Points, Sonnino said pointedly that "an underhand campaign of foreign propaganda has attempted to insinuate that Italian aspirations are inspired by conceptions of imperialism, of anti-democracy, of anti-nationalism, etc. This is all absolutely false." On the contrary, Italy's claims on Austrian territory were solidly based on "ethnography and legitimate defence by land and sea." Italians, he said, looked forward to good relations with their neighbors.[7]

During the war the European Allies, always willing to give away territory that was not theirs, promised the completion of Italy's national dream, as the popular slogan in Italy had it, from Trento to Trieste, across the vulnerable northeastern border that Austria-Hungary had menaced since Italy's birth. But in 1915, when the Treaty of London was drawn up, the British and the French threw in more: islands and a stretch of Dalmatia along Austria-Hungary's Adriatic coast; the port of Vlorë in Albania (Italian: Valona) as well as a protectorate over central Albania; the Dodecanese islands along the coast of Asia Minor; and shares of the Ottoman empire if it disappeared. (This caused a certain amount of difficulty at the Peace Conference, because Lloyd George had also promised part of the same territory, around Smyrna, to Greece.) Italy would have the same rights as Britain and France in the Arabian peninsula and the Red Sea. To Sonnino the Treaty of London represented a solemn agreement; for Britain and France by 1919 it had become an embarrassment.

The British and the French felt, rightly or wrongly, that Italy had not contributed much to the Allied victory. Italy's armies had delayed their attack on Austria-Hungary, and then made a mess of it. Italian ships had rarely ventured out of port, despite repeated promises to patrol the Mediterranean and Adriatic. The Italian government had squeezed resources out of its hard-pressed allies which it had then refused to use in the war effort. As Clemenceau put it, "the Italians met him with a magnifique coup de chapeau of the seventeenth century type, and then held out the hat for alms at the end of the bow." The attitude to Italy in Paris, the British ambassador reported, "has been one of supreme contempt up to now and now it is one of extreme annoyance. They all say that the signal for an armistice was the signal for Italy to begin to fight."[8]

Having bribed Italy to join the war with the promise of territory, Britain and France were outraged when their new ally continued to show what Lloyd George called "that huxtering spirit." When Italian armies moved rapidly at the end of the war to occupy all the territory, and more, that Italy had been promised around the Adriatic, Pichon, the French foreign minister, complained at length to the British ambassador that the Italian troops were deliberately provoking trouble with the local Slav population. "They would relish bloodshed as it would enable them to keep hold of territory which would certainly not be given to them by any Treaty of Peace."[9]

The likelihood, indeed by December 1918 the certainty, that Serbia would form some sort of state with the South Slav peoples of Austria-Hungary, was a fresh source of strain between Italy and its allies. Britain and France, for their own reasons, were sympathetic to the new state. Surely Italy could see that in the changed circumstances it no longer made sense to claim South Slav territory. After all, the promises had been based on the assumption that Austria-Hungary would still exist at the end of the war. It had made sense to deprive an enemy of its ports and naval bases. It did not make sense now to do the same to a friendly nation. "Every effort should be made," the British War Cabinet concluded, "to persuade Italy to take up a reasonable attitude on these questions." Clemenceau talked several times to Orlando to try to persuade him to give up the Treaty of London.[10]

The Italian government was not prepared to do so. Public opinion in Italy would have made it difficult. While liberals, faithful to the spirit of the great Giuseppe Mazzini, had hoped for the liberation of oppressed peoples, especially those under the tyranny of Italy's own former oppressor, most Italians saw the Croats and Slovenes as enemies who had fought loyally for Austria-Hungary and would probably do so again given the chance. When Italian forces moved in to occupy Croatia and Slovenia at the end of the war, they acted more as conquerors than as liberators. And were the Serbs any more trustworthy? General Pietro Badoglio, second-in-command of the Italian army, warned his government that the Croats and Slovenes, who were cleverer than the Serbs, would end up dominating them. Consequently he drew up an elaborate plan, which Sonnino and Orlando approved in December 1918, to destroy Yugoslavia and cement Italian control over the eastern side of the Adriatic by stirring up conflict among the Serbs, Croats and Slovenes and between peasants and their landlords. In Bosnia, Badoglio suggested, religious divisions could be used. He already had agents in place. Even ordinary Italian soldiers could do their bit by seducing the "susceptible" local women.[11]

The Italian navy had much the same attitude. It was furious when the Habsburg emperor, in one of his last acts, turned over his Adriatic navy and the huge naval base at Pula (Italian: Pola) to a provisional Yugoslav committee. The following day an Italian torpedo boat darted into Pula and sank the dreadnought *Viribus Unitis,* the pride of the Austrian navy, killing its Yugoslav captain and crew. After strenuous Italian objections, the remainder of the fleet was surrendered to the Allies, and Italian forces occupied Pula. The next months saw increasing friction between the Italian navy and the Allies, especially the Americans, over the Italian treatment of the local Slavs. The Italians defended themselves in a lengthy memorandum which argued that nature had played a cruel trick on Italy; while the western side of the Adriatic had few harbors and no natural defenses, "a wonderful advanced barrier of reefs and islands" protected the other side. "On the east, the sea is clear and deep and mines can be used with difficulty; on the west, the waters are muddy and shallow and seem made on purpose to favour the terribly insidious work of submarine weapons." It was quite simply a necessity for Italy to get that territory on the eastern side.[12]

The nationalists had still more arguments. Italy could not leave scattered Italian communities to the mercies of the Slavs. The press carried alarming, and untrue, stories of Italian women and children being murdered in the cities of Istria and along the Dalmatian coast. "Yugoslav oppression cuts the throats of the Italian population in Dalmatia and terrorizes them." Learned professors asserted that "what in Dalmatia is not Italian is barbaric!" The Italian military commander in Dalmatia was kinder: "This population is fundamentally good, good as simple and primitive people are. But the simple and primitive peoples are also extremely sensitive and suspicious and violent in their impulses." Italy's civilizing mission was clear. Italian newspapers ran photographs of local peasants going to church with the explanation that they were on their way to pay homage to the commander of the Italian forces, or of queues for food which, it was said, were Slavs lining up to demand that Italy stay.[13]

As 1918 came to an end, in Rome, Genoa and Naples enthusiastic crowds turned out on pro-Dalmatia days. The American ambassador believed that the government was behind the demonstrations. Sonnino said firmly, the ambassador reported, that Italy must put its safety in the Adriatic above all else and that meant controlling territory, not protection by a League of Nations. "Even the police required that people whom they protected should shut their doors in the evening so as at least to keep out intruders until the police could be summoned." Sonnino, like Orlando, thought Wilson's ideas foolish. "Is it possible to change the world from a room, through the actions of some diplomats? Go to the Balkans and try an experiment with the Fourteen Points."[14]

The Italian government did its best to bring its allies around to its way of thinking. In London in December 1918, Orlando told the British and the French that the Yugoslavs were carrying out "a veritable persecution" of Italians; Italian soldiers were being attacked, Italian women molested for wearing the Italian colors. He was firmly opposed to recognizing the new Yugoslav state. Britain and France reluctantly acquiesced. They felt obliged to respect the Treaty of London, but they did so resentfully. As Robert Cecil wrote to Britain's ambassador in Italy, "the fact is that the greediness of Italian foreign policy in all directions is leading Italy into serious difficulties. . . . The Yugoslavs have claimed far more than is their just due, but Sonnino's stubbornness and the extravagant nature of Italy's claims have had as a result that it is now literally true that Italy has not a friend in Europe except ourselves, and she is doing her best to make her isolation complete."[15]

That left the Americans. Wilson may have been shaky on some of the details of Italy's claims (apparently he thought at first that Trieste was a German city), but he knew where he stood on principles. He had made it clear that the United States was not bound by secret agreements. (The American president had been shown the Treaty of London during the war, although he later persuaded himself that he had never seen it.) His legal experts argued, and he agreed, that when Italy had sought armistices with the Central Powers on the basis of the Fourteen Points, it had implicitly accepted that these superseded the Treaty of London. The Fourteen Points had promised that "a readjustment of the frontiers of Italy should be effected along clearly recognizable lines of nationality." That would give Italy part of what it wanted on its northeast frontier but not much of Istria and none of Dalmatia. In the armistice negotiations, Orlando tried unsuccessfully to get on record an Italian reservation to the effect that Italy's frontiers must also take into account security needs. The Italians later claimed that their reservation had been noted; the Americans insisted that it had not.[16]

Orlando and Sonnino nevertheless awaited Wilson's arrival in Europe with considerable optimism. House encouraged them to think of the United States as a friend and, as Wilson's representative, he allowed the armistice with Austria-Hungary to be drawn up in such a way that Italian troops would be occupying all the territory promised under the Treaty of London. He advised Sonnino on negotiating techniques. If Italy waited to present its demands until Britain and France had gained what they wanted, it would be hard for the Peace Conference to refuse. "I did this," House confided to his diary, "in a spirit of sheer devilry. I shall enjoy being present when Sonnino and Orlando make their argument based upon the British and French claims." The Italians were also receiving misleading advice from Baron Macchi di Cellere, their ambassador in Washington, a man with an extraordinary capacity to ignore the facts, who assured them that Wilson was sympathetic to Italy and its aims. "A good man," Orlando admitted, "but absolutely inferior to the task and . . . the reason why we Italians went to the Conference in complete ignorance of Wilson's real sentiments." The American ambassador in Rome reported, "Baron Sonnino knows about America so little that it might almost be termed nothing and I do not believe that he is greatly in accord with what is our master motive."[17]

Wilson was inclined to be suspicious of the Italians, who, as he saw it, had gone into the war in a spirit of "cold-blooded calculation." One of the first things he did on arriving in Paris in December 1918 was to send for a copy of the Treaty of London. He met Sonnino and Orlando for the first time a few days before Christmas and had a long discussion of Italy's claims in the Adriatic. The Italians thought the meeting went well. The British ambassador, who talked to Wilson the following day, had a different impression: "He is very anti-Italian. . . . He was sick to death of Orlando and Sonnino and all their ways and he particularly did not want to have any conversation with them." With the delay in starting the Peace Conference, Wilson agreed to pay a state visit to Rome. This, sadly, only deepened the misunderstandings.[18]

He was received by enormous and enthusiastic crowds. "I had the impression of finding myself among real friends," Wilson observed. He concluded, mistakenly, that the people of Italy were behind his program. "The President said," reported his doctor, "that he felt the people of the country were primarily interested in bringing about a peace which would insure them against another war, such as they had just gone through. He felt that they had hit upon the league of nations idea as the means to the end desired." Four months later, when his relations with the Italian government were at their worst, he was to appeal directly to the Italian people.

For his part, Orlando persisted in his optimism. "I believe in Wilson and his ideas," he cheerfully told a friend. "I accept Wilsonianism in as much as it includes the rights and the interests of Italy." Sonnino was more suspicious. Wilson returned the feeling; Sonnino was, he concluded, "as slippery as an eel or an Italian." On January 13, Wilson informed Orlando that he had decided the Treaty of London was no longer valid. There the matter stood for some weeks, while the Supreme Council busied itself with the League of Nations and such difficult issues as whether the Bolsheviks should be invited to Paris.[19]

The Italian delegation settled in to the luxurious Hôtel Edward VII, near the Opéra. Only one delegate had been allowed to bring his wife, perhaps because he was very recently married. There was one telephone, and delegates needed Orlando's permission to use it. The delegation itself mirrored the political divisions in the government. "A little bit of Rome transported to Paris with all its attendant faults, alas" was the way one of the younger members described it. "Lack of organization, a prevalence of parliamentary alchemy (present and future) in the choice of staff, gossip and backbiting."[20]

It was not, it was widely agreed, a strong or effective delegation. As Macchi di Cellere, now brought over from Washington to lend his dubious assistance, explained grandly to an American, "Italy has no propaganda of her own; she is too old a country and too proud a race." Few of its members developed the informal contacts with other delegations that the British and the Americans did. Among the delegation's leaders, Antonio Salandra, a former prime minister, worried mainly about his health, while Orlando was affable but distracted. Sonnino remained aloof and secretive, guarding information even when it might have helped his fellow delegates. In his spare time he went for solitary walks. He refused to lobby on Italy's behalf: "To resort to such methods would be to sink to the level of the small nations which went around begging territory from world opinion." His relations with Orlando worsened as the months went on. There were furious scenes in which the normally controlled Sonnino went purple with rage.[21]

Divided among themselves, the Italians were also mistrustful of their allies. "They considered," said a British diplomat, "they were not being treated as equals by the other Powers; they were attacked and criticized on all sides; they were told what was good for them, but not taken into real discussions." Wilson, sniffed Sonnino, was a *specie di clergyman,* the United States, in Macchi di Cellere's word, a "usurer" which wanted to dictate the peace. Toward the end of January, Wickham Steed reported that Wilson had had "a stormy interview" with Sonnino, "who seems to have lost his temper and to have gone to the length of telling Wilson not to meddle in European affairs but to stick to his American last."[22]

Among the Europeans, the Italians got on best with the British. Orlando admired Lloyd George: "His Celtic blood made him like us Mediterraneans in cleverness." And there was little to divide their two countries. That was not the case with France. Italy owed its unification to France, but there was a feeling that France had exacted a high price when it took Nice and Savoy. Both countries aspired to be Mediterranean powers, and before the war they had clashed over Tunisia and Morocco. Italy had joined the Triple Alliance partly to find allies against France. As for those measurements which so preoccupied the world's statesmen, Italy lagged behind France in steel, coal and population production.

1. Woodrow Wilson's triumphal arrival in Paris before the start of the Peace Conference. His promise to establish a League of Nations to end war and to allow self-determination for nations raised tremendous expectations in Europe and farther afield, but disillusionment soon followed.

2. Georges Clemenceau (*center*) and David Lloyd George (*right*), prime ministers of France and Britain, walk past a guard of honor. (The gentleman with them may be Lord Beaverbrook.) Both men had held their countries together during the war. They came to the peace negotiations with much public support but also a heavy burden of expectations.

3. David Lloyd George (*center*) and the British empire delegation, which caused him considerable trouble at the Peace Conference. General Jan Smuts, the influential South African foreign minister, is second from the left in the front row. Lloyd George is flanked by Arthur Balfour, his foreign secretary (*left*), and the dyspeptic Billy Hughes of Australia (*right*). Winston Churchill is to the right of the table, and Henry Wilson, Lloyd George's cynical military adviser, stands behind his left shoulder.

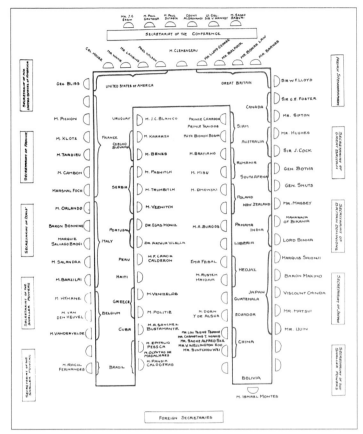

4. The seating plan at the Peace Conference. Thirty-two countries, from belligerents to neutrals, were invited to send delegates to Paris. The full Peace Conference met only eight times, which led to much grumbling from the smaller powers.

5. The real work of the conference was undertaken by special commissions and committees or by these four men and their advisers. *From left to right:* David Lloyd George (Britain), Vittorio Orlando (Italy), Georges Clemenceau (France) and Woodrow Wilson (United States). Until March they met, along with their foreign ministers and two Japanese delegates (Japan was included among the Great Powers as a courtesy), as the Supreme Council or Council of Ten.

6. The race between peace-making and revolution. While some commentators, then and since, have argued that the peacemakers were moved primarily by a fear of Russian Bolshevism, this is an oversimplification. The peacemakers were concerned about the spread of anarchy and about economic collapse in the center of Europe, but they also had considerable faith in their own ability to set the world right.

7. Woodrow and Edith Wilson at the races at St. Cloud. Although the Peace Conference was hard work, there was also time for relaxation.

8. Georges Clemenceau, the radical gadfly turned Father of Victory. Aged seventy-seven, he was the oldest of the Big Four. Although he recovered from an assassination attempt partway through the Peace Conference, some felt that he was never the same again.

9. Marshal Ferdinand Foch, French commander-in-chief and Supreme Allied Commander. He attacked Clemenceau for compromising too much on the German terms and in particular for accepting an Anglo-American guarantee to come to France's defense against a future German attack instead of holding out for French control of German territories west of the Rhine.

10. An artist's impression of the crowds waiting outside the French Foreign Ministry at the Quai d'Orsay to catch a glimpse of the peacemakers.

11. The peacemakers' chauffeurs.

12. When Woodrow Wilson returned in March 1919 from his brief trip to the United States, and David Lloyd George came back from London, it was decided to speed up the work of the Peace Conference by scrapping the Council of Ten in favor of a smaller and more informal group. The Council of Four, as it was known, generally met in Wilson's study. *From left to right:* Orlando, Lloyd George, Clemenceau, Wilson.

13. The peacemakers were besieged by petitioners. One of the more glamorous was Queen Marie of Rumania, who arrived in Paris with a large entourage, a huge wardrobe and demands for about half of Hungary.

14. Among the many peoples who looked to the Peace Conference to redress their grievances were the Poles, whose country had been carved up by its neighbors at the end of the eighteenth century. The collapse of Russia, Germany and Austria-Hungary by 1918 gave Poland its chance. Ignace Paderewski, the great pianist who became the newborn country's first prime minister, did much to win it support from the powers.

15. While Paderewski worked in Paris, General Józef Piłsudski struggled in Warsaw to re-create the Polish state and build a Polish army. Though his territorial ambitions did not extend as far as those of some Polish patriots, he nevertheless seized parts of southern Lithuania and moved eastward into Byelorussia and Ukraine, thereby clashing with the Bolsheviks.

16. Béla Kun, the Hungarian communist whose seizure of power in Budapest in March 1919 caused alarm in Paris. General Smuts, sent by the peacemakers on a fact-finding mission, concluded that Kun was unlikely to survive in office for long. In August 1919, the Hungarian was forced to flee as his enemies plotted against him and Hungary's neighbors Czechoslovakia and Rumania started to seize Hungarian territory.

17. The Arab delegation to the Peace Conference: Prince Feisal (*front*), who hoped for an independent Arab state under his family's rule, and, to his left, T. E. Lawrence in the Arab headdress that so infuriated the French. In spite of their wartime promises, neither the British nor the French were prepared to relinquish control of the Middle East, and the Arabs came to regard the Peace Conference as yet another betrayal by the Western powers.

18. The Italian prime minister, Vittorio Orlando, with stick in hand, leaves the Peace Conference. In April 1919, the Italians reached an impasse with their allies over Italy's claims in the Adriatic, in particular to the port of Fiume (Rijeka). Wilson refused to give way. The Italian walkout threatened the whole conference, because the Germans were about to be summoned to receive their terms.

19. Fiume, a small port at the head of the Adriatic where Slavs slightly outnumbered Italians, became a major nationalist issue in Italy. Having seized the city in September 1919, the poet Gabriele D'Annunzio remained there for fifteen months, defying his own government and making interminable nationalist speeches. Mussolini, the future Italian dictator, learned much from his example.

20. Eleutherios Venizelos, the Greek prime minister, who dreamed of a Greater Greece incorporating much of the old Ottoman empire. His enormous charm won him much support in Paris, especially from Lloyd George. As a result, Greece gained the European remnants of the Ottoman empire in Thrace and was allowed to send an army to occupy the largely Greek port of Smyrna (Izmir) on the coast of Asia Minor.

21. The peacemakers drew up a punitive treaty with the Ottoman empire, signed at Sèvres in 1921, but overlooked the awakening force of Turkish nationalism, which had by now found a leader in the distinguished general Kemal Atatürk.

22. Turkish crowds cheer the capture of Smyrna from the Greeks in 1922, which marked the end of Venizelos's dreams and of the Greek presence in what became modern Turkey.

23. Lord Curzon, foreign secretary after September 1919, watched Lloyd George's support for Greek ambitions with consternation and later had to negotiate a new treaty with the Turks to replace the collapsed Treaty of Sèvres.

24. The Turkish delegation to Lausanne in 1922–23. General Ismet, walking stick in hand, was Atatürk's trusted representative; he drove Curzon to distraction with his refusal to budge from his negotiating position. A treaty was eventually signed in 1923 that left Turkey in its present form.

25. The Peace Conference drew up treaties with the defeated powers of Austria, Bulgaria, Hungary and Ottoman Turkey, but that with Germany proved difficult. Because of disagreements among the Allies, what was to have been a preliminary meeting before negotiating with the enemy gradually turned into the Peace Conference proper. The German terms were not ready until May 1919. Count Ulrich Brockdorff-Rantzau (*third from right*) was Germany's foreign minister and leader of its delegation. The Germans never forgave the Allies for simply imposing their terms and declining to negotiate seriously.

26. An enormous protest demonstration in Berlin. The Germans were horrified by the peace terms, which they saw as a betrayal of a pledge they felt they had received from the Allies at the time of the armistice: that the peace would be negotiated on the basis of Wilson's new diplomacy, with no unjust retribution. The banner demands "Only the Fourteen Points," a reference to Wilson's famous speech.

27. The peacemakers made only a few minor changes in the terms in response to German objections and comments. They also gave the German government a deadline for signing, which plunged Germany into a political crisis. In Paris, Allied preparations for either the signing of the treaty or a resumption of the war went ahead. Here, French soldiers move furniture at the great palace at Versailles in preparation for the signing.

28. On June 23, 1919, shortly before the Allied deadline expired, the German government finally agreed to sign. The ceremony was scheduled for June 28 and there was a scramble for tickets. Some of those who could not get into the Hall of Mirrors were forced to peer through the windows.

29. The scene inside the Hall of Mirrors as the Treaty of Versailles was signed. The location had great significance for the French because it was here that the new nation of Germany had been proclaimed after France's defeat in the Franco-Prussian War of 1870–71.

30. The palace and grounds of Versailles on June 28, 1919. The fountains played and the guns were fired to announce to the waiting crowds that the German treaty had been signed. Although the Peace Conference continued until January 1920, this marked the end of its most important phase. Wilson left for the United States that night, and Lloyd George returned to Britain shortly afterward.

"Throughout the whole of my negotiations with the Italians," Lloyd George recalled, "I found that their foreign policy was largely influenced by a compound mixture of jealousy, rivalry, resentment, but more particularly, fear of France."[23] For France it was not so much a matter of fear (although there was some concern over the Italian birthrate) but of condescension tinged with contempt.

In December 1918, after the Allied meetings in London, Orlando and Sonnino had traveled to Paris with Clemenceau. "We did not see them a single time in the course of the long journey," reported Clemenceau's aide, "and, at the Gare du Nord, they disappeared without taking leave of M. Clemenceau, who was not only quite astonished but even quite offended." Clemenceau had a grudging respect for Sonnino but little use for Orlando: "all things to all men, very Italian."[24]

The collapse of Austria-Hungary opened up fresh areas for rivalry as France and Italy competed for influence in the center of Europe. In the Adriatic, France was torn between befriending Yugoslavia and keeping on reasonable terms with Italy. "I am so bored with Adriatic matters," wrote a French diplomat. "All the same we shouldn't abandon the Yugoslavs. They are as unreasonable as these others, but they are weak. How stupid they are in Rome!" As Clemenceau said wearily one day, much to Orlando's indignation, "My god, my god! Italy or Yugoslavia? The blonde or the brunette?" By April 1919 Clemenceau had gone firmly for the brunette. He was furious that the Italians had not supported France over the Saar or the issue of trying Germans for war crimes. He also took for granted that he had room to maneuver because, in the end, Italy would have to remain friendly to France.[25]

Orlando and Sonnino, suspicious of their allies, hostile to their Yugoslav neighbor and caught in an uneasy alliance which neither dared break for fear of bringing their government down, plowed on. Like a bomb with a slow-burning fuse, the official Italian memorandum went to the Peace Conference on February 7. It is an interesting document which, although it scarcely mentions the Treaty of London, repeats its provisions virtually unchanged, decked out this time in the ill-fitting clothes of the new diplomacy. "The Italian claims," it started, "show such a spirit of justice, rightfulness, and moderation that they come entirely within the principles enunciated and approved by President Wilson and should therefore be recognised and approved by everybody." Italy's demands were based almost entirely on self-determination, for Italians of course; the few small instances where it claimed land inhabited by other peoples were solely to make secure borders.[26]

Orlando and Sonnino concentrated, to the dismay of their own colo-

nialists, on Europe. The Italian Colonial Ministry had thrown itself enthusiastically into preparing grand schemes, particularly for Africa. For
Italian nationalists, the "year of shame" of 1896, with the defeat at Aduwa,
could be wiped out only by conquest. Britain and France must stand aside,
the colonial minister, Gaspare Colosimo, urged his government, and allow Italy to have exclusive influence over Ethiopia. Furthermore, in order
to cement Italy's control over the routes from the Red Sea and the Indian
Ocean into Ethiopia, Britain should add its share of Somalia to the piece
already in Italian hands and hand over the northeast part of Kenya. France
should relinquish its tiny piece of Somalia, as well as the railway from the
port of Djibouti into Addis Ababa. Colosimo also dreamed of a Libya enlarged by territory from British-run Egypt and from French possessions
and, if the Portuguese colonies went begging, of acquiring Angola as well.
Just before the end of the war he sent a memorandum to Balfour and
House outlining these goals. The wording was carefully chosen to sound
Wilsonian; the impact, however, was to leave an impression of Italian
greed.[27]

Orlando and Sonnino were not prepared to push the African claims
strongly in Paris and it is unlikely that Britain and France would have paid
much attention. They briskly divided up the German colonies without
consulting Italy and, as for handing over their own territory to Italy, each
country expressed itself perfectly willing to do so as long as the other did.
The Italians were left with yet another grievance and yet another frustrated dream.[28] Mussolini subsequently found that useful.

In Europe, the only one of Italy's claims that was settled easily was for
a piece of Austria-Hungary south of the Brenner Pass, the South Tyrol
and below that the Trentino. The Trentino, which was largely Italian-
speaking, was not a problem, but the Tyrol was overwhelmingly German.
The Tyrolese protested at the partition of a province with a long history of
self-government. So did the government of the new state of Austria: "It is
actually the Tyrol, till now, except Switzerland, the most burning centre of
liberty and resistance to all foreign domination, which will be sacrificed to
strategic considerations, as an offering on the altar of militarism." The
Italians argued that Italy could be safe only if it held the land sloping up to
the Brenner Pass. "Any other boundary to the south would merely be an
artificial amputation entailing the upkeep of expensive armaments contrary to the principles by which Peace should be inspired." Wilson, perhaps to show the Italians that he could be reasonable, let them know
before the Peace Conference opened that he would not object to the
change in Italy's northern frontier. His fellow peacemakers acquiesced.
Lloyd George briefly worried about the Tyrol, according to House, be-

cause he had once been on holiday there and it was one of the few parts of the continent he knew well. Wilson later regretted that he had handed over so many German-speaking Tyrolese—250,000 of them, to Italian rule. So did they, especially after 1922, when the Fascists decided to make them Italian. Suddenly, schools and government offices were run in Italian; children could not be given names that "offended Italian sentiment." It was only in the vastly changed Italy and Europe of the 1970s that the Tyrol finally regained some of its old autonomy.[29]

Wilson was prepared to accept an injustice to the Germans of the Tyrol but he would not accept Italy's claims where they ran up against those of the Yugoslavs. Outside the cities, the population along the eastern side of the Adriatic was almost entirely Slav: about 750,000 Croats, Slovenes, Serbs and Bosnians. Nevertheless, the Italians wanted to move the old border with Austria-Hungary between fifty and one hundred kilometers east into what is today Slovenia and Croatia, and south down the Dalmatian coast toward Split (Italian: Spalato). The result would take in the whole of the Istrian peninsula, including the naval base at Pula and Austria-Hungary's two major ports of Trieste and Fiume, with their railway links to central Europe; several key islands at the northeast end of the Adriatic; and chunks of Dalmatia around the cities of Zadar (Italian: Zara) and Šibenik (Italian: Sebenico). Italy also wanted Albania's port of Vlorë in the south. With these gains, Italy would dominate the Adriatic, and the new state of Yugoslavia would be left with a short coast, no decent port and only one railway line between the sea and the interior. This was precisely what Italy intended.

The Italians did not, of course, use that argument in Paris. They talked of strategic needs and they called on history. "The whole of Dalmatia was united to Italy in the centuries of Rome and Venice, for its own good fortune and the world's peace." They pointed to the Venetian lions, the Catholic churches, the Roman columns dotting the piazzas along the coast, the persistence of the Italian language despite Austrian oppression. They talked of the fearful injustice if Italians were made subject to "semi-barbaric" Slavs.[30]

Disturbing stories, however, were reaching Paris: tales of deportations of Slav nationalists, of arbitrary arrests, of Slav newspapers closed down and Yugoslav railway lines cut. A British officer sent a furious note to Balfour: "Dalmatia was being starved and the Italians only supplied food to those who signed a declaration of loyalty to Italy." Hoover, in charge of the Allied relief effort, reported that the Italian authorities were holding up food shipments in Trieste and that on February 22 they had suddenly stopped all communications to the interior. "This not only isolates the

Jugo-Slavs but cuts off the principal railway into Austria and Czecho-Slovakia." Wilson agreed with Hoover's conclusion that "the stoppage of American foodstuffs to starving people cannot be used as a political weapon" and accepted his recommendation that the United States retaliate by withholding aid to Italy. The issue poisoned Italian-American relations for the rest of the Peace Conference.[31]

Initially the Americans, with support from the British and French, encouraged Italy and Yugoslavia to work out their own border. The Yugoslavs were more than willing, they said, to compromise. Perhaps Wilson could arbitrate any areas of disagreement. The Italian delegation was appalled. Orlando confided to an American that "though the Southern Slav proposal embarrassed him horribly, he could not find a good reason for refusing it." In an interview with Wilson, he "moaned and wept, said that the Southern Slavs had taken him by the throat, but finally promised to give a reply as soon as he had been able to consult the King and his colleagues in Rome." When Wilson was on his way back to the United States in February, the Italians rejected his arbitration, claiming that they had done so only because the Yugoslavs, "in a brutal manner," had published the proposal prematurely.[32]

It was clear from the moment the Peace Conference opened that the Italians were in no mood to compromise with the Yugoslavs or anyone else. They refused to let anything affecting Italy's borders go to committees of experts. Clemenceau complained after a meeting in March: "This afternoon Orlando inflicted on us an interminable discourse to lay out Italy's demands and to indicate which frontiers he thought were necessary and just." And then "we had to submit to a second speech, no less boring from Sonnino." The covenant of the League of Nations and the German peace terms were worked out with scarcely a murmur from the Italians. (Orlando later argued, unconvincingly, that this was because Italy felt excluded.[33])

Italy's tactics were irritating, transparent and frequently inept. It opposed Yugoslavia's claims to territory from Bulgaria and Hungary and supported Rumania over the Banat. It sold arms to Hungary, and even signed a secret agreement with the government of the despised Béla Kun. Foolishly, Sonnino pushed Greece closer to Yugoslavia by refusing to consider Greek claims in Albania and by trying to hang on to the predominantly Greek Dodecanese islands along the coast of Asia Minor, which it had been occupying since the end of the Balkan wars. Sonnino petulantly refused to receive Venizelos when the Greek prime minister asked for an appointment. On committees the Italians were invariably anti-Yugoslav and doggedly uncooperative. If pressed, they usually claimed that their government had not given them instructions. Eyre Crowe from the British Foreign Office remonstrated with an Italian diplomat, who said merely, "You would not talk to us alone when we came to London in December, and you will not talk to us or make arrangements with us in Paris, and consequently we are not going to express any opinions on these questions."[34]

When the Italian demands finally came up for decision in April, the other powers were markedly less sympathetic. Bismarck's famous remark that Italy's appetite was invariably bigger than its teeth was quoted appreciatively. "The Italians," wrote Balfour wearily, "must somehow be mollified, and the only question is how to mollify them at the smallest cost to mankind." By now, the Italian delegates were desperate. Orlando was convinced, or so he said, that a secret society had pledged to kill him if he returned to Italy without Dalmatia. The nationalist press was campaigning ferociously for Italian control of the Adriatic, and politics was moving out of the council chambers onto the streets. The rapidly growing Socialist party, now dominated by radicals, sent out its squads, and the nationalist right its *fasci di combattimenti*. When Leonida Bissolati, a prominent opponent of Italy's demands, tried to speak at a huge League of Nations rally in La Scala in Milan, rabid nationalists, including Mussolini, were in the audience. An Italian journalist reported on a scene that was to become increasingly familiar:

> Then, at a given moment, as if an invisible baton had given the signal, the infernal symphony began. Squeaks, shrieks, whistles, grumbles, nearly human, and all the thinkable counterfeits of the wild pack's howling made up the bulk of the sound wave; but a human, nay, a patriotic cry became distinguishable now and then and ruled the inarticulate mass with the rhythm of a brutal march. They said: "Croati no! Croati no!" meaning that they wanted no friendship with Croats or Yugoslavs; and they meant too that Bissolati was a Croat.[35]

Fiume above all came to stand for both the Italian nationalist program and the determination of Wilson to resist it. It was an unlikely place to have caused such a crisis. Not particularly beautiful or distinguished, Fiume was a busy little port that had acted before the war as Hungary's outlet to the Adriatic. The population, as was so typical in central Europe, was mixed, with a small number of Hungarians, a prosperous Italian middle class and a largely Croat working class. In Fiume itself, Italians were in a slight majority but, if its suburbs of Sušak were added in, the Croats were. Before the war, the local Italians may have talked sentimentally of

Italy and grumbled at the Hungarian authorities, but it was only in 1918 that reunification with the motherland became a real possibility. Gangs of young men calling themselves the *giovani fiumani* suddenly appeared in the cafés, demanding that their orchestras play the Italian national anthem every fifteen minutes and forcing all the customers to stand up.[36]

Like so much of what was to happen in Fiume in the next two years, the events of that period at the end of the war became a matter of legend in Italy. Heroic volunteers—christened the Argonauts—braved Austrian gunfire, it was said, as they sped across the waters in fast boats to Venice to bring the Italian navy to Fiume's rescue. The facts, as reported by the American ambassador, that five young men from Fiume had chugged across in a commandeered tugboat and that the Italian navy had fired on them by mistake, were conveniently ignored. The Italian military who now occupied Fiume under the armistice agreements were determined that it should remain Italian. Diplomatic negotiations were irrelevant, said an admiral; "such discussions were merely debates of diplomats and political men; . . . Fiume was Italian and would remain so; . . . no intermeddling could in any way damage Italian rights."[37]

There was a practical reason for Italy's sudden attachment to Fiume. "It will be very difficult," one of the Italian delegates in Paris explained frankly, "for us to keep up the commerce of Trieste unless we control Fiume and are able to divert its trade to Trieste." It was as a symbol, though, that Fiume, "the jewel of the Adriatic," was important to Italian nationalists. "Why they have set their hearts on a little town of 50,000 people, with little more than half of them Italians, is a mystery to me," wrote House in his diary. In April 1919, when the uproar over Fiume was at its height, Orlando remarked pensively to House that it would have been better if Italy's demands could have been settled right at the end of the war: "Fiume never would have been injected into the terms by the Italians."[38]

Public opinion often fastens itself to trivial objects. In Italy in 1919 it also received a prod from an extraordinary figure—Gabriele D'Annunzio—who made Fiume his cause. He was short, bald, ugly and immensely charming. When he spoke to crowds, his oratory wove them into a single obedient mass. "Will you sacrifice your lives?" he would ask, and they would shout back "Yes!" That was what he expected. He was a leader, a *duce* before Mussolini; a superman, in the words of Nietzsche, with whom of course he agreed. D'Annunzio was also a great poet, playwright and filmmaker. His physical courage, his contempt for ordinary politicians and his devout nationalism spoke to his countrymen. His flouting of convention, his sense of drama and his passionate love affairs made him a romantic hero throughout Europe. Even at sixteen, when to sell his first book of verse he started the rumor that he was dead, he understood publicity. His life fed the legend: his mistress, the actress Eleonora Duse, waiting on the shore with a great purple robe as he emerged naked from his evening swim; the study, cluttered with beautiful and exotic objects, where the artist held his séances; the sudden flights from his creditors.

When Italy entered the war, D'Annunzio, then fifty-two, joined a cavalry regiment. He fought, however, where and as he pleased, at the front, in submarines and in the air. (He also took leave whenever it suited him.) He lost an eye but won medals for bravery. His most celebrated exploit came in August 1918, when he swooped over Vienna in his plane, filling the skies with leaflets in the Italian colors calling on Austria to surrender. In a war with few individual heroes, he stood out. Italy needed heroes.

D'Annunzio took up Italy's claims with enthusiasm. It was he who coined the phrase "the mutilated victory" and in January 1919 he published an inflammatory "Letter to the Dalmatians" in Mussolini's newspaper. The letter castigated the Allies, the "enfeebling transatlantic purgatives offered by Dr. Wilson" and the "transalpine surgery of Dr. Clemenceau," and boasted of Italy's valor during the war. "And what peace will in the end be imposed on us, poor little ones of Christ? A Gallic peace? A British peace? A star-spangled peace? Then no! Enough. Victorious Italy—the most victorious of all the nations—victorious over herself and over the enemy—will have on the Alps and over her sea the Pax Romana, the sole peace that is fitting."[39] (Although his writings were on the Vatican's Index, D'Annunzio reveled in Catholic imagery.)

While the clamor for Fiume and the rest of Italy's demands in the Adriatic mounted in Italy, the Peace Conference was preoccupied with other matters. Between February 14 and March 14, Wilson was back in the United States. Orlando too went home, where he made a bland speech to the Italian parliament that gave the impression that all was well in Paris. (When he mentioned Fiume, his audience rose to their feet with a cry of "Viva Fiume!"[40]) It was not until April, when tensions were still running high over the German terms, that the peacemakers got down to dealing with the borders between Italy and Yugoslavia.

At a meeting of the Council of Four on April 3, Lloyd George asked the Italians to explain their position on the Adriatic. Orlando did so at great length with the familiar arguments. He rejected a proposal to make Fiume a free state under the League of Nations. When the Yugoslavs were invited to present their views that afternoon, Orlando said stiffly that he would not attend because he did not care to deal with enemy nations. Over the next weeks, a series of private meetings between the Italians and their allies produced little but bad feeling. Rumors circulated that Orlando was thinking of walking out of the Peace Conference. On April 13, as the Council of Four tried to decide when to invite the German delegates to come to Paris, Orlando demanded that the Italian questions be settled first. "Italian public opinion is very excitable. I am doing what I can to calm it; but the consequences of a disappointment of this kind would be very grave." His government would probably fall if he could not report progress. His audience was sympathetic but unmoved. As Lloyd George said, "I am convinced that it is in the general interest to summon the German delegates straightaway and thus to prepare ourselves to negotiate with the only enemy state which is still standing." Wilson's suggestion, which was accepted, was to put off the summons to the Germans for a couple of days. In the meantime he undertook to have discussions with the Italians. Orlando accepted grudgingly. He was very bitter at what he saw as a betrayal by Clemenceau and especially Lloyd George, whom he described to House as a "slippery prestidigitator" and not a gentleman.[41]

Lloyd George and Clemenceau were equally annoyed. "I told Orlando," said Clemenceau, "that he thought I was the sainted King Stanislas of Poland who, when he was bitten by a dog, not only pardoned the animal but gave him a chunk of cheese in addition. Well, my name is Georges, not Stanislas. I am not giving cheese to the boys who scampered away from Caporetto. I shall live up to our treaty pledge, and in addition I shall convey a frank expression of my profound contempt. But I shall give no extras." Clemenceau privately asked the Italians to back down.[42] The Italians reiterated that the Treaty of London must be kept.

Wilson, not surprisingly, failed to produce a compromise. With his experts reminding him of his remark on the way over to Europe—"Tell me what's right and I'll fight for it"—he was digging in his heels. He repeatedly assured those close to him that he was not going to let the Italians get Fiume. When Baker, who saw him almost every evening, reported that he had told an Italian delegate that if Italy chose to leave the conference over Fiume, then the United States would feel under no obligation to continue its economic aid, Wilson replied: "That is exactly what you should have said."[43]

A meeting on April 14 between Wilson and Orlando was, according to the Italians, "very stormy." Wilson described it to House as one of the worst experiences of his life, comparable to the time when he had had to listen to the mother of a student he had expelled from Princeton tell him that her son was about to have an operation and would probably die. Wilson gave Orlando a memorandum in which he said he had made the German peace on the basis of the Fourteen Points and that he could not now

make the peace with Austria on a different one. Orlando told his delegation that the memorandum left no room for discussion.[44]

On April 19, the Saturday before Easter, what were to be six solid days of
discussions began. The Italians, almost at once, talked of Passion Week. "I
am indeed a new Christ," said Orlando, "and must suffer my passion for
the salvation of my country." He threatened to leave, whatever the consequences. "I understand the tragic solemnity of this moment. Italy will suffer from this decision. For her, it is only a question of choosing between
two deaths." Lloyd George asked: "On account of Fiume? On account of
a city where there are 24,000 Italians and where, if you count the population of the suburbs, the Italian majority is very doubtful?" He begged the
Italians to think of what would happen if the Americans responded by
pulling out. "I do not know how Europe can get back on its feet if the
United States does not stay with us and help us to oil the machinery."[45]

Wilson urged the Italians to think in new terms. "In America there is
disgust with the old order of things; but not only in America: the whole
world is weary of it." The Italians were unmoved. As Sonnino told Wilson, "after a war requiring such enormous sacrifices, in which Italy has
had 500,000 killed and 900,000 disabled, it is not conceivable that we
should return to a worse situation than before the war; certain islands on
the Dalmatian coast were conceded to us even by Austria-Hungary to secure our neutrality. You would not even grant us these; that could not be
explained to the Italian people." He regretted negotiating Italy's entry into
the war on the Allied side. "For my part, I see my death in all this—I mean
my moral death. I have ruined my country whilst believing that I was doing my duty."[46]

Orlando warned of civil wars in Italy. "What will happen in the country?" asked Sonnino. "We shall have, not Russian bolshevism, but anarchy." These were not idle threats, given the reports coming in from Italy:
of strikes, marches, riots, buildings sacked, demonstrators killed, violent
clashes between left and right. The rumors from Paris were inflaming the
situation: Orlando was giving way; the Allies had decided to build up
Yugoslavia as an anti-Bolshevik power; Wilson was determined to keep
Dalmatia out of Italian hands; Fiume was to be a free port. Cables came
back from Italy, exhorting the delegation to stand firm.[47]

Standing firm was all that Orlando and Sonnino could do at this point.
They had put themselves into a position where any compromise would
look like a major concession. Lloyd George and Clemenceau did their best
to bridge the gap between the Italians and the Americans: they were prepared to give Italy the islands but not the mainland of Dalmatia; Fiume

and perhaps all the cities on the Dalmatian coast could be free cities; Italy could be compensated in Asia Minor; maybe it could even have Fiume if a new port could be built for Yugoslavia somewhere else. Wilson agreed reluctantly to their attempts: "I don't much like to make a compromise with people who aren't reasonable. They will always believe that, by persisting in their claims, they will be able to obtain more." After a fruitless errand to the Italians with yet another set of proposals, Hankey confided to his diary: "We have now reached an impasse. The Italians say they won't sign the German Treaty unless they are promised Fiume and the whole Treaty of London. No one will give them Fiume, and President Wilson won't give them Dalmatia, which, he says, would contravene the ethnical principle." The Italians remained "absolutely inflexible." And now the Yugoslavs, who had been quietly watching the crisis develop, warned that they would fight if Italy got Fiume or the Dalmatian coast.[48]

Time was running out. The Germans were due to arrive on April 25 to receive their peace terms, and by now the Italians were not the only ones threatening to withdraw. The Japanese, usually so quiet, were pressing their claim to the former German possessions in China and were making one last attempt to get a clause on racial equality written into the covenant of the League of Nations. Japan's delegates, with their usual politeness, hinted that they might also be unable to sign the German treaty. Belgium was angry that its demands for reparations had not been met. The last thing Wilson, Lloyd George and Clemenceau wanted was the Germans to see the Allies quarreling among themselves.[49]

Everyone was showing the strain. In the seclusion of the Edward VII, the Italians accused each other of weakening. On Easter Sunday Orlando had his fit of weeping. Wilson looked haggard and his voice shook. Clemenceau was especially sarcastic and rude to the Italians. Even Lloyd George seemed nervous. Sonnino no longer bothered to conceal his dislike of Wilson; he told Lloyd George and Clemenceau, "Now President Wilson, after ignoring and violating his own Fourteen Points, wants to restore their virginity by applying them vigorously where they refer to Italy."[50]

The charge stung because it had some truth. Wilson had compromised his principle of self-determination over the Tyrol and the Polish Corridor. The week after Easter he reread his Fourteen Points and thought again about the new diplomacy he had hoped to bring the world. Issues, he reiterated, ought to be decided on the basis of facts. He went over the maps and the statistics with his experts. The ethnic mix did not entitle Italy to Fiume or Dalmatia: the Italian people were not being told the truth by their own government. Wilson now remembered, and misinterpreted, his trip to Italy four months previously. He had been deeply impressed by the crowds that had greeted him; they were, he was convinced, behind him. He resolved to make a direct appeal to the Italian people.[51]

On April 21 he showed Lloyd George and Clemenceau a statement that he had typed out himself. In clear and direct language it explained why the Treaty of London must be set aside. He reminded the Italians of how much their country was already gaining. "Her lines are extended to the great walls which are her natural defense." Italy had a chance to reach out in friendship to the new nation across the Adriatic. He called on the Italians to work with him to build a new order based on the rights of peoples and the right of the world to peace. Lloyd George and Clemenceau were impressed but cautious. Publication, Lloyd George remarked, "could indeed produce a helpful impression in Italy, but only after a certain period of time. For the moment, we must expect madness." With Clemenceau's support, he persuaded Wilson to wait while he made one final attempt to talk to the Italian delegation. When this failed too, Wilson sent his statement to the newspapers on the afternoon of April 23.[52]

When a special edition of *Le Temps* arrived at the Edward VII, there was intense indignation but no surprise. The Italians had known of the existence of Wilson's statement for a couple of days and had been contemplating their withdrawal from the conference for even longer. Orlando decided to return to Italy the following day. After a meeting of the Council of Four, at which he and Wilson spoke stiffly but politely to each other, he left to catch his train. Sonnino followed a couple of days later. "Well," said Lloyd George, "the fat is in the fire at last!"[53]

The Italian papers carried Wilson's statement beside Orlando's reply, the latter usually set in larger type. Cheering crowds welcomed Orlando's train as it passed. In Rome, the church bells rang out on his arrival, while overhead airplanes scattered patriotic pamphlets and demonstrators chanted, "Viva Orlando! Viva Fiume! Viva l'Italia!" The Italian government placed a guard around the American embassy. Walls throughout Italy were daubed with demands for the annexation of Fiume and caricatures of Wilson in an Austrian helmet. In Turin, students forced the owner of the President Wilson Café to take down his sign; they went up and down the Corso Wilson, renamed in honor of the president's recent visit, covering the street signs with new ones saying Corso Fiume. In Fiume itself, young Italians shouted, bizarrely, "Down with Wilson! Down with redskins!" The nationalist press demanded the immediate annexation of Fiume and Dalmatia.[54]

In a speech to the Italian parliament which started with a plea for "calm and serenity," Orlando blamed the situation on his allies and insisted:

"Italy firmly believes before everything else that the whole complex of her claims is based on such high and solemn reasons of right and justice that they ought to be recognised in their integrity." His government won a vote of confidence, 382 votes to 40. Nationalists, the fascists prominent among them, held mass meetings throughout the country. D'Annunzio was in his element, savaging the Allied treachery and mocking Wilson, the "Croatified Quaker," with "his long equine face," his mouth "of thirty-two false teeth." This was not a human being but an ugly puppet. Italy must not give in to criminal intrigues. "Down there, on the roads of Istria, on the roads of Dalmatia," cried D'Annunzio, "do you not hear the footsteps of a marching army?"[55]

The peacemakers watched with concern. The Belgians were threatening not to sign the German treaty and there was also a serious crisis over Japan's demands. The German delegates were arriving on April 29 and their terms had not been finalized. More worrying, could a Peace Conference in disarray force them to sign a treaty? "Chaos," said the headline in a Paris newspaper. "The various delegations," reported an American journalist, "are holding meetings to consider what shall be done, as it is suddenly being recognized that the very existence of the Peace Conference is threatened." The conference secretariat started going through the draft treaty with Germany to remove all references to Italy. In a plenary session, the delegate from Panama placed a black scarf on Orlando's empty chair. It was removed by a Portuguese delegate, who said it was too early for mourning.[56]

Behind the scenes both the Italian government and the Allies were looking for a way for Italy to come back. The Italians were shaken that the other powers seemed prepared to carry on without them. Clemenceau added pressure when he announced that the Austrian delegates had been invited to come to Paris by the middle of May. The members of the Italian delegation who remained in Paris sent Orlando urgent warnings that Italy's position was deteriorating rapidly. The United States was holding up a badly needed credit of $25 million. Britain and France were saying his withdrawal freed them from their obligation to respect the Treaty of London. They had gone ahead and divided up the African colonies. Only Lloyd George was hinting at a possible compromise.[57]

On May 5, the Italians announced that Orlando and Sonnino were returning. "Orlando looks very white and worn and says very little and without much pep," reported the American Seymour. "He looks ten years older. Sonnino is unchanged in appearance and preserves some truculence of manner, but is not aggressive."[58] The secretariat set about adding the words "Italy" and "Italian" by hand to the German terms.

The issue that had caused the rupture was still, however, a long way from being settled. Wilson was cool to any further negotiations with the Italians. "It is curious," he said, "how utterly incapable these Italians are of taking any position on principle & sticking to it." One faint hope, which House promoted, was that the Italians and the Yugoslavs might cut through the difficulties by dealing directly with each other. On May 16, the two sides came to House's suite at the Crillon, and, in a type of negotiation that became commonplace in the 1990s, sat in separate rooms while the Americans dashed back and forth between them. When Clemenceau asked Orlando the next day what had happened, his answer was gloomy: "Nothing. It is impossible." The fact that House was trying to bridge the Italian and American positions may have contributed to Wilson's growing antipathy to his old friend.[59]

The main part of the Peace Conference wound down in an atmosphere of mutual irritation. Wilson inveighed to Baker about the greedy Italians. The French complained that Italy was now trying to take over Austrian railways that French money had paid for. Clemenceau shouted: "France will resent it. She will not forget it. I don't expect fairness from you." When several French soldiers were lynched by nationalist mobs in Fiume, he loudly denounced the "peuple d'assassins" at the Council of Four. The Italians reserved their main venom for Wilson. When an assistant remarked to Sonnino, "Wilson seems affable this morning," his superior replied, "Who knows what new offers, what new blackmail have been contrived?" Orlando had become convinced, he said in his memoirs, that "Wilson had his own personal engagement with the Yugoslavs; what it was I don't know but there it was." The Italian press carried stories that Wilson had been bribed by the Yugoslavs or that he had a Yugoslav mistress. Sonnino and others believed rather that he was in the grip of American financial interests who wanted to develop the Adriatic for themselves, perhaps using the Red Cross as their cover.[60]

Before Wilson finally left for home at the end of June after signing the Versailles treaty, the Italians backed down very slightly by not insisting on quite all the territory promised them by the Treaty of London. But on Fiume they were as obstinate as before. Orlando and Sonnino were playing a dangerous game. Their main opponent, Wilson, would probably be out of office in eighteen months. On the other hand, Italian democracy might not last that long. As Orlando told Lloyd George, "I must have a solution. Otherwise I will have a crisis in parliament or in the streets in Italy." Lloyd George asked, "And if not, who do you see taking your place?" Orlando replied, "Perhaps D'Annunzio."[61]

On June 19 the Orlando government finally fell, but Sonnino and two others stayed on to sign the Treaty of Versailles on Italy's behalf. Orlando in later years took pride in the fact that he was not a signatory; in fact, he argued, Wilson had effectively excluded him from the Peace Conference with his appeal to the people of Italy. Although Italy had taken little part in drawing up the treaty, it did not do badly: it had a permanent seat on the League of Nations council, the Tyrol and a share in the reparations from Germany. That was not the view in Italy, however. As the British ambassador wrote to a friend: "They are I am sorry to say very sore and depressed here. Not less perhaps because they feel that their own representatives have in many ways mismanaged things."[62]

The government of Francesco Nitti, which succeeded Orlando's, was preoccupied with Italy's internal problems. Where it could settle outstanding foreign issues, it was more than willing to do so. The new foreign minister, Tommaso Tittoni, met Venizelos and worked out an agreement between Italy and Greece over Albania and the Dodecanese. There was even some movement on the Adriatic. In August 1919, Tittoni agreed with Lloyd George and Clemenceau that Fiume should become a neutral city under the League and that the whole of Dalmatia should go to Yugoslavia. The proposal was sent off to Wilson, by now back in the United States, but before an answer could come back, D'Annunzio decided to settle the matter his own way.

Various groups, some in the military, as well as veterans' associations, fascists and anarchists, had been plotting more or less openly all summer to seize Fiume. D'Annunzio, who was engrossed in a new love affair, was finally persuaded to lead them. On the evening of September 11 (chosen because he thought the number eleven lucky), he set off with about two hundred men. The next day, as the soldiers sent to stop him joined his force, he marched triumphantly into Fiume. The Italian military command withdrew without a murmur, the other Allied forces more reluctantly. The city, at least the Italian parts, went wild. That evening D'Annunzio made the first of his dramatic speeches from the balcony of the governor's palace.

For the next fifteen months, Fiume was caught up in a mad carnival of ceremonies, spectacles, balls and parties. The town's buildings were covered with flags and banners, its gardens ransacked for flowers to throw at the parades. In a fever of nationalism and revolution, fueled by drink and drugs, priests demanded the right to marry and young women stayed out all night. The city reverberated, said observers, with the sounds of lovemaking. A hospital was set aside to treat venereal diseases.[63] Volunteers and the merely curious from all over Italy and Europe dodged the ineffectual Allied blockade: E.F.T. Marinetti, the Futurist artist; the young Arturo Toscanini, with his orchestra; Guglielmo Marconi, the developer of the wireless; opposition politicians from Rome; gangsters and prostitutes; war aces with their planes; and Mussolini. Modern pirates on commandeered boats darted in and out of Fiume to seize supplies up and down the Adriatic. Armed men wandered the streets in uniforms of their own design. "Some had beards, and had shaved their heads completely," reported Osbert Sitwell. "Others had cultivated huge tufts of hair, half a foot long, waving out of their foreheads, and wore, balanced on the very back of the skull, a black fez." Most alarmingly for the Italian government, many of its own officers, from war heroes to distinguished generals, threw their lot in with D'Annunzio.[64]

D'Annunzio's oratory reached new heights. Fiume was sacred, the city of liberty, from which he would lead a crusade, to liberate first Dalmatia, then Italy, and finally the world. He made contacts with the Bolsheviks, with Egyptian nationalists, with Croats unhappy with the new Yugoslavia, and with Sinn Fein. Wild rumors, some of them true, came out of Fiume, of assassins dispatched to kill Nitti and Tittoni. And in Italy there were equally disturbing reports of planned military coups and armed uprisings. By the summer of 1921, large sections of northern Italy had become virtually ungovernable as fascist squads battled their left-wing and democratic enemies.[65]

It was an appalling and embarrassing situation for the Italian government, which desperately tried to find a resolution that did not further enrage either nationalist opinion at home or its allies abroad. Nitti tried to starve D'Annunzio out by putting an embargo on Fiume, though the terms allowed the Italian Red Cross to bring in basic supplies.[66] Mussolini watched and waited.

Discussions with Italy's allies produced ever more complex proposals but little else. From Washington, Wilson firmly ruled out any solution that gave Italy control of Fiume. Lloyd George pointed out acerbically that the United States was still trying to crack the whip in Europe but refusing to take any responsibility. Britain and France hesitated to put too much pressure on Italy. "There you have a country," said Clemenceau to Lloyd George, "where the King counts for nothing, where the army does not obey orders, where you have 180 Socialists on one side, & 120 men belonging to the Pope on the other!"[67]

Finally, in November 1920, Italy and Yugoslavia managed against all odds to reach an agreement. A new Italian government (Nitti had fallen in June) under the tough old realist Giovanni Giolitti wanted to restore order at home and extricate the country from damaging foreign adventures. Italy pulled its troops out of Albania, which helped to ease tensions with the Yugoslavs. For its part, the government in Belgrade badly needed to revive Yugoslavia's trade, something that could not be done as long as the Italians were being obstructive in the Adriatic ports. When the November presidential elections in the United States put a Republican into the White House, the Yugoslavs gave up any hope of a miraculous intervention by the Americans.[68] Shortly thereafter, Italian and Yugoslav delegates met at Rapallo and an astonished world learned that a treaty had been drawn up which settled the frontiers between their two countries. Italy gained virtually the whole of the Istrian peninsula, Zadar (the only town with an Italian majority on the Dalmatian coast) and a few small and insignificant islands in the Adriatic. Yugoslavia got the rest, while Fiume became a free state linked to Italy by a strip of land.

Many Italian nationalists, including Mussolini, saw the treaty as a triumph because it had, after all, kept Fiume out of Slav hands. In Yugoslavia, Croats and Slovenes complained that yet again their interests had been sacrificed by the Serbs. In Fiume itself, D'Annunzio withdrew into an embittered seclusion from which he emerged at intervals to insist that he would die rather than leave. On December 1, 1920, he declared war on Italy. The Italian military were finally stirred to action. On Christmas Eve their guns opened fire. When a shell narrowly missed him, D'Annunzio hastily negotiated a surrender, denounced the Italian people for their cowardice and "Christmas gluttony" and slunk back to Italy.[69]

Two years later, Mussolini showed how well he had learned the lessons of Fiume. He marched on Rome, and Italian democracy, weakened by the war and by the widespread disappointment with the "mutilated victory," gave way with scarcely a murmur. In January 1924, Mussolini annexed Fiume to Italy; in 1940, he did his best to wipe the hated Yugoslavia off the map. In 1945, the lines moved again and most of Istria, with the exception of Trieste, went to the reconstituted Yugoslavia. Some 300,000 Italians fled west into Italy. Fiume is now Rijeka and only the older generation still remember any Italian.

D'Annunzio lived on in his usual style at state expense. He was, the new *duce* complained, like a rotten tooth which had to be yanked out or plugged with gold. He played little further role in public life, preferring life on his estate with his magic, his women and his cocaine. He disapproved of Italy's growing friendship with Germany and died in 1938 in mysterious circumstances. A young German woman from the Tyrol who had worked as his assistant and mistress left the house abruptly and was next heard of working in the office of Hitler's foreign minister, Joachim von Ribbentrop.[70]

Sonnino, whose stubbornness had threatened to destroy the Paris Peace Conference, never replied to his critics and never spoke publicly again in Italy. He died at the end of 1922; his only request to the state he had served for so long was to be buried in a sarcophagus cemented into a cliff below his beloved house on the coast of Tuscany.[71] Orlando outlived almost everyone and went on to play a part in the overthrow of the fascists in 1944. He died, a revered senator, in the democratic Italy of 1952.

23

Japan and Racial Equality

I N THE SPRING of 1919, the French press was temporarily distracted from the Italian crisis by an intriguing question. Was Prince Kimmochi Saionji, the distinguished statesman at the head of the Japanese delegation, in Paris at all? He had scarcely been seen and it was rumored that he was seriously ill or had even gone back to Japan. Stephen Bonsal, House's ubiquitous eyes and ears, argued that this was typical Oriental behavior, that the prince preferred to stay in seclusion and "pull the wires that made the manikins dance."[1]

Westerners dealing with Japan tended to fall back on stereotypes about the mysterious East. So much about Japan was curious, including its status in the world. Was it a major power or not? And was it entitled to have the same number of delegates as the other Great Powers? There were arguments both ways. Japan was very new on the world scene and until 1914 had confined its attentions to nearby East Asia. Even though it had declared war on Germany, it had not made a major effort on the Allied side. On the other hand, it did have one of the world's three or four biggest navies (depending on whether the German one was counted), an impressive army and a very favorable balance of trade. In the view of Borden, the Canadian prime minister, there were "only three major powers left in the world: the United States, Britain and Japan." When the League of Nations finally came into existence, Japan had the dubious honor of being ranked fifth in terms of contributions expected.[2]

The Great Powers simply could not be consistent. At the insistence of Britain, Japan's ally, they gave Japan five delegates to the Peace Conference, just like themselves, but in the Supreme Council the Japanese were generally ignored or treated as something of a joke. "To think," said Clemenceau in an audible aside to his foreign minister during one meeting, "that there are blonde women in the world; and we stay closed up here with these Japanese, who are so ugly."[3] When it was decided to expedite business by setting up the Council of Four, Japan was not included. The excuse given, and it was just that, was that the Japanese delegation, unlike those of the other Great Powers, was not headed by a prime minister or president.

The Japanese delegation was like Prince Saionji—distinguished but retiring. Although the fashionable Hôtel Bristol was filled with experts covering everything from naval to labor questions, the Japanese represent-atives on the various bodies of the conference played, as one British com-mentator put it, "mainly a watching part." It did not help that many spoke only rudimentary English or French. When, on one committee, the chair-man asked the Japanese member whether he voted aye or nay, "Yes" came the reply. In any case, Japan was like Italy; it had certain goals in Paris, but not much interest in anything else. "They were the one-price traders of the Conference," wrote Wilson's press officer, Baker; "they possess the genius—perhaps the oriental genius—of knowing how to wait."[4]

The most public figures in the Japanese delegation were two experi-enced diplomats, Baron Nobuaki Makino, who had been foreign minister, and Viscount Sutemi Chinda, who was ambassador to Great Britain. House found them "silent, unemotional, watchful," and there were little jokes among the other peacemakers about how similar they looked. The two mikados, the Americans called them. But there were significant dif-ferences between the two men. Makino was a liberal who liked Wilson's new diplomacy and supported the League of Nations. Unfortunately, since his English was not very good, he failed to communicate this. Chinda's English was better and he appeared a hard-liner when awkward questions came up. All the Japanese delegates were tightly controlled from Tokyo, except Prince Saionji, who was too eminent to control.[5]

And he was in Paris, although he had arrived late, at the beginning of March. When Japan realized that Wilson, Lloyd George, Clemenceau and Orlando were leading their own delegations to Paris, its government hastily decided to send him, to compensate for not having sent their prime minister (whose political position was too shaky to risk the journey) or the foreign minister (who was too sick). Saionji's appointment was an indica-tion that Japan took the conference seriously. The government also hoped that, if Japan did not gain everything it wanted at the conference, his pres-tige would protect it from attacks from its enemies and from riots such as those that had followed the end of the Russo-Japanese War.[6] In Paris, Saionji chose to remain in the background, facilitating his colleagues' work through informal personal meetings much as he would have done in Japan.

On April 15 Bonsal paid a courtesy call on the elusive prince in his apartment near the Parc Monceau. He was renewing an old acquaintance, but his call was also an attempt to mend fences between Japan and its allies; relations had become rather strained. He was greeted by two formidable Japanese detectives, then led through a series of rooms to the inner sanctum. "A subdued, an almost religious light pervaded this room and some seconds elapsed before I caught sight of a tall, slim, and rather emaciated figure in Japanese dress advancing with outstretched hands toward me. . . . His countenance was as serene as that of the Great Buddha at Kamakura looking out to sea."[7]

The two men chatted amiably about past times in Japan and old friends. They touched on the problem of Russia and the Bolshevik government but they carefully stayed away from the tensions between Japan and the West—except for one oblique and highly telling exchange. Bonsal asked about an experiment that a Japanese foreign minister had conducted in the 1890s, when he had tried to graft cuttings from abroad onto a dwarf pine tree from the Ise shrine, the most sacred in the state-approved Shinto religion. The prince brought him up to date: "He grafted on the sacred stem shafts and cuttings of pines from Norway and from Scotland, from Russia and from California. As a result of these shocks there were temporary setbacks, but soon the noble Shinto type of pine from Ise prevailed."[8]

The prince knew well what message he was conveying. In his lifetime he had seen his country transformed from an insignificant collection of islands in the north Pacific into a major power. It is still difficult for the Japanese, let alone outsiders, to grasp the magnitude of that change. What had been an inward-looking nation ruled by a feudal nobility had been made into a modern power with all the underpinnings: an industrial economy which by 1919 was fast coming to rival that of France; a military that had exchanged its steel swords and pikes for machine guns and battleships; and an infrastructure of railways, telegraphs, schools and universities. The feudal lords, like the prince himself, had become diplomats, politicians and industrialists; their retainers had joined the army or the police.

The prince was a complex, enormously subtle man, as much a hybrid as his nation. His journey to Paris had been one not just of miles but of centuries. He was born in 1849, into a Japan still largely isolated from the outside world. His long family tree, kept with the utmost care, showed marriages with the other great houses and even the imperial family itself. By contrast, the Tokugawa clan, which had ruled Japan since the 1600s in the name of an impotent emperor, were vulgar parvenus. He had the usual education for a boy of his class: classical literature, in Chinese as well as Japanese; calligraphy; the traditional instruments and the cultivation of tiny, perfect bonsai trees. He also shocked his elders when he learned to ride, something considered demeaning for one of his rank. If things had gone in their customary procession, he would have lived out his life in the stifling, enclosed world of the old court, with an honorary position and a wife selected from among the small number of suitable girls. He would never have traveled abroad, because that was forbidden and, more important, unthinkable. He would never have enjoyed real power, because that lay in the hands of the military nobility.[9]

The Japanese have a myth that their islands are balanced on the back of a giant turtle; when the turtle moves, earthquakes result. In 1853 an earthquake of a different sort came. An aggressive American sailor, Commodore Matthew Perry, acting on behalf of the American government, appeared in Tokyo Bay demanding the opening up of trade between Japan and the United States. His expedition was followed by British, French and Russian gunboats bearing similar demands for trading privileges, for the right for their citizens to enter Japan, and for diplomatic relations. Japan's ruling circles argued for the next decade and a half over whether to refuse the impudent foreigners or try to cope with them, but the hard-line isolationists could not withstand an aggressive, expanding West. Even among the nobility, young radicals urged the Tokugawa rulers to open up to the outside world and let them travel abroad. Echoes of the debate made their way to the quiet, secluded court in Kyoto, and the young Saionji took the side of the radicals. He decided that he, too, would go abroad if he could.

In 1868 reforming nobles seized power from the old Tokugawa regime in the name of an old schoolmate of Saionji, now the Meiji emperor. Saionji fought on their side in the brief civil war that followed. When he returned to court, he caused a new scandal by appearing in Western dress with his hair cut short.[10] The Meiji Restoration (the misleading name given to the coup) saw the start of an extraordinary national effort as young Japanese were shipped abroad by the hundreds to study and Western experts were paid handsomely to come to Japan so that their brains could be picked. The government slogan summed up the goal: "Enrich the nation and strengthen the army." Japan chose Britain as a model for its navy, Prussia for its army and its constitution, the United States for its banking system and the world at large for its economy.

Saionji turned down offers of comfortable government jobs and set off to see the world. In 1870 he arrived in France, where he was to spend the next ten years. He took a degree in law at the Sorbonne, where one of his friends and classmates was the young Clemenceau, who remembered him as "amiable" and "impetuous." He met the Goncourt brothers and Franz Liszt. He loved the French, their culture and their liberal traditions. He even spoke French in his sleep. To the end of his life he drank Vichy water and used Houbigant cologne, which had to be imported specially for him.[11]

The elegant figure who arrived back in Japan was charming, ironic and slightly detached in his manner. He was also deeply puzzling to his fellow Japanese. One critic fell back on three English words to describe him: "intelligence, indolence, and indifference." For all his pride in his family, he never bothered to get married, although he had long liaisons with mistresses. (When he came to Paris in 1919, he brought a young woman nearly fifty years younger than himself; she was sent away because she was indiscreet.) He never had to worry about material wealth; a younger brother became head of one of Japan's enormous new industrial combines and as a matter of course provided for him.[12]

Saionji served the new Japan as a diplomat, foreign minister and then, in the 1900s, as prime minister. In 1913 the new emperor made him a *genro,* a term inadequately translated as "elder statesman." While *genro* had no official role under the new Japanese constitution, they wielded enormous influence, especially over the formation of new governments and foreign policy. In times of crisis, a word from the *genro* was usually enough to decide an issue. In American terms, it would have been as though William Howard Taft and Theodore Roosevelt had not only chosen Wilson as president but kept an eye on his policies.

Saionji's country was an amazing success story before 1914: it was the only Asian nation both to resist the Western imperialists and to join them. Its gross domestic product—the total value of all goods and services—increased almost three times between 1885 and 1920, mining and manufacturing by almost six times. Such rapid change brought strains as well as rewards; many Japanese looked back nostalgically to a simpler past. But Saionji urged his countrymen to look forward to a liberal democratic future and warned against relying on military strength alone. The warning was needed because as Japan grew more powerful, there were influential voices raised to argue that it must impose its will on its neighbors, by force if necessary.[13]

In the years before 1914, force seemed to be paying off, as Japan won a string of military victories, the first over China in 1895, when it acquired Taiwan and a dominant position in Korea. In 1902, in a tribute to Japan's growing power, Britain abandoned its long-standing hostility to alliances. The Anglo-Japanese naval alliance, still in effect in 1919, was a sign, especially to the Japanese, that Japan had arrived on the world scene. In 1904 Japan took on the formidable power of Russia in Manchuria, defeating its armies on land and sinking not one but two of its fleets. In the peace signed in 1905, Japan gained extensive rights in Manchuria. A few years later, in 1910, it formally annexed Korea, thus confirming what the world had conceded anyway. (A sad little delegation of Koreans appeared at the Peace Conference to ask for their independence.)

The other powers watched with a mixture of admiration and apprehension. By 1914, for example, a quarter of the world's cotton yarn exports were Japanese.[14] The British grew concerned about Japanese dominance of markets in China and India. The United States worried about its interests in Asia, which included not only the China trade but also its new possession, the Philippines. Among Asians, though, Japan was an inspiration, proof that it was possible to defeat the Western imperialists. Even the Chinese, who had most to lose from a strong Japan, saw hope in the Japanese example. Thousands of young Chinese sailed across the north Pacific to study in Japanese universities.

In all Asia, only Japan itself was skeptical of Japanese power. The war with Russia had been almost too much for the fledgling modern economy to bear. Was it worth it? What did the other powers think of Japan's victory? The Japanese could not help but see that the Western world was slow to accept them as equals. One leading statesman complained bitterly to a German friend, "Of course, what is really wrong with us is that we have yellow skins. If our skins were as white as yours, the whole world would rejoice at our calling a halt to Russia's inexorable aggression."[15]

The Japanese were painfully aware of their own vulnerability. They had very few resources of their own. What if other nations chose to cut their access to raw materials and markets? The nationalists' solution was for Japan to follow the example of other powers and establish an empire. There was talk of Japan's historic mission to lead Asia. China, in particular, offered an irresistible temptation. Its last ruling dynasty was moribund and the country was splintering in the face of uncontrolled corruption, regionalism and banditry. An abortive revolution in 1911 only led to more anarchy. China had so much that Japan needed, from raw materials to markets. And Manchuria, just beyond Korea, was so empty, an important consideration in a country whose population had increased by 45 percent between 1885 and 1920 and whose leaders feared that overpopulation would lead to social unrest, even revolution. But if the other powers were willing to give Japan a relatively free hand in Manchuria, they drew the line at China proper, where they had their own interests to protect.

Nationalist dreams worried liberals such as Saionji. "I am not worried about any general lack of patriotism," he said, "but afraid of where an abundance of patriotism might lead us." He was first and foremost an internationalist, who believed that a stable international order would allow Japan, along with other nations, to flourish peacefully. If expansion into Asia hurt Japan's good relations with the other powers, then it must be stopped.[16] The outbreak of the Great War only intensified the debate.

The Japanese watched the conflict itself with detachment—in the words of an elder statesman, "like a fire on the far bank of the river." The government initially hesitated over what it should do. Should it stay clear of the struggle? Back the Central Powers? (Many officers in the army had been trained in Germany and had a profound respect for its forces.) Back the Allies? (The view of the navy, which had close links with Britain.) The debates in the cabinet were largely pragmatic and revolved around where Japan would get the best deal. The decision was for the Allies. "Japan must take the chance of a millennium," said the government when it declared war on August 23, 1914, "to establish its rights and interests in Asia." In attacking Germany, Japan was choosing a low-risk way of advancing those interests. Germany had some concessions in China in the Shantung (Shandong) peninsula and a string of small islands in the north Pacific—the Marshalls, the Carolines, the Marianas—and no means of defending them. The campaign was over by November 1914.[17]

The rest of the war was equally good to Japan. It not only brought orders for Japanese manufacturers but handicapped much of the prewar competition. Japan's merchant marine doubled in size as exports to Britain and the United States doubled, those to China quadrupled and those to Russia sextupled. In 1918, Hughes warned Balfour that the industrious Japanese were moving in everywhere. "We too must work in like fashion or retire like my ancestors from the fat plains to the lean and rugged hills." And it was not just the economic threat that worried the British; at sea, Japan was more powerful than it had been in 1914, and on land, it was extending its influence over China and moving into Russian Siberia.[18]

The Japanese were worried by the resentment. During the war, the elder statesman Prince Aritomo Yamagata noted: "It is extremely important . . . to take steps to prevent the establishment of a white alliance against the yellow peoples." In 1917 the Japanese general staff said that it was out of the question to send troops to fight in Europe. They would be needed, when the war ended, to help Japan resist Western competition in China. Shortly before the war's end a Japanese journal asked leading figures what, in their opinion, Japan should get out of the war. The answers showed a considerable pessimism about Japan's international position and about the designs of Britain and the United States in Asia. The fears of an anti-Japan coalition of white powers were not as fanciful as they seemed.

By the end of the war even responsible Western leaders had reluctantly come to the conclusion that there might have to be a showdown one day. In 1917, in a memorandum to the War Cabinet, Balfour commented, almost as an aside, that Britain would almost certainly defend the United States if Japan attacked. Japan's dilemma, which was to become more acute by the 1930s, was whether to trust the white powers, work with them in strengthening the international order, or assume that it had better look out for itself.[19]

The government also had to listen to its own public opinion, which was demanding compensation for the costs of the attack on Germany, which in China alone amounted to two thousand Japanese lives and fifty million yen. And public opinion was something of which the élites who ran Japan were becoming afraid. The prosperity of the war had not touched all sections of society equally and there was significant resentment of the newly wealthy. The Russian Revolution gave a troubling example of what might happen. In the middle of 1918 serious riots over the cost of rice led to the fall of the government.[20]

The new government that took over was determined to hang on to Japan's gains but hoped to do so without alarming the other powers. Japan's delegation was dispatched to Paris with three clear goals: to get a clause on racial equality written into the covenant of the League of Nations, to control the north Pacific islands and to keep the German concessions in Shantung. Otherwise, according to instructions, it was to go along with Wilson's Fourteen Points. The prime minister personally told Makino to cooperate with the British and the Americans.[21] This was easier said than done.

The Pacific islands—the Marshalls, the Marianas and the Carolines—came up first at the Supreme Council. Thousands of tiny atolls and reefs dotting the vast stretch of the Pacific between Hawaii and the Philippines, they had passed the centuries in peaceful obscurity, and so had their peoples. Imperial rivalry, the spread of modern technology and the growth of modern navies had made them valuable to outsiders, first the Germans and now the Japanese. The Japanese military insisted that Japan should be able to control enough of the Pacific to protect itself and to control access to markets and raw materials on the mainland of Asia. That in turn meant being able to deal with other naval powers. Japan had defeated both China and Russia before 1914 and it had a naval treaty with Britain—but it had not come to a satisfactory accommodation with the United States. Nor was it likely to.

In 1898, during the Spanish-American War, the United States had taken charge of the Philippines and the important base of Guam to the east. Partly to protect its new acquisitions, it had also annexed Hawaii. At one step the United States had moved thousands of miles closer to Japan. Until the First World War, the American navy was still based in the Atlantic, but there were signals that American strategy was shifting to cope with its Asian responsibilities. In 1908, President Theodore Roosevelt sent a fleet steaming around the world. He pushed increased naval appropriations through Congress and started work on Pearl Harbor in Hawaii. By 1914 the United States had the third largest navy in the world, after Great Britain and Germany. The following year the Panama Canal, built with American money, opened, making it easy to move ships from one ocean to another. By 1916 the American government was openly committed to a "two-ocean" navy.[22] Some Americans were talking about manifest destiny, about how the United States was bound to go on expanding westward. Unfortunately, American destiny was bound to clash eventually with Japanese, and what looked like defensive moves by one country might well be seen as aggression by the other.

Both Japanese and American military planners were aware that their countries were starting to bump up against each other. Each side drew up plans for a possible war with the other, mainly as a precaution. On both sides, though, there were those who took the prospect of war quite seriously, even enthusiastically. In the United States, novels appeared in the years before 1914 to terrify their readers with the nightmare of a successful Japanese invasion. These sold particularly well on the West Coast. The sensational Hearst press made much of the "yellow peril" and had a field day with talk of plots by the Japanese government to build a naval base when a group of simple Japanese fishermen tried to take a lease on a bay in Mexico's Baja California. Japan experienced strangely similar scares, and the phrase "white peril" began to appear in the Japanese press. A retired Japanese naval officer wrote a novel, *Our Next War,* about a future in which Japan attacked the United States and seized American islands in the Pacific. When Japan prepared to move on the German concessions in China in 1914, many officers and men apparently thought that they were being mobilized to fight the United States. The Japanese navy advised its government that Japan must keep the islands as an outer perimeter to screen a hostile American advance or, conversely, as bargaining chips to exchange for an agreement on demilitarization in the Pacific.[23]

Japan could count on some support in Paris. In February 1917, in return for Japanese naval assistance, Britain had recognized Japan's claims to the islands, and Italy, France and Russia had followed suit. But the British dominions of New Zealand, Australia and, to a lesser extent, Canada were nervous, and vocal, about the growth of the Japanese presence in the Pacific. In Britain there was a feeling that Japanese help in the war had come slowly and reluctantly. The marmalade that the head of a large Japanese shipping company sent to British soldiers in the front lines and the more useful contribution of a squadron to the Mediterranean in 1917 did not entirely appease the British. (Their view of Japan's contribution was shared by the French; as Clemenceau told his fellow peacemakers in January 1919, "Who can say that in the war she played a part that can be compared for instance to that of France? Japan defended its interests in the Far East, but when she was requested to intervene in Europe, everyone knows what the answer of Japan was.") Few of the European statesmen, engaged as they were in a life-and-death struggle, had the detachment to see that there was no good reason for Japan to intervene in Europe. Relations were not improved by the peace feelers that Germany put out to Japan. Although Japan did not respond to them, the impression created was of an unreliable ally. The British navy started to contemplate a future war against Japan.[24]

Nevertheless, the official British position at the Paris Peace Conference was to support Japan's claims. Members of the British delegation made this quite clear when the Japanese asked anxiously for reassurance. Why did Britain only say that it would support Japanese claims, rather than guaranteeing that Japan would get the territories it wanted? Because that was all that Britain had promised to do in the secret agreement of 1917. Lloyd George himself said that Britain intended to stick by that promise.[25]

Wilson had no use for secret diplomacy and he made it quite clear that, as far as he was concerned, the 1917 agreement was a private arrangement that did not involve the United States. He was also under pressure to be tough with Japan. Anti-Japanese feeling was strong among the American public, partly because of Japanese immigration, a perennial irritant, but also because of the German peace moves. Mexico was another problem; Japan had sold weapons to what many Americans considered the wrong side in Mexico's bloody civil war, and then in 1917, in a clumsy attempt to win Japan to the side of the Central Powers, the German foreign minister, in the notorious Zimmerman telegram, had asked Mexico to invite Japan to join an alliance against the United States. Again, this left a bad impression. At the war's end, when Japan expanded enthusiastically into Siberia, under the mantle of Allied intervention against the Bolsheviks, Wilson shared the general distaste for what was seen as a conniving Japan. Now he worried that if Japan kept control of the north Pacific islands, it would have a series of stepping-stones across the Pacific toward Hawaii. His naval advisers warned of future Japanese bases and airfields.[26]

On January 27, 1919, Makino read a statement to the Supreme Council in which he reminded his audience how seizing the islands from Germany had kept the shipping lanes safe during the war. The locals, he said, sounding like any other imperialist, were a primitive people who could only benefit from Japan's protection and benevolence. Wilson mildly reiterated his preference for mandates as opposed to outright possession. He was not prepared to confront Japan on the islands, because he was disputing its other demands, for instance for the German concessions in China. He confined himself to saying that the United States could not accept a Japanese mandate over Yap, which lies at the western end of the Carolines and was a major nexus for international cables. The Americans were to raise the issue of some form of international control from time to time over the next few years, but with no success. When the mandates were finally divided in May 1919, Japan got all the islands it wanted.[27]

In the interwar years Japan did what the American navy had feared. Although the mandate terms forbade the establishment of military bases or the building of fortifications, this proved impossible to enforce. While foreigners found it increasingly difficult to visit the islands, Japan moved in settlers and the military. Japanese contractors built big new harbors and Truk, in the Carolines, was turned into Japan's main South Pacific naval base.[28] In the war to come, what had been obscure islands—Tinian, Saipan, Truk—became the sites of great battles.

What came to be known as "the racial equality clause" in the League covenant turned out to be far more problematic. In the years before the war, Japanese businessmen complained that they were frequently humiliated when they traveled abroad. In California, Japanese nationals first lost the right to buy land, then the right to lease it, and finally the right to bring their wives to join them. In 1906 the San Francisco School Board voted to send Chinese and Japanese children (of whom there were fewer than a hundred in total) to segregated classes lest they overwhelm the white children. Japanese (and Chinese and Indian) immigrants found it more and more difficult to get into Canada and the United States, and impossible to enter Australia. Even during the war, when Japan was fighting as an ally of the British empire, its nationals continued to be excluded.

The Japanese government had been conciliatory, offering to limit emigration, but it was under pressure from its own public opinion. In 1913, twenty thousand Japanese cheered when a speaker pronounced that Japan should go to war rather than accept the California laws on land ownership. In 1916 the government sent what was by Japanese standards a blunt message to Britain: "a general feeling of regret is prevalent in the Imperial Diet that anti-Japanese feeling is still strong in British colonies." As Japan prepared to take its place at the Peace Conference, Japanese newspapers were full of exhortations. "Now is the time," said one editorial, "to fight against international racial discrimination."[29]

Senior statesmen warned the government that Japan should approach the proposed League of Nations with great caution. What if it was simply another way to freeze the status quo and keep Japan in the second rank? Even Wilson's promises of a new diplomacy were suspect. Democracy and humanitarianism were nice sentiments, wrote a young patriot in an article that caused a considerable stir, but they were simply a cloak for the United States and Britain to maintain their control over most of the world's wealth. If Japan was to survive, wrote its author, Prince Fumimaro Konoe, it might have to be more aggressive. The Japanese delegation was dispatched to Paris with instructions to delay the creation of the League, and, if that were not possible, to make sure that the League's covenant contained a prohibition on racial discrimination. Konoe went along as an aide to Saionji. Years later he was to be Japan's prime minister when his country slid toward war with the United States. In 1945 he drank poison before he could be tried for war crimes.[30]

Since Wilson insisted that the League be the first item of business at the Peace Conference, the Japanese delegates worked quietly behind the scenes for the racial equality clause. At the start of February, Makino and Chinda called on House, who was, as usual, encouraging and friendly. He had always, he said, hated racial prejudice and would do his best to help them. When House met with Balfour a couple of days later, he was less optimistic. The British envoy had tried several different formulas but the difficulty was that the Japanese did not want completely anodyne wording, while for others—the Australians, for example—any mention of racial equality was unacceptable. Balfour was his usual detached self: the notion that all men were created equal was an interesting one, he found, but he did not believe it. You could scarcely say that a man in Central Africa was equal to a European. He also warned House that people in the United States and the British empire were seeing the proposed clause as a first step to outlawing restrictions on Japanese immigration. He was aware of this, House replied, but Japan did have a problem of overpopulation. Perhaps, he added hopefully, they could all go to Siberia—or Brazil.[31]

In the Commission on the League of Nations, Makino and Chinda discreetly let it be known that they were working on a clause that they would, in due course, bring forward. On February 13, as the first draft of the covenant was being readied, Makino read out a long statement. He wished to amend the "religious liberty" clause, which included a promise by League members not to discriminate against anyone within their jurisdiction on the basis of creed, religion or belief. He read his amendment:

The equality of nations being a basic principle of the League of Nations, the High Contracting Parties agree to accord, as soon as possible,

to all alien nationals of States members of the League equal and just
treatment in every respect, making no distinction, either in law or in
fact, on account of their race or nationality.

Makino recognized that racial prejudice ran deep, but the important
thing was to get the principle accepted and then let individual nations
work out their own policies. The League, he went on, would be a great
family of nations. They were all going to look out for each other. It was
surely unreasonable to ask nationals of one country to make sacrifices,
perhaps even give up their lives, for people who did not treat them as
equals. In the Great War, different races had fought side by side: "A common bond of sympathy and gratitude has been established to an extent
never before experienced."

It was a moving and liberal statement, and it made absolutely no difference. Cecil, speaking for Britain, said that, alas, this was a highly controversial matter. It was already causing problems within the British empire
delegation. He thought that it would be better to postpone the whole matter to a future date. There was a general murmur of agreement. Perhaps,
Venizelos suggested helpfully, they should drop the whole clause on religious liberty, since that was also a tricky subject. This brought a solitary
objection from the Portuguese delegate, who said that his government had
never yet signed a treaty that did not call on God. Cecil, in a rare moment
of humor, replied that this time they would all have to take a chance.
There was no mention of racial or religious equality in the draft which
now went forward to a full meeting of the Peace Conference for discussion. The Japanese made it clear that they intended to raise the issue
again.[32] The next day, February 14, Wilson left for the United States, and
the League was put to one side.

The racial equality clause, however, was starting to catch public attention. In Japan there were public meetings and demands to end "the badge
of shame." Along the West Coast of the United States political leaders
warned of the serious consequences to the white race if the clause passed.
The clause, Lloyd George said, repeating another common misunderstanding, was also aimed at the discrimination suffered by Japanese who
were already living in places such as Australia and the United States.[33]

The Japanese had, at best, lukewarm support in Paris. The Chinese,
whose nationals suffered from similar discrimination, felt they would
probably vote for the clause but, as one Chinese delegate told an American, they had much more important things to worry about—in particular,
Japan's claims in China. Wilson had to worry about opinion at home, and
he was becoming suspicious of the Japanese. Although he had trusted

them before, he told one of his experts, "in fact they had broken their agreement about Siberia." Moreover, Wilson himself was not especially enlightened when it came to race. He was a Southerner, after all, and although he had appealed for black votes in his first campaign for the presidency, he had done little for blacks once in office and had refused to allow black combat troops to fight alongside white Americans in the war, preferring to place them under French command.[34]

The loudest opposition to the racial equality clause came from the British empire delegation, in particular from Billy Hughes. Like many of his compatriots, Hughes firmly believed that the clause was the first breach in the dike protecting Australia. "No Govt. could live for a day in Australia if it tampered with a White Australia," wrote one of his subordinates from Paris. "The position is this—either the Japanese proposal means something or it means nothing: if the former, out with it; if the latter—why have it?" Hughes refused to accept any of the compromises House came up with. "It may be all right," he scribbled on one attempt. "But sooner than agree to it I would walk into the Seine—or the Folies Bergeres—with my clothes off." Massey of New Zealand followed in Hughes's wake.[35] This put the British in an awkward position. They wanted very much to maintain the alliance with Japan but, yet again, they had to pay attention to their dominions.

While Wilson was away in the United States, the British did their best to resolve the issue. The French, who had nothing at stake, watched with amusement. Borden and Smuts went back and forth between Hughes and the Japanese delegation. They arranged for Makino and Chinda to call on Hughes. (Saionji remained, as always, in the background.) The Japanese thought Hughes "a peasant"; he complained that they had been "beslobbering me with genuflexions and obsequious deference." The Australian allowed that he might accept the clause if it contained a proviso that it did not affect national immigration policies. It was the turn of the Japanese to refuse. Makino and Chinda appealed to House repeatedly for help, but they were looking in the wrong quarter. House was not prepared to fight for something that was bound to be unpopular in the United States. Privately, he was delighted that the British were taking the heat. "It has taken considerable finesse to lift the load from our shoulders and place it upon the British, but happily, it has been done."[36]

The Japanese delegates, under pressure from Tokyo, decided to go ahead with the clause. As Chinda told House, a defeat would at least show their own public that they had tried. On April 10, at a meeting of the Commission on the League of Nations, the Japanese let it be known that they would be introducing their amendment the next day. They had put it off so often, said House's son-in-law Gordon Auchincloss, that it had become something of a joke. On April 11, the commission met until late in the evening, trying to come up with a formula that would allow the United States to keep the Monroe Doctrine and join the League. Everyone was exhausted when the Japanese finally moved that a reference to racial equality be included in the preamble to the covenant. They had by now watered down their original proposal so that the clause would simply ask for "the principle of equality of nations and just treatment of their nationals." Makino and Chinda both spoke moderately and calmly. They made a very good impression. One by one the other delegates on the commission—Venizelos, Orlando, Wellington Koo from China, the French delegates, Bourgeois and Larnaude, and the Czech prime minister—spoke in favor of the amendment. Looking extremely uncomfortable, Cecil said briefly that he could not support it, then sat glumly with downcast eyes.

While the others were speaking, House slipped a note to Wilson, who was chairing the meeting: "The trouble is that if this Commission should pass it, it would surely raise the race issue throughout the world." Wilson knew that any reference to racial equality would alienate key politicians on the West Coast, and he needed their votes to get the League through Congress. He urged the Japanese to withdraw their amendment. It was a mistake, he said, to make too much fuss about racial prejudice. That would only stir up flames that would eventually hurt the League. Everyone in the room knew that the League was based on the equality of nations. There was no need to say anything more. He was speaking in the most friendly possible manner to the Japanese. He knew that they meant well, but he felt that he had to warn them that they were going about things the wrong way.

The Japanese delegates insisted on a vote. When a majority voted for the amendment, Wilson, with the dexterity he had no doubt learned as a university president, announced that because there were strong objections to the amendment it could not carry. The Japanese chose not to challenge this dubious ruling and so the racial equality clause did not become part of the covenant.[37]

The Japanese press was bitterly critical of the "so-called civilized world." Liberal, internationally minded Japanese were dismayed. They had played the game, they had shown themselves ready to participate in the international community, and yet they were still treated as inferiors. If nations were denied just and equal treatment, Makino warned a plenary session of the Peace Conference on April 28, they might well lose faith in the principles that guided the League: "Such a frame of mind, I am afraid, would be most detrimental to that harmony and co-operation, upon which foundation alone can the League now contemplated be securely built." He was right. The failure to get the racial equality clause was an important factor in the interwar years in turning Japan away from cooperation with the West and toward more aggressively nationalistic policies.[38]

In the short term, however, Japan was able to use its defeat to its advantage. "The Japanese told me with all oriental courtesy," Wilson reported to his fellow peacemakers toward the end of April, "that, if we didn't take their side on this article of the treaty, they couldn't sign the rest." Lloyd George appeared unperturbed. "Dear! Dear!" Clemenceau added, "If that doesn't bother you any more than that, I can't seem to be more bothered than you." In fact, they were all worried. The conference could not afford another defection. Wilson, desperate to save the League of Nations but unable to accept the racial equality clause, now faced giving Japan what it wanted in China. What made his position difficult was that China also had a strong case.[39]

A Dagger Pointed at the Heart of China

W‌HEN THE NEWS that the Great War was over reached China, the government declared a three-day holiday. Sixty thousand people, many of them nationalist students and their teachers, turned out for Peking's victory parade. To popular rejoicing, a monument put up by the kaiser's government to a German diplomat who had been killed during the Boxer Rebellion two decades earlier was torn down. The Chinese press was full of articles about the triumph of democracy over despotism and of enthusiasm for Wilson's Fourteen Points. Among young Chinese especially, there was an uncritical admiration for Western democracy, Western liberal ideals and Western learning. Many Chinese also hoped that the peace would bring an end to interference by the Great Powers in China's affairs.

China had declared war on Germany in the summer of 1917 and had made a substantial contribution to the Allied victory. The trenches of the Western Front required an enormous amount of digging and maintenance. By 1918 about 100,000 Chinese laborers had been shipped to France, where they freed valuable Allied soldiers to press the attack against the Germans. Many Chinese died in France, through shells or disease. More than five hundred were drowned when German submarines sank a French ship in the Mediterranean.

It was easier for China to find laborers for the war effort than experienced diplomats for the peace. Peking stripped its Foreign Ministry of its best talent, calling on its ambassadors from Washington, Brussels and London and the foreign minister. The delegation did not include either China's president or its prime minister, mainly because the political situation in China was so precarious that neither dared to leave. It did, however, hire several foreign advisers who were supposed to help explain China to the world and vice versa. (The American government, hoping to be the honest broker in Paris, would not let any of its nationals work for the Chinese—at least not officially.)

The group of some sixty Chinese and their five foreign advisers that finally assembled in Paris at the Hôtel Lutétia epitomized China itself, balanced uneasily between the old and the new, the north and the south, and with a strong hint of outside influence. It was not clear what they represented, for China was falling to pieces. While one set of soldiers and their supporters controlled the capital, Peking, and the north of China, another had proclaimed an independent government in the south, at Canton. Even as the Paris Peace Conference met, another peace conference was being held at Shanghai to try and reconcile the two governments. The delegation in Paris had been chosen by both sides and its members did not trust each other or their nominal government back in Peking.

Its leader, Lu Zhengxiang, a man in his late forties, epitomized how China was changing. He came from Shanghai, the great port which had grown under the stimulus of Western trade and investment. His father, a Christian, worked for foreign missionaries and sent him to Western-style schools, where he learned foreign languages, not the Chinese classics that so many generations of Chinese boys had studied.[1] Such men were anathema to the older generation of scholars (the mandarins, the West called them), who for centuries had run China. The minds of such scholars were subtle beyond the comprehension of most Westerners; their self-control and manners were impeccable. Their predecessors had governed China for centuries, but all their skills were no match for the guns and steamships of an aggressive West.

Lu had grown up at a time when the old civilization was fighting a losing battle against the forces of change. For centuries, China had run its own affairs in its own way. The Chinese called their country the Middle Kingdom—"middle" not in importance but because it was at the center of the known world. When the first Westerners—"long-nosed hairy barbarians"—had begun to appear in China's gaze, they made no more impression than a gnat might on an elephant. But in the nineteenth century the periphery had begun to disturb the center, selling opium, intruding through its traders, its missionaries and its ideas. The Chinese had resisted, bringing upon themselves a long series of defeats. By the end of the century, China's government had lost control of its own finances and tariffs, and China was dotted with foreign enclaves, ports, railways, factories and mines, and the foreign troops to guard them. The Great Powers threw the cloak of extraterritoriality around their subjects on the grounds that

Chinese laws and Chinese judges were too primitive to deal with the products of Western civilization. It was even said that the sign at the entrance to the park in the foreign concession area of Shanghai read, "No dogs. No Chinese." The Chinese have been trying to deal with the awful blows to their self-esteem and their established world order ever since.

As an eminent Chinese thinker famously asked, "Why are they small and yet strong? Why are we large and yet weak?" Gradually, for it was not easy to jettison the habits of two thousand years, the Chinese began to learn from the foreigners, sending students abroad and hiring foreign experts. New ideas and new techniques were already seeping in, through the missionaries who opened up colleges and schools, via the businessmen who settled in the big ports such as Canton and Shanghai, and from the increasing numbers of Chinese who went abroad to make their fortunes and came back to look for wives and to be buried.

Lu had the new sort of learning that China needed if it was to survive. He entered the diplomatic service, itself an innovation, and spent many of the years before the Great War in one European capital or another. He caused something of a scandal, first by marrying a Belgian woman, then by cutting his long pigtail. He also espoused increasingly radical views, blaming the dynasty for China's problems and arguing for a republic.

China's situation was grim. Foreign nationals were staking out their spheres of influence: the Russians in the north, the British in the Yangtze valley (the Yangtze ran for 3,500 miles from the China Sea to Tibet), the French in the south, the Germans in the Shantung peninsula—and the Japanese here, there and everywhere. The Americans, who did not join in—partly, said the cynics, because they did not have the resources—talked idealistically about an open door through which everyone could exploit the Chinese equally. The danger, as Chinese nationalists saw clearly, was that China would simply be carved up and the Chinese nation and what was left of Chinese civilization would disappear. If not for the fact that there was a standoff among the powers over how to do the carving, this might well have happened by the time of the Great War.

Fear stimulated the growth of modern Chinese nationalism. Terms such as "sovereign rights" and "nation" began to make their way into the Chinese language, which had never needed them before. Plays and songs told of a sleeping China awakening and sending its tormentors packing. Radicals formed shadowy and usually evanescent secret societies to overthrow the ruling dynasty, now seen as an obstacle to China's salvation. The first boycotts of goods produced by China's enemies, and the first demonstrations, began to shake China's great cities after 1900. There was a rash of patriotic suicides. These were tactics born of weakness, not of strength, but they showed the first stirrings of a powerful force. The Chinese increasingly settled on Japan as their major enemy.

In 1911 Lu and the other nationalists got part of their wish when a bloodless revolution toppled the last emperor, an eight-year-old boy. China became a republic mainly because modern institutions seemed necessary for dealing with the modern world. Few Chinese outside the cities had the slightest idea what a republic was. In the inland towns and villages, many did not even know that the dynasty had gone. (Indeed, a Red Guard who was sent out to the backwoods in the 1960s was startled to be asked by local farmers, "Tell us, who sits on the Dragon Throne these days?")

Lu served the new republic loyally as both foreign minister and prime minister. There were some hopeful signs. China's economy was beginning to stir—in the big cities, at any rate, where modern industries were coming to life. As the new knowledge permeated the schools and universities, China began to throw off some of the old repressive ways. Unfortunately China's first president, an imposing general called Yuan Shikai, came from the old conservative world. Within four years of the revolution, he was trying to make himself emperor. Although he died before he could get away with it, he left a deadly inheritance: a divided country, a weak and ineffectual parliament and, most ominous of all, a series of local armies headed by their own generals. China by 1916 was entering a period of internal chaos and warlord rule that was not to end until the late 1920s.

The great Chinese writer Lu Xun compared his countrymen to people sleeping in a house made of iron. The house was on fire and the sleepers would die unless they woke up. But if they did wake, would they be able to get out? Was it better to let them perish in ignorance or die in the full knowledge of their fate? For all their doubts, Lu Xun and the other radical intellectuals of his generation did try to wake China up. They made it their responsibility to speed change by clearing away the debris of the past and forcing the Chinese to look to the future. They published journals with names such as *New Youth* and *New Tide*. They wrote satirical plays and stories scorning tradition. Their prescription for China was summed up in the slogan "Mr. Science and Mr. Democracy"—science to represent reason, and democracy because that was what they thought China needed to bring unity between government and people and thus make China strong. They admired the Allies and hoped that they would treat China fairly, according to the principles Western leaders had so often enunciated during the war. Shantung would be the test.

A hilly, densely populated peninsula that juts into the north Pacific just below Peking, Shantung was as important to China as Alsace-Lorraine to

France. It was the birthplace of the great sage Confucius, whose ideas had for so long been part of the glue that held China together. (Even today, some twenty-six centuries after his birth, there are families in Shantung who claim to be his descendants.) Whoever held Shantung not only commanded the southern flank of Peking but also menaced the Yellow River and the Grand Canal which helped link north and south China. For Westerners, its name was synonymous with a popular soft silk fabric which was made there and, in more recent and horrifying memory, with the base from which the longhaired Boxer rebels had come with their mission of extirpating all Westerners and all Western influence from China.

It was inevitable that Shantung would attract the interest of outside powers during the general scramble for concessions and influence in China. Its population of some thirty million offered markets and cheap labor. It had coal and other mineral deposits that were crying out to be exploited. When the German traveler Ferdinand von Richthofen called the attention of his kaiser and the German navy to the fact that it possessed one of the finest natural harbors on the China coast—at Kiachow (Jiaozhou) on the south side of the peninsula—they listened with interest. Germany was on a search for world power, and in those days that meant colonies and bases. Providentially, two German missionaries were killed in local disturbances in 1897. "A splendid opportunity," said the kaiser, and sent a naval squadron to seize Kiachow. The Chinese government protested ineffectually and in 1898 signed an agreement giving Germany a ninety-nine-year lease on about a hundred square miles of Chinese territory around Kiachow harbor. Germany also got the rights to build railways, to open mines and to station German troops to protect its interests.

The German government lavished money on its new possession, far more than it spent on any of its much larger African colonies. It enticed German business, which was curiously reluctant to invest in Shantung, to build a railway and dig mines. (None ever showed a profit.) The navy took charge of the new port at Kiachow. Tsingtao (Qingdao), as it was known, was a model development with superb modern harbor facilities, neatly laid-out paved streets, piped water and sewage, an up-to-date telephone network, German schools, hospitals, and even a brewery that made excellent German beer, as it still does today. One admiring foreign visitor called Tsingtao "the Brighton of the East." By 1907 it was the seventh most important port in China. The only drawback was that it was many thousands of miles from the nearest German colonies and from Germany itself.[2]

For all the bluster with which the kaiser had demanded concessions in Shantung, the German government showed considerable tact in the years before 1914 in dealing with the Chinese authorities. It allowed Chinese troops to guard its railway line and mines when it could have insisted on its own soldiers; it gave up the right to build other lines; and it let Tsingtao become part of the Chinese customs system rather than keeping it as a free port. The result was that by 1914 German concessions were much more limited than they had been under the agreement of 1898 and Sino-German relations were relatively amicable. That fact did not help Germany when war broke out. The German chargé d'affaires in China sent a cable to Berlin saying "Engagement with Miss Butterfly very probable"— a message that the British, who were reading all the cables coming from the East, did not have much trouble decoding. The Chinese government was not in a position to intervene when Japan attacked, and there was nothing Germany itself could do. The kaiser had only his sympathy to spare: "God be with you! In the coming struggle I will think of you." And so the German concessions in Shantung, the railway, the neat little port and the mines passed into Japan's control.[3]

Japan talked about handing back the concessions to China, but the Chinese, not surprisingly, did not put much faith in this. During the war, Japan did what it could to ensure that it would hang on to its acquisition. Right from the start the occupation authorities had busied themselves building new railways, taking over the running of the telegraphs and the post office from the Chinese, and extracting taxes and labor from the local inhabitants. Japan achieved control of Shantung beyond anything Germany had enjoyed.[4]

Japan also did its best to tie up the ineffectual Chinese government in legal and other knots. It advanced large amounts of money to China, some of which came suspiciously close to bribes, to induce Chinese officials to support its goals. Private Japanese nationalist groups, factions within the military, and financiers pursued their own goals, often at cross-purposes to their own government. Arms went to southerners rebelling against the government in Peking, which Japan had recognized. In south Manchuria and the adjoining part of eastern Mongolia, the Japanese military authorities and adventurers intrigued with rebellious warlords. The consequence was that Japanese policy in China appeared extraordinarily devious when in fact it was more often simply confused and incoherent.

At an official level, successive Japanese governments tried, rather clumsily, to get China under their control. In January 1915, the Japanese minister in Peking paid a courtesy call on China's president. The minister talked about the close and friendly relationship of the two peoples over the centuries and said that it would be a shame if outside powers forced them apart. There were, he added, a few troublesome issues that it would be nice to settle. He then presented the astonished president with a list of twenty-one demands. If China refused to agree to them, Japan might have to take what he vaguely termed "vigorous methods." Some of the demands simply confirmed Japan's existing activities in China, but another set asked the Chinese government to agree in advance to whatever arrangements Japan and Germany should come to over the German concessions. Worse still was a final, secret set which would have virtually turned China into a Japanese protectorate. (Just in case the Chinese government had second thoughts, the paper on which the Japanese presented their list had a watermark of dreadnoughts and machine guns.[5])

The Chinese government stalled and quibbled on every point. It also leaked the demands, which produced nationalist protests throughout China. Japan reluctantly dropped the more drastic provisions but on May 25, 1915, forced the Chinese government to sign a treaty guaranteeing that Japan would get what it wanted in Shantung. The Chinese nationalists declared National Humiliation Day. In Tokyo, Saionji was so distressed at the blundering incompetence of his own government that he made his displeasure felt by blocking the foreign minister's attempt to become prime minister.[6]

Other nations watched with concern but did little. Britain badly needed Japan's help at sea. Japanese ships were already carrying out patrols in the Pacific, and the British hoped they might do the same for the route around the Cape of Good Hope and perhaps even in the Mediterranean.[7] France and Italy were content to follow the British, and Russia, which was taking terrible losses in Europe, had no desire to antagonize its powerful neighbor in the Far East. In its secret agreements of 1917 with Britain, France and Italy, Japan was assured support for its continued possession of the German possessions and privileges in Shantung.

The one power to object openly to Japan's activities in China was the United States, which was increasingly worried about Japan's growing power in the Pacific and on the mainland of Asia. Even before what Wilson called "the whole suspicious affair" of the Twenty-one Demands, there had been friction over such issues as the American navy's demand for a coaling station on the China coast and the high rates that the Japanese-run railway in Manchuria was charging for American goods.[8] American businessmen complained that Japanese competition was driving them out of the China market. During the long-drawn-out negotiations between China and Japan, the American government urged Japan to modify its position; in Peking, the firmly anti-Japanese American ambassador encouraged the Chinese to stand firm. The Americans sent a note to both the Chinese and the Japanese governments saying that it would not accept any agreement that undercut American treaty rights in China or China's own political or territorial integrity. (That reservation became very significant in 1931, when the United States used it as the basis for its objection to Japan's seizure of Manchuria.)

The Japanese government backed down in 1915, but it did not give up trying to establish the upper hand in China. In 1916, it signed a treaty with Russia under which Russia recognized Japan's special position in southern Manchuria and eastern Mongolia. At the same time, it sent Viscount Kikujiro Ishii to Washington to try to get American recognition of Japan's position in China. The talks between Ishii and Lansing resulted in an exchange of notes which each side interpreted to suit itself. The Americans believed they had simply recognized that Japan already had special interests in China because of geography; the Japanese maintained that the Americans had given their approval to Japan's special position in a much wider sense.[9]

The Russian Revolution of 1917 added to the Japanese determination to stay in China. As Ishii confided to his diary, "While foreign governments would not feel themselves endangered by calamity, epidemic, civil war or bolshevism in China, Japan could not exist without China and the Japanese people could not stand without the Chinese."[10] That was why the Japanese often referred to an "Asian Monroe Doctrine." Just as the United States for its own security treated Latin America as its backyard, so Japan had to worry about China and neighbors such as Korea and Mongolia.

In 1918, with the war nearly over, Japan made a final effort to get matters in China settled to its satisfaction. In May it signed a defense treaty with the Chinese government, and in September it exchanged secret notes reiterating the 1915 agreements on Shantung. In a phrase that was particularly damaging to China's case in Paris, the Chinese representative in Tokyo said that his government "gladly agreed" to the notes. In other words, the Chinese government compromised its own bargaining position before the war ended. Chinese delegates in Paris claimed that they knew nothing of the secret agreements until they were produced by the Japanese in January 1919.[11]

By 1919, Japan's maneuverings in China had left a bad impression on many outside observers. Even the British, who were committed to supporting Japan, were worried by what they perceived as Japanese arrogance and ambition. The British were particularly concerned about Japan's inroads into their economic sphere in the Yangtze valley. Their ambassador in Tokyo warned darkly, "Today we have come to know that Japan—the real Japan—is a frankly opportunistic, not to say selfish, country, of very moderate importance compared with the giants of the Great War, but with a very exaggerated opinion of her role in the universe." The British were further irritated by the way the Japanese press criticized the performance of British soldiers in the taking of the German concessions in China. The problem was that China seemed such a hopeless cause. Curzon, Balfour's successor as foreign secretary, drew a pointed comparison with Japan: "Within sight of their shores you have the great helpless, hopeless, and inert mass of China, one of the most densely populated countries in the world, utterly deficient in cohesion or strength, engaged in perpetual conflict between the North and the South, destitute of military capacity or ardour, an easy prey to a nation of the character I have described."[12] The French, on the China question at least, were in agreement with the British.

House also agreed. As he told Wilson during the war, it was unreasonable not to expect Japan to move into the mainland of China when so much of the white world was closed to the Japanese. "We cannot meet Japan in her desires as to land and immigration, and unless we make some concessions in regard to her sphere of influence in the East, trouble is sure, sooner or later to come." He added, with excessive optimism, "A policy can be formulated which will leave the door open, rehabilitate China, and satisfy Japan." The Japanese, when they analyzed the American delegation in Paris, put him down as a friend.[13] They could not find many others.

Years later Breckinridge Long, who was third assistant secretary of state with special responsibility for Far Eastern affairs before and during the Paris Peace Conference, told an interviewer that from 1917 onward suspicion of Japan was a constant factor in American thinking. Even Lansing, who prided himself on his reasonable approach to the world, felt the shift. In 1915, he argued for the need to conciliate Japan, even suggesting giving it the Philippines, and criticized people who had "hysterics about the deep and wicked schemes of Japan." But, as far as China was concerned, he became convinced that a line must be drawn. He sailed to Paris determined, he later said, "to have it out once and for all with Japan." He also took to referring to Japan as "Prussia," which was not meant as a compliment.[14]

As the Peace Conference started, it looked as though Wilson might take the same view. He was against secret treaties such as the ones Japan had made, and against handing out peoples and territories without consideration for their wishes. He was also deeply interested in China, an interest that had been fed by reports from the many American missionaries who worked there. One of his cousins edited a Presbyterian missionary weekly in Shanghai. He spoke of wanting to help China, of its moral regeneration, a task in which the United States stood ready to help as "friend and exemplar." Wilson's ambassador to Peking, Paul S. Reinsch, a progressive university professor from Wisconsin, showered Washington with accusations, some of which were true, that Japanese in China were stirring up rebellion, selling morphine and bribing officials, all with the aim of dominating the whole of East Asia. "Should Japan be given a freer hand and should anything be done which could be interpreted as a recognition of a special position of Japan," he warned, "either in the form of a so-called Monroe Doctrine or in any other way, forces will be set in action which make a huge armed conflict absolutely inevitable within one generation. There is no single problem in Europe which equals in its importance to the future peace of the world, the need of a just settlement of Chinese affairs."[15]

Wilson appeared to be listening. In 1918, he took the initiative in reviving a moribund multinational consortium for making loans to the Chinese government. Desultory talks dragged on throughout the Peace Conference, with Japan agreeing to enter the consortium while at the same time making sure that it did not lend money for any developments that might weaken its influence. That was just what the Americans hoped to do. "No mention was made," said a senior American official, "of *the ultimate objective, to drive Japan out of China.*"[16]

But was that what the United States really wanted? If Japan could not expand westward into Asia, would it turn to the Pacific, toward the Philippines, perhaps even farther east? Wilson and his advisers were torn, as indeed their successors would be in the 1920s, between the pragmatic goal of cooperation with Japan and the idealistic one of helping China. Could China be helped at all? Was it worth risking a conflict with Japan?

Just before he left for Paris Wilson summoned Wellington Koo, the Chinese ambassador in Washington, for a friendly chat. Koo, who was only thirty-two in 1919, was already a forceful and distinguished personality. Clemenceau, not usually given to praise, described him as "a young Chinese cat, Parisian of speech and dress, absorbed in the pleasure of patting and pawing the mouse, even if it was reserved for the Japanese." Koo knew the United States well. At Columbia University in New York, where he had earned both an undergraduate and a graduate degree, he had been an outstanding student. (In Paris he spent a happy afternoon singing old university songs with a former professor who was one of the American experts.) He had also been on the university debating team, as the Japanese delegates would learn to their cost. Koo came away from his meeting with Wilson convinced that the United States was going to support China at the Peace Conference. In a friendly way Wilson had suggested that Koo travel to France on the same boat as the Americans.[17] The Chinese saw this as a good sign.

Another good sign was the composition of the American delegation it-self. Lansing, in his early career in Washington, had acted as counsel for the Chinese government, and one of the delegation's experts, E. T. Williams, the head of the Far Eastern affairs division in the State Department during the war, had lived in China as both missionary and diplomat. The mood of the delegation was generally anti-Japanese. Even those who were prepared to consider the Japanese case had a visceral distaste for the mili-taristic, nationalist side of Japan which, they felt, had dominated Japanese war aims. Despite Wilson's often expressed wish that the United States should remain neutral in Asian matters, the American delegation showed a definite bias in Paris, helping the Chinese to draw up their demands and passing them information. The Chinese responded by asking the Ameri-cans for advice, and taking it.[18]

Because of its own internal dissension, the Chinese government did not brief its delegation to Paris very fully, but one instruction came through clearly: China must get back the German concessions in Shan-tung. In December 1918, as the delegation prepared to set off, it gave a press conference (itself a sign of how times were changing in China) with a wildly optimistic shopping list for the Peace Conference. China was going to ask for a sweeping settlement of relations with the powers, in-cluding the abolition of extraterritoriality, greater control of its own tariffs and of its railways, and the return of the German area in Shantung. In re-turn, China would allow foreign trade in Mongolia and Tibet.[19]

Unfortunately, the Chinese delegation mirrored all too well the coun-try's internal divisions. Its members suspected one another of selling out to the Japanese. Even on the way to Paris there had been some curious in-cidents. Lu had held a two-hour meeting with the Japanese foreign minis-ter in Tokyo. Versions of what took place at the meeting differ: the Japanese apparently believed that they got a promise that China would be cooperative at the Peace Conference; the Chinese later claimed, rather un-convincingly, that Lu merely recognized the existence of the secret agree-ments of 1918 between China and Japan, without accepting their validity. During the same stopover in Tokyo, a box in the Chinese luggage contain-ing important documents, including the full text of the secret agreements between China and Japan, was stolen. In Paris, C. T. Wang, a graduate of the Yale law school who represented the south China faction, sent a cable to Shanghai newspapers with dark accusations about "certain traitors" among his colleagues. He may have meant Koo, who was rumored to be engaged to a daughter of a notorious pro-Japanese official. (In fact Koo had fallen in love with a beautiful young Indonesian heiress who was in Paris.) Lu was dogged by reports that he had taken bribes from the Japanese. He became increasingly morose and withdrawn as the months went by.[20]

Shantung did not come up in Paris until the end of January. Wilson had still not decided what he should do. He explored possible alternatives. Perhaps, as he suggested to Koo, Britain might be persuaded to help China, in spite of the Anglo-Japanese alliance. Perhaps the Japanese would voluntarily give up their claims to Shantung. After all, various officials had suggested that Japan was willing to give the German concessions back to China. Perhaps Japan could save face by taking possession formally and then handing over sovereignty to China.[21]

The Japanese showed little disposition to compromise. On the morning of January 27, when the Supreme Council turned its attention to the fate of Germany's colonies in the Pacific, Makino tried to lump the Shantung concessions in with the various islands that had been seized from Germany. He argued that Shantung was merely a matter involving Japan and Germany and that there was no need for China to be there when it came up. He was clearly hoping that Shantung would be disposed of briskly, along with the Pacific islands, as part of the spoils of war. The other powers decided that Shantung should be discussed separately and that China should be invited to the discussion later that afternoon.[22]

In the break between the morning and afternoon sessions the Chinese did what they could to pressure their friends. Lu, their nominal leader, was nowhere to be seen; it was the young Koo who called on Lansing to ask whether China could expect support from the United States. Lansing was reassuring but added that he was worried about the European powers.[23]

That afternoon the Chinese perched on uncomfortable gilt chairs at the Quai d'Orsay to listen to Makino give a halting and unimpressive summary of Japan's case. (Koo claimed that Wilson told him afterward how disturbed he had been by the speech.) Koo replied for China the following morning. Although his voice shook at first, he tore into the Japanese in a dazzling speech replete with learned references to international law and Latin tags. It was true, he admitted, that China had signed agreements with Japan in 1915 and 1918 which seemed to promise that Japan would get the German rights in Shantung, but China had signed under duress and could not be held to the agreements. In any case, all questions dealing with German possessions had to be dealt with by the Peace Conference.[24]

China, Koo went on, was grateful to Japan for liberating Shantung from the Germans. "But grateful as they were, the Chinese delegation felt that they would be false to their duty to China and to the world if they did not object to paying their debts of gratitude by selling the birthright of their countrymen and thereby sowing the seeds of discord for the future." National self-determination and territorial integrity, those Wilsonian principles, obliged the powers to give Shantung back to China.[25]

Shantung was, said Koo, "the cradle of Chinese civilization, the birthplace of Confucius and Mencius, and a Holy Land for the Chinese." Moreover, to allow Shantung to fall under foreign control would be to leave a "dagger pointed at the heart of China." Ironically, that was very much how the Japanese military saw it: the war minister in Tokyo told his government that the railway running inland from the coast in Shantung was the "artery" pumping Japanese power into the Asian mainland. Borden called the Chinese presentation "very able," and Lansing thought that Koo had simply overwhelmed the Japanese. Clemenceau's warm congratulations, which were supposed to remain private, were common knowledge later the same evening.[26] On eloquence alone, the Chinese were the clear winners.

Unfortunately, the issue of Shantung was not decided in January. It had to wait until the frantic race in April, when the final clauses of the treaty with Germany were put together. By that time the peacemakers were juggling hundreds of decisions, giving way on one, insisting on another, trying to satisfy impossible demands so that there would be a treaty for the Germans that all the Allies would sign. The Chinese and their hopes were a small and insignificant part of the calculations. Wilson himself was being forced into the sort of horse-trading he hated, gaining Japan's assent to the League covenant, even without the racial equality clause, at the cost of his own principles. If the League was the best hope of the world, then perhaps the sacrifice of a small piece of China was worth it.

In the long hiatus, the Chinese and Japanese delegations were busy. Both sides showed that they had grasped an important element in the new international relations as they argued their case in public through speeches and interviews. While the Japanese delegation in Paris had a highly effective information section, most bystanders felt that China got the best of it, perhaps because their demands were more in tune with the mood of the times. During the first part of February, there was a very public dispute over the release of the secret agreements that China had signed with Japan. The Japanese delegation was taken aback when Clemenceau and the other leaders suggested that it might be a good idea to lay the documents before the Peace Conference. Koo, seeing a chance to embarrass Japan, agreed with alacrity and wired his government for copies. In Peking, the Japanese ambassador made a heavy-handed attempt to persuade the Chinese government not to release any documents without the consent of the Japanese government. News of this leaked into the press and not only further inflamed Chinese opinion but deepened American mistrust of Japan.[27]

The Chinese delegates wined and dined the experts and the foreign journalists. Lu arranged for the Chinese government to make donations to the French and Belgian governments to rebuild schools in Verdun and Ypres. But behind the scenes the Japanese did better. In private interviews that spring with Lloyd George and Balfour, with Clemenceau and his foreign minister, Pichon, they got the reassurance they wanted. Although they did not expect much from the American delegation, they had cordial interviews with House. As the Japanese explained it, the Chinese were attempting to renege on solemn promises. What helped Japan's case most of all was their willingness not to push the racial equality clause.[28]

On April 21, just before the Italians walked out of the Peace Conference, Makino and Chinda called on Wilson and Lansing to tell them that Japan wanted the dispute with China settled before the treaty with Germany was finished. They warned that failure to do so would create great resentment among the Japanese public. Wilson conferred that afternoon with Clemenceau and Lloyd George; the three leaders, who had hoped to postpone a decision on Shantung, recognized that they must give way to the Japanese demand. As Hankey put it, "It would be bad enough before handing over the German Treaty to lose the Italian Delegation, but if the fifth of the inviting Powers [Japan] had also withdrawn its representatives, the three remaining Powers responsible for the Treaty would be in a very awkward fix." Lansing complained that the mood in Paris was one of "selfish materialism tinctured with a cynical disregard of manifest rights" and asked, "Will American idealism have to succumb to this evil spirit of a past era?"[29]

On the morning of April 22, Makino addressed the Council of Four to restate Japan's claims. He also thoughtfully produced drafts of clauses for inclusion in the German treaty. Wilson appealed to Japan to consider the long-term interests of Asia and indeed of the world. Nations were going to have to think less of themselves and more of one another. That, after all, was what the League of Nations was all about. If Japan insisted on its rights in China, it would leave China bitter and mistrustful. And that would hurt everyone. "There was a lot of combustible material in China and if flames were put to it, the fire could not be quenched." The Japanese delegates listened politely but reminded the assembled statesmen that, if they did not get what they wanted, they could not sign the treaty.[30]

That afternoon was the turn of the Chinese. The Japanese delegates absented themselves, having decided, wisely, that they did not want to debate with the formidable Koo. The Chinese delegation listened to the peacemakers trying to justify what they were about to do. Lloyd George explained why the British had promised to support the Japanese claims. Remember, he urged, the desperate situation in which Britain had found itself in 1917. It had needed Japan's help to survive the German submarine campaign. "We had to ask Japan urgently to send us destroyers, and Japan made as advantageous a bargain as she could."[31]

Wilson offered reassurance. The League would ensure that the Chinese need not worry about future aggression from Japan or any other nation. And he, too, made a plea for understanding. The powers were in a very embarrassing position because of all the agreements that had been signed during the war. He was very sympathetic to the Chinese but they must recognize that treaties, including their own with Japan, were sacred. "Since this war began by the protest of the western nations against the violation of a treaty, we must, above all, respect treaties." Lloyd George agreed: "We cannot consider treaties as scraps of paper which can be torn up when one no longer needs them." With what one embittered Chinese observer described as "an air of innocence, ignorance and indifference," Clemenceau noted that whatever Lloyd George said went for him as well.[32]

Koo used all his eloquence and cleverness to reverse the tide. Again he denied that China's agreements with Japan had any validity. And in words that were prophetic, he warned his audience that China was at a parting of the ways. The majority of Chinese wished to cooperate with the West, but if the peacemakers failed to treat them justly they might turn away, perhaps toward Japan. "There is a party in China which favors Asia for the Asians." (In the 1930s, when Japan started to take over large parts of China, it did indeed find willing collaborators.) He finished with a warning. "It is a question of whether we can guarantee a peace of half a century to the Far East, or if a situation will be created which can lead to war within ten years." Koo achieved nothing except admiration for his effort and a decision to refer the Shantung question to a committee of experts. These were to report back by April 24 to the Council of Four on the relatively unimportant question of whether China would be better off if Japan got the German concessions as they had existed in 1914 or the concessions it had extracted in the wartime agreements. The committee produced a report in the record time of two days, opting for the former.[33]

The next few days were among the most tense at the Peace Conference. Italy had finally walked out. A worried Wilson reread his Fourteen Points for guidance. The principle of self-determination was clear: Italy should not have Fiume and Japan should not get Shantung. The crisis over Italy intensified the maneuverings over Shantung. The Chinese sent a memorandum and letters to Wilson; the Japanese delegates came to call. Makino and Chinda also visited Bonsal, House's assistant, to complain about the unkind things the Chinese press was saying about Japan and to threaten again that Japan would not sign the treaty. Makino, Bonsal noted, was in a fury. Saionji wrote a polite note to his old acquaintance Clemenceau, saying that Japan wanted the Shantung question settled as soon as possible.[34]

On April 25 the Council of Four (now reduced to three by Italy's defection) sent Balfour to talk to the Japanese about a possible compromise. Would they perhaps promise to hand back the German rights to China one day? On his own initiative, Wilson sent Lansing off on a similar mission. Neither Balfour nor Lansing got very far; the Japanese insisted on their rights. To Balfour, they suggested a bargain. If the powers accepted their claims on Shantung, Japan would promise not to make a fuss about the omission of racial equality when the League of Nations came up for final approval at the plenary session of the conference. To Lansing, they complained that the United States was always suspicious when Japan was merely acting in good faith.[35]

On Saturday, April 26, as Balfour was preparing his report on Japan's position, he received another visit from Makino, and a tentative bargain over Shantung was made. If Japan could take over Germany's economic rights in Shantung, the port at Tsingtao, railways (including those that had not yet been built) and the mines, it would be prepared to pull its occupation forces out. Japan, Balfour reported, would generously allow citizens of other nations to use the port and the railways. Moreover, it was prepared to hand back political control over the disputed area to the Chinese government soon. The Chinese understandably remained suspicious when they learned about this promise. By this stage, in any case, Shantung had become such a nationalist issue that it would have been difficult for them to accept any type of Japanese control. For their part, the Japanese felt that they could not make further concessions. Orders were coming from Tokyo to stand firm; Japan would lose prestige throughout the Far East if China were allowed to treat it with contempt.[36]

As Balfour reported to the Council of Four on Monday morning, Makino "with great delicacy but perfect clearness" pointed out that Japan's claims must be treated as a package. Japan had already lost on the racial equality clause; it would be "very serious" if it were to lose over Shantung as well. There was not much time; the plenary session of the Peace Conference was meeting that afternoon to give final approval to the League of Nations. It would be extremely embarrassing for the powers if Japan were to protest strongly at the omission of racial equality from its covenant. It would be worse if Japan were to vote against the League. With Wilson's reluctant acquiescence, the Council decided that Balfour should write to the Japanese accepting the bargain over Shantung.[37]

Baker, Wilson's press secretary, warned the president that world opinion supported China over the Shantung issue. "I know that too," Wilson replied, "but if Italy remains away & Japan goes home, what becomes of the League of Nations?" When Makino made a bland speech at the plenary session on April 28 in which he barely touched on the racial equality clause, Lansing, who had not been told of the final deal, knew immediately what had happened. He whispered to House that it was a betrayal of principle. House replied, "We have had to do it before." Lansing said angrily, "Yes, it has been done and it is the curse of this Conference." In the statement that he later drew up for the press, Wilson described the settlement as being "as satisfactory as could be got out of the tangle of treaties in which China herself was involved."[38]

The Chinese were shattered. Lu sent Wilson a dignified note. China had put its faith in the Fourteen Points and on the promise of a new way of conducting international relations. "She has relied, above all, on the justice and equity of her case. The result has been, to her, a grievous disappointment." Wilson's own advisers were almost unanimous in urging him to reject Japan's claims, whatever the consequences. Bliss considered resigning in order to avoid signing the treaty; with the support of his fellow delegates Lansing and White, he sent a stern letter to Wilson saying, "If it be right for a policeman, who recovers your purse, to keep the contents and claim that he has fulfilled his duty in returning the empty purse, then Japan's conduct may be tolerated." And he put his finger on the moral issue. If Japan got Shantung, why shouldn't Italy get Fiume? "Peace," he concluded, "is desirable, but there are things dearer than peace, justice and freedom."[39]

Wilson did what he could to limit the damage, and the effort nearly finished him. "Last night I could not sleep," he told his doctor, "my mind was so full of the Japanese-Chinese controversy." Grayson reported that he had never seen him so tired. Wilson insisted on detailed descriptions of what Japan was getting in China, right down to the composition of the railway police in Shantung. (They were to be Chinese with, where necessary, Japanese instructors.) When the Shantung clauses of the treaty came up for their final consideration at the meeting of the Council of Four on April 30, he also got a verbal assurance from the Japanese delegates that Japan would eventually give back sovereignty in Shantung to China. The Japanese steadfastly refused to put this in writing on the grounds that any appearance of giving way would inflame public opinion at home.[40]

By this point, the news that things were going badly for China had leaked out. Paris was full of rumors, which the press picked up. On the evening of April 29, Chinese students in Paris held a very stormy meeting in a hall in the Rue Danton. Speaker after speaker denounced the West. Wang Chingwei, who later won fame as the head of a Japanese puppet government in China, warned in fluent English of the reaction among the Chinese. A young woman art student called for an end to talk of peace: "We must go in for force." Eugene Chen, a journalist who was later to be China's foreign minister, introduced a resolution condemning the Big Four and singling out Wilson for particular mention. It was passed unanimously. That night Wilson's security was stepped up.[41]

The Chinese delegation got the full details of the settlement on April 30. One member threw himself to the floor in despair. When Baker arrived at the Hôtel Lutétia late that evening to convey Wilson's excuses and his sympathy, he found a very depressed group who blamed the president for letting them down. Some of them wanted to leave Paris at once rather than sign the treaty. (Koo later told Bonsal that he would sign only if his government gave him a direct order: "I hope they will not make me sign. It would be my death sentence.")[42]

The negotiations in Paris had been followed with intense interest on the other side of the world. The Chinese delegation had been bombarded with telegrams, from Chinese student organizations, chambers of commerce, even unions, all expressing their faith in Wilson's Fourteen Points and their confidence that the Peace Conference would respect China's claims.[43] By the first weekend in May, newspapers in China's major cities were reporting that the Shantung rights were going to be handed over to Japan. Chinese nationalists were bitterly critical of their own government but they were even angrier, if possible, with the Western powers.

On the night of May 3, a Saturday, students at Peking University, always a center of nationalist agitation, called together representatives from all the city's universities and colleges to plan a demonstration for the following morning in the great square of Tienanmen. The meeting was packed and highly emotional. The students agreed to send telegrams to the Chinese delegation in Paris asking them not to sign the treaty. One young man cut his finger and wrote on the wall in blood demanding the return of Tsingtao.[44]

The fury of the Chinese nationalists, significantly, went beyond merely condemning the Shantung decision. As one student recalled:

> When the news of the Paris Peace Conference finally reached us we were greatly shocked. We at once awoke to the fact that foreign nations

were still selfish and militaristic and that they were all great liars. I remember the night of May 2nd and very few of us slept. A group of my
friends and I talked almost the whole night. We came to the conclusion
that a greater world war would be coming sooner or later, and that this
great war would be fought in the East. We had nothing to do with our
Government, that we knew very well, and at the same time we could
no longer depend upon the principles of any so-called great leader like
Woodrow Wilson, for example. Looking at our people and at the piti-
ful ignorant masses, we couldn't help but feel that we must struggle.[45]

The morning of May 4 was cool and windy. By lunchtime more than
3,000 demonstrators had converged on Tienanmen Square. Most wore
the traditional silk gowns of scholars, but in a gesture to the Western
world some also had bowler hats. Marchers carried placards saying "Give
Us Back Tsingtao" or "Oppose Power Politics" or "China Belongs to the
Chinese." The leaders carried a manifesto which said dramatically, "This
is the last chance for China in her life and death struggle." By two P.M. the
crowd was growing bigger and was moving toward the foreign legation
quarter. When it reached the house of a minister widely suspected to be a
stooge of the Japanese, the mood turned nasty. Demonstrators rushed into
the house, smashed furniture and, when they could not find the minister
himself, beat up the Chinese ambassador to Japan, whom they found hid-
ing. The government tried to suppress the agitation by arresting the more
prominent student leaders, which only inflamed opinion further. The
dean of humanities from Peking University was seen handing out leaflets
on a street corner. Demonstrations spread to other big cities in China, and
nonstudents, from dockworkers to businessmen, began to join in. The
government was obliged to back down; in a humiliating reverse, it released the students with apologies.[46]

The disturbances finished off that other peace conference—the one in
Shanghai that was trying to reconcile north and south China. The southern faction tried to ride the wave of popular sentiment by demanding that
the Peking government reject all the wartime agreements with Japan and
refuse to accept the decision on Shantung. This was unacceptable to the
northern faction, who were by now dominated by pro-Japanese military,
and the Shanghai conference was suspended indefinitely.[47] With the collapse of even that faint hope, China was condemned to another nine years
of disunity and civil war.

The fourth of May was a landmark in the development of Chinese nationalism. It came to stand for the whole period of intellectual ferment;
but what was more important, it marked the rejection by many Chinese

intellectuals of the West. They had turned to Western democracy and liberalism before 1919, often because they could find no other model. Some had always felt uneasy with the Western stress on individualism and competition. The failure of the Chinese Republic and the spectacle of European nations tearing themselves apart in the war had deepened the unease. One distinguished scholar who was in Paris as an observer during the Peace Conference wrote home that Europeans "are like travelers in the desert and have lost their direction. . . . They are in utter despair. . . . They once had a great dream about the omnipotence of science. Now their talk is filled with its bankruptcy."[48]

Coincidence counts for more in history than some may care to think, and in 1919 an alternative presented itself to the Chinese. Not the alternative of returning to China's traditional ways, but the new order in Russia. The Russian Revolution offered an example of a traditional society, not unlike China's, which had apparently skipped ahead to the future in one bold and glorious move. The disillusionment with the West, their own dismal experience with Western-style democracy after 1911, and the clear alternative presented by Russia all came together to make communism seem the solution to China's problems. If further confirmation was needed, it came with an unprecedented gesture made by the new Bolshevik commissar for foreign affairs, who offered in the summer of 1919 to give up all the conquests and concessions squeezed out of China in the days of the tsars. (The Bolshevik government never actually delivered on the promise, but the Chinese at the time were deeply impressed by a generosity that no other power was showing.)

A year after the Paris Peace Conference, a group of Chinese radicals met to form the Chinese Communist Party. Many of the leading demonstrators from May 1919 were to become members. The dean of humanities who had handed out leaflets was the party's first chairman. Under the leadership of Mao Tse-tung and Chou En-lai, who had also been active in the May 4 agitation, the party went on to win power in China in 1949.[49]

In Paris, Koo made a valiant but doomed effort to modify the agreement in China's favor. At least he did not have to risk his life, for China did not sign the Treaty of Versailles in June 1919. The government in Peking could not make up its mind and so sent no orders. In any case, Chinese students in Paris surrounded the Hôtel Lutétia to prevent any of the delegates from leaving.[50] China eventually made its peace with Germany in September 1919.

Japan got Shantung through a determined use of pressure. Was it bluffing, or would it have refused to sign the treaty, as the other powers believed? The evidence is mixed. At the height of the negotiations over Shantung in April 1919, the government in Tokyo ordered its delegation not to agree to the League covenant if Japan's claims were denied. Whether the government realized that the covenant was part of the treaty with Germany is not clear. During the same period, however, internal government documents show that Japan was afraid of becoming isolated. It might have backed down in the face of a determined refusal to give it the Shantung rights. Before the Shantung clauses were finally agreed on by the Council of Four on April 30, the Japanese prime minister, Kei Hara, told his delegates in Paris to wait for further instructions in case of such a refusal.[51]

The Japanese greeted their victory in Paris with mixed feelings. When the delegation returned home, its members were greeted by a crowd protesting their failure to get the racial equality clause. Saionji apologized in his formal report to the emperor: "I am sad that we could not accomplish our wishes in total." He pointed out, however, that Japan's standing in the world was higher than it had been in 1914.[52] On the other hand, the delegates came away from Paris convinced that the United States was out to stop them in China. Perhaps they were right. In 1921 the election of Warren Harding as president brought a more anti-Japanese American administration. The already difficult relationship with the United States continued to be troubled in the 1920s by disagreements in China—over the loan consortium, for example, of which they were both members— and by continued discrimination against Japanese nationals in the United States.

The victory over Shantung proved costly in other ways. In China, nationalist agitation, far from dying down, grew in ferocity, proving a serious handicap to Japanese business. Moreover, Japan's relations with other powers were damaged. The British began to think seriously about the future of the Anglo-Japanese naval alliance. The notion that Japan was a "Yellow Prussia" took firm root in the West. In the summer of 1919, Curzon lectured Chinda, now the Japanese ambassador in London, about Japan's behavior in China. Japan had been unwise to insist on its rights in China; it had created hostility in China and apprehension in Britain. Curzon urged the Japanese ambassador to think of the future of the alliance between Britain and Japan, and of the more general question of security in the Far East.[53]

The Japanese government, which had not counted on the depth of opposition, began to think that it should keep the promise it had made in Paris to hand back its concessions in Shantung. At the beginning of 1920, it tried to open negotiations with the Chinese government to withdraw Japanese troops from the province. The Chinese declined to discuss the matter. In the autumn of 1921, Japan made a renewed effort; it suggested conditions under which it could give up its rights in Shantung. The Chinese government refused to give a clear answer.

Finally, at the Washington naval disarmament conference, with the British and the Americans acting as mediators, Japan got China to agree to a settlement under which China resumed full sovereignty in Shantung on February 4, 1922. The railway from the port of Tsingtao to the interior, which had caused such trouble, was sold back to China under a complicated scheme that effectively left Japan in control for the next decade. China was probably the loser in financial terms: the railway, as the Japanese had discovered, was unprofitable.[54] In Washington in 1922, Japan also signed a treaty with the other powers guaranteeing China's sovereignty and territorial independence. That guarantee ran out in 1937, when Japan invaded the mainland of China, and Shantung, along with all the coastal provinces right down to the south, passed under Japanese control.

The individuals who had played their roles at Paris went on to very different careers. After the debacle of June 1919, Lu Zhengxiang lost interest in diplomacy. He spent a few undemanding years as Chinese minister in Switzerland; then, when his beloved wife died in 1926, he entered a Benedictine monastery in Belgium, where he eventually rose to be abbot. He died in 1949 and is buried in Bruges. Koo continued to shine, serving China several times as its foreign minister, as its premier, and as ambassador in London, Washington and Paris. He represented China at the League of Nations and he was present at the founding of the United Nations. From 1966 to 1976, he sat as a judge on the International Court of Justice at The Hague. In 1977, Columbia University had a round of celebrations for his ninetieth birthday. In her memoirs, Madame Koo, the beautiful young heiress from Indonesia who had captivated him in 1919 in Paris, wrote rather sadly: "He was dedicated to his country. That he never saw me as an individual is not surprising. He was an honourable man, the kind China needed, but not a husband for me."[55] Wellington Koo died in 1985, at the age of ninety-eight.

Several junior members of the American delegation resigned over the American position on Shantung. Lansing hung on as secretary of state in spite of his distaste. He had always felt that the United States should avoid a confrontation over China. As he had warned on an earlier occasion, "It would be quixotic in the extreme to allow the question of China's territorial integrity to involve the United States in international difficulties." When Wilson fought unsuccessfully to persuade the American people to support the peace settlements, one of the issues that came up repeatedly at public meetings and in the Senate was the betrayal of China over Shantung. In the opinion of David Hunter Miller, the American legal expert at the Peace Conference, "most of the tears shed for the 'Rape of Shantung' were wept by Republican crocodiles, who cared no more for China than for Hecuba." In his last week in office, Wilson sent a note to buy tickets for a ball for the Chinese Famine Relief Fund. "I am very glad to be of any assistance," he wrote, "however slight."[56]

PART SEVEN

SETTING THE MIDDLE EAST ALIGHT

25

The Greatest Greek Statesman
Since Pericles

IN DECEMBER 1918, when the Greek delegation to the Peace Conference left Athens, members of Parliament lined up to kiss the hand of its leader, the prime minister, Eleutherios Venizelos. A curious display for a man who was seen, in Western Europe at least, as a great democrat. The delegation stopped in Rome, where Venizelos talked with the Italian prime minister and foreign minister about the competing Italian and Greek claims for Albanian and Turkish territory. No agreement was reached. The Italian press, hostile at the start of the visit, became even more so when the train carrying the Greeks from Italy to France accidently killed two railway workers. In Paris, the delegates took possession of three floors of the Hôtel Mercedes, close to the British. Although they numbered only nineteen, they had taken rooms for eighty people.[1] Greek demands at the Peace Conference demonstrated a similar optimism.

The Greek delegation included the foreign minister and a future president, but the only one who really counted was Venizelos. "A magnificent type of Greek," said Frances Stevenson, "cast in the classical mould mentally and physically." Energetic, persuasive, indefatigable, he won over the British, cajoled the French, reassured the Americans and almost neutralized the Italians. He worked fifteen-hour days in Paris; he wrote the memoranda and letters, gave the interviews and wooed the influential. Even the dour, self-important Hankey felt the spell at a lunch where Venizelos chatted "in abominable French" and was "deliciously indiscreet"; "a delightful old boy; a really big man." Only a few wondered whether his influence over the peacemakers was a good thing; "he has most certainly the good will of all who know him," said one American observer, "but is that really helpful? He enjoys the sympathy and the esteem of all the delegates and all the plenipotentiaries, but they also fear him because of his well-known and incontestable charm." Venizelos was Greece's greatest asset and, in the long run, its greatest liability. Without him Greece would never have won what it did at the conference table; without him it would not have tried to swallow so much of Asia Minor.[2]

Venizelos was born into privilege, the son of a wealthy merchant on Crete, at a time when much of Greek territory (including Crete itself) was still under Turkish rule. He was christened Eleuthcrios, "Liberator"; his father had fought for Greece's independence and three of his uncles had died in the cause. When Venizelos was only two, in 1866, a ghastly incident occurred which he never forgot. A rebellion, one of a series that shook the island repeatedly, ended in disaster when beleaguered Cretan rebels blew themselves up in a monastery. The survivors were massacred by the Turks.[3] His heritage, his history and his own character combined to produce a passionate Greek nationalist.

In 1881 Venizelos went to study law in Athens. Even then he was self-assured, haughty and a leader among his fellow students. He calmly contradicted his professors, refusing to back down even when it meant failing an examination. When a visiting British statesman, Joseph Chamberlain, was reported to have made a disparaging remark about Cretan nationalism, Venizelos demanded, and got, an interview. He informed Chamberlain that he was quite wrong and, in what was to become his style, showered him with facts and figures, all woven artfully together.[4]

The university of Athens, which had been founded just after Greece won its independence from the Ottomans, set out to revive classical culture; even the language of instruction was that of Socrates and Aristotle, not that of contemporary Greece. Many of its students, like Venizelos, saw themselves as missionaries of a Hellenic world to their fellows who still lived, unredeemed, under Turkish rule. One day, in his study, Venizelos gathered his friends around a large map. On it he drew the boundaries of the Greece he wanted: a good half of today's Albania and almost all of today's Turkey. Constantinople would be the capital.[5]

This was the *megali idea*—the "great idea." "Nature," said an early nationalist, "has set limits to the aspirations of other men, but not to those of the Greeks. The Greeks were not in the past and are not now subject to the laws of nature." The *megali idea* (the word "megalomania" comes from the same root) was made up of dreams and fantasies, of a reborn empire reflecting the golden age when Greek had been spoken from Rome to the Crimea.[6]

At the end of the century, as Crete first freed itself from Turkish rule and then joined Greece, Venizelos was prominent in the struggle. By 1910 he was prime minister. In the Balkan wars of 1912 and 1913, he maneuvered on the international stage with such success that Greece emerged with a large swath of territory in the north, from Epirus in the west to Macedonia and part of Thrace in the east. The new territories more than doubled its size. As soon as Venizelos signed the 1913 Treaty of Bucharest, which confirmed Greece's gains, he said, "And now let us turn our eyes to the East."[7]

The East meant Ottoman Turkey. So much of the Greek past lay there: Troy and the great city-states along the coast of Asia Minor—Pergamum, Ephesus, Halicarnassus. Herodotus, the father of history, was born there, and so was Hippocrates, the father of medicine. On Lesbos, Sappho had written her poetry, and at Sámos, Pythagoras had invented geometry. At the Hellespont (now the Dardanelles), Leander had drowned for love of Hero; Jason and his Argonauts had sailed to the eastern end of the Black Sea to retrieve the Golden Fleece from Colchis (in today's Georgia). The Byzantine empire and Christianity added another layer of memories and another basis for claims; for a thousand years, since Constantine became the first Christian emperor, his successors had sat in his city of Constantinople (today Istanbul), speaking Greek and keeping alive the great traditions. The Greek Orthodox patriarch still lived there, not in Athens. Santa Sophia, now a mosque, was the church built by the great Justinian in the sixth century. Centuries-old prophecies foretold that the city would be redeemed from the heathen Turks, who had taken it in 1453; generations of Greeks had longed for this.

Venizelos swore to the powers in Paris that Greece did not want Constantinople. Perhaps an American mandate might be desirable. Privately, he assured his intimates that Greece would soon achieve its dream; once the city was out of Turkish hands, the Greeks, with their natural industry and dynamism, would rapidly dominate it. "The Turks," he told Lloyd George, "were incapable of administering properly such a great city and port." During the Peace Conference Venizelos lost no opportunity to emphasize how very Greek the city was.[8]

For all that Greece, and Greek society, bore the imprint of the Ottoman past, Venizelos spoke for many Greeks when he insisted that his people were part of the modern, Western world. The Greeks would naturally civilize the backward Turks, just as the British or French were civilizing Africans and Asians. Why, he argued, one had only to look at the Greek birthrate (especially in Crete); the fact that it was the highest in the world demonstrated clearly the virility of the Greek nation. In 1919, he claimed, there were about two million Greeks living under Turkish rule.[9]

The correct figure was probably closer to one and a half million.[10] Not all of that number, however, despite what Venizelos claimed, thought of themselves as part of a greater Greece. All through Ottoman Turkey there were Greek colonies; some, like those in Pontus around Trebizond on the south shore of the Black Sea, had been founded so long ago that their inhabitants spoke a barely recognizable Greek. In the interior there was little difference between Greek and Turk. Perhaps as many as 400,000 nominal Greeks were distinguished from their Turkish neighbors solely by their religion and by the fact that they used Greek characters to write Turkish words. It was mainly in the great ports, Smyrna (today's Izmir) and Constantinople, that Greek nationalism meant something.

In the decades before 1914, thousands of Greeks migrated to Turkey looking for work and opportunity. They brought with them the hopes of their countrymen that the Turkish Greeks could be redeemed.[11] Changes in Turkey itself stimulated Greek nationalism. When the Young Turks seized power in 1908, the old easy tolerance the Ottomans had shown to minorities was doomed; in 1912 and 1913, when Muslim refugees fled from the Balkans back to Turkey, reprisals started there against Christian minorities. Even so, before the Great War Venizelos was cautious about talk of protecting the Turkish Greeks or of bringing them into union with Greece; his country had to recover from the Balkan wars and absorb its conquests. Indeed, in 1914 Venizelos was prepared to negotiate a peaceful exchange of populations, Greeks from Thrace and Asia Minor for Turks from Greece. The exchange, eight years later, was neither negotiated nor peaceful.

The First World War changed the picture completely. The Ottomans chose the losing side, Venizelos and Greece the winning one. By 1919 the Ottoman empire was in disarray and even Turkey seemed fated to disappear. The extent of the victory and the power of Greece's friends were intoxicating; Greek newspapers talked of "the realization of our dreams." Only Constantinople was not mentioned, because the censors forbade it. In reality, Turkey was defeated but far from finished; Greece's friends were neither as powerful nor as steadfast as Venizelos assumed; and Greece itself was deeply divided between supporters and enemies of Venizelos.[12]

The divisions were a legacy of Greece's entry into the war. Although Venizelos had been outspokenly pro-Ally from the start, King Constantine, who was married to the German emperor's sister and, more important, was a realist, wanted to keep Greece neutral. The king and his supporters were immune to the heady vision of a greater country; "a small but honourable Greece" was their preference.[13] A prolonged political crisis between 1915 and 1917 saw Venizelos driven from office; in 1916 he set up a provisional government in defiance of the king, which brought half of Greece into the war; and in 1917 Constantine was forced to leave Greece. A reunited Greece entered the war on the Allied side, but the unity was as thin as the excuses that Venizelos now used to round up his opponents. Government, judiciary, civil service, army, even the Orthodox church, were all purged, leaving a rift in Greek society that endured for a generation.

In the Allied camp these actions, if they were noticed at all, did little damage to Venizelos's reputation. He had bravely allowed British and French troops to land at Salonika (today Thessaloníki) when Greece was still neutral; he had spent millions that Greece could not afford on the military; and Greek troops had not only fought in the war but had gone off to help Allied anti-Bolshevik forces in Russia. He was a loyal ally, completely in sympathy with the West and its values, and opposed to German militarism. Venizelos quoted Wilsonian principles whenever possible; he became an enthusiastic supporter of the League of Nations.[14]

Venizelos was a star of the Peace Conference, the "biggest man he met," said Wilson with unwonted enthusiasm. He held dinner tables spellbound with stories of life as a guerrilla in the Cretan mountains, of how he had taught himself English by reading *The Times* with a rifle resting on his knees. And always the conversation included references to the glorious past and great future of Greece. "The whole," reported Harold Nicolson, "gives us a strange medley of charm, brigandage, welt-politik, patriotism, courage, literature—and above all this large muscular smiling man, with his eyes glinting through spectacles, and on his head a square skull-cap of black silk.[15]

On February 3, 1919, Venizelos got his chance to present Greece's case to the Supreme Council. He came with his notes, his statistics, even photograph albums showing happy Greek fishermen on the islands he wanted. That morning and the following day he was so reasonable, so persuasive. History, language, religion and of course, with a nod to the Americans, self-determination—he used them all. It was quite simple, he argued; in Europe, Greece must have the southern part of Albania (North Epirus, as he preferred to call it) and, farther east, between the Aegean and the Black Sea, Thrace (at the very least the western part), a few islands and a huge piece of Asia Minor stretching from a point halfway along the south shore of the Sea of Marmara almost four hundred miles down to the southern coast of Asia Minor to Smyrna. He pointed out that Greece was not asking for Constantinople. He complimented the Italians and made flattering references to the work of American teachers in his part of the world. It was a masterly performance: "such amazing strength & tact-

fulness of argument combined," in the opinion of a junior British diplomat. It was also dangerous—to Greece, to the Greeks and to the future
peace of the Middle East. In that moment of triumph at the Peace Conference, Venizelos lit a fuse that led to the catastrophic destruction of ancient Greek communities in Turkey and to a hostility between Greece and
Turkey that persists today.[16]

One look at a map (not something the great statesmen did often
enough) would also have showed that Venizelos was proposing a very
strange country, draped around the Aegean Sea. His Greece would stretch
one finger northward up the Adriatic, and another thin one along the top
of the Aegean toward Constantinople; then it would jump across a bit of
Turkish territory and the Dardanelles to take in about two thirds of the
coast of Asia Minor, with a big lunge inland at Smyrna. This Greece of
the "two continents and the five seas" was a country turned inside out, a
fringe of land around waters it did not control. It would have enemies:
Turkey certainly, and probably Bulgaria, both of which were down to
contribute land, and probably also Italy, which had its own plans for the
Adriatic, Albania and Asia Minor. Yes, agreed Venizelos, the shape was inconvenient. "But for thirty centuries Greeks had lived under these conditions, and had been able to surmount great catastrophes, to prosper and to
increase."[17]

Yet how could a country with fewer than five million people take on
such a burden? A country so poor that in the years before 1914 a sixth of
the population, almost all vigorous young men, had emigrated? So divided
that there had almost been a civil war in 1917? For all the talk of ancient
Greece, the country at the Peace Conference was new and shaky. As in the
dreams of the other Balkan countries, the glories of the past compensated
for the imperfections of the present.

Venizelos's arguments, so logically laid out before the Peace Conference, were as full of holes as the Greece he wanted. His statistics were as
dubious as any in the Balkans, a mix of outdated Ottoman numbers and
wishful thinking. In making his claim for southern Albania, for example,
he argued that people who looked like Albanians and spoke Albanian were
really Greek; if they were Orthodox, they were Greek to their very souls.
Why, the Greek military was full of men who were Albanian in origin.
Venizelos dealt with population figures like a conjurer: there were 151,000
Greeks in North Epirus, out of a total population of 230,000. Take away
the purely Albanian districts, and that left 120,000 Greeks and only 80,000
Albanians. Majority Greek areas should of course go to Greece (self-
determination) but so should all areas without a clear majority: "for it
would be contrary to all equity that, in a given people, a majority which

possesses a higher form of civilization should have to submit to a minority possessing an inferior civilization." The Albanians, indeed, were fortunate that Greece was willing to take them on.[18]

Its past gave modern Greece a ready-made circle of supporters. Clemenceau, in a rare burst of unqualified enthusiasm, told his secretary, Jean Martet, that humanity had reached its summit in ancient Greece: "Immerse yourself in Greece, Martet. It is something which has kept me going. Whenever I was fed up with all the stupidities and emptiness of politics, I turned to Greece. Others go fishing. To each his own." (Clemenceau had reservations about the modern Greeks, whom he found sadly ignorant about their own glorious history.[19]) The Greeks were the descendants of Homer and Pericles and Socrates. Serene temples, noble discus throwers, the golden light thrown by classical Greece and the Byzantine empire floated between the statesmen in Paris and the reality of a small, faction-ridden, backward nation. From Berlin to Washington, national parliaments, museums and galleries, even the whitewashed churches in small New England towns, showed the continuing power of classical Greece over the imagination of the West. Indeed, the young United States had nearly adopted classical Greek as its official language. The foreign services and governments of Britain, France and the United States were staffed by the products of classical education, their love for ancient Greece unimpaired by any close acquaintance with the modern nation.

Moreover, the struggle of the Greek people for freedom from Turkish rule which had started in the 1820s had been one of Europe's great liberal causes. Lord Byron gave his life, Delacroix some of his greatest paintings. And as long as Greeks were under Turkish rule, the cause lived on. In 1919, in cities all over Europe and the United States, supporters of Greece and its claims met to pass resolutions and raise money. The *Daily Telegraph* published Rudyard Kipling's translation of the Greek national anthem, the "Hymn to Liberty." For Jules Cambon, the Peace Conference brought "the best means of satisfying the ancient claims of the Hellenic nation and of at least completing the work of independence begun by the Liberal Nations of Europe a century ago."[20]

If Greece was golden, Turkey was shrouded in darker memories: a tangle of ferocious riders from Central Asia; the crescent flags waving outside Vienna; the massacres of the Bulgarians in the 1870s and, much more recently, of thousands of Armenians. Its sultan was the heir to the great and ruthless warlords who had made Europe tremble. (In fact, he was a shambling middle-aged man with rheumatism.) One of the Allied nightmares during the recent war had been that the sultan, who as caliph was the spiritual leader of Muslims all over the world, would call on all those millions to fight against Britain in India, or France in North Africa. Ottoman Turkey stood for Islam against Christianity, and now there was a chance to win a victory in that centuries-long clash of civilizations. In Britain, the archbishop of Canterbury and other notables hastened to form a Santa Sophia Redemption Committee.[21]

The world saw only a decaying, brutal, inefficient power which should not continue to exist. Its Arab provinces had already gone, freed by their own efforts or liberated by the Great Powers, depending on your point of view; the remnants of the Armenians had proclaimed an independent republic in May 1918, and the Kurds on the eastern borders were agitating for their own country. As for the fate of the Turkish-speaking heartland, of Thrace in Europe and of Anatolia in Asia Minor, that could be sorted out at the Peace Conference after Greek and Italian claims had been satisfied.

The British, who for so long had propped up Ottoman Turkey, now needed an alternative partner to keep the eastern end of the Mediterranean safe for their shipping. Clearly they did not want an extensive French empire there, and they did not want to spend their own money if they could help it. That made Greece, a strengthened Greece, quite appealing. Principles and interests conveniently overlapped. Greece was Western and civilized, Ottoman Turkey Asiatic and barbaric. And Venizelos was so admirable, "the greatest statesman Greece had thrown up since the days of Pericles," in Lloyd George's opinion. A stronger Greece, thought Lloyd George and many in the Foreign Office, would be a very useful ally. As Venizelos was quick to point out, Greece could provide ports for the British navy and airfields for what was clearly going to be an important new way of getting to India. Greek power could fill the vacuum left by the collapse of the Ottomans. Only the military, whose job it was to look at maps and assess strengths and weaknesses, tended to be skeptical, about both Greek military power and the extent to which Turkey really was finished. When the British general staff were asked to comment on Greek claims in Asia Minor, they warned that a Greek occupation "will create a source of continual unrest possibly culminating in an organised attempt by the Turks to reconquer this territory."[22]

Lloyd George, however, backed Venizelos as he backed few people. "He was," said Lloyd George, "essentially a liberal and a democrat, and all the reactionary elements hated and feared his ideals, his legislation and his personality." He could have been speaking of himself: the fighter, orator, iconoclast, the man who held out, as Lloyd George had done in the Boer War, against an unjust policy and his own government. The two men already knew and liked each other; at their first meeting, in 1912, it had been difficult to tell who had charmed the other more. To Venizelos, Lloyd George was like an Old Testament prophet, with "splendid capacities and clear insight of people and events"; to Lloyd George, his counterpart was "a big man, a very big man." Together they spun entrancing visions of a strong alliance among Greece and France and Britain, controlling the eastern Mediterranean to the benefit of all. Greece would flourish, while Ottoman Turkey would be reduced to a client state.[23]

During the war, the two men kept in touch. Lloyd George later claimed that he and Venizelos had plotted Constantine's overthrow together. In October 1918, when the war was in its last stages, Lloyd George took time out from a frantic schedule to discuss Greek claims with Venizelos over lunch. The meeting was friendly, and Lloyd George was encouraging, although at this stage he did not firmly commit himself to supporting all Greece's claims. Venizelos followed up with a memorandum and a private letter in which he stressed how anxious Greece was to be cooperative. On the one issue where he might have caused trouble for Britain, that of Cyprus, which was about 80 percent Greek, Venizelos was tact itself. If the British wanted to hand it over to Greece, why that would be delightful, and of course Greece would always let British forces use the bases there; if Britain wanted to keep it, that was also understandable.[24]

When Venizelos made his case to the Supreme Council, he was sure that the British stood behind him. He thought he could probably count on the French as well: Greek troops were fighting with the French against the Bolsheviks. The Americans were sympathetic; the Italians were his only major worry. From time to time Lloyd George prompted him with gentle questions; Wilson asked for minor clarification on Turkish atrocities, Clemenceau said virtually nothing; and Orlando referred delicately to differences between Greece and Italy which, he hoped, would be speedily resolved. (On that, as so much else, Orlando was wrong.) Venizelos wrote back to Athens full of confidence: "I think that the impression created by my exposé was a favourable one. Wilson, Clemenceau, Lloyd George and even Orlando reassured me of this when taking leave of them." The Greek foreign minister, who witnessed the performance, was equally delighted: "In principle we have all the Great Powers on our side—except Italy, who begins thinking of agreement and conciliation herself."[25]

The Italians may have been thinking of conciliation but they were also thinking of Albania and Asia Minor, where they had their eyes on some of what Greece wanted. They also hoped to keep the Dodecanese islands, even though their inhabitants were overwhelmingly Greek. Italian newspapers demanded everything that Italy had been promised, and more.

Writers inveighed against the barbarous Serbians and their friends the Greeks. The situation in Albania, where Greeks and Italians actually rubbed up against each other, made matters worse. Italy had occupied much of Albania during the war; local Greeks and the Greek government complained repeatedly about the behavior of the Italian forces. The Italians, it was said, were trying to win over the Albanians with extravagant promises, of no taxes for example. In Greece the papers carried lurid stories of Italian brutalities and rapes. "The whole population," in the opinion of the British ambassador in Athens, "would flock to the colours if mobilisation were ordered against Italy."[26]

During the war, Greece and Italy had talked in a desultory way about coming to a compromise, and early on in Paris, Sonnino and Venizelos, the charmless and the charming, met several times to see whether they could put together a deal. Sonnino suggested that Greece let Italy have all the coast of Albania and about half the interior; in return Greece could have the area around Korçë (Greek: Korytsa), the Dodecanese, and the area around Smyrna on the coast of Asia Minor. While the two men were prepared to bargain over Albania and the Dodecanese, neither would budge on Asia Minor. A deal would have saved much grief later on, but it never had a chance. Neither man trusted the other; both thought their countries could do better negotiating directly with the Great Powers.[27]

In February 1919 it looked as though Venizelos had been right to gamble. The only large question mark was the United States, and Venizelos had every reason to think that he could woo the Americans as successfully as he had wooed the British. He had long talks with House, who assured him that the United States would be helpful. Nicolson arranged for him to meet some of the younger Americans; "he is moderate, charming, gentle, apt. A most successful luncheon." Venizelos was always good at judging his audience. Seymour, the American expert, described another meeting to his family: "Realizing that his strongest asset would be our belief in his honesty, he determined to lay his cards on the table and speak with absolute frankness, and I think that he did. This policy was almost Bismarckian in cleverness." The Americans were sympathetic, but not blindly so. They had reservations about Greek claims in Albania and Thrace. When it came to Asia Minor, though, they preferred the Greek claims to the Italian. Even early on, American relations with Italy were deteriorating.[28]

As the Commission on Greek and Albanian Affairs began to meet in the second week of February, Venizelos kept up the pressure and his hectic pace of activities. He made another presentation: "He is overwhelmingly frank, genial, and subtle," reported Nicolson. The lunches and dinners went on; the letters and memoranda flowed from his pen. In the United States and Europe his sympathizers organized meetings; in the Balkans and Turkey, his agents stirred up Greek communities to send in petitions to the Peace Conference demanding that they be made part of Greece. Professors urged that Greeks should not be left under the rule of Albanians, "the one race which Europe has not been able to civilise." (For their part, Albanians begged the United States to take a mandate over their country.) Be careful, warned a member of the government back in Athens: "Trop de zèle can harm us."[29]

From its first meeting, the commission fell out on national lines, with the British and the French supporting Greece's claims, the Americans taking a more detached and moderate view and the Italians for denying virtually everything. Italy did not want a stronger Greece just across the Adriatic. The narrowest part of the Adriatic was at the heel of the Italian boot; sixty miles east, on the Albanian coast, was the superb natural harbor of Vlorë, guarded by the island of Sazan (Italian: Saseno). If Italy held both island and harbor, it could reach across and squeeze shut the entrance to the Adriatic. If an unfriendly power, though, sat on that eastern shore, Italy would always be at its mercy. When Serbia put in its claim for a slice of northern Albania, Italy opposed that as well. Italy had other interests too: the Catholic minority in the north, ministered to by Italian schools and Italian priests. From the Italian point of view, it would have been easiest to take over directly, or at least turn much of Albania into a protectorate.

As February and March wore on, the crisis between Italy and its allies made the commission's work even more difficult. The two Italian representatives tried to delay the meetings; they quibbled; they threatened to withdraw; they absented themselves, claiming illness (this caused awkward moments when other members met them dining out in Paris). The two, reported Nicolson, "are behaving like children and sulky children at that. They obstruct and delay everything."[30]

The Greek demands on Albania raised the wider issue of whether the little country, so recently created, would survive at all. Greece wanted most of the south on the basis of its own dubious nationality statistics. And, since little was simple in Paris, other issues lurked in the background. If Italy made gains in the southern Balkans, would it drop its demands at the top of the Adriatic? Would Greece back down in Albania in exchange for Asia Minor? Where did self-determination of peoples fit in?

Poor little Albania, with such powerful enemies and so few friends. It had almost no industry, little trade, no railways at all and only about two

hundred miles of paved road. Albania emerged just before the war, created out of four districts of the Ottoman empire. Few outsiders ever visited it; little was known about its history or its people. Only rarely had
Albanians—the great Roman emperors Diocletian and Constantine, for
example—popped up in Europe's history. According to some, the Albanians were the original Illyrian inhabitants of the Balkans, who had been
pushed into the poorest and most inaccessible parts by the slow sweep
south and west of the Slavs. Certainly their language was different from
those of their Montenegrin, Serbian and Greek neighbors. In the Ottoman empire, they were valued for their fighting abilities and their beauty.

History and geography—the tangle of mountains and valleys that
stretched inland from the coast—had produced a myriad of tribes, equally
suspicious of outsiders and each other. The Gegs of the north and the
Tosks of the south spoke different dialects and had different customs. As
elsewhere in the Balkans, the past had left in its wake religious divisions;
the 70 percent of the population that was Muslim was part Sunni and part
Shia; a minority were dervishes. The Christian minority was Catholic in
the north and Orthodox in the south. Rules about honor and shame, of a
dazzling complexity, governed daily life. In some areas, one man in five
died in a blood feud.

The rare travelers who made their way into Albania by foot or on
horseback tended to fall in love with the land and its people. Byron had
had himself painted in Albanian costume; perhaps inevitably, he also took
an Albanian mistress. At the end of the nineteenth century, the journalist
Edith Durham went there on the advice of her doctor. He had told her
travel was good for the nerves, but Albania was not what he had in mind.
She explored the country from end to end before the war, usually on her
own or with a single servant. The Albanians did not know what to make of
this strange dumpy creature; in the end, they decided to treat her as an
honorary man. When British soldiers were moving through eastern Albania during the war, they found that if they said "Durr-ham," it acted as a
passport.[31]

When Durham first encountered Albania, national feelings were stirring. An Austrian professor assembled an Albanian dictionary and grammar; this convinced literate Albanians that they might indeed be a people.
After much discussion the Latin alphabet was chosen in preference to
Greek or Arabic characters. Albanian books were published; folktales, histories, poetry. Albanian schools were opened, often surreptitiously. As
long as Turkish rule remained relatively light, many Albanians were content to work for the Ottomans, as soldiers or administrators. When the
Young Turks tried to reinvigorate the Ottoman empire just before the
Great War, their heavy-handed repression provided the missing stimulus;

nationalist uprisings broke out, with freedom from the Ottomans their goal. The large Albanian community abroad lent its enthusiastic support.

Independence became a matter of national survival in 1912, when it looked as if Albania's neighbors—Greece and Serbia prominent among them—were about to drive the Ottomans out of Europe altogether and divide up the spoils of war. This did not suit the Great Powers, who feared yet another war in the Balkans; so, in 1913, they created Albania. Its boundaries were drawn by an international commission, to the accompaniment of objections from the Serbs and the Greeks. When the commission visited southern Albania, a sharp-eyed journalist noticed the same people coming out at every stop carrying signs that read, "Welcome to a Greek Town." Greek troops who were temporarily in occupation made children sing Greek songs and householders were ordered to paint their houses in the Greek national colors. Even after Greece withdrew its troops, it continued to smuggle in irregulars, who tried to stir up rebellion.

Albania's short history had been an unhappy one. Tribal chieftains, brigands, Turkish loyalists, Greek, Serbian and Italian agents all pursued their own ends against the weak central government. One figure stood out: the sinister and beguiling Essad Pasha Toptani. It was said that, although he spoke no European language properly, he knew the value of money in all of them. He had worked variously for the Ottomans, as head of the police in Shkodër (Italian: Scutari); for the Young Turks; for the Montenegrins (who had designs on the north of Albania); and for the Italians, but always for himself. His compatriots feared and hated him. When his first wife threatened to poison him for taking a second wife (he was a poor Muslim but found his religion useful at times), she was widely admired.[32]

Into this maelstrom the Great Powers in their wisdom plunged Wilhelm of Wied, a German prince—"a feeble stick," in Durham's opinion, "devoid of energy or tact or manners and wholly ignorant of the country." In an act of stupendous foolishness, the new king made Essad his defense minister. Wilhelm lasted six months before he fled back to Germany, leaving five separate regimes each of which claimed to be the government of Albania. By that point the Great War had broken out and Albania, because of its position, was almost at once drawn in. Italy reached across the Adriatic to occupy Vlorë. Greece moved into the south. When the Serbian army fell back in 1915 before the Austrians, it marched through Albania. The long history of mutual suspicion between Serbs and Albanians now had a new chapter, as Albanian brigands harried the desperate Serbs on their way to the Adriatic.[33]

By the war's end, most of Albania was occupied: by Serbians in the north, Italians and Greeks in the south, Italians in most of the coastal towns and French in the interior around Shkodër in the north and Korçë in the southwest, where they flew a curious flag in which the French national colors were joined to a traditional Albanian design. In the south, Greece opened schools and held elections for deputies to the Greek parliament. Serbia and Greece talked in confidence about dividing Albania between them, but that ignored Italy, which had been promised Vlorë in the Treaty of London. (In 1917 Italy had tried to grab the whole of the country but was forced to back down.) The treaty hinted at yet another arrangement: Albania parceled out among Serbia, Montenegro and Greece, with a little statelet in the middle under Italian control.[34]

The Albanians, in the face of these threats to their country, attempted to pull themselves together. At a meeting in December 1918, representatives from different parts of the country elected a provisional government under Turkhan Pasha, an elderly gentleman who had once worked as an Ottoman diplomat. Essad, as usual, played his own game, insisting that he was the president of Albania or, alternatively, its king. (He had spent part of the war designing a dazzling uniform for himself and covering it with decorations of his own awarding.) When the provisional government sent a delegation to Paris led by Turkhan Pasha, Essad went on his own behalf and quarreled violently with the official delegates, whom he accused, in a case of the pot calling the kettle black, of intriguing with the Italians.[35] He was handicapped because he scarcely dared stir from his hotel for fear that one of his many enemies would try to assassinate him.

Albania's friends abroad, a motley crew, provided what help they could. One group hired a charming Hungarian aristocrat to lobby the Americans; unfortunately, it turned out that his main passion in life, and the subject of all his conversations, was the tooth structure of dinosaurs. The Pan-Albanian Federation of America dispatched an American missionary, who was equally ineffectual. Then there was Aubrey Herbert, a younger son of one of Britain's great aristocratic families. (His half-brother the earl of Carnarvon uncovered Tutankhamun's tomb.) He spent much of his time before the war traveling throughout the Ottoman empire, preferably, it seemed, in the most uncomfortable and dangerous conditions. He spoke several languages fluently, including Turkish and Albanian, and was an unpaid agent for the British Foreign Office. John Buchan used him as the model for the hero of *Greenmantle,* a man "who was blood brother to every kind of Albanian bandit." The Albanians offered him their throne. Herbert turned it down but created the Anglo-Albanian Society to work for Albania's independence. Edith Durham was its secretary.[36]

The Supreme Council granted an audience to Turkhan Pasha on February 24. "Very, very old and sad," reported Nicholson. "The Ten chatter and laugh while this is going on. Rather painful."[37] The Albanians threw themselves on the mercy of the Peace Conference and, in particular, on the Americans. "They trust," their written statement said, "that the principle of nationality so clearly and solemnly proclaimed by President Wilson and his great Associates will not have been proclaimed in vain, and that their rights—which have, up to now, been trampled underfoot—will be respected."

The Albanians challenged the Greek claims, producing their own statistics. Where Greece counted 120,000 Greeks in the south, the Albanians could find only 20,000. Religion was not an indicator of anything; Christian or Muslim, all Albanians were united in a love of their homeland, and had been for centuries. The Greeks claimed to be more civilized than Albanians, yet they had committed appalling atrocities. So had the Serbs. During the war, the Albanians had done whatever they could to help the Allies. Albania ought not to lose any territory; in fact, in strictest justice, it should be given the parts of Serbia, Montenegro and Greece where Albanians were in a clear majority.

The Albanian claim included Kosovo, a relatively prosperous farming area on Albania's northwest frontier, where, the Albanian delegates said, Albanians had been since "time immemorial"; the Serbs, who also claimed Kosovo, had not arrived until the seventh century. Moreover, Serbia, which had controlled Kosovo since 1913, had behaved appallingly. There would be trouble in the future if Albanians had to live under Serb rule.[38] (Serbs were saying the same thing about the Albanians.)

Whatever the rights and wrongs of the past (always a difficult matter to establish in the Balkans), it was clear that the Albanians had a good case. The majority of the population of Kosovo was Albanian. But for Serbs Kosovo was their Runnymede, their Valley Forge, and their Lorraine. Kosovo was where, in 1389, the Ottomans had defeated the Serbs and brought them under Muslim rule. It was at once a defeat and, paradoxically, the Serbs' great victory, celebrated annually down through the centuries. Legend had it that a saint, in the form of a falcon, offered the Serbian prince a choice between winning the battle on earth and winning in heaven; he chose the latter and, although he died, his salvation and that of the Christian Serbs was assured. "This region was undeniably a part of the great Serbian Empire in the thirteenth century," said House's assistant Bonsal. "Should it be restored to Belgrade now? Should California and New Mexico be restored to Spain or Mexico? I don't know." One solution might be a simple exchange of populations. "All would be well if friendly relations could be established between the disputants, but unfortunately all the experts say this is impossible; on this point at least they are in full agreement."[39]

Kosovo did not become an issue in 1919 because the powers saw no reason to enlarge Albania's borders in any direction. Albania was weak, its government ineffectual. What did it matter if some half-million Albanian farmers lived under Serbian or Yugoslav rule? Occasionally, in succeeding years, the world heard rumblings of discontent. Albanian priests appeared at the League of Nations to complain that their schools were being closed. During the Second World War, with German and Italian support, Albania at last seized Kosovo; but Tito, the new ruler of Yugoslavia, seized it back at the end of the war. Albania grumbled but dared not do anything openly. And Tito's rule was relatively light compared with what came later. In 1989, seventy years after the Paris Peace Conference, Albania revived the old claims to Kosovo.

The Greek commission ignored Albania and its claims and spent most of its time trying to sort out the competing demands of Italy and Greece. Various schemes were floated; for Italy to have a mandate over the whole of Albania, or Greece one over the south. The French, mainly to block Italy's expansion, urged that Korçë in the south must go to Greece because it controlled the only road joining the Adriatic side of Greece to Greek Macedonia. There were rumors that Greece and Italy were talking again about a separate deal; that Italy was arming friendly Albanian gangs; that the French intended to remain in occupation of Korçë unless it were given to Greece. The Americans were curiously passive, perhaps because the inner circle around Wilson was absorbed with the German treaty and the worsening relations with Italy. In desperation, Nicolson came up with an absurd scheme: for Albania to be divided up, with the north linked to Serbia, a Muslim state in the center under an Italian mandate, the south under Greek rule, and Korçë the home of a Central Albanian University under American protection.[40]

The Albanians were horrified, reported Wilson, who had received a number of petitions, at the thought of an Italian mandate. Perhaps they should have their independence. "I really don't know what they would do with it," replied Lloyd George, "except cut each other's throats." Albania would be just like the Scottish highlands in the fifteenth century. "Don't speak ill of the mountains of Scotland," said Wilson, "it is my family's place of origin." And that was the end of the matter as far as the Council of Four was concerned.[41]

In the summer of 1919, when a new and more conciliatory government came to power in Italy, it made an agreement with Venizelos, himself under pressure to settle Greece's disputed claims. The deal was a matter of old-style horse-trading: Italy would support Greek claims, including those to Thrace, if Greece gave up its claims to the territory Italy wanted in the southern part of Asia Minor. Italy would also hand over all of the Dodecanese islands except the most important one, Rhodes. (This was not as much of a sacrifice as it sounded, because Italy had no legal claim to them.) In the case of Albania, Italy agreed that Greece should have the south; in return, Greece would recognize Italy's possession of the port of Vlorë and its hinterland, and an Italian mandate over what was left. As a symbol of the new spirit of compromise, a railway would be built from Vlorë to Athens.

Almost immediately, other powers raised objections. The French refused to leave Korçë until a more general settlement was achieved. The new state of Yugoslavia was agitated at the thought of so much Italian territory along its borders. And if Greece and Italy were getting pieces of Albania, then it wanted some in the north.

The final blow to the agreement came in February 1920 from an unexpected quarter. President Wilson, defeated in his struggle to get the Treaty of Versailles accepted by Congress, still clung to his principles. The United States, he said in a note to his European allies, was not prepared to do an injustice to the people of Albania. By the spring, the Albanians were in full-scale revolt against the Italian occupation. By August, Italy was prepared to sign an armistice that left it with only the island of Sazan, facing the port of Vlorë. "It is very sad," commented an Italian newspaper, "to witness this debacle after so much noble and generous Italian blood has been given and so many millions have been expended for a great work of civilisation and for the security of our frontiers."[42] The French pulled out of Korçë, and Greece and Yugoslavia, for the time being, dropped their demands. At the end of 1920 Albania was admitted to the League of Nations as an independent state, its boundaries virtually the same as they had been in 1913.

Not for nothing was Albania the birthplace of the king who gave his name to the Pyrrhic victory. Internal politics continued in their turbulent fashion. Essad briefly achieved his dream of being king, but he never sat on his throne. In spite of his bodyguards and Browning revolvers, as he left the Hôtel Continental in Paris an old enemy gunned him down. The assassin was killed in turn, on the orders of Essad's nephew Zog, who duly became king.

Italy never completely abandoned its designs. Under Mussolini, Italian influence continued to grow; finally, on the eve of the Second World

War, Italy annexed Albania. After the war, a former teacher of French, Enver Hoxha, set up one of the stranger and more reactionary communist regimes. Repeated attempts by the Albanian resistance and their Western supporters to restore King Zog came to nothing, largely because they were betrayed by the leading Soviet mole in the West, Kim Philby. In the 1990s, after the end of the Cold War, Essad's great-nephew, an arms dealer from South Africa, revived his claim to the throne.

Greece did much better in Thrace, where Venizelos claimed almost the whole. What he glossed over, with much clever juggling of statistics, was the population mix. Eastern Thrace probably had a Greek majority; in the western part, which had belonged to Bulgaria since 1913, Turks outnumbered Greeks by almost three to one. There was also a significant Bulgarian minority. This was awkward; if the principle of nationality were to apply, something the Americans always favored, then Greece could claim only eastern Thrace. Western Thrace should go back to Turkey or possibly stay with Bulgaria, which needed its seaports. The Italians, who were rumored to be intriguing with the Bulgarian government against Serbia, supported the latter solution. In either case, another country would sit between the main part of Greece and its new province of eastern Thrace. The Greeks argued that the Bulgarians, and many of the Turks, were really Greek. As one delegate assured Bonsal, "They are of straight Attic descent and the land is full of them; but to pacify their ferocious Slav neighbors, and so that they may be understood in their daily life and pursuits, many of them have lost all knowledge of their mother tongue." The Greek fallback position was that the Muslim majority in western Thrace, whether Bulgarian- or Turkish-speaking, would prefer rule by Greece. Conveniently, Venizelos produced a pleading letter from local Muslims: "It would not be just to allow us to suffer under the hardest and most unpitying yoke that one can imagine—under the Bulgarian yoke."[43]

In any case, the Greeks urged, why should defeated enemies be given consideration? Venizelos was prepared to allow Ottoman Turkey a small slice of Thrace just to the north of Constantinople. (He hoped, of course, that the city and its surroundings would soon be Greek.) As for western Thrace, it would be better for the future safety of the world, not to say the Balkans, if Bulgaria relinquished the whole to Greece. "Whatever concessions might be made would be useless, for Bulgaria would never rest until the whole of the Balkans were handed over to her. Bulgaria claimed complete hegemony over the whole of the Peninsula, and she would seize every opportunity to fulfil her ambitions. Bulgaria represented in the Balkans, the Prussia of Western Europe."[44] The British and French, who disliked Bulgaria, agreed. Apart from any other considerations, Greece needed a land link to eastern Thrace.

To objections raised by the Americans and the Italians that Bulgaria would suffer economically if it lost all its ports on the Mediterranean, Venizelos, as always, had an answer: "The principle of nationality should take precedence over economic considerations. Bulgaria had excellent ports on the Black Sea." And, given Bulgaria's past record, it was quite capable of building submarine bases on the Aegean and menacing Greece. If Bulgaria really needed an outlet, Greece would allow it to use a port. (When such a provision was eventually drawn up, Bulgaria rejected it outright: "A Bulgarian outlet to the sea through Turkish and Greek territory is not only impossible, but also unacceptable psychologically."[45])

Although the Greek commission finally recommended giving both parts of Thrace to Greece, the Peace Conference postponed making any decision at all on the grounds that it was premature, since the fate of Constantinople had not yet been settled. (There was talk of the United States taking a mandate.) When Thrace came up before the Peace Conference again in the summer of 1919, the United States had given up the idea of the mandate and was now also firmly opposed to giving western Thrace to Greece. Instead, the Americans argued for leaving it with Bulgaria, much to the irritation of the British, who pointed out that if one of Greece's claims were denied, the whole lot would have to be reviewed. Venizelos was coming under attack at home; he told Lloyd George that his position would be very dangerous unless he could show some solid gains.[46]

The gradual withdrawal of the United States from Europe made it possible for the European powers to ignore its wishes. In the Treaty of Neuilly with Bulgaria, which was signed in November 1919, Bulgaria lost western Thrace. The Bulgarian delegation made one last futile appeal: "The exclusion of Bulgaria from Western Thrace, of which even our enemies the Greeks and the Serbians, who were our conquerors in the war of 1912–1913, did not have the courage to deprive us, . . . will further separate Bulgaria geographically from France and the great sea powers."[47] In 1920, western and eastern Thrace, which had by now been taken from Turkey, were handed over by the Allies to Greece. The Greeks were to enjoy their new acquisition in peace for precisely two years. Far to the south, in Asia Minor, the "great idea" was crashing rudely against reality. Greece had stretched too far; in doing so it had awoken the forces of Turkish nationalism.

The End of the Ottomans

F AR AWAY FROM PARIS, at the southeast tip of Europe, another great
city had been lamenting the past and thinking uneasily about the future. Byzantium to the Greeks and Romans, Constantinople to the peacemakers, Istanbul, as it was to the Turks, had once been the capital of the
glorious Byzantine empire and then, after 1453, of the victorious Ottoman
Turks. Now the Ottoman empire in its turn was on a downward path.
The city was crammed with refugees and soldiers from the defeated
armies, short of fuel, food and hope. Their fate—indeed, that of the whole
empire—appeared to depend on the Peace Conference.

Layers of history had fallen over Constantinople, leaving churches,
mosques, frescoes, mosaics, palaces, covered markets and fishing villages.
The massive city walls had seen invaders from Europe and the East, Persians, Crusaders, Arabs and finally the Turks. The last Byzantine emperor
had chosen death there in 1453, as the Ottoman Turks completed their
conquest of his empire. Underneath the streets of Istanbul lay the shards
of antiquity; walls, vaults, passageways, a great Byzantine cistern where
Greek and Roman columns held up the roof. Above, the minarets of the
mosques—some of them, such as the massive Santa Sophia, converted
from Christian churches—and the great tower built by the Genoese
brooded over the city's hills. Across the deep inlet of the Golden Horn,
the old city of Stamboul, with its squalor and its magnificence, faced the
more spacious modern quarter where foreigners lived. It was a city with
many memories and many peoples.

All around was the water. To the northwest, the Bosphorus stretched
up into the Black Sea toward Russia and central Asia; southwest, the Sea of
Marmara led into the Dardanelles and the Mediterranean. Geography had

created the city, and geography had kept it important through the centuries. From antiquity, when Jason sailed through and Alexander the Great won a great victory over the Persians nearby, to more modern times, when Catherine the Great of Russia and Wilhelm II of Germany both reached out to grasp it, the city had always been a prize.

Much of the diplomacy of the nineteenth century had revolved around controlling vital waterways such as this. Russia longed for warm-water ports with access to the world's seas. Britain in turn bolstered an ailing Ottoman empire to keep the Russians safely bottled up in the Black Sea. (Only in the most desperate moments of the war had the British conceded Russian control over the straits; fortunately, owing to the revolutions of 1917, Russia would not be collecting its prize.) The Ottoman Turks, who had once reached the gates of Vienna, had little to say. Even the Young Turk revolt just before the Great War did little to arrest their decline. Their empire shrank, in the Balkans and across North Africa.

In 1914, the Ottoman leaders decided to confront Russia, now allied to their old friend Britain: the empire joined the war on the side of Germany and Austria-Hungary. It was a gamble that failed. The Ottoman empire fought astonishingly bravely, given its relative weakness. In Mesopotamia and at Gallipoli, Turkish soldiers humiliated the Allies, who had expected quick victories. But by 1918, Ottoman luck had run out. The collapse of Bulgaria in September opened the road to Constantinople from the west, while British and Indian troops pushed in from the south and east. Out on the eastern end of the Mediterranean, Allied warships gathered in ominous numbers. Only on its northeastern borders, where the old Russian empire was disintegrating, was there respite, but the Ottomans were too weak to benefit. Their empire had gone piecemeal before the war; now it melted like snow. The Arab territories had gone, from Mesopotamia to Palestine, from Syria down to the Arabian peninsula. On the eastern end of the Black Sea, subject peoples—Armenians, Georgians, Azerbaijanis, Kurds—struggled to establish new states in the borderlands with Russia. "General attitude among Turks," reported an American diplomat, "is one of hopelessness, waiting the outcome of the Peace Conference." Like so many other peoples, they hoped the Americans would rescue them; self-determination might salvage at least the Turkish-speaking areas in eastern Thrace and Anatolia. In Constantinople, intellectuals founded a "Wilsonian Principles Society."[1]

The men who had led the empire into the war resigned in the first week of October and fled on a German warship, and a caretaker government sent word to the British that it wanted peace. The British government agreed to open talks promptly at the Aegean island of Mudros, partly to keep the French on the sidelines. Although the British had consulted with the French on the armistice terms, they made the dubious argument that since the Ottoman empire had contacted them first, it was Britain's responsibility to handle negotiations. The French government and the senior French admiral at Mudros both protested in vain. All negotiations were handled by the British commander, Admiral Arthur Calthorpe.[2]

The Ottoman delegates were led by Hussein Rauf, a young naval hero and the new minister of the navy. On October 28 they arrived at Calthorpe's flagship, the *Agamemnon*. The negotiations were civil, even friendly. Rauf found Calthorpe honest and straightforward—and reassuring when he promised that Britain would treat Turkey, for that was all that remained of the empire, gently. Constantinople probably would not be occupied; certainly no Greek or Italian troops, particular bugbears of the Turks, would be allowed to land. When Rauf arrived home, he told a reporter: "I assure you that not a single enemy soldier will disembark at our Istanbul." The British had treated them extraordinarily well: "The armistice we have concluded is beyond our hopes." Even though they had accepted all the clauses put forward by the British, Rauf trusted Calthorpe, who promised that the armistice terms would not be used unfairly. The British were really only interested in free passage through the straits; why would they want to occupy Constantinople, or indeed anywhere else? Rauf told himself that, after all, the British had already taken the Arab territories: "I could think of no other area they would want from the point of view of their national interests and so might try to seize."[3]

When the two men put their signatures to the armistice on October 30, they cheerfully toasted each other in champagne. Rauf, the *Agamemnon*'s captain wrote to his wife, "made me a very graceful little speech thanking me for my hospitality and consideration to him as a technical enemy." The photograph of the captain's young twin sons, said Rauf, had been a source of inspiration to him. "Wasn't that nice?"[4]

In London, the British cabinet received the news of the armistice with delight and fell to discussing how Constantinople ought to be occupied, given "the mentality of the East." The British and their allies had every intention of enforcing the armistice rigorously. All Turkish garrisons were to surrender; all the railways and telegraphs would be run by the Allies; and Turkish ports were to be available for Allied warships. But the most damaging clause was the seventh, which read simply: "The Allies have the right to occupy any strategic points in the event of a situation arising which threatens the security of the Allies." Years later Rauf looked back: "There was a general conviction in our country that England and France were countries faithful not only to their written pacts, but also to their promises. And I had this conviction too. What a shame that we were mistaken in our beliefs and convictions!"[5]

From his post far away to the south, by the Syrian border, a friend of Rauf's who was also a war hero wrote to his government with dismay: "It is my sincere and frank opinion that if we demobilize our troops and give in to everything the British want, without taking steps to end misunderstandings and false interpretations of the armistice, it will be impossible for us to put any sort of brake on Britain's covetous designs." Mustafa Kemal—better known today as Atatürk—dashed north to Constantinople and urged everyone he could see, from leading politicians to the sultan himself, to establish a strong nationalist government to stand up to the foreigners. He found sympathy in many quarters, but the sultan, Mehmed VI, preferred to placate the Allies. In November 1918, Mehmed dissolved parliament and tried to govern through his own men.[6]

The great line of sultans that had produced Suleiman the Magnificent had dwindled to Mehmed VI. His main achievement was to have survived the rule of three brothers: one who was deposed when he went mad; his paranoid and cruel successor, so fearful of enemies that he employed a eunuch to take the first puff of every cigarette; and the timid old man who ruled until the summer of 1918. Mehmed VI was sane but it was difficult to gauge whether there were many ideas in his bony head. He took over as sultan with deep misgivings. "I am at a loss," he told a religious leader. "Pray for me."[7]

The power of the throne, which had once made the world tremble, had slipped away. Orders from the government, reported the American representative, "often receive but scant consideration in the provinces and public safety is very poor throughout Asia Minor." Although Constantinople was not officially occupied at first, Allied soldiers and diplomats "were everywhere—advising and ordering and suggesting." Allied warships packed the harbor so tightly that they looked a solid mass. "I am ill," murmured the sultan, "I can't look out the window. I hate to see them." Atatürk had a very different thought: "As they have come, so they shall go."[8]

Atatürk was a complicated, brave, determined and dangerous man whose picture, with its startling blue eyes, is still everywhere in Turkey today. In 1919 few foreigners had ever heard of him; four years later he had humbled Britain and France and brought into existence the new nation-state of Turkey. The tenth of November, the anniversary of his death, is a national day of remembrance. He could be ruthless, as both his friends and his enemies found; after his great victories, he tried some of his oldest associates, including Rauf, for treason. He could also be charming, as the many women in his life discovered. Children loved him, and he loved them; he always said, however, that it was just as well he was childless since the sons of great men are usually degenerates. He had a rational and scientific mind, but in later life grew fascinated by the esoteric. He refused to allow Ankara radio to play traditional Turkish music; it was what he listened to with his friends. He wanted to emancipate Turkish women, yet when he divorced the only woman he ever married, he did so in the traditional Muslim way. He was a dictator who tried to order democracy into existence. In 1930 he created an opposition party and chose its leaders; when it started to challenge him, he closed it down. He was capricious, but in his own way fair. His subordinates knew that any order he had given at night during one of his frequent drinking bouts should be ignored.[9]

The man who made Turkey was born on the fringes of the old Ottoman empire in the Macedonian seaport of Salonika. His mother was a peasant who could barely read and write, his father an unsuccessful merchant. Like the Ottoman empire itself, Salonika contained many nationalities. Even the laborers on the docks spoke half a dozen languages. About half of Salonika's people were Jews; the rest ranged from Turks to Greeks, Armenians to Albanians.[10] Western Europeans dominated the trade and commerce, just as European nations dominated the Ottoman empire.

Early on Atatürk developed a contempt for religion that never left him. Islam—and its leaders and holy men—were "a poisonous dagger which is directed at the heart of my people." From the evening when, as a student, he saw sheikhs and dervishes whipping a crowd into a frenzy, he loathed what he saw as primitive fanaticism. "I flatly refuse to believe that today, in the luminous presence of science, knowledge, and civilization in all its aspects, there exist, in the civilized community of Turkey, men so primitive as to seek their material and moral well-being from the guidance of one or another sheikh."[11]

Over his mother's objections, he insisted on being educated in military schools. In those days these were not only training leaders of the future; they were centers of the growing nationalist and revolutionary sentiment. Atatürk's particular aptitudes were for mathematics and politics. He learned French so that he could read political philosophers such as Voltaire and Montesquieu. When he was nineteen, Atatürk won a place in the infantry college in Constantinople. He found a worldly, cosmopolitan capital. Less than half its population was Muslim. The rest were a mix of Sephardic Jews whose ancestors had escaped from Christian Spain centuries before, Polish patriots fleeing tsarist rule, and Orthodox Armenians, Rumanians, Albanians and Greeks. Despite four centuries of Ottoman rule, the Greeks still dominated commerce. (Even after the Second World

War, over half the members of Istanbul's chamber of commerce had Greek names.) Europeans ran the most important industries, and Western lenders kept the government solvent and supervised its finances. The Ottomans were now so weak that they were forced to give Westerners even more of the special privileges, which first started in the sixteenth century capitulations, which included freedom from Turkish taxes and Turkish courts. As a Turkish journalist wrote sadly: "We have remained mere spectators while our commerce, our trades and even our broken-down huts have been given to the foreigners."[12]

The infantry college where Atatürk studied was on the north side of the Golden Horn, in the newer part of the city, with its wide streets, gas lighting, opera house, cafés, chamber of commerce, banks, shops with the latest European fashions, even brothels with pink satin sofas just like those in Paris. Atatürk explored it with enthusiasm, carousing and whoring and reading widely, but he always remained ambivalent about Constantinople. It was a place to be enjoyed but dangerous to governments.[13] He later moved the capital far inland to the obscure city of Ankara.

Like many young officers in the years before 1914, Atatürk dabbled in secret societies which swore to give the empire a modern constitution. He shared the hopes of the revolution of 1908, and the disappointments when it failed to make the empire stronger.[14] In 1908 Austria annexed Bosnia and Herzegovina and Bulgaria declared its independence. In 1911 Italy, the weakest of the European powers, declared war and seized Libya. After the Balkan wars of 1912 and 1913, Albania, Macedonia and part of Thrace, including Salonika, were gone. By 1914 the European part of the empire, which had once stretched into Hungary, was reduced to a small enclave in Thrace tucked under Bulgaria. In six years, 425,000 square miles had been lost.

When the Great War started, Atatürk was enjoying life as a diplomat in Bulgaria. He went to his first opera in Sofia; fifteen years later, he put an opera house into the plans for his new capital of Ankara. He took up ball-room dancing; later, in his new republic, civil servants were made to dance at official balls because "that was how they do it in the West." At the beginning of 1915, he was offered command of a new division which was being thrown into the defense of the Gallipoli peninsula. Many Allied reputations were destroyed at Gallipoli; his was made. As the author of the official British history later wrote, "Seldom in history can the exertions of a single divisional commander have exercised, on three separate occasions, so profound an influence on the course of a battle, but perhaps on the fate of a campaign and even the destiny of a nation."[15]

The Constantinople Atatürk found at the end of the war was very different from the city he remembered. There was no coal and very little

food. A Turk who was a boy at the time remembered his mother struggling to feed the family: "It seemed to us that we had lived forever on
lentils and cabbage soup and the dry, black apology for bread." The government was bankrupt. On street corners distinguished officers sold
lemons because their pensions were worthless. And more refugees were
pouring in: Russians fleeing the civil war, Armenians searching desperately for safety, and Turks abandoning the Middle East and Europe. By the
end of 1919 perhaps as many as 100,000 were sleeping on the streets of the
city. The only Turks who prospered were black marketeers and criminals.
Crazy rumors swept through the city: one day crowds rushed to Santa
Sophia because it was whispered that Christian bells were being hung
again.[16]

Local Greeks, intoxicated by the hope of restored Hellenic rule, hung
out the blue-and-white flag of Greece; a giant picture of Venizelos went
up in one of the main squares. The Greek patriarch sent aggressive demands to Paris, denouncing the Turks and demanding that Constantinople be made Greek again. His office told Greek Christians to stop
cooperating with the Turkish authorities. The Greeks were, said an English diplomat, "apt to be uppish."[17] Some hotheads jostled Turks in the
streets and made them take off their fezzes.

Allied officers and bureaucrats arrived in increasing numbers to supervise the armistice. "Life," recalled a young Englishman, "was gay and
wicked and delightful. The cafes were full of drinking and dancing." In
the nightclubs, White Russians sang melancholy songs and pretty young
refugees sold themselves for the price of a meal. You could race motor-
boats across the Sea of Marmara, ride to hounds on the Asian side of the
Bosphorus and pick up wonderful antiques for pennies. The Allies unofficially divided up Constantinople into spheres of influence and took over
much of its administration; they ran the local police and set up their own
courts. When the Turkish press was critical of their guests, the Allies took
over press censorship as well. When Constantinople was officially occupied in March 1920, it was hard to tell the difference.[18]

Outside the city, in Thrace and Asia Minor, Allied officers fanned out
to monitor the surrender. The French occupied the important southern
city of Alexandretta (today Iskenderun) and by early 1919 were moving inland. On the whole, the British were more popular; as one lady in the
south commented, "Les anglais ont envoyés les fils de leurs 'Lords,' mais
les français ont envoyés leurs valets" ("The English sent the sons of their
lords, but the French sent their valets").[19] The sultan's government, as
weak and demoralized as its figurehead, did nothing, seeking only to placate the Allies.

The Allies were not in a mood to be placated. Some, such as Curzon, who chaired the cabinet committee responsible for British policy in the East, thought the time had come to get rid of "this canker which has poisoned the life of Europe." Corruption, nameless vices and intrigue had spread out from Constantinople to infect the innocent Europeans. The Peace Conference was the chance to excise the source of such evil once and for all: "The presence of the Turks in Europe has been a source of unmitigated evil to everybody concerned. I am not aware of a single interest, Turkish or otherwise, that during nearly 500 years has benefited by that presence." Although as a student of history he should have known better, Curzon argued: "Indeed, the record is one of misrule, oppression, intrigue, and massacre, almost unparalleled in the history of the Eastern world." His prime minister shared his sentiments; like many Liberals, Lloyd George had inherited his hostility to the Turks from the great Gladstone.[20]

For Curzon the question was, What would replace the Ottoman empire? Britain still wanted to ensure that hostile warships did not use the straits. It still needed to protect the route to India through the Suez Canal. There was a new factor, too: the increasingly important supplies of oil from Mosul in the Ottoman empire and from Persia. Britain did not want to take on the whole responsibility itself, and Greece certainly could not; on the other hand, it did not want another major power moving in, such as its ally France. After all, the two countries had fought for centuries, over Europe, North America, India, Africa and the Middle East. Their friendship, by comparison, was a recent affair. It had stood the test of the war but it was not clear that it would stand the test of peace. There had already been trouble over the Arab parts of the Ottoman empire. Did Britain really want French ships at the eastern end of the Mediterranean, French bases up and down the coast? Curzon was quite sure that it did not:

A good deal of my public life has been spent in connection with the political ambitions of France, which I have come across in Tunis, in Siam, and in almost every distant region where the French have sway. We have been brought, for reasons of national safety, into an alliance with the French, which I hope will last, but their national character is different from ours, and their political interests collide with our own in many cases. I am seriously afraid that the great Power from whom we may have most to fear in the future is France.

It would be a great mistake, he went on, to allow the French to acquire influence in the Middle East: "France is a highly organised State, has boundless intrepidity, imagination, and a certain power of dealing with Eastern peoples."[21]

The French did not trust the British any more than the British trusted them. And France had considerable interests in the Ottoman empire, from the protection of fellow Christians to the extensive French investments. For France, though, what happened to the Ottoman empire or in the Balkans was much less important than dealing with Germany. Clemenceau, whatever his colonial lobby thought, would compromise with Britain because he needed its support in Europe. While he did not want to see the Asian part of Turkey disappear completely, Clemenceau did not, at least initially, have strong views about Greek claims there. As far as Europe was concerned, he supported Greek claims to Thrace. If Greece blocked Italian claims, so much the better for France.[22]

During the war, Britain, France and Russia had held a number of discussions about the future of the Ottoman empire. In 1916, the British and French representatives, Sir Mark Sykes and Georges Picot, had agreed that their two countries would divide up the Arab-speaking areas and that, in the Turkish-speaking parts, France would have a zone extending north into Cilicia from Syria. The Russians, who had already extracted a promise that they would annex Constantinople and the straits, gave their approval on condition that they got the Turkish provinces adjacent to their borders in the Caucasus. The decision of the new Bolshevik government to make peace with the Central Powers effectively canceled that agreement. Britain and France were now left as the major powers in the Middle East, and as the war wound down, they circled suspiciously around each other.

In the Supreme Council on October 30, Lloyd George and Clemenceau quarreled angrily over Britain's insistence on negotiating the Turkish truce on their own. "They bandied words like fish-wives," House reported. Lloyd George told Clemenceau:

> Except for Great Britain no one had contributed anything more than a handful of black troops to the expedition in Palestine. I was really surprised at the lack of generosity on the part of the French Government. The British had now some 500,000 men on Turkish soil. The British had captured three or four Turkish Armies and had incurred hundreds of thousands of casualties in the war with Turkey. The other Governments had only put in a few nigger policemen to see that we did not steal the Holy Sepulchre! When, however, it came to signing an armistice, all this fuss was made.

It was an unfair argument; as Clemenceau pointed out on a later occasion, the British had sent correspondingly fewer troops to the Western Front.

"My opinion was and remains that if the white troops which you sent over there had been thrown against the Germans, the war could have been ended some months earlier." The French nevertheless backed down on the armistice, as Pichon said, "in the spirit of conciliation which the French government always felt to apply in dealing with Britain." There was not to be much of that spirit when it came to dividing the spoils.[23]

The peacemakers did not get around to the Ottoman empire until January 30, 1919, and then it was only in the course of that difficult discussion over mandates for the former German colonies. Lloyd George, who had spent the previous week bringing the Americans and his recalcitrant dominions to agreement, mentioned the Ottoman empire briefly as an example of where mandates were needed. Because the Turks had been so bad at governing their subject peoples, they should lose control of all their Arab territories—Syria, Mesopotamia, Palestine and Arabia itself. Since the Arabs were civilized but not yet organized, they would need outside guidance. The Ottomans also ought to lose territory on their northeast frontier. They had behaved appallingly to the Armenians, and clearly an Armenian state should come into existence, probably as a mandate of an outside power. There might have to be a Kurdistan, south of Armenia. That still left the predominantly Turkish-speaking territories, the slice in Europe, the straits and Anatolia in Asia Minor. Those, Lloyd George said airily, could be settled "on their merits." (He did not mention the parcels of land stretching inland from the coast of Asia Minor that had been promised to the French, the Italians or the Greeks.)

The other important thing, Lloyd George argued, was to keep all the various groups within the empire from attacking each other. This was not a responsibility Britain wanted. As Lloyd George pointed out, the Allies had over a million troops scattered across the Ottoman empire and Britain was paying for the lot. "If they kept them there until they had made peace with Turkey, and until the League of Nations had been constituted and had started business and until it was able to dispose of this question, the expense would be something enormous, and they really could not face it."[24] He had to answer to Parliament.

Lloyd George hoped that Wilson would take the hint and offer the United States as the mandatory power at least for Armenia and the straits. Better still, the Americans might decide to run the whole of the Turkish areas. House certainly hinted at the possibility. However, the Americans had not really established a clear position on the Ottoman empire beyond an antipathy toward the Turks. American Protestant missionaries, who had been active in Ottoman Turkey since the 1820s, had painted a dismal picture of a bankrupt regime. Much of their work had been among the Armenians, so they had reported at first hand the massacres during the war. Back in the United States large sums of money had been raised for Armenian relief. House had cheerfully chatted with the British about ways of carving up the Ottoman empire, and Wilson had certainly considered its complete disappearance.[25]

The United States had never declared war on the Ottoman empire, which put it in a tricky position when it came to determining the empire's fate. The only one of Wilson's Fourteen Points that dealt with it was ambiguous: "The Turkish portions of the present Ottoman Empire should be assured a secure sovereignty, but the other nationalities which are now under Turkish rule should be assured an undoubted security of life and an absolutely unmolested opportunity of autonomous development." What were the Turkish portions? Who should have autonomous development? The Arabs? The Armenians? The Kurds? The scattered Greek communities?

When the Inquiry, that collection of American experts, produced its memorandum in December 1918, it said both that Turkey proper (undefined) must be justly treated and that subject races must be freed from oppression and misrule, which in turn meant "autonomy" for Armenia and "protection" for the Arab parts. Oddly contradicting this, the official commentary on the Fourteen Points, which had come out in October 1918, talked about international control of Constantinople and the straits, perhaps a Greek mandate on the coast of Asia Minor, where it was incorrectly said that Greeks predominated, and possibly American mandates for Constantinople, Armenia, even Macedonia in the Balkans. Before the Peace Conference started, it was generally assumed that, at the very least, the United States would take a mandate for Armenia and the straits. Not everyone was pleased. British admirals, having got rid of the Russian menace, did not want to see a strong United States at the eastern end of the Mediterranean. The India Office was also concerned. Mehmed VI was not only the Ottoman sultan but also the caliph, the nearest thing to a spiritual leader of all Muslims. Turning him out of Constantinople, even putting him under the supervision of an outside power, might enrage Indian Muslims. Lloyd George simply ignored their objections.[26]

As so often, the Peace Conference delayed difficult decisions. At that January meeting, Wilson suggested that the military advisers look at how the burden of occupying the Turkish territories could best be shared out. "This would clarify the question," said Lloyd George. Of course, it did not. The report duly came in and was discussed briefly on February 10; it was put on the agenda for the following day but in the event the boundaries of Belgium proved to be much more interesting.[27]

On February 26, the appearance of an Armenian delegation before the Supreme Council briefly reminded the peacemakers that the Ottoman empire remained to be settled. Boghos Nubar Pasha was smooth, rich and cultivated; his father had been prime minister of Egypt. His partner, Avetis Aharonian, was a tough, cynical poet from the Caucasus. Boghos spoke for the Armenian diaspora, Aharonian for the homeland in the mountains where Russia, Persia and Turkey met. In what was by now a familiar pattern they appealed to history—the centuries that Armenians had lived there, the persistence of Armenian Christianity—to their services to the Allies (some Armenians had fought in Russia's armies) and to Allied promises. And, like other delegations, they staked out a claim for a huge area of land, stretching south and west from the Caucasus down to the Mediterranean. Less typically, they also asked for the protection of an outside power, a wise request for a country with such neighbors and such a past. They placed their hopes on the United States. "Scarcely a day passed," said an American expert, "that mournful Armenians, bearded and black-clad, did not besiege the American delegation or, less frequently, the President, setting forth the really terrible conditions in their own native land."[28]

The Armenians brought one of the saddest histories to the conference. Between 1375, when the last independent Armenian state was conquered, and the spring of 1918, when nationalist forces had proclaimed the republic of Armenia on what had been Russian territory, they had lived under alien rule. After the Russians had advanced down into the Caucasus at the start of the nineteenth century, the Armenian lands were divided up among Russia itself, Ottoman Turkey and Persia. The Armenians, many of them simple farmers, had become Russian, Turkish or Persian, but as ideas of nationalism and self-determination swept eastward, the vision of a reborn Armenian nation took shape. It was not a coherent vision—Christian, secular, conservative, radical, pro-Turkish or pro-Russian, there was no agreement as to what Armenia might be—but it was increasingly powerful. Unfortunately, however, Armenian nationalism was not the only nationalism growing in that part of the world.

"Who remembers the Armenians today?" Hitler asked cynically. At the Paris Peace Conference, the horrors of what the Turks had done to the Armenians were still fresh, and the world had not yet grown used to attempts to exterminate peoples. The killings had started in the 1890s, when the old regime turned savagely on any groups that opposed it. Ottoman troops and local Kurds, themselves awakening as a nation, had rampaged through Armenian villages. The Young Turks, who took over the government in 1908, promised a new era with talk of a secular, multi-ethnic state, but they also dreamed of linking up with other Turkish peoples in central

Asia. In that Pan-Turanian world, Armenians and other Christians had no place.

When the Ottoman empire entered the war, Enver Pasha, one of the triumvirate of Young Turks who had ruled in Constantinople since 1913, sent the bulk of its armies eastward, against Russia. The result, in 1915, was disaster; the Russians destroyed a huge Ottoman force and looked set to advance into Anatolia just when the Allies were landing at Gallipoli in the west. The triumvirate gave the order to deport Armenians from eastern Anatolia on the grounds that they were traitors, potential or actual. Many Armenians were slaughtered before they could leave; others died of hunger and disease on the forced marches southward. Whether the Ottoman government's real goal was genocide is still much disputed; so is the number of dead, anywhere from 300,000 to 1.5 million.[29]

Western opinion was appalled. In Britain, Armenia's cause attracted supporters from the duke of Argyll to the young Arnold Toynbee. British children were told to remember the starving Armenians when they failed to clean their plates. In the United States, huge sums of money were raised for relief. Clemenceau wrote the preface for a book detailing the atrocities: "Is it true that at the dawn of the twentieth century, five days from Paris, atrocities have been committed with impunity, covering a land with horror—such that one cannot imagine worse in time of the deepest barbarity?" The usually restrained Lansing wrote to Wilson, who was strongly pro-Armenian, "It is one of the blackest pages in the history of this war." "Say to the Armenians," exclaimed Orlando, "that I make their cause my cause." Lloyd George promised that Armenia would never be restored to "the blasting tyranny" of the Turks. "There was not a British statesman of any party," he wrote in his memoirs, "who did not have it in mind that if we succeeded in defeating this inhuman Empire, our essential condition of the peace we should impose was the redemption of the Armenian valleys for ever from the bloody misrule with which they had been stained by the infamies of the Turks."[30]

Fine sentiments—but they amounted to little in the end. At the Peace Conference, even heartfelt agreement on principle faltered in the face of other considerations. Armenia was far away; it was surrounded by enemies and the Allies had few forces in the area. Moving troops and aid in, at a time when resources were stretched thin, was a major undertaking; what railways there were had been badly damaged and the roads were primitive. Help was far away, but Armenia's enemies were close at hand. Russians, whether the armies of the Whites or the Bolsheviks, who were advancing southward, would not tolerate Armenia or any other independent state in the Caucasus. On Armenia's other flank, Turks deeply resented the loss of Turkish territory, and the further losses implied in the Armenian claims.

In Paris, Armenia's friends were lukewarm and hesitant. The British, it is true, saw certain advantages for themselves in taking a mandate for Armenia: the protection of oil supplies coming from Baku on the Caspian to the port of Batum on the Black Sea, and the creation of a barrier between Bolshevism and the British possessions in the Middle East. (In their worst nightmares, the British imagined Bolshevism linking up with a resurgent Islam and toppling the British empire.) On the other hand, as the War Office kept repeating, British resources were already overstretched. The French Foreign Office, for its part, toyed with ideas of a huge Armenia under French protection which would provide a field for French investment and the spread of French culture. Clemenceau, however, had little enthusiasm for the notion. The Italians, like the French, preferred to concentrate their efforts on gains on the Mediterranean coast of Turkey and in Europe. That left the Americans.[31]

On March 7, House assured Lloyd George and Clemenceau that the United States would undoubtedly take on a mandate. Lloyd George was delighted at the prospect of the Americans taking on the "noble duty," and relieved that the French were not taking on a mandate. House, as he often did, was exaggerating. Wilson had warned the Supreme Council that "he could think of nothing the people of the United States would be less inclined to accept than military responsibility in Asia." It is perhaps a measure of how far Wilson's judgment had deteriorated that, on May 14, when Armenia came up at the Council of Four, he agreed to accept a mandate, subject, he added, to the consent of the American Senate. This ruffled the French because the proposed American mandate was to stretch from the Black Sea to the Mediterranean, taking in the zone in Cilicia promised to France under the Sykes-Picot Agreement. While Clemenceau, who took little interest in the Turkish-speaking territories, did not raise an objection, his colleagues were furious. From London, Paul Cambon complained: "They must be drunk the way they are surrendering . . . a total capitulation, a mess, an unimaginable shambles." Although no one suspected it at the time, no arrangement made in Paris was going to make the slightest difference to Armenia.[32]

Many other schemes for the Ottoman empire were floating around the conference rooms and dinner tables in Paris that spring. "Let it be a *manda* [buffalo]," said one wit in Constantinople, "let it be an ox, let it be any animal whatsoever; only let it come quickly." If all the claims, protectorates, independent states and mandates that were discussed actually had come into existence, a very odd little Turkey in the interior of Anatolia would have been left, with no straits, no Mediterranean coast, a truncated Black Sea coast, and no Armenian or Kurdish territories in the northeast. What was left out of the calculation in Paris, among other things, was the inability of the powers to enforce their will. Henry Wilson, chief of the British Imperial General Staff, thought the politicians completely unrealistic: "They seem to think that their writ runs in Turkey in Asia. We have never, even after the armistice, attempted to get into the background parts." Also overlooked were the Turks themselves. Almost everyone in Paris assumed that they would simply do as they were told. When Edwin Montagu, the British secretary of state for India, cried, "Let us not for Heaven's sake, tell the Moslem what he ought to think, let us recognize what they do think," Balfour replied with chilling detachment, "I am quite unable to see why Heaven or any other Power should object to our telling the Moslem what he ought to think." That went for the Arab subjects of the Ottoman empire as well.[33]

27

Arab Independence

ONE DAY DURING the Peace Conference, Arnold Toynbee, an adviser to the British delegation, had to deliver some papers to the prime minister. "Lloyd George, to my delight, had forgotten my presence and had begun to think aloud. 'Mesopotamia . . . yes . . . oil . . . irrigation . . . we must have Mesopotamia; Palestine . . . yes . . . the Holy Land . . . Zionism . . . we must have Palestine; Syria . . . h'm . . . what is there in Syria? Let the French have that.' "[1] Thus the lineaments of the peace settlement in the Middle East were exposed: Britain seizing its chance; the need to throw something to the French; a homeland for the Jews; oil; and the calm assumption that the peacemakers could dispose of the former Ottoman territories to suit themselves. For the Arab Middle East, the peace settlements were the old nineteenth-century imperialism again. Britain and France got away with it—temporarily—because the United States did not choose to involve itself and because Arab nationalism was not yet strong enough to challenge them.

At their meeting in London in December 1918, just before Wilson arrived in Europe, Lloyd George and Clemenceau found time to agree on a division of the Ottoman empire's vast Arab territories, stretching from Mesopotamia on the borders of the Persian empire to the Mediterranean. Both men were still buoyed up by their victory over Germany and by the novel but apparently warm friendship between their two nations. Clemenceau was delighted at his reception as the London crowds went mad, cheering, whistling and throwing hats and walking sticks into the air. "Really," said Mordacq, Clemenceau's aide, "among such a phlegmatic and cold people, that spoke volumes." The conversation on the Middle East was short and good-humored. "Well," said Clemenceau, "what are we to discuss?" Lloyd George replied, "Mesopotamia and Palestine." Clemenceau: "Tell me what you want." Lloyd George: "I want Mosul." Clemenceau: "You shall have it. Anything else?" Lloyd George: "Yes I want Jerusalem too." Clemenceau: "You shall have it but Pichon will make difficulties about Mosul."[2] (Mosul was about to become important because of oil.)

Lloyd George apparently gave Clemenceau promises in return: that Britain would support France, even against the Americans, in its demand for control over the Lebanese coast and the interior of Syria, and that France would have a share of whatever oil turned up in Mosul. Clemenceau was so generous, the French later claimed, because Lloyd George had also assured him that he could count on British support for his demands in Europe, particularly along the Rhine. Lloyd George does not mention that part of the deal in his memoirs. Were the French wrong or the British being perfidious (again)? Unfortunately there was no official record of the conversation. It was an ill-omened start for an issue that was to poison French-British relations during the Peace Conference and for many years after.[3]

What came to be called the Syrian Question (although it really related to all the Ottoman Arab territories) need not have done so much damage. Britain and France had already made their deal on the Middle East with the secret Sykes-Picot Agreement of 1916. The unexpected collapse of the Ottoman empire, however, stirred up old dreams and old rivalries. The bickering, which dragged on through 1919, was about more than territory. It was about Joan of Arc and William the Conqueror, the Heights of Abraham and Plassy, about the Crusades, about Napoleon in Egypt and Nelson's destruction of his fleet at the Battle of the Nile, about the scramble for Africa, which had so nearly led to war over Fashoda, Sudan, in 1898, and about the competition for influence between French and Anglo-Saxon civilization.

Lloyd George, a Liberal turned land-grabber, made it worse. Like Napoleon, he was intoxicated by the possibilities of the Middle East: a restored Hellenic world in Asia Minor; a new Jewish civilization in Palestine; Suez and all the links to India safe from threat; loyal and obedient Arab states along the Fertile Crescent and the valleys of the Tigris and Euphrates; protection for British oil supplies from Persia and the possibility of new sources under direct British control; the Americans obligingly taking mandates here and there; the French doing what they were told. At a private dinner just before the end of the war his closest advisers found him "in a very *exalté* frame of mind," "very intransigent." He wanted to exclude France as much as possible from the Middle East, even at the cost of breaking previous promises. And that meant above all Sykes-Picot, "that unfortunate Agreement," as Curzon put it, "which has been hanging like a millstone round our necks ever since."[4]

Like so many of the other deals that haunted the Peace Conference as unwelcome guests, Sykes-Picot was made in the midst of the war, when promises were cheap and the prospect of defeat very real. In 1916, the war was going badly for the Allies. In the east the Gallipoli landings had failed and in Mesopotamia a large force from India had surrendered. The British wanted to start a new offensive against the Ottomans from Egypt but to divert resources from the Western Front they had to have French agreement. What they offered as bait was an agreement on the future disposition of the Ottoman empire.

The two negotiators were both Catholic, and both knew the Middle East at first hand. Picot had been consul-general in Beirut before the war, and Sykes had traveled widely from Cairo to Baghdad. Picot was born into that French upper middle class which produced so many of France's diplomats, colonial governors and high-ranking bureaucrats. Tall and pompous, conservative and devout, he cared equally for his own dignity and that of France. He was close to powerful colonial lobby groups in France; his brother was treasurer of the Comité de l'Asie Française, which in spite of its name was much concerned with the Middle East.[5]

Sykes, by contrast, was one of those wealthy, aristocratic dilettantes who fluttered around the fringes of British diplomacy. He never had much formal schooling—tutors on the great estate in Yorkshire, brief interludes at boarding schools and a couple of years at Cambridge, where he distinguished himself in amateur theatricals. He was enthusiastic, energetic and frequently impractical. T. E. Lawrence said of him: "He saw the odd in everything, and missed the even. He would sketch out in a few dashes a new world, all out of scale, but vivid as a vision of some sides of the thing we hoped." He loved practical jokes, drawing caricatures, the Yorkshire countryside and the British empire. He hated cities, routine and pacifists. He was devoted to his wife and six children, perhaps because of his own unhappy childhood with a drunken and promiscuous mother and a neurasthenic and cold father. He adored the old, unspoiled Middle East of the desert and simple peasants; he blamed the French and international finance for modernizing and corrupting the old society. He admired French culture but thought France did not deserve its empire. "The French," he said after visiting French North Africa, "are incapable of commanding respect, they are not sahibs, they have no gentlemen, the officers have no horses or guns or dogs."[6]

Curiously, Picot and Sykes managed to work well together. Their plan, which was approved by their respective governments in May 1916, was reasonable enough, if you were a Western imperialist. The Syrian coast, much of today's Lebanon, was to go to France, while Britain would take direct control over central Mesopotamia, around Baghdad, and the southern part around Basra. Palestine, a thorny issue because of the intense interest of other Christian powers (Russia in particular), would have an international administration. What was left, a huge area that included what is now Syria, Mosul in the north of Iraq, and Jordan, would have local Arab chiefs under the supervision of the French in the north and the British in the south. (The Arabian peninsula was not mentioned, presumably because no one thought all those miles of sand worth worrying about.) The agreement appeased the French, who had considerable investments along the Syrian coast and who saw themselves as protectors of the area's large Christian communities, such as the Maronites around Mount Lebanon. It suited the British equally well, and they had cleverly placed the French between themselves and the Russian empire as it reached southward.[7]

Almost as soon as the deal was made, the British nevertheless began to regret it. Would it not be wiser to control Palestine, so close to the Suez Canal, directly? This was much urged by British officials in Egypt. Why should the French get Mosul? When Russia dropped out of the war in 1917, it suddenly seemed less essential to have France as a buffer. Sykes, reported a colleague as news of the Ottoman surrender came in, "has evolved a new and most ingenious scheme by which the French are to clear out of the whole Arab region except the Lebanon and in return take over the protectorate of the whole Kurdo-Armenian region from Adana to Persia and the Caucasus."[8]

In France, a heterogeneous colonialist lobby—fabric manufacturers in Lyon, who wanted Syrian silk; the Chamber of Automobile Manufacturers, who noted that Mosul was wonderful country for driving; Jesuit priests, whose order ran a university in Beirut; the financiers, officials and intellectuals in the Comité de l'Asie Française—urged their government to stand firm. Syria, for this lobby, was invariably Greater Syria, stretching south to the Sinai and east into Mosul. Parliamentary groups pointed out the strategic imperatives. France already had Algeria and Tunisia along the south shore of the Mediterranean; now it must add Morocco. It was too late, alas, for Egypt, snaffled away by the British in a devious maneuver in 1882. But it was not too late for Lebanon and its Syrian hinterland and Palestine. The Quai d'Orsay sent memoranda to Clemenceau on "this heavy but glorious burden." France's connection with Syria went back to the Crusades. It had already done much to protect Christians and bring

civilization to all the Arabs. Now the locals were counting on France to repair the damage done by years of Turkish rule. France must not give up
Syria. French public opinion would be rightly enraged if "after such a war
and such a victory, which has consecrated the preeminent role of France
in the world, its position [were] inferior to what it was before August
1914."[9]

The British position hardened. The Eastern Committee of the War
Cabinet, set up in 1918 to work out British policy in the Middle East, returned repeatedly to the need to contain their ally. If France got Palestine
and Syria, Britain, according to Curzon, the committee's chairman and
moving spirit, would be obliged to keep a large force in Egypt to protect
the Suez Canal and the vital route to India. And there were other routes,
overland or by air (a new possibility), from the eastern end of the Mediterranean through Syria and Mesopotamia, or farther north along the
Black Sea and past the Caucasus. Balfour pointed out that this was a dangerous argument: "Every time I come to a discussion—at intervals of, say,
five years—I find there is a new sphere which we have got to guard, which
is supposed to protect the gateways of India. Those gateways are getting
further and further from India, and I do not know how far west they are
going to be brought by the General Staff." His colleagues remained determined to destroy Sykes-Picot.[10]

Even before the French realized this, British actions aroused their suspicions. French Catholics had been dismayed when British forces under
General Sir Edmund Allenby swept the Turks out of Jerusalem just before
Christmas 1917. The "Protestant peril" was taking over the Holy Land.
The French colonial lobby watched anxiously as the Egyptian pound became the currency first in Palestine and then in Syria, and trade flowed
south. When Picot rushed to Palestine to try to protect French interests,
he found Allenby and his staff uncooperative. In the summer of 1918, as
the last great German offensive battered the Western Front and the British
prepared another major offensive into Syria, the Quai d'Orsay warned
that French public opinion would not accept that "France be deprived of
benefits which were rightfully hers by those who diverted their troops at
the crucial moment." French anxiety was not allayed by the subsequent
refusal of the British military authorities to hand over full powers to
French representatives in the areas of Syria earmarked for France under
Sykes-Picot. The British also kept an ominous silence about their long-
term plans. Picot, less hard-line than many of his colleagues, tried to warn
Sykes of the mood in France: "The spiteful see it as evidence of hidden
intentions. Even the others are becoming anxious." The British refused to
take French concerns or Picot himself seriously: "rather a vain and weak

man," said one officer, "jealous of his own position and of the prestige of France."[11]

Although the British and the French acted as though the Middle East was theirs to quarrel over, they did have to pay some attention to their allies. The vague promises that had been made to Italy during the war—promises of access to ports such as Haifa and Acre; of a say in the administration of Palestine; of equal treatment in the Arabian peninsula and the Red Sea—could be safely ignored and generally were. The United States was a different matter. While Wilson assumed that the Arabs would need guidance, presumably from Britain and France, he took seriously the idea of consulting the wishes of the locals. "Every territorial settlement involved in this war," he had said to Congress in his "Four Principles" speech of February 11, 1918, "must be made in the interest and for the benefit of the populations concerned." Gaston Domergue, a former minister of colonies and vice chairman of the official French committee to formulate France's colonial aims, quite rightly exclaimed, "The obstacle is America!"[12]

With a smooth shift of gears, the Europeans began to talk the language of the Americans. It was quite clear, said Domergue, that "we need a colonial empire to exercise, in the interests of humanity, the civilizing vocation of France." The British were equally adept at putting old imperial goals in appealing new clothes. It would not do to upset the Americans; as Smuts told his colleagues on the Eastern Committee: "You do not want to divide the loot; that would be a wrong policy for the future." On the other hand, if the Americans could be persuaded that the British were respecting Arab wishes, they might put pressure on the French to give up some of what they had been promised under Sykes-Picot. Cecil, high-minded and devious, warned that "the Americans will only support us if they think we are going in for something in the nature of a native Government." Curzon concurred: "If we cannot get out of our difficulties in any other way we ought to play self-determination for all it is worth, wherever we are involved in difficulties with the French, the Arabs, or anybody else, and leave the case to be settled by that final argument knowing in the bottom of our hearts that we are more likely to benefit from it than is anybody else."[13]

The British and French governments, in a declaration that was circulated widely in Arabic, conveniently discovered that their main goal in the war on Ottomans had been "the complete and definite emancipation of the peoples so long oppressed by the Turks and the establishment of national governments and administrations deriving their authority from the initiative and free choice of the indigenous populations." Words were cheap. The British, as Curzon had said, were confident that Arabs would willingly choose Britain's protection. The French did not take Arab nationalism seriously at all. "You cannot," said Picot, "transform a myriad of tribes into a viable whole." Both powers overlooked the enthusiasm with which their declaration had been received in the Arab world; in Damascus, Arab nationalists had cut electric cables and fired off huge amounts of ammunition in celebration.[14] The British and the French who had summoned the djinn of nationalism to their aid during the war were going to find that they could not easily send it away again.

At the end of November 1918, a dark, handsome young man who claimed, with some justification, to speak for the Arabs boarded a British warship in Beirut bound for Marseille and the Paris Peace Conference. Feisal, descendant of the Prophet and member of the ancient Hashemite clan, was clever, determined and very ambitious. He was also dazzling. No matter that he had been brought up in Constantinople; he was everyone's image of what a noble desert Arab should be. Lansing, normally so prosaic, thought of frankincense and gold. "He suggested the calmness and peace of the desert, the meditation of one who lives in the wide spaces of the earth, the solemnity of thought of one who often communes alone with nature." Allenby, the tough old British general, saw "a keen, slim, highly strung man. He has beautiful hands like a woman's; and his fingers are always moving nervously when he talks." With "the cavalry of St. George" (gold sovereigns), British weapons and advisers, Feisal had led an Arab revolt against the Turks.[15]

The British had gambled in backing him, and in so doing they had given undertakings that sat uneasily with that other set of promises in Sykes-Picot. In 1915 Sir Henry McMahon, a senior official in Cairo, had opened conversations with Feisal's father, Hussein, the sharif of Mecca. "A small neat old gentleman of great dignity and, when he liked, great charm," Hussein was interested more in the fortunes of his own family than in Arab self-determination. Immensely proud of his ancestry, which he could trace back for dozens of generations (and frequently did), he was head of one of the Arab world's most ancient and distinguished families, guardian of Islam's holiest sites throughout the Hejaz, and proud owner of the phone number Mecca 1. McMahon, in what has remained a highly controversial correspondence with the sharif, promised that, if the Arabs rose against the Turks, they would have British assistance and, more important, their independence. To safeguard French and British interests a few areas were specifically exempted from Arab rule: the area west of a line stretching more or less from Aleppo in the north to Damascus in the south—in other words, the coast of Syria and Lebanon—as well as the old Turkish provinces of Baghdad and Basra. The boundaries between the exempted territories and the rest were not made clear. The British later argued, in defiance of geography, that Palestine also lay west of the Aleppo–Damascus line. And what did independence mean? Hussein and his supporters assumed that, even in the exempted areas, the government would be Arab under European supervision; the rest, from the Arabian peninsula, up through Palestine to the interior of Syria and to Mosul in the north of Mesopotamia, would be an independent Arab state. This was not quite how the British envisaged it.[16]

In 1915 the details of what was an exchange of promises, not a firm treaty, did not matter that much. Perhaps it is also fair to say that neither side was negotiating in entirely good faith. Hussein wildly exaggerated his own influence when he hinted at vast Arab conspiracies waiting for his signal. In 1915, his position was precarious. He had spent much of his life waiting in Constantinople for the Ottomans to appoint him sharif and he recently had learned that they were thinking of deposing him.[17] Close at hand, he faced a formidable rival in Ibn Saud, who was welding together the tribes of the interior to challenge him. From the British point of view it was not at all clear that the Arabs would ever rise, or that the Ottoman empire would collapse, or even that the Allies could win the war. Like the Sykes-Picot agreement, the Hussein-McMahon letters were a short-term expedient rather than a part of a long-term strategy. And there was yet another promise made in those war years that was going to cause trouble to the peacemakers. The Balfour Declaration, telling the Jews of the world that they could have a homeland in Palestine, was issued by the British government and subscribed to by the French and later the Americans. It was not clear how it meshed with the agreements with the Arabs.

Promissory notes given in wartime are not always easy to collect in peace but in June 1916, when the Arab revolt started, the British had every reason to feel pleased with their diplomacy. The sharif promptly proclaimed himself king of the Arabs, although the British would only recognize him as king of the Hejaz. Four of his sons fought the Turks, but the one who stood out was Feisal. Riding at Feisal's side was his fair-haired, blue-eyed British liaison officer, later to become even more famous as Lawrence of Arabia.

A distinguished scholar and a man of action, a soldier and a writer, a passionate lover of both the Arabs and the British empire, T. E. Lawrence was, in Lloyd George's words, "a most elusive and unassessable personality." He remains a puzzle, surrounded by legend, some based in reality, some created by himself. It is true that he did brilliantly at Oxford, that he could have been a great archaeologist and that he was extraordinarily brave. It is not true that he created the Arab revolt by himself. His great account, *The Seven Pillars of Wisdom,* is part history, part myth, as he himself admitted. He claimed that he passed easily as an Arab, but Arabs found his spoken Arabic full of mistakes. He shuddered when the American journalist Lowell Thomas made him famous, but he came several times in secret to the Albert Hall to hear his lectures. "He had," said Thomas, "a genius for backing into the limelight." When he chose, Lawrence was enormously charming. His friends ranged across worlds and classes, from the desert Arabs to E. M. Forster. He could also be brutally rude. When his neighbor at a dinner party during the Peace Conference said nervously, "I'm afraid my conversation doesn't interest you much," Lawrence replied, "It doesn't interest me at all."[18]

In *The Seven Pillars of Wisdom,* the description of Lawrence's first meeting with Feisal is epic: "I felt at first glance that this was the man I had come to Arabia to seek—the leader who would bring the Arab Revolt to full glory." His impressions at the time give a more human Feisal: "He is hot tempered, proud, and impatient, sometimes unreasonable, and runs off easily at tangents. Possesses far more personal magnetism and life than his brothers, but less prudent. Obviously very clever, perhaps not overscrupulous."[19]

That last was equally true of Lawrence. To Feisal he held out the vision of the throne in an independent Syria, one that included Lebanon, and played down the other promises the British had made, to the French or to the Jews. He made sure that Feisal's forces got credit for the capture of Damascus, much to the annoyance of the Australians who actually did the work. Feisal was appointed the chief administrator of Syria. Lawrence did all this for the Arabs but also for the British. He himself did not know which were the more important to him. Sometimes he talked of the Arabs as "we" and the British as "you." Like other pro-Arabists, he hoped that the Arabs would happily and willingly choose limited self-government under the benevolent supervision and control of the British. Self-determination, he told Curzon's Eastern Committee, was "a foolish idea in many ways. We might allow the people who have fought with us to determine themselves." Britain's imperial needs would thus neatly mesh with Arab nationalism—and he would not have to choose between them.[20]

The French saw Lawrence as Feisal's "evil genius" who had turned the simple Arab against them. When Lawrence arrived with Feisal at Marseille in November 1918, wearing, as a French colonel noted in disgust, "his strange white oriental dress," they told him he was welcome only as a British officer. Lawrence left France in a fury, but turned up for the start of the

Peace Conference, still in Arab dress. While he was fêted by the British and the Americans, the French muttered darkly about his unreasoning hatred of their country. He had taken, it was said, his Croix de Guerre and paraded it on a dog's collar. Clemenceau, hoping to avoid a confrontation with Britain over Syria, agreed to see him. He reminded Lawrence that the French had fought there in the crusades. "Yes," replied Lawrence, "but the Crusaders had been defeated and the Crusades had failed."[21]

The French, who suspected that the British hoped to use Feisal to weaken their own case for Syria ("British imperialism with Arab head-gear," in the words of one French diplomat), did not want him or Lawrence in France at all and would have stopped them in Beirut if they had known in time. But they hesitated to turn Feisal away at Marseille; there was always a faint chance that he could be detached from the British. Feisal was greeted correctly but coolly and informed that he had no official standing and that he had been badly advised in making his trip. He was dragged off on a tour of the battlefields to keep him away from Paris and it was only when he threatened to leave that he was given an audience with Poincaré. The French also doled out a Légion d'Honneur, which Feisal received, as fate would have it, from General Henri Gouraud, who was later to turn him off his throne in Syria.[22]

When he went on to London, Feisal found a warmer welcome but with undercurrents that unsettled him. The British suggested that he might have to accept French overlordship in Syria. They also wanted him to agree that Palestine was not part of Syria, as the Arabs maintained, and to sign an agreement with Chaim Weizmann, leader of the World Zionist Organization, recognizing the Zionist presence there. Feisal was lonely and at sea in an unfamiliar world. He needed British support in the face of French hostility. He signed at the beginning of January; the validity of the document, like that of so many others dealing with the Middle East, has been debated ever since.[23]

When the Peace Conference opened, the French tried to drive a wedge between Feisal and the British. His name was omitted from the list of official delegates. When Feisal complained, a French Foreign Ministry official said bluntly: "It is easy to understand. You are being laughed at: the British have let you down. If you make yourself on our side, we can arrange things for you." After the British protested, the French grudgingly allowed Feisal to attend as an official delegate, but only as representing his father's Hejaz. Lawrence was close at his side, chaperon, translator and, because Feisal was receiving a subsidy from the Foreign Office, paymaster. The French press attacked Feisal as a British puppet; French intelligence opened his letters and delayed his telegrams back to the Middle East. In an ultimately unsuccessful gambit, the Quai d'Orsay also nurtured the Central Syrian Committee, which claimed to speak for Syrians around the world and which wanted, it said, a greater Syria, including the Lebanon, under French protection. The main effect was to make Arab nationalists even more suspicious of the French.[24]

On February 6, the delegation from the Hejaz finally got its chance to address the Supreme Council. Feisal, in white robes embroidered with gold, a scimitar at his side, spoke in Arabic while Lawrence translated. It was rumored that Feisal merely recited the Koran while Lawrence extemporized. The Arabs, Feisal said, wanted self-determination. While he was prepared to respect the exemptions of the Lebanon and Palestine, the rest of the Arab world should have its independence. He invited Britain and France to live up to the promises they had made. While Lloyd George posed questions designed to show the contribution the Arabs had made to the Allied victory, Wilson asked only whether the Arabs would prefer to be part of one mandate or several. Feisal tried to dodge what was an awkward question, stressing that the Arabs preferred unity and independence. If the powers decided on mandates, then, he hinted, his people would prefer the Americans to anyone else. When Feisal, with Lawrence, called on Wilson privately, they found him reserved and noncommittal, although years later, when things had gone badly for Feisal, he maintained that Wilson had promised that, if Syria really established its independence, the United States would protect it.[25]

The French foreign minister tried to catch Feisal out. As a British observer reported maliciously, "Pichon had the stupidity to ask what France had done to help him." Feisal at once praised the French while managing to point out the very limited amount of aid France had sent. "He said it all in such a way that no one could possibly take offence and of course Pichon looked a fool, as he is." A few days later the French returned to the attack, producing Arabs who claimed that their people, whether Christian or Muslim, wanted nothing so much as French help. Unfortunately, as the gray-bearded spokesman for the Central Syrian Committee was launching into his two-hour oration, an American expert slipped Wilson a note pointing out that the speaker had spent the previous thirty-five years in France. Wilson stopped listening and wandered about the room. Clemenceau whispered angrily to Pichon, "What did you get the fellow here for anyway?" Pichon replied with a shrug, "Well, I didn't know he was going to carry on this way." Clemenceau's own view was that Feisal's demands were absurdly extravagant, but he still hoped to avoid an open confrontation with the British, especially since the discussions on the terms to be offered Germany were reaching an acute stage.[26]

The French also brought in a delegation asking for a separate Lebanon under the protection of France, whose praises they sang. "Her liberal principles," said its leader, "her time-honoured traditions, the benefits Lebanon never failed to receive from her in hard times, the civilisation she diffused throughout made her prominent in the eyes of all the inhabitants of Lebanon." France had historically been the protector of the Christian communities throughout the Ottoman empire but it had particularly close ties to the Maronites, who probably formed a majority in the wild country around Mount Lebanon. In 1861 France had forced the Ottomans to set up an autonomous province there. Maronites had fought side by side with French Crusaders; they claimed, improbably, a family connection with Charlemagne; like French Catholics, they looked to the pope in Rome rather than to the Orthodox patriarch in Constantinople; and, most important perhaps, they admired French culture almost as much as the French themselves. When Maronite leaders outlined a greater Lebanon, to include the Bekáa Valley and most of the coast from Tripoli to Sidon, as well as a large number of Muslims, France was sympathetic.[27]

Although Clemenceau himself was mainly concerned at the Peace Conference with France's security in Europe, he could not entirely ignore his own colonial lobby. He told Kerr, Lloyd George's assistant, that he "personally was not particularly concerned with the Near East. France, however, had always played a great part there, and from the economic point of view a settlement which would give France economic opportunities was essential, especially in view of their present financial condition. He further said that French public opinion expected a settlement which was consonant with France's position. He could not, he said, make any settlement which did not comply with this condition." He was prepared, as he had shown at that famous disputed conversation in December 1918, to go a long way to accommodate the British; he could not give them everything in the Middle East.[28]

In the press of urgent business before Wilson left for his short trip home on February 14, nothing was decided about the Arab territories and the issue continued to fester. The main source of the trouble was that the British were still undecided about what they wanted. Should they keep their hands off and let the French have Syria, as they had promised in Sykes-Picot and as the Foreign Office preferred? Curzon's Eastern Committee and the military hastened to point out the dangers if France should end up controlling a swath of former Turkish territory from Armenia in the north to the borders of Palestine in the south. Then there were those, like Lawrence himself, who felt that Britain had an obligation to the Arabs and to Feisal in particular and could not therefore simply abandon them to the French. Lloyd George tended to agree; as he told the British empire delegation, "we could not face the East again if we broke faith." He would give France Syria only if there was no alternative. On the other hand, he did not really want to alienate the French. As on other issues, Lloyd George tried to keep his options open. He delayed withdrawing British occupation troops from Syria, thereby persuading the French, if they needed persuading, that the British were untrustworthy. As Balfour complained:

> We have got into an extraordinary muddle over the whole subject, partly owing to the unreasonableness of the French, partly owing to the essentially false position in which we have placed ourselves by insisting on a military occupation of a country which we do not propose under any circumstances to keep ourselves, while excluding those whom we recognise are to have it, and partly owing to the complicated and contradictory character of the public engagements into which we have entered.[29]

While Wilson was away, the British floated various schemes, all of which would leave France with nothing like what it would have had under Sykes-Picot. Lloyd George urged Clemenceau to accept Feisal as ruler of Syria and warned him that if he did not, there could be war in Syria. The British further infuriated the French with a plan to rectify the borders of Palestine, which would have taken, the French complained, almost a third of Syrian territory in the south. "The notes coming in from the French government," said the British ambassador in Paris, "could hardly be worse if we were enemies instead of allies."

Lord Milner, the British colonial secretary who had been given responsibility for the Syrian issue, arrived in Paris to reassure the French that "we did not want Syria and had not the slightest objection to France's being there." He even persuaded Clemenceau, an old friend, to meet Feisal and see if they could work something out. Unfortunately, the attempt to assassinate Clemenceau came on February 19, before the meeting could take place. Milner, claiming he did not want to bother Clemenceau, never followed up; Clemenceau refused to have anything more to do with Milner. A few weeks later, Lloyd George apparently went back to Sykes-Picot, but three days later he produced yet another map leaving France with Lebanon and the port of Alexandretta in the north and Syria virtually independent under Feisal. Clemenceau complained bitterly to House that Lloyd George always broke his promises. The French government was under intense pressure from French colonialists; even the Quai d'Orsay was stirring up a press campaign to demand the Syrian mandate. "I won't give way on anything any more," Clemenceau assured Poincaré. "Lloyd George is a cheat. He has managed to turn me into a 'Syrian.' "[30]

On March 20, with Wilson back in Paris, Pichon and Lloyd George went over the whole history again in the Council of Four. Sykes-Picot, said Wilson in disgust afterward, sounded like a type of tea; "a fine example of the old diplomacy." Sykes himself was dead by this time, carried off in the great flu epidemic, and Picot was in Beirut, trying valiantly to uphold his country's interests in the face of a hostile British military administration. Allenby, who had been summoned to Paris from Damascus, warned that the Arabs would violently oppose a French occupation. Wilson tried to find a compromise. After all, as he pointed out, his only interest was in peace. Why not send a fact-finding inquiry to ask the Arabs themselves what they wanted? The Peace Conference, he said, using a favorite formula, would find "the most scientific basis possible for a settlement." To annoy the British, Clemenceau slyly suggested that the commission look at Mesopotamia and Palestine as well. With the insouciance that drove the French colonial lobby mad, he told Poincaré that he had agreed to the commission only to be nice to Wilson and that, in any case, the commissioners would find nothing but support for France in Syria, "where we have traditions of 200 years." The French president was horrified. As he told his diary, "Clemenceau is a man for catastrophes; if he cannot prevent them, he will also provoke them." Lloyd George agreed to the commission, but privately thought it a dreadful idea, and so, on second thought, did Clemenceau. The two stalled when it came to naming their representatives, with the result that Wilson, in exasperation, finally decided in May to go ahead unilaterally and send his own commissioners out to the Middle East.[31]

When Feisal heard the initial news that a commission was to be appointed, he drank champagne for the first time in his life. He was confident, as was the ubiquitous Lawrence, that it would confirm Syrian independence under his rule. The months in Paris had been frustrating and boring for both men. A flight over the city helped relieve their feelings. "How dreadful, to have no bombs to throw upon these people," Feisal exclaimed. "Never mind, here are some cushions." Lawrence became increasingly difficult, playing silly practical jokes such as throwing sheets of toilet paper down a stairwell at Lloyd George and Balfour one evening. In April, Feisal and Clemenceau had their long-delayed meeting, at which they discussed yet another plan providing for a mild form of French mandate, which had been drawn up by British and French experts. Clemenceau found Feisal friendlier and more reasonable than before and believed that Feisal had accepted the terms. In fact, Feisal was stalling, on Lawrence's advice. By May, when it was quite clear that there was no agreement and no serious Allied commission of inquiry, Feisal was safely back in Damascus.[32]

In Paris the wrangling between Britain and France went on, culminating, on May 21, with a violent scene between Clemenceau and Lloyd George over the whole Ottoman empire. Clemenceau pointed out that France had agreed to the incorporation of Cilicia into an Armenian mandate under the United States. He reminded Lloyd George that he had given up Mosul the previous December. "I have thus abandoned Mosul and Cilicia; I made the concessions you asked of me without hesitation, because you told me that, afterwards, no difficulty would remain. But I won't accept what you propose today; my government would be overthrown the next day, and even I would vote against it." Clemenceau threatened to go back on his offer of Mosul. That put before the Peace Conference the question of not just Mosul but the whole area stretching south to the Persian Gulf, now known as Iraq, an issue the British had managed to avoid up to this point.[33]

Mesopotamia—the term the British used loosely to refer to the old Ottoman provinces of Mosul, Baghdad and Basra—had scarcely been mentioned at the conference except as a possible mandate to be held, everyone assumed, by Britain. British troops were in occupation, British administrators from India were running it and British ships were sailing up and down the Tigris. No power was likely to challenge the British claim: Russia and Persia were too weak, the United States uninterested. France, until that stormy session of the Council of Four in May, had apparently given up any claim. Clemenceau spoke in anger but he may have also begun to realize just what he had given up so blithely: oil.

Coal had been the great fuel of the Industrial Revolution, but by 1919 it was becoming clear that oil was the fuel of the future. Tanks, aircraft, lorries and navies all needed oil. British petroleum imports alone quadrupled between 1900 and 1919 and most of the increase, worryingly, came from outside the British empire: from the United States, Mexico, Russia and Persia. Control of oilfields, refineries and pipelines was clearly going to be important in the future, as it had been in the Great War, when "the Allied cause," according to Curzon, "floated to victory upon a wave of oil." No one knew for certain whether Mesopotamia had oil in any quantity, but when black sludge seeped out of the ground and lay in pools around Baghdad, or gas fires flared off swamps in Mosul, it was easy to guess. By 1919, the British navy was arguing, without awaiting further evidence, that the Mesopotamian oilfields were the largest in the world. It seemed foolish to hand over control of any part to the French, whatever Sykes-Picot said. As Leo Amery, one of Lloyd George's bright young men, wrote: "The greatest oil-field in the world extends all the way up to and beyond Mosul, and even if it didn't we ought as a matter of safety to control sufficient ground in front of our vital oil-fields to avoid the risk of having them rushed at the outset of the war."[34]

Clemenceau, who had once said, "When I want some oil, I'll find it at my grocer's," had by now grasped the importance of the new fuel. He had given up formal control over Mosul but he insisted to Lloyd George that France should have its share of whatever was in the ground. Walter Long, the British minister of fuel, and Henry Bérenger, his French counterpart, a man who believed that oil was the "blood of victory," were put to work. They produced an agreement under which France would have a quarter-share of the Turkish Petroleum Company and in return would allow two pipelines to be built across Syria from Mosul to the sea. Both sides agreed that they did not want the Americans, who were starting to take an interest in Middle East oil, muscling in. Unfortunately, what was a reasonable compromise got caught up in the confrontation over Syria. "There was a first-class dogfight," Henry Wilson noted in his diary, "during which the Tiger said Walter Long had promised the French half the Mesopotamian oil! Lloyd George asked me if I had ever heard of this. Of course, never. Whereupon Lloyd George wrote at once to Tiger and said that arrangement was cancelled." The Foreign Office did not find this out until some months later, which shows the confusion in British policymaking at this period. It was only in December 1919, after Britain and France had finally settled their dispute over Syria, that the oil issue was put to rest, on very much the same terms that Long and Bérenger had agreed. As part of the deal, the French government also agreed permanently to abandon France's claim to Mosul.[35]

The British knew that they did not want the French to have Mosul, but beyond that their own policy toward Mesopotamia developed by fits and starts. The initial British campaign there in 1914 had been defensive, designed only to protect the Persian Gulf from the Turks. Once they had secured their bridgehead, they had been drawn north toward Baghdad. A young political officer, Arnold Wilson, wrote to his parents: "The only sound thing is to go on as far as possible and not try to look too far ahead." Four years later the British had gone very far indeed, up to the Kurdish areas on the borders of Turkey, and Wilson was now head of the British administration.[36]

Arnold Wilson was handsome, courageous, stubborn and stoical. His school report said: "He has fought his faults bravely and the worst of them are perhaps exaggerated virtues. His talent is for management and organization and he is capable of a great deal of work for others and unselfishness. His manners are his worst foe." He loathed dancing, gossip and idleness. He quoted scripture freely; his finger never hesitated on the trigger. He had, in short, the qualities of a great proconsul of empire at a time when proconsuls were becoming obsolete.[37]

When the war started, Wilson was in the north of Turkey, near Mount Ararat, completing an immense project to map the boundary between Persia and Ottoman Turkey. (The border has stood with scarcely a change.) He and a colleague made their way back to Britain via Russia and Archangel. As he was about to join his regiment in France, he was ordered back to the Middle East, to join the Mesopotamian campaign as assistant to Sir Percy Cox, the chief political officer. When, at the end of the war, Cox was called away to deal with Persian matters, Wilson was his obvious replacement. From April 1918 to October 1920 he governed Mesopotamia.[38]

Wilson, like most of the other British there, assumed that Britain was acquiring a valuable new property. With oil, if Mosul had any worth exploiting, and wheat, if irrigation was done properly, the new acquisition could be self-sufficient; indeed, it might even return money to the imperial treasuries. Wilson urged the government in London to make Mosul part of its war aims and, just after the Turkish armistice, he made sure that British forces moved in. Mosul was, he argued, important for the defense of Baghdad and Basra.[39] With the collapse of the Ottomans and the Russian Revolution, it had also gained wider strategic importance. The British were backing anticommunist forces in Russia as well as the little independent republics that had sprung up in the Caucasus. One way of doing this, and of preventing the spread of Bolshevism farther south, was to open up communications between Persia and the Caucasus, and that meant through Mosul.

Wilson had firm ideas about how the area should be ruled. "Basra, Baghdad, and Mosul should be regarded as a single unit for administrative purposes and under effective British control." It never seems to have occurred to him that a single unit did not make much sense in other ways. In 1919 there was no Iraqi people; history, religion, geography pulled the people apart, not together. Basra looked south, toward India and the Gulf; Baghdad had strong links with Persia; and Mosul had closer ties with Turkey and Syria. Putting together the three Ottoman provinces and expecting to create a nation was, in European terms, like hoping to have Bosnian Muslims, Croats, and Serbs make one country. As in the Balkans, the clash of empires and civilizations had left deep fissures. The population was about half Shia Muslim and a quarter Sunni, with other minorities from Jews to Christians, but another division ran across the religious one: while half the inhabitants were Arab, the rest were Kurds (mainly in Mosul), Persians or Assyrians. The cities were relatively advanced and cosmopolitan; in the countryside, hereditary tribal and religious leaders still dominated.[40] There was no Iraqi nationalism, only Arab. Before the war, young officers serving in the Ottoman armies had pushed for greater autonomy for the Arab areas. When the war ended, several of these, including Nuri Said, a future prime minister of Iraq, had gathered around Feisal. Their interest was in a greater Arabia, not in separate states.

Arnold Wilson did not foresee the problems of throwing such a diverse population into a single state. He was a paternalist who thought the British would remain for generations. "The average Arab, as opposed to a handful of amateur politicians in Baghdad, sees the future as one of fair dealing and material and moral progress under the aegis of Great Britain." He urged his government to move quickly: "Our best course is to declare Mesopotamia to be a British Protectorate under which all classes will be given forthwith the maximum degree of liberty and self-rule compatible with good and safe government." His superiors in London ruled that out. They preferred indirect rule, something the British had used in the Indian princely states and Egypt. It had the advantage of being cheaper than direct control—an important consideration, especially in 1919. As Balfour pointed out, when the Eastern Committee was talking away about all the glorious possibilities that lay before Britain: "We consider the advantage to the natives, the advantage to our prestige; we consider certain things connected with trade and commerce, and all the rest of it; but money and men I have never seen referred to, and they seem to me to be the governing considerations." And indirect rule did at least bow in the direction of Arab self-determination and liberal opinion. "What we want," said a senior official at the India Office, "is some administration with Arab institutions which we can safely leave while pulling the strings ourselves; something that won't cost very much, which Labour can swallow consistent with its principles, but under which our economic and political interests will be secure."[41]

This was easier said than done. There was a new spirit stirring in the Arab world and farther afield. In India, nationalists were rallying behind Gandhi; in Egypt, the Wafd party was growing day by day. Arab nationalism was still weak in Iraq, but it was already a potent force in Syria and Egypt. Arnold Wilson's oriental secretary and trusted adviser realized this, even if he did not.

Gertrude Bell was the only woman to play a key figure in the peace settlements in her own right. Thin, intense, chain-smoking, with a voice that pierced the air, she was accustomed to being out of the ordinary. Although she came from a rich, well-connected family, she had broken with the usual pattern of her class—marriage, children and society—by going to Oxford and becoming the first woman to receive a first-class degree in history. She climbed the Matterhorn and pioneered new routes in the Alps. She was a noted archaeologist and historian. She was also arrogant, difficult and very influential. In November 1919, when the British commander-in-chief in Baghdad held a reception for eighty notables, they left their seats to crowd around her.[42]

With only her servants and guides for company, Gertrude Bell had traveled all over the Middle East before the war, from Beirut to Damascus and from Baghdad to Mosul. She loved the desert: "Silence and solitude fall round you like an impenetrable veil; there is no reality but the long hours of riding, shivering in the morning and drowsy in the afternoon, the bustle of getting into camp, the talk around Muhammad's fire after dinner, profounder sleep than civilization contrives, and then the road again."[43] By 1914, she was widely recognized as one of Britain's leading authorities on the Middle East. In 1915, she became the first woman to work for British military intelligence and the only woman officially part of the British expedition to Mesopotamia.

She herself did not believe in rights for women. Nor did she like most of her own sex. "It is such a pity," she said loudly in front of a young English bride, "that promising young Englishmen go and marry such fools of women." Her best friends were men: Lawrence, St. John Philby (father of a notorious son), Feisal and, for a time, Arnold Wilson. She loved passionately but never married. When her first great love turned out to be a gambler, her father refused his permission, and her second was already married. On Christmas Day in 1920 she wrote to her father: "As you know I'm rather friendless. I don't care enough about people to take trouble about them, and naturally they don't trouble about me—why should they? Also all their amusements bore me to tears and I don't join in them."[44]

She threw herself into her work in Mesopotamia. "We shall, I trust," she wrote to her father, "make it a centre of Arab civilisation and prosperity." The Arabs, she assumed at first, would play little part in their own government. "The stronger the hold we are able to keep here the better the inhabitants will be pleased." She got on well with Arnold Wilson in those early days. He was, she reported enthusiastically to her parents, "a most remarkable creature, 34, brilliant abilities, a combined mental and physical power that is extremely rare." Wilson in turn admired her "unwearying diligence" in dealing with paperwork. She was, he told his family, "extraordinarily vigorous and helpful in many ways." Together they waited for word from their superiors about what would happen to Mesopotamia. It did not come. "I presumed," said Wilson, "that if their oracles were dumb it was because their doubts were even greater than ours." As they waited, Bell began to change her mind about the sort of government Mesopotamia needed. Arabs would have to play a larger role than she had at first thought.[45]

In January 1919, Arnold Wilson sent Bell off to Cairo, London and Paris to try to find out what was happening. In February, he followed her to Paris, where she was putting the case for a country in Mesopotamia. As she wrote rather grandly to her family, "I'm lunching tomorrow with Mr. Balfour who, I fancy, really doesn't care. Ultimately I hope to catch Mr. Lloyd George by the coat tails, and if I can manage to do so I believe I can enlist his sympathies. Meanwhile we've sent for Colonel Wilson from Baghdad." She was convinced, rightly as it turned out, that the fate of Mesopotamia was linked to settlement of the dispute over Syria: "We can't consider one without the other, and in the case of Syria it's the French attitude that counts." She had been spending a great deal of time with Lawrence and Feisal and now shared their hope that the French might be persuaded to have Feisal as king of an independent Syria. Arnold Wilson disapproved strongly of Lawrence and his views: "He seems to have done an immense amount of harm and our difficulties with the French seem to me to be mainly due to his actions and advice."[46]

The talking and the lobbying accomplished little. As Montagu, secretary of state for India, wrote plaintively to Balfour: "We have now collected in Paris Miss Bell and Colonel Wilson. They are responsible to me. They come to me and say 'We are here. What do you want of us?' I can give them no information of what is going on." While the peacemakers prevaricated, in Mesopotamia unrest was spreading: among Kurds and Persians, who were restless under Arab domination; among the Shia, who resented Sunni influence; among tribal leaders challenged by British power; among high-ranking officers and bureaucrats who had lost their status with the collapse of the Ottomans; and among the increasing numbers of Arab nationalists. Bell worried from the sidelines. In April she wrote to her old friend Aubrey Herbert, himself anxious about Albania, "O my dear they are making such a horrible muddle of the Near East, I confidently anticipate that it will be much worse than it was before the war—except Mesopotamia which we may manage to hold up out of the general chaos. It's like a nightmare in which you foresee all the horrible things which are going to happen and can't stretch out your hand to prevent them."[47]

· · ·

That spring Egypt blew up. Egyptians had never taken happily to British rule, even though the British tried to disguise it by governing through a khedive. By the time the war started, Egypt had the foundations for a strong national movement: powerful religious leaders, local magnates and a growing professional class, who were building links to each other and downward, into the huge peasant population of the Nile delta. The war itself brought fresh trouble. When the Ottoman empire, still nominally the overlord of Egypt, declared war on Britain in 1914, the British declared a protectorate. That infuriated many Egyptians, as did the influx of quantities of British and Australian troops, and the accompanying rise in prices. The British sent out contradictory messages about the future: on the ground, their hold over the country tightened, but the government in London used Woodrow Wilson's language. The Fourteen Points themselves were received enthusiastically in Egypt.[48]

In November 1918, just after the Anglo-French declaration to the Arabs used precisely that language of self-determination, a prominent Egyptian nationalist led a delegation to speak to Sir Reginald Wingate, the head of the British administration in Egypt. Said Zaghlul was a distinguished lawyer, a literary man and a former minister of education. He had come out of traditional Egypt, from a landowning family in the delta, but with the patronage of a princess from the royal family he had moved into the more modern, cosmopolitan world of Cairo. The British had initially counted him as one of their supporters. "He should go far," thought Lord Cromer, the first British proconsul in Egypt: "He possesses all the qualities necessary to serve his country. He is honest; he is capable; he has the courage of his convictions." By 1914, however, the British were less enthusiastic. Zaghlul, perhaps because he had not been made prime minister, perhaps out of genuine conviction, was moving into the nationalist camp.[49]

In his interview with Wingate, Zaghlul demanded complete autonomy for the Egyptians. They were, he told Wingate, "an ancient and capable race with a glorious past—far more capable of conducting a well-ordered government than the Arabs, Syrians and Mesopotamians, to whom self-government had so recently been promised." He asked permission for a delegation (or *wafd*) to travel to London and Paris to present the nationalists' demands. When Wingate refused, Egyptians protested furiously: "Extremist Indians had been given a hearing by Mr. Montagu; the Arab Emir Feisal was allowed to go to Paris. Were Egyptians less loyal? Why not Egypt?"[50]

By the start of the Peace Conference, petitions were circulating about Egypt; thousands, then hundreds of thousands, signed. The protests coalesced into a movement, appropriately called the Wafd. Zaghlul urged the khedive to demand complete independence. On March 9, the British authorities arrested Zaghlul and three other leading nationalists and deported them to Malta. The following day, strikes and demonstrations broke out all over Egypt. In an unprecedented gesture, upper-class women poured out of their seclusion; "I did not care if I suffered sunstroke," said one; "the blame would fall on the tyrannical British authority."[51] The protests turned violent; the telegraph wires were cut and railway tracks torn up. On March 18, eight British soldiers were murdered by a mob. The British suddenly faced losing control of Egypt altogether.

In something of a panic, the British government hastily imposed martial law and dispatched Allenby to bring the Egyptians into line. To London's considerable surprise, he rapidly concluded that he must release the nationalist leaders from detention in Malta and allow them, if they wished, to travel abroad if he was to have any hope of working with the Egyptians. Zaghlul made his way to Paris, where he apparently had little success in winning support from the other powers.[52] He had, however, impressed on the British that changes had to be made in the way they ran Egypt. Although it took many months of negotiations, in 1922 the British government finally conceded Egypt's independence. (It kept control, however, of the Suez Canal and foreign policy.) Zaghlul became prime minister in 1924.

India, the reason the British were in Egypt at all, also worried the British in 1919. Indian nationalism was even further developed than Egyptian. What had once been polite requests for limited self-government had now turned into demands for home rule. During the war, Mohandas Gandhi had arrived from South Africa with the tools of political organization and civil disobedience which he had perfected to transform the largely middle-class Indian National Congress into a formidable mass movement. Rapid inflation, the collapse of India's export trade and the revelations of how British military incompetence had wasted the lives of Indian soldiers in Mesopotamia disillusioned even those Indians who had thought that at least British rule provided good government. Although Britain promised a gradual move toward self-rule in 1917, it was being outflanked and outwitted.

Indian nationalists noted President Wilson's talk of self-determination with approval but at first they paid little attention to the Peace Conference. India had no territorial claims, or at least not ones that the Indians themselves cared about. (The British officials in the India Office tried, unsuccessfully, to put in claims for Indian mandates over Mesopotamia and German East Africa.[53]) It was represented not by its own leaders but by

Montagu, the secretary of state for India, and two carefully chosen Indians: Lord Satyendra Sinha, a distinguished judge who was useful on committees, and the Maharajah of Bikaner, who said very little but gave nice dinner parties. The peacemakers were taken by surprise, and the British alarmed, when a seemingly minor matter—the abolition of the caliphate in Constantinople—suddenly became a major cause in India.

Indian Muslims, who made up a quarter of British India's population, had been quietly unhappy for some time at the prospect that the end of the Ottoman empire might bring the end of the spiritual leadership that the sultan exercised over the world's Muslims. Mosques throughout India prayed for him as caliph in their weekly observances. The war had pulled Indian Muslims in two directions. A small minority openly sided with the Ottomans and were put in jail for saying so; the rest, sullenly or sadly, remained quiescent. When rumors floated back from Paris to India in 1919 that the powers were planning to divide up the Ottoman empire, depose the sultan and abolish the caliphate, Muslim newspapers published articles beseeching the British to protect him, and local notables formed caliphate committees. Petitions poured in to the British authorities, claiming, inaccurately, that Wilson had promised to protect the caliphate. The government of India urged the British government to leave the sultan in Constantinople with some sort of authority over Muslim holy places throughout the Middle East. In Paris, Montagu warned his colleagues repeatedly of the risks of alienating a large group of Indians who had been notably loyal to the British. His warnings, and his prickly personality, merely produced irritation. Lloyd George wrote to him: "In fact throughout the Conference your attitude has often struck me as being not so much that of a member of the British Cabinet, but of a successor on the throne of Aurangzeb!"[54]★

On May 17 Lloyd George grudgingly agreed to bring before the Council of Four a deputation, which included the Aga Khan, to ask that the Turkish parts of the Ottoman empire not be parceled out among different powers, and that the caliphate be allowed to continue. Lloyd George himself was impressed: "I conclude that it is impossible to divide Turkey proper. We would run too great a risk of throwing disorder into the Mohammedan world."[55] Unfortunately, four days later, on May 21, he and Clemenceau had their violent argument over the Middle East settlement and the whole issue, including the caliphate, was put off indefinitely.

In India, the Muslims were increasingly anxious. The local committees

★Aurangzeb was the last effective Mughal emperor in India.

organized themselves into a central caliphate committee. The chief Muslim political organization, the Muslim League, sent a deputation to see Lloyd George. What was much more serious, Gandhi decided to throw his and Congress's support behind the movement. Skinny, introverted, obsessed equally with his bowels and his soul, attuned always to the political currents in India but listening as much to his own complicated heart, Gandhi was an unlikely political genius. In the caliphate agitation he saw an opportunity to build bridges between Hindus and Muslims and to embarrass the British authorities.

India was already uneasy. The great flu epidemic had carried off twelve million Indians (Gandhi used it as an example of Britain's moral unfitness to rule India). Muslims were incensed over the caliphate, workers were striking and peasants were protesting about their rents. The government of India made matters worse by introducing legislation to increase its arbitrary powers. In March and April, the big cities saw huge demonstrations and public meetings. On April 6 Gandhi called for a general strike across India. Although he urged his followers to refrain from violence, there were sporadic outbreaks of looting and rioting. The worst trouble came in the Punjab where, on April 13, at Amritsar, a panicking British officer ordered his troops to fire point-blank into a large crowd. The Amritsar Massacre, as it came to be known, galvanized even moderate Indian opinion against the British. The British, especially those in India, started to panic. Was there, a local English-language newspaper asked, "some malevolent and highly dangerous organization which is at work below the surface?" Were the disturbances caused by Bolsheviks? Infiltrators from Egypt? Or perhaps a worldwide Muslim conspiracy? Perhaps it was more than coincidence that a war had just broken out with Muslim Afghanistan and that Ibn Saud's forces, largely drawn from a puritanical Islamic movement, were sweeping across the Arabian peninsula.[56]

Their Egyptian and Indian troubles shook British confidence and brought home yet again the limits of British power. Henry Wilson, chief of the Imperial General Staff, had tried repeatedly to make his government aware of this; as he wrote to a friend in April 1919, "My whole energies are now bent to getting our troops out of Europe and Russia and concentrating all our strength in our coming storm centres, viz. England, Ireland, Egypt and India. There you are, my dear." Even if they pulled troops back from areas such as the Caucasus and Persia, the military were not sure that they could deal with the "storm centres." Britain's armies were melting away. In the Middle East alone, Allenby was demobilizing an average of 20,000 men a month during the spring of 1919.[57]

The troubles also brought home the costs. "Do please realize,"

Churchill—now colonial secretary—wrote to his private secretary in the Colonial Office on November 12, 1921, "that everything that happens in the Middle East is secondary to the reduction of expense." As Curzon reported gloomily to Balfour after a particularly inconclusive cabinet discussion in the summer of 1919: "This fact did emerge; the burden of maintaining an English and an Indian Army of 320,000 men in various parts of the Turkish Empire and in Egypt, or of 225,000 men excluding Egypt, with its overwhelming cost, is one that can no longer be sustained." Lloyd George, who had seen no urgent need to make the peace settlement for the Ottoman empire, finally started to pay attention. In August 1919, just before he went on holiday, Balfour provided him with an admirably lucid summary of the problems although, typically, he offered no solutions: "The unhappy truth . . . is that France, England and America have got themselves into a position over the Syrian problem so inextricably confused that no really neat and satisfactory issue is now possible for any of them." Lloyd George was also becoming uncomfortably aware of the depth of French anger.

To complicate matters further, Feisal had been displaying an unwelcome independence since his return to Syria in May. In one of his first speeches in Damascus, he told his Arab audience, "It now remains for you to choose to be either slaves or masters of your own destiny." He was rumored to be talking to Egyptian nationalists about a common front against the British and to Turkish ones about a possible reunion with Turkey. His agents were spreading propaganda into Mesopotamia. In a conversation with Allenby, Feisal claimed that Woodrow Wilson had told him to follow the example of the American Revolution: "If you want independence recruit soldiers and be strong." If Feisal did decide to lead an uprising, the British military authorities in Syria warned Lloyd George, they could not contain it.[58]

In September, Lloyd George, who moved quickly once he had made up his mind, decided that Britain would pull its troops out of Syria and let the French move in. After difficult conversations, Lloyd George and Clemenceau agreed on the handover of power. (There was still to be trouble over the border between Syria and Palestine, which was not finally settled until 1922.[59]) The Americans protested weakly and talked of self-determination, but they were no longer a serious factor. By the end of 1919 the other outstanding issues between Britain and France had been settled: Mosul's oil was to be shared, more or less along the lines that had been agreed six months earlier.

At the San Remo Conference in April 1920, where the terms of the treaty with the Ottoman empire were approved, the British and French, their differences temporarily forgotten, awarded themselves mandates, the British for Palestine and Mesopotamia, the French for Syria. In theory these were not valid until they were confirmed by the League of Nations. Not surprisingly, a League dominated by Britain and France did this in 1922.

The Arabs were consulted, but only by the Americans. Wilson's Commission of Inquiry, which Clemenceau and Lloyd George had declined to support, had duly gone ahead. Henry King, the president of Oberlin, and Charles Crane, who had done so much to help Czechoslovakia's cause, doggedly spent the summer of 1919 traveling through Palestine and Syria. They found that an overwhelming majority of the inhabitants wanted Syria to encompass both Palestine and Lebanon; a similar majority also wanted independence. "Dangers," they concluded, "may readily arise from unwise and unfaithful dealings with this people, but there is great hope of peace and progress if they be handled frankly and loyally."[60] Their report was not published until 1922, long after the damage had been done.

In September 1919 Feisal was baldly informed that Britain and France had reopened their discussions on the Middle East. The British made sure that he did not arrive in London until after Lloyd George and Clemenceau had reached their agreement. Feisal protested; he was not going to submit to French rule. The British, perhaps with some embarrassment, merely urged him to talk to the French. From Oxford, Lawrence watched helplessly as his government abandoned his old friend and the Arabs. He read and reread a poem about the expulsion of Adam and Eve from the Garden of Eden and often, his mother recalled, he sat in her house, "the entire morning between breakfast and lunch in the same position, without moving, and with the same expression on his face."[61]

In Paris, Feisal got a cool welcome. "After having covered him with flowers and sung his praises in every key, the French press," reported Mordacq, "practically drew him through the mud and heaped lies and insults on him." Clemenceau was sympathetic but firm; the French would accept Feisal as ruler in Damascus, so long as he could maintain order. He would, of course, call on French troops in any emergency. Feisal, in a grand gesture, presented Clemenceau with his horses; two were beautiful Thoroughbreds, reported Mordacq, the rest only so-so. The Tiger, in any case, was on his way out, and French official views, never sympathetic to Arab nationalism, were hardening. French rule needed to be consolidated in Syria, especially with Turkish nationalists attacking French forces in Cilicia. The new government in France, elected in November 1919, was much more interested in empire than Clemenceau's had been. Poincaré's successor as president, Paul Deschanel, was later to assure a deputation of fellow colonialists that the Mediterranean and the Middle East were cornerstones of French policy. (Shortly afterward he was found talking to the trees in the gardens at the Elysée Palace.) Although Feisal lingered on in Paris until January 1920, he failed to get a firm agreement with the French. He went home to Damascus, disappointed not only in the French but also in the British; in his words, "he had been handed over tied by feet and hands to the French."[62]

Back in Damascus, Feisal found a deteriorating situation. The French high commissioner, General Gouraud, the man who in happier days had given Feisal his decoration, believed in being firm with the Arabs. Arab nationalists themselves were increasingly belligerent, encouraged in part by the example of D'Annunzio in Fiume, who appeared to be getting away with defying the powers. In the wide Bekáa Valley with its great ruined Roman city at Baalbek, Arab irregulars sniped at French troops. (In the 1970s, radical guerrillas from around the world found the valley similarly convenient.) Behind the scenes, there was tremendous pressure on Feisal to make a declaration of independence, even if it meant war with France. Feisal reluctantly went along with the current. On March 7, 1920, the Syrian Congress proclaimed him king of Syria, and not of the circumscribed Syria agreed upon by Britain and France, but of Syria within its "natural boundaries," including Lebanon and Palestine and stretching east to the Euphrates. There were clashes with French troops. Shortly afterward, another congress claiming to speak for Mesopotamians also met in Damascus. It declared independence, proclaimed Feisal's brother Abdullah king, and demanded that the British end their occupation.[63]

Even within Syria, however, Feisal did not have complete support. Lebanese Christians, who did not want to get caught in a dispute with France, proclaimed their separate independence at a huge meeting on March 20, 1920, and chose as a flag the French tricolor with a Lebanese cedar in the center.[64] Meanwhile, Arab radicals accused Feisal of being too complaisant with the French. In July, Gouraud sent Feisal an ultimatum, demanding, among other things, unconditional acceptance of the French mandate over Syria and punishment of those who had attacked the French. Feisal appealed desperately to the other powers, who responded with nothing more than murmurs of sympathy. On July 24, on the road to Damascus, French troops swept aside a poorly armed Arab force. Feisal and his family went into exile in Palestine and then Italy.

To bring Syria under control, the French shrank it. They rewarded their Christian allies by swelling the borders of Mount Lebanon with the Bekáa Valley, the Mediterranean ports of Tyre, Sidon, Beirut and Tripoli, and the land in the south, north of Palestine. Thousands of Muslims now joined a state dominated by Christians. The result was a Syria which even after the French finally left still remembered what it had lost, and a Lebanon dancing uneasily around unresolved religious and ethnic tensions. In the 1970s, Lebanon blew up; to no one's surprise but the outside world's, the Syrian government took the opportunity to send in its troops, which have stayed ever since.

For the Arabs, 1920 remains the year of disaster: Palestine gone, then Syria, Lebanon and finally Mesopotamia. In the summer of 1920, rebellions broke out over about a third of Mesopotamia, up and down the Euphrates valley and in the Kurdish areas of Mosul. Bell, who had long since come around to the view that Mesopotamia must have self-government, had warned of this. Arnold Wilson, with whom she was no longer on speaking terms, blamed it all on outside agitators and the influence of his namesake's Fourteen Points.[65] Railway lines were cut and towns besieged; British officers were murdered. The British reacted harshly, sending punitive expeditions across the land to burn villages and exact fines. In a new but very effective tactic, their aircraft machine-gunned and bombed from the air. By the end of the year, order had been restored and Wilson had been replaced by his old mentor, the more diplomatic Cox.

The events in Mesopotamia shook the British government badly. "We are at our wits' end," said Churchill, "to find a single soldier." Critics asked whether Mesopotamia was worth the cost. Curzon, Churchill and Lloyd George all wanted to keep it if they could. The practical, and cheap, solution, which Bell and Cox had been urging, was to find a pliable Arab ruler. Conveniently, they had Feisal, to whom, after all, they did owe something. At a conference in Cairo in March 1921, Churchill, as colonial secretary, agreed to make him king. As a second prize, his older brother Abdullah, "a sensualist, idle, and very lazy," would get the little state of Transjordan. Feisal was duly invited to visit Mesopotamia, where the stage management of Cox and Bell produced a stream of supplicants asking him to stay as their king. St. John Philby, who favored a republic and said so loudly, was sent packing. An election produced a vote of 96 percent in favor of Feisal. Bell designed his flag, his coronation and his kingship. "I shall have to set about getting proper ceremonial for Feisal's court," she sighed. On August 23, 1921, in the cool of the early morning, Feisal was crowned king of what was henceforth known as "the well-rooted country": Iraq. "It was an amazing thing to see all Iraq, from North to South, gathered together," reported Bell. "It is the first time it has happened in history."[66]

Gertrude Bell remained close to Feisal at first but, as he grew in experience and confidence, he chafed under the stream of advice.[67] He was proving generally to be less amenable than the British had hoped. He pushed for the independence of his new country, and in 1932 Iraq joined the League of Nations as an independent state. Feisal died the following year. His son, a cheerful playboy, died in a car crash in 1939. His successor, Feisal's grandson, was killed in the coup of 1958 which made Iraq a republic. Hussein, Feisal's father, who had hoped to found a great Hashemite dynasty to run the Arab world, lost first his reason and then his throne in the Hejaz in 1924, when Ibn Saud finally overran it and created the kingdom that still bears his name. The only Hashemite kingdom that still survives is Jordan, where Abdullah, much to everyone's surprise, proved a very effective ruler. Abdullah's great-grandson is now king.

T. E. Lawrence, never really happy again after the war in the desert, also died in a crash, in 1935, when he swerved on his motorcycle to avoid two boys. Gertrude Bell committed suicide in 1926. Arnold Wilson left public service to work for Anglo-Persian Oil. At the age of fifty-five he was killed in action as an air force gunner over Dunkirk. Picot, whose agreement with Sykes had caused such trouble between France and Britain, ended his career under a cloud. Replaced in Syria in 1920, he was shipped off to Bulgaria, where he caused a scandal by an open affair with a woman of dubious reputation. Another posting in Buenos Aires brought more scandal and stories of unpaid bills. He retired from the French diplomatic service in 1932 and disappeared from history.[68]

Britain and France paid a price for their role in the peace settlements in the Middle East. The French never completely pacified Syria, and it never paid for itself. The British pulled back in Iraq and Jordan as quickly as they could, but they found they were stuck with Palestine and an increasingly poisonous atmosphere between Arabs and Jews. The Arab world as a whole never forgot its betrayal and Arab hostility came to focus on the example of Western perfidy nearest at hand, the Zionist presence in Palestine. Arabs also remembered the brief hope of Arab unity at the end of the war. After 1945, those resentments and that hope continued to shape the Middle East.

28

Palestine

A T THE END of February 1919 a middle-aged British research chem-
ist wrote to his wife from Paris: "Yesterday, the 27th February, at 3:30
p.m. at the Quai d'Orsay there took place an historic session." It was, he
told her, "a marvellous moment, the most triumphant of my life!" Chaim
Weizmann had been at the Supreme Council with a deputation of fellow
Zionists to make the case for a Jewish home in Palestine. That day in Paris
he had spoken briefly, with his customary clarity and energy. He appealed
to the self-interest of the powers: millions of Jews were trying to leave the
former Russian and Austrian empires. Where could they go? "The Great
Powers would naturally scrutinize every alien who claimed to enter their
countries, and the Jew would be regarded as a typical wandering alien."
The obvious solution was to let them go to Palestine; it was underpop-
ulated, with plenty of empty space. With money and work, both of which
the world's Jews were ready to provide, it could support millions more.
All that was needed was the signal from the peacemakers. He was demanding this, he said proudly, "in the name of the people who had suffered martyrdom for eighteen centuries." As he finished speaking, he told
his wife, "Sonnino got up and congratulated me there and then, so did Mr.
Balfour and all the others, except the French."[1]

There were many such delegations in Paris and many demands. The
Zionists did not have the influence or power of the Czechs or the Poles,
nor was there in the public mind a Jewish cause like the Armenian one.
They had some friends in powerful places, but they also faced hostility
and indifference. Yet Weizmann was right to feel triumphant. He knew
that, even if the French were hostile, the Americans and British were behind him; indeed, he had previously vetted his statements with members

of their delegations.[2] Both Weizmann and Zionism had come a long way from their origins and would go a long way yet.

The son of a modest timber merchant, Weizmann was born in Russia in 1874, in a tiny hamlet in, as he said, one of the "darkest and remote corners of the Pale of Settlement." Almost half the world's Jews, some seven million, lived in Russia, most forced into the Pale, in what is today Belarus, Ukraine and eastern Poland. The country was flat and marshy— "mournful and monotonous," said one Jewish writer—bitterly cold in the winter and stifling in the summer. The Jews were rich in tradition and faith, desperately poor in almost every other way. While their numbers were increasing, the land and resources allowed them by the tsarist government were not. "It was as if," said an observer, "all the Jews of Russia were to be violently crowded in and piled on top of one another like grasshoppers in a ditch." The government, which veered between indifference and brutality, offered no way out and no protection from anti-Jewish riots and pogroms. "It is an ugly life," said a Jewish poet, "without pleasure of satisfaction, without splendour, without light, a life that tastes like lukewarm soup, without salt or spice."[3]

Even in that world, though, ideas were stirring, ideas of socialism, democracy, nationalism. Some Russian Jews, such as Trotsky, turned to revolution; far more, hundreds of thousands, left for North America and Western Europe. In the years before 1914, the Jewish population in the United States went from 250,000 to 3 million; in Britain, from 60,000 to 300,000. Among the Russian Jews who moved westward was the young Weizmann. In Western Europe, he discovered a different world, where the ghettos and the old legal discrimination against Jews had vanished. Jews were able to live as British or French or Germans, with simply a different religion from most of their compatriots. Weizmann acquired a wife, a young medical student, herself from Russia, and two lifelong passions— for chemistry and Zionism.

At first Zionism—the struggle for a Jewish homeland, perhaps even a Jewish state, where Jews would be in a majority, where they would be safe and would be able to live with dignity—appealed to only a small number, to cranks or visionaries. By 1900, however, much had changed. Nationalism, which itself helped to produce Zionism, had also brought fresh dangers to Jews, when other nationalists turned a suspicious eye on the minorities among them. There was a bewildering and horrifying resurgence of the old dark European hatred for the Jews, even integrated, secular Jews. Sigmund Freud's father had his hat knocked off his head by a stranger who shouted, "Jew, get off the pavement." Surprising numbers of French, in the home of liberty, equality and fraternity, showed themselves ready to believe a trumped-up charge of treason because the officer in question, Alfred Dreyfus, was Jewish. In prewar Vienna, the mayor was a notorious anti-Semite and in the charming coffeehouses the Viennese told crude anti-Jewish jokes. In 1897 Theodor Herzl, a journalist from Vienna, held the world's first Zionist congress. Weizmann attended the next one, and every one that followed.

Tall, balding, looking with his goatee like "a well-nourished Lenin," Weizmann even then carried himself with great assurance. He criticized his seniors in the Zionist movement for being too timid. He publicly disagreed with Herzl over the scheme to buy Uganda from the British government and set up a Jewish state there. For Weizmann—and, in the end, for the overwhelming majority of Zionists—the only possible location was Palestine, in those days a small backward province of the Ottoman empire. That was where the holy places were and the reminders of the last Jewish kingdom, destroyed by the Romans. When Weizmann was once asked why the Jews had a right to Palestine, he simply replied: "Memory is right."

Weizmann despised assimilated Jews and those who would not support Zionism. They were blind; worse, they were unpatriotic. "The essential point which most Jews overlook," he said about the German Jews he had known as a student, "and which forms the very crux of the Jewish tragedy, is that those Jews who are giving their energies and their brains to the Germans are doing it in their capacity as Germans, and are enriching Germany and not Jewry, which they are abandoning." A Jewish home in Palestine was essential. "Palestine," he insisted, "and the building up of a Jewish nation from within, with its own forces and its own traditions, would establish the status of the Jews, would create a type of 100% Jew."[4]

By 1914 Weizmann had established himself in Manchester as a reader (assistant professor) in biochemistry at the university. He had also risen in the Zionist organization, which now had 130,000 paid-up members, but he did not have the position he felt he deserved. Jews from the East felt he had become too Anglicized, English Jews that he was too Russian. He had offended too many of the older generation with his criticism of Herzl and too many of his contemporaries with his sarcasm and lack of tolerance for bores. His speeches were lectures, from a platform of superiority. Abba Eban, later Israel's foreign minister, worked for him as a young man: "He revealed a scientist's economy of phrase and emotion, a hard sense of realities, and an almost cruel insistence on telling his Jewish audiences how difficult and complex their Zionist task was going to be." Weizmann became Zionism's leader in the end because there was no one else who could do the job. He frequently grew discouraged, often threatened to resign, but he never gave up on his long-term goal to establish a Jewish state in Palestine. Perhaps his greatest contribution to Zionism was his extraordinary ability to win over key figures, both within the Jewish community and among the world's leaders. "Starting with nothing," he told an opponent, "I, Chaim Weizmann, a *yied* from Pinsk and only *almost* a Professor at a provincial university, have organized the *flower* of Jewry in favour of a project which probably by Rothschild (Lord) and his satellites is considered as mad."[5]

With the war, Weizmann moved up a gear. By his own estimate he had 2,000 meetings with politicians, civil servants, diplomats: anyone who could be useful in gaining Palestine for the Jews. He overcame the offhand distaste for foreigners and Jews among the British upper classes. One forgot, said Cecil, with surprise, his "rather repellent and even sordid exterior" in the face of his "subdued enthusiasm" and "the extraordinary impressiveness of his attitude."[6] Weizmann made a conquest of Cecil; more important, he made one of Cecil's cousin Balfour, foreign secretary after 1916. It was a strange friendship—the intense, committed Jew from the Pale and the charming, worldly Englishman who had drifted through life with such ease—but for Weizmann and Zionism it was crucial.

Balfour has always been hard to pin down: a philosopher who became a politician; an aesthete who loved tennis and golf; ruthless, as the Irish learned to their cost, but invariably kind and polite to his subordinates. When he forgot the name of a favorite thriller writer, he was mildly distressed. "That's always the way," he said sadly, "so ungrateful; so ungrateful." Languid, dressed with casual elegance, with a smile, said one, "like moonlight on a tombstone," he rarely seemed to take himself or anything else seriously. He was a great parliamentary speaker, but he made light of it. "I say what occurs to me," he told Churchill, "and sit down at the end of the first grammatical sentence." He told a lunch party that, alas, he had a strange mental quirk when it came to decisions: "I can remember every argument, repeat all the pros and cons, and even make quite a good speech on the subject. But the conclusion, the decision, is a perfect blank in my mind." His defenders called this a pose, just as his habit of staying in bed all morning was his way of working hard. Others were not so sure. "If you wanted nothing done," said Churchill, "A.J.B. was undoubtedly the best man for the task." Lloyd George was once asked what he thought Balfour's place in history would be. His answer: "He will be just like the scent on a pocket handkerchief."[7]

From his father Balfour inherited a fortune that made him one of the richest men in Britain; from his mother, a deeply religious woman, the

Cecil family tradition of public service and Conservative politics. Like Curzon, who succeeded him in the Foreign Office, he was part of that cosy, aristocratic world where everyone was somehow connected to everyone else. He once nearly got engaged, but the girl he had chosen died of typhoid fever. He never married, and one of his devoted sisters kept house for him. He was attached to his family and friends, but he did not really need them. As he wrote to one, "You are as necessary as you ever were—but how necessary is that? How necessary are any of us to any of us?"[8]

He was clever, fascinated by ideas, and with a great ability to grasp the essence of an argument. He was also curiously, even alarmingly, detached. At the height of German submarine warfare, which threatened to strangle Britain economically, his only response to the daily list of sinkings was "It is very tiresome. These Germans are intolerable." In cabinet meetings, Lloyd George said, Balfour would present a case persuasively and then, after a pause, the other side with equal eloquence, ending with a sigh: "But if you ask me what course I think we ought to take then I must say I feel perplexed." Curzon, who knew him well, came to regard him as an evil and dangerous man:

> His charm of manner, his extraordinary intellectual distinction, his seeming indifference to petty matters, his power of dialectic, his long and honourable career of public service, blinded all but those who knew him from the inside to the lamentable ignorance, indifference and levity of his regime. He never studied his papers, he never knew the facts, at the Cabinet he had seldom read the morning's Foreign Office telegrams, and he never looked ahead. He trusted to his unequalled powers of improvisation to take him through any trouble and enable him to leap lightly from one crisis to another.[9]

It is strange, therefore, that Balfour not only made a commitment to Zionism but that he persisted with it. One of his subordinates thought that he had never really cared about anything else. Was it his early religious upbringing that left him, as it did Lloyd George, with an intimate knowledge of Jewish history? His fascination with the intellectual abilities of Jews? He told Nicolson that Jews were "the most gifted race that mankind has seen since the Greeks of the fifth century." Did he see in Zionism, as he once said, "guardians of a continuity of religious and racial tradition that made the unassimilated Jew a great conservative force in world politics"? In a conversation with House, Balfour remarked that "someone told him, and he was inclined to believe it, that nearly all Bolshevism and disturbances of a like nature, are directly traceable to the Jews of the world.

They seem determined either to have what they want or to upset present civilization." While he found anti-Semitism vulgar, even deplorable, he also grumbled to a close woman friend that he had spent a weekend with too many Jews: "I believe the Hebrews were in an actual majority—and though I have no prejudice against the race (quite the contrary) I began to understand the point of view of those who object to alien immigration." As with so much about Balfour, the workings of his mind and heart remain a mystery. Shortly before he died, one of his favorite nieces heard him say that "on the whole he felt that what he had been able to do for the Jews had been the thing he looked back upon as the most worth his doing."[10]

Balfour met Weizmann for the first time in 1906: "It was from that talk with Weizmann that I saw that the Jewish form of patriotism was unique. Their love of their country refused to be satisfied by the Uganda scheme." In 1914 the two met again and, according to Weizmann, Balfour said with evident emotion, "It is a great cause you are working for; I would like you to come again and again."[11] Balfour was not Weizmann's only conquest. Churchill, Sykes and C. P. Scott all became his supporters. Most important, so did Lloyd George.

Like Balfour, Lloyd George had grown up with the Bible. "I was taught far more about the history of the Jews than about the history of my own land. I could tell you all the kings of Israel. But I doubt whether I could have named half a dozen of the kings of England, and not more of the kings of Wales." And were not the Welsh and the Jews really quite alike: religious, gifted and with a love of learning? Lloyd George was thrilled when British forces captured Jerusalem, "something which generations of the chivalry of Europe failed to attain." His geography of Central Europe may have been shaky but he knew the Holy Land. (Indeed, his sweeping statement that the British mandate of Palestine must run from "Dan to Beersheba" caused endless problems at the Peace Conference as the experts poured over biblical atlases to try to find out what he really meant.)[12]

In his time as minister of munitions during the war, Lloyd George liked to say that he had incurred a particular debt to Weizmann. Britain had been running desperately short of acetone, essential for making explosives. By chance, Weizmann was working on a process for producing it on a large scale. In a grand gesture he made it available to the British for the duration of the war without payment. When Lloyd George asked Weizmann to accept an honor from the king, the answer was "There is nothing I want for myself." When Lloyd George pressed him, Weizmann asked for support for the Zionist cause. "That," claimed Lloyd George in his memoirs, "was the fount and origin of the famous declaration about

the National Home for the Jews in Palestine." (The French had yet another theory; that Lloyd George had a mistress who was the wife of a
prominent Jewish businessman.)[13]

Weizmann and his acetone made a wonderful story but British statesmen, for all their sentiment, would not do anything against Britain's interests. By 1917, these appeared to be converging with Zionist goals.
Weizmann wanted a Jewish Palestine and, as he pointed out, it would need
protection for some years to come. He did not trust the French and was
cool toward the Americans. Britain was not only powerful, but just and
fair; in addition, "the fact that England is a biblical nation accounts for the
spiritual affinity between them and the Jews." With Jewish immigration,
Palestine would become "an Asiatic Belgium" and an important strategic
asset for the British empire. "Palestine is a natural continuation of Egypt
and the barrier separating the Suez Canal from . . . the Black Sea."[14] That
argument made sense to Lloyd George, to the War Office, and to at least
some in the Foreign Office. So much the better if it removed Palestine
from the French, who had been promised it under the Sykes-Picot Agreement, that wartime arrangement among the Allies to divide up the Arab
Middle East. From 1917, with Lloyd George's encouragement, Sykes met
privately with Weizmann and other Zionists. The final, and perhaps most
important, factor in swinging British support behind the Zionists was to
make propaganda among Jews, particularly in the United States, which
had not yet come into the war, and in Russia, where Jews for obvious reasons were lukewarm toward their own government. When alarming
rumors reached London that Germany was thinking of making a public
declaration in favor of Zionism, the British government moved with
speed.

Curzon, who unlike most of his colleagues had actually been to Palestine, thought the Zionist dream absurd. "I cannot conceive a worse
bondage," he said, "to which to relegate an advanced and intellectual community." He also asked an awkward question: "What is to become of the
people of the country?" A much more passionate argument came from
Montagu, the highly strung secretary of state for India, who thought
Zionism a "mischievous political creed, untenable by any patriotic citizen
of the United Kingdom." He himself was a Jew by faith but an Englishman by nationality. Was he now to be told that his true loyalty lay in Palestine? And what would that mean for the rights of Jews as citizens of other
countries? The cabinet discounted these objections and by the end of
October 1917 it had agreed on a formula. Sykes rushed out of the meeting
waving a piece of paper: "Dr. Weizmann, it's a boy!" Balfour announced
British policy in a brief letter to Lord Rothschild, a leading British Jew:

"His Majesty's Government view with favour the establishment in Palestine of national home for the Jewish people, and will use their best endeavours to facilitate the attainment of this object." The words had been chosen with great care. "National home," as the British government insisted repeatedly, did not mean a state. Weizmann and other Zionist leaders were equally careful. There was no intention, they said, of creating a Jewish state right away. It might be different, of course, in some distant future, when more Jews had emigrated to Palestine. Few people were convinced, and perhaps it was not expected that they would be. The day after the declaration was made public, *The Times*'s headline read, "Palestine for the Jews. Official Sympathy." From the start, Jews and non-Jews alike, politicians, diplomats and journalists, talked in terms of a Jewish state.[15]

In the next months, as British forces moved north from Egypt to capture Jerusalem and then the whole of Palestine, what everyone called the Jewish Legion—units of the Royal Fusiliers that had been specially recruited among Jews—went with them. (Vladimir Jabotinsky, the brilliant, abrasive and extremist Russian journalist who had brought the Jewish Legion into existence, marched in its ranks as a second lieutenant.)

When Allenby set up his military administration in Palestine, his first proclamation and all official documents were translated into Hebrew as well as Arabic. In the summer of 1918, with the approval of the British government, the Zionists purchased an estate on a hill in Jerusalem and, in the presence of a crowd that included Allenby and all the senior Allied commanders, Weizmann laid the foundation stones for the Hebrew University. In 1918, too, the British government authorized the dispatch to Palestine of a Zionist commission, headed by Weizmann. Although its instructions were vague—it was to act as a link with the British military administration as well as organizing the local Jews—the commission took on the character of official representative of the Jewish community in Palestine. Moreover, it acted, as British officers sometimes complained, like a government in the making.[16]

Weizmann himself moved cautiously. He easily resisted pressure from a minority of radicals, including Jabotinsky, who demanded an immediate Jewish state. He maneuvered to ensure that the British or the Americans, not the French, who were too imperialistic and too Catholic, became the mandatory power for Palestine. His task was complicated by divisions and rivalries within Zionism. In an echo of the Peace Conference itself, the Americans in the Zionist movement challenged the dominance of the Europeans. The American Zionist delegation to the Peace Conference complained that Weizmann was dictatorial and undemocratic, his draft memorandum on Palestine "too meagre." They demanded a "Jewish

Commonwealth," even a "Jewish state," with a Jewish governor and Jews throughout the administration and a Jewish majority on the executive and legislative councils. Weizmann found the Americans legalistic and politically naïve. "I urge again, our demands not to be a matter of a formula of the Peace Conference, but to be insistently and tirelessly pursued from day to day and from month to month." He got his way partly by threatening, yet again, to resign, partly because the British government made it quite clear that it would not take on the mandate under such conditions. At that stage the Americans were not prepared to challenge him openly. As Felix Frankfurter, the future Supreme Court justice, pointed out: "He has a sway over English public men and over English permanent officials who will continue to govern England when Lloyd George and Balfour will be no more—such as no other Jew in England or on the continent has or can easily acquire."[17]

Most of the leading Zionists went to Paris for the conference. Weizmann kept up his customary rounds of interviews with the powerful and influential. House, as usual, was sympathetic, Wilson gave him forty minutes and Balfour assured him that Palestine would be given generous borders. The French were less forthcoming. "I speak French fluently," Weizmann told Wilson, "but the French and I speak a different language." Weizmann was careful not to talk of a future Jewish state or a Jewish majority in Palestine. On one occasion, though, he used a phrase that came back to haunt the Zionists: that Palestine should "be as Jewish as England was English."[18]

When the Zionist mission appeared before the Supreme Council on February 27, Weizmann was not the only speaker. No American Zionist spoke, partly because their chief spokesman had not arrived from London, but several Europeans did. The Polish writer Nahum Sokolow reminded his listeners of the dreadful plight of the Jews of Eastern Europe: "The hour of deliverance of his unhappy people had struck." Weizmann, who stood watching him, later recalled, "I could see Sokolow's face and without being sentimental, it was as if two thousand years of Jewish suffering rested on his shoulders." Menachem Ussishkin, a forceful Russian Jew, spoke in Hebrew, the ancient language which was now coming to life again. The final speakers—André Spire, a poet and leading figure in French Zionism, and Sylvain Lévy, a distinguished scholar—had been added to the delegation at the insistence of the French government and over the strenuous objections of Weizmann and his colleagues. What they feared happened: where the Zionist mission claimed to speak for the vast majority of Jews, Spire and Lévy showed a more complicated picture. They pointed out, quite correctly, that only a minority of French Jews were Zionists.

They themselves were proud to be French (as Lévy said, "Jewish in senti-ment, but French above all"). They requested that France's ancient rights in Palestine, which included acting as protector for Catholics, be main-tained and suggested that France, as a Mediterranean nation and a great force for civilization in the world, would be the most suitable nation to take on the mandate.[19]

French Foreign Ministry officials looked on approvingly. (Lévy, said Weizmann contemptuously, looked as if he had been hypnotized.) The French had supported the idea of a Jewish homeland during the war, mainly for propaganda reasons, but there was no need in peacetime to give up French claims in Palestine, claims that, as colonialists never tired of pointing out, went back to the Crusades. French officials attached to the military occupation in Palestine were conspicuously devout. The British had no idea, Picot told Ronald Storrs, the military governor of Jerusalem, of the rejoicing in France when the Holy City had been taken from the Turks. Storrs replied briskly: "Think what it must have been for us who took it." Before the Zionist mission presented its case to the Supreme Council, a senior official informed Spire, "we are anxious for a French Zionist to make a statement favourable to Zionism, but you should try to make it clear that France must have Palestine."[20]

Lévy did even better, at least from the French point of view. Speaking at considerable length, he said firmly that he was not a Zionist at all. He pointed to the problems that would be caused if all the Jews in Eastern Europe, who Weizmann claimed were simply waiting for the signal to move to Palestine, actually did so. The country was not yet capable of sup-porting a large population. (In fact, although he would not have admitted it publicly, Weizmann shared this concern.) Lévy also raised a serious question: Was a Jewish home the right thing for Jews? "It seemed to him shocking that the Jews, as soon as their rights of equality were about to be recognised in all countries of the world, should already seek to obtain ex-ceptional privileges for themselves in Palestine." How could Jews around the world, as some Zionist leaders had suggested, share in the government of Palestine? "It would be dangerous to create a precedent whereby cer-tain people who already possessed the rights of citizenship in one country would be called upon to govern and to exercise other rights of citizenship in a new country." Jews already came under suspicion; "as a Frenchman of Jewish origin, he feared the results." The argument was the same as Mon-tagu had made in his attack on the Balfour Declaration. "A shameful spec-tacle," Weizmann had said of Montagu and now he turned on Lévy, hissing "Je ne vous connais plus. Vous êtes un traître." ("I no longer know you. You are a traitor.")[21]

No decision was made on Palestine that day, or for months to come, and it barely came up at subsequent meetings of the Peace Conference. As so often happened in Paris, an issue that was to cause increasing trouble over the years was scarcely considered at all. "The Palestinians are very bitter over the Balfour Declaration," reported an American intelligence officer in 1917. "They are convinced that the Zionist leaders wish and intend to create a distinctly Jewish community and they believe that if Zionism proves to be a success, their country will be lost to them even though their religious and political rights be protected." The Balfour Declaration had promised such protection for what it called "the existing non-Jewish communities in Palestine," a curious formulation when Palestinian Arabs, most of them Muslim but including some Christians, made up about four fifths of a population of some 700,000. It also reflected a tendency on the part of both the world's statesmen and Zionist leaders to see Palestine as somehow empty. "If the Zionists do not go there," said Sykes firmly, "some one will, nature abhors a vacuum." A British Zionist is supposed to have coined the phrase "The land without people—for the people without land."[22]

Even those who recognized that there were Arabs living in Palestine tended to view them through the spectacles of Western imperialism. The Zionist settlers who arrived there before the war were frequently surprised at how "Oriental" and primitive their new land was. They and their leaders talked hopefully, for many of them were progressive and liberal, of how their presence would tug the Arabs out of their tradition-bound lives and help them to move forward. Herzl assured a member of a prominent Arab family that prosperity would grow throughout Palestine. "If one looks at the matter from this point of view, and it is the correct view, one inevitably becomes a friend of Zionism." There would be no need for Arabs to think of self-government. Yet even before 1914, there were signs that nationalism and a corresponding unease at the Zionist presence were starting to stir among the Palestinian Arabs. Weizmann, who when he talked about the Palestinians sometimes sounded like a British district officer in India, at first discounted this: "The Arabs, who are superficially clever and quickwitted, worship one thing, and one thing only— power and success." The innocence, and the incomprehension, were breathtaking—and dangerous.[23]

Even in 1919, the British in Palestine were finding themselves caught between Zionists and Arabs. The Zionists complained, with some truth, that the military authorities were at best insensitive, at worst anti-Semitic. Jabotinsky, from the Jewish Legion, said that the British could deal with the Arabs, "just the same old 'natives' whom the Englishman has ruled and led for centuries, nothing new, no problems." The Zionists were a different matter: "a problem from top to toe, a problem bristling with difficulties in every way—small in numbers, yet somehow strong and influential, ignorant of English, yet imbued with European culture, claiming complicated claims."[24] (Jabotinsky's own contribution to the problems was to organize an underground army.)

The British, of course, had created their own dilemma by making promises during the war that they could not now fulfill. On the one hand they had supported a Jewish homeland on land largely inhabited by Arabs, and on the other they had encouraged the Arabs to revolt against their Ottoman rulers with the promise of Arab independence. When the Arabs pointed out that Palestine had not been exempted from the land to come under Arab rule, the British accused them of ingratitude. "I hope," noted Balfour, "remembering all that, they will not begrudge that small notch, for it is no more geographically, whatever it may be historically—that small notch in what are now Arab territories being given to the people who for all these hundreds of years have been separated from it."[25]

The Arabs did begrudge it, particularly the Palestinian Arabs. The Balfour Declaration in 1917 and the arrival of the Zionist commission in 1918, the waving of the blue and white Zionist flag throughout Palestine, the tactless demand of a Zionist conference in Jaffa that the name of the area immediately be changed to Eretz Israel ("the Land of Israel"), all worried them exceedingly. Curzon had warned about this: "If we were supposed to have identified ourselves with the Jews, and the whole Arab force backed by Feisal on the other side were thrown into the scale against us, that would produce complications."[26] Complications there were to be.

In an attempt to avoid the consequences of their own actions, the British encouraged the Zionists and Arab nationalists to come to terms. When Weizmann visited Palestine in 1918, the Foreign Office urged him to remember that "it is most important that everything should be done to . . . allay Arab suspicions regarding the true aims of Zionism." When Storrs, the military governor of Jerusalem, gave a dinner party for the Zionist visitors and local notables, Weizmann made a gracious speech: "There was room for both to work side by side; let his hearers beware of treacherous insinuations that Zionists were seeking political power—rather let both progress together until they were ready for joint autonomy." That summer, Weizmann and Feisal met in Feisal's camp near the Gulf of Aqaba. The meeting was amiable, even friendly, and Weizmann put on Arab headdress for a photograph of the two of them. Both agreed that they did not trust the French. Feisal appeared well disposed toward a Zionist presence in Palestine but warned that he had to be careful of Arab opinion. He could not, in any case, make a definite commitment without consulting his father. Weizmann left with the impression that Feisal did not place much value on Palestine: "He is contemptuous of the Palestinian Arabs whom he doesn't even regard as Arabs!"[27]

Later in the year, after the war had ended, they met again, this time in London. Again all went well. Weizmann assured Feisal that the Zionists could use their influence to get American support for the Arabs, and Feisal in return indicated that he did not foresee any trouble over Palestine. "It was curious there should be any friction between Jews and Arabs," he told Weizmann. After all, there was plenty of land to go around. On January 3, 1919, the two signed their agreement full of expressions of goodwill and hope for the future: Jewish immigration to Palestine would be encouraged, while the Zionists would lend their assistance to developing the independent Arab state which presumably was about to be set up by the Peace Conference. Feisal scrawled a brief proviso to the effect that his consent depended on the British carrying out their promises to the Arabs. The agreement, always improbable, vanished into the widening gulf between Feisal and the British and between Jews and Arabs in Palestine.[28]

The fate of Palestine rested, as it had done for centuries, with outside powers and in 1919 that meant mainly Britain and France. Italy tried to smuggle in some Italian priests disguised as soldiers during the military occupation to further its halfhearted claims to protect Christians in the Holy Land. The main Italian concern, however, was to ensure that France did not get anything that Italy did not.

The United States, in contrast to what happened after the Second World War, played a minor role. The American government had quietly approved the Balfour Declaration and Wilson himself was sympathetic to Zionism. "To think," he told a leading New York rabbi, "that I the son of the manse should be able to help restore the Holy Land to its people." It would do the Jews good, he thought, to enjoy their own nationality. He even contemplated, although only briefly, an American mandate for Palestine. But then there was the sacred tenet of self-determination. Why should the wishes of a minority of Jews prevail over those of a much larger number of Arabs? Balfour and Louis Brandeis, a Supreme Court justice and the leading American Zionist, came up with an ingenious solution. It was wrong to use mere "numerical self-determination": a great many potential inhabitants of the Jewish home in Palestine still lived outside its borders. "And Zionism," said Balfour, "be it right or wrong, good or bad, is rooted in age-long traditions, in present needs, in future hopes of far profounder import than the desires and prejudices of the 700,000 Arabs who now inhabit that ancient land." In any case, he pointed out, reverting to the language of the old diplomacy, the Great Powers were behind Zionism. Wilson nevertheless insisted that his Commission of Inquiry into the Middle East include Palestine. The two American commissioners, Charles Crane and Henry King, the businessman and the professor, reported back at the end of the summer of 1919 that the Arabs in Palestine were "emphatically against the entire Zionist program" and recommended that the Peace Conference limit Jewish immigration and give up the idea of making Palestine a Jewish homeland. Nobody paid the slightest attention.[29]

Where Palestine was concerned, the main issue by this point was its future borders. Lloyd George's airy talk of a land stretching from Dan to Beersheba worried the French, who saw it as enlarging Palestine in the north at the expense of Syria. Did Dan include the Litani River and the upper reaches of the Jordan? Water was always an important consideration in the Middle East. The Zionists pushed for the most generous border. "It is absolutely essential," Weizmann argued, "for the economic development of Palestine that this line be drawn so as to include the territories east of the Jordan which are capable of receiving and maintaining large Jewish mass settlements." His borders would have included part of today's Jordan. The British government supported him for its own ends: to limit French influence and to protect railway routes (even though the railways did not yet exist) between Mesopotamia and the Mediterranean. The Quai d'Orsay protested: Palestine would stretch right up to the suburbs of Damascus.[30] Clemenceau refused to concede any more to the Zionists or, as he saw it, to Britain. The border between Syria and Palestine remained substantially where it had been set by the Sykes-Picot Agreement. The French conceded only that Palestine could use surplus water from Syria; this has caused trouble down to the present day.

In April 1920, at San Remo, Britain and France set the final terms of their agreements on the Middle East. Britain got the Palestine mandate. (Its terms included carrying out the Balfour Declaration.) The French made one last attempt to keep their old rights to protect Christians. With an alacrity that suggests a previous deal with the British, the Italians said that, with the disappearance of the Ottoman empire and a "civilized nation" taking over in Palestine, it was no longer necessary to have special arrangements. At the end of the conference Lloyd George said to Weizmann, who had rushed over from Palestine: "Now you have got your start, it all depends on you."[31] The Palestinian Arabs were not represented in San Remo but they had made their feelings clear in the riots against Jews that had broken out in Palestine two weeks earlier.

All that remained was to draw up the details of the mandate and get it ratified by the League of Nations. This took another two years, mainly because it proved impossible to sign a treaty with Ottoman Turkey. The British simply carried on as though Palestine were officially theirs. Mindful of its promises to the Arabs, the British government, at the urging of Churchill, now colonial secretary, divided the mandate in two, with Palestine confined to the area west of the Jordan and a new little Arab state of Transjordan under the rule of Feisal's brother Abdullah. Weizmann was disappointed. He had stressed to Churchill that the lands east of the Jordan had always been "an integral and vital part of Palestine." The soil was rich, the climate "invigorating," and there was plenty of water. "Jewish settlement," he concluded optimistically, "could proceed on a large scale without friction with the local population."[32] The Zionists, however, were not prepared to antagonize the British over the issue. It was much more important to ensure that the terms of the mandate were written in their favor.

This was not easy. Among the British, the realization was dawning that a Jewish homeland in Palestine meant trouble for Britain. Curzon spoke for many in the Foreign Office when he told Balfour, "Personally, I am so convinced that Palestine will be a rankling thorn in the flesh of whoever is charged with its Mandate, that I would withdraw from this responsibility while we yet can." Zionism had produced what had not previously existed, an organized Palestinian Arab opinion, which learned rapidly to use letters of protest, petitions and the language of self-determination. On the streets of Jerusalem mobs took more direct action; from 1920 on the British authorities had to deal with sporadic outbreaks of violence there and elsewhere against Jews. Churchill was usually sympathetic to Zionism, but he warned Lloyd George: "Palestine is costing us 6 millions a year to hold. The Zionist movement will cause continued friction with the Arabs. The French ensconced in Syria with *4 divisions* (paid for by not paying us what they owe us) are opposed to the Zionist movement & will try to cushion the Arabs off on to us as the real enemy."[33]

The British grasped at one expedient after another. Perhaps the Arabs and the Zionists might still come to an understanding. In the summer of 1921 a delegation of Palestinian Arabs traveled to London. Churchill listened with a certain amount of impatience to their rambling complaints about the Zionists. (He dodged the awkward question posed by their leader, "What is this promise that you made and what does it mean?") "Have a good talk with Dr. Weizmann," he advised the Arabs. "Try to arrange something with him for the next few years." Neither side was prepared to talk seriously to the other. "Political blackmailers" and "trash" was Weizmann's view.[34] The Arabs simply repeated that they refused to recognize the Balfour Declaration and anything done in its name.

At this point the British toned down the language of the mandate to imply that the Jewish national home would merely be in Palestine rather than occupying the whole. In place of the duty of the mandatory power to develop a self-governing commonwealth, they substituted "self-governing institutions." Weizmann, traveling endlessly, firing off telegrams and letters, calling on all his extensive contacts, struggled to prevent the British government from making the terms even weaker. He wrote in despair to Albert Einstein: "All the shady characters of the world are at work, against us. Rich servile Jews, dark fanatic Jewish obscurantists, in combination with the Vatican, with Arab assassins, English imperialist anti-Semitic reactionaries—in short, all the dogs are howling." He was not as alone as he felt. Support kept coming, often from unexpected quarters such as German Zionists, Anglican clergy or Italian Catholics. The United States Congress roused itself from its introspective, isolationist mood to pass resolutions in favor of the Jewish national home. And Weizmann's chief British allies remained firm. In a private meeting at Balfour's house on July 22, 1921, Lloyd George and Balfour assured him that "they had always meant an eventual Jewish state." When the awkward issue of Zionist gunrunning into Palestine came up, Churchill winked: "We won't mind it, but don't speak of it." All present agreed that the Palestinian Arab delegation was a nuisance. Why not bribe them, Lloyd George suggested cheerfully? The prime minister was full of helpful ideas. "You ought," he told Balfour, "to make a big speech again in the Albert Hall on Zionism."[35]

In July 1922 the League of Nations approved the Palestine mandate brought before it by the British government. In Palestine, an Arab congress rejected the mandate completely. Weizmann was elated: the mandate gave official recognition to the Jews as a people. This was, however, only the end of the first chapter of the Jewish struggle; "if only we go on working and working in Palestine, the time will come when there will be another opportunity of giving the Mandate its true value."[36] That opportunity was to come in a terrible and unexpected fashion with the rise of Hitler and the Second World War.

Balfour visited Palestine for the first time in 1925, with Weizmann and his wife. In Jerusalem, he opened the new Hebrew University with a stirring speech in which he talked proudly of his own share in the establishment of a Jewish home. He was touched by the reception he received throughout Palestine from Jews but failed to notice the Arabs in mourning and the shops closed in protest. His private secretary destroyed the hundreds of angry telegrams he received from Arabs before he could see them. When he and his party moved on to Syria to do some sightseeing, the French authorities mounted a guard around him, much to his annoyance. In Damascus, his hotel was surrounded by an excited crowd of 6,000

Arabs. As the paving stones started to fly and the French cavalry fired back, Balfour watched bemused. A young Arab attached to his party tried to explain why there was such opposition to Zionism. Balfour merely replied that he found the results of his experiment "extraordinarily interesting." He sailed back to Europe on the *Sphinx*.[37]

Atatürk and the Breaking of Sèvres

A T THE BEGINNING of May 1919, the fitful discussions about the Ottoman empire received an unwelcome jolt from Italian moves in Asia Minor. The Italians had landed forces in Turkey for brief periods during the winter, ostensibly to protect Italian nationals, or, on one occasion, a convent. Now their troops appeared to be settling in at the ports of Adalia (Antalya) in the south and at Marmaris, facing the island of Rhodes, both on territory that Italy was claiming under its wartime agreements. Reports came in of an Italian battleship at the port of Smyrna (Izmir) and on May 11 Eleutherios Venizelos told the Council of Four that Italian working parties were building jetties at Scala Nuova (Kuşadası), slightly to the south. He also alleged that the Italians had done a secret deal with the Turks. The peacemakers were ready to believe the worst. "I am not inclined to let the Italians do what they want in that part of the world," said Wilson. "I distrust their intentions. If I published in America all that we know about their activity and intrigues, it would cause their infernal machine to hang fire."[1]

Lloyd George and Clemenceau shared Wilson's irritation but were constrained by their wartime commitments. In the Treaty of London of 1915, which had brought Italy into the war, they had promised that, if Turkey were divided up, Italy would get "a just share." The language was dangerously vague, suggesting that Italy might get a large piece of the coast of Asia Minor, certainly the Turkish province of Adalia and territories around it, and perhaps as far north as Smyrna and south to Adana, just where the coast of Asia Minor curves south again. That is certainly what the Italians assumed. It was awkward that, under the Sykes-Picot Agreement between Britain and France, the French also had a claim to the area around Adana. The Italian government had not seen the agreement when it was made, but it had heard enough to make it uneasy. Sonnino had asked repeatedly for clarification; he finally got it at the little Alpine town of St.-Jean-de-Maurienne in April 1917. Lloyd George remembered the meetings as being as cool as the snow which still lay on the ground. Sonnino was "flushed with suppressed anger." Britain and France grudgingly conceded a bigger share of the Turkish territories; Italy was to have direct control of a great rectangle in the south of Asia Minor which included the important port of Smyrna, and a large wedge to the north of Smyrna would be an Italian zone of influence. Lloyd George said sharply to Sonnino, "You want us to do the work and hand it over to you at the end of the war." Although both Britain and France subsequently claimed that the agreement was invalid on the grounds that it depended on Russian consent (which did not come because of the revolution), the Italian government insisted that it was still owed its share of Asia Minor.[2]

Italian nationalists called on the memory of the great Roman empire to bolster their claims (although when the Greeks recalled their even older empire, Italians dismissed it as "empty Hellenic megalomania"). They pointed to Italy's need for raw materials (the coal mines at Erëgli, or Heracleum as the Italians preferred to call it, were a particular favorite) and for outlets for investment and goods. Italy would protect Christians generally and Italian settlers in particular, and would civilize the Turks. The chief of the general staff in 1918 painted a lyrical picture of the future Italian zone: "The climate there is suitable for our emigrants, the fertility is well known, as the corn bears fiftyfold; finally the existence of immense uncultivated areas is proved by the population density, which, including the towns is at present less than twenty-seven persons per square km; the population itself would then have everything to gain and nothing to lose by Italian colonization." In reality, most Italians preferred to invest their money safely at home; and emigrants, as the experience of Italy's few colonies had shown, preferred the Americas. "Italians," admitted Orlando, "generally did not care a bit about Asia Minor, nor about colonies in Africa."[3]

Sonnino took the straightforward view that Asia Minor was part of the spoils of war and Italy would take its share. As he put it, either all the powers got something or no one did. He told the Italian high commissioner in Constantinople that Italy's rivals were cunningly using the doctrine of self-determination to deny Italian claims for annexation and spheres of influence. This must be countered by getting locals to demand Italian protection; Sonnino urged his high commissioner to do this carefully and quietly. His main concern, however, was the Adriatic, and he was prepared to bargain away far-off claims for solid gains closer to home.[4]

As the crisis with Italy over Fiume and the Adriatic worsened at the end of April, Lloyd George and Clemenceau were prepared to use Asia Minor as bait. As Lloyd George told Wilson, "What would perhaps bring M. Sonnino towards us would be a concession in Asia." It was dangerous, murmured Balfour, but it was important to appease the Italians: "Unfortunately, this necessity haunts and hampers every step in our diplomacy." Wilson resisted. "Italy," he pointed out, "lacks experience in the administration of colonies." Furthermore, the Turks would dislike Italian rule. Lloyd George fell back on history—"The Romans were very good governors of colonies"—and a surprising view of the Turks as "a docile people, who have never cut railroads, nor anything of the kind." Wilson was unimpressed: "Unfortunately the modern Italians are not the Romans." He also pointed out that the Greeks, who presumably would get some sort of mandate in Asia Minor, did not like the Italians: "The Patriarch of Constantinople, who came to see me the other day, expressed to me, with the reserve of an ecclesiastic, a very marked feeling against the possibility of seeing the Italians become his neighbours."[5]

During the first week of May, by which time the Italians were boycotting the Peace Conference, the British and French cooled on the idea of tempting them back with morsels of the Ottoman empire. On May 2, when the Big Three met, more reports of Italian moves along the coast of Asia Minor were coming in. "Madness," said Lloyd George. Clemenceau was for a tough line: "If we don't take precautions, they will hold us by the throat." Wilson threatened to send an American battleship to either Fiume or Smyrna. Lloyd George said that Venizelos had offered to send a Greek warship.[6]

Venizelos was in his element, stirring up feeling against the Italians and offering help to the powers. He had been working hard from the start of the Peace Conference to press Greek claims, with mixed success; the crisis was, as he recognized, Greece's great opportunity. Although Venizelos tried to argue that the coast of Asia Minor was indisputably Greek in character, and the Turks in a minority, his statistics were highly dubious. For the inland territory he was claiming, where even he had to admit that the Turks were in a majority, Venizelos called in economic arguments. The whole area (the Turkish provinces of Aidin and Brusa [Bursa] and the areas around the Dardanelles and Ismid) was a geographic unit that belonged to the Mediterranean; it was warm, well watered, fertile, opening out to the world, unlike the dry, Asiatic plateau of the hinterland. "The Turks were good workers, honest in their relations, and a good people as subjects," he told the Supreme Council at his first appearance in February. "But as rulers they were insupportable and a disgrace to civilisation, as was proved by their having exterminated over a million Armenians and 300,000 Greeks during the last four years." To show how reasonable he was being, he renounced any claims to the ancient Greek settlements at Pontus on the eastern end of the Black Sea. He would not listen to petitions from the Pontine Greeks, he assured House's assistant, Bonsal: "I have told them that I cannot claim the south shore of the Black Sea, as my hands are quite full with Thrace and Anatolia." There was a slight conflict with Italian claims, but he was confident the two countries could come to a friendly agreement. They had, in fact, already tried and it had been clear that neither was prepared to back down, especially on Smyrna.[7]

The thriving port of Smyrna lay at the heart of Greek claims. It had been Greek in the great Hellenic past, and in the nineteenth century had become predominantly Greek again as immigrants from the Greek mainland had flocked there to take advantage of the new railways which stretched into the hinterland and opportunities for trade and investment. The population was at least a quarter of a million before the war and more Greeks lived there than in Athens itself. They dominated the exports—from figs to opium to carpets—which coursed down from the Anatolian plateau in Asia Minor. Smyrna was a Greek city, a center of Greek learning and nationalism—but it was also a crucial part of the Turkish economy.

When Venizelos reached out for Smyrna and its hinterland, he was going well beyond what could be justified in terms of self-determination. He was also putting Greece into a dangerous position. Taking the fertile valleys of western Asia Minor as they sloped up toward the dry Anatolian highlands was perhaps necessary, as he argued, to protect the Greek colonies along the coast. From another perspective, though, it created a Greek province with a huge number of non-Greeks as well as a long line to defend against anyone who chose to attack from central Anatolia. His great rival General Ioannis Metaxas, later dictator of Greece, warned of this repeatedly: "The Greek state is not today ready for the government and exploitation of so extensive a territory."[8] Metaxas was right.

The Commission on Greek and Albanian Affairs, which was expected to come up with a rational solution to all the competing claims on Ottoman territory, not surprisingly failed to do so. The Italians opposed Greek claims outright and the British and French were sympathetic. The American experts, who were prepared to admit Greece's claims in Europe, felt they could not, in good conscience, do so in Asia Minor. The Turks were in the majority in the area as a whole and, even though Smyrna was Greek, it would be wrong on economic grounds to sever it from Turkey. As the American expert William Linn Westermann said, "Smyrna and its harbor are the eyes, the mouth, and the nostrils of the people of Anatolia." Nor did the Americans accept the argument that the Turks were so backward that they needed outside rule. "It is the consensus of opinion," said an American expert, "of American missionaries, who know him through and through, of American, British, and French archeologists who have worked for years beside and with him, of British merchants who have traded with him, of British soldiers who have fought against him, that the Anatolian Turk is as honest as any other people of the Near East, that he is a hard-working farmer, a brave and generous fighter, endowed fundamentally with chivalrous instincts."[9]

The commission's report simply presented both views. Wilson might well have backed the position of his own experts if his exasperation with the Italians had not made him willing to listen to Venizelos, who was making sure that the Big Three, as they now were, received alarming reports of dubious veracity of Greeks being massacred by Turks and of the way in which the Italians were, so he said, working hand in glove with the Turks. To Nicolson, one of the British experts on the commission, Venizelos boasted happily, "I have received assurances of comfort and support from Lloyd George and Wilson." Lloyd George had already agreed that a Greek cruiser should go to Smyrna, and Venizelos saw an opening to send Greek forces into Asia Minor as a counterbalance to the Italians. He and Venizelos had a private dinner in early May. Frances Stevenson, who was present, noted in her diary: "The two have a great admiration for each other, & D. is trying to get Smyrna for the Greeks, though he is having trouble with the Italians over it." What Venizelos remembered from the evening was that Lloyd George was hopeful he could get Constantinople as well for the Greeks.[10]

On the morning of May 6, the Allies casually took the decision that set in train the events that destroyed, among many other things, Smyrna itself, Venizelos's great dream and Lloyd George's governing coalition. In the Council of Four, Lloyd George pressed for a decision on Smyrna. If they did not act, he said, the Italians would get away with grabbing a piece of Asia Minor. Greek troops were available; they could be told to land wherever there was a danger of disturbances or massacres. "Why not tell them to land now?" replied Wilson. "Do you have any objection?" "None," said Lloyd George. Clemenceau put in: "I don't have any either. But must we notify the Italians?" "Not in my opinion," said Lloyd George. The Italians, who returned to the Peace Conference the following day, were told that their allies had been obliged to take action in their absence to prevent imminent massacres. When Sonnino asked why the Great Powers had not sent their own contingents, Clemenceau claimed that it would be difficult to place them under a Greek general. He assured

Sonnino that "today Smyrna belongs to no one; it is not a question of determining the fate of that city, but of carrying out a temporary operation with a well-defined objective." Clemenceau had in fact temporarily fallen under Venizelos's spell: "Ulysses," he told Mordacq, "is only a small man beside him. He is a diplomat of the first rank, very sensible, very well prepared, very shrewd, always knowing what he wants."[11]

The afternoon after that fateful decision Lloyd George asked Venizelos for a quick interview before the Council of Four met. Venizelos wrote in his diary that Lloyd George started with a simple question:

> LLOYD GEORGE: Do you have troops available?
> VENIZELOS: We do. For what purpose?
> LLOYD GEORGE: President Wilson, M. Clemenceau and I decided today
> that you should occupy Smyrna.
> VENIZELOS: We are ready.

Venizelos was full of optimism as he met with the Big Three and their military advisers to arrange the details. His troops were ready, the Turks would offer no resistance and the Greek inhabitants of Smyrna would welcome them. Lloyd George and Venizelos agreed that it would be best if French and English troops occupied the forts at the entrance to the harbor and then turned them over to the Greeks. Clemenceau went along, with some reluctance; he was beginning to have cold feet, especially about antagonizing the Italians needlessly. Wilson was torn between his wish to act within the letter of the law and his distaste for the Italians. In the end he supported the occupation, which was scheduled for May 15. "The whole thing," wrote Henry Wilson, the British military expert, "is mad and bad."[12]

In Smyrna itself the mood was tense. Agents of the Greek government had been there since the end of the war, trying to stir up popular enthusiasm for Greek rule. The British and French representatives watched sympathetically, the Italians with hostility. The Turkish minority was deeply uneasy. When news spread that the Greeks were coming, the city erupted with demonstrations. Several thousand Turks banged drums during the night in protest; a much larger number of excited Greeks gathered along the waterfront on the morning of May 15. The Orthodox bishop stood ready to bless the soldiers. The blue-and-white flag of Greece flew everywhere. As the first Greek troops marched into town, the crowds cheered and wept. It was like a holiday, until suddenly a shot was fired by somebody outside a Turkish barracks. Greek soldiers started firing wildly, and when Turkish soldiers stumbled out of the barracks in surrender, the

Greeks beat them and prodded them along toward the waterfront with bayonets. The Greek onlookers went wild and joined in. Some thirty Turks died. All over Smyrna mobs sprang up, killing and looting. By the evening, between 300 and 400 Turks and 100 Greeks were dead. The disorder spread out into the surrounding countryside and towns in the following days.[13] It was a disaster for the Greeks and Greek claims, and a foretaste of what was to come.

Throughout Turkey the news of the landings was received with consternation. They seemed to many a first step to the partition of the Turkish parts of the Ottoman empire. "After I learned about the details of the Smyrna occupation," a woman who was an early supporter of Atatürk remembered, "I hardly opened my mouth on any subject except when it concerned the sacred struggle which was to be." In Constantinople, crowds marched with black flags. A delegation of upper-class women made an unprecedented call on the British high commissioner. "A slice had been cut," said their spokeswoman, "from the living body of the Ottoman Empire of which she was a member and by that act a bleeding member." In his palace, the sultan wept. His ministers talked impotently about making a protest. Atatürk, who happened to be there, asked, "Do you think your protest will make the Greeks or the British retire?" When the ministers shrugged, he added: "There are perhaps more definite measures that might be taken."[14]

Atatürk had by now decided that the place to be was the interior, where there were troops and officers loyal to nationalist ideals. The problem was how to get there. His dilemma was solved inadvertently by the British occupation authorities, who insisted that the government send out an officer to restore law and order. Atatürk managed to get himself appointed with sweeping powers for the whole of Anatolia. He felt, he would later say, "as if a cage had been opened, and as if I were a bird ready to open my wings and fly through the sky." The day after the Greeks landed in Smyrna, he left Constantinople with a visa from the British. Four days later, on May 19, he and his small party landed at the Black Sea port of Samsun. That day is now a national public holiday in the Turkey he created. Few people in Constantinople had any idea of what he intended, and it was to be many months before the first hints of what was brewing in Anatolia reached Paris. Lloyd George later claimed that "no information had been received as to his activities in Asia Minor in reorganising the shattered and depleted armies of Turkey. Our military intelligence had never been more thoroughly unintelligent."[15]

Atatürk and his friends took a terrific gamble, one that might have failed had it not been for the help that the Allies unwittingly gave them in

the next months. Allied policies were confused, inept and risky—and created the ideal conditions for Turkish nationalism to flourish. The decision
to allow Italian and then Greek forces to land on the coast of Asia Minor,
the indications that Armenia and Kurdistan would be set up as separate
states, and the possibility that the whole area around the straits, including
Constantinople itself, would be stripped away from Turkey, left Turkish
nationalists with their backs to the wall. Their country was vanishing; they
had little to lose by resistance. Every delay in Paris in settling the treaty
with the Ottoman empire saw Allied forces grow weaker and Atatürk's
stronger.

Across the sun-baked Anatolian plateau that summer of 1919 Atatürk
moved incessantly, sometimes in his old car, sometimes by train, more
often by horseback, gathering like-minded officers about him and weav-
ing the independent groups that had sprung up to protest the Allied occupation into the basis of a nationalist movement. "If we have no weapons
to fight with," he promised, "we shall fight with our teeth and nails." In
June, he announced the start of national resistance, against the Greeks in
Smyrna, the French in the south and the Armenians in the east. "We must
pull on our peasant shoes, we must withdraw to the mountains, we must
defend the country to the last rock. If it is the will of God that we be defeated, we must set fire to all our homes, to all our property; we must lay
the country in ruins and leave it an empty desert." As reports filtered back
to Constantinople, the British pressed the sultan's government to recall
their inspector-general. When Atatürk received the order on June 23 to return to Constantinople, he resigned his commission and called a congress
at Erzurum, which issued what became the national pact. Its key provision
was that the lands inhabited by Turks, including of course Constantinople, must remain a whole.[16]

From June 1919 onward, the fate of the remainder of the Ottoman
empire depended less and less on what was happening in Paris and more
and more on Atatürk's moves. Two different worlds—one of international
conferences, lines on maps, peoples moving obediently into this country
or that, and the other of a people shaking off their Ottoman past and
awakening as a Turkish nation—were heading toward collision. In Paris,
the powers continued on their way, largely unaware of what was stirring
to the east. The horse-trading of hypothetical mandates went merrily on.

On May 13, two days before the Greek invasion, Harold Nicolson was
summoned with his map to Lloyd George's flat in the Rue Nitot to explain to him how much he could offer to the Italians. Orlando and Sonnino arrived and the party sat around the dining room table. Nicolson
said, "The appearance of a pie about to be distributed is thus enhanced."

The Italians asked for land to the south of Smyrna. "Oh no!" said Lloyd George, "you can't have that—it's all full of Greeks!" Nicolson realized with consternation that Lloyd George had mistaken the colors indicating contours for population distribution. "Ll.G. takes this correction with great good humour. He is as quick as a kingfisher." When someone pointed out that mandates must be with "the consent and wishes of the people concerned," there was great jollity. "Orlando's white cheeks wobble with laughter and his puffy eyes fill up with tears of mirth."[17]

Later that afternoon, Nicolson's map lay on the carpet in front of Clemenceau, Wilson and Lloyd George as its owner waited outside reading *The Picture of Dorian Gray*. Inside, in Wilson's study, Lloyd George sketched out an Italian mandate in southern Anatolia in glowing terms: "Where the Turks made a wilderness, the Italians can build roads, railways, irrigate the soil and cultivate it." The French could take the north of Anatolia and the Greeks would have Smyrna and its surroundings, as well as the Dodecanese islands, and, said Lloyd George magnanimously, he would give them Cyprus as well. Clemenceau, who had been sitting silently by, expressed some doubts about the Greeks' ability to run a mandate: "I covered the entire Peloponnese without seeing a single road." Wilson was for giving them a chance: "By showing them our confidence, we will give them the ambition to do well." Caught up in the spirit of things, Wilson even said that he felt hopeful that the United States would take the mandate for Armenia. Clemenceau said he assumed that the Americans would then take Constantinople as well. Nicolson was called in to take instructions. When Balfour saw these, he was moved to a rare display of anger: "I have three all-powerful, all-ignorant men sitting there and partitioning continents with only a child to take notes for them." He sent a strong memorandum to Lloyd George saying how dangerous it would be to partition Turkey.[18]

Lloyd George also heard from his military advisers, who were almost unanimously opposed. So were Churchill and Montagu, who rushed over from London to warn yet again that cutting up Turkey meant "eternal war" with the Muslim world, including that in India. Lloyd George agreed to receive an Indian delegation, but when it arrived posthaste from London by special train, it found that the prime minister had gone off on a motor tour.[19]

The arrangements made on May 13 fell apart almost immediately. The Italians irritated both Lloyd George and Wilson with new troop landings. Lloyd George completely changed his mind on an Italian mandate: "I believe that to put the Italians into Asia Minor would be to introduce a source of trouble there." He had also been impressed by Montagu's warnings. "I conclude," he told the other leaders when they met on May 19, "that it is impossible to divide Turkey proper. We would run too great a risk of throwing disorder into the Mohammedan world." Wilson agreed that there was such a danger. He also worried that the mandates might look like a division of the spoils, and, as he pointed out, since the Turks themselves had made it clear that they wanted a single state, it would be awkward if not wrong to divide Anatolia between an Italian and a French mandate. There was no justification for destroying Turkey's sovereignty: "I am forced to remind myself that I, myself, used this word in the Fourteen Points, and that these have become a kind of treaty which binds us." Perhaps, he suggested, France could take on the responsibility for advising a Turkish state, and they might avoid the word "mandate." They could even leave the sultan in Constantinople, without of course letting him have any power over the straits. Lloyd George was at first amenable but two days later, after meeting with appalled members of the British cabinet, who had come over to Paris especially, he came back with a suggestion for American control, rather than French, over the whole of Anatolia, as well as the straits and Armenia.[20]

This infuriated Clemenceau, who had been watching with some bewilderment. He was already angry with Lloyd George over Syria. "You say that France mustn't be in Asia Minor because that would displease Italy: do you think there is no public opinion in France? France is, moreover, of all Europe, the country with the greatest economic and financial interests in Turkey—and here she is thrown out to please first the Mohammedans, and then Italy." He and Lloyd George got into a furious argument about the division of not just Turkey but the whole of the Middle East. "Both lost their tempers violently and made the most absurd accusations. Clemenceau tried hard to recover his temper at the end, and when they parted said 'You are the very baddest boy.' " At one point, so it has been claimed, Clemenceau, who after all had considerable experience in such matters, offered Lloyd George a choice of pistols or swords.[21]

Wilson tried to smooth things over. "Perhaps," he said, "we have the impression today of a greater disagreement than actually exists." But he had little to offer by way of a solution. He doubted that the United States would be able to take on a mandate for Anatolia, although he still hoped that it might do so for Armenia, and, as with other issues, fell back on the hope that further study would provide a solution. His fellow peacemakers let the matter drop: the treaty with Germany was far more urgent.[22]

The Ottoman empire was discussed only once more before President Wilson sailed back to the United States at the end of June. The discussion came in response to the appearance of representatives of the sultan's government. Perhaps to while away the time as they waited for the German response, the powers did what they had not done with Germany and allowed a defeated nation to appear before they had drawn up its treaty. It was an indication of how casually the powers were treating the fate of the Ottoman empire. On June 17 three representatives of the Ottoman Turks spoke to a group that included Clemenceau, Lloyd George, Wilson and their foreign ministers. Damad Ferid, the Turkish prime minister, an amiable, rich man whose main achievement had been to marry the sultan's sister, made Turkey's plea. He threw the blame for Turkey's entry into the war and responsibility for the horrific slaughter of Armenian Christians on his predecessors, and he assured his listeners that his country's fondest hope was to become a useful member of the League of Nations. He begged them to leave the Ottoman empire intact. He also had a written statement, which, unfortunately, was not quite ready. Clemenceau offered him little encouragement. "There is no case to be found either in Europe or Asia or Africa," he said, "in which the establishment of Turkish rule in any country has not been followed by a diminution of material prosperity, and a fall in the level of culture; nor is there any case to be found in which the withdrawal of Turkish rule has not been followed by a growth in material prosperity and a rise in the level of culture. Neither among the Christians of Europe nor among the Moslems of Syria, Arabia and Africa, has the Turk done other than destroy wherever he has conquered."[23]

The peacemakers agreed that Damad's performance was pathetic. Wilson thought he had "never seen anything more stupid." He suggested that the delegation be sent packing: "They had exhibited a complete absence of common sense and a total misunderstanding of the West." Lloyd George found it "the best proof of the political incapacity of the Turks." The delegation and its memorandum were jokes. No one could suggest how a reply to them could be worded; Wilson wondered whether it was necessary to reply at all. Lloyd George was for drawing up peace terms that sorted out the Arab lands, Smyrna and Armenia but left aside the Turkish territories in Thrace and Anatolia; those could be dealt with when the Americans had made up their minds about what mandates they would take on. He assumed this would happen in the next couple of months. Wilson confined himself to saying that he now had come around to thinking that the Turks should be removed from control of Constantinople. Clemenceau commented merely: "As for the way we will dispose of the territories of the Turkish Empire, after our last conversations, I must say I no longer know where we are." The three abandoned the subject, with Lloyd George saying, "If we could only make peace summarily and finish with it." "I fear," said Clemenceau, "that is not possible."[24]

· · ·

In London, someone who knew more about the Ottoman empire than anyone in Paris had been watching all this with alarm and despair. Curzon, who had been left in charge of the Foreign Office in Balfour's absence, sent a stream of memoranda and letters warning that it was dangerous to assume that the Turks were finished, and folly to delay a comprehensive settlement. Lloyd George paid him as little attention as he did most professional diplomats. Curzon represented so much that he disliked: the pedigreed aristocrat, the landowner, the polished product of Oxford and of London drawing rooms. He confided to Frances Stevenson how much "he loathed the Curzon set, and all that they stood for— loathed their mannerisms, their ideals, their customs, their mode of life." In time the loathing mellowed into derision mixed with a grudging respect for Curzon's knowledge and ability.[25] In the end, though, it was Curzon who brought Lloyd George down.

And it was Curzon who, with Atatürk and his armies, set the borders of the modern Turkey. The two men, the English statesman and the Turkish soldier, were adversaries but they never met. Both were stubborn, clever and proud, both had moments of profound insecurity, and both were more complex than they appeared. Curzon, the great viceroy of India, was also the man who was booed by his countrymen in Delhi because he had dared to punish a British regiment for killing an Indian; an English snob who preferred American wives; a statesman who adored paintings and furniture; and the arch-imperialist who knew the non-European world better than most of his contemporaries. Just as his frock coats concealed the pain of an injured back and the steel brace that held him upright, so his pomposity hid the man who wept when his feelings were hurt. He knew that some saw him as a caricature. He told the story against himself that, when he saw a crowd of ordinary soldiers bathing, his reaction was "Dear me! I had no conception that the lower classes had such white skins."[26]

George Curzon was born into the class that, in the years before the Great War, dominated Britain and through Britain the world. His family had occupied an estate in Derbyshire for centuries, and he could have drifted through life if he had chosen. "My ancestors," he once said, "have held Kedleston for 900 years, father and son, but none of them ever distinguished himself. They were just ordinary country gentlemen—M.P.s, Sheriffs, and so on. I made up my mind I would try to get out of the groove." His parents, as was usual, left his upbringing to others, in his case a governess who hated toys but loved punishments, often for wholly imaginary sins. In later life Curzon came to the conclusion that she had been insane. It was only at Eton that he finally started to blossom. He made friends, some for life, and with, as he admitted, "a passionate resolve to be head of the class," he won all the major prizes available. By the time he left he was a personage: flamboyant, popular, successful and more than a touch arrogant. Oxford merely confirmed these characteristics, but while there he also learned to speak in public, although some found his style too orotund. He also gained a reputation as a leading Conservative and dashed into a hectic social life. His failure to gain a first in his finals was a mere temporary setback in what most people agreed was a brilliant start.[27]

He had been given much. Yet there was also something missing: a toughness, perhaps, common sense, balance. His feelings were too easily bruised and his self-pity too readily aroused. He worked too hard, at the wrong things. At the height of an international crisis he sat up into the night adding up his bills. Montagu, his colleague in the War Cabinet, wrote to a friend: "He amuses me, interests me, irritates me. Extraordinarily easy to deal with in the upshot, but, Oh!, what a process!" Curzon bombarded them all with questions and letters. "It will amuse you that on a day when I know that he had two meetings of the War Cabinet and a meeting of the Eastern Committee, every paper relevant to all three of which he had read, my wife said that she discovered him at Harrod's Stores registering for tea!" He drew up the timetables for his daughters' lessons and questioned their nanny closely on the cost of their bloomers; he told the gardeners how to weed and the foresters how to cut down trees; he insisted on hanging his own pictures. Servants in London put him on a blacklist.[28]

He never quite achieved what he wanted. His time in India should have been glorious, but it ended in ignominy when he was forced out by Lord Kitchener, the commander-in-chief of the Indian army. Even when he finally became foreign secretary in the autumn of 1919, he had to play second fiddle to Lloyd George. When Lloyd George fell, he waited in vain for the summons to be prime minister. People found him difficult to work with, especially his subordinates. "He suffered," said one, "from absurd megalomania in regard to his knowledge of art, his worldly possessions and his social position: but I have seen him display a humility about people and things, which was almost pathetic." He was wildly inconsistent: "He abused us like pickpockets one day and wrote us ecstatic letters of appreciation the next."[29]

Curzon devoted his life to the service of Britain and its empire, both of which he saw as forces for good in the world. Like many British statesmen, he saw Europe as dangerous only when its balance of power was disturbed. "His ideal world," said Nicolson, who came to know him well, "would have been one in which England never intervened in Europe and Europe never intervened in Africa or Asia. America, as a distant, even if rebellious, plantation, was in either case not expected to intervene at all." He disliked most foreigners, especially the French. He preferred, at least in the abstract, simple peasants like the Turk of Anatolia, "a simple-minded, worthy fellow . . . who would much prefer living his own simple existence detached from Europe." He knew the world east of Suez well; he had traveled from the old Ottoman empire to Japan and written massive studies of central Asia, Persia and India. His colleagues in the cabinet were often reminded that he was the only one present who had been to some remote place. He was brilliant, if overbearing, in discussion; less successful in coming up with concrete policies.[30]

The dilatory proceedings in Paris in 1919 drove Curzon nearly mad. He had no love for the Ottoman empire but he warned repeatedly against stirring up Turkish nationalism:

> That the Turks should be deprived of Constantinople is, in my opinion, inevitable and desirable as the crowning evidence of their defeat in war; and I believe that it will be accepted with whatever wrathful reluctance by the Eastern world. But when it is realized that the fugitives are to be kicked from pillar to post and that there is to be practically no Turkish Empire and probably no Caliphate at all, I believe that we shall be giving a most dangerous and most unnecessary stimulus to Moslem passions throughout the Eastern world and that sullen resentment may easily burst into savage frenzy.

He strongly opposed mandates for Italy either in the south of Anatolia or anywhere else, as well as the award of Smyrna to Greece, "who cannot keep order five miles outside the gates of Salonika." The landing in Smyrna, he said a few months later, "was the greatest mistake that had been made in Paris."[31]

His warnings went largely unheeded, and Curzon turned his pent-up energies to reorganizing the Foreign Office. He changed the official ink-stand, taught the secretaries how to pull the blinds and, with much damage to official fingers, introduced a new filing system with large, sharp pins. In October 1919 he at last became foreign secretary. He argued for lenient peace terms for Turkey but he had to contend with Lloyd George and his private staff, who had taken on much of the responsibility for foreign affairs. The prime minister was still determined that Greece would have Smyrna and perhaps much more, and Curzon, for all his doubts, was not prepared to stand up to him. Although he threatened resignation from time to time, he had waited too long to be foreign secretary. Lloyd George joked that Curzon always sent his letter of resignation by a slow messenger and his withdrawal of the offer by a much faster one.[32]

While the British disagreed among themselves, Allied policy on the Turkish settlement, never particularly coherent, was in disarray. With its failure to ratify the Treaty of Versailles, the United States was clearly withdrawing from overseas involvement; American mandates for Anatolia, the straits or even Armenia would be out of the question. The British were curiously reluctant to face this, perhaps because Lloyd George hoped to buy time for Greece to strengthen its position in Asia Minor. When Wilson left Paris, Lloyd George claimed, the Allies were convinced that he would be able to persuade the American people to take on mandates, and so they waited. Then Wilson fell sick in September 1919. "We could not rush to assume the President's practical demise," Lloyd George later recalled, "in the face of official medical assurances of his probable restoration to health after a period of complete rest." Still the Allies waited. "We were in despair as to what action we could take without risking a breach with America."[33]

Italian interest in Turkey, never strong, was also waning. The Italian troops on the coast of Asia Minor seemed to be doing little beyond clashing with the Greek forces. Although Italy had promised in May 1919, under considerable pressure from Britain, to send a force to replace British troops in the Caucasus, it had delayed doing so. On June 19, 1919, the Orlando government fell, taking along with it Sonnino. Nitti, the new prime minister, preferred to concentrate on Italy's formidable internal problems. He immediately canceled the expensive, and hazardous, expedition to the Caucasus. As far as Asia Minor was concerned, both he and his foreign minister, Tittoni, were more interested in concessions, for coal mines for example, than in territory. They were prepared to leave Italian forces there only as long as there was no trouble. The British began to suspect that the Italians were now collaborating with Turkish nationalists.[34]

France continued to take an interest in Turkey, but it was in no mood to work with Britain. The Syrian issue festered on, and many French feared that the British were trying to maneuver them out of the Turkish territories as well. Clemenceau had always been lukewarm in his support for Greece and he was under considerable pressure from his own financiers to come to terms with the Turks. French interests held 60 percent of the Ottoman debt; if Turkey was partitioned, it might well be impossible to salvage the debt.[35]

Curzon recognized that, in the absence of the United States, it was essential to deal with the French over Turkey. In November 1919 he contacted his opposite number in Paris, Pichon, and suggested confidential discussions. He was convinced that time was running out. In October he had dispatched Lieutenant Colonel Alfred Rawlinson, who knew Atatürk slightly, to find out what peace terms Atatürk might accept. The Turkish nationalists now controlled more than a quarter of the interior; by the end of the year, Atatürk had established a rival capital to Constantinople, in Ankara. When the British, followed reluctantly by the French and Italians, took over the full control of Constantinople on March 16, 1920, in the name of law and order and arrested a number of leading nationalists, Atatürk simply responded by arresting all Allied officers within his reach, including the unfortunate Rawlinson, and by calling his own parliament. The center of power was now clearly in Ankara. Curzon was coming to the conclusion that the best thing might be to allow a new Turkey to emerge, with Atatürk at its head. Unfortunately, he could not convince Lloyd George.[36]

After a series of Allied meetings, which culminated in April 1920 with the conference at San Remo (like "a second-class English watering-place," in Curzon's view[37]), a draft treaty was finally cobbled together and presented to representatives of the government in Constantinople. Turkey was to be small and subservient. The hodgepodge of outside financial controls from the nineteenth century was rationalized and indeed strengthened. Although the Turks were to remain in Constantinople, the straits were placed under an international regime. France and Italy each had a sphere of influence in Anatolia; Greece was to have Smyrna and Thrace. There would be an independent Armenia (although no provisions were made for ensuring this) and something called Kurdistan would be autonomous within Turkey.

By this point it was too late for Armenia. The collapse of tsarist Russia and then the withdrawal of Ottoman forces had opened a window that was starting to close. Armenia, Daghestan, Georgia and Azerbaijan had all declared their independence in the spring of 1918. The new states, shaky, poor, struggling to cope with refugees, might have survived the brigands, the deserters from the Turkish armies, the White Russian forces, disease and hunger. They might have settled the differences that led them to war with each other. They might have held off General Denikin, the White Russian, because he had to deal with the Bolsheviks as well. What they could not withstand was the combination of a determined Russian assault from the north and a resurgent Turkey in the south.

Even then, with some support from outside, they might have had a hope. Of all the powers, Britain was best placed to provide immediate aid. At the end of 1918, British forces from Mesopotamia had moved into the Caucasus on the Caspian side to occupy Baku and its oilfields. Three further divisions had been sent out from Constantinople across the Black Sea to take charge of its eastern end with the important port of Batum, in Georgia. By the start of 1919, British forces controlled the railway that ran across the Caucasus and linked the two cities. British intentions, though, even to the British themselves, were not clear. Access to Caspian Sea oil, protecting a possible route to India, keeping the French out, furthering self-determination: all were reasons for Britain to occupy the Caucasus. By 1919, the Bolshevik menace had been thrown into the mix; Curzon warned about putting the region "at the mercy of a horde of savages who know no restraint and are resolved to destroy all law." But many of his colleagues were for staying out. What did it matter, Balfour asked, if the Caucasus were misgoverned? "That is the other alternative," said Curzon sarcastically. "Let them cut each other's throats." Balfour replied, "I am all in favour of that."[38]

Despite Curzon's insistence, by the spring of 1919 the British government was finding its involvement in the area too onerous. "The sooner we get out of the Caucasus the better," Henry Wilson told Lloyd George. In June the cabinet decided to withdraw all troops by the end of the year. Denikin was to be given weapons in return for a promise not to touch the independent republics. The Italians were meant to be taking over but, as Wilson advised Lloyd George, that was highly unlikely.

The decision troubled many. Hankey, secretary to the cabinet, wrote to Lloyd George that autumn about "the strong feeling which exists in many circles in the British Empire in favour of the Armenians and the natural repugnance to leave to their fate a nation whose cause we have so often espoused in the past. It cannot be denied that there is a certain callousness in withdrawing our forces from Transcaucasia at the very moment when massacres are reported to be in progress."[39] (In parts of Azerbaijan and in Armenia itself, local Muslims were burning Armenian villages and killing the inhabitants.)

The British troop withdrawal nevertheless continued, and, lest Denikin be upset, Britain held off on granting the Caucasian republics recognition. Only in January 1920, when it was clear that the White Russians were finished and that the Bolsheviks were poised to sweep southward, did Britain finally recognize the little states and send them some weapons. The War Office took the opportunity to offload surplus Canadian Ross rifles, famous for their ability to jam even under perfect conditions.[40]

Meanwhile, a threat was emerging to the south as Atatürk and his forces strengthened their hold on Anatolia. The Turks had never concealed their determination to keep their Armenian provinces and to take back part of independent Armenia. Tentative communications between the Bolsheviks and the Turkish nationalists had already started. Atatürk was no communist but the Bolsheviks, after all, were the enemies of his enemy Britain. Only the independent republics—Armenia, Georgia and Azerbaijan—kept the Turks and the Bolsheviks from linking up to form a common front against the imperialists, who were trying to dismember both their countries.[41] The Bolsheviks, as friendless as Atatürk, responded with enthusiasm, shipping arms and gold down to Anatolia.

While the Allies discussed Armenia in San Remo, the Bolsheviks took its neighboring republic of Azerbaijan. Communist-inspired rebellions broke out in Armenia itself. The Allies contacted the League of Nations to ask it to protect the larger Armenian state they were thinking of setting up; the League, which was then in its early months, replied that since the League itself was not really in existence it could not do so. The Allies then addressed themselves to the United States, where the issue of an American mandate for Armenia had been moribund since Wilson's return from Europe. The invalid president took the request to Congress, which turned it down by a decisive majority in May. Senator Lodge told a friend: "Do not think I do not feel badly about Armenia. I do, but I think there is a limit to what they have a right to put off on us."[42]

Kurdistan had even less chance than Armenia of finding a protector. The issue had come up only once at the Paris Peace Conference. When Lloyd George had first produced his list of possible mandates for the Ottoman territories on January 30, he had forgotten to mention it. When he hastily added Kurdistan to his list, he cheerfully admitted that his geography had been faulty. He had thought that it would be covered by Mesopotamia or Armenia, but his advisers had told him he was wrong. Wisely, he did not try to specify the borders of the new mandate: like so much else about Kurdistan, they were rather hazy.[43]

The Kurds were far away, on the eastern side of the Ottoman empire, and, at that date, had made little impact on world opinion. Mark Sykes, who had traveled in Kurdish territory before the war, liked them because they were tough and good fighters. The American expert, who had never been there, did not: "In some respects the Kurds remind one of the North American Indians. . . . Their temper is passionate, resentful, revengeful, intriguing and treacherous. They make good soldiers, but poor leaders. They are avaricious, utterly selfish, shameless beggars, and have a great propensity to steal."[44]

The Kurds lived in a dangerous neighborhood. Beyond the mountains to the north and east lay Russia and Persia, to the west the Turks and to the south the Arabs of Mesopotamia. During the Great War, Ottoman and Russian armies had battled on their northern edge and the British had pushed up from the south. Perhaps as many as 800,000 Kurds had died fighting in the Ottoman armies or of starvation and disease.[45] Estimating Kurdish numbers was always difficult. Since Kurdish culture blurred into Arab, Persian, Turkish, even Armenian, it was impossible to say how many Kurds there really were. About three quarters of them—perhaps a million or even two million—lived in the Ottoman empire, the majority in what later became Turkey, the rest in Iraq, with a scattering in Syria. The remainder were in Persia.

It was difficult to say what the Kurds really were. Their name itself originally meant "nomad." They had little coherent history, merely conflicting myths about their origin. There had been no great Kurdish kingdoms and few Kurdish heroes except Saladin. Kurds were divided by tribes, by religion (most were Sunni Muslims, but there were Shias and Christians as well), by language and by the fact that they were scattered among different nations. They had a reputation for being unruly. A German ethnographer was forgiving: "At bottom their vices are chiefly those of the restless life they lead in a land in which organized government has been unknown for the past eight centuries." They fought each other, outside authority, whether Ottoman or Persian, and other peoples. The Ottomans had used Kurdish Muslims in their slaughter of Armenians. At the end of the war, the British and Indian troops who occupied the area managed to keep an uneasy peace.[46]

Unlike other emerging nations, Kurdistan had no powerful patrons in Paris, and the Kurds were not yet able to speak effectively for themselves. Busy with their habitual cattle raids, abductions, clan wars and brigandage, with the enthusiastic slaughter of Armenians or simply with survival, they had not so far demonstrated much interest even in greater autonomy within the Ottoman empire, where the majority lived. Before the Great War, the nationalisms stirring among the other peoples of the Middle East had produced only faint echoes among the Kurds. Even the main center of Kurdish nationalism, consisting of a few small societies and a handful of intellectuals, was in Constantinople. The only Kurdish spokesman in Paris in 1919, a rather charming man, had lived there so long that he was nicknamed Beau Sharif. He did his best, drawing up claims for a vast country that would stretch from Armenia (if it came into existence) down to the Mediterranean. Much of that territory was also being claimed by the Armenians and by Persia.[47]

Britain was the only one of the powers with more than a passing interest in seeing a Kurdistan on the map. The United States, sympathetic to the Armenians, had no love for the Kurds. The French had put in a claim for a mandate mainly as a bargaining tool; when Britain confirmed its possession of Syria in the autumn of 1919, France dropped any pretense of interest. It continued, however, to oppose a British mandate over Kurdistan.[48]

Lloyd George and his advisers were primarily concerned with getting and protecting their mandate of Mesopotamia, with its promise of important oil deposits; they would have preferred not to have a slice of Ottoman territory running across the north. A Kurdistan would have the advantage of protecting the southern boundary of Armenia, if it survived, and so providing yet another barrier between Bolshevism and British interests. It would also neatly block the French in Syria and southern Anatolia from extending their influence north. The British assumed Kurdistan could be run cheaply, under local chiefs, on the pattern of the northern frontiers of India. They argued that the Kurds themselves wanted British protection; the Kurds disobligingly spent much energy in 1919 rebelling against British occupation forces and murdering British agents.[49]

Throughout 1919 and 1920, as they tried to settle the Turkish treaty, the British funded various Kurdish groups that claimed to be able to bring the Kurds under British protection. A Major Noel, the "Kurdish Lawrence," went on a mysterious mission to the Kurdish areas in the summer of 1919 to stir up an independence movement. He only infuriated the nationalist Turks and his own colleagues. As the British political adviser in Constantinople complained, "I made it as clear as words five times repeated can make things clear that we were *not* out for intrigues against the Turks, and that I could promise *nothing whatsoever* as regards the future of Kurdistan."[50]

British support was at best lukewarm in 1919 and was tied, at least partly, to the United States taking on a mandate for Armenia. By the autumn it was clear that was not going to happen. It was also clear that the Turks were far from finished. Atatürk was rapidly building his forces in the east, close to the Kurdish areas. The idea of Britain's propping up a separate Kurdistan became increasingly unattractive from both financial and military points of view. By the summer of 1919, British forces in the Ottoman empire were down to only 320,000 men. In Mesopotamia British authorities argued for incorporating part of the Kurdish territory in the new mandate of Iraq. The Ottoman provincial boundaries had never been really firm in that part of the world, so it could be argued that the old province of Mosul stretched north into the Kurdish hills and mountains.[51]

The Kurds themselves were divided as ever. Should they put their trust in the Turks or the British? Try to make amends with the Armenians? Ask the Bolsheviks for help? The Greek threat helped many to make up their minds, at least temporarily. When Greek forces first landed at Smyrna in the spring of 1919 and then struck inland toward Atatürk and his forces in the summer of 1920, the Muslim Kurds, generally deeply religious, saw it as a conflict between Islam and Christianity. Atatürk, whatever his private feelings, was adroit enough to use the appeal to Islam when he approached the Kurdish chiefs for their support. Rumors that Britain was planning to seize the southern Kurdish territories drove even Kurdish nationalists to throw their lot in with Atatürk.[52]

By this point, Curzon and Lloyd George were in agreement for once: an independent Kurdish state was out of the question, even if it meant leaving some Kurdish territories under Turkish control. At San Remo in April 1920, Lloyd George admitted that

he himself had tried to find out what the feelings of the Kurds were. After inquiries in Constantinople, Bagdad and elsewhere, he found it impossible to discover any representative Kurd. No Kurd appeared to represent anything more than his own particular clan. . . . On the other hand, it would seem that the Kurds felt they could not maintain their existence without the backing of a great Power. . . . But if neither France nor Great Britain undertook the task—and he hoped neither would—they appeared to think it might be better to leave them under the protection of the Turks. The country had grown accustomed to Turkish rule, and it was difficult to separate it from Turkey unless some alternative protector could be discovered.

In the peace terms drawn up for Turkey, the status of Kurdistan was left up in the air: perhaps autonomy within Turkey, a mandate under a power or complete independence. Also undecided were Kurdistan's borders, to be settled by a fact-finding mission. (The British made sure that the territories they wanted were firmly placed in the new state of Iraq.) There was a faint promise: perhaps, if the Kurds could convince the League they were ready for independence, and really wanted it, they might one day join with their fellows in Iraq.[53]

When details of these and other terms filtered out in the spring of 1920 after the San Remo Conference, the reaction among the Turks was entirely predictable. "They were received on all sides," reported Curzon's emissary to Atatürk, "with derisive shouts of laughter, and the activity of the military preparations was immediately much increased." In Ankara,

the nationalist parliament rejected both the terms and the sultan's government. A steady stream of nationalists slipped away from Constantinople
and made their way inland to Atatürk's forces. The Allied high commissioners sent strong warnings that Turkish opinion, already inflamed,
would not accept the loss of Smyrna, where the Greeks were digging in.
Curzon had feared this. As he wrote to Lloyd George, "I am the last man
to wish to do a good turn to the Turks . . . but I do want to get peace in Asia
Minor, and with the Greeks in Smyrna, and Greek divisions carrying out
Venizelos's orders and marching about Asia Minor I know this to be impossible."[54]

As the situation deteriorated, the Allies, or rather the British, decided
on a step that was ultimately to be fatal to their position in Turkey. Venizelos, who feared that his government would fall unless he could show some
successes, and whose forces had been chafing in Smyrna under repeated
nationalist attacks, finally got approval in June 1920 from Lloyd George
to move inland. As a sort of quid pro quo, Venizelos also sent troops to
support the occupying forces at Constantinople. The Supreme Council,
which was still in existence, provided a thin cover of legality; Greek troops
were simply responding, on behalf of the Allies, to Turkish attacks. The
British high commissioner in Constantinople wrote angrily to Curzon:
"The Supreme Council, thus, are prepared for a resumption of general
warfare; they are prepared to do violence to their own declared principles;
they are prepared to perpetuate bloodshed indefinitely in the Near East;
and for what? To maintain M. Veniselos in power in Greece for what cannot in the nature of things be more than a few years at the outside." Curzon agreed completely: "Venizelos thinks his men will sweep the Turks
into the mountains. I doubt it will be so."[55]

And so the last stage of peacemaking in Turkey started with war. Greek
troops moved out of Smyrna on a wide front, up the valleys to the edge of
the Anatolian plateau. The Turkish nationalists melted back into the inte-
rior. In Europe, another Greek army swept aside a weak and disorganized
Turkish force in Thrace. Venizelos expressed great confidence; to Henry
Wilson, he foretold the collapse of Atatürk's forces and the spread of
Greek power inland, to Constantinople, even perhaps to Pontus on the
Black Sea. Privately, the Greek prime minister had moments of panic but,
by this point, he had little choice but to go on.[56] By August 1920, the
Greeks were 250 miles into the interior.

That same month, the Allies and Damad Ferid, representing the sultan's government, signed a peace treaty in a showroom at the Sèvres
porcelain factory on the outskirts of Paris: not a thing of beauty, but as easily smashed. Allied military advisers warned that it would take at least

twenty-seven divisions to enforce the terms, divisions they did not have. In Turkey, there was a national day of mourning; newspapers had black borders, shops were closed and prayers were recited all day. Atatürk fought on. By now he had most of the nationalist forces in Turkey under his control, and in the north he and the Bolsheviks were stamping out the troublesome Caucasian republics.[57]

In September 1920, less than a month after the Treaty of Sèvres had promised an independent Armenia incorporating part of Turkey, Atatürk's forces attacked from the south. Despite their best efforts and the attacks of their tiny air force of three planes, the Armenians were gradually forced back. When Aharonian, the Armenian poet who had spoken for his country in Paris, tried to see Curzon in London, he was brushed off with a letter. "What we want to see now is concrete evidence of some constructive and administrative ability at home, instead of a purely external policy based on propaganda and mendicancy," wrote Curzon. On November 17, the Armenian government signed an armistice with Turkey which left only a tiny scrap of country still free. Five days later, a message arrived from President Wilson. Under the Treaty of Sèvres he had been asked to draw Armenia's boundaries; he decided it should have 42,000 square kilometers of Turkish territory.[58]

With his nation abandoned by the world and crushed between two enemies, the Armenian prime minister said, "Nothing remains for the Armenians to do but choose the lesser of two evils."[59] In December, Armenia became a Soviet republic; the Bolshevik commissar for nationalities, Joseph Stalin, was active in bringing it to heel. The following March, the Treaty of Moscow between Turkey and the Soviet Union confirmed the return of the Turkish provinces of Kars and Ardahan to Turkey. (Stalin was the negotiator for the Bolsheviks.) The border has lasted to this day.

Kurdistan was finished too. By March 1921 the Allies had backed away from the vague promises in the Treaty of Sèvres. As far as Kurdistan was concerned, they said, they were ready to modify the treaty in "a sense of conformity with the existing facts of the situation."[60] The "existing facts" were that Atatürk had denounced the whole treaty; he had successfully kept part of the Armenian territories within Turkey; and he was about to sign a treaty giving the rest to the Soviet Union. Kurdish nationalists might protest, but the Allies no longer had any interest in an independent Kurdish state.

Stability on his northern and eastern flanks enabled Atatürk to deal with the Greek invasion in the west. Here, too, the current of events was running in his favor. In November 1920, Venizelos, much to everyone's surprise (including his own), was defeated in an election. That left the way open for the return of his old enemy King Constantine, which in turn finished off what was left of the Allied policy on Turkey. Italy and France argued that they were no longer under any obligation to support Greece and that the Treaty of Sèvres must be revised. The Italians hinted that they would be willing to work with Atatürk to modify its terms.

The treaty was also unpopular in France, where the colonial lobby denounced it as a sellout. The French government, for its part, could no longer afford the 500 million francs per year for France's zone of occupation in the southern part of Asia Minor—or the losses. By the start of 1920 the Turks were waging an increasingly effective guerrilla war. Over 500 French soldiers were casualties in the first two weeks of February alone. The French were forced to abandon one post after another and this threatened their hold on Syria to the south. In October 1921, France signed a treaty with Atatürk's government which provided for the withdrawal of all French forces from Cilicia in the south. France got economic concessions, while Atatürk gained something much more important—recognition by a leading power. Curzon was furious: "We seem to be reverting to the old traditional divergence—amounting almost to antipathy—between France and ourselves, fomented by every device that an unscrupulous Govt and a lying Press can suggest."[61]

In Greece, Constantine's return led to a purge of pro-Venizelos officers in the army, throwing it into confusion just as the spring campaigning season of 1921 opened in Asia Minor. The new Greek government nevertheless felt honor bound to try to hang on to what Greece had been promised. Lloyd George, over the objections of Curzon, encouraged the Greeks with many nods and winks to attack the Turks. That summer the Greek forces pushed far inland toward Ankara, an extraordinary military accomplishment across parched wastelands. It was the farthest extent of Greece's advance, and beyond its capacity to sustain. Along the 400 miles of Greek lines, the soldiers knew that they were done for. "Let us go home and to hell with Asia Minor," they were saying the following spring.[62]

The Greek government, which had appealed in vain to its allies for money and military support, resigned itself to a negotiated peace with Turkey and the loss of at least some of the territory it was occupying. In April 1922 Atatürk refused an offer brokered by Britain, France and Italy. Turkey would accept an armistice only if Greece started to evacuate its forces at once from Asia Minor, something that was politically impossible for the Greek government. Throughout the summer, Greece's political and military leaders hesitated over what to do next. On the front lines, the Greek soldiers dug in and waited.

On August 26, 1922, the Turkish counterattack finally came toward

Smyrna. The orders were simple: "Soldiers, your goal is the Mediterranean."[63] The Greek forces were shattered and on September 10, Atatürk rode in triumph into Smyrna. The city was packed with stragglers and refugees who had fled from Greek villages inland. On the quays a great crowd struggled to get onto the ships and to safety. In the back streets and alleys, the looting and killing had begun. The conquering soldiers and the Turks of Smyrna had many scores to settle. Like their masters in Rome, Paris and London, the representatives of the powers now abandoned the Greeks to their lot. As foreign troops watched from their ships, the city started to burn.

The first fire may have broken out by accident, but eyewitnesses later saw Turks going through the Armenian and Greek quarters with cans of petrol. "It was a terrifying thing to see even from a distance," a British officer recalled. "There was the most awful scream one could ever imagine. I believe many people were shoved into the sea, simply by the crowds nearest the houses trying to get further away from the fire." Atatürk watched the flames impassively; "a disagreeable incident" was his reaction.[64] When the fires died out, Greek Smyrna was no more.

The collapse of the Greek army left the small Allied occupation forces in Constantinople and guarding the straits suddenly exposed. As Atatürk's forces advanced north toward the Sea of Marmara and Constantinople, the British government decided that it must stand firm at Chanak and Ismid on the Asiatic side. It called on the British empire and its allies, but little beyond excuses and reproaches came back. Of the dominions, only New Zealand rallied to the flag. The Italians hastily assured Atatürk of their neutrality. The French ordered their troops out of Chanak. Curzon rushed over to Paris and had a dreadful scene with Poincaré, now French prime minister, in which he talked of "abandonment" and "desertion." When Poincaré shouted back, Curzon rushed out of the room in tears. He grasped the British ambassador's arm: "I can't bear that horrid little man. I can't bear him." Only a stiff brandy enabled him to resume what proved to be fruitless negotiations.[65]

Lloyd George was for war, but cooler heads, including Curzon's and those of the military on the spot, finally prevailed. Atatürk was at last ready for negotiations. The armistice of Mudanya, of October 11, provided for the Turks to take over eastern Thrace from the Greeks. In return, Atatürk promised not to move troops into Constantinople, Gallipoli or Ismid until a peace conference could decide their fate.

All over Asia Minor and Thrace the Greeks were moving out, more than a million of them. Greek shopkeepers, farmers, priests, old men and women, Muslim Greeks, Greeks who did not speak a word of Greek, stumbled into a country unable to feed and house them. The young Ernest Hemingway, reporting for a Toronto newspaper, saw the Greek soldiers going home: "All day long I have been passing them, dirty, tired, unshaven, wind-bitten soldiers, hiking along the trails across the brown, rolling, barren Thrace countryside. No bands, no relief organizations, no leave areas, nothing but lice, dirty blankets, and mosquitos at night. They are the last of the glory that was Greece. This is the end of their second siege of Troy."[66]

The Greek adventure in Asia Minor had already brought down Venizelos; now it destroyed his great patron, Lloyd George. The Chanak crisis was too much for a shaky coalition government. Curzon discreetly abandoned his old colleagues. When a new Conservative government under Bonar Law took office in November 1922, Curzon was reappointed foreign secretary. He left almost immediately for Lausanne, where the Turkish peace was now at last to be concluded.

A few of those who assembled there had been at the Paris Peace Conference—Curzon himself, Poincaré, a subdued Venizelos, who had been invited by the new government to represent Greece, Stamboliski of Bulgaria with his glamorous interpreter, the only woman at the conference. There were new faces too, among them Mussolini, in white spats and black shirt, ill at ease at his first major international conference, and Georgi Chicherin, the Soviet commissar of foreign affairs, with his thin red beard and "furtive old-clothes-man slouch." Turkey was now represented by the nationalists, led by Inönü Ismet, a trusted general of Atatürk. When the Allies had tried to invite the Constantinople government as well, Atatürk had simply abolished the sultanate. The Americans, in their new mood of detachment from European affairs, sent only observers: Richard Child, an amiable former journalist, and Joseph Grew, later American ambassador to Tokyo at the time of Pearl Harbor. Grew found, to his surprise, that Curzon was really quite charming: "Never have I enjoyed anything more than the small dinners of three or four which he appeared to love and where, after the table was swept and the port brought on, he would sit hour after hour telling stories, anecdotes, and experiences in a delightful vein seldom seen in present-day society."[67]

Curzon had many things to try his patience in Lausanne: his drunken valet, who hid his dress trousers; his back brace, which broke and cut into him; above all, the French and the Italians, "overflowing with unctuous civility to the Turks and showing an inclination to bolt at every corner from the course"; and of course the Turks themselves. Ismet, "a little dark man, absolutely without magnetism," who looked "more like an Armenian lace-seller than a Turkish general," stonewalled, played up his deafness, and obstinately reiterated his demands. He had come with firm instructions from Atatürk: to negotiate an independent Turkey, free of outside interference. As a good soldier, he intended to follow them. "You remind me," Curzon snapped one day, "of nothing so much as a music box. You play the same old tune day after day until we are heartily sick of it—sovereignty, sovereignty, sovereignty." With heavy sarcasm Curzon poked holes in Ismet's arguments. Ismet shrugged and simply ignored him. Curzon, he said, "treated us like schoolboys but we did not mind. He treated the French and the Italians just the same." In the evenings the Turk took solace in his favorite green chartreuse; one of the Americans who unwisely joined him swore off the drink for life. Adding to Curzon's frustration with the Turks was his knowledge that he was struggling against an unseen adversary. Far off in Ankara, Atatürk was watching the conference closely and cabling his orders to Ismet.[68]

After endless haggling and a dramatic walkout by Curzon designed to put pressure on the Turks, a peace was worked out by July 1923. Ismet, with "deep circles under his eyes," signed for Turkey, the British ambassador to Constantinople for Britain. The Treaty of Lausanne was unlike Versailles, Trianon, St. Germain, Neuilly and Sèvres, those products of the Paris Peace Conference. "Hitherto we have dictated our peace treaties," Curzon reflected. "Now we are negotiating one with the enemy who has an army in being while we have none, an unheard of position."[69]

Very little remained of the Sèvres terms. There was no mention of an independent Armenia or Kurdistan and, although Curzon tried to add clauses to the new treaty giving protection to minorities, the Turks refused on the grounds of sovereignty. Turkey's borders now included virtually all the Turkish-speaking territories, from eastern Thrace down to Syria. The straits remained Turkish, but with an international agreement on their use. The old humiliating capitulations were swept away. The Lausanne treaty also provided for a compulsory transfer of populations, Muslims for Christians. Most Greeks had already left Turkey; now Muslim families from Crete to the borders of Albania were forcibly uprooted and dumped in Turkey, "a thoroughly bad and vicious solution," warned Curzon, "for which the world will pay a heavy penalty for a hundred years to come." The only exceptions to the transfer, by special agreement, were the Turks in western Thrace and the Greeks in Constantinople and on a couple of small islands. Communities have lingered on, harassed by a myriad of petty regulations and used as convenient scapegoats whenever relations have worsened between Greece and Turkey, as they did in the 1960s over Cyprus and in the summer of 1999 over Kosovo.[70]

The one unreconciled dispute at Lausanne was over Mosul, in the north of Iraq. The Turkish delegation, arguing along lines that Turkish governments have used ever since, claimed it, on the grounds that its Kurds were really Turks. After all, said the chief Turkish negotiator triumphantly, the *Encyclopaedia Britannica* said so. Curzon, who was determined to hang on to Mosul, for the sake of its oil rather than its Kurds, was withering: "It was reserved for the Turkish delegation to discover for the first time in history that the Kurds were Turks. Nobody has ever found it out before."[71] The issue of Mosul came close to breaking up the conference; both sides eventually agreed to refer it to the League of Nations, which finally awarded it to Iraq in 1925.

The Kurds were left under different governments—Atatürk's in Turkey, Reza Shah's in Persia, and Feisal's in Iraq—none of which had any tolerance for Kurdish autonomy. Within Iraq, the British for a time toyed with the idea of a separate administration for the Kurdish areas, recognizing that the Kurds did not like being under Arab rule. In the end, the British preferred to do nothing; Iraq became independent in 1932 without promising any special consideration to the Kurds. In Turkey, Atatürk and the nationalists dropped their earlier emphasis on all Muslims together and moved to establish a secular and Turkish state, to the dismay of many Kurds. The language of education and government was to be Turkish; indeed, between 1923 and 1991 Kurdish was first discouraged then outlawed. In 1927, the Turkish foreign minister assured the British ambassador that the Kurds were bound to disappear like what he described as "Red Hindus"; if the Kurds showed any disposition to turn nationalist, Turkey would expel them, just as it had done with the Armenians and Greeks.[72]

The Kurds have never accepted their fate quietly, and Kurdish nationalism, a tenuous force at the time of the Paris Peace Conference, grew stronger over the years under repression. The promises made in Paris and by that first Treaty of Sèvres became part of Kurdish memories and hopes. In the summer of 1919, the leader of the first of a series of uprisings in Kurdish territory strapped a Koran to his arm; on a blank page were written Allied promises—including the one of Wilson's Fourteen Points which talked about autonomous development for the non-Turkish nationalities.[73]

Ismet returned from Lausanne to a hero's welcome, and the treaty is still seen as modern Turkey's greatest diplomatic victory. In the autumn of 1923, the last foreign troops left Constantinople. The sultan had gone the year before, spirited out of his palace in a British military ambulance and carried by British warship to Malta. He died in exile in San Remo, impoverished and lonely. His cousin, a gentle artist, became caliph for just over a year until Atatürk abolished the caliphate as well. What was left of the royal family was sent into exile, where they gradually dissipated what

meager funds they had left. A handful have made their way back to
Turkey; one princess runs a hotel, and a prince works in the archives in the
Topkapi palace.

Curzon died in 1925, worn out by years of overwork. Atatürk died in
1938, of cirrhosis of the liver, and Ismet succeeded him as president. In
1993, on the seventieth anniversary of the Treaty of Lausanne, Ismet's son
and Curzon's grandson laid a wreath together on Atatürk's grave.[74]

PART EIGHT

FINISHING UP

30

The Hall of Mirrors

O N SUNDAY, May 4, 1919, the Council of Four, after dictating some
last-minute changes, gave orders that the German treaty should go
to the printers. Lloyd George went off to a picnic at Fontainebleau, the
others to rest. Two days later, a rare plenary session was called to vote on
the terms. Since there was no final version ready, the delegates had to listen to André Tardieu reading a lengthy summary in French; many of the
English-speakers nodded off. "So," wrote Henry Wilson in his diary, "we
are going to hand out terms to the Boches without reading them ourselves
first. I don't think in all history this can be matched." The Portuguese
complained that their country was not getting any reparations; the Chinese objected to the clauses giving German concessions in China to Japan;
and the Italian delegate pointed out that his colleagues might have something to say about the clauses which had been decided in their absence.
Then, to general amazement, Marshal Foch asked to be heard. He made
one last plea for the Rhine as a barrier between Germany and France. Clemenceau crossly demanded why he had made such a scene. "C'était pour
faire aise," Foch answered, "à ma conscience." ("It was to ease my conscience.") To *The New York Times* he said: "The next time, remember, the
Germans will make no mistake. They will break through into Northern
France and seize the Channel ports as a base of operations against England." Fortunately, perhaps, he was dead by the time Hitler did precisely
that twenty years later.[1]

Foch's warnings did not trouble the peacemakers. "Everyone seems
delighted with the peace terms," reported Frances Stevenson, "& there is
no fault to find with them on the ground that they are not severe enough."
Wilson looked at the printed treaty with pride: "I hope that during the rest

of my life I will have enough time to read this whole volume. We have completed in the least time possible the greatest work that four men have ever done." Even Clemenceau was pleased. "In the end, it is what it is; above all else it is the work of human beings and, as a result, it is not perfect. We all did what we could to work fast and well." When Wilson asked him whether they should wear top hats to their meeting with the Germans, the old man replied: "Yes, hats with feathers."[2]

At Versailles, in the cold and gloomy Hôtel des Réservoirs, the German delegates, some 180 experts, diplomats, secretaries and journalists, were waiting with increasing impatience. They had set off on April 28 from Berlin, as an American observer warned, in an "excited and almost abnormal frame of mind," convinced that they were going to be treated as pariahs; their treatment in France had confirmed their worst fears. The French had slowed down their special trains as they entered the areas devastated by the war: it was, said one German, a "spiritual scourging," but also an omen. "Ours, therefore, the sole responsibility for all the shattered life and property of these terrible four and a half years." When they arrived the following day they had been brusquely loaded onto buses and sent under heavy escort to Versailles; their luggage had been unceremoniously dumped in the hotel courtyard and they were told rudely to carry it in themselves. The hotel itself was where French leaders had stayed in 1871 while they negotiated with Bismarck. It was now surrounded by a stockade—for the Germans' safety, the French claimed. The Germans grumbled that they were being treated "like the inhabitants of a Negro village in an exposition."[3]

The delegation's leader was Germany's foreign minister, Ulrich von Brockdorff-Rantzau. He was the obvious choice. He had served with distinction in the old imperial diplomatic service, but unlike many of his colleagues, he had accepted the new order and established good relations with the socialists who now held office. During the war he had been highly critical of German policies and had urged a compromise peace. He was also a bad choice. Haughty, monocled, slim, immaculately turned out, he looked as though he had just stepped out of the kaiser's court. (Indeed, his twin brother managed the kaiser's estates.) The family was an old and distinguished one: Rantzaus had served Denmark; Germany; even, in the seventeenth century, France. A Marshal Rantzau was rumored to have been the real father of Louis XIV. When a French officer asked Brockdorff-Rantzau about it, the count replied: "Oh yes, in my family the Bourbons have been considered bastard Rantzaus for the past three hundred years." He was witty, cruel and capricious, and most people were afraid of him. He loved champagne and brandy, some said to excess. The head of the British military mission in Berlin believed that he took drugs.[4]

Like many of his compatriots in 1919, Brockdorff-Rantzau put his faith in the Americans. He thought that, in the long run, the United States would see that its interests, economic or political, lay with a revived Germany. The two might work together with Britain, perhaps even with France, to block Bolshevism in the east. And if the British and the Americans fell out, as they almost certainly would, the United States would see the value of having a strong Germany on its side. Like so many Germans, Brockdorff-Rantzau thought President Wilson would ensure that the peace terms were mild. After all, Germany had done as Wilson himself had suggested and become a republic. That alone showed its good faith.

Their country, most Germans believed, had surrendered on the understanding that the Fourteen Points would be the basis for the peace treaty. "The people," reported Ellis Dresel, an American diplomat sent to Berlin, "had been led to believe that Germany had been unluckily beaten after a fine and clean fight, owing to the ruinous effect of the blockade on the home morale, and perhaps some too far reaching plans of her leaders, but that happily President Wilson could be appealed to, and would arrange a compromise peace satisfactory to Germany." The country would undoubtedly have to pay some sort of indemnity, but nothing toward the costs of the war. It would become a member of the League of Nations. It would keep its colonies. And the principle of self-determination would work in its favor. German Austria should be allowed to decide whether to join its German cousins. German-speaking areas in West Prussia and Silesia would, of course, remain German. In Alsace-Lorraine, the predominantly German parts would also be able to vote on their future.[5]

In the first months of the peace the Germans clutched the Fourteen Points like a life raft, with very little sense that their victors might not see things the same way. So many of the familiar landmarks—kaiser, army, bureaucracy—had been obliterated. That brought unsettling hopes and fears. The country was less than fifty years old; why should it continue to exist? Bavarians, as well as Rhinelanders, contemplated regaining the independence they had lost in 1870, when Germany was created. On the far left, revolutionaries dreamed of another Russian revolution and for a time, as insurrections flared up unpredictably in first one city and then another, it looked as though they might get their wish. Thomas Mann talked of the end of civilization with something close to exhilaration. Political parties across the spectrum floundered as they tried to redefine themselves. There was a widespread fear that German society was done for; the old moral standards had dissolved. There was also, perhaps understandably, a reluctance to think seriously about the future, especially the one that was being shaped in Paris. "The people at large," according to Dresel, "are strangely apathetic on questions connected with peace. A feverish desire to forget the trouble of the moment in amusements and dissipation is everywhere noticeable. Theatres, dance halls, gambling dens, and race tracks are crowded as never before." A distinguished German scholar remembered "the dreamland of the armistice period."[6]

A few Germans made it their business to find out what was going on in Paris during the months of waiting. The Foreign Office studied the Allied press, looking for divisions among the victors. There were some direct contacts with Allies, in the negotiations over the lifting of the blockade or over the terms of the armistice. From time to time, Allied representatives talked about the larger issues. An American intelligence officer, a Colonel Arthur Conger, hinted that he was acting for a higher authority in Paris. A Harvard graduate who had specialized in classics, Eastern religions and music, Conger told his German counterparts about the tensions between the Americans and the French over the armistice and assured them that Wilson would oppose excessive French demands. He also gave the Germans much advice. They should follow the American model when they drew up their new constitution and give their president considerable power. The German Foreign Office duly passed this on to the framers of what became the Weimar constitution. In March 1919, Professor Emile Haguenin, ostensibly a low-ranking diplomat but in fact head of the French secret service in Switzerland, held secret conversations in Berlin with leading Germans. He left the misleading impression that the French were prepared to be moderate on reparations and Silesia if Germany would acquiesce in French control of the Saar mines and the occupation of the Rhineland.

The German government tried to use such men as messengers. When the American Dresel told Brockdorff-Rantzau in April 1919 that Germany must accept French control of the Saar and a free city in Danzig, the German exploded. "Under no circumstances would I sign the peace treaty." He added what was by now a familiar warning: "If the Entente insisted on these conditions, in my opinion Bolshevism would be unavoidable in Germany." Like others in Europe in 1919, the Germans found the bogey of revolution useful as a way of putting pressure on the peacemakers. The evidence suggests that the German government did not itself take the threat particularly seriously.[7]

What it did take very seriously were its preparations for the expected peace conference with the Allies. In November 1918, the government set up a special peace agency which labored away through the winter, producing volume after volume of detailed studies, maps, memoranda, arguments and counterarguments for use by the German delegates. When the special trains rolled off toward Versailles, they carried packing crates full of material for negotiations the Germans were never to have.

As the days went by in Versailles, the Germans worked away doggedly. Because they were convinced, with reason, that the French were listening in, all their meetings took place to music, as one delegate after another took turns playing one of Liszt's Hungarian rhapsodies or "The Pilgrim's Chorus" from *Tannhäuser* or winding up the gramophones which had been specially brought from Berlin. In the spirit of the new, democratic Germany, members of the delegation took their meals together at long tables, aristocrats beside working-class socialists, generals next to professors. They all celebrated May Day. The French press carried wild reports: the Germans were eating huge numbers of oranges; they were demanding quantities of sugar.[8]

Outside the hotel, curious crowds of French waited to see the enemy. Occasionally they jeered and whistled, but mostly they were quiet, even friendly. The Germans went out for excursions in cars provided by the French, to the shops in Versailles or out into the country. They walked in the Trianon park. "Old magnolias and crab-apple trees are in full bloom," wrote a member of the Foreign Office to his wife, "and the rhododendrons and lilacs will soon be in bloom." The birds, finches, thrushes, even an oriole, were wonderful. "But in the background of all this loveliness the shadow of fate, as if reaching out for us, grows constantly darker and comes steadily closer."[9]

Finally, after the Germans had been in Versailles for a week, the summons to a meeting at the Trianon Palace Hotel came. On May 7 (the anniversary, perhaps by coincidence, of the German sinking of the *Lusitania*), the Allies would hand over the peace terms. The Germans would have two weeks to submit their comments in writing. Late that night, until two A.M., and again the next morning the Hôtel des Réservoirs rang with debates over how the German representatives should behave. Brockdorff-Rantzau, who would be the chief spokesman, was determined not to stand up; he had seen diagrams in the French newspapers of the meeting room which referred to the seats set aside for the Germans as the prisoners' dock. Deciding what he should say was much more difficult. This might be his only chance to speak directly to the peacemakers. The delegation had already prepared several alternate drafts for speeches. When he drove through the park on May 7, Brockdorff-Rantzau had two texts with him, one very short and noncommittal, the other much longer and more defiant. He had not decided which to use.[10]

The room was packed: delegates from all nations, secretaries, generals, admirals, journalists. "Only Indians and Australian aborigines were absent among the races of the earth," said a German journalist. "Every shade of skin apart from these: the palest ivory yellow, coffee-coloured brown, deep black." In the middle of the room, facing the Great Powers, was a table for the Germans. All eyes turned to the door as they entered, "stiff, awkward-looking figures." Brockdorff-Rantzau, said a witness, "looked ill, drawn and nervous" and was sweating. There was a brief hesitation and the crowd, observing a courtesy from the vanished world of 1914, rose to its feet. Brockdorff-Rantzau and Clemenceau bowed to each other.[11]

Clemenceau opened the proceedings. Without the slightest sign of nerves he spoke coldly, outlining the main headings of the treaty. "The hour has struck for the weighty settlement of our account," he told the Germans. "You asked us for peace. We are disposed to grant it to you." He threw out his words, said one of the German delegates, "as if in concentrated anger and disdain, and . . . from the very outset, for the Germans, made any reply quite futile." When the interpreters had finished the English and French versions, Clemenceau asked if anyone else wanted to speak. Brockdorff-Rantzau held up his hand.[12]

He chose the longer speech. Although he said much that was conciliatory, the ineptitude of his interpreters, his decision to remain seated and his harsh, rasping voice left an appalling impression. Clemenceau went red with anger. Lloyd George snapped an ivory paper knife in two. He understood for the first time, he told people afterward, the hatred the French felt for Germans. "This is the most tactless speech I have ever heard," said Wilson. "The Germans are really a stupid people. They always do the wrong thing." Lloyd George agreed: "It was deplorable that we let him talk." Only Balfour, detached as always, failed to share the general indignation. He had not noticed Brockdorff-Rantzau's behavior, he told Nicolson. "I make it a rule never to stare at people when they are in obvious distress." As he left the Trianon Palace Hotel, Brockdorff-Rantzau stood for a moment on the steps and nonchalantly lit a cigarette. Only those close to him noticed that his lips were trembling.[13]

Back at their hotel, the Germans fell on their copies of the treaty. The separate sections were torn out and handed over to teams of translators. By morning, a German version had been printed and sent off. A delegate phoned Berlin with the main points: "The Saar basin . . . Poland, Silesia, Oppeln . . . 123 milliards to pay and for all that we are supposed to say 'Thank you very much.'" He was shouting so loudly that the French secret service could scarcely make out the words. When the Germans met at midnight for a hasty meal, the dining room buzzed with comments: "all our colonies"; "Germany to be left out of the League"; "almost the whole merchant fleet"; "if that's what Wilson calls open diplomacy." One delegate, a former trade unionist, staggered into the room: "Gentlemen, I am drunk. That may be proletarian, but with me there was nothing else for it. This shameful treaty has broken me, for I had believed in Wilson until today." (In the rumors that spread through Paris this incident was magnified: "the delegates, secretaries, and translators lying drunk, in all stages of dress and undress, in the rooms and even on the stairs of the Hotel.") "The worst act of world piracy ever perpetrated under the flag of hypocrisy," said the banker Max Warburg. Brockdorff-Rantzau himself merely said with disdain: "This fat volume was quite unnecessary. They could have expressed the whole thing more simply in one clause—'L'Allemagne renonce à son existence.'" ("Germany surrenders all claims to its existence.")[14]

The shock was echoed in Germany. Why should Germany lose 13 percent of its territory and 10 percent of its population? After all, had Germany lost the war? Since the armistice, the military and its sympathizers had been busily laying the foundations of the stab-in-the-back theory: that Germany had been defeated not on the battlefield but by treachery at home. Why should Germany alone be made to disarm? Why, and this was the question that became the focus of German hatred of the treaty, should Germany be the only country to take responsibility for the Great War? Most Germans still viewed the outbreak of hostilities in 1914 as a necessary defense against the threat from the barbaric Slavs to the east. The treaty was completely unacceptable, said Philipp Scheidemann, the chancellor. "What hand would not wither which placed this chain upon itself and upon us?" What had happened to Wilson's promises? "Well, I'll give you some open diplomacy," said Gustav Noske, the tough, crude minister of defense, to an American journalist. "You Americans go back home and bury yourself [sic] with your Wilson." Where Wilson had been seen to this point as Germany's savior, he overnight became the wicked hypocrite. When he died in 1924, the German embassy, alone among the foreign embassies in Washington, refused to lower its flag.[15]

What is striking at this distance is the outrage—and the surprise. In its preparations for the peace negotiations, the Foreign Office had anticipated many of the terms: on disarmament; the demilitarization and occupation of the Rhineland; the loss at the very least of the Saar mines; considerable losses, probably including Danzig, on Germany's eastern frontier; and reparations of at least 60 billion marks. The best explanation for what was an inexplicable reaction comes from an American observer who said in April 1919: "The Germans have little left but Hope. But having only that I think they have clung to it—the Hope that the Americans would do something, the Hope that the final terms would not be so severe as the Armistice indicated and so on. Subconsciously, I think the Germans have been more optimistic than they realized." And, he added prophetically, "when they see the terms in cold print, there will be intense bitterness, hate and desperation."[16]

It was in that mood that the German delegation prepared its observations on the peace terms. By the end of May it had produced pages of closely reasoned objections and counterproposals. The overall thrust was that the treaty was not the just and fair one the Allies had promised. In the territory being taken from Germany, Germans were being denied the right of self-determination. The reparations were condemning the German people to "perpetual slave labor." Germany alone was being asked to disarm. Brockdorff-Rantzau had decided to pursue a particular strategy that was to have dangerous consequences. Germany, he insisted, was not going to accept all the guilt for the war. "Such a confession in my mouth," he had told his audience at the Trianon Palace, "would be a lie." But neither he nor Germany was being asked to make such a confession. The notorious Article 231 of the treaty, which the Germans inaccurately called the "war guilt" clause, had been put in to establish German liability for reparations. There were similar clauses in the treaties with Austria and Hungary; they never became an issue, largely because the governments concerned did not make them so.[17]

The Germans' reaction was different partly because they had been nervously anticipating the accusation for months. Liberals, who had criticized their own government during the war, had been arguing that Germany should not have to carry the burden of guilt. The great sociologist Max Weber and a group of leading professors issued a public manifesto: "We do not deny the responsibility of those in power before and during the war, but we believe that all the great powers of Europe who were at war are guilty."[18] By the time the peace terms appeared, Germans of all political persuasions saw their worst fears being realized.

Although his own government doubted its wisdom, Brockdorff-Rantzau pushed stubbornly ahead with his attack on Article 231, partly to undermine the Allied case for reparations but mostly out of a sense of honor. On May 13 he wrote to the Allies, "The German people did not will the war and would never have undertaken a war of aggression." He returned to the question again and again in other, lengthy, memoranda. The Allies merely dug in their heels. "I could not accept the German point of view," wrote Lloyd George in his memoirs, "without giving away our whole case for entering into the war." Wilson said sharply, "It is enough to reply that we don't believe a word of what the German government says."

Germany accepted its aggression and its responsibility when it sued for the armistice, said Clemenceau on behalf of the Council of Four. "It is too late to seek to deny them today." And so Article 231, a clause that the young John Foster Dulles helped to draft as a compromise over reparations, became the great symbol of the unfairness and injustice of the Treaty of Versailles in Weimar Germany, in much subsequent history—and in the English-speaking world.[19]

At four o'clock in the morning of May 7, the day the Germans got the terms, Herbert Hoover, the American relief administrator, had been woken by a messenger carrying a copy of the treaty fresh from the presses. Like everyone else, he had never before seen it as a whole. The sheer scope, the cumulative impact of all the provisions, worried him. Unable to get back to sleep, he wandered out into the empty Paris streets. There, as day was breaking, he ran into Jan Smuts and John Maynard Keynes. "We agreed," Hoover recalled years later, "that the consequences of many parts of the proposed Treaty would ultimately bring destruction."[20]

The publication of the treaty crystallized the unease of many of the peacemakers but whether it was caused by the peace terms themselves, the nature of the Peace Conference, the future of the world, or their own future, is not always easy to distinguish. Lansing, the American secretary of state, who had been sitting resentfully on the sidelines, found that the treaty confirmed his worst fears about Wilson as a negotiator. He dashed off a vehement memorandum: "The terms of the peace appear immeasurably harsh and humiliating, while many of them are incapable of performance." Bullitt, still smarting from the failure of his Russian diplomacy, organized a meeting of the younger members of the American delegation at the Crillon. "This isn't a treaty of peace," he said. They must all resign. About a dozen agreed. Bullitt pulled the table decorations to pieces to award red roses to those who joined him and yellow jonquils to those who did not. The letters of resignation spoke of disillusionment, of how Wilson's great principles and the idealism of the United States had been sacrificed to serve the interests of the greedy Europeans. Bullitt, typically, made sure that his letter went directly to the press.[21]

In the British delegation, the reaction was similar. Nicolson caught the mood. "We came to Paris confident that the new order was about to be established; we left it convinced that the new order had merely fouled the old. We arrived as fervent apprentices in the school of President Wilson; we left as renegades." The British pardoned themselves for having created an "imperialistic peace"; it was all the fault of the Italians and the French. In Britain, the emotions of the "khaki" election of the previous December had dissipated and more tolerant feelings toward Germany were emerging. The archbishop of Canterbury declared himself "very uncomfortable" with the treaty. He spoke, he said, for "a great central body which is ordinarily silent and which has no adequate representation in the ordinary channels of the Press."[22]

The French reaction, of course, was different. Critics complained that the treaty was too weak, apart from some on the left who found it too harsh. Their complaints made little impact on the public. Many French thought Clemenceau had got the best terms he could: "glorious and comforting" was how one journalist described them. In any case, there was little appetite for reopening the whole weary round of negotiations. After the Germans sent their detailed counterproposals on May 29, the French press was scathing: "monument of impudence," "odious piece of buffonery," "arrogance." A noted liberal exclaimed that the only words he could find for the German note were "indecency and lack of conscience."[23]

The British and the Americans, by contrast, were impressed. Henry Wilson, no friend of the Germans, wrote in his diary: "The Boches have done exactly what I forecast—they have driven a coach and four through our Terms, and then have submitted a complete set of their own, based on the 14 points, which are much more coherent than ours." At that moment, the separatists in the Rhineland, with support from some of the French military, staged a futile bid for independence. On June 1 placards went up in several cities along the Rhine. Where they were not immediately torn down by angry crowds, they met with a profound silence. Attempts to seize government offices failed ignominiously. Brockdorff-Rantzau immediately sent a strong protest to Clemenceau. On June 2 Wilson and Lloyd George showed Clemenceau reports they had received from their own generals in the Rhineland complaining about French intrigues. Lloyd George suggested that the Allies might have to rethink their fifteen-year occupation of the Rhineland.[24]

Lloyd George was in fact rethinking the whole treaty. He was well aware that, in the long run, it was not in Britain's best interests to have a weak and possibly revolutionary Germany at the heart of Europe. It also did not seem to be in his own political interest. In a by-election in Central Hull, the candidate advocating "a good, an early and non-revengeful peace" crushed the coalition candidate. His closest colleagues warned that the British public would not support a harsh treaty. The detailed German comments on the treaty, which the Allies received on May 30, echoed many of the concerns that Lloyd George had discussed with his British colleagues. The deputy prime minister, Bonar Law, found the German objections "in many particulars very difficult to answer." Lloyd George agreed. The Germans were in effect saying to the Allies: "You have a set of principles which, when they suit you, you apply, but which, when they suit us, you put by."[25]

The most eloquent critic of all was Smuts. "I am grieved beyond words," he wrote, "that such should be the result of our statesmanship." And his words rolled on: "an impossible peace, conceived on the wrong basis," "our present panic policy," "shocking," "drastic." It would be "practically impossible for Germany to carry out the provisions of the Treaty." The reparations clauses were unworkable "and must kill the goose which is to lay the golden eggs." (Yet it was Smuts himself who had pumped up the figure for reparations by adding in pensions for the widows and orphans of Allied soldiers.) The occupation of the Rhineland and the handing over of German territory to Poland were "full of menace for the future of Europe." He doubted very much that he would be able to sign the treaty as it stood. Lloyd George rather sharply asked him if South Africa was prepared in the same spirit of conciliation to hand back German Southwest Africa. "In this great business," came the reply, "South West Africa is as dust in the balance compared to the burdens now hanging over the civilised world."[26] But Smuts did not offer to give it up.

Sufficiently disturbed by all this, Lloyd George called the British empire delegation together on June 1. Several key ministers from the British government, including Austen Chamberlain, the chancellor of the exchequer; Montagu, the secretary of state for India; and Churchill, secretary of state for war, who had come over from London the night before, joined the meeting. Smuts made an impassioned speech. The peace terms "would produce political and economic chaos in Europe for a generation and in the long run it would be the British Empire which would have to pay the penalty." There was, he added, "far too much of the French demands in that settlement." There was a general murmur of agreement. "The hatred of France for Germany," said Churchill, "was something more than human." General Botha, the prime minister of South Africa, who rarely spoke, reminded them that it was the anniversary of the day, seventeen years ago, when he and Lord Milner had signed the peace that ended the Boer War. "On that occasion it was moderation which had saved South Africa for the British Empire, and he hoped on this occasion that it would be moderation which would save the world." The meeting unanimously authorized Lloyd George to go back to the Council of Four and ask for modifications of the terms on Germany's frontiers with Poland, on reparations, on the Rhineland occupation and on the scores of smaller but irritating "pin pricks." In addition, he would request a promise to Germany that it could enter the League of Nations soon.[27]

The following day Lloyd George told the Council of Four that his colleagues would not authorize him to sign the treaty in its present form; nor would they agree to having the British army march into Germany or the British navy resume the blockade. Wilson and Clemenceau were horrified at the prospect of redoing the work that had been so painfully accomplished. Both concluded that Lloyd George had lost his nerve. "It makes me a little tired," Wilson told the American delegation, "for people to come and say now that they are afraid the Germans won't sign, and their fear is based upon things that they insisted upon at the time of the writing of the treaty." Privately, he said that Lloyd George appeared "to have no principles whatever of his own, that he reacted according to the advice of the last person who had talked with him: that expediency was his sole guiding star." Wilson, for all his earlier reservations, was not now prepared to budge. Clemenceau would give way only on minor matters. As he pointed out in the Council of Four, he had fought his own people to get to this point; if he made any further concessions his government would fall. Lloyd George's view, at least as he reported it in his memoirs, was that he was not suggesting major changes, only ones to bring the treaty more into line with Wilson's own principles.[28]

Two weeks of frequently acrimonious discussions followed. (At one point Wilson is reported to have said to Lloyd George, "You make me sick!") In the end, Lloyd George got one substantial concession: it was agreed that the people of Upper Silesia would decide by plebiscite whether to stay with Germany or join Poland. Otherwise, he achieved little beyond irritating his allies. On the Rhineland occupation, which he proposed to shorten, he faced the implacable opposition of Clemenceau, who, as he told House, would not agree to even fourteen years and 364 days. Eventually some small changes were made to minimize friction between the occupying forces and the German administration and civilians. On the League, the Allies merely assured Germany that they would admit it when they thought that it was behaving properly.[29]

Lloyd George made very little headway on the reparations clauses, partly because he himself still did not know just what he wanted. He had argued strenuously in the past against putting a fixed sum in the treaty. Now he hesitated. Possibly some sort of amount could be mentioned to cover pensions and so on, and the Germans could undertake to repair the damage to Belgium and France. Or perhaps the Germans could say how much the repairs would cost and then the Allies could tell them if it was not enough. He thought at least they should look into it again. Wilson, who had only given way on the fixed sum in the face of opposition from the French and the British, exclaimed to Baker, his press secretary, that Lloyd George was arrogant and intolerable.[30]

Nevertheless, the reparations commission was asked to look at the whole matter again. Again it failed to agree. The French and the British found it impossible to fix a sum; the Americans suggested 120 billion gold marks and even drafted a note to the Germans. Wilson said firmly that justice demanded that the Germans bear a heavy burden, but that the Allies must not drive the German economy to ruin. "I rather like the crust and the sauce of this pie," said Lloyd George, "but not the meat." Wilson replied, "You must however prepare your stomach for meat that will be able to sustain you." Certainly, said Lloyd George, but under one condition: "it is that you give me enough of it." Clemenceau interjected, "And especially, I would like to be sure that it will not go into someone else's stomach." Lloyd George proposed a variety of ingenious schemes to give the impression of a fixed sum without actually naming a figure. "This is your reply to the American proposal about fixing the figure," said Wilson incredulously. "Have you read the rest of the American report?"[31] The clauses were left as they were.

On June 16 the Germans were informed that they had three days to accept the treaty (the deadline was later extended until June 23)—or the Allies would take the necessary steps. Brockdorff-Rantzau and his chief advisers left that night for Weimar. An angry crowd whistled and jeered as their cars rolled toward the railway station. A secretary was knocked out by a rock. The French authorities were unrepentant—remember, said a report, what the Germans did to Belgium—although they later paid the unfortunate woman, who never recovered, a substantial amount.[32]

Reports from Allied agents indicated that it was highly likely that the German government would reject the treaty. The German public was strongly against signing, although it was not clear if it was prepared to fight. Brockdorff-Rantzau, as the Allies knew from intercepted telegrams, was urging rejection and his delegation was behind him. "If Germany refuses," said Clemenceau at the Council of Four, "I favour a vigorous and unremitting military blow that will force the signing." Wilson and Lloyd George agreed without hesitation. On May 20, Foch, as supreme Allied commander, gave the order for a massive drive by forty-two divisions into central Germany. The British prepared to renew the naval blockade.[33]

Two days before the deadline an event occurred that further hardened Allied determination. Far from Paris, at Scapa Flow, the officers of the interned German fleet had been listening to the news from Paris with increasing dismay. The winter had been long and gloomy. The crews had not been allowed to go ashore, a disappointment in particular for the radical sailors who had volunteered for duty so that they could spread the revolution to Britain. The men, bored and mutinous, obeyed routine orders only after prolonged discussions and the ships that had been the pride of the German navy were now filthy. The admiral in charge determined to salvage something of German naval honor. At noon on June 21 British sailors noticed that all the enemy ships had simultaneously raised the German ensign. When one after another the dreadnoughts and destroyers began to list, it was obvious what was happening. The British were too late to save more than a few; by five that afternoon, 400,000 tons of expensive shipping had gone. (Most of the German sailors took to their lifeboats but ten were killed when the British fired at the German ships in a last-ditch attempt to stop the scuttling.) The Germans were delighted; and so was House, who told his diary, "Everyone is laughing at the British Admiralty." The peacemakers were annoyed. "There was no doubt," said Lloyd George, "that the sinking of these ships was a breach of faith." Wilson agreed: "He shared Mr. Lloyd George's suspicions to the full, and did not trust the Germans." There should certainly be no further extension of the deadline, as the German government had requested. In fact, there was some relief that a possible source of conflict between Britain and the United States had been removed.[34]

In Germany, the political situation was chaotic. The coalition government was deeply divided over whether to sign the treaty. Political leaders in the west, along the Allied invasion route, were for peace at all costs, as were the premiers of most of the German states, who saw themselves having to make separate treaties with the victors. The nationalists talked bravely of defiance without making any useful suggestions about how to put it into practice. Among the military, wild schemes circulated: to set up a new state in the east which would be a fortress against the Allies; to have a mass revolt by the officers against the government; or to assassinate the leading advocate of signing, the centrist politician Matthias Erzberger.[35]

The son of a village postman from the Catholic south, Erzberger was bold, cheerful and pragmatic. During the war, his had been the most influential voice for a moderate, negotiated peace. His enemies, and they were many, loathed him for his red face and little eyes, his maddening smile and his habit of saying the unthinkable. Brockdorff-Rantzau, his opposite in almost every respect, could barely be civil to him. In 1919, Erzberger was Germany's armistice commissioner. He was convinced that Germany could not afford to start fighting again. Public opinion, for all the noisy demonstrations from the nationalists, seemed to agree with him. Yes, he told his colleagues in the cabinet, the treaty will place terrible burdens on the German people; and, yes, the right might try a military coup. But there would be a chance for Germany to survive. With the state of war ended, factories would start producing again, unemployment would go down, exports would rise and Germany could afford imports. "Bolshevism will lose its attraction." If Germany did not sign, then the picture would be very different. The Allies would occupy the Ruhr, Germany's industrial heartland; their advance eastward would cut the country in half; the Poles would probably attack from the east; the economy and the transportation system would collapse. "Plunder and murder will be the order of the day." Germany would break up into "a crazy patchwork quilt" of states, some under Bolshevik rule, others under right-wing dictatorships. Germany must sign.[36]

That was not how Brockdorff-Rantzau saw it. He asserted, without much solid evidence, that the Allies were bluffing. They did not want to have to occupy Germany. They were bound to make concessions, even negotiate seriously, if only Germany stood firm. Britain and the United States would probably break with France. His delegation passed a unanimous recommendation: "The conditions of peace are still unbearable, for Germany cannot accept them and continue to live with honour as a nation." The military took the same view. He could not, said Field Marshal Paul von Hindenburg, hold out any hope of success against the Allies, "but as a soldier I can only prefer honourable defeat to a disgraceful peace."[37] The cabinet, which had been leaning toward acceptance of the terms, was deadlocked and resigned on June 20. Brockdorff-Rantzau resigned as head of the German delegation and left politics altogether. (In 1922 he returned as ambassador to Moscow, where his imperious manners deeply impressed the Bolsheviks and where he worked, with considerable success, for closer relations between his country and the Soviet Union.)

Germany now had no government and no spokesman. It almost did not have a president, but Ebert was persuaded that he had a duty to stay on. The deadline of seven P.M. on June 23 drifted closer. On June 22, Ebert finally managed to put together a government. After another lengthy debate, the National Assembly voted in favor of signing, with the reservation that Germany did not recognize the articles dealing with the surrender and trial of those responsible for the war and the "war guilt" clause. The response from Paris was swift: "The German government must accept or refuse, without any possible equivocation, to sign the treaty within the fixed period of time." In Weimar there was fearful confusion. Many deputies and cabinet ministers had left for home, confident that their work was done. The German government asked Paris for an extension of the deadline and then met all night without, however, reaching a decision. Word came from Paris on the morning of June 23 that the deadline would not be extended. At the eleventh hour, after the German army had let it be known that it was in favor of signing, the government managed to get a

resolution through the National Assembly. Many of the right-wing nationalists, vociferous opponents of signing, were privately relieved at the
decision. In another resolution they voted that they did not doubt the patriotism of those who had supported the government. The session closed
as the assembly's chairman said, "We commend our unhappy country to
the care of a merciful God."[38]

The peacemakers waited tensely for the final German word. At about
4:30 in the afternoon a secretary rushed into the Council of Four to say
that the German reply was on the way. "I am counting the minutes," said
Clemenceau. At 5:40 the note arrived. The statesmen crowded around as a
French officer translated the German. Lloyd George broke into smiles,
Wilson grinned and Clemenceau dashed off orders to Foch to stay his advance and to the military in Paris to fire their guns. No more work was
done at the Peace Conference that day.[39]

The signing ceremony was set for June 28, the anniversary of the assassination of the archduke and his wife at Sarajevo; the place was the Hall of
Mirrors at the Palace of Versailles, where the German empire had been
proclaimed in 1871. Clemenceau took personal charge of the arrangements. In great good humor he marched a party through the immense
formal rooms of the palace, amusing them with ancient scandals about
French kings. Look at those two, he whispered, pointing to Wilson and
Balfour: "I bet they are speaking filth; see the look of an old satyr that Balfour has." He ordered magnificent furniture and tapestries to be brought
in to add grandeur and an offending inkwell to be taken away. (Eminent
French officials scoured the museums and antique stores of Paris for one
that met with his approval.[40])

Many of the plenipotentiaries were also in the antique shops, looking
for seals in metal, stone, whatever they could find. (It was a diplomatic tradition that signatures have a personal stamp.) Hughes of Australia had to
be talked out of one showing Hercules slaying a dragon; he finally used a
button from an Australian army uniform. (He had his way, however, with
a four-foot-high marble replica of the Venus de Milo, which he bought
for his long-suffering assistant.) Lloyd George thought he might use a
gold pound. "Then leave it for me," said Clemenceau. "I don't have any
more," Lloyd George replied. "They've all gone to America." On June 27,
as a secretary carefully dripped red wax through a funnel, the plenipotentiaries duly wielded their seals on the treaty in preparation for the next
day's signing.[41]

There was also a hunt for tickets. Each of the Big Five had sixty places
in the Hall of Mirrors. "A very awkward number," said Wilson. "If it were

restricted to say ten it would be easy to make a selection, but if one has to select sixty there are certain to be many heart-burnings." One enterprising American businessman managed to get into the grounds outside the palace by claiming his cigarette case stamped with the manufacturer's coat of arms was a pass. The glamorous red-haired writer Elinor Glyn charmed Lloyd George into letting her attend as a reporter. There were stories of places going for exorbitant prices.[42]

Other, more alarming, rumors circulated. In Berlin, a party of German soldiers had seized flags from the Franco-Prussian War due to be returned to France and burnt them in front of the monument to Frederick the Great while a crowd sang patriotic anthems. Could the Germans refuse to sign, even at this late date? On June 25, the French reported that the skeleton German delegation at the Hôtel des Réservoirs was in high spirits: only low-ranking officials would be sent to sign the treaty. When the Council of Four sent an emissary to inquire, the delegate in charge reported that his government was having great difficulty in finding any minister who would take the responsibility of signing. It was only on June 27 that word came that two representatives were on their way: the new foreign minister, Hermann Müller, and Johannes Bell, the minister of transport. The German delegates arrived at three in the morning, after the customary slow trip by train through the battlefields. New rumors buzzed around Paris: the two would sign, but then they would shoot themselves, possibly Lloyd George and Clemenceau as well, or perhaps simply throw a bomb.[43]

The twenty-eighth of June dawned as a glorious summer day. That morning, the Anglo-American guarantee to come to France's defense if she were attacked by Germany was given formal shape as the French signed separate treaties with the British and the Americans. How much the guarantee was worth was another matter. House doubted that it would get Senate approval: he had always seen it as a useful sop to the French, not a serious commitment. Wilson tended to agree: "We yielded," he told a press conference, "in a certain measure, to meet this French viewpoint." He confidently expected that the guarantee would be unnecessary once the League was up and running, long before Germany became a menace again.[44]

Cars took the peacemakers out to Versailles. (The female secretaries from the British delegation were less fortunate; they were packed, "like sardines," into lorries.[45]) The mile-long drive from the gates to the palace itself was lined with motionless French cavalry in their blue uniforms and steel helmets, the red-and-white pennants on their lances fluttering in the breeze. From the courtyard, filled with more troops, the invited passed up the Grand Staircase lined with members of the élite Garde Républicaine in their white trousers, black boots, dark blue coats and shining silver helmets with long plumes of horsehair, sabers held up in salute.

In the Hall of Mirrors, the crowd—statesmen, diplomats, generals, reporters, some handpicked ordinary soldiers (the French ones bore the scars of terrible injuries), a scattering of women—buzzed and chattered as they took their places on red upholstered benches. The press corps jostled at one end of the room. This was to be the first time that a major treaty was filmed. Frances Stevenson was indignant: "How can you concentrate on the solemnity of a scene when you have men with cameras in every direction, whose sole object is to get as near as they can to the central figures?" There were several conspicuous absences. Foch had gone to his headquarters in the Rhineland. He never forgave Clemenceau: "Wilhelm II lost the war. . . . Clemenceau lost the peace." The Chinese seats were empty because China was refusing to sign the treaty, in protest against the decision to award Shantung to Japan.[46]

One by one the main figures made their way in and found their seats at a huge table flanked by two shorter ones. Clemenceau was beaming. "This is a great day for France," he told Lansing. A copy of the treaty in a special leather box lay on a small Louis XV table. Overhead portraits of Louis XIV—as Roman emperor, great ruler and victor over foreign powers—surveyed the latest chapter in the long struggle between the French and the Germans. At three P.M., the ushers called for silence. "Bring in the Germans," ordered Clemenceau. An Allied guard came through the door and behind them the two German delegates, dressed in formal suits. "They are deathly pale," reported Nicolson. "They do not appear as representatives of a brutal militarism." Many of the audience, including Nicolson himself, felt deeply sorry for them.[47]

Clemenceau opened the proceedings with a brief statement. The German delegates walked forward, conscious of the thousand pairs of eyes. They pulled out the fountain pens which they had carefully brought so that they need not use the pens provided by French patriotic societies, and put their signatures to the treaty with trembling hands. Otherwise they showed little emotion. A signal flashed out from the room to the outside world. Guns around Versailles boomed and the noise spread out to France as other guns took up the chorus. One by one, the Allies and associated powers added their signatures to the treaty and then queued to sign two other agreements, a protocol on the administration of the Rhineland and a treaty with Poland.[48]

Paul Cambon thought the whole affair disgraceful. "They lack only music and ballet girls, dancing in step, to offer the pen to the plenipotentiaries for signing. Louis XIV liked ballets, but only as a diversion; he signed treaties in his study. Democracy is more theatrical than the great king." House thought it more like a Roman triumph, with the defeated being dragged behind their conqueror's chariots: "To my mind it is out of keeping with the new era which we profess an ardent desire to promote. I wish it could have been more simple and that there might have been an element of chivalry, which was wholly lacking. The whole affair was elaborately staged and made as humiliating to the enemy as it well could be." Perhaps, thought a young American more optimistically, the old vicious cycle of revenge and more revenge in Europe had finally been broken.[49]

The audience at first watched in respectful silence, but as the minutes dragged by the noise of conversation rose. Delegates who had finished signing wandered off to chat to friends. Others took copies of their programs around to get autographs. The Germans sat in solitude until finally a daring Bolivian, and then two Canadians, came up to ask for their signatures. After three quarters of an hour there was a call for silence and Clemenceau pronounced the meeting over. The Germans were escorted out. Müller had promised himself that he would be businesslike: "I wanted our ex-enemies to see nothing of the deep pain of the German people, whose representative I was at this tragic moment." Back at the hotel he collapsed. "A cold sweat such as I had never known in my life before broke out all over my body—a physical reaction which necessarily followed the unutterable psychic strain. And now, for the first time, I knew that the worst hour of my life lay behind me." He and the rest of his party insisted on leaving for Germany that night.[50]

The peacemakers walked down to the terrace overlooking the great formal gardens as the fountains spurted into the air. A huge and enthusiastic crowd surged around them. Wilson was nearly pushed into a fountain. Lloyd George was rescued, angry and disheveled, by a squad of soldiers. "A similar thing would never have happened in England," he told an Italian diplomat. "And if it had happened, someone would have had to pay." Afterward Lloyd George, much to his annoyance, was made to sit down and write a letter to the king announcing that the peace had been concluded.[51]

Wilson left by train that night for Le Havre and the United States. Clemenceau came to see him off and, according to one reporter, said with unusual emotion, "I feel as though I were losing one of the best friends I ever had." A small crowd uttered a few listless cries to speed the Americans on their way. At the Hôtel Majestic the British were given a special celebratory dinner, with one more course than usual and free champagne. Afterward there were dances, one for the hotel staff and another for the guests.

Smuts, perhaps as yet another protest against the treaty, joined the staff dance. Paris itself became a giant party, as the streets filled with people singing and dancing. Along the Grands Boulevards the buildings blazed with lights and cars towed the captured German cannon about. (It took the authorities days to collect them all again.) Late that night, as Lansing finished up his account of the day, he could still hear the noise of celebrations outside.[52]

While Paris rejoiced, Germany mourned. In its cities and towns the flags flew at half-mast. Even good socialists now talked of "a peace of shame." Off in the Baltic, where German volunteers were fighting against Bolshevism (and to reassert German power), the news came like a thunderclap. "We shivered," said one, "from the terrible cold of abandonment. We had believed our country would never betray us." Nationalists blamed the traitors at home who had stabbed Germany in the back, and the governing coalition which had signed the treaty.

The Weimar Republic never recovered from that double burden. The nationalists blithely ignored their own promise not to doubt the patriotism of those who voted for the treaty, and did their best to stigmatize them in the eyes of the German people. In 1921, when he was on holiday in the Black Forest, Erzberger was assassinated by two former army officers. "The man," said a leading nationalist paper, "whose spirit unhappily still prevails in many of our government offices and laws, has at last secured the punishment suitable for a traitor." His murderers fled to Hungary but returned to Germany in triumph as "Erzberger's judges" when Hitler came to power. Both were finally tried after the Second World War.[53]

In England, meanwhile, John Maynard Keynes considered his future. He had resigned from the Treasury and left Paris in disgust before the treaty was signed. "I've gone on hoping even through these last dreadful weeks," he wrote to Lloyd George on June 5, "that you'd find some way to make of the Treaty a just and expedient document. But now it's apparently too late. The battle is lost." Keynes was in a curious mood. He told Virginia Woolf that Europe, and in particular the governing classes of which he was a part, were doomed, yet he wrote to another friend that he was tremendously happy to be back at Cambridge. In personal terms he was extremely successful, both professionally and socially, but he felt guilty about his part in the war when so many of his Bloomsbury friends had been pacifists. They in turn laughed at his worldly success, his new friends, his experiments in heterosexuality. Perhaps *The Economic Consequences of the Peace* was something of an act of atonement. Perhaps, too, as Lamont, the American expert on reparations, said, "Keynes got sore because they wouldn't take his advice, his nerve broke, and he quit."[54]

Keynes spent much of the summer writing. In October he met the German banker Melchior again at a conference in Amsterdam. He read him a draft; Melchior was very impressed. This was not surprising, because Keynes echoed much of what the Germans themselves were saying about the Treaty of Versailles. *The Economic Consequences of the Peace* came out just before Christmas in 1919 and has remained in print ever since. It sold over 100,000 copies and was translated into eleven languages, including German, within a year of its appearance. Extracts were read out in the U.S. Senate by a leading opponent of the treaty. The book was wildly successful in Germany, and in the English-speaking world it helped to turn opinion against the peace settlements and against the French. In 1924, a cabinet minister in the Labour government in Britain referred to the treaty as "a treaty of blood and iron which betrayed every principle for which our soldiers thought they were fighting."[55]

Among Germans, as memories faded of the desperate state of affairs in 1919, the belief spread that Germany could have resisted the peace terms if only weak and venal politicians had stood firm. The treaty was, as a popular song put it, "only paper." In 1921, a French diplomat reported to Paris that "a violent campaign using the press, posters and meetings is underway in Germany to undermine the legal basis of the Versailles treaty: German guilt in the war." The German Foreign Office set up a special "war guilt" section which poured out critical studies. In the beer halls of Bavaria, the young Hitler drew crowds with his ringing denunciations of the "peace of shame."[56]

Public opinion in Britain and the United States increasingly swung round to the view that the peace settlements with Germany were deeply unfair. During the next decade, memoirs and novels such as the German *All Quiet on the Western Front* (which sold 250,000 copies in the first year of its English edition) showed that soldiers on both sides had suffered equally from the horrors of trench warfare. The publication of confidential documents from prewar archives undermined the assumption that Germany alone was responsible for the war. Books on the origins of the war apportioned the blame more evenly, to the vanished regimes in Russia or Austria-Hungary, to arms manufacturers or capitalism generally.[57]

In Germany itself, grievances were kept fresh by the myriad of nationalist groups who made much of the fact that millions of German-speakers now found themselves under alien rule, in the Sudetenland of Czechoslovakia, in Poland and in the free city of Danzig. The disarmament clauses were seen as hypocritical and the prohibition on union between Germany and Austria a clear violation of the principle of self-determination. Reparations were "punitive" and "savage," their unfairness compounded by the fact that Germany had to sign the Treaty of Versailles without knowing what the final amount would be. In Germany the *Diktat* ("dictated treaty") took the blame for all that was wrong with the economy: high prices, low wages, unemployment, taxes, inflation. Without the burden of reparations, life would go back to normal; the sun would shine and there would be happy afternoons in the beer gardens, wine cellars and parks. Germans ignored the fact that fighting the Great War had been expensive, and that losing it had meant they could not transfer the costs to anyone else.[58] Like most people since, they also did not grasp that reparations payments never amounted to anything like the huge amounts mentioned in public discussions.

The final figure was set in London in 1921 at 132 billion gold marks (about £6.6 billion or $33 billion). In reality, through an ingenious system of bonds and complex clauses, Germany was committed to pay less than half that amount. It would pay the remainder only when circumstances permitted, such as an improvement in Germany's export figures. Germany also got generous credit for payments in cash or in kind it had already made, such as replacing the books in the Louvain library in Belgium that German troops had burned at the beginning of the war, or for German railways in the territory transferred to Poland. (It tried unsuccessfully to claim the ships scuttled at Scapa Flow.) Even when the payment schedules were revised downward several times, however, the Germans continued to argue that reparations were intolerable. With a unanimity rare in Weimar politics, Germans felt they were paying too much. Germany regularly defaulted on its payments—for the last time and for good in 1932. Orlando had warned of this in 1919, when he said that the capacity to pay was related to the will of the debtor. "It would be dangerous," he added, "to adopt a formula which would, as it were, reward bad faith and a refusal to work."[59]

In the final reckoning, Germany may have paid about 22 billion gold marks (£1.1 billion, $4.5 billion) in the whole period between 1918 and 1932. That is probably slightly less than what France, with a much smaller economy, paid Germany after the Franco-Prussian War of 1870–71.[60] In one way the figures matter; in another they are completely irrelevant. The Germans were convinced that reparations were ruining them. If Germany was not prepared to pay reparations, the Allies were not prepared to enforce their will. While the Treaty of Versailles provided for sanctions— specifically, prolonging the occupation of the Rhineland—the Allies had to want to use them. By the 1930s neither the British nor the French government was prepared to do so over reparations or anything else.

In 1924, a British member of the Inter-Allied Commission of Control, which was established by the Treaty of Versailles to monitor Germany's compliance with the military terms, published an article in which he complained that the German military had systematically obstructed its work and that there were widespread violations of the disarmament clauses of the treaty. There was a storm of protest in Germany at this calumny. (Years later, after Hitler had come to power, German generals admitted that the article had been quite right.[61]) Where, said the Germans, was the general disarmament so often talked about? Why should Germany be the only nation in the world to disarm? The Americans, who had retreated so visibly from world affairs with the repudiation of the League, could scarcely disagree. Nor could the British. The French found themselves increasingly isolated when they complained that Germany was disobeying the military clauses.

The extent of the violations was not completely known at the time, even to the French. Flying clubs were suddenly very popular and were so effective that when Hitler became chancellor he was able to produce a German air force almost at once. The Prussian police force, the largest in Germany, became more and more military in its organization and training. Its officers could easily have moved into the German army, and some did. The self-appointed Freikorps, which had sprung up in 1918, dissolved and its members reformed with dazzling ingenuity as labor gangs, bicycle agencies, traveling circuses and detective bureaus. Some moved wholesale into the army. The Treaty of Versailles limited the number of officers in the army itself to 4,000 but it said nothing about the noncommissioned officers. So the German army had 40,000 sergeants and corporals.[62] Foch had been right; a volunteer army could provide the backbone for rapid expansion.

Factories that had once produced tanks now turned out inordinately heavy tractors; the research was useful for the future. In the Berlin cabarets, they told jokes about the worker who smuggled parts out of a baby carriage factory for his new child only to find when he tried to put them all together he kept getting a machine gun. All over Europe, in safe neutral countries such as the Netherlands and Sweden, companies whose ultimate ownership was in German hands worked on tanks or submarines. The safest place of all, farthest from the prying eyes of the Control Commission, was the Soviet Union. In 1921 the two pariah nations of Europe realized they had something to offer each other. In return for space and secrecy for experiments with tanks, aircraft and poison gas, Germany provided technical assistance and training.[63]

When historians look, as they have increasingly been doing, at the other details, the picture of a Germany crushed by a vindictive peace cannot be sustained. Germany did lose territory; that was an inevitable consequence of losing the war. If it had won, we should remember, it would have certainly taken Belgium, Luxembourg, parts of the north of France and much of the Netherlands. The Treaty of Brest-Litovsk showed the intentions of the German supreme command for the eastern frontiers. Despite its losses Germany remained the largest country in Europe west of the Soviet Union between the wars. Its strategic position was significantly better than it had been before 1914. With the reemergence of Poland, there was now a barrier between it and the old Russian menace. In place of Austria-Hungary, Germany had only a series of weaker and quarreling states on its eastern frontier. As the 1930s showed, Germany was well placed to extend its economic and political sway among them.

The separation of East Prussia from the rest of Germany was an irritation, but such separations were nothing new in the history of Prussia, which for most of its existence had been a series of noncontiguous parcels of territory. Is such a separation necessarily bound to bring trouble? Alaska is separated from the rest of the United States by a large piece of Canada. When was the last time Washington and Ottawa complained to each other about transit rights?[64] The real problem with the Polish Corridor was that many, perhaps a majority, of Germans in the interwar years did not accept it, for all sorts of reasons to do with attitudes toward the Poles and resentment of the Treaty of Versailles. If relations between Poland and Germany had been better, that land barrier need not have been troublesome. Danzig became a free city, but it was still open to German investment and German shipping.

In the west, Germany also faced an advantageous situation. France was gravely depleted by the war, unwilling and, by the 1930s, increasingly unable to summon up the determination to oppose Germany. The guarantee from the United States and Britain was worthless after the failure of the American Senate to ratify it. France's attempts to build alliances with the weak and quarreling nations in Central Europe were a measure of its desperation. It got little support from the British, who made it clear that their empire was their primary concern. The clearest demonstration that the peacemakers had not emasculated Germany came after 1939.

With different leadership in the Western democracies, with stronger democracy in Weimar Germany, without the damage done by the Depression, the story might have turned out differently. And without Hitler to mobilize the resentments of ordinary Germans and to play on the guilty consciences of so many in the democracies, Europe might not have had another war so soon after the first. The Treaty of Versailles is not to blame. It was never consistently enforced, or only enough to irritate German nationalism without limiting German power to disrupt the peace of Europe. With the triumph of Hitler and the Nazis in 1933, Germany had a government that was bent on destroying the Treaty of Versailles. In 1939, von Ribbentrop, the German foreign minister, told the victorious Germans in Danzig: "The Führer has done nothing but remedy the most serious consequences which this most unreasonable of all dictates in history imposed upon a nation and, in fact, upon the whole of Europe, in other words repair the worst mistakes committed by none other than the statesmen of the western democracies."[65]

Conclusion

WITH THE SIGNING of the Treaty of Versailles on June 28, 1919, the world government in Paris dissolved. Wilson left that night, Lloyd George and what was left of the British empire delegation the following morning in a special train. (The British government later discovered to its annoyance that the French had sent a large bill for the train.) Orlando, whose government had fallen, had already gone. Clemenceau, alone of the Big Four, remained in Paris. He spent the summer shepherding the German treaty through the National Assembly and supervising the preparations for a national day of celebration in July. His only break was a brief visit to the devastated regions in the north. The Paris hotels reopened for normal business as the journalists and delegations went home. The prostitutes complained that business was off.[1] At the end of the summer, the British gave up the Majestic. Two decades later, it became the headquarters of another foreign delegation, this time the German army in occupation in Paris.

The Peace Conference continued until January 1920, but it was like a theatrical production whose stars had gone. The foreign ministers and the diplomats took over again but they never regained their old grip on foreign relations. The important decisions were always referred back to their political superiors in Rome or London or Washington and the difficult issues were hammered out in special conferences, of which Lloyd George alone attended thirty-three between 1919 and 1922.

Between January and June 1919, the peacemakers had accomplished an enormous amount: a League of Nations and an International Labour Organization, mandates handed out, the Germany treaty finished, the treaties with Austria, Hungary, Bulgaria and Ottoman Turkey nearly done—but there were many loose ends. Russia's borders were still fluctuating and it was not clear which of its states along the periphery would keep their new independence. Finland? Ukraine? Georgia? Armenia? In the wreckage of empires in the center of Europe the borders were still being disputed. And the decision, taken so lightly, to let the Greeks land in Smyrna had set off a chain of explosions that would not end until 1923.

Moreover, some of the great problems that had faced the peacemakers at the start of the Peace Conference had only been shelved. Russian Bolshevism had been contained, perhaps, but the longer war between the capitalist West and the communist East was only just starting. The German question was still there to trouble Europe. The Allied victory had not been decisive enough and Germany remained too strong.

Nationalism, far from burning itself out, was still gathering momentum. There was much fuel to hand in Central Europe and farther afield, in the Middle East and in Asia. In many cases the peacemakers found themselves dealing with faits accomplis. Yugoslavia, Poland and Czechoslovakia all existed before the Peace Conference started. The best the peacemakers could do was to try to prevent the decomposition of Europe and the Middle East into further and further subdivisions based on nationality and to draw borders as rational as possible. The demand for nation-states based on single nationalities was not itself rational in the world of 1919. It was not possible, then, to put all the Poles in Europe into Poland and all the Germans into Germany. In Europe alone, 30 million people were left in states where they were an ethnic minority, an object of suspicion at home and of desire from their co-nationals abroad.[2]

In that grim winter of 1919, a young American diplomat in Vienna received a delegation of gray-bearded men from Slovenia in the northwest of the Balkans. They spoke German. Their whole town of 60,000 people had spoken German for over 700 years. Now Slovenia was to become part of the new state of Yugoslavia. They were reluctant to be ruled by people they felt to be inferior. Would the United States please annex them? Nicholas Roosevelt, a young cousin of the great Teddy, passed the request on to his superiors but received no reply.[3] Although neither Roosevelt nor the elderly Germans knew it, their community was fated to disappear, along with many others, when the Germans were forcibly expelled from much of Central Europe after the Second World War.

In 1919 the world still shrank from the expulsion of minorities and frowned on forcible assimilation. That left, it seemed, only toleration, of the minority by the majority, a quality that was in short supply in many countries. The peacemakers did their best to impose obligations on governments to treat their minorities well. The new states and some of the smaller powers in the center of Europe had to sign treaties that bound them to treat their minorities equally, to tolerate their religions and to allow them such rights as using their own languages. Both the Rumanians and the Yugoslavs protested. What about similar provisions for the blacks in the United States or the Irish in Britain?, Queen Marie of Rumania asked Wilson. Why, demanded Brătianu, the Rumanian prime minister, was his country being singled out in this way? Italy had minorities but it was not being asked to sign. East Europeans were different, Clemenceau told him unhelpfully. Although both Rumania and Yugoslavia eventually signed, it was not an auspicious start.[4]

The minorities' treaties remained a feeble gesture in the face of growing national chauvinism. The League gave up trying to supervise them by 1934 and the Great Powers had enough else to worry about besides obscure minorities. There were a few hopeful signs: little Estonia voluntarily gave autonomy to its minorities. The mainly Swedish-speaking Åland islands remained under Finnish rule after 1919, but a special treaty guaranteed both language and culture. The Second World War and its aftermath showed yet another solution—the expulsion and murder of unwanted minorities. Some twelve million Germans went westward and seven million Poles, Czechs, Slovaks and Ukrainians were forced to return to what now became their native lands. Europe was left with only minuscule national minorities, less than 3 percent of its total population. Self-determination, that noble ideal, produced dreadful offspring when it was wedded to ethnic nationalism.[5]

The peacemakers in 1919 felt that they had done their best, but they had no illusions that they had solved the world's problems. As he left Paris on June 28, Wilson said to his wife, "Well, little girl, it is finished, and, as no one is satisfied, it makes me hope we have made a just peace; but it is all in the lap of the gods."[6] It was also in the laps of those who came next to lead the world, some of whom had been in Paris—such as Prince Konoe of Japan and Franklin Delano Roosevelt—some of whom had been watching from afar. In Italy, Mussolini was rising fast in nationalist politics, as the old liberal order crumbled under assaults from men such as D'Annunzio. The young Adolf Hitler was in Munich that June, taking congenial courses on the glories of German history and the evils of international Jewish capital. Already he was discovering his own talents as an ideologue and an orator.

Lloyd George had three more years in power. After he was forced to resign in November 1922 he never again held office, although he remained a member of Parliament until his death in 1945. His memoirs of the Peace

Conference, published in 1938, are entertaining, frequently inaccurate, and tend to blame the French or the Americans for everything that went wrong. Clemenceau unwisely ran for president of France at the end of 1919. Expecting to be acclaimed, he withdrew in a rage when it became clear that he would face opposition. He left France almost immediately and spent the next years traveling. He continued to write, a huge and almost unreadable two-volume work on philosophy and a short study of the ancient Athenian orator Demosthenes, who warned his civilized and comfort-loving fellow citizens that they were in danger from the barbarian Philip of Macedon. He refused to write his memoirs and destroyed most of his papers in 1928. He had made his contribution to history, he told a British journalist, but he disdained all discussion of the past. Stung by the posthumous publication of an attack by Foch, he finally took up his pen and drafted a defense of his work during the war and at the Peace Conference. He died in November 1929, before he could complete it. Whatever secrets he had about the inner workings of the Peace Conference, he took with him.[7]

Wilson's end was the saddest. Exhausted by the Peace Conference, he plunged into a wrenching and debilitating fight with the Senate over ratification of the Treaty of Versailles and, more specifically, the League of Nations. His supporters and his opponents had both been busy while he was away. The League to Enforce the Peace was energetically lobbying for ratification. Wilson, unfortunately, did not much care for them, dismissing them as "butters-in" and "wool-gatherers." The League for the Preservation of American Independence, inspired, so it frequently said, by George Washington's and Thomas Jefferson's repeated warnings against permanent or entangling alliances, did its best to thwart the president. As for the ninety-six members of the Senate, it became apparent that they were dividing into roughly four groups. At least six Republicans would not have the League in any form—they came to be known as the Irreconcilables. A few Democrat mavericks would probably vote with them. Some nine Republicans were Mild Reservationists who would have accepted the League so long as their reservations to protect American sovereignty were registered. (Reservations were the well-established diplomatic practice of accepting an international agreement with qualifications; so long as all parties to the treaty agreed, the reservations stood.) This left three dozen Republicans who were not yet fully committed. Most Democrats still followed their president, although many privately hoped he would come to terms with the Mild Reservationists. If Wilson did compromise, there was a good chance that there would be enough votes to get the treaty passed. Would the European powers accept reservations? Lloyd

George claimed in his memoirs that they had always expected they might have to. But they were never put to the test.[8]

Wilson could have built his own coalition. The Republicans only had a majority of two in the Senate and he could have won over the moderates among them by accepting some reservations. When Lansing urged him to compromise, the president was unmoved: "His face took on that stubborn and pugnacious expression which comes when anyone tells him a fact which interferes with his plans." His opponents, Wilson told an intimate, were moved by the basest instincts. "They are going to have the most conspicuously contemptible names in history."[9]

The president arrived back in Washington at midnight on July 8, 1919. A crowd of 100,000, enormous for those days, waited at the train station. Two days later he presented the Treaty of Versailles, with the League covenant at its start, to the Senate in person. "Dare we reject it," he asked them, "and break the heart of the world?" His speech, it was generally agreed, was poor. Unusually, he read parts of it and he lost his thread in places. Washington, and the country, readied themselves for the next step—the Senate's consideration of the treaty.[10]

At first Wilson chose to work largely behind the scenes, meeting with Republican senators in an effort to persuade them that American independence was not compromised by membership in the League or by Article X, in particular, which was the heart of collective security. (Signatories promised "to respect and preserve as against external aggression the territorial integrity and existing political independence of all Members of the League.") He was confident, he told a British diplomat, that the treaty would go through the Senate. He was not prepared, he reiterated, to accept any changes; the treaty must be ratified as they had written it in Paris.[11]

At the end of his first week in Washington, Wilson escaped the summer heat with a cruise on the Potomac on the presidential yacht. He was already looking tired. The impending treaty fight was not the only problem facing his administration that summer. Food prices were going up sharply; racial tensions were exploding into race riots; key unions threatened strikes. The weather broke, with violent thunderstorms, and the president took to his bed for several days. A touch of dysentery, was Admiral Grayson's explanation. There has been much speculation since that it was in fact a minor stroke. Whatever the case, and we will never know for certain, Wilson was clearly not the man he had been. He was easily confused and forgot things he should have known. He lost his temper frequently, often over small matters. Wilson's deteriorating mental and physical health contributed, perhaps, to his refusal to face the reality that he did not have the votes to get the treaty as it stood through the Senate and also to making his well-known stubbornness something more like blind obstinacy. Grayson and Mrs. Wilson, loyal and protective to a fault, did their best to persuade him to rest. They also downplayed the problems with his health.[12]

On July 14 a Democrat who supported the treaty made the first of what were to be five months of speeches in the Senate. On July 31 the Senate Foreign Relations Committee under Lodge's chairmanship started six weeks of hearings. Not surprisingly, the questioning from the Republican majority focused on the League's covenant, especially the by now notorious Article X. On August 19, in an extraordinary breach with convention, Wilson appeared before the committee. He gave no indication that he was prepared to compromise. Four days later, the committee voted on the first of what were to be numerous amendments and reservations to the treaty. The issue they chose was Shantung—to reverse its award to Japan and hand it back to China. An angry Wilson decided the time had come to reach beyond the senators to the American people.[13]

On September 2, 1919, he left Washington for a trip across the country. His closest advisers begged him not to go. Wilson was adamant. The treaty must be saved, even if he had to give his life for it. "In the presence of the great tragedy which now faces the world," he told them, "no decent man can count his personal fortunes in the reckoning."[14] Grayson heard the decision with dread: "There was nothing I could do except to go with him and take such care of him as I could." As Wilson boarded his special train, he complained about the dreadful headaches that he had been having. For almost a month Wilson made speech after speech, sometimes two, even three a day. He hammered at the same themes. The treaty was a great document for peace and for humanity, dearly bought with the sacrifice of the young American men who had gone over to fight in Europe. Those who opposed it back in Washington were partisan, shortsighted, selfish, ignorant, perhaps something worse. "When at last in the annals of mankind they are gibbeted, they will regret that the gibbet is so high." He was glad, he told an audience in St. Louis, that he was away from the capital. "The real voices of the great people of America sometimes sound faint and distant in that strange city!" The crowds grew larger and more enthusiastic as he headed west. Supporters of the treaty grew moderately confident that it might get through if only Wilson would accept some of the milder reservations.[15]

Wilson's headaches grew worse and he looked more and more exhausted. Bad news came in from Washington. Sentiment was growing in favor of reservations. William Bullitt, still smarting from the repudiation of his trip to Russia, now took his revenge, making a dramatic appearance before the Senate hearings to paint a picture of one blunder after another in Paris. Worse, he said that Lansing, the secretary of state, shared his criticisms. Lansing issued an unconvincing denial. "My God!" exclaimed Wilson. "I did not think it was possible for Lansing to act in this way." Grayson noticed with alarm that the president turned pale and saliva appeared in the corners of his mouth. In San Francisco, Wilson told an old friend, a woman whom he had once been close to, that the attacks on the treaty were simply personal. "If *I* had nothing to do with the League of Nations, it would go through just like that!"[16]

On September 25 Wilson was in Colorado. By now he was having repeated coughing attacks which Grayson attributed to asthma. He had to sit propped up at nights and could not sleep for more than two hours at a time. He spoke in Pueblo that afternoon, his fortieth speech in twenty-one days. "Disloyalty," he said of the League's opponents. There would be no compromise with them, no reservations to the covenant: "We have got to adopt it or reject it."[17]

Wilson never spoke in public again. At two the next morning, Mrs. Wilson woke Grayson. He found the president in a pitiable state, ill, gasping for air, the muscles in his face twitching. Wilson feebly insisted that he must carry on. His wife and doctor overruled him. "The doctor is right," Wilson told his secretary with tears in his eyes. "I have never been in a condition like this, and I just feel as if I am going to pieces." The president was suffering, Grayson said in a public statement, from physical exhaustion and a nervous reaction affecting his stomach. The rest of the tour was canceled and the president's train headed back to Washington.[18]

On October 2, at the White House, Wilson had a massive stroke that left him partly paralyzed on his left side. Although he would make a limited recovery over time, he was not physically or mentally the man he had been. He never effectively functioned as president again, although he continued to influence the battle over the treaty from his sickroom. Mrs. Wilson and Grayson took it upon themselves to conceal the full extent of his illness and to carry out his wishes. In the first weeks after the stroke, when it was not clear that Wilson would survive, they kept everyone except Wilson's daughters and the essential nurses and doctors from seeing the president. The leader of the Senate Democrats, Gilbert Hitchcock of Nebraska, was shocked when he finally saw Wilson on November 7. "As he lay in bed slightly propped up by pillows with the useless arm concealed beneath the covers I beheld an emaciated old man with a thin white beard which had been permitted to grow."[19]

The treaty continued to make its way through the Senate for the rest of

October and part of November 1919. Amendments, twelve in all, were defeated by a combination of Democrats and moderate Republicans. Lodge managed, however, to hold most of the Republicans together, and their votes, along with those of the few Democrats who crossed party lines, were sufficient to attach a number of reservations to the treaty. The most crucial reservation involved Article X; the United States would not act to protect the territorial integrity or independence of any League member unless Congress approved. Lodge put forward a motion of ratification incorporating the reservation. When Hitchcock went to Wilson's bedside for a second time on November 17 to discuss this, he found the president significantly more alert—but also more determined than ever. Wilson adamantly opposed the reservation in any form. "That cuts the very heart out of the treaty." He told Hitchcock to let the Republicans take the responsibility for defeating the treaty; they would have to answer to the people of the United States. The following day Mrs. Wilson sent Hitchcock a letter she had written at her husband's dictation. The reservations of Senator Lodge and his cronies amounted to a nullification of the treaty. "I sincerely hope," Wilson said unequivocally, "that the friends and supporters of the League will vote against the Lodge resolution of ratification." The next day the Senate voted on Lodge's motion. It was defeated by a combination of those Democrats, the majority, who still followed Wilson's bidding and Republican Irreconcilables. Four weeks later, Wilson learned that he had won the Nobel Peace Prize.[20]

Moderate Republicans and Democrats made a last-ditch effort to find a compromise. From the White House an embittered Wilson did his best to block them. Even so the moderates came close; when the Senate voted for the final time on March 19, 1920, on a fresh resolution to ratify the treaty, with slightly modified reservations, the new resolution passed. Twenty-three Democrats defied their president to vote in favor. The necessary two-thirds majority, however, remained just out of reach so the Senate failed to give its consent to the treaty. "Doctor," Wilson said to Grayson that night, "the devil is a busy man."[21]

He never changed his view that he had been right to reject compromise. The United States later signed separate treaties with Germany, Austria and Hungary, but it never joined the League. Wilson, who had briefly contemplated running for president again, lingered on until 1924. Mrs. Wilson survived to go to John F. Kennedy's inauguration in 1960.

Wilson's efforts, and those of the many other peacemakers who shared his ideals, were not completely wasted. The Treaty of Versailles, and the other treaties with the defeated that used it as a model, certainly contained provisions about territory and reparations that could have been written in earlier centuries, but they were also imbued with a new spirit. The covenant of the League came at the start, not as an afterthought, and the League itself was woven into the later clauses, supervising the plebiscites, governing the Saar and Danzig, and monitoring the mandates. The provisions for an International Labour Organization, for treaties to protect minorities, to set up a permanent court of justice or to try men such as the kaiser for offenses against international morality, underlined the idea that there were certain things that all humanity had in common and that there could be international standards beyond those of mere national interest. And when those treaties were attacked in the interwar years it was generally because they had failed to match those standards.

Later it became commonplace to blame everything that went wrong in the 1920s and 1930s on the peacemakers and the settlements they made in Paris in 1919, just as it became easy to despair of democracy. Pointing the finger and shrugging helplessly are effective ways of avoiding responsibility. Eighty years later the old charges about the Paris Peace Conference still have a wide circulation. "The final crime," declared *The Economist* in its special millennium issue, was "the Treaty of Versailles, whose harsh terms would ensure a second war."[22] That is to ignore the actions of everyone—political leaders, diplomats, soldiers, ordinary voters—for twenty years between 1919 and 1939.

Hitler did not wage war because of the Treaty of Versailles, although he found its existence a godsend for his propaganda. Even if Germany had been left with its old borders, even if it had been allowed whatever military forces it wanted, even if it had been permitted to join with Austria, he still would have wanted more: the destruction of Poland, control of Czechoslovakia, above all the conquest of the Soviet Union. He would have demanded room for the German people to expand and the destruction of their enemies, whether Jews or Bolsheviks. There was nothing in the Treaty of Versailles about that.

The peacemakers of 1919 made mistakes, of course. By their offhand treatment of the non-European world, they stirred up resentments for which the West is still paying today. They took pains over the borders in Europe, even if they did not draw them to everyone's satisfaction, but in Africa they carried on the old practice of handing out territory to suit the imperialist powers. In the Middle East, they threw together peoples, in Iraq most notably, who still have not managed to cohere into a civil society. If they could have done better, they certainly could have done much worse. They tried, even cynical old Clemenceau, to build a better order. They could not foresee the future and they certainly could not control it. That was up to their successors. When war came in 1939, it was a result of twenty years of decisions taken or not taken, not of arrangements made in 1919.

Of course things might have been different if Germany had been more thoroughly defeated. Or if the United States had been as powerful after the First World War as it was after the Second—and had been willing to use that power. If Britain and France had not been weakened by the war—or if they had been so weakened that the United States had felt obliged to step in. If Austria-Hungary had not disappeared. If its successor states had not quarreled with each other. If China had not been so weak. If Japan had been more sure of itself. If states had accepted a League of Nations with real powers. If the world had been so thoroughly devastated by war that it was willing to contemplate a new way of managing international relations. The peacemakers, however, had to deal with reality, not what might have been. They grappled with huge and difficult questions. How can the irrational passions of nationalism or religion be contained before they do more damage? How can we outlaw war? We are still asking those questions.

Woodrow Wilson's Fourteen Points

I. Open covenants of peace, openly arrived at, after which there shall be no private international understandings of any kind but diplomacy shall proceed always frankly and in the public view.

II. Absolute freedom of navigation upon the seas, outside territorial waters, alike in peace and in war, except as the seas may be closed in whole or in part by international action for the enforcement of international covenants.

III. The removal, so far as possible, of all economic barriers and the establishment of an equality of trade conditions among all the nations consenting to the peace and associating themselves for its maintenance.

IV. Adequate guarantees given and taken that national armaments will be reduced to the lowest point consistent with domestic safety.

V. A free, open-minded, and absolutely impartial adjustment of all colonial claims, based upon a strict observance of the principle that in determining all such questions of sovereignty, the interests of the populations concerned must have equal weight with the equitable claims of the government whose title is to be determined.

VI. The evacuation of all Russian territory and such a settlement of all questions affecting Russia as will secure the best and freest cooperation of the other nations of the world in obtaining for her an unhampered and unembarrassed opportunity for the independent determination of her own political development and national policy and assure her of a sincere welcome into the society of free nations under institutions of her own choosing; and, more than a welcome, assistance also of every kind that she may need and may herself desire. The treatment accorded Russia by her sister nations in the months to come will be the acid test of their good will, of their comprehension of her needs as distinguished from their own interests, and of their intelligent and unselfish sympathy.

VII. Belgium, the whole world will agree, must be evacuated and restored without any attempt to limit the sovereignty which she enjoys in common with all other free nations. No other single act will serve as this will serve to restore confidence among the nations in the laws which they have themselves set and determined for the government of their relations with one another. Without this healing act the whole structure and validity of international law is forever impaired.

VIII. All French territory should be freed and the invaded portions restored, and the wrong done to France by Prussia in 1871 in the matter of Alsace-Lorraine, which has unsettled the peace of the world for nearly fifty years, should be righted, in order that peace may once more be made secure in the interest of all.

IX. A readjustment of the frontiers of Italy should be effected along clearly recognizable lines of nationality.

X. The peoples of Austria-Hungary, whose place among the nations we wish to see safeguarded and assured, should be accorded the freest opportunity of autonomous development.

XI. Rumania, Serbia, and Montenegro should be evacuated; occupied territories restored; Serbia accorded free and secure access to the sea; and the relations of the several Balkan states to one another determined by friendly counsel along historically established lines of allegiance and nationality; and international guarantees of the political and economic independence and territorial integrity of the several Balkan states should be entered into.

XII. The Turkish portions of the present Ottoman Empire should be assured a secure sovereignty, but the other nationalities which are now under Turkish rule should be assured an undoubted security of life and an absolutely unmolested opportunity of autonomous development, and the Dardanelles should be permanently opened as a free passage to the ships and commerce of all nations under international guarantees.

XIII. An independent Polish state should be erected which should include the territories inhabited by indisputably Polish populations, which should be assured a free and secure access to the sea, and whose political and economic independence and territorial integrity should be guaranteed by international covenant.

XIV. A general association of nations must be formed under specific covenants for the purpose of affording mutual guarantees of political independence and territorial integrity to great and small states alike.

Bibliography

ABBREVIATIONS

FRUS   *Papers Relating to the Foreign Relations of the United States:*
       The Paris Peace Conference 1919

PWW   *The Papers of Woodrow Wilson*

UNPUBLISHED SOURCES

Bodleian Library, Oxford
    Alfred Milner Papers
British Library, London
    Arthur Balfour Papers
    George Nathaniel Curzon Papers
    Edwin Montagu Papers
Churchill College, Cambridge
    Archives of Lord Hankey of the Chart
    Winston S. Churchill Papers, Charwell Group
    Alan Leeper Papers
House of Lords Record Office
    Lloyd George Papers
Library of Congress, Washington, D.C.
    The Ray Stannard Baker Papers
    George Louis Beer Collection
    Tasker H. Bliss Papers
Ministère des Affaires Etrangères, Paris
    Jules Cambon Papers
    Paul Cambon Papers
    Georges Mandel Papers
    André Tardieu Papers
    Série à Paix, 1914–1920
    Europe, 1918–1929
Ministère de la Défense, Archives d'Armée de Terre, Château de Vincennes
    Clemenceau Papers
National Archives of Canada, Ottawa
    Oliver Mowat Biggar Papers
    Robert Laird Borden Papers
    Loring Christie Papers

National Library of Australia, Canberra
    Frederic William Eggleston Papers
    William Morris Hughes Papers
    J. G. Latham Papers
    R. R. Garran Papers
Public Record Office, London
    Cabinet Papers, CAB 29/Peace Conference and Other International Conferences
Scottish Record Office, Edinburgh
    Lothian (Philip Kerr) Papers
St. Antony's College, Oxford
    Ian Malcolm Papers
University Microfilms International
    Sidney Sonnino Papers
Yale University Library, New Haven
    Gordon Auchincloss Papers
    Edward Mandel House Papers
    Charles Seymour Papers
    Sir William Wiseman Papers

OTHER SOURCES

Adam, M. "France and Hungary at the Beginning of the 1920s," *War and Society in East Central Europe,* ed. B. K. Kiraly, P. Pastor and I. Sanders, vol. 6, *Essays on World War I: Total War and Peacemaking, A Case Study on Trianon,* ed. B. K. Kiraly, P. Pastor and I. Sanders. New York, 1982.

Adamthwaite, A. *Grandeur and Misery: France's Bid for Power in Europe, 1914–1940.* London, 1995.

Adelson, R. *Mark Sykes: Portrait of an Amateur.* London, 1967.

Ahmad, F. "The Late Ottoman Empire," *The Great Powers and the End of the Ottoman Empire,* ed. M. Kent. London, 1984.

Alastos, D. *Venizelos: Patriot, Statesman, Revolutionary.* London, 1942.

Albrecht-Carrié, R. "Fiume: Nationalism versus Economics," *Journal of Central European Affairs* (1942).

———. *Italy at the Paris Peace Conference.* Hamden, Connecticut, 1966.

Alcock, A. "Trentino and Tyrol: From Austrian Crownland to European Region," *Europe and Ethnicity,* ed. S. Dunn and T. G. Fraser. London, 1996.

Aldcroft, D. H. *From Versailles to Wall Street, 1919–1929.* London, 1987.

———. "The Versailles Legacy," *History Review,* 29 (December 1997).

Aldrovandi Marescotti, L. *Guerra diplomatica: ricordi e frammenti di diario.* Milan, 1936.

———. *Nuovi ricordi e frammenti di diario per far seguito a "Guerra diplomatica" (1914–1919).* Milan, 1938.

Allizé, H. *Ma mission à Vienne.* Paris, 1933.

Almond, N., and R. H. Lutz, eds. *The Treaty of St. Germain: A Documentary History of Its Territorial and Political Clauses.* Stanford, California, 1935.

Ambrosius, L. E. *Woodrow Wilson and the American Diplomatic Tradition: The Treaty Fight in Perspective.* Cambridge, Massachusetts, 1990.

Amery, L. S. *The Leo Amery Diaries,* ed. J. Barnes and D. Nicholson, 2 vols. London, 1980.

Anderson, M. S. *The Eastern Question, 1774–1923: A Study in International Relations.* London, 1966.

Andrew, C. M., and A. S. Kanya-Forstner. *France Overseas: The Climax of French Imperial Expansion, 1914–1924.* Stanford, California, 1981.

Antonius, G. *The Arab Awakening: The Story of the Arab National Movement.* New York, 1965.

Apponyi, A. *The Memoirs of Count Apponyi.* London, 1935.

Armstrong, H. F. *Peace and Counterpeace: From Wilson to Hitler: Memoirs of Hamilton Fish Armstrong.* New York, 1971.

Ashmead-Bartlett, E. *The Tragedy of Central Europe.* London, 1923.

Azan, P. *Franchet d'Esperey.* Paris, 1949.

Baerlein, H. P. *The Birth of Yugoslavia,* 2 vols. London, 1922.

Bailey, T. A. *Woodrow Wilson and the Lost Peace.* Chicago, 1963.

Baker, R. S. *What Wilson Did at Paris.* New York, 1919.

———. *Woodrow Wilson and World Settlement: Written from His Unpublished Material,* 2 vols. London, 1923.

———. *Woodrow Wilson: Life and Letters,* 8 vols. Garden City, New York, 1927–39.

Banac, I. *The National Question in Yugoslavia: Origins, History, Politics.* Ithaca and London, 1984.

Bandholtz, H. *An Undiplomatic Diary by the American Member of the Inter-Allied Military Mission to Hungary, 1919–1920.* New York, 1966.

Barcsay, T. "The Karolyi Revolution in Hungary, October 1918–March 1919," unpublished DPhil. thesis. University of Oxford, 1971.

Barker, E. *Austria 1918–1972.* London, 1973.

Bartlett, V. *Behind the Scenes at the Peace Conference.* London, 1920.

Baruch, B. M. *The Making of the Reparation and Economic Sections of the Treaty.* New York, 1920.

Bauer, O. *The Austrian Revolution.* London, 1925.

Beadon, R. H. *Some Memories of the Peace Conference.* London, 1933.

Beaverbrook, Lord. *The Decline and Fall of Lloyd George.* London, 1963.

Beers, B. F. *Vain Endeavor: Robert Lansing's Attempts to End the American-Japanese Rivalry.* Durham, North Carolina, 1962.

Bell, P.M.H. *France and Britain 1900–1940: Entente and Estrangement.* London and New York, 1996.

Bennett, G. *Cowan's War: The Story of British Naval Operations in the Baltic, 1918–1920.* London, 1964.

Bessel, R. *Germany After the First World War.* Oxford, 1993.

———. "Why Did the Weimar Republic Collapse?" *Weimar: Why Did German Democracy Fail?,* ed. I. Kershaw. New York, 1990.

Birdsall, P. *Versailles: Twenty Years After.* London, 1941.

Block, R. "City of the Future," *New York Review of Books,* June 9, 1994.

Boemeke, M., G. D. Feldman, and E. Glaser, eds. *The Treaty of Versailles: A Reassessment After 75 Years.* Cambridge and Washington, 1998.

Bonsal, S. *Unfinished Business.* Garden City, New York, 1944.

———. *Suitors and Suppliants: The Little Nations at Versailles.* New York, 1946.

Borden, R. L. *Robert Laird Borden: His Memoirs,* ed. H. Borden, 2 vols. London, 1938.

Borsanyi, G. *The Life of Communist Revolutionary, Bela Kun.* Highland Lakes, New Jersey, 1993.

Bosworth, R.J.B. "Italy and the End of the Ottoman Empire," *The Great Powers and the End of the Ottoman Empire,* ed. M. Kent. London, 1984.

Bothwell, R. *Loring Christie.* New York and London, 1988.

Boyce, R., ed. *French Foreign and Defence Policy, 1918–1940: The Decline and Fall of a Great Power.* London and New York, 1998.

Brecher, F. W. "French Policy Towards the Levant, 1914–18," *Middle Eastern Studies,* 29/4 (1993).

Bridge, F. R. "The Foreign Policy of the Monarchy 1908–1918," *The Last Years of Austria-Hungary,* ed. M. Cornwall. Exeter, 1990.

Brown, J. M. *Gandhi's Rise to Power.* Cambridge, U.K., 1972.

———. *Gandhi: Prisoner of Hope.* New Haven and London, 1989.

Brown, R. C. *Robert Laird Borden,* 2 vols. Toronto, 1975–80.

Brownell, W., and R. N. Billings. *So Close to Greatness: A Biography of William C. Bullitt.* New York and London, 1987.

Bruun, G. *Clemenceau.* Cambridge, Massachusetts, 1943.

Bunselmeyer, R. *The Cost of War, 1914–1919: British Economic War Aims and the Origins of Reparation.* Hamden, Connecticut, 1975.

Burgwyn, H. J. *Italian Foreign Policy in the Interwar Period, 1918–1940.* Westport, Connecticut, 1987.

———. *The Legend of the Mutilated Victory: Italy, the Great War, and the Paris Peace Conference, 1915–1919.* Westport, Connecticut, 1993.

Burnett, P. M. *Reparation at the Paris Peace Conference from the Standpoint of the American Delegation,* 2 vols. New York, 1965.

Burns, M. "Disturbed Spirits: Minority Rights and New World Orders, 1919 and the 1990s," *New European Orders, 1919 and 1991,* ed. S. F. Wells and P. Bailey Smith. Washington, D.C., 1996.

Busch, B. C. *Mudros to Lausanne: Britain's Frontier in West Asia, 1918–1923.* Albany, 1976.

———. *Britain, India and the Arabs, 1914–1921.* Berkeley, 1971.

Butler, H. *The Lost Peace.* London, 1941.

Butler, J.R.M. *Lord Lothian, Philip Kerr, 1882–1940.* London, 1960.

Cairns, J. C. "A Nation of Shopkeepers in Search of a Suitable France: 1919–1940," *American Historical Review,* 3 (1974).

Calder, K. J. *Britain and the Origins of the New Europe.* Cambridge, U.K., 1976.

Callimachi, A.-M. *Yesterday Was Mine.* New York, London and Toronto, 1949.

Callwell, C. E. *Field Marshal Sir Henry Wilson: His Life and Diaries,* 2 vols. London, 1927.

Cambon, P. *Correspondance, 1870–1924,* 3 vols. Paris, 1946.

Cambridge History of Japan, 6 vols. Cambridge, 1989.

Campbell, F. G. "The Struggle for Upper Silesia, 1919–1922," *Journal of Modern History,* 42/3 (September 1970).

Campbell, J. *F. E. Smith, First Earl of Birkenhead.* London, 1983.

Cannadine, D. *The Decline and Fall of the British Aristocracy.* New Haven and London, 1990.

Carls, S. D. *Louis Loucheur and the Shaping of Modern France, 1916–1931.* Baton Rouge and London, 1993.

Carsten, F. L. *Revolution in Central Europe, 1918–19.* Berkeley and Los Angeles, 1972.

Carton de Wiart, A. *Happy Odyssey: The Memoirs of Lieutenant-General Sir Adrian Carton de Wiart.* London, 1950.

Cecil, R. *A Great Experiment: An Autobiography.* London, 1941.

———. *All the Way.* London, 1949.

Chernow, R. *The Warburgs.* New York, 1993.

Chi, M. S. *China Diplomacy, 1914–1918.* Cambridge, Massachusetts, 1970.

———. "Ts'ao Ju-lin (1876–1966): His Japanese Connections," *The Chinese and the Japanese: Essays in Political and Cultural Interactions,* ed. A. Iriye. Princeton, New Jersey, 1980.

Chow, T. *The May Fourth Movement: Intellectual Revolution in Modern China.* Cambridge, Massachusetts, 1960.

Chu, P. *V. K. Wellington Koo: A Case Study of China's Diplomat and Diplomacy of Nationalism, 1912–1966.* Hong Kong, 1981.

Churchill, W. S. *The Aftermath.* New York, 1929.

———. *Great Contemporaries.* London, 1959.

Cienciala, A. M. "The Battle of Danzig and the Polish Corridor at the Paris Peace Conference of 1919," *The Reconstruction of Poland, 1914–23,* ed. P. Latawski. London, 1992.

———, and T. Komarnicki. *From Versailles to Locarno: Keys to Polish Foreign Policy, 1919–1925.* Lawrence, Kansas, 1984.

Clemenceau, G. *Grandeur and Misery of Victory.* Toronto, 1930.

Clogg, R. *A Concise History of Greece.* Cambridge, U.K., 1992.

Cohen, W. I. *The American Revisionists: The Lessons of Intervention in World War I.* Chicago and London, 1967.

Connors, L. *The Emperor's Advisor: Saionji Kinmochi and Pre-war Japanese Politics.* London, 1987.

Constant, S. *Foxy Ferdinand: Tsar of Bulgaria.* London, 1979.

Cook, G. L. "Sir Robert Borden, Lloyd George, and British Military Policy, 1917–1918," *Historical Journal,* 14/2 (1971).

Coolidge, H. J., and R. H. Lord. *Archibald Cary Coolidge.* Boston and New York, 1932.

Cooper, J. M. *Breaking the Heart of the World: Woodrow Wilson and the Fight for the League of Nations.* Cambridge, U.K., and New York, 2001.

Cornwall, M. "The Dissolution of Austria-Hungary," ed. M. Cornwall, *The Last Years of Austria-Hungary.* Exeter, 1990.

Craig, G. A., and F. Gilbert, eds. *The Diplomats: 1919–1939.* New York, 1963.

Crampton, R. J. *A Short History of Modern Bulgaria.* Cambridge, U.K., 1987.

Crozier, A. J. "The Establishment of the Mandates System, 1919–25," *Journal of Contemporary History,* 14/3 (1979).

Cruttwell, C.R.M.F. *A History of the Great War, 1914–1918.* London, 1982.

Curry, G. "Woodrow Wilson, Jan Smuts and the Versailles Settlement," *American Historical Review,* 66/4 (July 1961).

Curry, R. W. *Woodrow Wilson and Far Eastern Policy, 1913–1921.* New York, 1968.

Czernin, F. *Versailles 1919.* New York, 1964.

Darwin, J. *Britain, Egypt and the Middle East: Imperial Policy in the Aftermath of War, 1918–1922.* New York, 1981.

Davies, N. "Great Britain and Polish Jews, 1918–1920," *Journal of Contemporary History,* 8/2 (April 1973).

———. "Lloyd George and Poland, 1919–20," *Journal of Contemporary History,* 6/3 (1971).

———. *White Eagle, Red Star: The Polish-Soviet War, 1919–1920.* London, 1972.

———. *God's Playground: A History of Poland,* 2 vols. New York, 1982.

Deák, F. *Hungary at the Paris Peace Conference: The Diplomatic History of the Treaty of Trianon.* New York, 1942.

Debo, R. K. *Revolution and Survival: The Foreign Policy of Soviet Russia, 1917–18.* Toronto and Buffalo, 1979.

Department of External Affairs, Ottawa. *Documents on Canadian External Relations,* vol. 2, *The Paris Peace Conference.* Ottawa, 1969.

Department of State. *Papers Relating to the Foreign Relations of the United States: The Paris Peace Conference 1919,* 13 vols. Washington, D.C., 1942–47.

———. *Papers Relating to the Foreign Relations of the United States: The Robert Lansing Papers, 1914–1920,* 2 vols. Washington, D.C., 1939–40.

———. *The Treaty of Versailles and After.* Washington, D.C., 1947.

Desmond, R. W. *Windows on the World: World News Reporting, 1900–1920.* Iowa City, 1980.

Deutscher, I. *The Prophet Armed: Trotsky: 1879–1921.* New York, 1965.

Dillon, E. J. *The Inside Story of the Peace Conference.* New York and London, 1920.

Dingman, R. *Power in the Pacific: The Origin of Naval Arms Limitations, 1914–1922.* Chicago, 1976.

Dockrill, M. L., and J. D. Goold. *Peace Without Promise: Britain and the Peace Conferences, 1919–1923.* Hamden, Connecticut, 1981.

Dockrill, M. L., and Z. Steiner. "The Foreign Office at the Paris Peace Conference in 1919," *International History Review,* 2/1 (January 1980).

Dominian, L. *The Frontiers of Language and Nationality in Europe.* New York, 1917.

Dontas, D. V. "Troubled Friendship: Greco-Serbian Relations, 1914–1918," *The Creation of Yugoslavia,* ed. D. Djordjevic. Santa Barbara and Oxford, 1980.

Dragnich, A. N. *Serbia, Nikola Pasic, and Yugoslavia.* New Brunswick, New Jersey, 1974.

———. "The Serbian Government, the Army and the Unification of Yugoslavs," *The Creation of Yugoslavia, 1914–1918,* ed. D. Djordjevic. Santa Barbara and Oxford, 1980.

Duchêne, F. *Jean Monnet: The First Statesman of Independence.* New York, 1994.

Dugdale, B. *Arthur James Balfour, 1906–1930.* New York, 1937.

Dunn, S., and T. G. Fraser, eds. *Europe and Ethnicity: The First World War and Contemporary Ethnic Conflict.* London, 1996.

Durham, M. E. *Twenty Years of Balkan Tangle.* London, 1920.

Duroselle, J.-B. *Clemenceau.* Paris, 1988.

Duus, P. *The Rise of Modern Japan.* Boston, 1976.

Dyer, G. "The Turkish Armistice of 1918: 1—The Turkish Decision for a Separate Peace, Autumn 1918," *Middle Eastern Studies,* 8/2 (May 1972).

———. "The Turkish Armistice of 1918: 2—A Lost Opportunity: The Armistice Negotiations of Moudros," *Middle Eastern Studies,* 8/3 (October 1972).

Dziewanowski, M. K. *Joseph Pilsudski: A European Federalist, 1918–1922.* Stanford, 1969.

Eban, A. *An Autobiography.* New York, 1977.

Eckelt, F. "The Internal Policies of the Hungarian Soviet Republic," *Hungary in Revolution, 1918–19,* ed. I. Volgyes. Lincoln, Nebraska, 1971.

Egerton, G. W. "Britain and the 'Great Betrayal': Anglo-American Relations and the Struggle for United States Ratification of the Treaty of Versailles, 1919–1920," *Historical Journal,* 21/4 (1978).

———. *Great Britain and the Creation of the League of Nations.* Chapel Hill, North Carolina, 1978.

———. "The Lloyd George Government and the Creation of the League of Nations," *American Historical Review,* 79/2 (April 1974).

Ekmecic, M. "Serbian War Aims," *The Creation of Yugoslavia,* ed. D. Djordjevic. Santa Barbara and Oxford, 1980.

Elcock, H. *Portrait of a Decision: The Council of Four and the Treaty of Versailles.* London, 1972.

Elon, A. *The Israelis: Founders and Sons.* New York, 1972.

Epstein, K. *Matthias Erzberger and the Dilemma of German Democracy.* New York, 1971.

Esposito, D. M. "Imagined Power: The Secret Life of Colonel House," *Historian,* 60/4 (Summer 1998).

Eubank, K. K. *Paul Cambon: Master Diplomatist.* Norman, Oklahoma, 1960.

Eyck, E. *A History of the Weimar Republic,* 2 vols. New York, 1970.

Farnsworth, B. *William C. Bullitt and the Soviet Union.* Bloomington and London, 1967.

Farwell, B. *The Great War in Africa, 1914–1918.* New York and London, 1986.

Ferguson, N. "Keynes and German Inflation," *English Historical Review,* 110/436 (April 1995).

———. *The Pity of War.* New York, 1999.

Fifield, R. H. "Disposal of the Carolines, Marshalls, and Marianas at the Paris Peace Conference," *American Historical Review,* 51/3 (April 1946).

———. *Woodrow Wilson and the Far East: The Diplomacy of the Shantung Question.* New York, 1952.

Figes, O. *A People's Tragedy: The Russian Revolution, 1891–1924.* London, 1996.

Fischer, L. *The Soviets in World Affairs: A History of the Relations between the Soviet Union and the Rest of the World, 1917–1929.* New York, 1960.

Fisher, J. *Curzon and British Imperialism in the Middle East, 1916–19.* London, 1999.

Fitzhardinge, L. F. "Hughes, Borden, and Dominion Representation at the Paris Peace Conference," *Canadian Historical Review,* 49/2 (June 1968).

———. *The Little Digger, 1914–1952: William Morris Hughes. A Political Biography,* 2 vols. London and Sydney, 1979.

———. "W. M. Hughes and the Treaty of Versailles, 1919," *Journal of Commonwealth Political Studies,* 5 (July 1967).

Fitzherbert, M. *The Man Who Was Greenmantle: A Biography of Aubrey Herbert.* London, 1983.

Floto, I. *Colonel House in Paris: A Study of American Policy at the Paris Peace Conference, 1919.* Princeton, New Jersey, 1973.

Foch, F. *The Memoirs of Marshal Foch.* Garden City, New York, 1931.

Fogelsong, D. S. *America's Secret War Against Bolshevism.* Chapel Hill and London, 1995.

French, D. " 'Had We Known How Bad Things Were in Germany, We Might Have Got Stiffer Terms': Great Britain and the German Armistice," *The Treaty of Versailles: A Reassessment after 75 Years,* ed. M. Boemeke, G. D. Feldman and E. Glaser. Cambridge, U.K., and Washington, D.C., 1998.

Fried, A., ed. *A Day of Dedication: The Essential Writings and Speeches of Woodrow Wilson.* New York, 1965.

Friedman, I. "The McMahon–Hussein Correspondence and the Question of Palestine," *Journal of Contemporary History,* 5/2 (1970).

————. *The Question of Palestine, 1914–1918: British-Jewish-Arab Relations.* Oxford, 1973.

Fromkin, D. *A Peace to End All Peace: The Fall of the Ottoman Empire and the Creation of the Modern Middle East.* New York, 1989.

————. *In the Time of the Americans: FDR, Truman, Eisenhower, Marshall, MacArthur—The Generation That Changed America's Role in the World.* New York, 1995.

Fry, M. G. *Lloyd George and Foreign Policy,* 2 vols. Montreal and London, 1977.

Garnett, D., ed. *The Essential T. E. Lawrence.* New York, 1951.

Garran, R. *Prosper the Commonwealth.* Sydney, 1958.

Geddes, D. "The Mandate for Yap," *History Today* (December 1993).

Gelfand, L. E. *The Inquiry.* New Haven, Connecticut, 1963.

Genov, G. P. *Bulgaria and the Treaty of Neuilly.* Sofia, 1935.

George, A. L., and J. L. George. *Woodrow Wilson and Colonel House: A Personality Study.* New York, 1964.

Gerson, L. *Woodrow Wilson and the Rebirth of Poland, 1914–1920: A Study in the Influence on American Policy of Minority Groups of Foreign Origin.* Hamden, Connecticut, 1972.

Gidney, J. A. *A Mandate for Armenia.* Kent, Ohio, 1967.

Gilbert, M. *Winston S. Churchill,* 8 vols. London, 1966–88.

————. *Sir Horace Rumbold: Portrait of a Diplomat, 1869–1941.* London, 1973.

Gilmour, D. *Curzon.* London, 1994.

Glazebrook, G. P. de T. *Canada at the Peace Conference.* London, Toronto and New York, 1942.

Glyn, A. *Elinor Glyn.* London, 1968.

Gokay, B. "Turkish Settlement and the Caucasus, 1918–20," *Middle Eastern Studies,* 32/2 (April 1996).

Goldstein, E. "Great Britain and Greater Greece, 1917–1920," *Historical Journal,* 32/2 (1989).

————. *Winning the Peace: British Diplomatic Strategy, Peace Planning, and the Paris Peace Conference, 1916–1920.* Oxford, 1991.

Gollin, A. M. *Proconsul in Politics: A Study of Lord Milner in Opposition and in Power.* London, 1964.

Grayson, C. T. *Woodrow Wilson.* Washington, D.C., 1960.

Gregory, J. D. *On the Edge of Diplomacy: Rambles and Reflections, 1902–1928.* London, 1928.

Grew, J. C. *Turbulent Era: A Diplomatic Record of Forty Years, 1904–1945.* Boston, 1952.

Grigg, J. *The Young Lloyd George.* London, 1973.

————. *Lloyd George: From Peace to War, 1912–1916.* London, 1985.

————. *Lloyd George: The People's Champion.* Berkeley and Los Angeles, 1978.

Griswold, A. W. *The Far Eastern Policy of the United States.* New Haven, Connecticut, 1938.

Groueff, S. *Crown of Thorns.* Lanham, Maryland, 1987.

Guhin, M. A. *John Foster Dulles: A Statesman and His Times.* New York and London, 1972.

Guiral, P. *Clemenceau et son Temps.* Paris, 1994.

Hall, H. D. *Mandates, Dependencies and Trusteeship.* London, 1948.

Hancock, W. H. *Smuts: The Sanguine Years, 1870–1919.* Cambridge, U.K., 1962.

————, and J. Van der Poel, eds. *Selections from the Smuts Papers,* 7 vols. Cambridge, U.K., 1966.

Hankey, M. P. *The Supreme Control at the Paris Peace Conference 1919: A Commentary.* London, 1963.

Hardach, G. *The First World War, 1914–1918.* Berkeley and Los Angeles, 1977.

Hardinge, C. *Old Diplomacy: The Reminiscences of Lord Hardinge of Penshurst.* London, 1947.

Harington, C. *Tim Harington Looks Back.* London, 1940.

Harris, H. W. *Peace in the Making.* London, 1920.

Harrod, R. F. *The Life of John Maynard Keynes.* London, 1951.

Haskins, C. H., and R. H. Lord. *Some Problems of the Peace Conference.* Cambridge, Massachusetts, 1920.

BIBLIOGRAPHY

Headlam-Morley, J. *A Memoir of the Peace Conference 1919,* ed. A. Headlam-Morley, R. Bryant and A. Cienciala. London, 1972.
Heater, D. *National Self-Determination: Woodrow Wilson and His Legacy.* New York, 1994.
Hecksher, A. *Woodrow Wilson.* New York, 1991.
Helmreich, P. C. *From Paris to Sèvres: The Partition of the Ottoman Empire at the Peace Conference of 1919–20.* Columbus, Ohio, 1974.
Henig, R. B., ed. *The League of Nations.* New York, 1973.
Hess, R. L. "Italy and Africa: Colonial Ambitions in the First World War," *Journal of African History* (1963).
Hiery, H. J. *The Neglected War: The German South Pacific and the Influence of World War I.* Honolulu, 1995.
Hoensch, J. K. *A History of Modern Hungary, 1867–1986.* London and New York, 1988.
Holborn, H. "Diplomats and Diplomacy in the Early Weimar Republic," *The Diplomats, 1919–1939,* ed. G. A. Craig and F. Gilbert. New York, 1963.
Hoover, H. *The Ordeal of Woodrow Wilson.* Baltimore and London, 1992.
House, E. M. *The Intimate Papers of Colonel House Arranged as a Narrative by Charles Seymour,* 4 vols. Boston and New York, 1926–28.
———, and C. Seymour, eds. *What Really Happened at Paris: The Story of the Peace Conference, 1918–1919, by American Delegates.* New York, 1921.
Hovi, K. *Cordon sanitaire or barrière de l'est?* Turku, 1975.
Howard, E. *Theatre of Life: Life Seen from the Stalls, 1905–1936.* London, 1936.
Howard, H. N. *The Partition of Turkey: A Diplomatic History, 1913–1923.* New York, 1966.
———. *Turkey, the Straits and U.S. Policy.* Baltimore and London, 1974.
Howard, M. *War and the Liberal Conscience.* Oxford, 1981.
Huddleston, S. *Peace-making at Paris.* London, 1919.
Hudson, G. "The Far East at the End of the First World War," *Journal of Contemporary History,* 4/2 (April 1969).
Hudson, W. J. *Billy Hughes in Paris: The Birth of Australian Diplomacy.* West Melbourne, Victoria, 1978.
Hugessen, H.M.K. *Diplomat in Peace and War.* London, 1949.
Hughes, W. H. *Policies and Potentates.* Sydney, 1950.
———. *The Splendid Adventure.* Toronto, 1928.
Hunter, J. *The Emergence of Modern Japan.* London and New York, 1989.
Hunter Miller, D. *My Diary at the Conference of Paris, with Documents,* 21 vols. New York, 1928.
———. *The Drafting of the Covenant,* 2 vols. New York, 1928.
Huntford, R. *Nansen: The Explorer as Hero.* London, 1998.
James, L. *The Golden Warrior: The Life and Legend of Lawrence of Arabia.* London, 1990.
———. *Imperial Warrior: The Life and Times of Field-Marshal Viscount Allenby, 1861–1936.* London, 1993.
Jaszi, O. *The Dissolution of the Habsburg Monarchy.* Chicago and London, 1929.
Jedrezejewicz, W. *Pilsudski: A Life for Poland.* New York, 1982.
Jelavich, B. *History of the Balkans,* 2 vols. Cambridge, U.K., and New York, 1983.
Jelavich, C. "Nicholas P. Pasic: Greater Serbia or Jugoslavia?" *Journal of Central European Affairs,* 11/2 (July 1951).
Jones, T. *Whitehall Diary,* vol. 1, *1916–1925.* London, 1969.
Károlyi, M. *Memoirs of Michael Károlyi: Faith Without Illusion.* London, 1956.
Kawamura, N. "Wilsonian Idealism and Japanese Claims at the Paris Peace Conference," *Pacific Historical Review,* 66/4 (1997).
Kedourie, E. *The Chatham House Version and Other Middle-Eastern Studies.* London, 1970.
———. "The End of the Ottoman Empire," *Journal of Contemporary History,* 3/4 (October 1968).
Keegan, N. M. "From Chancery to Cloister: The Chinese Diplomat Who Became a Benedictine Monk," *Diplomacy and Statecraft,* 10/1 (1999).
Keiger, J. *Raymond Poincaré.* Cambridge, U.K., 1997.

Kenez, P. *Civil War in South Russia, 1919–1920.* Berkeley and Los Angeles, 1977.

Kennedy, A. L. *Old Diplomacy and New.* London, 1922.

Kennedy, M. D. *The Estrangement of Great Britain and Japan, 1917–1935.* Berkeley and Los Angeles, 1969.

Kent, B. *The Spoils of War: The Politics, Economics, and Diplomacy of Reparations, 1918–1932.* Oxford, 1989.

Kent, M. *Oil and Empire: British Policy and Mesopotamian Oil, 1900–1920.* London, 1976.

———. *Moguls and Mandarins: Oil, Imperialism and the Middle East in British Foreign Policy, 1900–1940.* London, 1993.

———, ed. *The Great Powers and the End of the Ottoman Empire.* London, 1984.

Kershaw, I., ed. *Hitler, 1889–1936: Hubris.* London and New York, 1998.

———. *Weimar: Why Did German Democracy Fail?* New York, 1990.

Kessler, H. *In the Twenties: The Diaries of Harry Kessler.* New York, 1971.

Keylor, W. R. "Versailles and International Diplomacy," *The Treaty of Versailles: A Reassessment after 75 Years,* ed. M. Boemeke, G. D. Feldman and E. Glaser. Cambridge, U.K., and Washington, D.C., 1998.

———. *The Legacy of the Great War.* Boston and New York, 1998.

Keynes, J. M. *Two Memoirs: Dr. Melchior, a Defeated Enemy, and My Early Beliefs.* London, 1949.

———. *The Economic Consequences of the Peace.* New York, 1971.

Khoury, P. *Syria and the French Mandate.* Princeton, 1987.

King, J. C. *Foch Versus Clemenceau: France and German Dismemberment, 1918–1919.* Cambridge, U.K., 1960.

King, W. [Wen-ssu Chin]. *China at the Paris Peace Conference in 1919.* Jamaica, N.Y., 1961.

———. *V. K. Wellington Koo's Foreign Policy.* Shanghai, 1931.

Kinross, P. B. *Ataturk: A Biography of Mustafa Kemal, Father of Modern Turkey.* London, 1964.

Kiraly, B. K., P. Pastor and I. Sanders, eds. *War and Society in East Central Europe,* vol. 6, *Essays on World War I: Total War and Peacemaking: A Case Study on Trianon.* New York, 1982.

Kissinger, H. *Diplomacy.* New York, 1994.

Klein, F. "Between Compiègne and Versailles: The Germans on the Way from a Misunderstood Defeat to an Unwanted Peace," *The Treaty of Versailles: A Reassessment After 75 Years,* ed. M. Boemeke, G. D. Feldman and E. Glaser. Cambridge, U.K., and Washington, D.C., 1998.

Kleine-Ahlbrandt, W. L. *The Burden of Victory: France, Britain and the Enforcement of the Versailles Peace, 1919–1925.* Lanham, Maryland, New York and London, 1995.

Klieman, A. *Foundations of British Policy in the Arab World: The Cairo Conference of 1921.* Baltimore and London, 1970.

Klingaman, W. *1919: The Year Our World Began.* New York, 1987.

Klotz, L. L. *De la guerre à la paix: souvenirs et documents.* Paris, 1924.

Knock, T. J. *To End All Wars: Woodrow Wilson and the Quest for a New World Order.* New York and Oxford, 1992.

Komarnicki, T. *Rebirth of the Polish Republic: A Study in the Diplomatic History of Europe, 1914–1920.* London, 1957.

Krüger, P. "German Disappointment and Anti-Western Resentment, 1918–19," *Confrontation and Cooperation: Germany and the United States in the Era of World War I, 1900–1924,* ed. H.-J. Schröder. Providence and Oxford, 1993.

Kumao, H. *Saionji-Harada Memoirs: Fragile Victory, Prince Saionji and the 1930 London Treaty Issue,* trans. T. F. Mayer-Oakes. Detroit, 1968.

Lacey, R. *The Kingdom.* New York and London, 1981.

La Fargue, T. E. *China and the World War.* Stanford, California, 1937.

Laffan, R.G.D. *The Serbs: The Guardians of the Gates.* New York, 1989.

Landau, Z. "The Economic Integration of Poland 1918–23," *The Reconstruction of Poland, 1914–23,* ed. P. Latawski. London, 1992.

Langer, W. L. "The Well-Spring of Our Discontents," *Journal of Contemporary History*, 3/4 (October 1968).

Lansing, R. *The Big Four and Others of the Peace Conference*. Boston, 1921.

———. *The Peace Negotiations: A Personal Narrative*. Boston and New York, 1921.

Laroche, J. *Au Quai d'Orsay avec Briand et Poincaré, 1913–1926*. Paris, 1957.

Latawski, P. "Roman Dmowski, the Polish Question, and Western Opinion, 1915–1918: The Case of Britain," *The Reconstruction of Poland, 1914–23*, ed. P. Latawski. London, 1992.

Latham, J. G. *The Significance of the Peace Conference from an Australian Point of View*. Melbourne, 1920.

Lauren, P. G. "Human Rights in History: Diplomacy and Racial Equality at the Paris Peace Conference," *Diplomatic History*, 2/3 (1978).

Lazo, D. D. "A Question of Loyalty: Robert Lansing and the Treaty of Versailles," *Diplomatic History*, 9/1 (Winter 1985).

Lebow, R. N. "Woodrow Wilson and the Balfour Declaration," *Journal of Modern History*, 40/4 (1968).

Ledeen, M. *The First Duce: D'Annunzio at Fiume*. Baltimore, 1977.

Lederer, I. J. *Yugoslavia at the Peace Conference: A Study in Frontiermaking*. New Haven and London, 1963.

Lentin, A. *Lloyd George, Woodrow Wilson and the Guilt of Germany*. Leicester, 1984.

———. "Lord Cunliffe, Lloyd George, Reparations and Reputations at the Paris Peace Conference, 1919," *Diplomacy and Statecraft*, 10/1 (1999).

———. "Trick or Treat? The Anglo-French Alliance, 1919," *History Today*, 42 (December 1992).

Levene, M. "The Balfour Declaration: A Case of Mistaken Identity," *English Historical Review* (January 1992).

———. "Nationalism and Its Alternatives in the International Arena: The Jewish Question at Paris, 1919," *Journal of Contemporary History*, 28 (1993).

———. *War, Jews, and the New Europe: The Diplomacy of Lucien Wolf, 1914–1919*. Oxford and New York, 1992.

Levin, P. L. *Edith and Woodrow: the Wilson White House*. New York, 2001.

Lewis, D. L. *W.E.B. Du Bois: Biography of a Race, 1868–1919*. New York, 1993.

Liddell Hart, B. *Foch: The Man of Orleans*. London, 1931.

Lieven, A. *The Baltic Revolution: Estonia, Latvia, Lithuania and the Path to Independence*. New Haven and London, 1994.

Link, A. S. *Wilson: The Road to the White House*. Princeton, New Jersey, 1947.

———. *Wilson: The New Freedom*. Princeton, New Jersey, 1956.

———. *Wilson the Diplomatist*. Chicago, 1963.

———. *Wilson: Confusions and Crises, 1915–1916*. Princeton, New Jersey, 1964.

Lloyd George, D. *The Truth About Reparations and War Debts*. London, 1932.

———. *War Memoirs*, 6 vols. London, 1934.

———. *The Truth About the Peace Treaties*, 2 vols. London, 1938.

Lloyd George, F. *The Years That Are Past*. London, 1967.

Louis, W. R. *British Strategy in the Far East, 1919–1939*. Oxford, 1971.

———. *Great Britain and Germany's Lost Colonies, 1914–1919*. Oxford, 1967.

Lovin, C. R. *A School for Diplomats: The Paris Peace Conference of 1919*. Lanham, Maryland, 1997.

Lowe, C. J., and M. L. Dockrill. *The Mirage of Power*, 3 vols. London and Boston, 1972.

Lowe, C. J., and F. Marzari. *Italian Foreign Policy, 1870–1940*. London and Boston, 1975.

Lowry, B. *Armistice 1918*. Kent, Ohio, and London, 1996.

Luckau, A. *The German Delegation at the Paris Peace Conference*. New York, 1971.

Lundgreen-Nielsen, K. *The Polish Problem at the Paris Peace Conference: A Study in the Policies of the Great Powers and the Poles, 1918–1919*. Odense, 1979.

———. "Aspects of American Policy towards Poland at the Paris Peace Conference and the Role of Isiah Bowman," *The Reconstruction of Poland, 1914–23*, ed. P. Latawaski. London, 1992.

————. "The Mayer Thesis Reconsidered: The Poles and the Paris Peace Conference, 1919," *International History Review*, 7/1 (February 1985).

Macartney, C. A. *Hungary and Her Successors: The Treaty of Trianon and Its Consequences 1919–1937.* London and New York, 1937.

————. *National States and National Minorities.* New York, 1934.

Macfie, A. L. "The British Decision Regarding the Future of Constantinople, November 1918–January 1920," *Historical Journal*, 18/2 (1975).

————. *The End of the Ottoman Empire, 1918–1923.* London and New York, 1998.

Mackay, R. F. *Balfour: Intellectual Statesman.* Oxford and New York, 1985.

MacMillan, M. "Canada and the Origins of the Imperial War Cabinet," *Imperial Canada, 1867–1917,* ed. C. M. Coates. Edinburgh, 1997.

Magosci, P. R. *Historical Atlas of East Central Europe.* Toronto, 1993.

Maier, C. S. *Recasting Bourgeois Europe.* Princeton, 1975.

————. "The Truth about the Treaties?" *Journal of Modern History,* 51 (March 1979).

Malcolm, I. *Lord Balfour: A Memory.* London, 1930.

Mamatey, V. S. *The United States and East Central Europe, 1914–1918: A Study in Wilsonian Diplomacy and Propaganda.* Princeton, New Jersey, 1957.

————, and R. Luza, eds. *A History of the Czechoslovak Republic, 1918–1948.* Princeton, 1973.

Mansel, P. *Constantinople: City of the World's Desire, 1453–1924.* New York, 1995.

Mansergh, N. *The Commonwealth Experience,* 2 vols. Toronto and Buffalo, 1983.

Mantoux, E. *The Carthaginian Peace.* London, 1946.

Mantoux, P. *The Deliberations of the Council of Four,* 2 vols., ed. and trans. A. S. Link. Princeton, New Jersey, 1992.

Marder, A. J. *From the Dreadnought to Scapa Flow: The Royal Navy in the Fisher Era, 1904–1919,* 5 vols. London, 1970.

Marks, S. *Innocent Abroad: Belgium at the Paris Peace Conference of 1919.* Chapel Hill, 1981.

————. "The Myths of Reparations," *Central European History,* 11/3 (1978).

————. "Reparations Reconsidered: A Reminder," *Central European History* 2/4 (1969).

————. "Smoke and Mirrors," *The Treaty of Versailles: A Reassessment After 75 Years,* ed. M. Boemeke, G. D. Feldman and E. Glaser. Cambridge, U.K., and Washington, D.C., 1998.

Marlowe, J. *Late Victorian: The Life of Sir Arnold Talbot Wilson.* London, 1967.

Marston, F. S. *The Peace Conference of 1919: Organisation and Procedure.* London, 1944.

Martel, G. "The Prehistory of Appeasement: Headlam-Morley, the Peace Settlement and Revisionism," *Diplomacy and Statecraft,* 9/3 (November 1998).

Masaryk, T. G. *The Making of a State: Memories and Observations, 1914–1918.* New York, 1969.

Maxwell, E. *R.S.V.P.: Elsa Maxwell's Own Story.* Boston and Toronto, 1954.

May, A. J. *The Passing of the Hapsburg Monarchy, 1914–1918,* 2 vols. Philadelphia, 1966.

Mayer, A. J. *Politics and Diplomacy of Peacemaking: Containment and Counterrevolution at Versailles, 1918–1919.* New York, 1967.

Mazower, M. "Minorities and the League of Nations in Interwar Europe," *Daedalus,* 126/2 (1997).

————. "Two Cheers for Versailles," *History Today,* 49/7 (July 1999).

McCrum, R. "French Rhineland Policy at the Paris Peace Conference, 1919," *Historical Journal,* 21/3 (1978).

McDougall, W. A. *France's Rhineland Diplomacy, 1914–1924: The Last Bid for a Balance of Power in Europe.* Princeton, New Jersey, 1978.

————. "Political Economy Versus National Sovereignty: French Structures for German Economic Integration after Versailles," *Journal of Modern History,* 51 (March 1979).

McDowall, D. *A Modern History of the Kurds.* London and New York, 1996.

Mee, C. L. *The End of Order: Versailles 1919.* New York, 1980.

Ministero degli Affari Esteri. *I documenti diplomatici italiani,* 6th ser., ed. R. Mosca. Rome, 1956–.

Miquel, P. *La paix de Versailles et l'opinion publique française.* Paris, 1972.

Mitchell, D. *1919: Red Mirage.* New York, 1970.

Mitrovic, A. "The 1919–1920 Peace Conference in Paris and the Yugoslav State: An Historical Evaluation," *The Creation of Yugoslavia, 1914–1918,* ed. D. Djordjevic. Santa Barbara and Oxford, 1980.

Mommsen, W. J. "Max Weber and the Peace Treaty of Versailles," *The Treaty of Versailles: A Reassessment After 75 Years,* ed. M. Boemeke, G. D. Feldman and E. Glaser. Cambridge, U.K., and Washington, D.C., 1998.

Monroe, E. *Britain's Moment in the Middle East.* Baltimore, 1963.

Montgomery, A. E. "The Making of the Treaty of Sèvres of 10 August 1920," *Historical Journal,* 25/4 (1972).

Mordacq, G. H. *Clemenceau au soir de sa vie,* 2 vols. Paris, 1933.

———. *Le ministère Clemenceau,* 4 vols. Paris, 1931.

Morgan, K. O. *David Lloyd George: Welsh Radical as World Statesman.* Westport, Connecticut, 1982.

Mosley, L. *Curzon: The End of an Epoch.* London, 1961.

Napier, H. D. *The Experiences of a Military Attaché in the Balkans.* London, 1924.

Nassibian, A. *Britain and the Armenian Question, 1915–1923.* New York, 1984.

Nekrich, A. M. *Pariahs, Partners, Predators: German-Soviet Relations, 1922–1941.* New York, 1997.

Nelson, H. I. *Land and Power: British and Allied Policy on Germany's Frontiers 1916–19.* London and Toronto, 1963.

Neu, C. E. *The Troubled Encounter: The United States and Japan.* New York, 1975.

Nevakivi, J. *Britain, France and the Arab Middle East, 1914–1920.* London, 1969.

Newman, B. *Secret Servant.* London, 1935.

Nicolson, H. *Curzon: The Last Phase.* London, 1934.

———. *Peacemaking, 1919.* London, 1964.

Nicolson, N., ed. *Vita and Harold: The Letters of Vita Sackville-West and Harold Nicolson.* London, 1993.

Nish, I. H. *Alliance in Decline: A Study in Anglo-Japanese Relations, 1908–23.* London, 1972.

———. *Japanese Foreign Policy, 1869–1942: Kasumigaseki to Miyakezaka.* London, 1977.

Nitti, F. *Rivelazioni: dramatis personae.* Naples, 1948.

Noble, G. B. *Policies and Opinions at Paris, 1919: Wilsonian Diplomacy, the Versailles Peace, and French Public Opinion.* New York, 1935.

Nordholt, J.W.S. *Woodrow Wilson: A Life For World Peace.* Berkeley, 1991.

Northedge, F. S. "1917–1919: The Implications for Britain," *Journal of Contemporary History,* 3/4 (October 1968).

Nowak, K. F. *Versailles.* London, 1928.

Orga, I. *Portrait of a Turkish Family.* London and New York, 1988.

Orlando, V. E. *Memorie (1915–1919).* Milan, 1960.

Ormos, M. "The Hungarian Soviet Republic and Intervention by the Entente," *War and Society in East Central Europe,* vol. 6, *Essays on World War I: Total War and Peacemaking. A Case Study on Trianon,* ed. B. K. Kiraly, P. Pastor and I. Sanders. New York, 1982.

Orpen, W. *An Onlooker in France, 1917–1919.* London, 1921.

Pakula, H. *Queen of Rumania.* London, 1989.

Palmer, A. W. *The Decline and Fall of the Ottoman Empire.* London, 1993.

Palmer, F. *Bliss, Peacemaker.* Freeport, New York, 1970.

Paloczi-Horvath, G. *The Undefeated.* London, 1993.

Pandey, B. N. *The Break-up of British India.* London and New York, 1969.

Pastor, P. *Hungary Between Wilson and Lenin: The Hungarian Revolution of 1918–1919 and the Big Three.* New York, 1976.

Perman, D. *The Shaping of the Czechoslovak State: A Diplomatic History of the Boundaries of Czechoslovakia.* Leiden, 1962.

Petsalis-Diomidis, N. *Greece at the Paris Peace Conference (1919).* Thessaloniki, 1978.

Pipes, R. *Russia Under the Bolshevik Regime.* New York, 1995.

Poincaré, R. *Au service de la France XI: A la recherche de la paix, 1919.* Paris, 1974.

Pope, N., and H. Pope. *Turkey Unveiled: Ataturk and After.* London, 1997.

Pugach, N. H. *Paul S. Reinsch: Open Door Diplomat in Action.* Millwood, New York, 1979.

Pugh, M. *Lloyd George.* London and New York, 1988.

Raffo, P. "The Anglo-American Preliminary Negotiations for a League of Nations," *Journal of Contemporary History,* 9/4 (1974).

Rattigan, F. *Diversions of a Diplomat.* London, 1924.

Rawlinson, A. *Adventures in the Near East 1918–1922: In Three Parts.* London and New York, 1924.

Reinharz, J. *Chaim Weizmann: The Making of a Statesman.* New York and Oxford, 1993.

Renouvin, P. *War and Aftermath, 1914–1929.* New York, 1968.

Repington, C. *After the War: London, Paris, Rome, Athens, Prague, Vienna, Budapest, Bucharest, Berlin, Sofia, Coblenz, New York, Washington: A Diary.* Boston and New York, 1922.

Reynolds, D. *Britannia Overruled.* London and New York, 1991.

Ribot, A. *Journal d'Alexandre Ribot et correspondances inédites, 1914–1922.* Paris, 1936.

Riddell, G. *Lord Riddell's Intimate Diary of the Peace Conference and After 1918–1923.* London, 1933.

————, et al. *The Treaty of Versailles and After.* New York, 1935.

Rodd, J. R. *Social and Diplomatic Memories,* 3 vols. London, 1925.

Röhl, J.C.G. *The Kaiser and His Court: Wilhelm II and the Government of Germany.* Cambridge, U.K., 1996.

Roosevelt, N. *A Front Row Seat.* Norman, Oklahoma, 1953.

Rose, K. *King George V.* London, 1983.

Roskill, S. *Hankey: Man of Secrets,* 3 vols. London, 1972.

Roszkowski, W. "The Reconstruction of the Government and State Apparatus in the Second Polish Republic," *The Reconstruction of Poland, 1914–23,* ed. P. Latawski. London and Basingstoke, 1992.

Rothschild, J. *East Central Europe Between the Two World Wars.* Seattle and London, 1974.

Rowland, P. *Lloyd George.* London, 1975.

Rowley, C. D. *The Australians in German New Guinea, 1914–1921.* Carlton, Victoria, 1958.

Rudin, H. *Armistice, 1918.* New Haven, Connecticut, 1944.

Ryan, A. *The Last of the Dragomans.* London, 1951.

Ryder, A. J. *The German Revolution of 1918.* Cambridge, 1967.

Sakmyster, T. L. "Great Britain and the Making of the Treaty of Trianon," *War and Society in East Central Europe,* vol. 6, *Essays on World War I: Total War and Peacemaking. A Case Study on Trianon,* ed. B. K. Kiraly, P. Pastor and I. Sanders, New York, 1982.

————. *Hungary's Admiral on Horseback: Miklòs Horthy, 1918–1944.* New York, 1994.

Saladino, S. "In Search of Sidney Sonnino," *Reviews in European History* (1976).

Salter, A. *Slave of the Lamp; A Public Servant's Notebook.* London, 1967.

Sanders, R. *The High Walls of Jerusalem: A History of the Balfour Declaration and the Birth of the British Mandate for Palestine.* New York, 1983.

Sayer, D. *The Coasts of Bohemia: A Czech History.* Princeton, New Jersey, 1998.

Schachtman, T. *Edith and Woodrow.* New York, 1981.

Schiff, V. *The Germans at Versailles 1919.* London, 1930.

Schrecker, J. E. *Imperialism and Chinese Nationalism; Germany in Shantung.* Cambridge, Massachusetts, 1971.

Schröder, H.-J. *Confrontation and Cooperation: Germany and the United States in the Era of World War I, 1900–1924.* Providence and Oxford, 1993.

Schuker, S. A. *American "Reparations" to Germany, 1919–33: Implications for the Third-World Debt Crisis.* Princeton, 1988.

————. *The End of French Predominance in Europe: The Financial Crisis of 1924 and the Adoption of the Dawes Plan.* Chapel Hill, North Carolina, 1976.

————. "The Rhineland Question," *The Treaty of Versailles: A Reassessment After 75 Years,* ed. M. Boemeke, G. D. Feldman and E. Glaser. Cambridge, U.K., and Washington, D.C., 1998.

Schüller, R. *Unterhändler des Vertrauens: aus den nachgelassenen Schriften von Sektionschef Dr. Richard Schüller,* ed. J. Nautz. Munich, 1990.

Schwabe, K. "Germany's Peace Aims and the Domestic and International Constraints,"
    The Treaty of Versailles: A Reassessment After 75 Years, ed. M. Boemeke, G. D. Feldman
    and E. Glaser. Cambridge, U.K., and Washington, D.C., 1998.
———. *Woodrow Wilson, Revolutionary Germany, and Peacemaking, 1918–1919: Missionary
    Diplomacy and the Realities of Power.* Chapel Hill and London, 1985.
Schwarcz, V. *The Chinese Enlightenment: Intellectuals and the Legacy of the May Fourth Move-
    ment of 1919.* Berkeley, 1986.
Scott, C. P. *The Political Diaries of C. P. Scott, 1911–1928,* ed. T. Wilson. London, 1970.
Seton-Watson, C. *Italy From Liberalism to Fascism, 1870–1925.* London, 1967.
———. "1919," *Review of International Studies* (1989).
Seton-Watson, H., and C. Seton-Watson. *The Making of a New Europe: R. W. Seton-Watson
    and the Last Years of Austria-Hungary.* London, 1981.
Seymour, C. *Letters from the Paris Peace Conference.* New Haven and London, 1965.
Sforza, C. *Fifty Years of War and Diplomacy in the Balkans.* New York, 1940.
———. "Sonnino and His Foreign Policy," *Contemporary Review* (1929).
Shaarawi, H. *Harem Years: The Memoirs of an Egyptian Feminist (1879–1924).* New York,
    1986.
Shanafelt, G. W. "An English Lady in High Albania: Edith Durham and the Balkans," *East
    European Quarterly,* 30/3 (1996).
Sharp, A. "The Genie That Would Not Go Back Into the Bottle: National Self-
    Determination and the Legacy of the First World War and the Peace Settlement," *Eu-
    rope and Ethnicity: The First World War and Contemporary Ethnic Conflic,* ed. S. Dunn and
    T. G. Fraser. London, 1996.
———. *The Versailles Settlement: Peacemaking in Paris, 1919.* London, 1991.
Shotwell, J. T. *At the Paris Peace Conference.* New York, 1937.
Silverman, D. P. *Reconstructing Europe After the Great War.* Cambridge, Massachusetts, 1982.
Skidelsky, R. *John Maynard Keynes: A Biography,* 2 vols. London, 1983.
Sluglett, P. *Britain in Iraq, 1914–1932.* London, 1976.
Smith, M. L. *Ionian Vision: Greece in Asia Minor, 1919–1922.* New York, 1973.
Snelling, R. C. "Peacemaking, 1919: Australia, New Zealand and the British Empire Del-
    egation at Versailles," *Journal of Imperial and Commonwealth History,* 4/1 (1975).
Sonyel, S. R. *Turkish Diplomacy 1918–1923: Mustafa Kemal and the Turkish National Movement.*
    London and Beverly Hills, 1975.
Soutu, G.-H. "The French Peacemakers and Their Home Front," *The Treaty of Versailles:
    A Reassessment After 75 Years,* ed. M. Boemeke, G. D. Feldman and E. Glaser. Cam-
    bridge, U.K., and Washington, D.C., 1998.
Spector, S. *Rumania at the Paris Peace Conference: A Study of the Diplomacy of Ioan I. C. Bra-
    tianu.* New York, 1962.
Spence, J. D. *The Search for Modern China.* New York and London, 1990.
Stadler, K. R. *The Birth of the Austrian Republic, 1918–1921.* Leyden, 1966.
———. "The Disintegration of the Austrian Empire," *Journal of Contemporary History,* 3/4
    (October 1968).
Steed, H. W. *Through Thirty Years, 1892–1922: A Personal Narrative,* 2 vols. Garden City, New
    York, 1924.
Steffens, L. *The Autobiography of Lincoln Steffens.* New York, 1931.
Stein, L. *The Balfour Declaration.* London, 1961.
Stevenson, D. *The First World War and International Politics.* Oxford, 1991.
———. "France at the Paris Peace Conference," *French Foreign and Defence Policy,
    1918–1940: The Decline and Fall of a Great Power,* ed. R. Boyle. London and New York,
    1998.
———. "French War Aims and the American Challenge, 1914–1918," *Historical Journal,*
    22/4 (1979).
Stevenson, F. *Lloyd George: A Diary,* ed. A.J.P. Taylor. London, 1971.
Stickney, E. P. *Southern Albania or Northern Epirus in European International Affairs, 1912–1923.*
    Stanford, California, 1926.

Stone, N. *The Eastern Front 1914–1917.* London, 1998.

Storrs, R. *Orientations.* London, 1937.

Sugar, P. F., and I. J. Lederer, eds. *Nationalism in Eastern Europe.* Seattle and London, 1994.

Suny, R. G. *Looking Toward Ararat: Armenia in Modern History.* Bloomington and Indianapolis, 1993.

Suval, S. *The Anschluss Question in the Weimar Era: A Study of Nationalism in Germany and Austria, 1918–1932.* Baltimore and London, 1974.

Sykes, C. *Crossroads to Israel: 1917–1948.* Bloomington and London, 1973.

Tanner, M. *Croatia: A Nation Forged in War.* New Haven and London, 1997.

Tardieu, A. *The Truth about the Treaty.* Indianapolis, 1921.

Taylor, A.J.P. *The Habsburg Monarchy 1809–1918.* London, 1964.

———. *The Troublemakers.* London, 1993.

Taylor, E. *The Fall of the Dynasties: The Collapse of the Old Order, 1905–1922.* New York, 1963.

Temperley, H.W.V., ed. *A History of the Peace Conference of Paris,* 6 vols. London, 1920–24.

———. "How the Hungarian Frontiers Were Drawn," *Foreign Affairs,* 6 (1928).

Thompson, C. T. *The Peace Conference Day by Day.* New York, 1920.

Thompson, J. M. *Russia, Bolshevism, and the Versailles Peace.* Princeton, New Jersey, 1966.

Tihany, L. C. "The Baranya Republic and the Treaty of Trianon," *War and Society in East Central Europe,* vol. 6, *Essays on World War I: Total War and Peacemaking. A Case Study on Trianon,* ed. B. K. Kiraly, P. Pastor and I. Sanders. New York, 1982.

Tillman, S. P. *Anglo-American Relations at the Paris Peace Conference of 1919.* Princeton, 1961.

Tokes, R. L. "Bela Kun: The Man and the Revolutionary," *Hungary in Revolution 1918–19,* ed. I. Völgyes. Lincoln, Nebraska, 1971.

Toynbee, A. *Acquaintances.* London, 1967.

Trachtenberg, M. *Reparation in World Politics: France and European Economic Diplomacy, 1916–1923.* New York, 1980.

———. "Reparations at the Paris Peace Conference," *Journal of Modern History,* 51 (March 1979).

———. "Versailles After Sixty Years," *Journal of Contemporary History,* 17 (1982).

Tumulty, J. P. *Woodrow Wilson as I Knew Him.* New York, 1921.

Ullman, R. H. *Anglo-Soviet Relations, 1917–1921,* 3 vols. Princeton, 1961–72.

Unterberger, B. M. "The United States and National Self-Determination: A Wilsonian Perspective," *Presidential Studies Quarterly,* 26/4 (Fall 1996).

———. *The United States, Revolutionary Russia, and the Rise of Czechoslovakia.* Chapel Hill, 1989.

———. "Woodrow Wilson and the Bolsheviks: The 'Acid Test' of Soviet-American Relations," *Diplomatic History,* 11/2 (Spring 1987).

Vansittart, R. *The Mist Procession: The Autobiography of Lord Vansittart.* London, 1958.

Vermes, G. "The October Revolution in Hungary: From Karolyi to Kun," *Hungary in Revolution, 1918–19,* ed. I. Völgyes. Lincoln, Nebraska, 1971.

Villard, O. G. *Fighting Years: Memoirs of a Liberal Editor.* New York, 1939.

Vivarelli, R. *Storia delle origini del fascismo,* 2 vols. Bologna, 1991.

Vopicka, C. J. *Secrets of the Balkans; Seven Years of a Diplomatist's Life in the Storm Centre of Europe.* Chicago, 1921.

Waite, R.G.L. *Vanguard of Nazism: The Free Corps Movement in Postwar Germany, 1918–1923.* Cambridge, Massachusetts, 1952.

Walker, C. J. *Armenia: The Survival of a Nation.* London, 1990.

Wallace, W. S. *The Memoirs of The Rt. Hon. Sir George Foster, P.C., G.C.M.G.* Toronto, 1933.

Wallace, W. V. "Czechs and Slovaks," *Europe and Ethnicity: The First World War and Contemporary Ethnic Conflict,* ed. S. Dunn and T. G. Fraser. London, 1996.

Wallach, J. *Desert Queen: The Extraordinary Life of Gertrude Bell: Adventurer, Adviser to Kings, Ally of Lawrence of Arabia.* New York, 1996.

Walworth, A. *Wilson and His Peacemakers: American Diplomacy at the Paris Peace Conference, 1919.* New York, 1986.

———. *Woodrow Wilson,* 2nd ed. Baltimore, Maryland, 1965.

Wambaugh, S. *Plebiscites since the World War,* 2 vols. Washington, 1933.

Wandycz, P. S. *France and Her Eastern Allies, 1919–1925; French-Czechoslovak-Polish Relations from the Paris Peace Conference to Locarno.* Minneapolis, 1962.

———. *The Lands of Partitioned Poland, 1795–1918.* Seattle and London, 1974.

———. *The United States and Poland.* Cambridge, Massachusetts, 1980.

———. "Dmowski's Policy and the Paris Peace Conference: Success or Failure?" *The Reconstruction of Poland, 1914–23,* ed. P. Latawski. London and Basingstoke, 1992.

Watson, D. *Georges Clemenceau: A Political Biography.* New York, 1974.

Watt, R. M. *The Kings Depart.* New York, 1968.

Webster, C. *The Congress of Vienna, 1814–1815.* London, 1963.

Weinberg, G. L. "The Defeat of Germany in 1918 and the European Balance of Power," *Central European History,* 2/3 (1969).

———. *The Foreign Policy of Hitler's Germany: Diplomatic Revolution in Europe 1933–36.* Highlands, New Jersey, 1994.

Weintraub, S. *A Stillness Heard Around the World.* New York and Oxford, 1985.

Wemyss, W. *The Life and Letters of Lord Wester Wemyss.* London, 1935.

West, R. *Black Lamb and Grey Falcon: A Journey Through Yugoslavia.* New York, 1941.

Wheeler-Bennett, J. *Brest-Litovsk.* London, 1963.

———. *The Nemesis of Power: The German Army in Politics, 1918–1945.* London, 1956.

White, W. *Dateline: Toronto. The Complete Toronto Star Dispatches, 1920–1924.* New York, 1985.

White, W. A. *The Autobiography of William Allen White.* New York, 1946.

Widenor, W. C. *Henry Cabot Lodge and the Search for an American Foreign Policy.* Berkeley, 1980.

Willert, A. *The Road to Safety: A Study in Anglo-American Relations.* New York, 1953.

Williams, W. *The Tiger of France: Conversations with Clemenceau.* New York, 1949.

Wilson, J. *Lawrence of Arabia: The Authorised Biography of T. E. Lawrence.* London, 1989.

Wilson, W. *The Papers of Woodrow Wilson,* ed. A. S. Link, 69 vols. Princeton, New Jersey, 1966–.

Windisch-Grätz, L. *My Adventures and Misadventures,* ed. and trans. C. Kessler. London, 1965.

Winstone, H.V.E. *Gertrude Bell.* London, 1980.

Wolff, R. L. *The Balkans in Our Time.* New York, 1967.

Woodhouse, J. *Gabriele D'Annunzio: Defiant Archangel.* Oxford, 1998.

Wormser, G. M. *Clemenceau vu de près.* Paris, 1979.

Yapp, M. *The Making of the Modern Near East, 1792–1923.* London and New York, 1987.

———. *The Near East Since the First World War.* London and New York, 1991.

Yearwood, P. " 'On the Safe and Right Lines': The Lloyd George Government and the Origins of the League of Nations, 1916–1918," *Historical Journal,* 32/1 (1989).

Yergin, D. *The Prize: The Epic Quest for Oil, Money, and Power.* New York, 1991.

Zamir, M. "Faisal and the Lebanese Question, 1918–20," *Middle Eastern Studies,* 27/3 (1991).

Zamoyski, A. *Paderewski.* London, 1982.

Zebel, S. H. *Balfour: A Political Biography.* Cambridge, U.K., 1973.

Zeine, Z. N. *The Emergence of Arab Nationalism, with a Background Study of Arab-Turkish Relations in the Near East.* Beirut, 1966.

Zeman, Z. *The Masaryks: The Making of Czechoslovakia.* London and New York, 1990.

Zimmern, A. *The Third British Empire.* London, 1926.

Zinner, P. E. "The Diplomacy of Eduard Benes," *The Diplomats: 1919–1939,* ed. G. A. Craig and F. Gilbert. New York, 1963.

Zivojinovic, D. R. *America, Italy and the Birth of Yugoslavia, 1917–1919.* Boulder, 1972.

Notes

INTRODUCTION

1. Cambon, vol. 3, p. 292.
2. Temperley, *History,* vol. 1, pp. 243–46.
3. Webster, p. 15.
4. Ribot, p. 255.
5. Callwell, vol. 2, p. 197.

CHAPTER 1: WOODROW WILSON COMES TO EUROPE

1. Beers, p. 148; Seymour, p. 8; Shotwell, pp. 67–69.
2. Willert, p. 166.
3. FRUS, vol. 1, pp. 128–37; Walworth, *Woodrow Wilson,* vol. 2, p. 215.
4. Link, *Road to the White House,* pp. 2–4; Nordholt, pp. 13, 33.
5. Villard, p. 226; Library of Congress, Baker Papers, Group 1, notebooks, 8.3.19.
6. C. T. Thompson, p. 190; F. Palmer, p. 400.
7. Beers, pp. 52–53, 100; Armstrong, p. 104; Walworth, *Wilson and His Peacemakers,* p. 9; F. Palmer, p. 363.
8. Bailey, pp. 87, 92–101; House, *Intimate Papers,* vol. 4, pp. 220–26.
9. Nordholt, p. 195; Library of Congress, Baker notebooks, 18.10.18.
10. Fried, p. 309.
11. PWW, vol. 55, p. 120; vol. 56, p. 128; Scott, p. 386.
12. Seymour, pp. 9–10.
13. Link, *Confusions and Crises,* pp. 11–14.
14. National Archives of Canada, Biggar Papers, vol. 2, letter of 20.3.19; Yale University Library, Auchincloss Papers, Group 580, series I, diary, 22.12.18; Hecksher, pp. 347–53, 498–99.
15. Seymour, pp. 22–26; Shotwell, pp. 75–78; Hunter Miller, *Drafting of the Covenant,* vol. 1, pp. 41–44.
16. Scott, p. 367; C. T. Thompson, p. 369.
17. Seymour, p. 24.
18. Link, *The New Freedom,* pp. 324–27; Department of State, *Lansing Papers,* vol. 2, p. 461.
19. Department of State, *Lansing Papers,* vol. 2, pp. 461–62; Link, *The New Freedom,* pp. 375, 386.
20. Link, *The New Freedom,* pp. 67, 398; British Library, Balfour Papers, 49734/186–192.
21. Zivojinovic, p. 44; Hunter Miller, *Drafting of the Covenant,* vol. 1, p. 46.
22. Seymour, p. 25.
23. Roosevelt, p. 97; Fried, pp. 309, 318, 332; Sharp, "The Genie," *passim;* Bonsal, *Suitors and Suppliants,* p. 275; PWW, vol. 55, p. 463; Hunter Miller, *Drafting of the Covenant,* vol. 1, p. 294.

24. Lansing, *Peace Negotiations,* pp. 97–98; Temperley, *History,* vol. 1, p. 439.
25. Sharp, "The Genie," p. 10; Wambaugh, vol. 1, pp. 3–5, 13–14, 17; Davies, *White Eagle, Red Star,* p. 35; FRUS, vol. 12, p. 515.
26. Temperley, *History,* vol. 4, p. 429; Spector, p. 243.
27. Seymour, p. 25.
28. Link, *Wilson the Diplomatist,* pp. 14–15, 96–97; Yale University Library, Auchincloss diary, 5.11.18.
29. FRUS, vol. 1, pp. 296, 407.
30. Hunter Miller, *Drafting of the Covenant,* vol. 1, p. 43; Seymour, p. 23; D. Lloyd George, *Truth About the Peace Treaties,* vol. 1, pp. 223–24.
31. Zeine, p. 85, n. 11; H. Nicolson, *Peacemaking,* pp. 35–42; Nordholt, pp. 285–86; Bailey, pp. 27–28; PWW, vol. 54, p. 432; R. W. Curry, pp. 210–11; Schwabe, *Wilson, Revolutionary Germany, and Peacemaking,* pp. 180–81.
32. PWW, vol. 53, pp. 378–79, 397; Seymour, pp. 38–39; Shotwell, pp. 81–84.
33. Shotwell, pp. 85–88; PWW, vol. 53, pp. 382–84.

CHAPTER 2: FIRST IMPRESSIONS

1. Library of Congress, Baker notebooks, 23.12.18.
2. George and George, pp. 76–79.
3. Link, *New Freedom,* p. 95; Library of Congress, Baker notebooks, 16.12.18; Esposito, pp. 741–56; George and George, p. 231.
4. Link, *New Freedom,* pp. 93–94; George and George, pp. 92–93.
5. House, *Intimate Papers,* vol. 4, p. 88; Yale University Library, House Papers, series II, c, diary.
6. Mordacq, *Le ministère Clemenceau,* vol. 1, pp. 93–95; Riddell, *Intimate Diary,* p. 78; D. Lloyd George, *Truth About the Peace Treaties,* vol. 1, pp. 245–46; Yale University Library, House diary, 1.4.19; Library of Congress, Baker notebooks, 3.4.19.
7. See D. Lloyd George, *War Memoirs,* vol. 6, chapter 85; D. Stevenson, *First World War,* pp. 225–35; Rudin, pp. 271–83.
8. Floto, p. 78; FRUS, vol. 1, p. 333.
9. House, *Intimate Papers,* vol. 4, pp. 252–53.
10. Walworth, *Woodrow Wilson,* vol. 2, p. 217; Tillman, p. 66; D. Lloyd George, *Truth About the Peace Treaties,* vol. 1, pp. 181–82.
11. PWW, vol. 53, p. 520; D. Lloyd George, *Truth About the Peace Treaties,* vol. 1, pp. 185–201.
12. D. Lloyd George, *Truth About the Peace Treaties,* vol. 1, pp. 149–50, pp. 193–94.
13. PWW, vol. 53, pp. 707–8; vol. 54, p. 175.
14. FRUS, vol. 1, pp. 386–96; House, *Intimate Papers,* vol. 4, p. 243, n. 1; PWW, vol. 54, p. 235; Ministère de la Défense, Clemenceau Papers, 6N72, Conférence de la Paix, memorandum of 18.12.18; C. T. Thompson, pp. 56–58; Shotwell, p. 100, n. 2.
15. Bonsal, *Suitors and Suppliants,* p. 132; Bonsal, *Unfinished Business,* p. 68; F. Stevenson, p. 192; Riddell, *Intimate Diary,* p. 41; Watson, pp. 401–7; D. Stevenson, "France at the Peace Conference," p. 13.
16. *Times,* 21.12.18.
17. Seymour, p. 42; Shotwell, p. 88; FRUS, vol. 11, p. 498; H. Nicolson, *Peacemaking,* p. 225; Toynbee, pp. 200–2.
18. House, *Intimate Papers,* vol. 4, pp. 269–71; Yale University Library, Auchincloss diary, 18.12.18.

CHAPTER 3: PARIS

1. National Archives of Canada, Biggar Papers, letter of 14.1.19; Shotwell, pp. 112, 115.
2. House, *Intimate Papers,* vol. 4, pp. 218–19; FRUS, vol. 1, pp. 119–23; Ministère de la Défense, Clemenceau Papers, 6N72, Conférence de la Paix, Pichon to Jusserand, 7.11.18; D. Lloyd George, *Truth About the Peace Treaties,* vol. 1, pp. 147–48; Yale University Library, Wiseman Papers, series I, 7/178, Peace Conference diary, 19.1.19.

3. Williams, p. 246; Watson, p. 220.
4. Kleine-Ahlbrandt, p. 39.
5. Aldcroft, *Versailles to Wall Street,* pp. 13–19.
6. Nevakivi, p. 109; Laroche, pp. 58–60; Keylor, "Versailles and International Diplomacy," p. 483, n. 41; Guiral, p. 309.
7. Mordacq, *Le ministère Clemenceau,* vol. 3, p. 118; Riddell, *Intimate Diary,* p. 20; Yale University Library, House diary, 28.4.19; Orlando, p. 369.
8. F. Stevenson, p. 286.
9. Williams, p. 28.
10. Ibid., pp. 16, 280–82.
11. Ibid., p. 278.
12. Watson, p. 136; F. Stevenson, p. 212; D. Lloyd George, *War Memoirs,* vol. 5, p. 2675.
13. Williams, pp. 249, 254–55.
14. D. Lloyd George, *War Memoirs,* vol. 5, p. 2681; Williams, pp. 72–74, 165; Mordacq, *Le ministère Clemenceau,* vol. 2, p. 343, vol. 3, p. 5.
15. Trachtenberg, *Reparation in World Politics,* p. 30; Mordacq, *Le ministère Clemenceau,* vol. 3, p. 206; P. Mantoux, vol. 2, p. 274; Watson, pp. 338–39; Ministère des Affaires Etrangères, Série à Paix, 60 (Conditions de la Paix), notes préliminaires sur la réorganisation de l'Allemagne, 27.10.17.
16. Churchill College, Hankey Papers, 4/11, Hankey to Esher, 10.2.19; Headlam-Morley, p. 102; Library of Congress, Beer Collection, diary, 1.3.19; Yale University Library, House diary, 24.1.19.
17. Riddell, *Intimate Diary,* p. 20.
18. Mordacq, *Le ministère Clemenceau,* vol. 3, p. 106; Watson, pp. 278–79, 341; Williams, pp. 203–4; PWW, vol. 57, p. 513; F. Lloyd George, p. 155.
19. Hardinge, p. 242; F. Stevenson, p. 192; Nitti, p. 95.
20. Repington, p. 389; Williams, p. 286; Keiger, pp. 92, 98, 210, 223; Adamthwaite, p. 8; Hughes, *Policies and Potentates,* pp. 223–27; Watson, pp. 250–58.
21. Keiger, pp. 234–36, 246–47, 251–52, 255, 256–59.
22. Mordacq, *Le ministère Clemenceau,* vol. 3, p. 191; Duroselle, pp. 721–28.

CHAPTER 4: LLOYD GEORGE AND THE BRITISH EMPIRE DELEGATION

1. Watson, p. 226; D. Lloyd George, *War Memoirs,* vol. 5, pp. 2678–79, 2686; Mordacq, *Clemenceau au soir de sa vie,* vol. 1, pp. 256–57.
2. Rowland, p. 419; Cecil, *Great Experiment,* p. 67.
3. Grigg, *Young Lloyd George,* pp. 100–2.
4. Grigg, *From Peace to War,* p. 225; Churchill, *Aftermath,* pp. 4–5.
5. Grigg, *Young Lloyd George,* pp. 210–12.
6. Harrod, p. 257.
7. Grigg, *Young Lloyd George,* p. 67.
8. Ibid., pp. 33–36.
9. Grigg, *The People's Champion,* p. 338; Harrod, p. 240.
10. Grigg, *The People's Champion,* p. 77.
11. Ibid., p. 358.
12. Ibid., p. 125, n. 3.
13. Ministère des Affaires Etrangères, Europe, 1918–1929, EU18–40, Grande Bretagne, vol. 7, Les comptes-courants, 1.3.23; PWW, vol. 58, p. 103; Grigg, *The People's Champion,* pp. 327–30.
14. Grigg, *From Peace to War,* pp. 212, 478; Dugdale, pp. 131–33.
15. Beaverbrook, p. 303; Grigg, *From Peace to War,* p. 477.
16. Dockrill and Steiner, pp. 55–86; Dugdale, p. 199.
17. Fry, vol. 1, pp. 246–48, 255; Amery, vol. 1, p. 240; Vansittart, p. 248; Grigg, *From Peace to War,* p. 420.
18. Dockrill and Steiner, p. 77.
19. Riddell, *Intimate Diary,* p. 42.

20. Grigg, *Young Lloyd George,* pp. 212, 285, 296–97.

21. D. Lloyd George, *War Memoirs,* vol. 4, pp. 1731–32.

22. Cook, p. 385; MacMillan, pp. 67–69, 72–73; Fitzhardinge, *The Little Digger,* vol. 2, pp. 91–94, 300; D. Lloyd George, *War Memoirs,* vol. 4, p. 1744.

23. Fitzhardinge, *Little Digger,* vol. 2, p. 354; House of Lords Record Office, Lloyd George Papers, F/28/2/9; Roskill, vol. 2, pp. 29–30; R. C. Brown, vol. 2, p. 152.

24. FRUS, vol. 1, pp. 482–86, 531–33; Public Record Office, CAB29/28, British empire delegation minutes, 1 (13.1.19).

25. Zimmern, p. 30; Hunter Miller, *Drafting of the Covenant,* vol. 1, 490; House of Lords Record Office, Lloyd George Papers, F/5/5, Botha to Lloyd George, 15.5.19; Nicolson, *Peacemaking,* p. 240; Ministère des Affaires Etrangères, Série à Paix, 1914–1920, vol. 287, travaux préparatoires de la conférence, Paul Cambon to Pichon 6.11.18; see, for example, Yale University Library, House diary, entries for 28.10.18 and 6.2.19.

26. Garran, p. 257; Steed, vol. 2, p. 265; H. Nicolson, *Peacemaking,* pp. 44–45.

27. National Archives of Canada, Biggar Papers, letter of 9.2.19.

28. Shotwell, p. 170.

29. National Archives of Canada, Christie Papers, vol. 4, file 9; H. Nicolson, *Peacemaking,* p. 45; Toynbee, p. 205.

30. E. Howard, p. 288.

31. National Archives of Canada, Christie Papers, vol. 7, file 20; Borden, vol. 2, p. 844.

32. D. Lloyd George, *War Memoirs,* vol. 4, p. 1754; House of Lords Record Office, Lloyd George Papers, F/5/2/28, Borden to Lloyd George, 23.11.18.

33. Louis, *Great Britain and Germany's Lost Colonies,* pp. 82–83.

34. Fitzhardinge, *Little Digger,* vol. 2, pp. 74–75.

35. Bonsal, *Suitors and Suppliants,* pp. 113, 229; National Archives of Canada, Biggar Papers, vol. 2, letter to Mrs. Biggar, 7.3.19.

CHAPTER 5: WE ARE THE LEAGUE OF THE PEOPLE

1. H. Nicolson, *Peacemaking,* pp. 253–54; Shotwell, pp. 175–77; Seymour, pp. 154–55; House and Seymour, p. 181; Riddell et al., *The Treaty of Versailles,* p. 15; PWW, vol. 54, p. 5.

2. House, *Intimate Papers,* vol. 4, p. 469.

3. Churchill, *Aftermath,* pp. 13–14; Gelfand, pp. 227–28, 259.

4. National Archives of Canada, Borden Papers, vol. 431, file 53; H. Nicolson, *Peacemaking,* p. 26; FRUS, vol. 3, pp. 535–37; Tardieu, pp. 88–91.

5. Hankey, pp. 29–31; FRUS, vol. 3, pp. 553–56.

6. FRUS, vol. 3, pp. 492, 537.

7. Ibid., pp. 600, 607, 618.

8. White, *Autobiography,* p. 555.

9. FRUS, vol. 3, pp. 609–13; Mordacq, *Le ministère Clemenceau,* vol. 3, p. 106; Villard, pp. 387–88.

10. FRUS, vol. 3, pp. 546–47, 551.

11. Aldrovandi Marescotti, *Nuovi ricordi,* p. 102; FRUS, vol. 3, pp. 614, 620–22.

12. D. Lloyd George, *Truth About the Peace Treaties,* vol. 1, p. 91.

13. Mazower, "Minorities," p. 50; Library of Congress, Bliss Papers, box 244, letter of 26.2.19.

14. R. W. Curry, p. 211.

15. National Archives of Canada, Borden Papers, 444/158; FRUS, vol. 3, pp. 1022–23; Shotwell, p. 179.

16. Shotwell, pp. 144–45; Seymour, p. 128.

17. Hoover, p. 88; Mitchell, pp. 92–96; FRUS, vol. 2, p. 635; vol. 3, p. 513.

18. FRUS, vol. 3, p. 516.

19. Hoover, pp. 91–99; FRUS, vol. 2, pp. 658–61; Ministère des Affaires Etrangères, Tardieu Papers, 166/195, "Conférence interallié de Londres, 2 et 3 décembre 1918"; Trachtenberg, *Reparation in World Politics,* pp. 23–24.

20. Hoover, pp. xv–xx; D. Lloyd George, *Truth About the Peace Treaties,* vol. 1, pp. 305–6; FRUS, vol. 2, pp. 713–14.
21. Temperley, *History,* vol. 1, pp. 304–8; Hoover, pp. 99–114.
22. Aldcroft, "Versailles Legacy," pp. 8–14; Silverman, chapters 7 and 8.

CHAPTER 6: RUSSIA

1. Mordacq, *Le ministère Clemenceau,* vol. 3, p. 88; FRUS, vol. 3, pp. 159–64; H. Nicolson, *Peacemaking,* p. 243.
2. Ullman, vol. 2, p. 111, n. 22; pp. 174–75.
3. D. Lloyd George, *Truth About the Peace Treaties,* vol. 1, pp. 326–27.
4. Watson, pp. 315, 372.
5. Headlam-Morley, pp. 7–8.
6. Baker, *Woodrow Wilson and World Settlement,* vol. 2, p. 64; National Archives of Canada, C1864, Borden diary, 13.2.19; P. Mantoux, vol. 1, p. 46.
7. Klein, *passim;* National Archives of Canada, Biggar Papers, vol. 2, letters of 20.1.19, 4.4.19, 5.2.19.
8. J. M. Thompson, pp. 175–76; Ullman, vol. 2, pp. 141–42.
9. Gilbert, *Churchill,* vol. 4, pp. 227, 277–79, 355–56, 375; D. Lloyd George, *Truth About the Peace Treaties,* vol. 1, pp. 325.
10. Ullman, vol. 1, pp. 68–70; FRUS, vol. 3, p. 583; PWW, vol. 56, p. 247; D. Lloyd George, *Truth About the Peace Treaties,* vol. 1, pp. 330–31; Davies, *White Eagle, Red Star,* p. 90.
11. Duroselle, p. 809; FRUS, vol. 3, pp. 591–92; Shotwell, p. 77; Ashmead-Bartlett, p. 201.
12. D. Lloyd George, *Truth About the Peace Treaties,* vol. 1, p. 321; FRUS, vol. 3, p. 491.
13. Watson, pp. 48–55; House of Lords Record Office, Lloyd George Papers, F3/4/5, Balfour to Lloyd George, 18.1.19.
14. D. Lloyd George, *Truth About the Peace Treaties,* vol. 1, p. 369; Bonsal, *Suitors and Suppliants,* p. 20.
15. FRUS, vol. 3, pp. 581–84; Yale University Library, Wiseman diary, 19.1.19.
16. Public Record Office, Cabinet Papers, CAB 29/28, British empire delegation minutes, 2 (20.1.19).
17. Churchill, *Aftermath,* pp. 243–44.
18. Gilbert, *Churchill,* vol. 4, p. 231.
19. Mamatey, p. 297; J. M. Thompson, pp. 5–6, 46–50; Knock, pp. 156–57.
20. Noble, p. 270; Ullman, vol. 2, chapter 1.
21. Gilbert, *Churchill,* vol. 4, pp. 226–27, 230–33; Public Record Office, Cabinet Papers, CAB 29/28, British empire delegation minutes, 8 (17.2.19).
22. Azan, p. 239; Kenez, pp. 180–91; Pipes, pp. 74–75.
23. FRUS, vol. 3, pp. 471–73; vol. 4, pp. 122–23, 379–82; F. Palmer, p. 378.
24. Hovi, pp. 216–17 and *passim;* FRUS, vol. 4, p. 121; Gilbert, *Churchill,* vol. 4, p. 254; Public Record Office, Cabinet Papers, CAB 29/28, British empire delegation minutes, 8 (17.2.19).
25. Ministère de la Défense, Clemenceau Papers, 6N72, notes of a conversation at 10 Downing Street, London, 11.12.19; Churchill College, Churchill Papers, Charwell Group, Char 16/20, Lloyd George to Churchill, 16.2.19; Churchill, *Aftermath,* pp. 266–67; Scottish Record Office, Lothian Papers, 771, 19.2.19, Lloyd George to Kerr, 19.2.19.
26. Figes, p. 575; Ullman, vol. 2, pp. 212–14.
27. Gilbert, *Churchill,* vol. 4, pp. 264, 286; House of Lords Record Office, Lloyd George Papers, F/89/2/20, Lloyd George to Kerr, 16.2.19.
28. FRUS, vol. 3, pp. 647–53; Riddell, *Intimate Diary,* p. 13; C. T. Thompson, p. 133.
29. Debo, p. 18.
30. Fischer, pp. 101–3.
31. J. M. Thompson, pp. 90–91; FRUS, vol. 3, pp. 643–46.

32. National Archives of Canada, Borden diary, 23.1.19; J. M. Thompson, pp. 115–16.
33. J. M. Thompson, pp. 119–22; E. Howard, p. 300.
34. J. M. Thompson, pp. 110–11, 122; Yale University Library, Wiseman diary. 19.1.19; Poincaré, p. 131; Scottish Record Office, Lothian Papers, 1216, Kerr to Lloyd George, 11.2.19.
35. D. Lloyd George, *Truth About the Peace Treaties,* vol. 1, p. 368; Gilbert, *Churchill,* vol. 4, pp. 239–43; Churchill, *Aftermath,* p. 173; FRUS, vol. 3, pp. 1041–44.
36. Public Record Office, Cabinet Papers, CAB 29/28, British empire delegation minutes, 8 (17.2.19); FRUS, vol. 4, pp. 10–21, 28; Yale University Library, House diary, 17.2.19; Callwell, vol. 2, p. 170; Riddell, *Intimate Diary,* p. 21.
37. Churchill, *Aftermath,* pp. 176–77; Churchill College, Churchill Papers, Char 16/20, Lloyd George to Churchill, 16.2.19; J. M. Thompson, pp. 141–43; Tillman, p. 141.
38. J. M. Thompson, pp. 149–52.
39. Brownell and Billings, pp. 18–21, 29–33; Farnsworth, pp. 30–33.
40. Steffens, p. 791; Farnsworth, pp. 35–39; J. M. Thompson, pp. 152–58.
41. Farnsworth, p. 40; Steffens, pp. 797–98.
42. Steed, vol. 2, p. 302–6.
43. Ullman, vol. 2, pp. 153–57.
44. Brownell and Billings, pp. 93–98; Farnsworth, pp. 62–63.
45. Hoover, pp. 118–19, 247–49.
46. Ibid., pp. 120–22.
47. Huntford, pp. 488–89; J. M. Thompson, pp. 263–67.
48. Pipes, pp. 9–14.
49. Churchill, *Aftermath,* p. 186; P. Mantoux, vol. 2, pp. 193–95, 333–34.

CHAPTER 7: THE LEAGUE OF NATIONS

1. Yale University Library, Auchincloss diary, 28.1.19, 29.1.19.
2. Henig, pp. 164–66.
3. Kissinger, p. 161; M. Howard, chapters 1–3.
4. H. Nicolson, *Peacemaking,* pp. 31–32.
5. House of Lords Record Office, Lloyd George Papers, F/117/1/3, Imperial War Cabinet, 1918, minutes of meetings, 46 (24 December 1918); Egerton, "The Lloyd George Government," p. 431; Cecil, *All the Way,* pp. 153–56.
6. Noble, pp. 99–104; PWW, vol. 54, p. 235; Cecil, *Great Experiment,* p. 59.
7. Temperley, vol. 1, p. 447.
8. Willert, pp. 152–53; Hunter Miller, *Drafting of the Covenant,* vol. 1, p. 122.
9. Egerton, *Great Britain and the Creation of the League of Nations,* pp. 65–69; Willert, pp. 152–53.
10. National Archives of Canada, Biggar Papers, letter of 30.3.19; Jones, vol. 1, p. 28.
11. Hancock, pp. 1–51.
12. Hancock and van der Poel, vol. 4, pp. 10–16.
13. Clemenceau, p. 141; Public Record Office, CAB 29/12, memorandum of 3.12.18.
14. Hunter Miller, *Drafting of the Covenant,* vol. 2, pp. 23–60; Hancock and van der Poel, vol. 4, p. 34.
15. Hunter Miller, *Drafting of the Covenant,* vol. 1, pp. 34–36; Hancock and van der Poel, vol. 4, pp. 41–42; PWW, vol. 55, p. 266; Tillman, p. 73.
16. Clemenceau, p. 138; Cecil, *Great Experiment,* pp. 11–16; Cecil, *All the Way,* pp. 13–18.
17. Cecil, *Great Experiment,* p. 63; Raffo, p. 166; PWW, vol. 54, p. 152.
18. FRUS, vol. 3, pp. 176–201.
19. PWW, vol. 54, pp. 152–54; Hunter Miller, *Drafting of the Covenant,* vol. 1, pp. 120–21, 124–26; Temperley, vol. 6, pp. 434–35; Yale University Library, House diary, 4.2.19.
20. Baker, *Woodrow Wilson and World Settlement,* vol. 1, 242–43; House and Seymour, p. 403.
21. Cecil, *Great Experiment,* pp. 64–65.
22. Ministère de la Défense, Clemenceau Papers, 6N72, Conférence de la Paix, memorandum of 18.12.1918; Yale University Library, House diary, 28.4.19; Bonsal, *Unfin-*

ished Business, p. 30; PWW, vol. 54, p. 489; Mordacq, *Le ministère Clemenceau,* vol. 3, pp. 256–57; Poincaré, p. 283.

23. Willert, p. 152; Egerton, *Great Britain and the Creation of the League of Nations,* pp. 134–35; Hunter Miller, *Drafting of the Covenant,* vol. 1, pp. 209–10, 216–17.

24. Lansing, *Peace Negotiations,* p. 49; Widenor, pp. 306–7; Steed, vol. 2, p. 282; Cecil, *Great Experiment,* p. 78; Egerton, *Great Britain and the Creation of the League of Nations,* p. 142; Egerton, "The Lloyd George Government," pp. 432–33; Callwell, vol. 1, pp. 184, 213.

25. D. Lloyd George, *Truth About the Peace Treaties,* vol. 1, pp. 195–96; House of Lords Record Office, Lloyd George Papers, F5/5/28, Borden to Lloyd George, 23.11.18; Brown, vol. 2, pp. 155–56; Department of External Affairs, Ottawa, vol. 2, pp. 58–63.

26. C. T. Thompson, pp. 187–88; Steed, vol. 2, p. 282; Hunter Miller, *Drafting of the Covenant,* vol. 1, pp. 209–10, 216–17, 344–46; PWW, vol. 56, pp. 164–65; Poincaré, p. 150.

27. PWW, vol. 55, p. 120; Cecil, *Great Experiment,* p. 72.

28. FRUS, vol. 3, p. 1002; Hunter Miller, *Drafting of the Covenant,* vol. 1, pp. 279–80.

29. Public Record Office, Cabinet Papers, CAB 29/28, British empire delegation minutes, 17 (3.4.19. P.M.); House, *Intimate Papers,* vol. 4, p. 285; Mayer, pp. 378–80.

30. D. Lloyd George, *Truth About the Peace Treaties,* vol. 1, p. 656.

31. FRUS, vol. 3, pp. 210–15; PWW, vol. 55, p. 160.

32. Public Record Office, Cabinet Papers, CAB 29/28, British empire delegation minutes, 27 (21.4.19); Tillman, pp. 280–83.

33. Tillman, pp. 287–94; Hunter Miller, *Drafting of the Covenant,* vol. 1, pp. 337–38; Public Record Office, Cabinet Papers, CAB 29/28, British empire delegation minutes, 27 (21.4.19).

34. Hunter Miller, *Drafting of the Covenant,* vol. 1, pp. 442–50; Walworth, *Woodrow Wilson,* vol. 2, pp. 302–3.

35. FRUS, vol. 3, pp. 285–319; Hunter Miller, *Drafting of the Covenant,* vol. 1, pp. 497; Cecil, *All the Way,* p. 152.

36. Tillman, p. 133.

CHAPTER 8: MANDATES

1. Scottish Record Office, GD 40, Lothian Papers, 883/2, notes by Headlam-Morley, 2.4.19.

2. Temperley, vol. 3, p. 221.

3. Louis, *Great Britain and Germany's Lost Colonies,* pp. 7–9; D. Lloyd George, *Truth About the Peace Treaties,* vol. 1, pp. 622–25; Louis, *Great Britain and Germany's Lost Colonies,* p. 119; Public Record Office, Cabinet Papers, CAB 29/28, British empire delegation minutes, 5 (28.1.19).

4. C. T. Thompson, p. 160.

5. Poincaré, p. 104; Mordacq, *Le ministère Clemenceau,* vol. 3, p. 192.

6. FRUS, vol. 3, pp. 803–4; Hunter Miller, *Drafting of the Covenant,* vol. 1, pp. 115–16, 501–3; Hankey, pp. 143–44; Marston, pp. 185–86.

7. Farwell, pp. 73–75; Bodleian Library, Milner Papers, dep. 380/2/8–10 and 380/3/11.

8. FRUS, vol. 3, pp. 722–23, 740–45.

9. Walworth, *Wilson and His Peacemakers,* p. 71; FRUS, vol. 3, pp. 720–22; W. J. Hudson, pp. 17, 78; Rowley, pp. 276–79.

10. Hiery, pp. 157–59, 177, 206.

11. C. T. Thompson, pp. 159–61; National Library of Australia, Eggleston Papers, 423/6/58–92, private Peace Conference diary, 29.1.19.

12. FRUS, vol. 3, pp. 759–63, 768.

13. Ibid., pp. 743, 765–66, 771; PWW, vol. 54, p. 308; House, *Intimate Papers,* vol. 4, p. 297.

14. Roskill, p. 53; Public Record Office, Cabinet Papers, CAB 29/28, British empire delegation minutes, 4 (27.1.19); D. Lloyd George, *Truth About the Peace Treaties,* vol. 1, p. 538; Yale University Library, House diary, 27.1.19, 29.1.19; Hunter Miller, *Drafting of the Covenant,* vol. 1, p. 109; Garran, p. 265.

15. Borden, pp. 906, 908; Sharp, *Versailles Settlement,* p. 162.

16. Riddell, *Intimate Diary*, pp. 16–18; Fitzhardinge, "Hughes and the Treaty of Versailles," pp. 136–37; House, *Intimate Papers*, vol. 4, p. 299; D. Lloyd George, *Truth About the Peace Treaties*, vol. 1, p. 542; National Archives of Canada, Borden diary, 30.1.19; Bonsal, *Unfinished Business*, p. 37; National Library of Australia, Eggleston Papers, 423/6/8–31, "The Paris Peace Conference."

17. D. Lloyd George, *Truth About the Peace Treaties*, vol. 1, pp. 542–46; FRUS, vol. 3, pp. 797–802.

18. Mordacq, *Le ministère Clemenceau*, vol. 3, pp. 106–7.

19. Lewis, pp. 574–76, 577–78.

20. National Archives of Australia, Borden Papers, vol. 431, file 5; House of Lords Record Office, Lloyd George Papers, F 28/3/34, Hughes to Milner, 3.5.19; F 28/3/35 and F 28/3/37, Hughes to Lloyd George, 9.5.19; F36/4/10, Allen to Massey, 15.5.19; F36/4/15, Massey to Milner, 15.5.19; *Guardian Weekly*, 4.7.93; 11.7.93; 4.11.99.

21. Bodleian Library, Milner Papers, 390, Costa to Clemenceau, 4.5.19; Louis, *Great Britain and Germany's Lost Colonies*, pp. 151–52.

22. FRUS, vol. 5, p. 420; Marks, *Innocent Abroad*, pp. 46–47; Louis, *Great Britain and Germany's Lost Colonies*, pp. 64–66.

23. Marks, *Innocent Abroad*, p. 320.

CHAPTER 9: YUGOSLAVIA

1. Banac, pp. 89–90.

2. PWW, vol. 54, p. 149.

3. Bonsal, *Suitors and Suppliants*, p. 247; Mitrovic, pp. 207–8.

4. Dragnich, *Serbia, Pasic and Yugoslavia*, p. 226; Sforza, *Fifty Years*, pp. 113, 146–47; D. Lloyd George, *Truth About the Peace Treaties*, vol. 2, p. 802; Banac, pp. 158–59.

5. Scottish Record Office, Lothian Papers, 925, notes of an interview between Lloyd George and Pašić, 15 October 1918.

6. Banac, p. 59; Armstrong, p. 261.

7. Sforza, *Fifty Years*, pp. 8–9; Durham, p. 95.

8. Block, p. 51; Durham, pp. 209, 232–33.

9. Lederer, p. 92.

10. Armstrong, p. 364; West, p. 366.

11. Lederer, p. 86; C. A. Macartney, *Hungary and Her Successors*, p. 365; Sforza, *Fifty Years*, p. 157; Tanner, p. 125.

12. Albrecht-Carrié, *Italy at the Paris Peace Conference*, pp. 30–31.

13. Tanner, p. 115; Steed, vol. 2, pp. 165–66; House of Lords Record Office, Lloyd George Papers, 56/2/18, Rennell Rodd to Arthur Balfour, 11 November 1918.

14. Tanner, p. 116.

15. Dragnich, "Serbian Government," pp. 43–44; Steed, vol. 2, pp. 235–39.

16. Seton-Watson and Seton-Watson, pp. 313, 319; Temperley, vol. 4, pp. 202–3.

17. Tanner, pp. 119–20; FRUS, vol. 12, p. 475.

18. FRUS, vol. 12, pp. 487–88.

19. B. Jelavich, vol. 2, pp. 150–52.

20. Lederer, p. 113; Bonsal, *Suitors and Suppliants*, p. 88; FRUS, vol. 3, pp. 488, 503.

21. Shotwell, p. 146.

22. Cruttwell, p. 235; West, p. 1051; Durham, p. 118; Banac, p. 276.

23. Department of State, *Lansing Papers*, vol. 2, p. 123; Calder, p. 232, n. 63.

24. Lederer, chapters 4 and 5 *passim*, p. 165.

25. FRUS, vol. 4, pp. 45–53; Seton-Watson and Seton-Watson, p. 150.

26. House and Seymour, p. 142.

27. Dockrill and Goold, pp. 89–92.

28. House, *Intimate Papers*, vol. 3, p. 333.

CHAPTER 10: RUMANIA

1. FRUS, vol. 1, pp. 265–66.

2. H. Nicolson, *Peacemaking*, p. 227.

3. FRUS, vol. 3, pp. 813–15.
4. Callimachi, p. 266; H. Nicolson, *Peacemaking*, p. 248; Spector, pp. 18–19; Walworth, *Wilson and His Peacemakers*, p. 102, n. 90.
5. H. Nicolson, *Peacemaking*, p. 254.
6. FRUS, vol. 3, pp. 818–34.
7. Ibid., pp. 827, 854.
8. Ibid., pp. 850–51.
9. Wolff, p. 36; Dillon, pp. 215, 237.
10. Callimachi, pp. 56–58.
11. Gregory, pp. 52–53, 122; Cruttwell, p. 293; Callimachi, p. 49.
12. Seymour, pp. 97–98.
13. Lederer, p. 100.
14. Spector, p. 230; Anderson, p. 332, n. 2.
15. Rattigan, p. 192; Cruttwell, p. 295; Spector, pp. 44, nn. 96, 97; FRUS, vol. 2, p. 844; Lederer, p. 142.
16. Spector, p. 89; FRUS, vol. 3, pp. 851–54.
17. Dockrill and Goold, p. 93; H. Nicolson, *Peacemaking*, p. 269.
18. Marston, p. 117; Macartney, *Hungary and Her Successors*, pp. 380–90, 393–94.
19. Seymour, pp. 158, 241.
20. Tihany, pp. 297–320; Seymour, pp. 173, 268; Spector, pp. 72, 125; Yale University Library, House Papers, 2/570 26.4.19, minutes of a conversation with Brătianu; Bonsal, *Suitors and Suppliants*, pp. 169–71.
21. Pakula, p. 274.
22. Callimachi, p. 98; Wolff, p. 127; Pakula, p. 276; British Library, Balfour Papers, Add. MS 49744, correspondence, 267–68.
23. Yale University Library, House diary, 8.3.19; British Museum, Balfour Papers, Add. MS 49744, correspondence, 267–68; F. Stevenson, p. 171; Spector, p. 112, n. 46.
24. Pakula, pp. 285–87; Walworth, *Wilson and His Peacemakers*, p. 455.
25. Macartney, *Hungary and Her Successors*, pp. 404, 410–25.

CHAPTER 11: BULGARIA

1. FRUS, vol. 4, pp. 717–18, 749–51.
2. Dockrill and Goold, pp. 94–95.
3. Wolff, p. 41.
4. Roosevelt, p. 382; Constant, p. 187; Petsalis-Diomidis, p. 160, n. 29; Groueff, p. 59; Dockrill and Goold, p. 95.
5. Fitzherbert, p. 235; Repington, p. 356; Groueff, p. 68.
6. Groueff, p. 75.
7. Groueff, pp. 61, 68, 78; Petsalis-Diomidis, pp. 87, 167; See, for example, Ekmecic, p. 20; Lederer, p. 125.
8. FRUS, vol. 2, pp. 246–47, 254.
9. Ibid., p. 249; Genov, p. 20; Temperley, vol. 4, p. 450.
10. Genov, p. 33.
11. Ibid., p. 31; Spector, p. 72; FRUS, vol. 2, pp. 264–66.
12. Genov, pp. 25, 49.
13. FRUS, vol. 8, p. 84.
14. Temperley, vol. 4, pp. 412–15; Bowman, pp. 163–64; Groueff, p. 65.
15. Petsalis-Diomidis, p. 264.
16. Groueff, p. 100; Crampton, pp. 96–98.
17. B. Jelavich, vol. 2, p. 255.

CHAPTER 12: MIDWINTER BREAK

1. PWW, vol. 55, pp. 152–53, 480.
2. Shotwell, pp. 108, 153–55, 167; Cecil, *Great Experiment*, p. 69; Seymour, pp. 152–57; H. Nicolson, *Peacemaking*, pp. 104–8, 257.
3. Churchill College, Hankey Papers, 4/11, Hankey to Esher, 10.2.19; Scottish Record

Office, Lothian Papers, 1240, Kerr to Lloyd George, 3.3.19; Yale University Library, House diary, 24.2.19; 25.2.19; House of Lords Record Office, Lloyd George Papers, 52/3/11, Derby to Lloyd George, 14.3.19; Silverman, pp. 20–39.

4. PWW, vol. 54, p. 235; Villard, p. 389; Klotz, p. 105; Hardinge, p. 231; National Archives of Canada, Biggar Papers, letter of 20.3.19; Shotwell, p. 157.

5. PWW, vol. 55, pp. 1, 41, 153; vol. 56, pp. 86–87.

6. Shotwell, pp. 136, 187; Seymour, p. 161; E. Howard, p. 301.

7. Temperley, vol. 1, pp. 243–44; Hugessen, p. 22; H. Nicolson, *Peacemaking*, p. 142; A. L. Kennedy, p. 364.

8. Glyn, pp. 256–57; Fromkin, *Time of the Americans*, pp. 225–27; F. Lloyd George, p. 155.

9. Maxwell, pp. 133, 136.

10. Seymour, p. 144; Churchill College, Hankey Papers, 3/24 3–29, 18.1.19; Villard, pp. 398–99; Glynn, p. 245.

11. Mee, p. 106; National Archives of Canada, Biggar Papers, letter of 26.1.19; PWW, vol. 57, pp. 502–3; Maxwell, p. 142.

12. Huddleston, pp. 113–14; F. Stevenson, p. 172.

13. Maxwell, pp. 137–38, 162; Villard, p. 454; Mordacq, *Le ministère Clemenceau*, vol. 3, p. 287.

14. Yale University Library, Auchincloss diary, 25.1.19; Hugessen, p. 25; Armstrong, p. 71; F. Lloyd George, p. 149.

15. E. Howard, p. 308; Dillon, p. 31; F. Stevenson, p. 175.

16. Seymour, p. 138; Shotwell, pp. 189–90; White, *Autobiography*, p. 556.

17. Yale University Library, Auchincloss diary, 21.4.19; Shotwell, pp. 234–39, 270–93, 280; Seymour, pp. 195–200.

18. Lansing, *Peace Negotiations*, p. 107; Bonsal, *Unfinished Business*, p. 42; Beers, p. 149; White, *Autobiography*, p. 566; PWW, vol. 57, p. 141.

19. Hankey, chapter 9; Seymour, p. 169.

20. H. Nicolson, *Peacemaking*, pp. 175–76 [my translation].

21. Mordacq, *Le ministère Clemenceau*, vol. 3, pp. 133–35; C. T. Thompson, p. 218; F. Stevenson, p. 172.

22. Scottish Record Office, Lothian Papers, 771, Lloyd George to Kerr, 19.2.19.

23. Mee, p. 101; Repington, p. 189; Mordacq, *Le ministère Clemenceau*, vol. 3, pp. 138–43; Poincaré, pp. 167, 177; PWW, vol. 57, p. 332; Steed, vol. 2, p. 325.

24. Jones, vol. 1, pp. 76, 79; Rowland, pp. 507–9.

25. Cooper, pp. 55, 57–59, 70; Hecksher, pp. 537–38.

26. Nordholt, pp. 317–21.

27. Walworth, *Wilson and His Peacemakers*, pp. 182–83; Widenor, pp. 283–87, 305.

28. Bonsal, *Unfinished Business*, p. 59; Bonsal, *Suitors and Suppliants*, p. 264; PWW, vol. 55, p. 410; Nordholt, pp. 322–23; Yale University Library, Auchincloss Papers, 002–029, Wilson to House, 4.3.19.

29. Ambrosius, pp. 93–96; Bonsal, *Suitors and Suppliants*, p. 256.

30. Fried, pp. 367–68.

CHAPTER 13: PUNISHMENT AND PREVENTION

1. Rudin, p. 370.

2. Ministère des Affaires Etrangères, PA-AP 42, Paul Cambon papers, vol. 68, report of interview between Paul Cambon and Lloyd George, 12.11.18; Steed, vol. 2, p. 252; French, p. 79 and *passim*.

3. Schwabe, *Woodrow Wilson, Revolutionary Germany*, p. 156.

4. FRUS, vol. 3, pp. 705–14, 895–925, 950, 978.

5. House of Lords Record Office, Lloyd George Papers, F/147/3/4, note from Foch, Bliss, Wilson and Diaz, 9.4.19; St. Antony's College, Oxford, Malcolm Papers, 1/12, diary entries for 20.4.19, 21.4.19, 25.4.19; P. Mantoux, vol. 2, pp. 493–500.

6. F. Lloyd George, p. 162; FRUS, vol. 3, pp. 933–34.

7. Temperley, vol. 1, p. 321; FRUS, vol. 3, pp. 904–5; PWW, vol. 55, p. 161; Keynes, *Two Memoirs*, pp. 61–62.

8. Epstein, pp. 293–94; Temperley, vol. 1, pp. 313–17; Marks, "Smoke and Mirrors," p. 352, n. 62; FRUS, vol. 4, pp. 274–93.
9. PWW, vol. 53, p. 708.
10. Fried, p. 324; Trachtenberg, *Reparation in World Politics,* p. 51.
11. Röhl, chapter 1.
12. Rose, p. 229.
13. Rowland, pp. 463, 466–69; Callwell, vol. 2, p. 149; Rose, p. 231; Lentin, *Lloyd George,* p. 29; J. Campbell, pp. 449–59; House of Lords Record Office, Lloyd George Papers, F/117/1/3, minutes of the Imperial War Cabinet, 37 (20.11.18); Goldstein, *Winning the Peace,* p. 224.
14. P. Mantoux, vol. 1, pp. 189, 193.
15. Walworth, *Wilson and His Peacemakers,* p. 215, n. 51; House and Seymour, pp. 231–58; P. Mantoux, vol. 1, p. 110.
16. Mordacq, *Le ministère Clemenceau,* vol. 3, p. 27; Aldrovandi Marescotti, *Nuovi ricordi,* p. 92.
17. Röhl, pp. 210–11; Eyck, vol. 1, pp. 187–88.

CHAPTER 14: KEEPING GERMANY DOWN

1. Tillman, pp. 164–65; Reynolds, p. 121.
2. FRUS, vol. 3, p. 930; House of Lords Record Office, Lloyd George Papers, F23/4/39, Hankey to Lloyd George, 19.3.19.
3. Seymour, p. 159; Riddell, *Intimate Diary,* p. 190; Yale University Library, House diary, 24.1.19; PWW, vol. 53, p. 410; Library of Congress, Baker notebooks, 21.3.19.
4. FRUS, vol. 3, p. 905; Guiral, p. 291; Mordacq, *Le ministère Clemenceau,* vol. 3, p. 265; Yale University Library, House diary, 14.4.19.
5. Liddell Hart, p. 413; Mordacq, *Le ministère Clemenceau,* vol. 3, pp. 65, 90–91; Scottish Record Office, Lothian Papers, 1214/1; Ribot, p. 256.
6. See, for example, FRUS, vol. 3, pp. 704–14; PWW, vol. 54, pp. 178, 275, 301–2.
7. Lowry, pp. 20–22; Walworth, *Wilson and His Peacemakers,* pp. 48–49, 86–87; FRUS, vol. 3, pp. 896–908, 970–79; House of Lords Record Office, Lloyd George Papers, F23/4/22, Hankey to Lloyd George, 23.2.19.
8. FRUS, vol. 4, p. 186; House of Lords Record Office, Lloyd George Papers, F3/4/15, Balfour to Lloyd George, 5.3.19.
9. FRUS, vol. 4, pp. 213–30.
10. F. Palmer, p. 375; House of Lords Record Office, Lloyd George Papers, F/147/1, "Notes of an interview between M. Clemenceau, Colonel House and myself, 7.3.19"; Callwell, vol. 2, p. 173.
11. FRUS, vol. 4, pp. 69–71.
12. Keiger, p. 258; British Library, Balfour Papers, 49744/184–190, 14.12.18, Derby to Balfour, 14.12.18; Mordacq, *Le ministère Clemenceau,* vol. 3, p. 191; Trachtenberg, *Reparation in World Politics,* pp. 86–87.
13. Lloyd George, *Truth About the Peace Treaties,* vol. 1, pp. 387–9; Tardieu, p. 146.
14. House of Lords Record Office, Lloyd George Papers, F3/4/2, Foch to Lord Robert Cecil, 8.1.19; Callwell, vol. 2, p. 153; Liddell Hart, p. 411; McCrum, p. 631.
15. McCrum, pp. 629–31; J. C. King, p. 80.
16. J. C. King, p. 41.
17. McCrum, pp. 628–32; Yale University Library, Auchincloss diary, 23.2.19; Scottish Record Office, Lothian Papers, 1229/2, Hankey memorandum 22.2.19; House of Lords Record Office, Lloyd George Papers, F 89/2/29, Kerr to Lloyd George, 22.2.19.
18. House of Lords Record Office, Lloyd George Papers, 52/2/52, Derby to Balfour, 14.12.18; Keiger, pp. 251, 256–57; J. C. King, chapter 1.
19. Yale University Library, House diary, 9.2.19; Scott, p. 372; House of Lords Record Office, Lloyd George Papers, 60/2/42, notes of an interview with the president, 23.1.18; F/147/1, "Notes of an interview between M. Clemenceau, Colonel House and myself, 7.3.19."
20. Nelson, p. 113 [my translation].

21. McCrum, p. 626, n. 10.
22. D. Lloyd George, *Truth About the Peace Treaties,* vol. 1, pp. 386, 398–99; Tardieu, p. 171; Mordacq, *Le ministère Clemenceau,* vol. 3, p. 118; Duroselle, p. 748; Scottish Record Office, Lothian Papers, 1217, Lloyd George to Kerr, 12.2.19.
23. Churchill College, Hankey Papers, 1/5 diary, 27.8.18; PWW, vol. 56, p. 86; Nelson, pp. 204–5; Seymour, p. 226.
24. Tardieu, pp. 147–67; D. Lloyd George, *Truth About the Peace Treaties,* vol. 1, p. 396; PWW, vol. 55, p. 480; Nelson, p. 209.
25. Scottish Record Office, Lothian Papers, 1174, notes of a conversation of 11.3.19.
26. PWW, vol. 55, pp. 488, 499.
27. D. Lloyd George *Truth About the Peace Treaties,* vol. 1, pp. 247–48; PWW, vol. 55, pp. 152–53.
28. PWW, vol. 55, p. 530; Walworth, *Wilson and His Peacemakers,* p. 204; Callwell, vol. 2, p. 174.
29. D. Lloyd George, *Truth About the Peace Treaties,* vol. 1, pp. 601–3.
30. FRUS, vol. 4, p. 249; PWW, vol. 55, p. 522; Marder, vol. 5, p. 251.
31. FRUS, vol. 4, pp. 224–25, 365; Marder, vol. 5, p. 254; Yale University Library, House Papers, series I/10 0293, Grey to House, 3.6.19; Scottish Record Office, Lothian Papers, 65/49–54, notes on Heligoland, 14.4.19; P. Mantoux, vol. 1, pp. 252–56.
32. FRUS, vol. 3, p. 475; Marder, pp. 257–62.
33. Dingman, p. 84; P. Mantoux, vol. 1, p. 377; PWW, vol. 55, pp. 515–21; vol. 57, p. 92.
34. PWW, vol. 55, p. 458; vol. 57, p. 91; Marder, vol. 5, pp. 228–30, 263–64; House of Lords Record Office, Lloyd George Papers, F/147/1, "Notes of an interview between M. Clemenceau, Colonel House and myself, 7.3.19."
35. PWW, vol. 56, pp. 338, 518–19; Marder, vol. 5, pp. 231–34.
36. Marder, vol. 5, p. 269.

CHAPTER 15: FOOTING THE BILL

1. House and Seymour, p. 259.
2. Public Record Office, Cabinet Papers, CAB 29/28, British empire delegation minutes, 34 (1.6.19, P.M.).
3. See, for example, Schuker, *American "Reparations"*; Marks, "Reparations Reconsidered"; Marks, "The Myths of Reparations."
4. Keynes, *Economic Consequences,* pp. 41–45; Skidelsky, vol. 1, p. 389.
5. Keynes, *Economic Consequences,* p. 36; Keynes, *Two Memoirs,* p. 20.
6. Keynes, *Economic Consequences,* p. 7.
7. Skidelsky, vol. 1, pp. 384–91.
8. Burnett, vol. 1, pp. 1011–14, 1018; Silverman, p. 145, and chapter 5, *passim;* Schuker, *The End of French Predominance,* p. 9.
9. Trachtenberg, *Reparation in World Politics,* pp. 1–10; Ministères des Affaires Etrangères, Série à Paix, 59, "Conditions de la Paix: Notes et études sur les conditions de la paix à obtenir et les clauses à insérer dans les traités de paix à signer. Résumé des voeux et avis du Bureau d'Etudes Economiques"; Duchêne, p. 40.
10. PWW, vol. 54, pp. 196, 431, 494; House of Lords Record Office, Lloyd George Papers, F6/6/49, Cecil to Lloyd George, 31.5.19, and F89/2/35, Kerr to Lloyd George, 28.2.19; D. Lloyd George, *Truth About Reparations and War Debts,* chapter 9; House and Seymour, p. 484; Silverman, pp. 32–35; Kent, pp. 40–43.
11. Rowland, p. 494; C. T. Thompson, p. 236; Yale University Library, House diary, 21.2.19.
12. Burnett, vol. 1, pp. 31–32; Public Record Office, Cabinet Papers, CAB 29/28, British empire delegation minutes, 13 (13.3.19).
13. Baruch, pp. 5–7.
14. Burnett, vol. 1, p. 34; Hardach, pp. 156–60; Schuker, *American "Reparations,"* p. 20.
15. Burnett, vol. 1, pp. 33, 514; Public Record Office, Cabinet Papers, CAB 29/28, British empire delegation minutes, 33 (1.6.19, A.M.).
16. Burnett, vol. 1, pp. 4–8, 21; B. Kent, p. 69.

17. Bunselmeyer, p. 174, n. 9; Public Record Office, Cabinet Papers, CAB 29/28, British empire delegation minutes, 33 (1.6.19, A.M.).
18. Silverman, p. 39; Burnett, vol. 1, p. 61; House of Lords Record Office, Lloyd George Papers, F/45/9/25, Smuts to Lloyd George, 4.12.18; F45/9/29, Smuts to Lloyd George, 26.3.19; F 45/9/33, Smuts to Lloyd George, 5.5.19; Hancock, pp. 539–41.
19. Burnett, vol. 1, p. 777.
20. House of Lords Record Office, Lloyd George Papers, F/117/1/3, Imperial War Cabinet, 1918, minute 38 (26.11.18); W. S. Wallace, pp. 193–95.
21. Lentin, "Lord Cunliffe," pp. 50–86, 52, n. 12; Headlam-Morley, p. 180; H. Nicolson, *Peacemaking,* p. 350; Seymour, p. 276; D. Lloyd George, *Truth About the Peace Treaties,* vol. 1, p. 474; Burnett, vol. 1, 711; Yale University Library, House diary, 24.3.19, 4.4.19.
22. Burnett, vol. 1, pp. 43–44; Lentin, "Lord Cunliffe," pp. 50–86; House of Lords Record Office, Lloyd George Papers, F/213/5/6, Lamont to Wiseman, n.d.
23. Public Record Office, Cabinet Papers, CAB 29/28, British empire delegation minutes, 34 (1.6.19, P.M.); Riddell, *Intimate Diary,* p. 31; Trachtenberg, *Reparation in World Politics,* pp. 48–51.
24. British Library, Balfour Papers, 49744/258–263, notes of a conversation between Briand and Lloyd George, 18.3.19; Yale University Library, House diary, 6.3.19; PWW, vol. 56, p. 285.
25. Bunselmeyer, p. 141.
26. Ibid., pp. 129–33; Pugh, p. 128; F. Stevenson, p. 180; Rowland, p. 490.
27. House of Lords Record Office, Lloyd George Papers, F28/2/16, Hughes to Lloyd George, 10.12.18.
28. A. J. P. Taylor, *Troublemakers,* p. 159.
29. Yale University Library, House diary, 28.4.19; D. Lloyd George, *Truth About the Peace Treaties,* vol. 1, pp. 473, 498; Trachtenberg, *Reparation in World Politics,* pp. 41–43; Mordacq, *Le ministère Clemenceau,* vol. 3, p. 218; Riddell, *Intimate Diary,* p. 38; FRUS, vol. 13, p. 205; Keynes, *Two Memoirs,* p. 61; Noble, pp. 201–5; Poincaré, p. 286; PWW, vol. 56, p. 502; vol. 59, p. 314.
30. Noble, pp. 186–93, 195.
31. FRUS, vol. 3, p. 976; Trachtenberg, *Reparation in World Politics,* p. 43; D. Lloyd George, *Truth About the Peace Treaties,* vol. 1, pp. 441–44.
32. Trachtenberg, *Reparation in World Politics,* p. 42, n. 49.
33. Tardieu, *Truth,* p. 290; Trachtenberg, *Reparation in World Politics,* pp. 55, 64–66, 71; chapter 2, *passim.*
34. Trachtenberg, *Reparation in World Politics,* pp. 35–36; House of Lords Record Office, Lloyd George Papers, F/89/2/37, Kerr to Lloyd George, 2.3.19; Scottish Record Office, Lothian Papers, 1236, Kerr to Lloyd George, 1.3.19.
35. Burnett, vol. 1, p. 59; PWW, vol. 56, p. 501.
36. FRUS, vol. 6, p. 796; See article 234 and annex 1, Treaty of Versailles.
37. Guhin, pp. 30–32; P. Mantoux, vol. 1, pp. 106, 147.

CHAPTER 16: DEADLOCK OVER THE GERMAN TERMS

1. Yale University Library, House diary. 12.3.19; Walworth, *Wilson and His Peacemakers,* p. 203; PWW, vol. 56, p. 62.
2. Tardieu, pp. 176–82; PWW, vol. 56, p. 81; House of Lords Record Office, Lloyd George Papers, F 3/4/19, Balfour to Lloyd George, 18.3.19.
3. Tardieu, p. 182; Nelson, pp. 232–40.
4. Riddell, *Intimate Diary,* p. 41; Temperley, vol. 2, p. 178; Headlam-Morley, p. 33.
5. Callwell, vol. 2, p. 176; Hankey, pp. 98, 101.
6. F. Stevenson, p. 174.
7. D. Lloyd George, *Truth About the Peace Treaties,* vol. 1, pp. 404–16; P. Mantoux, vol. 1, p. 31; Tardieu, p. 443; Nelson, p. 227.
8. PWW, vol. 56, pp. 247, 444.
9. P. Mantoux, vol. 1, pp. 33–34, 88; Mordacq, *Le ministère Clemenceau,* vol. 3, p. 202.
10. PWW, vol. 56, p. 312.

11. Ibid., pp. 347–54; P. Mantoux, vol. 1, pp. 49–68; Mordacq, *Le ministère Clemenceau,* vol. 3, pp. 195, 205; Library of Congress, Baker notebooks, 1.4.19.

12. Callwell, vol. 2, p. 180; Shotwell, p. 255; National Archive of Canada, Biggar Papers, letter of 7.4.19; C. T. Thompson, p. 287; Noble, p. 315.

13. Library of Congress, Baker notebooks, 3.4.19; PWW, vol. 56, pp. 408, 540; Noble, pp. 315–16; Callwell, vol. 2, p. 180.

14. F. Stevenson, p. 178; PWW, vol. 57, pp. 50–51, 63.

15. Noble, pp. 322, 324–28; C. T. Thompson, p. 291; Mordacq, *Le ministère Clemenceau,* vol. 3, p. 217; PWW, vol. 57, p. 99.

16. Liddell Hart, pp. 420–23; Mordacq, *Le ministère Clemenceau,* vol. 3, pp. 226–31.

17. Keiger, pp. 258–62; Poincaré, pp. 315–24.

18. Riddell, *Intimate Diary,* p. 45; C. T. Thompson, p. 288.

19. C. T. Thompson, p. 292; PWW, vol. 57, pp. 98–101, 146.

20. Yale University Library, House diary, 12.4.19 and 14.4.19; Yale University Library, Auchincloss diary, 15.4.19; Schuker, "The Rhineland Question," pp. 302–4.

21. Mordacq, *Le ministère Clemenceau,* vol. 3, pp. 220–21; Yale University Library, House diary, 15.4.19; Noble, pp. 331–32.

22. Lloyd George, *Truth About the Peace Treaties,* vol. 1, p. 427; Schuker, "The Rhineland Question," p. 304.

23. Mordacq, *Le ministère Clemenceau,* vol. 3, pp. 221, 245; Ribot, p. 274; Keiger, p. 262.

24. Watson, p. 361.

CHAPTER 17: POLAND REBORN

1. Davies, *God's Playground,* vol. 2, p. 122, and chapter 3, *passim.*

2. Zamoyski, p. 178.

3. Jedrezejewicz, pp. 4–10.

4. Davies, *God's Playground,* vol. 2, p. 385.

5. Roszkowski, p. 158; E. Howard, p. 342, n. 1.

6. Shotwell, p. 305; Wandycz, *Lands of Partitioned Poland,* pp. 291–93; Davies, *God's Playground,* pp. 52–53; Gregory, p. 170.

7. Davies, *White Eagle, Red Star,* p. 62; Wandycz, *Lands of Partitioned Poland,* pp. 340–41; Scottish Record Office, Lothian Papers, 879/1, Esmé Howard, 17.2.19; Landau, pp. 146–47.

8. Kessler, p. 23; Wandycz, "Dmowski's Policy," pp. 119–20.

9. Lundgreen-Nielsen, *Polish Problem,* pp. 54–57; Wandycz, "Dmowski's Policy," p. 118.

10. FRUS, vol. 12, p. 370; Cienciala and Komarnicki, pp. 91–92.

11. Lundgreen-Nielsen, *Polish Problem,* p. 121, n. 163; Latawski, pp. 4–7; Headlam-Morley, p. xxviii.

12. Bonsal, *Suitors and Suppliants,* p. 131; Duroselle, p. 814.

13. Wandycz, *The United States and Poland,* p. 109; Gerson, pp. 62–63; P. Mantoux, vol. 1, p. 108.

14. Komarnicki, pp. 253–59; Gerson, p. 102–3; E. Howard, p. 339.

15. H. Nicolson, *Peacemaking,* p. 332.

16. Komarnicki, p. 145; Lundgreen-Nielsen, *Polish Problem,* pp. 80–81.

17. Gerson, pp. 105–6.

18. Lundgreen-Nielsen, *Polish Problem,* pp. 131–34, 231–33; FRUS, vol. 3, pp. 670–75.

19. FRUS, vol. 3, pp. 772–82; Churchill College, Hankey Papers, 3/24, Hankey to Adeline Hankey, 29.1.19; Lundgreen-Nielsen, "Aspects of American Policy," p. 100, n. 21; Ministère des Affaires Etrangères, Tardieu Papers, 356, "Conférence de la Paix 1919: Pologne: Problèmes politiques et économiques (notes, correspondances), Décembre 1918–Octobre 1919."

20. Library of Congress, Bliss Papers, box 244, diary, 1.1.19; House and Seymour, p. 70; Bonsal, *Suitors and Suppliants,* pp. 118–20; P. Mantoux, vol. 2, p. 150; FRUS, vol. 3, pp. 672–74.

21. House and Seymour, p. 72.

22. Temperley, vol. 6, p. 220.

23. Nelson, pp. 147–51, 152–54; Wandycz, *France and Her Eastern Allies*, pp. 34–37; House and Seymour, p. 71.
24. FRUS, vol. 4, pp. 414–19.
25. Komarnicki, *Rebirth of the Polish Republic*, pp. 319–49; Davies, "Lloyd George and Poland, 1919–20," pp. 132–33; Wandycz, "Dmowski's Policy," pp. 123–24.
26. F. Stevenson, p. 38; F. Lloyd George, p. 153; Scottish Record Office, Lothian Papers, 911/2, Kerr to Horace Rumbold, 15.12.19.
27. P. Mantoux, vol. 1, pp. 33–34.
28. PWW, vol. 56, p. 313; Tillman, pp. 207–9; Headlam-Morley, pp. 169–71; P. Mantoux, vol. 1, pp. 105–9, 118, 201, 233; Nelson, pp. 187–91.
29. Cienciala and Komarnicki, pp. 106–10; Weinberg, *Foreign Policy*, pp. 13–14.
30. House and Seymour, p. 80; FRUS, vol. 6, pp. 833–35; St Antony's College, Malcolm Papers, 1/12, diary, 8.5.19.
31. Riddell, *Intimate Diary*, pp. 83–84.
32. Public Record Office, Cabinet Papers, CAB 29/28, British empire delegation minutes, 33 (1.6.19, A.M.); PWW, vol. 60, p. 20.
33. P. Mantoux, vol. 2, pp. 278–86, 312, 389–92; Mordacq, *Le ministère Clemenceau*, vol. 3, pp. 304–5.
34. F. G. Campbell, pp. 361–85.
35. E. Howard, p. 333.
36. Temperley, vol. 6, p. 297; Bennett, pp. 70–71, 77, 83.
37. FRUS, vol. 4, p. 592; Waite, pp. 97–98.
38. Waite, pp. 101–2, 111–15, 120; P. Mantoux, vol. 1, p. 258.
39. P. Mantoux, vol. 2, p. 550; Waite, pp. 123–30.
40. Cienciala and Komarnicki, pp. 114–16; Lieven, pp. 52–53.
41. Cienciala and Komarnicki, pp. 122, 126; Lieven, p. 60.
42. P. Mantoux, vol. 2, p. 309; Lundgreen-Nielsen, *Polish Problem*, pp. 206, 291–98.
43. FRUS, vol. 3, p. 782; vol. 6, pp. 199–200; Wandycz, *United States and Poland*, pp. 138–39.
44. P. Mantoux, vol. 2, pp. 143–47.
45. Ibid., vol. 1, p. 44; Lundgreen-Nielsen, *Polish Problem*, pp. 222–23, 279–88.
46. FRUS, vol. 4, p. 410; vol. 6, p. 198–99; Scottish Record Office, Lothian Papers, 911/2, Kerr to Rumbold, 15.12.19.
47. Cienciala and Komarnicki, pp. 165–73; Gilbert, *Rumbold*, pp. 186; Carton de Wiart, pp. 112–14.
48. Dziewanowski, p. 202.
49. Ibid., pp. 190–91, 305; Carton de Wiart, p. 96; Davies, *God's Playground*, vol. 2, p. 396; Gilbert, *Rumbold*, p. 206; Wandycz, *France and Her Eastern Allies*, pp. 154–56; Scott, p. 386.
50. Davies, *God's Playground*, vol. 2, p. 397; Carton de Wiart, pp. 106–7; Gilbert, *Rumbold*, pp. 209–10, 216.
51. Zamoyski, pp. 204–10.

CHAPTER 18: CZECHS AND SLOVAKS

1. FRUS, vol. 12, p. 236.
2. House and Seymour, p. 94.
3. F. Lloyd George, p. 152; D. Lloyd George, *Truth About the Peace Treaties*, vol. 2, pp. 941–42.
4. Hovi, pp. 109–11; Ministère des Affaires Etrangères, Série à Paix 344 (Tchécoslovaquie), Les Frontières de la Tchécoslovaquie, 22.2.19.
5. Zinner, vol. 1, pp. 100–4; Laroche, pp. 39–40; Zeman, pp. 84–85, 156–58; Bonsal, *Suitors and Suppliants*, pp. 151–52.
6. Ministère des Affaires Etrangères, Série à Paix 299, Beneš to Pichon, 7.11.18; British Museum, Balfour Papers, 184–190, Derby to Balfour, 14.12.18; Perman, pp. 35–40; Zinner, pp. 102–3.
7. Zeman, pp. 21–2, 43–44, 50–59.

8. Steed, vol. 2, p. 100.
9. Zeman, p. 117.
10. Mamatey, pp. 316–17, 342–43.
11. Ibid., pp. 282–84; Masaryk, p. 208.
12. Zeman, pp. 110–12; Mamatey, pp. 285–86.
13. Mamatey, p. 317.
14. Perman, p. 70; Ministère des Affaires Etrangères, Série à Paix 299, "Travaux préparatoires de la conférence, politiques des petites nations alliées," note from Edward Beneš, received 3.11.18; Perman, pp. 73–75.
15. Perman, pp. 126–30.
16. FRUS, vol. 3, pp. 877–87.
17. Ibid., 886–87; D. Lloyd George, *Truth About the Peace Treaties,* vol. 2, p. 940; Ministère des Affaires Etrangères, Série à Paix 299, "Travaux préparatoires de la conférence, politiques des petites nations alliées," Beneš to Pichon, 7.11.18.
18. D. Lloyd George, *Truth About the Peace Treaties,* vol. 2, p. 931; Seymour, pp. 155–56.
19. FRUS, vol. 3, pp. 877–87; vol. 12, p. 273.
20. House and Seymour, p. 97; Seymour, p. 176; H. Nicolson, *Peacemaking,* pp. 272–73; Laroche, pp. 81–82.
21. H. Nicolson, *Peacemaking,* p. 280.
22. FRUS, vol. 4, pp. 543–46; Mamatey, pp. 306–7; Perman, pp. 132, 162–63; D. Lloyd George, *Truth About the Peace Treaties,* vol. 2, pp. 937–38, 941; FRUS, vol. 3, p. 402; Headlam-Morley, p. xxvi; Seton-Watson and Seton-Watson, pp. 367–68.
23. Perman, pp. 178–79; Rothschild, pp. 76–84.
24. Sayer, pp. 150–51, 169–79.
25. Perman, pp. 220–23; P. Mantoux, vol. 2, pp. 351, 378–80.
26. Komarnicki, p. 356; Temperley, vol. 4, pp. 350–51; FRUS, vol. 3, pp. 777, 881–83; vol. 4, p. 608; vol. 8, pp. 118–24.
27. Temperley, vol. 4, p. 355; FRUS, vol. 12, pp. 318–22, 327.
28. Temperley, vol. 4, p. 357; H. Nicolson, *Peacemaking,* p. 25; FRUS, vol. 3, pp. 782–84; E. Howard, p. 305.
29. P. Mantoux, vol. 1, p. 234; Wandycz, *France and Her Eastern Allies,* pp. 93–94; FRUS, vol. 4, pp. 327–30.
30. FRUS, vol. 4, pp. 608–12; House and Seymour, pp. 82–83.
31. Davies, *White Eagle, Red Star,* p. 182.
32. D. Lloyd George, *Truth About the Peace Treaties,* vol. 2, p. 945; W. V. Wallace, pp. 55–57; Sayer, pp. 172–75.
33. FRUS, vol. 12, pp. 238, 345–46, 349; Scottish Record Office, Lothian Papers, 68/1–23, memorandum on the position in Hungary by E. Ashmead-Bartlett, 7.6.19.
34. Bonsal, *Suitors and Suppliants,* pp. 156–64.
35. W. V. Wallace, pp. 58–59.

CHAPTER 19: AUSTRIA

1. Mordacq, *Le ministère Clemenceau,* vol. 3, p. 300.
2. A.J.P. Taylor, *Habsburg Monarchy,* p. 250; Stone, pp. 124–47.
3. Bridge, p. 24.
4. Cornwall, pp. 120–23.
5. P. Mantoux, vol. 2, p. 231.
6. Almond and Lutz, eds., pp. 62–63; Headlam-Morley, pp. 126–30; P. Mantoux, vol. 2, pp. 228–31; FRUS, vol. 6, pp. 26–30.
7. Coolidge and Lord, p. 200; House and Seymour, p. 109; P. Mantoux, vol. 2, p. 229; Almond and Lutz, p. 226.
8. D. Lloyd George, *War Memoirs,* vol. 4, chapter LXI; D. Lloyd George, *Truth About the Peace Treaties,* vol. 2, p. 291; Duroselle, pp. 809–12; Schüller, pp. 234–35.
9. FRUS, vol. 12, p. 309.
10. Almond and Lutz, p. 88; FRUS, vol. 4, pp. 775–77; vol. 2, pp. 254–56.

11. Ashmead-Bartlett, pp. 20–26, 30–31; FRUS, vol. 12, pp. 228–32, 285–89; H. Nicolson, *Peacemaking*, pp. 293–94; E. Taylor, pp. 366–67.
12. Almond and Lutz, pp. 92, 109; FRUS, vol. 12, pp. 286, 290, 305–7.
13. P. Mantoux, vol. 1, 428–9; FRUS, vol. 5, pp. 368–69; Hankey, p. 137.
14. Allizé, pp. 48, 135; Schüller, p. 228; Stadler, *Birth of the Austrian Republic*, pp. 41–42.
15. Allizé, pp. 138, 142–43; Schüller, pp. 232–33; PWW, vol. 60, p. 19; Beadon, p. 200.
16. P. Mantoux, vol. 2, pp. 230, 236, 239; D. Lloyd George, *Truth About the Peace Treaties*, vol. 2, p. 943.
17. Schüller, pp. 234–35.
18. Suval, pp. 3–8; Barker, pp. 8–9; Stadler, *Birth of the Austrian Republic*, pp. 62–64.
19. Stadler, *Birth of the Austrian Republic*, pp. 62–69; FRUS, vol. 12, pp. 231, 240–44, 263.
20. Stadler, *Birth of the Austrian Republic*, pp. 70–71; FRUS, vol. 12, pp. 278–79; Bauer, pp. 110–11.
21. House, *Intimate Papers*, vol. 4, 335; Ministère des Affaires Etrangères, Série à Paix 60, Conditions de la Paix, memorandum of 25.10.18; Bonsal, *Unfinished Business*, pp. 87, 95; Bauer, p. 116; P. Mantoux, vol. 1, pp. 34, 459–60; Stadler, *Birth of the Austrian Republic*, p. 73; Nelson, pp. 309–11; FRUS, vol. 12, pp. 278–79.
22. Temperley, vol. 4, p. 393; Headlam-Morley, p. 147.
23. Hankey, p. 160; Marston, pp. 208–9; Beadon, p. 201; H. Nicolson, *Peacemaking*, p. 356.
24. P. Mantoux, vol. 2, pp. 6, 470–71; FRUS, vol. 7, pp. 173–74; Dockrill and Goold, p. 113.
25. Almond and Lutz, p. 64; Schüller, p. 236; Stadler, *Birth of the Austrian Republic*, p. 48; Howard, p. 382.
26. Schüller, pp. 237–42.
27. FRUS, vol. 12, pp. 501–10.
28. Steed, vol. 2, p. 333.
29. Lederer, p. 223; Seymour, p. 250; Laroche, p. 77.
30. Wolff, pp. 155–56.
31. Lederer, p. 297.
32. FRUS, vol. 12, pp. 600–601; Temperley, vol. 4, pp. 382–85; Stadler, *Birth of the Austrian Republic*, pp. 136–41.

CHAPTER 20: HUNGARY

1. Shotwell, p. 225.
2. May, vol. 2, chapter 15; P. Mantoux, vol. 1, p. 49.
3. Károlyi, pp. 24–25; Paloczi-Horvath, chapters 1–3; Jaszi, pp. 220–39.
4. Károlyi, pp. 20–25; Mitchell, p. 59; Windischgrätz, p. 48.
5. Károlyi, pp. 31–32; Windischgrätz, p. 102.
6. FRUS, vol. 12, pp. 380–82.
7. P. Mantoux, vol. 1, p. 97; Ashmead-Bartlett, p. 201; Ministère des Affaires Etrangères, Jules Cambon Papers, folder 88; Scottish Record Office, Lothian Papers, 3–18, Stephen Barczy to Lloyd George, 21.12.18; Barcsay, pp. 293–94.
8. FRUS, vol. 12, pp. 234, 372–77, 380–83, 387–88.
9. Pastor, pp. 50–51; H. Nicolson, *Peacemaking*, p. 127.
10. Azan, pp. 231–32; Károlyi, pp. 146–47.
11. FRUS, vol. 3, pp. 248–51, 845; Macartney, *Hungary and Her Successors*, pp. 276–77; Barcsay, p. 298.
12. Deák, pp. 46–48; D. Lloyd George, *Truth About the Peace Treaties*, vol. 2, p. 920; Pastor, pp. 131–32; FRUS, vol. 12, pp. 395, 405, 408–10; Ministère des Affaires Etrangères, Jules Cambon Papers, folder 88, "Documents relatifs à l'Autriche allemande et à la Hongrie."
13. Barcsay, p. 304, n. 1; Károlyi, pp. 146–47; FRUS, vol. 4, p. 158.
14. FRUS, vol. 12, pp. 414–16.
15. Tokes, pp. 170–76; Borsanyi, chapter 2; Bonsal, *Unfinished Business*, p. 124.
16. Vermes, pp. 53–54.

17. FRUS, vol. 12, pp. 416–17; P. Mantoux, vol. 1, pp. 11–15.
18. D. Lloyd George, *Truth About the Peace Treaties,* vol. 1, p. 406; Mantoux, 1, 11–15, 75–76.
19. H. Nicolson, *Peacemaking,* p. 293; Churchill College, Cambridge. Leeper Papers, 3/88, Allen Leeper to Rex Leeper, 10.4.19; F. Stevenson, p. 179; Bonsal, *Unfinished Business,* p. 75.
20. Károlyi, p. 160; H. Nicolson, *Peacemaking,* p. 298.
21. H. Nicolson, *Peacemaking,* p. 304.
22. Bonsal, *Unfinished Business,* pp. 78, 141; FRUS, vol. 5, pp. 41–43; Hancock, pp. 518–9.
23. Ashmead-Bartlett, pp. 101, 123, 134; Károlyi, pp. 159, 163; FRUS, vol. 12, pp. 440–41.
24. Deutscher, p. 434; Ormos, pp. 132–35; Ashmead-Bartlett, pp. 125–27, 162–71; Sakmyster, *Hungary's Admiral,* pp. 18–19.
25. Eckelt, *passim.*
26. Deák, p. 78; Armstrong, pp. 73, 79, n. 115; P. Mantoux, vol. 2, pp. 349–50, 352, 375–82; Ormos, pp. 142–43; Mayer, p. 781.
27. Deák, p. 78; Scottish Record Office, Lothian Papers, 68/1–23 memorandum on the position in Hungary by E. Ashmead-Bartlett, 7.6.19; Churchill College, Leeper Papers 3/8, Allen Leeper to Rex Leeper, 10.4.19.
28. P. Mantoux, vol. 1, p. 386.
29. Ashmead-Bartlett, pp. 200–202.
30. P. Mantoux, vol. 2, pp. 362, n. 1, 376; Spector, pp. 136–37.
31. FRUS, vol. 6, pp. 133, 411–16; P. Mantoux, vol. 2, pp. 338–39, 354; F. Palmer, *Bliss,* p. 399.
32. P. Mantoux, vol. 2, p. 420; House of Lords Record Office, Lloyd George Papers, F/89/3/2, memorandum from Balfour, 2.7.19; Tokes, pp. 202–3.
33. Deák, pp. 112–28; Bandholtz, pp. 303–4.
34. Bandholtz, pp. 26–28, 42–43, 70–71, 76, 90, 107.
35. Spector, pp. 197–219; Apponyi, p. 256.
36. Apponyi, *passim* and p. 253; Károlyi, pp. 44–45.
37. Laroche, p. 99.
38. Deák, pp. 539–49; D. Lloyd George, *Truth About the Peace Treaties,* vol. 2, pp. 962–70.
39. Apponyi, p. 270; Deák, pp. 210, 214–15, 238–42, 251–52, 253–77; Adam, pp. 148–55; Temperley, vol. 4, p. 421; Sakmyster, "Great Britain," p. 125.
40. Hoensch, pp. 103–4; Sakmyster, *Hungary's Admiral,* pp. 74–76.

CHAPTER 21: THE COUNCIL OF FOUR

1. PWW, vol. 58, p. 275.
2. Bonsal, *Suitors and Suppliants,* p. 179; Aldrovandi Marescotti, *Guerra diplomatica,* p. 407.
3. Hunter Miller, *Drafting of the Covenant,* vol. 1, p. 131; Mordacq, *Le ministère Clemenceau,* vol. 3, pp. 178–79; Tardieu, p. 100; Steed, vol. 2, p. 298.
4. Marston, p. 166; E. Howard, p. 279; Tardieu, p. 102.
5. National Archives of Canada, Borden Papers, 428/9; Dillon, p. 123; Cambon, p. 318.
6. Marston, pp. 168–69; P. Mantoux, vol. 1, pp. xiii–xvii.
7. PWW, vol. 59, pp. 419–20; Riddell, *Intimate Diary,* p. 55; P. Mantoux, vol. 2, p. 358; Aldrovandi Marescotti, *Nuovi ricordi,* p. 53; D. Lloyd George, *Truth About the Peace Treaties,* vol. 1, p. 228.
8. P. Mantoux, vol. 1, pp. 80–99; vol. 2, pp. 193–203; Yale University Library, Auchincloss diary, 31.3.19; Library of Congress, Baker notebooks, 31.3.19; PWW, vol. 56, p. 436; National Archives of Canada, Borden Papers, C1864, diary 31.3.19; F. Stevenson, p. 267; Poincaré, p. 292; Riddell, *Intimate Diary,* pp. 40–41; Noble, pp. 316–22.
9. F. Lloyd George, p. 165; Riddell, *Intimate Diary,* pp. 168–69.
10. PWW, vol. 58, p. 276; vol. 60, p. 197; vol. 61, p. 112, n. 1; Library of Congress, Baker notebooks, 17.5.19; Hecksher, pp. 555–56.

11. Walworth, *Wilson and His Peacemakers,* p. 390; Marston, pp. 182–83, 185–86; Hankey, pp. 134–38, 143–44.
12. Library of Congress, Baker notebooks, 17.5.19; Marks, *Innocent Abroad,* pp. 197–99.
13. Marks, *Innocent Abroad,* pp. 170–77.
14. PWW, vol. 59, p. 247; Riddell, *Intimate Diary,* p. 43; House of Lords Record Office, Lloyd George Papers, F 3/4/21, Hardinge to Balfour, 4.4.19.
15. Marks, *Innocent Abroad,* pp. 93–95; PWW, vol. 61, p. 375.
16. Marks, *Innocent Abroad,* pp. 9–11, 149–51.
17. Ibid., pp. 144–46; Temperley, vol. 2, pp. 190–91; Nelson, pp. 312–18.
18. P. Mantoux, vol. 1, pp. 135–38; Marks, *Innocent Abroad,* pp. 183–205.

CHAPTER 22: ITALY LEAVES
 1. F. Stevenson, pp. 181–82; Roskill, vol. 2, p. 8; Churchill College, Hankey Papers, 3/25, letter to wife, 23.4.19; Scott, p. 386.
 2. Yale University Library, Auchincloss diary, 13.5.19; H. Nicolson, *Curzon,* p. 106, n. 1.
 3. Albrecht-Carrié, p. 82; Vivarelli, vol. 1, pp. 382–83.
 4. D. Lloyd George, *Truth About the Peace Treaties,* vol. 1, p. 253; vol. 2, p. 819; Yale University Library, Auchincloss diary, 15.4.19; 003–0031, House to Wilson, 27.2.19.
 5. D. Lloyd George, *Truth About the Peace Treaties,* vol. 1, p. 253; Sforza, 'Sonnino', p. 724; Saladino, p. 623; Aldrovandi Marescotti, *Guerra diplomatica,* p. 369.
 6. Mordacq, *Le ministère Clemenceau,* vol. 3, p. 277, n. 1; Vivarelli, vol. 1, pp. 84–85.
 7. FRUS, vol. 1, pp. 422–23.
 8. British Library, Balfour Papers, 49734/186–192; 49744/123–128, Derby to Balfour, 15.11.18; Duroselle, pp. 782–84; Repington, p. 13.
 9. D. Lloyd George, *Truth About the Peace Treaties,* vol. 2, pp. 768–69; British Library, Balfour Papers, 49744/161–3, Derby to Balfour, 21.11.18.
10. Lloyd George, *Truth About the Peace Treaties,* vol. 2, p. 794; Bonsal, *Suitors and Suppliants,* p. 117.
11. Vivarelli, vol. 1, p. 386; Lederer, pp. 71–75.
12. See Zivojinovic, chapters 8–10; FRUS, vols. 1, pp. 475–87.
13. Baerlein, vol. 1, p. 87; vol. 2, pp. 49, 75, 80, 141; Zivojinovic, pp. 230–31.
14. FRUS, vol. 1, pp. 472–73; Mamatey, p. 315; Aldrovandi Marescotti, *Guerra diplomatica,* p. 250.
15. Ministère de la Défense, Clemenceau Papers, 6N72, minutes of a meeting of the allies, 2.12.18; Zivojinovic, p. 275, n. 26.
16. Library of Congress, Beer diary 30.3.19; Albrecht-Carrié, pp. 80, 90–94; P. Mantoux, vol. 1, p. 293; Bonsal, *Suitors and Suppliants,* p. 102.
17. Mamatey, pp. 199, 361–62; Yale University Library, House diary, 15.11.18; Vivarelli, vol. 1, pp. 398–99; Orlando, p. 388.
18. Baker, *Life and Letters,* vol. 7, p. 513; British Library, Balfour Papers, 49744/217–219, Derby to Balfour, 22.12.18.
19. PWW, vol. 53, p. 621; vol. 54, p. 50; Vivarelli, vol. 1, p. 386, n. 107; Library of Congress, Baker notebooks, 19.5.19.
20. Lovin, p. 27.
21. Hunter Miller, *My Diary,* vol. 1, p. 55; Lovin, pp. 33–34; Seton-Watson, *Italy,* p. 532, n. 1; Orlando, p. 387.
22. Headlam-Morley, p. 16; Rodd, vol. 3, p. 377; Mamatey, p. 118; Steed, vol. 2, p. 273.
23. Orlando, p. 356; D. Lloyd George, *Truth About the Peace Treaties,* vol. 2, p. 806.
24. Mordacq, *Le ministère Clemenceau,* vol. 3, pp. 30, 277, n. 1; Clemenceau, p. 140; Orlando, p. 360.
25. Duroselle, pp. 787–88; Orlando, p. 370.
26. Albrecht-Carrié, pp. 370–87.
27. Hess, pp. 105–26.
28. Seton-Watson, *Italy,* p. 534; Bodleian Library, Milner Papers, 389, meeting of Colonial Committee, 15.5.19, 19.5.19; Milner to Lloyd George, 16 May 1919.

29. Temperley, vol. 4, pp. 281, 283; Albrecht-Carrié, pp. 81, 85, 375; Yale University Library, House diary, 10.3.19; Baker, *Woodrow Wilson and World Settlement,* vol. 2, p. 146; Library of Congress, Baker Papers, notebook, 28.5.19; Alcock, pp. 71–73, 79–81.

30. Albrecht-Carrié, p. 379; FRUS, vol. 1, p. 478.

31. Zivojinovic, p. 231, n. 49; chapter 9; Hoover, p. 106.

32. Albrecht-Carrié, pp. 107–8; Steed, vol. 2, pp. 280–81, Yale University Library, House Papers, series III, box 201, 2/566.

33. Mordacq, *Le ministère Clemenceau,* vol. 3, p. 172; Orlando, pp. 482–83.

34. Ministère de la Défense, Clemenceau Papers, 6N75, copy of a treaty, 13.6.19; Orlando, pp. 386–87; House of Lords Record Office, Lloyd George Papers, F/23/4/22, Hankey to Lloyd George, 23 February 1919.

35. British Library, Balfour Papers, 49752 (vol. 2), "The Problem of Italy and Turkey in Anatolia," 16 May 1919; Yale University Library, House Papers, series III, box 201, 2/567; Mayer, pp. 219–20.

36. Baerlein, vol. 1, p. 62.

37. Ledeen, p. 28; FRUS, vol. 1, pp. 449, 462.

38. Baker, *Woodrow Wilson and World Settlement,* vol. 2, p. 135; Yale University Library, House diary, 3.4.19; House, *Intimate Papers,* vol. 4, p. 441.

39. Woodhouse, p. 321; Mayer, p. 222.

40. Albrecht-Carrié, p. 116; Vivarelli, vol. 1, p. 391, n. 120.

41. Aldrovandi Marescotti, *Guerra diplomatica,* p. 214; P. Mantoux, vol. 1, pp. 243–44; Yale University Library, House diary, 15.4.19.

42. Bonsal, *Suitors and Suppliants,* pp. 101, 117.

43. Albrecht-Carrié, p. 129; Library of Congress, Baker notebooks, 7.4.19.

44. Yale University Library, House diary, 15.4.19; Albrecht-Carrié, pp. 126–28, 445–47; Aldrovandi Marescotti, *Guerra diplomatica,* p. 215.

45. Seton-Watson, *Italy,* p. 532, n. 3; P. Mantoux, vol. 1, p. 288; Aldrovandi Marescotti, *Guerra diplomatica,* pp. 247–48.

46. Albrecht-Carrié, pp. 464–65; P. Mantoux, vol. 1, p. 295.

47. P. Mantoux, vol. 1, p. 301; Albrecht-Carrié, p. 479; Mayer, pp. 687–88.

48. P. Mantoux, vol. 1, pp. 290-312; Albrecht-Carrié, pp. 160–62; Hankey, pp. 125–26.

49. P. Mantoux, vol. 1, p. 306.

50. Aldrovandi Marescotti, *Guerra diplomatica,* pp. 239, 250, 255, 257, 262.

51. Library of Congress, Baker notebooks, 25.4.19; Baker, *Woodrow Wilson and World Settlement,* vol. 2, p. 129.

52. P. Mantoux, vol. 1, pp. 308, 315–7; Riddell, *Intimate Diary,* p. 56.

53. Aldrovandi Marescotti, *Guerra diplomatica,* pp. 257–65; Mordacq, *Le ministère Clemenceau,* vol. 3, p. 231; Riddell, *Intimate Diary,* p. 56.

54. Steed, vol. 2, p. 329; Mayer, pp. 701–2; Ministère des Affaires Etrangères, Série à Paix, vol. 317, report from the French consul in Turin, 28.4.19; Baerlein, vol. 1, p. 138.

55. Scottish Record Office, Lothian Papers, 66, 6–15; Mayer, pp. 707–8, 710–11; Woodhouse, p. 319.

56. C. T. Thompson, pp. 335, 342; Seton-Watson, *Italy,* p. 532, n. 2.

57. University Microfilms International, Sonnino Papers, reel 40, 479, 486, 488; Albrecht-Carrié, pp. 153–55.

58. Seymour, p. 266.

59. Library of Congress, Baker notebooks, 30.5.19; Aldrovandi Marescotti, *Guerra diplomatica,* p. 357; Albrecht-Carrié, p. 168.

60. Library of Congress, Baker notebooks, 19.5.19; Aldrovandi Marescotti, *Nuovi ricordi,* pp. 100, 106; Seton-Watson, *Italy,* p. 539; Orlando, p. 484; Baerlein, vol. 1, p. 139; House of Lords Record Office, Lloyd George Papers, 56/2/27, Rodd to Lloyd George, 6.5.19.

61. Albrecht-Carrié, pp. 167–73; Seton-Watson, *Italy,* p. 533; Aldrovandi Marescotti, *Nuovi ricordi,* p. 33.

62. Orlando, pp. 482–83; See Bodleian Library, Milner Papers, 46/2, Rodd to Milner, 30.6.19; Seton-Watson, *Italy,* p. 535.
63. Ledeen, pp. 102–3, 148–49; Woodhouse, p. 341.
64. Ledeen, pp. 145–46.
65. Ibid., pp. 88, 95–97; Seton-Watson, *Italy,* pp. 546–47.
66. Ledeen, p. 108.
67. Tillman, pp. 382–83; F. Stevenson, p. 192.
68. Temperley, vol. 4, pp. 329–30.
69. Seton-Watson, *Italy,* p. 582.
70. Woodhouse, pp. 371, 379.
71. Rodd, p. 384.

CHAPTER 23: JAPAN AND RACIAL EQUALITY
1. Bonsal, *Suitors and Suppliants,* p. 239.
2. Nish, *Japanese Foreign Policy,* pp. 4–5.
3. Aldrovandi Marescotti, *Guerra diplomatica,* p. 337.
4. Temperley, vol. 1, p. 259; Seymour, pp. 177–78; Baker, *What Wilson Did,* p. 73.
5. House, *Intimate Papers,* vol. 4, p. 304; Curry, p. 251; Nish, *Japanese Foreign Policy,* p. 117; Nish, *Alliance in Decline,* p. 267.
6. Connors, pp. 60–61.
7. Bonsal, *Suitors and Suppliants,* pp. 231–32.
8. Ibid., p. 233.
9. Kumao pp. 24–25; Connors, p. 3.
10. Kumao, pp. 24–25; Connors, p. 3.
11. Clemenceau, p. 140; Kumao, pp. 26, 40.
12. Kumao, pp. 23–4, 26, 38, 63.
13. *Cambridge History of Japan,* vol. 6, pp. 386, 433; Connors, pp. 14–16.
14. Hunter, p. 119.
15. Duus, p. 134.
16. Connors, pp. 15, 18–19, 22, 109–10.
17. Yamagata Aritomo, quoted in Nish, *Alliance in Decline,* p. 255; Nish, *Alliance in Decline,* pp. 127–31; *Cambridge History of Japan,* vol. 6, p. 279.
18. Curry, p. 197; Nish, *Alliance in Decline,* pp. 258–59.
19. Nish, *Japanese Foreign Policy,* p. 282; Chi, *China Diplomacy,* p. 86; Dingman, p. 57; Nish, *Alliance in Decline,* p. 217.
20. La Fargue, p. 46.
21. Dingman, p. 76.
22. Ibid., p. 43.
23. Neu, pp. 127–29, 131–32; Chi, "Ts'ao Ju-lin," p. 103; M. D. Kennedy, pp. 41, 44; Dingman, p. 58.
24. Nish, *Alliance in Decline,* pp. 196, 227, n. 48, 232; Fifield, *Woodrow Wilson and the Far East,* p. 111; FRUS, vol. 3, p. 506.
25. Nish, *Alliance in Decline,* p. 267.
26. Fifield, *Woodrow Wilson and the Far East,* p. 141, 191; Nish, *Alliance in Decline,* p. 267; Curry, pp. 131–32, 137–38; Beers, p. 70; Hunter Miller, *My Diary,* vol. 1, p. 100.
27. FRUS, vol. 3, pp. 739–40; Geddes, pp. 32–37; P. Mantoux, vol. 1, p. 312.
28. Fifield, "Disposal of the Carolines," pp. 472–79.
29. Nish, *Alliance in Decline,* p. 172; Lauren, pp. 260–61.
30. FRUS, vol. 1, p. 494; Kawamura, pp. 51–52.
31. Yale University Library, House diary, 4.2.19; Scottish Record Office, Lothian Papers, 37–40, notes dictated on Monday 10 February, 1919; Hunter Miller, *Drafting of the Covenant,* vol. 1, pp. 183–84; Bonsal, *Unfinished Business,* p. 33.
32. Hunter Miller, *Drafting of the Covenant,* vol. 2, pp. 323–25; Bonsal, *Unfinished Business,* p. 33; FRUS, vol. 3, pp. 224–25.
33. Lauren, p. 268; PWW, vol. 55, p. 489; Scottish Record Office, Lothian Papers, 37–40,

notes dictated on Monday 10 February, 1919; D. Lloyd George, *Truth About the Peace Treaties,* vol. 1, pp. 636.

34. Hunter Miller, *Drafting of the Covenant,* vol. 1, p. 336; Hunter Miller, *My Diary,* vol. 1, p. 100; Link, *Wilson: The New Freedom,* pp. 243–54.

35. Snelling, p. 23; W. J. Hudson, pp. 55–57; National Library of Australia, Hughes Papers, series 24/2, folder 11: 1538/24/902; House of Lords Record Office, Lloyd George Papers, F 6/6/29, Cecil to Lloyd George, 15.4.19.

36. Ministère de la Défense, Clemenceau Papers, 6N74, Société des Nations, letter of 18.4.19; Nish, *Alliance in Decline,* p. 271; W. J. Hudson, p. 57; Garran, p. 265; House of Lords Record Office, Lloyd George Papers, F 6/6/29, Cecil to Lloyd George, 15.4.19; National Archives of Canada, Christie Papers, vol. 5, file 16; Borden diary, 31.3.19; Public Record Office, Cabinet Papers, CAB 29/28, British empire delegation minutes, 29 (28.4.19); Bonsal, *Unfinished Business,* p. 154; Yale University Library, House diary, 13.2.19.

37. House, *Intimate Papers,* vol. 4, p. 313; Yale University Library, Auchincloss diary, 10.4.19; Hunter Miller, *Drafting of the Covenant,* vol. 1, pp. 461–66; vol. 2, pp. 387–93.

38. Lauren, pp. 274–75; FRUS, vol. 3, p. 291.

39. P. Mantoux, vol. 1, p. 314.

CHAPTER 24: A DAGGER POINTED AT THE HEART OF CHINA

1. Keegan, p. 173.
2. Schrecker, pp. 215–17, 231.
3. Ibid., pp. 168–203, 247.
4. Chi, *China Diplomacy,* p. 26; Schrecker, p. 248.
5. Fifield, *Woodrow Wilson and the Far East,* p. 25.
6. Connors, p. 110.
7. Nish, *Alliance in Decline,* pp. 158–59.
8. Curry, pp. 127–28.
9. Nish, *Japanese Foreign Policy,* p. 116.
10. Ibid., p. 286.
11. Chow, p. 87; Fifield, *Woodrow Wilson and the Far East,* p. 187.
12. Chi, *China Diplomacy,* p. 25; Nish, *Alliance in Decline,* pp. 156, 193; Quoted in Louis, *British Strategy,* p. 19.
13. Curry, pp. 127, 182, 253–54; Fifield, *Woodrow Wilson and the Far East,* p. 141.
14. Curry, p. 155; Beers, pp. 109, 121, 149, 154.
15. Fifield, *Woodrow Wilson and the Far East,* p. 134; Curry, pp. 15, 30; Pugach, pp. 241, 261.
16. Curry, p. 194.
17. Clemenceau, p. 140; Shotwell, pp. 136–37, 161; W. King, *China at the Peace Conference,* p. 3.
18. Fifield, *Woodrow Wilson and the Far East,* pp. 230–31, 191–94; Beers, p. 153; Shotwell, pp. 136–37.
19. Chu, p. 15; La Fargue, p. 178; W. King, *China at the Peace Conference,* p. 2.
20. Fifield, *Woodrow Wilson and the Far East,* pp. 140, 144; Chow, p. 86; Curry, p. 251; Bonsal, *Suitors and Suppliants,* p. 237; Chu, p. 30, n. 66.
21. W. King, *China at the Peace Conference,* p. 26; Fifield, *Woodrow Wilson and the Far East,* p. 126, n. 55.
22. Fifield, *Woodrow Wilson and the Far East,* pp. 124–25.
23. W. King, *China at the Peace Conference,* p. 5.
24. Ibid., pp. 9–11; Fifield, *Woodrow Wilson and the Far East,* pp. 130–31.
25. W. King, *China at the Peace Conference,* p. 7.
26. Fifield, *Woodrow Wilson and the Far East,* pp. 197–98; Shotwell, p. 151; Kawamura, p. 50.
27. Fifield, *Woodrow Wilson and the Far East,* pp. 143–55.
28. Keegan, p. 178; W. King, *China at the Peace Conference,* p. 12; Fifield, *Woodrow Wilson and the Far East,* pp. 141–42.

29. Curry, pp. 265–67; Fifield, *Woodrow Wilson and the Far East*, p. 243; PWW, vol. 57, pp. 582–83; Hankey, p. 131.
30. Fifield, *Woodrow Wilson and the Far East*, pp. 247–49; Curry, p. 268; P. Mantoux, vol. 1, pp. 319–28.
31. P. Mantoux, vol. 1, p. 330; La Fargue, p. 217.
32. Fifield, *Woodrow Wilson and the Far East*, p. 253; W. King, *China at the Peace Conference*, p. 21; P. Mantoux, vol. 1, pp. 329–36.
33. Hankey, p. 132; P. Mantoux, vol. 1, pp. 334–36; La Fargue, p. 218.
34. Library of Congress, Baker notebooks, 25.4.19; Fifield, *Woodrow Wilson and the Far East*, p. 260, 268; Bonsal, *Suitors and Suppliants*, p. 235.
35. Curry, p. 274; Fifield, *Woodrow Wilson and the Far East*, pp. 267–71.
36. PWW, vol. 57, p. 583; Shotwell, p. 196, n. 1; Kawamura, pp. 523–24.
37. Fifield, *Woodrow Wilson and the Far East*, pp. 269–70; Curry, pp. 275–76; P. Mantoux, vol. 1, 399–401.
38. Library of Congress, Baker notebooks, 25.4.19; Beers, p. 160; La Fargue, p. 231.
39. Curry, pp. 272, 277, 279; Keegan, p. 178; La Fargue, p. 222; Floto, p. 233; Fifield, *Woodrow Wilson and the Far East*, pp. 298–301; Beers, p. 158.
40. PWW, vol. 58, p. 244; Library of Congress, Baker notebooks, 30.4.19; Heckscher, p. 567; Fifield, *Woodrow Wilson and the Far East*, pp. 277–80; P. Mantoux, vol. 1, pp. 425–27.
41. Chow, p. 90; Bonsal, *Suitors and Suppliants*, pp. 242–43.
42. Curry, p. 280; Fifield, *Woodrow Wilson and the Far East*, p. 287; Bonsal, *Suitors and Suppliants*, p. 244.
43. Chow, p. 90.
44. Ibid., p. 101.
45. Ibid., p. 93.
46. Schwarcz, pp. 14, 18, 22.
47. Fifield, *Woodrow Wilson and the Far East*, p. 303.
48. Schwarcz, p. 12.
49. Ibid., pp. 15–22; Chow, p. 189.
50. Spence, p. 294.
51. Fifield, *Woodrow Wilson and the Far East*, p. 243; Chi, "Ts'ao Ju-lin," p. 181, n. 138.
52. Nish, *Japanese Foreign Policy*, pp. 123, 287–88; Curry, p. 282.
53. Fifield, *Woodrow Wilson and the Far East*, pp. 346–47.
54. Griswold, p. 327; Nish, *Japanese Foreign Policy*, p. 138.
55. Chu, p. 80.
56. Fifield, *Woodrow Wilson and the Far East*, pp. 298–300; Beers, p. 26; Curry, p. 309.

CHAPTER 25: THE GREATEST GREEK STATESMAN SINCE PERICLES

1. Petsalis-Diomidis, p. 109 and Appendix B.
2. F. Lloyd George, p. 167; Petsalis-Diomidis, pp. 123, 135; Churchill College, Hankey diary, 17.10.18; Bonsal, *Suitors and Suppliants*, p. 176.
3. Alastos, pp. 11–12.
4. Ibid., pp. 14–18.
5. Ibid., p. 13.
6. Clogg, p. 33.
7. Petsalis-Diomidis, p. 17.
8. Ibid., p. 187; House of Lords Record Office, Lloyd George Papers, 55/1/10.
9. Petsalis-Diomidis, p. 177; House of Lords Record Office, Lloyd George Papers, 55/1/32, Venizelos to Lloyd George, 23.7.20; 92/12/1, interview between Lloyd George and Venizelos; FRUS, vol. 3, pp. 863–73.
10. Magosci, p. 97.
11. Smith, pp. 25–27.
12. Petsalis-Diomidis, p. 679.
13. Clogg, p. 89.

14. D. Lloyd George, *Truth About the Peace Treaties,* vol. 2, pp. 1203–4; Dillon, p. 75.
15. PWW, vol. 55, p. 266; H. Nicolson, *Peacemaking,* p. 251.
16. FRUS, vol. 3, pp. 859–66, 868–75; Churchill College, Leeper Papers, 3/8, Allen Leeper to Rex Leeper, 3.2.19.
17. FRUS, vol. 3, p. 874.
18. Stickney, p. 79.
19. Duroselle, p. 777; P. Mantoux, vol. 2, p. 56.
20. Smith, pp. 63–64; Goldstein, "Great Britain and Greater Greece," p. 344.
21. Goldstein, "Great Britain and Greater Greece," p. 343; Churchill College, Hankey diary, 27.12.18.
22. D. Lloyd George, *Truth About the Peace Treaties,* vol. 2, p. 204; Petsalis-Diomidis, p. 129; Smith, p. 253; Goldstein, "Great Britain and Greater Greece," pp. 346–47.
23. D. Lloyd George, *Truth About the Peace Treaties,* vol. 2, p. 1216; Smith, p. 18.
24. Riddell, *Intimate Diary,* p. 27; House of Lords Record Office, Lloyd George Papers, 55/1/10; Petsalis-Diomidis, pp. 72–73, 132–34.
25. Alastos, pp. 188, nn. 1 and 2; Petsalis-Diomidis, p. 135.
26. Petsalis-Diomidis, pp. 49–52, 76–78.
27. Ibid., pp. 62–63, 116–18; House of Lords Record Office, Lloyd George Papers, F3/4/6, Hardinge to Balfour, 21.1.19.
28. Yale University Library, House diary, 8.1.19; Bonsal, *Suitors and Suppliants,* p. 177; H. Nicolson, *Peacemaking,* p. 24; Seymour, p. 56.
29. H. Nicolson, *Peacemaking,* p. 268; Stickney, pp. 88, 95; Petsalis-Diomidis, pp. 162–63, 164, n. 41.
30. National Archives of Canada, Borden diary, 8.2.19; H. Nicolson, *Peacemaking,* pp. 262, 266.
31. Durham, pp. 246, 260–61; Shanafelt, pp. 283–300.
32. Bonsal, *Suitors and Suppliants,* p. 74; Durham, p. 181.
33. Fitzherbert, pp. 125–26; Laffan, pp. 223–28.
34. Dontas, p. 105; Stickney, p. 68.
35. Stickney, pp. 91–92.
36. Roosevelt, p. 95; Cannadine, p. 383; Fitzherbert, *passim.*
37. H. Nicolson, *Peacemaking,* p. 268.
38. FRUS, vol. 4, pp. 111–16.
39. Bonsal, *Suitors and Suppliants,* p. 185.
40. H. Nicolson, *Peacemaking,* p. 260; Goldstein, "Great Britain and Greater Greece," p. 348; Petsalis-Diomidis, pp. 150–51.
41. P. Mantoux, vol. 1, p. 495.
42. Stickney, p. 125.
43. Temperley, vol. 6, pp. 39–40; Petsalis-Diomidis, p. 88; Bonsal, *Suitors and Suppliants,* p. 180; FRUS, vol. 7, p. 397.
44. FRUS, vol. 3, p. 866.
45. Ibid., vol. 7, pp. 246, 379–80; Genov, p. 62.
46. Helmreich, pp. 153–55; Goldstein, "Great Britain and Greater Greece," p. 349; House of Lords Record Office, Lloyd George Papers, 92/12/1, interview between Lloyd George and Venizelos, 5 September 1919.
47. Genov, p. 56.

CHAPTER 26: THE END OF THE OTTOMANS

1. FRUS, vol. 2, p. 282; Ahmad, p. 18.
2. Dyer, "The Turkish Armistice of 1918: 2," pp. 316, 323–24.
3. Ibid., pp. 327, 335–36.
4. Ibid., p. 334.
5. Ibid., pp. 319, 335, 345, n. 45.
6. Kinross, p. 153.
7. Ibid., p. 134.

8. FRUS, vol. 2, p. 281; Orga, p. 194; Kinross, p. 159.
9. Kinross, pp. 481, 531, 542.
10. Mazower, "Minorities," p. 47.
11. Kinross, pp. 16, 437, 468.
12. Suny, p. 107; Pope and Pope, p. 116; Mansel, pp. 286–88.
13. Kinross, p. 21.
14. Ibid., chapters 2 and 3.
15. Ibid., pp. 72, 111; Pope, p. 163.
16. Orga, pp. 164, 209; Kinross, p. 158; A. W. Palmer, pp. 244–45.
17. Mansel, pp. 384–85; Ryan, p. 139.
18. Mansel, pp. 398–400; Busch, *Mudros to Lausanne,* pp. 64–67.
19. Walker, p. 294.
20. British Library, Curzon Papers, F112/274, War Cabinet, Eastern Committee minutes, 46 (23.12.18).
21. British Library, Curzon Papers, Eastern Committee minutes, 40 (2.12.18).
22. Anderson, p. 268 n. 1; Petsalis-Diomidis, p. 75; P. Mantoux, vol. 2, p. 56.
23. Watson, pp. 367–68; D. Lloyd George, *War Memoirs,* vol. 6, p. 3314; P. Mantoux, vol. 2, p. 164.
24. FRUS, vol. 3, p. 806.
25. Helmreich, p. 13; Scottish Record Office, Lothian Papers, 1173, "Notes of an interview between M. Clemenceau, Colonel House and myself," 7.3.19; Walker, pp. 125–26; H. N. Howard, *The Partition,* pp. 135, 424.
26. FRUS, vol. 1, p. 52; H. N. Howard, *Turkey, the Straits and U.S. Policy,* p. 47; Hunter Miller, *My Diary,* vol. 1, pp. 27–28, 74; C. T. Thompson, p. 76; H. Nicolson, *Peacemaking,* p. 226; Macfie, "The British Decision," p. 391; British Library, Curzon Papers, F112/274, Eastern Committee minutes, 46 (23.12.18); House of Lords Record Office, Lloyd George Papers, F40/2, Montagu to Lloyd George, 28.2.19.
27. Helmreich, pp. 29–30; FRUS, vol. 3, pp. 956–69.
28. FRUS, vol. 4, pp. 147–57; Baker, *Woodrow Wilson and World Settlement,* vol. 2, p. 24.
29. Suny, p. 114 and chapter 6, *passim.*
30. FRUS, vol. 1, p. 42; Duroselle, p. 822 [my translation]; D. Lloyd George, *Truth About the Peace Treaties,* vol. 2, pp. 1257–58; Walker, pp. 263–64; House, *Intimate Papers* vol. 4, p. 199; Hoover, p. 141.
31. British Library, Curzon Papers, Eastern Committee minutes, 42 (9.12.18); Andrew and Kanya-Forstner, pp. 170–71, 194.
32. Helmreich, p. 50; House of Lords Record Office, Lloyd George Papers, 1173, "Notes of an interview between M. Clemenceau, Colonel House and myself, 10.30 A.M., 7.3.19"; D. Lloyd George, *Truth About the Peace Treaties,* vol. 2, p. 1262; FRUS, vol. 3, p. 807; vol. 5, p. 614; Andrew and Kanya-Forstner, p. 194.
33. Ryan, p. 130; Kinross, p. 241; Helmreich, p. 335, n. 38.

CHAPTER 27: ARAB INDEPENDENCE

1. Toynbee, pp. 211–12.
2. Mordacq, *Le ministère Clemenceau,* vol. 3, pp. 25, 28–29; Churchill College, Hankey diary, 4.12.18, note added 11.12.20.
3. Temperley, vol. 6, p. 182; Andrew and Kanya-Forstner, pp. 174–75; D. Lloyd George, *Truth About the Peace Treaties,* vol. 2, p. 1038.
4. Churchill College, Hankey diary, 6.10.18; Nevakivi, p. 118; British Library, Curzon Papers, Eastern Committee minutes, 39 (27.11.18).
5. Fromkin, *A Peace to End All Peace,* p. 190; Storrs, pp. 316, 324.
6. Sanders, p. 268; Adelson, p. 135; Nevakivi, p. 32.
7. D. Stevenson, *First World War and International Politics,* pp. 129–30.
8. Amery, vol. 1, p. 237.
9. Andrew and Kanya-Forstner, pp. 46, 69; Ministère de la Défense, Clemenceau Pa-

pers, 6N72, memoranda of 18.12.18, annex III; "Plan de règlement des questions d'Orient 12.12.18"; 6N76, note 1.2.19.

10. British Library, Curzon Papers, F112/274, Eastern Committee minutes, 41 (5.12.18); Eastern Committee minutes, 42 (9.12.18).

11. Andrew and Kanya-Forstner, pp. 152, 158–59; Nevakivi, pp. 65, 78–79.

12. Temperley, vol. 1, p. 439; Andrew and Kanya-Forstner, p. 149.

13. Andrew and Kanya-Forstner, p. 147; British Library, Curzon Papers, F112/274, Eastern Committee minutes, 39 (27.11.18), minutes 40 (2.12.18).

14. Zeine, p. 46; Nevakivi, pp. 59, 83; Andrew and Kanya-Forstner, p. 90.

15. Lansing, *The Big Four,* pp. 164–65, 169; James, *Imperial Warrior,* p. 173.

16. Lacey, p. 83; Yapp, *Making of the Modern Near East,* pp. 281–86.

17. Fromkin, *Peace to End All Peace,* pp. 174, 176–87.

18. D. Lloyd George, *Truth About the Peace Treaties,* vol. 2, p. 1028; Antonius, p. 321; Garnett, p. 20; James, *Golden Warrior,* p. 311.

19. Garnett, p. 89.

20. Fromkin, *Peace to End All Peace,* pp. 339–41; Garnett, pp. 117–18; Library of Congress, Beer Collection, diary, 8.1.19; British Library, Curzon Papers, Eastern Committee minutes, 41 (5.12.18); Nevakivi, p. 85.

21. Mordacq, *Le ministère Clemenceau,* vol. 3, p. 102; Zeine, pp. 51, 62; Bell, p. 128.

22. Zeine, pp. 50–52.

23. Ibid., p. 59; Antonius, pp. 280–86.

24. James, *Golden Warrior,* pp. 304, 599; Andrew and Kanya-Forstner, p. 131.

25. Hughes, *Policies and Potentates,* pp. 221–23; FRUS, vol. 3, pp. 889–94; Library of Congress, Bliss Papers, box 244, diary, 25.1.19; Beer Collection, diary, 7.1.19; Bonsal, *Suitors and Suppliants,* p. 40; Zeine, p. 144.

26. Andrew and Kanya-Forstner, p. 186; Shotwell, p. 178; Mordacq, *Le ministère Clemenceau,* vol. 3, pp. 113, 118–9.

27. FRUS, vol. 4, p. 3; Zamir, pp. 408–9.

28. Watson, p. 371.

29. Zeine, p. 59; Nevakivi, p. 98; Public Record Office, London, CAB 29/28; British empire delegation minutes, 7 (7.2.19); British Library, Balfour Papers, 49734/164–67, Balfour to Curzon, 8.9.19.

30. Yale University Library, House diary, 7.3.19, 12.3.19; Nevakivi, pp. 119, 128–29; Andrew and Kanya-Forstner, pp. 189, 194–98, 205.

31. Baker, *Woodrow Wilson and World Settlement,* vol. 1, p. 74; James, *Imperial Warrior,* p. 185; FRUS, vol. 5, p. 12; Poincaré, pp. 286–87.

32. Antonius, p. 288; Nevakivi, pp. 138, 143; Fitzherbert, p. 219; James, *Golden Warrior,* p. 311; Mordacq, *Le ministère Clemenceau,* vol. 3, p. 233.

33. P. Mantoux, vol. 2, p. 133.

34. Yergin, pp. 183, 189; Nevakivi, p. 91; Amery, vol. 1, p. 232.

35. Sluglett, p. 32; Callwell, vol. 2, p. 194; M. Kent, *Oil and Empire,* p. 148.

36. Marlowe, p. 92.

37. Ibid., p. 13.

38. Ibid., p. 113.

39. Ibid., p. 132.

40. Sluglett, appendix 1.

41. Marlowe, pp. 136–38; British Library, Curzon Papers, Eastern Committee minutes, 43 (16.12.18); Sluglett, p. 37.

42. Wallach, pp. 213–14.

43. Ibid., p. 108.

44. Ibid., p. 290–91.

45. Ibid., p. 207; Marlowe, p. 112; Sluglett, p. 22; Winstone, pp. 195, 198, 202; Zamir, pp. 408–9.

46. Winstone, pp. 209–10.

47. Sluglett, p. 34; Fitzherbert, p. 219.

48. Darwin, chapter 3, *passim;* Kedourie, *Chatham House Version,* p. 90.
49. Storrs, p. 54; Kedourie, *Chatham House Version,* pp. 84–88.
50. Zeine, p. 189.
51. Shaarawi, p. 114.
52. Darwin, pp. 83–84; Temperley, vol. 6, p. 198.
53. Public Record Office, CAB 29/2, Indian desiderata for the peace settlement.
54. J. M. Brown, *Prisoner of Hope,* pp. 140–41; J. M. Brown, *Gandhi's Rise to Power,* p. 192; House of Lords Record Office, Lloyd George Papers, F/23/4 "The Future of Constantinople," 5.2.19; Public Record Office, Cabinet Papers, CAB 29/28, British empire delegation minutes, 16 (3.4.19); Busch, *Britain, India and the Arabs,* p. 390.
55. P. Mantoux, vol. 2, pp. 95–100.
56. *The Englishman* (Calcutta), 8.4.19; Pandey, p. 107; Darwin, p. 247.
57. Callwell, vol. 2, p. 182; Darwin, pp. 30–32; James, *Imperial Warrior,* pp. 184, 194.
58. Gilbert, *Churchill,* vol. 4, p. 638; British Library, Balfour Papers, 49734/154–60, Curzon to Balfour, 20.8.19; Nevakivi, pp. 178, 181; Scottish Record Office, Lothian Papers, 74/19–21, 12.8.19; James, *Imperial Warrior,* pp. 194–95; Temperley, vol. 6, pp. 155–56; Andrew and Kanya-Forstner, p. 200.
59. Mordacq, *Le ministère Clemenceau,* vol. 4, pp. 97–98.
60. FRUS, vol. 12, pp. 751–863.
61. Nevakivi, p. 199; Wilson, p. 621.
62. Mordacq, *Le ministère Clemenceau,* vol. 4, pp. 134, 141, 203; Andrew and Kanya-Forstner, p. 213; Keiger, p. 268; Nevakivi, p. 208.
63. Andrew and Kanya-Forstner, pp. 201–2, 215; Zeine, pp. 120, n. 6, 146–47; Marlowe, pp. 212–3.
64. Zeine, pp. 136–37.
65. Marlowe, pp. 162, 204, 215.
66. Gilbert, *Churchill,* vol. 4, p. 495; Callwell, vol. 2, p. 273; British Library, Curzon Papers, F111/274, Eastern Committee minutes, 39 (27.11.18); Wallach, pp. 311, 321.
67. Wallach, p. 364.
68. Brecher, p. 656.

CHAPTER 28: PALESTINE

1. Reinharz, p. 298; FRUS, vol. 4, pp. 164–65; Andrew and Kanya-Forstner, p. 187.
2. Shotwell, p. 170.
3. Elon, pp. 62–63, 67; Sanders, p. 81.
4. Sanders, pp. 120–21, 418.
5. Eban, p. 12; Stein, pp. 121–22; Reinharz, p. 36.
6. Sanders, p. 318.
7. House of Lords Record Office, Lloyd George Papers, 60/2/26; Mansergh, vol. 2, p. 27; Churchill, *Great Contemporaries,* p. 250; Gilmour, pp. 503–4; Riddell, *Intimate Diary,* p. 325; Jones, vol. 1, p. 201.
8. Malcolm, p. 110.
9. D. Lloyd George, *War Memoirs,* vol. 2, pp. 1014, 1017; Mosley, p. 207.
10. Vansittart, p. 232; Mackay, p. 317; Yale University Library, House diary, 31.12.18; Sanders, p. 119; Dugdale, vol. 2, p. 171.
11. Stein, p. 152; Dugdale, vol. 2, p. 163; Sanders, pp. 119–21.
12. Sanders, p. 73; Rowland, p. 424.
13. D. Lloyd George, *War Memoirs,* vol. 2, p. 586; Ministère des Affaires Etrangères, Europe 1918–1929, EU18–40, Grande Bretagne, vol. 7, 4.4.19.
14. Sanders, p. 518; Stein, p. 127.
15. Gilmour, p. 481; Adelson, p. 243; Friedman, *Question of Palestine,* pp. 311–24.
16. Reinharz, pp. 223, 242; Sykes, p. 23.
17. Reinharz, pp. 291–95, 303–4.
18. Ibid., p. 296; Gilbert, *Churchill,* vol. 4, p. 639; FRUS, vol. 4, pp. 161–70.
19. Reinharz, p. 298; FRUS, vol. 4, pp. 161–70.

20. Andrew and Kanya-Forstner, p. 187; Storrs, pp. 326, 349, n. 1.
21. Reinharz, pp. 194, 199, 301; FRUS, vol. 4, p. 168.
22. Reinharz, p. 220; Yapp, *The Near East Since the First World War,* p. 116; Adelson, p. 243; Elon, p. 195.
23. Elon, pp. 209, 225–26; chapter 5, *passim;* Scottish Record Office, Lothian Papers, 64–78, Weizmann to Balfour, 30.5.18.
24. Reinharz, p. 278.
25. Dugdale, p. 161.
26. Sanders, p. 652; Storrs, p. 414; British Library, Curzon Papers, Eastern Committee minutes, 41 (5.12.18).
27. Wilson, p. 512; Storrs, p. 400; Reinharz, pp. 255–56.
28. Wilson, p. 593; Antonius, pp. 285–86, appendix F.
29. Lebow, pp. 501–23; PWW, vol. 54, pp. 432–33; Tillman, p. 226; Dockrill and Goold, p. 163; FRUS, vol. 12, pp. 793–95.
30. Klieman, p. 70; Nevakivi, pp. 119–23.
31. Nevakivi, p. 274; Reinharz, pp. 318, 387.
32. Gilbert, *Churchill,* vol. 4, p. 541.
33. British Library, Balfour Papers, 49734/154–60, Curzon to Balfour, 20.8.19; Sykes, pp. 49–50; Gilbert, *Churchill,* vol. 4, pp. 484–85.
34. Ibid., p. 625–27; Reinharz, pp. 357–58.
35. Sanders, p. 657; D. Lloyd George, *Truth About the Peace Treaties,* vol. 2, p. 1194; Reinharz, p. 392; Gilbert, *Churchill,* vol. 4, p. 621; Sykes, pp. 58–61.
36. Reinharz, pp. 394–95.
37. Sykes, pp. 72–73.

CHAPTER 29: ATATÜRK AND THE BREAKING OF SÈVRES

1. P. Mantoux, vol. 1, p. 454; vol. 2, pp. 37–38.
2. Temperley, vol. 6, p. 21; Petsalis-Diomidis, p. 47; D. Lloyd George, *Truth About the Peace Treaties,* vol. 2, pp. 774–83.
3. Bosworth, pp. 52–55, 67–69; Smith, pp. 69–79; Lowe and Marzari, p. 172.
4. Bosworth, p. 53; University Microfilm International, Sonnino Papers, reel 40/47, telegram of 26.1.19; Aldrovandi Marescotti, *Guerra diplomatica,* p. 365.
5. P. Mantoux, vol. 1, p. 305; vol. 2, p. 40; FRUS, vol. 5, p. 582; British Library, Balfour Papers, 49752, vol. 2, "The Problem of Italy and Turkey in Anatolia," 16.5.19.
6. P. Mantoux, vol. 1, pp. 448–55.
7. FRUS, vol. 3, pp. 868–75, 872; Bonsal, *Suitors and Suppliants,* p. 183; Llewellyn Smith, p. 70.
8. Llewellyn Smith, p. 51.
9. House and Seymour, pp. 192–93; House of Lords Record Office, Lloyd George Papers, F23/4/22, Hankey to Lloyd George, 23.2.19.
10. P. Mantoux, vol. 2, p. 31; H. Nicolson, *Peacemaking,* pp. 321–22; F. Stevenson, p. 183; Smith, p. 80.
11. P. Mantoux, vol. 2, pp. 47–48; Mordacq, *Le ministère Clemenceau,* vol. 3, p. 278.
12. Smith, p. 79; P. Mantoux, vol. 1, pp. 495–96; vol. 2, pp. 29–31, 36; Callwell, vol. 2, p. 192.
13. Smith, pp. 86–91.
14. Kinross, pp. 181–82; Ryan, p. 128.
15. Kinross, p. 177; D. Lloyd George, *Truth About the Peace Treaties,* vol. 2, p. 1285.
16. Kinross, pp. 199, 671–72.
17. H. Nicolson, *Peacemaking,* pp. 333–35.
18. P. Mantoux, vol. 2, pp. 55, 70; N. Nicolson, p. 84; British Library, Balfour Papers, Add. MS 49752, vol. 2, "The Problem of Italy and Turkey in Anatolia," 16.5.19.
19. Callwell, vol. 2, p. 193; N. Nicolson, p. 84.
20. P. Mantoux, vol. 2, pp. 72, 100, 106, 109–13.
21. Ibid., pp. 133–34; Roskill, vol. 2, p. 91; Churchill College, Hankey diary, 21.5.19; Andrew and Kanya-Forstner, p. 197; Steed, vol. 2, p. 330.

22. P. Mantoux, vol. 2, p. 137; Helmreich, pp. 75–79; Baker, *Woodrow Wilson and World Settlement,* vol. 2, p. 203.
23. H. N. Howard, *Partition of Turkey,* p. 237.
24. Helmreich, p. 110; FRUS, vol. 6, p. 711; P. Mantoux, vol. 2, pp. 552–56.
25. F. Stevenson, p. 76; Gilmour, pp. 491, 534–35.
26. H. Nicolson, *Curzon,* p. 47, n. 1.
27. Riddell, *Intimate Diary,* p. 184; Gilmour, pp. 7–8.
28. H. Nicolson, *Curzon,* p. 20; British Library, Montagu Papers, 15.6.18/31; Vansittart, p. 273.
29. Gregory, p. 254.
30. H. Nicolson, *Curzon,* p. 193; Gilmour, p. 510.
31. H. Nicolson, *Curzon,* p. 80; Gidney, p. 113.
32. Gilmour, p. 502; H. Nicolson, *Curzon,* pp. 74, 214.
33. Gidney, pp. 196–99; D. Lloyd George, *Truth About the Peace Treaties,* vol. 2, pp. 1264–67.
34. Lowe and Marzari, pp. 172–73; House of Lords Record Office, Lloyd George Papers, notes of an interview between Lloyd George and Tittoni, 31.8.19, F200/1/12; Helmreich, p. 197, n. 6.
35. Duroselle, pp. 778–79; Montgomery, p. 776.
36. A. L. Macfie, "The British Decision," p. 393; Rawlinson, pp. 190, 250–52; Scottish Record Office, Lothian Papers, 1–9, memorandum, "America and the League of Nations," 14.11.19.
37. Gilmour, p. 521.
38. Gilbert, *Churchill,* vol. 4, p. 305; British Library, Curzon Papers, Eastern Committee meeting, 42 (9.12.18).
39. Gilmour, p. 516; House of Lords Record Office, Lloyd George Papers, F47/8/13, Wilson to Lloyd George, 12.5.19 and 14.5.19; F/24/1/10 Hankey to Lloyd George, 4.9.19; Gilbert, *Churchill,* vol. 4, pp. 265, 305.
40. Nassibian, pp. 152–54, 229; Walker, p. 290, n.
41. Walker, pp. 275, 279; Gokay, pp. 59–66.
42. Walker, p. 281; Suny, p. 129.
43. FRUS, vol. 3, p. 806.
44. Adelson, p. 65; Gelfand, p. 243.
45. McDowall, pp. 108–9.
46. Ibid., pp. 3–5; Dominian, p. 296; Nassibian, pp. 19–20, 25.
47. McDowall, p. 3; Sonyel, pp. 6–8.
48. McDowall, p. 130; Busch, *Mudros to Lausanne,* p. 178.
49. McDowall, pp. 120–21; Helmreich, p. 204.
50. McDowall, pp. 121–29.
51. Ibid., pp. 120–21, 134–37, 143; Fromkin, *Peace to End All Peace,* p. 404.
52. McDowall, pp. 125–28, 132.
53. Helmreich, pp. 301–2; Temperley, vol. 6, pp. 90–91; McDowall, pp. 450–51.
54. Rawlinson, pp. 295–96; Busch, *Mudros to Lausanne,* p. 207; Smith, p. 122; M. Kent, *Moguls and Mandarins,* p. 100.
55. Dockrill and Goold, p. 210.
56. Smith, p. 127; Callwell, vol. 2, pp. 213, 248–49.
57. Dockrill and Goold, p. 210; Sonyel, p. 82.
58. Walker, pp. 315–6.
59. Ibid., p. 315.
60. Temperley, vol. 6, p. 91.
61. Sonyel, pp. 83–84; Adamthwaite, p. 94; Dockrill and Goold, p. 222.
62. Smith, pp. 191–97, 266.
63. Kinross, p. 354.
64. Smith, p. 309; Kinross, p. 372.
65. H. Nicolson, *Curzon,* pp. 273–74; Gilmour, p. 544.
66. W. White, *Dateline,* p. 245.
67. N. Nicolson, p. 121; W. White, *Dateline,* pp. 244–45, 254; Grew, vol. 1, p. 525, n. 45.

68. Dockrill and Goold, pp. 241, 246; W. White, *Dateline,* p. 254; Grew, vol. 1, pp. 525, 542–43; Gilbert, *Rumbold,* p. 290.
69. Grew, vol. 1, p. 584; Gilmour, p. 556.
70. Dockrill and Goold, p. 239; C. A. Macartney, *National States,* p. 444; Pope and Pope, pp. 116–18.
71. Kinross, p. 407.
72. McDowall, pp. 171–78; Mansel, p. 421.
73. McDowall, p. 158.
74. Sonyel, p. 225; Pope and Pope, pp. 22–23; Gilmour, p. 567.

CHAPTER 30: THE HALL OF MIRRORS
1. Hankey, pp. 143–44, 146; Marston, pp. 185–86; Callwell, vol. 2, p. 189; FRUS, vol. 3, p. 386; H. Nicolson, *Peacemaking,* p. 327; P. Mantoux, vol. 2, p. 473, n. 2.
2. F. Stevenson, p. 183; Aldrovandi Marescotti, *Guerra diplomatica,* pp. 299, 318; Mordacq, *Le ministère Clemenceau,* vol. 3, p. 264.
3. FRUS, vol. 12, p. 85; Schiff, pp. 51–52; Lovin, p. 58; Scottish Record Office, Lothian Papers, 70/5, notes by M. Massigli, 8.5.19.
4. Schiff, pp. 34–39; Nowak, pp. 184–86; Wheeler-Bennett, *Nemesis of Power,* p. 49, n. 2; St. Antony's College, Malcolm Papers, 1/2, diary, 25.4.19.
5. FRUS, vol. 12, p. 119; Schwabe, *Woodrow Wilson, Revolutionary Germany,* pp. 185–88.
6. Klein, p. 206; Bessel, *Germany After the First World War,* chapter 8; FRUS, vol. 12, pp. 86, 92, 99; Schwabe, "Germany's Peace Aims," p. 42.
7. See Schwabe, *Woodrow Wilson, Revolutionary Germany,* pp. 157–59, 310–17, 319, n. 51; Epstein, pp. 305–6, 319; Soutu, pp. 179–80; Nowak, pp. 240–44; Walworth, *Woodrow Wilson and His Peacemakers,* p. 385; Klein, pp. 211–12.
8. Schiff, pp. 32–33; Nowak, pp. 178–82; Lovin, 57–60.
9. Luckau, p. 116.
10. Luckau, pp. 62–65.
11. Schiff, p. 67; Riddell, *Intimate Diary,* p. 71; Hankey, pp. 151–53.
12. Hankey, p. 153; Luckau, p. 119.
13. F. Stevenson, p. 183; Hankey, pp. 154–55; Riddell, *Intimate Diary,* pp. 73–74; Aldrovandi Marescotti, *Guerra diplomatica,* p. 306; H. Nicolson, *Peacemaking,* pp. 329–30; Nowak, p. 225.
14. Sharp, *Versailles Settlement,* p. 127; Schiff, pp. 75–77; Luckau, p. 124; Steed, vol. 2, p. 336; Nowak, p. 228.
15. Mommsen, p. 535; Eyck, vol. 1, p. 98; Schwabe, *Woodrow Wilson, Revolutionary Germany,* p. 336; Krüger, pp. 323–35.
16. Luckau, pp. 182–88; FRUS, vol. 12, p. 96.
17. FRUS, vol. 6, pp. 795–901; Holborn, pp. 140–44; Marks, "Smoke and Mirrors," pp. 356–59; Luckau, pp. 81–84; Mommsen, pp. 537–39.
18. Luckau, p. 47, 81.
19. Luckau, pp. 130–31, 242, 254, 268–72; 287–99; 306–14; Nowak, p. 244; D. Lloyd George, *Truth About the Peace Treaties,* vol. 1, p. 684; P. Mantoux, vol. 2, p. 403.
20. Hoover, p. 234.
21. Lansing, p. 272; Fromkin, *In the Time of the Americans,* pp. 260–63; Walworth, *Wilson and His Peacemakers,* pp. 394–95.
22. H. Nicolson, *Peacemaking,* p. 187; Lentin, *Lloyd George, Woodrow Wilson,* p. 92.
23. Noble, pp. 353–58, 362–63; Miquel, pp. 548–55.
24. Callwell, vol. 2, p. 195; J. C. King, pp. 96–102; McDougall, *France's Rhineland Diplomacy,* pp. 70–72; Mordacq, *Le ministère Clemenceau,* vol. 3, pp. 298–99.
25. Lentin, *Lloyd George, Woodrow Wilson,* pp. 89–93; House of Lords Record Office, Lloyd George Papers, F 6/6/47, Cecil to Lloyd George, 27.5.19; Public Record Office, Cabinet Papers, CAB 29/28, British empire delegation minutes, 32 (30.5.19).
26. House of Lords Record Office, Lloyd George Papers, F 45/9/29, Smuts to Lloyd George, 26.3.19; F45/9/33, Smuts to Lloyd George, 5.5.19; F 45/9/34, Smuts to Lloyd

George 14.5.19; F 45/9/35, Smuts to Lloyd George, 22.5.19; F45/9/39, Smuts to Lloyd George, 2.6.19; F45/9/4, Lloyd George to Smuts, 3.6.19; F45/9/41, Smuts to Lloyd George, 4.6.19.

27. Public Record Office, Cabinet Papers, CAB 29/28, British empire delegation minutes, 33 (1.6.19, A.M.); 34 (1.6.19, P.M.).

28. P. Mantoux, vol. 2, pp. 268–72, 274; Mordacq, *Le ministère Clemenceau*, vol. 3, p. 303; FRUS, vol. 11, pp. 222; Library of Congress, Baker notebooks, 9.6.19; D. Lloyd George, *Truth About the Peace Treaties*, vol. 1, pp. 678–79.

29. Lentin, *Lloyd George, Woodrow Wilson*, p. 100; Yale University Library, House diary, 31.5.19; P. Mantoux, vol. 2, pp. 428–37; FRUS, vol. 6, pp. 341–42.

30. P. Mantoux, vol. 2, p. 276; Library of Congress, Baker notebooks, 3.6.19.

31. P. Mantoux, vol. 2, pp. 358–61; 363–75.

32. Ministère de la Défense, Clemenceau Papers, 6N73, "Incidents de Versailles"; Schiff, pp. 124–26.

33. British Library, Balfour Papers, Add. MS 49750/231–236, memorandum from Sir Ian Malcolm; Scottish Record Office, Lothian Papers 466/26 3.6.19; St. Antony's College, Malcolm Papers, 8.5.19; P. Mantoux, vol. 2, pp. 401, 462, 459–75; Schiff, pp. 114–34; Klein, p. 214, n. 35; Holborn, pp. 145–47.

34. Rudin, p. 316; Marder, vol. 5, pp. 270–82; FRUS, vol. 6, pp. 613–14; Yale University Library, House diary. 23.6.19.

35. Epstein, pp. 311–24.

36. Ibid., pp. 314, n. 51, 315–17, chapter 12, *passim;* Nowak, p. 267; Schiff, p. 143.

37. Epstein, pp. 325–26; Luckau, p. 91; Nowak, p. 266.

38. P. Mantoux, vol. 2, p. 513; Eyck, vol. 1, p. 104; Luckau, pp. 109–12; Wheeler-Bennett, *Nemesis of Power,* pp. 55–59; Epstein, pp. 320–23.

39. Aldrovandi Marescotti, *Nuovi ricordi,* pp. 83–84; Hankey, p. 181.

40. Aldrovandi Marescotti, *Nuovi ricordi,* p. 89; Ministère des Affaires Etrangères, Jules Cambon Papers, folder 100 (correspondence), Jules Cambon to Paul Cambon, 26.6.19.

41. Garran, p. 271; Aldrovandi Marescotti, *Nuovi ricordi,* p. 96; National Archives of Canada, Christie Papers, vol. 7, file 21, "The Dominions and the Peace Conference: A New Page in Constitutional History," by Clement Jones, p. 184.

42. Riddell, *Intimate Diary,* p. 99; Shotwell, p. 382; Amery, vol. 1, p. 260; Lovin, p. 70.

43. Aldrovandi Marescotti, *Nuovi ricordi,* p. 87; Hankey, pp. 182–85; Garran, p. 270.

44. Yale University Library, House diary, 20.3.19; C. T. Thompson, p. 411.

45. Headlam-Morley, p. 178.

46. Marks, "Smoke and Mirrors," p. 370, n. 138; F. Stevenson, p. 187; Duroselle, p. 886.

47. H. Nicolson, *Peacemaking,* p. 368; Shotwell, p. 383.

48. FRUS, vol. 11, pp. 597–604; H. Nicolson, *Peacemaking,* pp. 365–71; Schiff, pp. 167–71; Hankey, pp. 188–89; Callwell, vol. 2, p. 201.

49. Eubank, p. 193; House, *Intimate Papers,* vol. 4, p. 487; Shotwell, p. 383.

50. Schiff, pp. 170–72.

51. Aldrovandi Marescotti, *Nuovi ricordi,* p. 110; Rowland, p. 495.

52. C. T. Thompson, p. 421; Headlam-Morley, p. 180; Garran, p. 272; F. Lloyd George, p. 145; FRUS, vol. 11, pp. 603–4; Ashmead-Bartlett, pp. 208–10.

53. Ryder, p. 224; Waite, p. 129; Epstein, pp. 388–89.

54. Skidelsky, vol. 1, pp. 348–53, 374–75, 378–89; Keylor, "Versailles and International Diplomacy," p. 485, n. 51.

55. Ferguson, "Keynes and German Inflation," p. 375; Schuker, *End of French Predominance,* p. 296.

56. Schuker, *American "Reparations" to Germany,* p. 12; Keiger, p. 271; Kershaw, *Hitler,* pp. 148–53.

57. See, for example, Cohen.

58. Bessel, "Why Did the Weimar Republic Collapse?", pp. 126–28.

59. Schuker, *American "Reparations" to Germany,* pp. 16–17; Marks, "Reparations Recon-

sidered," *passim;* Marks, "The Myths of Reparations," pp. 233–34; Eyck, vol. 1, pp. 174–75; P. Mantoux, vol. 1, p. 151.

60. Schuker, *American "Reparations" to Germany,* pp. 106–8; Marks, "The Myths of Reparations," p. 233; Marks, "Smoke and Mirrors," p. 348; Temperley, vol. 2, p. 54.

61. Eyck, vol. 1, p. 318.

62. Waite, chapter 8; Wheeler-Bennett, *Nemesis of Power,* p. 98.

63. Wheeler-Bennett, *Nemesis,* pp. 145–46; Eyck, vol. 1, 223–24; Nekrich, chapter 1, *passim.*

64. See Weinberg, "The Defeat of Germany," pp. 252–53.

65. Department of State, *The Treaty of Versailles and After,* p. 27.

CONCLUSION

1. Ministères des Affaires Etrangères, Georges Mandel Papers, 234/2, 22.7.19; Steffens, p. 803.

2. Sharp, "The Genie," p. 25.

3. Roosevelt, p. 97.

4. FRUS, vol. 3, pp. 394–410.

5. Ibid., pp. 403–5, 408–9; Burns, pp. 47–50.

6. Schachtman, p. 189.

7. Repington, p. 187; Watson, pp. 388–94, 438.

8. Cooper, pp. 26–27, 81–84, 123, 126–30; D. Lloyd George, *Truth About the Peace Treaties,* vol. 2, pp. 1412–13; Tillman, pp. 394–97.

9. Tumulty, p. 378; PWW, vol. 62, pp. 258–59.

10. Fried, p. 395; Hecksher, pp. 582–83; Cooper, pp. 119–21.

11. Hecksher, p. 586.

12. Cooper, pp. 12–23; Levin, pp. 309–10; Hecksher, pp. 591–93; PWW, vol. 62, Appendix, pp. 628–38.

13. Cooper, pp. 141–53; PWW, vol. 62, p. 507.

14. Tumulty, p. 435.

15. Grayson, p. 95; PWW, vol. 63, *passim* for speeches; pp. 50, 72, 235, 267–68.

16. PWW, vol. 63, pp. 3, 65, 152, 275, 308, 397, 446 (health); also pp. 63, 337–39, 420, 444–45; Tumulty, p. 447–48; Hecksher, pp. 609–22.

17. PWW, vol. 63, pp. 500–513.

18. Ibid., pp. 518–20, 522.

19. Levin, pp. 342–44, chapter 26, *passim;* Cooper, pp. 198–205, 258.

20. Cooper, pp. 260–62.

21. Ibid., chapter 8, *passim;* Grayson, p. 106; Hecksher, p. 631.

22. *Economist,* 31.12.99.

Index

ABOUT THE AUTHOR

MARGARET MACMILLAN received her Ph.D. from Oxford University and is provost of Trinity College and professor of history at the University of Toronto. Her previous books include *Women of the Raj,* a selection of the Book-of-the-Month Club and the History Book Club, and *Canada and NATO. Paris 1919,* published in the United Kingdom as *Peacemakers,* won the Duff Cooper Prize, the Samuel Johnson Prize, and the PEN Hessell Tiltman Prize. Margaret MacMillan is the great-granddaughter of David Lloyd George. She lives in Toronto.

ABOUT THE TYPE

This book was set in Bembo, a typeface based on an old-style Roman face that was used for Cardinal Bembo's tract *De Aetna* in 1495. Bembo was cut by Francisco Griffo in the early sixteenth century. The Lanston Monotype Machine Company of Philadelphia brought the well-proportioned letterforms of Bembo to the United States in the 1930s.